Computational Finance 1999

Computational Finance 1999

edited by Yaser S. Abu-Mostafa, Blake LeBaron, Andrew W. Lo, and Andreas S. Weigend

The MIT Press
Cambridge, Massachusetts
London, England

Second printing, 2001

© 2000 Massachusetts Institute of Technology

All rights reserved. No part of this book may be reproduced in any form by any electronic or mechanical means (including photocopying, recording, or information storage and retrieval) without permission in writing from the publisher.

This book was set in Computer Modern by Windfall Software using LATEX and was printed and bound in the United States of America.

Library of Congress Cataloging-in-Publication Data

Computational finance 1999 / edited by Yaser S. Abu-Mostafa ... [et al.].
   p. cm.
  Includes bibliographical references and index.
  ISBN 0-262-01178-6 (hc.: alk. paper)
  ISBN 0-262-51107-X (pbk.: alk. paper)
  1. Finance—Data processing Congresses. 2. Finance—Mathematical models Congresses. I. Abu-Mostafa, Yaser S., 1957–
  HG174 .C64 2000
  332'.0285—dc21   99-30172
                                                   CIP

Contents

Preface

This volume contains a selection of the papers presented at Computational Finance '99 at the Stern School of Business, New York University, in January 1999. This conference is an annual refereed meeting, which was previously called "Neural Networks in the Capital Markets."

I would like to thank the other editors, especially Andreas Weigend, for their help in arranging the conference and these proceedings. I would also like to acknowledge the following people for their help in refereeing the many papers submitted to this conferences and for making valuable comments and suggestions to the authors of the papers in these proceedings.

The CF99 program committee included:

A. Atiya, Cairo University

J. Cowan, University of Chicago

F. X. Diebold, NYU Stern and University of Pennsylvania

R. Gencay, University of Windsor

M. Jabri, Sydney University

J. E. Moody, Oregon Graduate Institute

C. E. Pedreira, Catholic University PUC-Rio

A.-P. N. Refenes, London Business School

M. Steiner, Universitaet Augsburg

D. Tavella, Align Risk Analysis

A. Timmermann, University of California, San Diego

H. White, University of California, San Diego

L. Xu, Chinese University of Hong Kong

The following people were of assistance as outside referees:

C. Neely, Federal Reserve Bank of St. Louis

T. Poggio, Massachusetts Institute of Technology

Blake LeBaron
December 1999

Contributors

Filippo Altimisso
Banca d'Italia

Edoardo Amaldi
Cornell University

Amir F. Atiya
California Institute of Technology

Giuseppe Ballocchi
Olsen & Associates

Mark A. Bedau
Reed College

Andrea Beltratti
University of Turin

N. Burgess
London Business School

André de Carvalho
University of Guelph

Mikhail Chernov
Pennsylvania State University

Yiu-ming Cheung
The Chinese University of Hong Kong

Lew Clewlow
Warwick Business School

N. K. Chidambaran
Tulane University and New York University

Peter Christofferson
McGill University

Michel Dacorogna
Olsen & Associates

Peter Dayan
University College London

Engelbert Dockner
University of Vienna

Georg Dorffner
Austrian Research Institute for Artificial Intelligence

Jeff Fleming
Rice University

J. Galindo-Flores
Harvard University

Ramazan Gençay
Olsen & Associates

Eric Ghysels
Pennsylvania State University

Paul Glassman
Columbia University

David Goldbaum
Rutgers University

Russell Grimwood
Warwick Business School

Jinyong Hahn
University of Michigan

Zac Harland
Krueger Research

Philip Heidelberger
T.J. Watson Research Center

Thomas Hellström
Malardalen University

Kenneth Holmström
Malardalen University

Juan del Hoyo
Universidad Autonoma de Madrid

David A. Hsieh
Duke University

Tor Jacobson
Sueriges Riksbank

George J. Jiang
York University

Shareen Joshi
Santa Fe Institute

Christian Keber
University of Vienna

Chris Kirby
Australian Graduate School of Management

Zhi-bin Lai
The Chinese University of Hong Kong

Paul Lajbcygier
Monash University

Chi-Wen Jevons Lee
Tulane Unversity

Juan K. Lin
Massachusetts Institute of Technology

J. Guillermo Llorente
Alvarez Universidad Autonoma de Madrid

Cornelis A. Los
University of Adelaide

Malik Magdon-Ismail
California Institute of Technology

Edmar Martinelli
University of Sao Paulo

Alberto Matias
University of Sao Paulo

Michael de la Maza
Redfire Capital Management Group

John Moody
Oregon Graduate Institute

Claudio Morana
Heriot-Watt University

Matthew R. Morey
Smith College

Ralph Neuneier
Siemens AG

Dirk Ormoneit
Stanford University

Barbara Ostdiek
Rice University

Art Owen
Stanford University

Jeffrey Parker
Reed College

Olivier Pictet
Olsen & Associates

Jean-François Pusztaszeri
Cornell University

Min Qi
Kent State University

T.S. Raghu
Arizona State University

H.R. Rao
SUNY Buffalo

Solange Rezende
University of Sao Paulo

Kasper F. Roszbach
Stockholm School of Economics / De Nederlandesche Banke

Dirk W. Rudolph
Bankakademie

Matthew Saffell
Oregon Graduate Institute

Christian Schittenkopf
Austrian Research Institute for Artificial Intelligence

Sebastian Schneider
University of Augsberg

P.K. Sen
SUNY Buffalo and Georgia State University

Perwez Shahabuddin
Columbia University

Catherine Shenoy
University of Kansas

Prakash P. Shenoy
University of Kansas

Spyros Skouras
University of Cambridge

Pieter J. van der Sluis
University of Amsterdam

Manfred Steiner
University of Augsberg

Peter Tiňo
Austrian Research Institute for Artificial Intelligence

Neville Towers
London Business School

Joaquin Trigueros
Tulane University

Raymond Tsang
National Australia Bank Group

Benjamin Van Roy
Stanford University

H. D. Vinod
Fordham University

Yangru Wu
Rutgers University

Lei Xu
The Chinese University of Hong Kong

Howard Yang
Oregon Graduate Institute

Yi Zhou
Goldman Sachs

Computational Finance 1999

1 Introduction

Blake LeBaron

This volume consists of a subset of the papers that were presented at Computational Finance '99 at the Stern School of Business at New York University in January 1999.

This is the second year of the conference called "Computational Finance," but this is the sixth in a series of conferences originally called "Neural Networks in the Capital Markets." As with last year's program the name change has continued to broaden the scope of this meeting to include all aspects of computational finance. The early emphasis on artificial neural networks and financial forecasting has given way to a wide range of topics, from advanced Monte-Carlo methods for derivative pricing to agent-based computational models. The contents of this volume reflects this in its coverage of many of these topics.

The conference has seen several subtler changes in its audience as well. In earlier conferences the boundaries between researchers coming out of the economics/finance areas and the hard sciences were often very clear. As more interdisciplinary centers are started and more researchers are crossing boundaries, these distinctions are becoming less clear. Also, the emphasis on raw computing power seems to be lessening. In an era when fast computing is becoming steadily more ubiquitous, it is no longer impressive to use many compute cycles. Indeed, one presenter bragged of running models in a spreadsheet. Technique now dominates over raw computing in this field.

The conference was held for three days, with the first day dedicated to tutorials. The second and third days had oral presentations along with poster sessions. The conference was very well attended with over 300 participants.

The proceedings are divided by field into several sections.

1.1 Risk Management/Portfolio Optimization

The first section contains papers dealing with issues related to risk management. This work now commands equal attention to financial forecasting, and is becoming an integral part of investment management operations. Papers include summaries of improved monte-carlo methods and value-at-risk estimation. New methods for assessing old portfolio performance measures are introduced as well.

1.2 Volatility

A major feature of most financial time series is the forecastability of volatility. The edge gained in certain markets from having a better volatility model can be quite significant. Papers in this section look at issues involved in volatility forecasting and timing, mean-variance optimization, and improved estimation methods for stochastic volatility models.

1.3 Time Series Methods

This section highlights methods that come from a more traditional time series approach to financial forecasting. However, there is nothing traditional about the methods which include neural networks, independent component analysis, and other nonparametric techniques applied to several different financial series. Methods are also proposed for estimating parameter stability and data snooping biases which often accompany large nonlinear models.

1.4 Dynamic Trading Strategies

The final test of many forecasting models is the generation of useful dynamic trading strategies. It is always important to test any model in how it performs with live trading. The papers in this section take a trading perspective to computational finance problems. These involve advanced computational learning techniques such as genetic algorithms, dynamic programming, and reinforcement learning, along with more traditional technical trading strategies. The analysis again covers a wide range of series from the Dow Jones Industrials to minute by minute foreign exchange rates, mutual fund rebalancing, and hedge fund analysis.

1.5 Heterogeneous Agents

This section presents one of the newer areas of computational finance: the modeling of markets as sets of many interacting agents. These papers may not be as practically oriented as some of the others in this volume, but they may be the key to unlocking what is really going on in the dynamics of markets. Papers in this section look at the interactions of technical and fundamental strategies and problems related to delegated portfolio management. All are done from the perspective of individual agents interacting in markets with no global coordination.

1.6 Credit Risk

One of the more successful applications of advanced pattern recognition in finance
has been in analyzing problems of credit risk. The papers in this section combine
symbolic and neural network based methods for generating better assessments of
defaults and credit risk.

1.7 Option Pricing

Much of the activity in computational finance has been in the fast changing world
of options pricing. This section highlights papers with strong connections to options
pricing and trading. Computational methods range from genetic programming to
efficient method of moments estimation. Empirical frameworks for handling volatility issues include stochastic volatility models along with ARCH approaches.

I Risk Management and Portfolio Optimization

2   Importance Sampling and Stratification for Value-at-Risk

Paul Glasserman, Philip Heidelberger, and Perwez Shahabuddin

This paper proposes and evaluates variance reduction techniques for efficient estimation of portfolio loss probabilities using Monte Carlo simulation. Precise estimation of loss probabilities is essential to calculating value-at-risk, which is simply a percentile of the loss distribution. The methods we develop build on delta-gamma approximations to changes in portfolio value. The simplest way to use such approximations for variance reduction employs them as control variates; we show, however, that far greater variance reduction is possible if the approximations are used as a basis for importance sampling, stratified sampling, or combinations of the two. This is especially true in estimating very small loss probabilities.

2.1   Introduction

Value-at-Risk (VAR) has become an important measure for estimating and managing portfolio risk [Jorion 1997, Wilson 1999]. VAR is defined as a certain quantile of the change in a portfolio's value during a specified holding period. To be more specific, suppose the current value of the portfolio is $V(t)$, the holding period is Δt, and the value of the portfolio at time $t + \Delta t$ is $V(t + \Delta t)$. The loss in portfolio value during the holding period is $L = -\Delta V$ where $\Delta V = [V(t + \Delta t) - V(t)]$ and the VAR, x_p, associated with a given probability p is defined by the relationship

$$P\{L > x_p\} = p, \tag{2.1}$$

i.e., the VAR x_p is the $(1 - p)$'th quantile of the loss distribution. Typically Δt is one day or two weeks, and $p \leq 0.05$; often $p \approx 0.01$ is of interest. To evaluate (2.1), Monte Carlo simulation is often used; changes in the portfolio's risk factors are simulated, the portfolio is re-evaluated, and the loss distribution is estimated. However, obtaining accurate VAR estimates can be computationally expensive because:

1. there may be a large number of instruments in the portfolio thereby making each portfolio evaluation costly, and

2. when p is small, a large number of simulation runs may be required to obtain accurate estimates of the tail probability.

The purpose of this paper is to describe variance reduction techniques that offer the potential to dramatically reduce the number of runs required to achieve a given precision. These techniques build on [Glasserman et al 1999a, Glasserman et al 1999b]. The key to reducing the variance of an estimate of the VAR x_p is to obtain accurate estimates of $P\{L > x\}$ for values of x that are close to x_p, and this is the issue that we focus on.

Our approach is to exploit knowledge of the distribution of an approximation to the loss to devise more effective Monte Carlo sampling schemes. The specific loss approximations employed are first and second order Taylor series expansions of L; these are the well known delta and delta-gamma approximations, respectively (see, e.g., [Jorion 1997], [Rouvinez 1997], and [Wilson 1999]). When the risk factors have a multivariate normal distribution, as is often assumed, the distribution of the delta approximation is known in closed form while the distribution of the delta-gamma approximation can be computed numerically [Imhof 1961] and [Rouvinez 1997].

These approximations are not always sufficiently accurate to provide precise VAR estimates. Nevertheless, because of correlation between the approximation and the actual loss, knowledge about the approximation can be put to great advantage for the purpose of variance reduction. This correlation is illustrated in Figure 2.1, which is a scatter plot of the actual loss and the delta-gamma approximation to the loss for one of the portfolios described in Section 2.4. Clearly, the value of the delta-gamma approximation tells us a great deal about the value of the loss. The most obvious way to try to exploit this correlation for variance reduction is to use the delta-gamma approximation as a control variate. But the approximation can also be used as a basis for importance sampling and stratified sampling. (See, e.g., [Hammersley and Handscomb 1964] for background on variance reduction techniques.) In control variates, only the mean of a correlated variable is used to achieve variance reduction whereas importance sampling and stratified sampling can make use of the full distribution.

If one is interested in estimating $P\{L > x\}$, then one can use $I(Q > x)$ as a control variate where Q is the approximation to the loss and $I()$ is the indicator function. Specifically, this means replacing the standard estimator $I(L > x)$ with

$$I(L > x) - \beta[I(Q > x) - P\{Q > x\}]$$

where L and Q are evaluated in the same price scenario and $P\{Q > x\}$ is computed numerically. The coefficient β can be estimated from the simulation to minimize variance, or—as seems preferable in this setting—fixed at 1 to avoid the bias introduced when β is estimated. Independent of our work, [Cárdenas et al 1999] have also suggested using the delta-gamma approximation as a control variate. The effectiveness of such a control decreases as we go further out in the tail because the correlation between $I(L > x)$ and $I(Q > x)$ typically decreases as x increases. For example, for the portfolio of Figure 2.1, the estimated correlation between L and

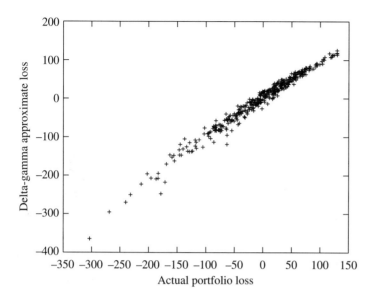

Figure 2.1
A scatter plot showing delta-gamma approximate losses versus actual portfolio losses. The portfolio is short ten at-the-money calls and puts on each of ten underlying assets. The assets are
uncorrelated and each has a volatility of 0.30; the options expire in 0.10 years and the losses are
measured over 0.04 years. Negative losses are gains.

Q is 0.99, but the correlation between $I(L > x)$ and $I(Q > x)$ is 0.85 for $x = 90$
and it drops to 0.50 for $x = 125$. [Cárdenas et al 1999] have also suggested using a
simple form of stratified sampling in which there are two strata defined by $\{Q \leq x\}$
and $\{Q > x\}$ and in which the fraction of samples drawn from each stratum is
proportional to the probability of the stratum. Note that for large x, the fraction
of samples drawn from the important region in which $Q \approx x$ remains small.

Examination of Figure 2.1 reveals that the problem in estimating $P\{L > x\}$
for a large value of x is that very few samples drawn actually have $L > x$. Thus
most samples are "wasted" in the sense that $I(L > x) = 0$ with high probability.
Importance sampling (IS) [Hammersley and Handscomb 1964, Glasserman et al
1999a, Glasserman et al 1999b] is well-suited to such "rare event" simulations.
Suppose the joint density of the changes in risk factors is f. Rather than simulating
with this density, a different joint density g is used. Write

$$P\{L > x\} = \int I(L > x)f(z)dz = \int I(L > x)\frac{f(z)}{g(z)}g(z)dz = \tilde{E}[I(L > x)\ell(Z)] \quad (2.2)$$

where $\tilde{E}$ denotes expectation when sampling is done under density g and $\ell(Z) = f(Z)/g(Z)$ is the likelihood ratio. That is, an unbiased estimate of $P\{L > x\}$ can be obtained by drawing samples with density g and multiplying the output (in this case $I(L > x)$) by the likelihood ratio. The key is picking a good IS density g, and this topic has been the subject of much research in a wide variety of application areas; see, e.g., [Glasserman et al 1999a] and [Heidelberger 1995] and the numerous references therein. Roughly speaking, we want to pick g so as to make the rare event of interest more likely to occur, but extreme care needs to be exercised; see [Glasserman and Wang 1997] for some cautionary examples. In this paper we describe how the delta and delta-gamma approximations can be used to guide the selection of an effective IS distribution. As described in [Glasserman et al 1999a], IS can be effectively combined with stratified sampling to obtain further variance reduction when pricing a class of European-style options. In this paper we consider effective IS-stratification combinations for VAR estimation. In addition, stratified sampling on the approximation, without IS, can also be used to great effect, provided many strata are defined and a greater fraction of samples are drawn from the strata in which the event $\{L > x\}$ is more likely to occur.

The application of these variance reduction techniques does involve some overhead. However, because the per sample cost to evaluate a large portfolio can be enormous, substantial pre-simulation overhead can often be justified so long as it produces even modest variance reduction. Indeed, the overhead of these methods is quite small. Assuming that the delta-gamma approximation is given, the only overheads are:

1. a one time cost to compute an IS change of measure,

2. a one time cost to compute quantities related to the stratified sampling, and

3. a small additional per sample cost to generate risk factors from the required conditional (stratified) distribution and to compute the likelihood ratio; this cost is negligible compared to the cost of evaluating even a modest-sized portfolio.

For the sample portfolios considered in this paper, the variance is typically reduced by more than an order of magnitude, thereby making this overhead well worthwhile.

In this paper, our emphasis is on describing algorithms and providing initial indications of the factors affecting their performance. For these purposes, we use synthetic portfolios of options whose characteristics are easily controlled (e.g., a perfectly delta-hedged portfolio). Theoretical properties of the algorithms and further numerical studies will be described in a subsequent paper.

The rest of the paper is organized as follows. The delta and delta-gamma approximations are reviewed in Section 2.2. Preliminaries on the basic variance reduction techniques employed in this paper are given in Section 2.3. Variance reduction techniques based on the delta and delta-gamma approximations are discussed in Sections 2.4 and 2.5, respectively. Section 2.6 considers stratified sampling in further detail (both with and without IS) and in particular focuses on issues related to the effective allocation of samples to strata.

2.2   The Delta and Delta-Gamma Approximations

In this section, we express the delta and delta-gamma approximations as sums of terms involving independent standard normal random variables (mean zero, variance one). This facilitates the computation of the required quantities for control variates, importance sampling, and stratification. Our development is similar to that of [Rouvinez 1997], but is included to introduce key notation.

We assume that there are m risk factors, and that $S(t) = (S_1(t), \ldots, S_m(t))$ denotes the value of these factors at time t. Define $\Delta S = [S(t + \Delta t) - S(t)]'$ to be the change in the risk factors during the interval $[t, t + \Delta t]$. The delta-gamma approximation is given by

$$\Delta V = -L \approx \Theta \Delta t + \delta' \Delta S + \tfrac{1}{2} \Delta S' \Gamma \Delta S \qquad (2.3)$$

where $\Theta = \frac{\partial V}{\partial t}$, $\delta_i = \frac{\partial V}{\partial S_i(t)}$, and $\Gamma_{ij} = \frac{\partial^2 V}{\partial S_i(t) \partial S_j(t)}$ (all partial derivatives being evaluated at $S(t)$). The delta approximation is $\Delta V = -L \approx \Theta \Delta t + \delta' \Delta S$.

Assume now that ΔS has a multivariate normal distribution with mean vector zero and covariance matrix Σ. To draw samples of ΔS we can set $\Delta S = CZ$ where Z is a vector of m independent standard normals and C is any matrix for which $CC' = \Sigma$. (Shortly, we make a more specific choice of matrix.) Thus, for the delta approximation,

$$P\{L > x\} \approx P\{b'Z > x + \Theta \Delta t\} \equiv P\{Y > y_x\} \qquad (2.4)$$

where

$$b' = -\delta'C, \qquad Y = b'Z, \qquad \text{and} \qquad y_x = x + \Theta \Delta t. \qquad (2.5)$$

For the delta-gamma approximation, we seek to express $L \approx c + b'Z + Z'\Lambda Z \equiv c + Q$ where the Z's are independent standard normals and Λ is a diagonal matrix. To this end, choose C so that

$$CC' = \Sigma \quad \text{and} \quad \tfrac{1}{2}C'\Gamma C \text{ is diagonal.} \tag{2.6}$$

To see that such a choice is possible, start with an arbitrary C for which $CC' = \Sigma$ and write

$$\tfrac{1}{2}C'\Gamma C = -U\Lambda U',$$

where U is an orthogonal matrix whose columns are eigenvectors of $\tfrac{1}{2}C'\Gamma C$ and $-\Lambda$ is a diagonal matrix of eigenvalues of $\tfrac{1}{2}C'\Gamma C$ (hence also of $\tfrac{1}{2}\Gamma\Sigma$). Now replace the original C with CU and observe that the new choice satisfies (2.6). Hence, with (2.6) in force, we have

$$L \approx -\Theta\Delta t - \delta'CZ + Z'\Lambda Z = -\Theta\Delta t + b'Z + Z'\Lambda Z \tag{2.7}$$

where $b' = -\delta'C$ and Z is a vector of independent standard normals. Thus

$$P\{L > x\} \approx P\{Q > x + \Theta\Delta t\} = P\{Q > y_x\} \tag{2.8}$$

where $Q = b'Z + Z'\Lambda Z = \sum(b_i Z_i + \lambda_i Z_i^2)$ is the stochastic part of the quadratic approximation to L. By completing the square, the distribution of Q can be related to that of the sum of noncentral chi-squared random variables. [Imhof 1961] gives expressions that are suitable for numerical integration for computing the distribution function of Q.

2.3 Variance Reduction Preliminaries

Because the use of control variates is straightforward, we focus on importance sampling, stratified sampling, and combinations of the two. As described in (2.2) we can write $P\{L > x\} = \tilde{E}[I(L > x)\ell(Z)]$ where $\tilde{E}$ denotes expectation using the IS distribution for Z and $\ell(Z)$ is the likelihood ratio. With Z a vector of standard normals, we consider two types of IS, changing either just the mean of Z or both the mean and covariance matrix. If the mean of Z is changed from 0 to v, then

$$\ell(Z) = \exp\left(\tfrac{1}{2}v'v - v'Z\right), \tag{2.9}$$

while if the mean is changed from 0 to v and the covariance matrix is changed from I to B, $B > 0$, then

$$\ell(Z) = \frac{\exp(-\tfrac{1}{2}Z'Z)}{|B|^{-\frac{1}{2}}\exp\left\{-\tfrac{1}{2}(Z-v)'B^{-1}(Z-v)\right\}} \tag{2.10}$$

where $|B|$ is the determinant of B. If n samples $(Z^{(1)}, \ldots, Z^{(n)})$ are drawn and associated losses $(L_1, \ldots, L_n)$ computed, the IS estimate of $P\{L > x\}$ is

$$\hat{P}_x = \frac{1}{n} \sum_{j=1}^{n} I(L_j > x)\ell(Z^{(j)}). \tag{2.11}$$

It is straightforward to incorporate a control variate with IS. If X is a random variable with known mean, the control variate under IS would be $X\ell(Z)$, which has the same mean.

In stratified sampling, we identify a stratification variable X and partition the range of X into k intervals (strata) $(\mathcal{S}_1, \ldots, \mathcal{S}_k)$. Write

$$P\{L > x\} = \sum_{i=1}^{k} P\{L > x | X \in \mathcal{S}_i\} P\{X \in \mathcal{S}_i\}. \tag{2.12}$$

We typically have in mind using from $k = 25$ to $k = 100$ equiprobable strata (i.e., $P\{X \in \mathcal{S}_i\} = 1/k$). Draw n_i samples of X from stratum i. Let X_{ij} denote the j'th sample in stratum i, let $Z^{(ij)}$ be a sample of Z having the conditional distribution of Z given $X = X_{ij}$, and let L_{ij} be the portfolio loss corresponding to the sample $Z^{(ij)}$. Then $P\{L > x\}$ is estimated by

$$\hat{P}_x = \sum_{i=1}^{k} P\{X \in \mathcal{S}_i\} \times \frac{1}{n_i} \sum_{j=1}^{n_i} I(L_{ij} > x). \tag{2.13}$$

We are free to allocate samples to the strata (i.e., choose the n_i's) in an essentially arbitrary manner, and the optimal allocation is well known: for a given total number of samples and equiprobable strata, the optimal n_i is proportional to the standard deviation of $I(L_{ij} > x)$.

When combining IS and stratified sampling, we can think of applying either stratified sampling or importance sampling first. Applying stratified sampling first, write

$$\begin{aligned} P\{L > x\} &= \sum_{i=1}^{k} P\{L > x | X \in \mathcal{S}_i\} P\{X \in \mathcal{S}_i\} \\ &= \sum_{i=1}^{k} \tilde{E}[I(L > x)\ell(Z) | X \in \mathcal{S}_i] P\{X \in \mathcal{S}_i\}, \end{aligned} \tag{2.14}$$

i.e., X is drawn from its original distribution and then Z is drawn from the IS distribution, given X. The estimator associated with (2.14) is

$$\hat{P}_x = \sum_{i=1}^{k} P\{X \in \mathcal{S}_i\} \times \frac{1}{n_i} \sum_{j=1}^{n_i} I(L_{ij} > x)\ell(Z^{(ij)}). \tag{2.15}$$

Applying importance sampling first, write

$$P\{L > x\} = \tilde{E}[I(L > x)\ell(Z)] = \sum_{i=1}^{k} \tilde{E}[I(L > x)\ell(Z)|X \in \mathcal{S}_i]\tilde{P}\{X \in \mathcal{S}_i\}, \tag{2.16}$$

where $\tilde{P}$ denotes the probability under IS. In this method, both X and Z (given X) are drawn from the IS distribution. The estimator associated with (2.16) is

$$\hat{P}_x = \sum_{i=1}^{k} \tilde{P}\{X \in \mathcal{S}_i\} \times \frac{1}{n_i} \sum_{j=1}^{n_i} I(L_{ij} > x)\ell(Z^{(ij)}). \tag{2.17}$$

To see the distinction between (2.14) and (2.16), suppose each method employs k equiprobable strata (under P and $\tilde{P}$, respectively). If $X = b'Z$ and $L \approx X$, then using (2.14), the mean of X is 0 and only a few strata will have positive indicators, $I(L > x)$, for a large x. If, using (2.16), the mean of Z is shifted from 0 to v where $b'v = x$, then the mean of X is x and approximately half the strata will have positive indicators. Hence, when we combine IS and stratification, we apply IS first, i.e., we use (2.16) and (2.17).

An efficient sampling scheme for a linear stratification variable $X = b'Z$ is described in [Glasserman et al 1999a]. Briefly, let $v = b/\sqrt{(b'b)}$, let Φ^{-1} denote the inverse of the standard normal distribution; then if U is uniformly distributed over the unit interval and ξ is an m-vector of independent standard normals,

$$Z = \Phi^{-1}(U)v + (I - vv')\xi$$

is also a vector of independent normals. Replacing independently sampled U's with a stratified sample (using subintervals of the unit intervals as strata) has the effect of stratifying $v'Z$ and hence also $b'Z$. See [Glasserman et al 1999a] for details.

2.4   Variance Reduction Based on the Delta Approximation

The most obvious variance reduction technique based on the delta approximation is to use the tail probability of the delta approximation itself as a control variate. Specifically, (2.4) suggests using $I(Y > y_x)$ as a control variate where $Y = b'Z$ and $y_x = x + \Theta\Delta t$. The mean of this control variate is easily calculated. However, as discussed earlier the effectiveness of this approach diminishes as x increases. Note also that there may be some other $y' \neq y_x$ for which the control variate $I(Y > y')$ yields more variance reduction.

Stratified sampling on $Y = b'Z$ uses more information about the delta approximation and avoids some of the difficulties involved in applying control variates (e.g., selecting the best y' and estimating the optimal control variate multiplier, which can introduce bias and even lead to negative estimates of the probability). However, unless the strata allocation $\{n_i\}$ is designed so as to assign most samples to "promising" strata, most samples will result in $L < x$.

In estimating a rare event probability such as $P\{L > x\}$, one heuristic for choosing an IS distribution is based on a large deviations analysis that states that (under appropriate technical conditions) the probability of a rare event is approximately equal to the probability of "the most likely path" to the rare event (see, e.g., [Bucklew 1990]). With this heuristic, the IS distribution is selected so as to make this most likely path to the rare event the most likely path selected under IS. For multivariate Gaussian distributions this approach has been studied in [Chen et al 1993] and developed for option pricing in [Glasserman et al 1999a, Glasserman et al 1999b]. To apply this heuristic we change the means of the Gaussian random variables from 0 to $\mu = (\mu_1, \ldots, \mu_m)$ where μ is the point that maximizes the probability of the rare event. Using the delta approximation in (2.4), we find μ by solving the optimization problem:

$$\max \quad -\frac{1}{2}\sum_{i=1}^{m} z_i^2 \qquad \text{such that} \qquad \sum_{i=1}^{m} b_i z_i \geq y_x \qquad (2.18)$$

The solution to this optimization problem is $\mu = b y_x / (b'b)$.

The appropriate likelihood ratio is given by (2.9) with $v = \mu$. The per sample second moment of this estimator is $\tilde{E}[I(L > x)\ell(Z)^2] = E[I(L > x)\ell(Z)]$, so a sufficient condition for variance reduction is $\ell(Z) \leq 1$ for all points Z such that $L > x$. The condition $\ell(Z) \leq 1$ is equivalent to $\frac{1}{2}\mu'\mu - \mu'Z \leq 0$, which, by completing the square, is equivalent to the condition that every point $Z \in \{L > x\}$ is closer to μ than it is to 0. In fact, we obtain a variance reduction by shifting the mean to any vector v (not just μ) provided each point in $\{L > x\}$ is closer to v than it is to 0. Similarly, if $\ell(Z) \leq f$ for all Z in $\{L > x\}$, then the second moment of the IS estimate is reduced by at least a factor of f.

The variance of the IS estimator could further be reduced by using a control variate, most obviously $I(Y > y_x)\ell(Z)$.

To combine IS with stratification, one could stratify upon virtually any random variable. For normal distributions, it is particularly convenient to stratify upon a linear combination of the Z's. Note that when the mean of the IS distribution is μ, then $\ell(Z) = c_1 \exp(-\mu'Z) = c_1 \exp(-c_2 b'Z)$ for some constants c_1 and c_2. This strongly suggest stratifying upon $\mu'Z$ (equivalently $b'Z$), since this simultaneously removes essentially all the variability in the likelihood ratio and much of the variability in the indicator $I(L > x)$, provided the delta approximation is close to the loss L.

Numerical Examples

We now illustrate the performance of the estimators described above. Our examples consist of portfolios of options on ten underlying assets. Even in this restricted setting there are far too many possible variations to attempt an exhaustive comparison here. Instead, we choose simple examples illustrating general principles. We keep the properties of the underlying assets particularly simple to make the effect of the portfolio structure more transparent. Thus, all ten assets have an initial value of 100 and an annual volatility of 0.30, and all pairs of distinct assets have a common correlation of ρ, with either $\rho = 0$ or $\rho = 0.2$. We consider three portfolios: (1) a portfolio short ten at-the-money calls on each underlying asset, each call having an expiry of 0.5 years; (2) a portfolio short ten calls struck at 100 and long ten calls struck at 105 (a "bear spread") on each underlying asset, each call having an expiry of 0.1 years; (3) a portfolio short ten at-the-money calls and five at-the-money puts on each underlying asset, each option having an expiry of 0.1 years. We assume 250 trading days in a year and use a continuously compounded risk-free interest rate of 5%.

Table 2.1 compares three methods on these portfolios. For each case we estimate losses over ten days (.04 years). Since the relevant magnitude of losses varies widely across models, we specify the loss threshold x as x_{std} standard deviations above the mean loss according to the delta-gamma approximation and vary x_{std}:

$$x = \left(\sum_i \lambda_i - \Theta\Delta t\right) + x_{std} \sqrt{\sum_i b_i^2 + 2\sum_i \lambda_i^2}.$$

This makes it easier to compare loss thresholds across models. In the examples of Table 2.1 we chose values of x_{std} that would result in loss probabilities close to 1% or 5% with $\rho = 0$ and then used the same values of x_{std} with $\rho = 0.2$.

We evaluate the performance of the methods by estimating the ratio of the variance using standard Monte Carlo (no variance reduction) to the variance obtained with each method based on an equal number of samples. Thus, the larger the ratio the greater the variance reduction. Assuming roughly equal computing time per sample with and without variance reduction (which is the case in these examples), the variance ratio is a measure of computational speed-up: a method with a variance ratio of 10, say, produces as precise an estimate as standard Monte Carlo in 1/10 as much computing time.

The last three columns of the table report variance ratios using a delta-gamma control variate, using IS based on the delta approximation and combining IS with stratification in the direction determined by the delta approximation. (We could have used a delta control variate but we wanted to compare the IS methods with the best available control variate.) The first portfolio, consisting solely of calls far from expiration, has a strong linear component and, not surprisingly, all three methods result in notable variance reduction; but the combined IS-stratification method substantially outperforms the control variate, particularly at small loss probabilities. The second portfolio is far less linear because of the form of the payoff on each asset (it is neither convex nor concave) and because the options are much closer to expiration. The control variate is much less effective in this case, but the other two methods remain very effective. Losses in this portfolio occur only in one direction for each underlying asset, and the IS scheme takes advantage of this property even in the absence of linearity. This property fails to hold in the third portfolio—losses can now occur from large movements in the underlying assets in either direction. The IS scheme makes losses from the calls more likely (since they have greater weight) but in so doing makes losses from the puts rarer and thus fails to reduce variance effectively. Indeed, the rarity of losses from the puts results in a highly skewed distribution for the estimator which can therefore appear to underestimate the loss probability in small samples. These effects are less pronounced at $\rho = 0.2$, where the common correlation across assets turns out to magnify the linear term in the portfolio value.

The results in Table 2.1 suggest that the potential gains from the combination of IS and stratification are very substantial, but that the delta approximation alone does not provide a consistently reliable basis for implementation—particularly when movements of an underlying risk factor in more than one direction can result in portfolio losses. The delta-gamma based methods in the next section address this shortcoming.

2.5 Variance Reduction Based on the Delta-Gamma Approximation

We now show how the full delta-gamma approximation can be used to derive variance reduction techniques. First, (2.8) suggests using $I(Q > y_x)$ as a control

Table 2.1
Comparison of variance reduction methods. Variance ratios are estimated from 120,000 replications; the stratified estimator uses 40 strata and 3000 samples per strata. Variance ratios are estimates of the computational speed-up relative to standard Monte Carlo.

					Variance Ratios		
	Portfolio	x_{std}	$P\{L > x\}$	δ-Γ CV	δ-IS	δ-IS-Strat.
$\rho = 0$	ATM Calls	1.7	4.7%	16.1	7.9	23.4
		2.5	.8%	10.2	40.0	96.5
	Spreads	1.7	4.8%	3.1	8.6	19.8
		2.4	1.1%	2.1	30.8	58.9
	Calls & Puts	1.7	5.3%	5.1	0.6	0.5
		2.5	1.3%	3.0	0.4	0.6
$\rho = 0.2$	ATM Calls	1.7	5.0%	22.7	10.0	62.3
		2.5	1.0%	10.6	38.0	220.0
	Spreads	1.7	5.3%	5.1	8.8	35.3
		2.4	1.0%	3.0	33.4	86.2
	Calls & Puts	1.7	5.9%	7.5	5.9	10.2
		2.5	2.1%	4.5	10.4	18.6

variate, or using Q as a stratification variable. To stratify on Q, we must be able to sample Q and also sample Z given Q. Since $P\{Q \in \mathcal{S}_i\}$ can be computed numerically, one can in principle sample Q using the inverse transform method. However, we do not know of a direct method to sample Z given the quadratic form Q. (A method based on acceptance-rejection will be described elsewhere.) However, a simple method for generating Z's from the correct conditional distribution is as follows. First, generate a vector Z of independent standard normals and compute Q. If $Q \in \mathcal{S}_i$, then this Z has the distribution of Z given $Q \in \mathcal{S}_i$. If there are fewer than n_i samples from stratum i, then use this Z to evaluate the portfolio, otherwise discard it. Continue sampling until there are the required number of samples from each stratum. Like a rejection method, this wastes some samples. However, our experience has been that except for the most skewed $\{n_i\}$, this sampling overhead is modest (especially compared to the cost of evaluating the portfolio). Analysis of this overhead will be described elsewhere.

Stratification upon other variables is also possible. First, suppose $\lambda_1 \gg \lambda_i (i > 1)$ and $\lambda_1 > 0$. Then much of the variability in the positive part of Q is explained by Z_1^2. This suggests stratifying on Z_1^2, which has a chi-square distribution (or Z_1, which has a normal distribution). This distribution can be easily sampled using the inverse transform. If the λ_i's are all approximately equal, then much of the variability in Q is explained by $R^2 = Z_1^2 + \cdots + Z_m^2$ which suggests stratifying upon R^2 ("radial stratification"). Note that R^2 has a chi-square distribution with m degrees of freedom. To accomplish the stratified sampling, first draw R^2 using the inverse transform. Now draw independent standard normals $X_1, \ldots, X_m$ and set $Z_i = X_i\sqrt{R}/\sqrt{X_1^2 + \ldots + X_m^2}$ (see page 234 of [Fishman 1996]). The primary advantage of stratifying on R^2 rather than Q is this direct method of sampling R^2 and then Z given R^2. However, stratifying on Q is typically more effective than stratifying on R^2.

We can use the delta-gamma approximation in a variety of ways to select an IS distribution. First, as in Section 2.4, we could apply the "most likely path" approach in which only the mean vector is changed. In this approach, we would solve the same optimization problem as in (2.18), except that the constraint is $\sum(b_i z_i + \lambda_i z_i^2) \geq y_x$ which is derived from the quadratic approximation rather than the linear (delta) approximation. The optimal mean vector now has the form $\mu_i = \beta b_i/(1 - 2\beta\lambda_i)$ for some normalization constant β. However, this approach will suffer from the same problem as that described in Section 2.4: poor results will be obtained unless the event $\{L > x\}$ is dominated by the point μ.

We now examine IS changes of measure in which both the mean and the covariance matrix of Z are changed. We restrict ourselves to a particular form of the mean and covariance matrix, which are arrived at by considering "exponential twisting" of the quadratic form Q. Such exponential twisting arises frequently in the study of rare events and associated IS procedures (see, e.g., [Bucklew 1990]). Let θ be a twisting parameter and define

$$B_\theta = (I - 2\theta\Lambda)^{-1} \qquad \text{and} \qquad \mu_\theta = \theta B_\theta b. \tag{2.19}$$

When IS is done by setting the mean vector to μ_θ and the covariance matrix to B_θ, then the likelihood ratio of (2.9) simplifies to

$$\ell(Z) = \exp\left\{-\theta(b'Z + Z'\Lambda Z') + \psi(\theta)\right\} = \exp\left\{-\theta Q + \psi(\theta)\right\} \tag{2.20}$$

where

$$\psi(\theta) = \frac{1}{2}\sum_{i=1}^m \left(\frac{(\theta b_i)^2}{1 - 2\theta\lambda_i} - \log(1 - 2\theta\lambda_i)\right) \tag{2.21}$$

is the logarithm of the moment generating function of the random variable Q. Notice that when importance sampling is done this way, the only random term in the likelihood ratio is Q. How should θ be chosen? Suppose that the delta-gamma approximation is exact. Then the per sample second moment of the estimator is

$$
\begin{aligned}
E_\theta[\ell(Z)^2 I(Q > y_x)] &= E_\theta[\exp(-2\theta Q + 2\psi(\theta))I(Q > y_x)] \\
&\leq \exp(-2\theta y_x + 2\psi(\theta))
\end{aligned} \tag{2.22}
$$

where E_θ denotes expectation under IS when the twisting parameter is θ. Picking $\theta = \theta_x$ to minimize the right side of (2.22) yields the best possible upper bound for the second moment (although not necessarily the smallest second moment). While there is no closed form expression for θ_x, it may be easily found by solving the non-linear equation $\psi'(\theta_x) = y_x$. (The function ψ is strictly convex with $|\psi'(\theta)| \to \infty$ as $|\theta|$ increases, ensuring that a unique solution exists and is easily found numerically.) With this value of θ_x, the mean of Q under IS is equal to y_x. Furthermore, as will be shown in a subsequent paper, selecting the twisting parameter in this fashion yields an "asymptotically optimal" IS technique as $x \to \infty$, provided the delta-gamma approximation is exact. Roughly speaking, "asymptotically optimal" means that the second moment goes to zero at twice the rate that the first moment goes to zero, which is the best possible rate since the variance is non-negative. Although simulation would not even be required if the delta-gamma approximation were exact, this analysis indicates that the IS procedure should be very effective in practice.

Let the λ_i's be ordered so that $\lambda_1 \geq \cdots \geq \lambda_m$. To avoid unininteresting cases, we assume $\lambda_1 > 0$. Then it may be shown that $0 < \theta_x < \lambda_1/2$. Under IS, the variance of Z_i is changed from 1 to $1/(1 - 2\theta_x\lambda_i)$. Therefore, if $\lambda_i > 0$, the variance of Z_i is increased, but if $\lambda_i < 0$, the variance of Z_i is decreased. Thus, under IS, stochastic variables that increase the quadratic part of delta-gamma are made more variable while those that decrease the quadratic part are made less variable.

Because the likelihood ratio takes the form $\ell(Z) = \exp(-\theta_x Q + \psi(\theta_x))$, stratification on the quadratic form Q is particularly attractive. It removes essentially all of the variability due to the likelihood ratio, and much of the variability in $I(L > x)$ provided the delta-gamma approximation (essentially Q) is close to the loss L.

Combining IS with stratification on Z_1 (or Z_1^2) or with radial stratification (on R^2) is also possible, although these methods are usually not as effective as stratification on Q. IS can also be combined with stratification on a linear combination of the Z's, most obviously upon $b'Z$.

Numerical Examples

We test the performance of some of the methods described above on a variety of portfolios. As in the previous examples, we mainly consider portfolios of options on ten underlying assets; the assets all have annual volatilities of 0.30, and in all but two cases we take them to be uncorrelated. Our experience (as well as some of the experiments in this paper) indicate that varying the covariance structure does not have a marked effect on the relative performance of the methods beyond the differences that can be observed by varying the structure of the portfolio; varying the portfolio makes the qualitative features more transparent. One of the correlated cases uses a covariance matrix of 10 international equity indices downloaded from the RiskMetrics^{TM} web site, but the others are purely hypothetical.

Table 2.3 shows results for the following portfolios:

1. *0.5yr ATM*: short ten at-the-money calls and five at-the-money puts on each asset, all options having a half-year maturity;

2. *0.1yr ATM*: same as previous but with maturity of 0.10 years;

3. *Delta hedged:* same as previous but with number of puts on each asset increased to result in a delta of zero;

4. *0.25yr OTM*: short ten calls struck at 110 and ten puts struck at 90, all expiring in 0.25 years;

5. *0.25yr ITM*: same as previous but with calls struck at 90, puts at 110;

6. *Large λ_1*: same as "Delta hedged" but with number of calls and puts on first asset increased by a factor of 10;

7. *Linear λ*: same as "Delta hedged" but with number of calls and puts on ith asset increased by a factor of i, $i = 1, \ldots, 10$;

8. *100, $\rho = 0.0$*: short ten at-the-money calls and ten at-the-money puts on 100 underlying assets, all options expiring in 0.10 years;

9. *100, $\rho = 0.2$*: same as previous but with correlations of distinct assets set to 0.20.

10. *Index*: short fifty at-the-money calls and fifty at-the-money puts on 10 underlying assets, all options expiring in 0.5 years. We use the covariance matrix in Table 2.2. The initial asset prices are taken as (100, 50, 30, 100, 80, 20, 50, 200, 150, 10).

The first two portfolios are similar to one considered in Section 2.4. Shortening the time to expiration as in the second portfolio increases the quadratic terms relative to the linear terms. In the third portfolio, the linear terms are eliminated completely. The next two are similar to the second portfolio but with all options out-of and in-the-money, respectively. The sixth portfolio has one dominant eigenvalue and the seventh portfolio has linearly increasing eigenvalues. The eighth and ninth portfolios are designed to test the effect of increasing the number of underlying assets. As mentioned before, the last portfolio is designed to test the effect of using a real covariance matrix.

Table 2.2
The covariance matrix used for Portfolio 10 (rounded to three decimal places).

$$
\begin{pmatrix}
0.289 & 0.069 & 0.008 & 0.069 & 0.084 & 0.085 & 0.081 & 0.052 & 0.075 & 0.114 \\
0.069 & 0.116 & 0.020 & 0.061 & 0.036 & 0.088 & 0.102 & 0.070 & 0.005 & 0.102 \\
0.008 & 0.020 & 0.022 & 0.013 & 0.009 & 0.016 & 0.019 & 0.016 & 0.010 & 0.017 \\
0.069 & 0.061 & 0.013 & 0.079 & 0.035 & 0.090 & 0.090 & 0.051 & 0.031 & 0.075 \\
0.084 & 0.036 & 0.009 & 0.035 & 0.067 & 0.055 & 0.049 & 0.029 & 0.022 & 0.062 \\
0.085 & 0.088 & 0.016 & 0.090 & 0.055 & 0.147 & 0.125 & 0.073 & 0.016 & 0.112 \\
0.081 & 0.102 & 0.019 & 0.090 & 0.049 & 0.125 & 0.158 & 0.087 & 0.016 & 0.127 \\
0.052 & 0.070 & 0.016 & 0.051 & 0.029 & 0.073 & 0.087 & 0.077 & 0.014 & 0.084 \\
0.075 & 0.005 & 0.010 & 0.031 & 0.022 & 0.016 & 0.016 & 0.014 & 0.143 & 0.033 \\
0.114 & 0.102 & 0.017 & 0.075 & 0.062 & 0.112 & 0.127 & 0.084 & 0.033 & 0.176
\end{pmatrix}
$$

Table 2.3 compares five methods in estimating loss probabilities over a 10-day horizon. Their performance is indicated by the variance ratios in the last five columns of the table: "δ-Γ CV" is the delta-gamma control variate, "IS" is importance sampling as described in (2.19)–(2.22), "ISS-Lin" combines IS with stratification along the eigenvector of the quadratic approximation associated with the largest eigenvalue, "ISS-Rad" combines IS with stratification of the radius R, "ISS-Q" combines IS with stratification of Q. (All the stratification methods use equiprobable strata and an equal number of samples per stratum.) Stratifying R is equivalent to stratifying Q when $b = 0$ and the λ_i are all equal (e.g., Portfolio 3); otherwise, it is a simple but potentially crude approximation to stratifying Q.

The results in Table 2.3 suggest some consistent patterns. At a loss probability near 5% the first four methods give broadly similar improvements, but as the loss probability decreases the effectiveness of the importance sampling and stratified sampling methods can increase dramatically whereas the control variate becomes less effective. In the presence of a strong linear component (especially the first portfolio) or a dominant eigenvalue (the sixth portfolio), linear stratification can produce substantial improvement beyond IS. When the quadratic terms dominate and are symmetric (as in the third and eighth portfolios), radial stratification provides substantial benefit. In the absence of symmetry in the quadratic terms (due to variations in the number of options in portfolios six and seven and due to correlation in the ninth portfolio), radial stratification is much less effective. Stratifying the approximation Q gives consistently impressive results and appears to be the best method overall, achieving the best variance reduction in all but one case. Finally, the eighth and ninth portfolios suggest that increasing the number of

Table 2.3
Comparison of variance reduction methods based on delta-gamma approximations. Variance ratios are estimated from 120,000 replications; the stratified estimator uses 40 strata and 3000 samples per strata. Variance ratios are estimates of the computational speed-up relative to standard Monte Carlo.

Portfolio	x_{std}	$P\{L > x\}$	δ-Γ CV	IS	ISS-Lin	ISS-Rad	ISS-Q
					Variance Ratios		
0.5yr ATM	1.65	5.3%	10.3	7.8	15.3	8.0	86.0
	2.5	1.0%	4.7	29.5	52.1	29.9	271.0
	2.8	0.5%	4.1	54.1	94.0	56.6	454.0
0.1yr ATM	1.75	5.0%	5.3	7.3	8.8	7.6	30.0
	2.6	1.1%	2.5	21.9	25.7	22.1	69.9
	3.3	0.3%	1.5	27.1	29.2	29.4	173.0
Delta hedged	1.9	4.7%	3.0	6.0	6.8	13.3	13.8
	2.8	1.1%	1.9	17.6	17.8	30.6	30.3
	3.2	0.5%	1.9	28.5	29.3	45.4	48.1
0.25yr OTM	2.7	1.1%	2.5	23.0	23.0	24.2	60.2
0.25yr ITM	2.7	1.1%	2.5	23.0	23.0	24.2	60.3
Large λ_1	3.5	1.2%	2.5	9.6	28.1	9.8	22.8
Linear λ	3.0	1.0%	2.1	17.3	18.3	17.9	29.2
100, $\rho = 0.0$	2.5	1.0%	2.6	26.9	27.7	43.5	45.4
100, $\rho = 0.2$	2.5	1.0%	2.0	10.3	20.5	10.3	23.4
Index	3.2	1.1%	3.1	18.3	54.0	18.3	119.0

underlying assets or risk factors does not in itself entail a loss of effectiveness of the methods.

2.6 Effective Allocation of Samples to Strata

Suppose there are k strata and a limit n on the total number of samples that can be drawn ($n = n_1 + \cdots + n_k$). As is well known, there is an easily derived optimal allocation of samples to strata: for equiprobable strata, the optimal n_i is proportional to σ_i, the standard deviation of a stratum i sample. Whereas our earlier experiments used a uniform allocation (i.e., equal n_i's), in this section we briefly explore what further gains can be obtained by using an optimal, or near optimal allocation $\{n_i\}$. We limit this study to two methods: stratification on Q with and without the asymptotically optimal IS (i.e., the mean and covariance are given by (2.19) with $\theta = \theta_x$). To estimate the appropriate σ_i's, pilot studies are performed (with and without IS, respectively). Then the portfolio is simulated using the estimated optimal allocations.

We experimented with these methods on Portfolio 10 of the last section. The pilot runs used 100 samples for each of the 40 strata. From these we estimated optimal allocations and then used these allocations for a full run of 120,000 samples for each case, as in the previous numerical results. Using the estimated optimal allocations without IS reduced variance by a factor of 70, compared with a factor of 119 reported for ISS-Q in Table 2.3. But using the estimated optimal allocations with IS reduced variance by a factor of 1397, about 12 times greater that that achieved with ISS-Q.

2.7 Summary

We have proposed a variety of ways of using delta-gamma approximations as a basis for variance reduction in Monte Carlo estimation of portfolio loss probabilities. The simplest of these methods uses the delta-gamma approximation as a control variate. Numerical results suggest, however, that far greater variance reduction can be achieved by using the delta-gamma approximation with importance sampling and stratified sampling. An exponential change of measure based on the delta-gamma approximation together with stratified sampling of the approximation appears to be especially effective.

References

Bucklew, J. A.. 1990. *Large Deviation Techniques in Decision, Simulation and Estimation.* John Wiley & Sons, Inc., New York.

Cárdenas, J., E. Fruchard, J.-F. Picron, C. Reyes, K. Walters, and W. Yang. 1999. Monte Carlo within a day. *Risk*, 12 (Feb):55 – 59.

Chen, J.-C., D. Lu, J. Sadowsky, and K.Yao. 1993. On importance sampling in digital communications - part i: Fundamentals. *IEEE J. Selected Areas in Communications*, 11:289 – 299.

Fishman, G. S.. 1996. *Monte Carlo Concepts, Algorithms, and Applications.* Springer, New York.

Glasserman, P., P. Heidelberger, and P. Shahabuddin. 1999a. Asymptotically optimal importance sampling and stratification for pricing path-dependent options. *Mathematical Finance*, 9:117–152.

Glasserman, P., P. Heidelberger, and P. Shahabuddin. 1999b. Importance sampling in the Heath-Jarrow-Morton framework. Technical report, IBM Research Report RC 21367, Yorktown Heights, NY.

Glasserman, P. and Y. Wang. 1997. Counterexamples in importance sampling for rare event probabilities. *The Annals of Applied Probability*, 7:731–746.

Hammersley, J. and D. Handscomb. 1964. *Monte Carlo Methods.* Methuen & Co., Ltd., London.

Heidelberger, P.. 1995. Fast simulation of rare events in queueing and reliability models. *ACM Transacations on Modeling and Computer Simulation*, 5:43 –85.

Imhof, J.. 1961. Computing the distribution of quadratic forms in normal variables. *Biometrika*, 48:419 – 426.

Jorion, P.. 1997. *Value at Risk: The New Benchmark for Controlling Derivatives Risk.* McGraw-Hill, New York.

Rouvinez, C.. 1997. Going Greek with VAR. *Risk*, 10 (Feb):57 – 65.

Wilson, T.. 1999. Value at risk. In Alexander, C., editor, *Risk Management and Analysis, Vol 1*, pages 61 – 124. Wiley, Chichester, England.

3   Confidence Intervals and Hypothesis Testing for the Sharpe and Treynor Performance Measures: A Bootstrap Approach

H. D. Vinod and Matthew R. Morey

The Sharpe (1966) and Treynor (1965) portfolio performance measures are widely cited and used in the literature and pedagogy of finance. However, due of the presence of random denominators in the definitions of the performance measures and the difficulty in determining the sample size needed to achieve asymptotic normality, they do not easily allow for the construction of confidence intervals and hypothesis testing. This paper uses the various forms of the bootstrap methodology including the single, studentized, and double bootstrap to construct confidence intervals and conduct hypothesis testing on these performance measures. This paper improves upon the previous efforts of Jobson and Korkie (1981) who use the delta method to develop hypothesis tests for these performance measures. We illustrate our methodology with several actual mutual funds.

3.1   Introduction

The Sharpe (1966) and Treynor (1965) portfolio performance measures are widely used and cited in the literature and pedagogy of finance. However, due of the presence of random denominators in their definitions and the difficulty in determining the sample size needed to achieve asymptotic normality, they do not easily allow for the construction of confidence intervals and hypothesis testing. This paper uses various forms of the bootstrap methodology including the single, studentized, and double bootstrap to construct confidence intervals and conduct hypothesis testing on these performance measures. In this way, the paper improves upon the previous efforts of Jobson and Korkie (JK) who use the delta method to develop hypothesis tests for these performance measures.

The paper is organized as follows. Section I of the paper discusses the Sharpe and Treynor measures and provides some motivation for the use of confidence intervals and hypothesis testing on the performance measures. Section II explains the bootstrap and then applies this methodology to constructing confidence intervals. Section III describes JK (1981) hypothesis testing approach and explains how our methodology improves upon their efforts. Section IV concludes the paper.

3.2   The Sharpe and Treynor Performance Measures

Consider the following scenario in which the relative performance of n portfolios is to be evaluated.[1] In this scenario, $r_{i,t}$ represents the excess return from the i-th

---

1. The notation in this section is the same as Jobson and Korkie (1981).

portfolio in period t, where $i = 1, 2, \ldots, n$. A random sample of T excess returns on the n portfolios is then illustrated by $r'_t = [r_{1t}, r_{2t}, \ldots r_{nt}]$, where $t = 1, 2, \ldots, T$ and where r_t is assumed to be multivariate normal random variable, with mean $\mu = \{\mu_i\}, = 1, 2, \ldots, n$ and a covariance matrix $\sum = (\sigma_{ij})$ where $i, j = 1, 2, \ldots n$. It is well-known that the unbiased estimators of the mean vector and the covariance matrix are

$$\bar{r} = \frac{1}{T} \sum_{t=1}^{T} r_t, \text{ and } S = \{s_{ij}\} \frac{1}{T-1} \sum_{t=1}^{T} (r_t - \bar{r})(r_t - \bar{r})'. \tag{3.1}$$

These two estimators are then used to form the estimators of the traditional Sharpe and Treynor performance measures.

The population value of the Sharpe (1966) performance measure for portfolio i is defined as $Sh_i = \frac{\mu_i}{\sigma_i}, i = 1, 2, \ldots, n$. It is simply the mean excess return over the standard deviation of the excess returns for the portfolio. The population value of the Treynor (1965) performance measure is $Tr = \frac{\mu_i \sigma_m^2}{\sigma_{im}}, i = 1, 2, \ldots, n$, where m is the market proxy portfolio often denoted by the Standard and Poor's 500 index (S&P 500) and is the familiar Beta from the Capital Asset Pricing Model (CAPM). The conventional sample-based point estimates of the Sharpe and Treynor performance measures used in (1) are then

$$\hat{Sh}_i = \frac{\bar{r}_i}{s_i} \text{ and } \hat{Tr}_i = \frac{\hat{r}_i s_m^2}{s_{im}} \text{ for } i = 1, 2, \ldots, n. \tag{3.2}$$

The Sharpe and Treynor measures do not permit small-sample confidence intervals, because of the presence of s_i, s_n in their definitions of (2). Moreover, the sample size needed achieve asymptotic normality is difficult to determine.

Despite this difficulty, the ability to construct confidence intervals on these performance measures is valuable. A confidence interval provides additional information for comparing portfolios. For example, consider an investor who uses the Sharpe measure to evaluate portfolios. Such an investor will identify two different portfolios as having very similar performance, because they have similar Sharpe point estimates. However, such an appraisal does not at all consider the range of uncertainty behind these point estimates; one portfolio may have a very narrow confidence interval on its Sharpe measure while the other has a wide confidence interval. Such knowledge, may sway an investor to prefer the portfolio with the shorter interval.

Furthermore, there is a possibly serious problem with the use of the Sharpe and Treynor measures in cases of sampling in a bear market.[2] For example, if we are comparing portfolios, the following scenario can arise. A portfolio which has a higher risk and a more negative return can have a higher Sharpe measure than a portfolio which has a lower risk and a higher (but still negative) mean return. Due to the possibility of such results occurring, confidence intervals and hypothesis testing have further merit, as they clarify the situation and allow for a rational comparison of portfolios despite perverse ranking by point estimates.

3.3   Creating Confidence Intervals using the Bootstrap

A confidence interval around a population parameter is a well-known method of statistical inference. Traditional small-sample parametric confidence intervals start with the assumption that the sampling distribution of the test statistic is normal, at least asymptotically. However, since the small-sample sampling distributions of the Sharpe and Treynor measures are non-normal in that they have significant skewness and kurtosis, the usual method based on ratio of the statistic to its standard errors is biased and unreliable. Various bootstrap resampling techniques can help solve the non-normality problem. These techniques have only recently become available due to declining costs of computing. For a survey of the bootstrap literature see Davison and Hinkley (1997) and Vinod (1993).

To understand the basic idea behind the bootstrap consider the following. Consider a statistic $\hat{B}$, based on a sample of size, T. In the bootstrap methodology, instead of assuming the shape of the sampling distribution of $\hat{B}$, one empirically approximates the entire sampling distribution of $\hat{B}$ by investigating the variation of $\hat{B}$ over a large number of pseudo samples obtained by resampling. For the resampling, a Monte-Carlo type procedure is used on the available sample values. This is conducted by randomly drawing, with replacement, a large number of resamples of size T from the original sample. Each resample has T elements, however any given resample could have some of the original data points represented more than once and some not at all. Note that each element of the original sample has the same probability, $(1/T)$, of being in a sample. The initial idea behind bootstrapping was that a relative frequency distribution of $\hat{B}$'s calculated from the resamples can be a good approximation to the sampling distribution of $\hat{B}$. This idea has since been

---

2. Jobson and Korkie (1981) p. 891, also make this point.

extended to achieve better approximations and to conditional models and one-step conditional moments.[3]

In this paper we use three variations of the bootstrap to arrive at confidence intervals for the Sharpe and Treynor performance measures. These are the single bootstrap (s-boot), the studentized bootstrap (boot-t) and the double bootstrap (d-boot). Efron's original bootstrap, described in numerous journal articles and econometrics textbooks, is called the s-boot here.[4]

In terms of the s-boot, the resampling for the Sharpe measure is done "with replacement" of the original excess returns themselves for $j = 1, 2, \ldots, J$ or 999 times. Thus we calculate 999 Sharpe measures from the original excess return series. The choice of the odd number 999 is convenient, since the rank-ordered 25-th and 975-th values of estimated Sharpe ratios arranged from the smallest to the largest, yield a useful s-boot 95% confidence interval.

For the Treynor measure we obtain J estimates of the numerator μ, similar to the Sharpe measure described above. However, the denominator is the Beta estimated by the regression of $R_i = \alpha_i + \beta_i R_m + e_i$, where R_i is the portfolio return and R_m is the market return (we use the S&P500 index returns as the market proxy). Hence the s-boot for the Treynor measure needs resampling of the residuals of the above regression $J(= 999)$ times. Replacing the original residuals by the resampled residuals, keeping the original ordinary least squares (OLS) estimates of intercept, slope coefficients, and using the same right hand side regressors, yields J versions of the dependent variable. The procedure then creates J separate regression problems for which the intercept and slopes can be again estimated, as explained in Judge et al (1988). These J estimates of Beta yield the J denominators of the Treynor measures. Again we rank-order these measures from the smallest to the largest and choose the 25-th and 975-th order statistics to yield the simple s-boot 95% confidence interval.

Unfortunately, a typical 95% s-boot confidence interval for non-standard sample statistics similar to (2) may not cover the true parameter with the coverage probability of 0.95. Consider a standard statistic similar to the sample mean or a regression coefficient b, which estimates β with the standard error S. Now the quantity $q = (b - \beta)/S$ is pivotal in the sense that its distribution does not depend on β.

---

3. For example, let b* denote resampled regression coefficients, b the original coefficients, and the unknown parameters. The extended bootstrap approximates the properties of (b*) by the observable (b*−b). See Davison and Hinkley (1997) for recent references and Vinod (1993) for references to earlier attempts.

4. Judge et al (1988, p.416) or Greene (1997, p.184).

Under normality of regression errors, q has the well-known t-distribution leading to the usual confidence intervals. If we wish to relax the normality assumption, simple s-boot can provide good confidence intervals that are first-order correct, i.e., correct to order $(1/\sqrt{T})$ when T is the sample size. For further improvements, especially for non-standard statistics similar to (2), bootstrap theory suggests that a 95% s-boot confidence interval may need further adjustments to make sure that it covers the unknown parameter with the correct coverage probability of 0.95

One such adjustment called studentized bootstrap (boot-t) has been developed.[5] It is implemented as follows. The first step is to convert the $J = 999$ s-boot values into a studentized scale by subtracting the mean and dividing by the standard deviation of the J resampled values. Next, we select the 25-th and 975-th ordered values from the studentized transformed scale. Finally, we undo the studentization by multiplying 25-th and 975-th values by the standard deviation and adding the mean. Davison and Hinkley (1997, p. 212) offer an elegant proof that the boot-t is second-order correct, in the sense that the error in coverage by the estimated confidence interval of the true parameter is of order $(1/T)$. This second-order accuracy result depends on availability of a reliable estimate of the standard deviation used as the denominator of the studentization transformation.

Another method of improving the coverage probability of confidence intervals for nonstandard statistics similar to those in (2) is bootstrapping the bootstrap, or d-boot.[6] The d-boot involves K further replications of each $j = 1, 2, \ldots J$. We choose $K = 174$ replications based on optimal choice suggested in the literature and described in McCullough and Vinod (1998) who give a step-by-step description of the d-boot. Clearly, the d-boot is computationally intensive, since it will require 174 times 999 computations of the underlying statistic; indeed a supercomputer may be needed to study the properties of d-boot by simulation.[7]

Roughly speaking, the method used in the d-boot is the following. If the original estimate is $\hat{\theta}$ and the single bootstrap estimate is denoted by θ_j we resample each $\theta_j K$ times and denote the resampled estimates as θ_{jk}. One keeps track of the proportion of times θ_{jk} is less than or equal to $\hat{\theta}$. The theory of d-boot proves that under ideal conditions, the probability distribution of the proportions in which θ_{jk} is less than or equal to $\hat{\theta}$ must be a uniform random variable. The appeal of the double

---

5. An excellent up-to-date description of the related theory with examples is given in Davison and Hinkley (1997).

6. Vinod (1995) is one of the first applications of d-boot in econometrics.

7. Letson and McCullough (1998) have implemented such a simulation and shown its superiority. Vinod (1998) also uses d-boot for refined inference.

bootstrap method is that when conditions are not ideal, the resulting non-uniform distribution remains easy to handle. All that happens is that the probabilities 0.025 and 0.975 occur at some nearby numbers (0.028 and 0.977, say). For adjusting the s-boot confidence interval the d-boot involves choosing the nearby (e.g., 28-th and 977-th) order statistics instead of the 25-th and 975-th values indicated by s-boot. The point in using the d-boot is that one does not need to try to know the form of the non-normal sampling distribution of the statistic. In fact the distribution need not have any known form. The statistics based on (2) may not have any known form when the normality assumption is relaxed.

We now turn to an application of our approach where we examine the confidence intervals on the Sharpe and Treynor performance measures for several well-known mutual funds. In order to illustrate the usefulness of the procedure we examine the confidence intervals of similarly rated funds. Hence, we use two sets of "growth" mutual funds for our data.[8] Our first set is made from two mutual funds, the Fidelity Magellan and The Neuberger/Berman Partners, which have similar Sharpe measures. Our second set also has two funds, Putnam Vista and Elfun Trust, which have similar Treynor measures. Excess monthly returns for the funds were calculated by subtracting the monthly three-month T-Bill rates of returns from the monthly mutual fund returns. The data spans from January 1978 to December 1997 (240 monthly observations) and is taken from the Morningstar Principia program.

3.3.1 The Sharpe Measure

Table 1 reports estimates of the mean monthly excess returns, $\bar{r}_i$; standard deviation of the excess monthly returns, s_i; the Sharpe measure point estimates, $\hat{Sh}_i$; and the confidence intervals for the three bootstrap methods for the of the first set of funds (Fidelity Magellan and Neuberger/Berman Partner). On the basis of the Sharpe measure, the Fidelity Magellan Fund performance would be ranked just slightly higher than the Neuberger/Berman Fund. In terms of confidence intervals, the two funds have similar 95 percent confidence interval widths for both the single bootstrap and studentized bootstrap approaches. Only with the double bootstrap is a considerable difference revealed: the confidence interval width of the Neuberger/Berman Fund is twenty percent larger than the Magellan fund. Hence, the Magellan fund not only has a higher performance measure, but also we can be slightly more confident in the accuracy of this point estimate.

---

8. We follow Morningstar's (1998) definition of a growth fund.

Table 3.1
Confidence Intervals (C.I.) for the Sharpe Performance Measure

Sharpe Performance Measures			
Fund Name	$\bar{r}_i$	s_i	$\hat{S}h_i$
Fidelity Magellan	1.3868	5.4104	0.2563
Neuberger/Berman Partners	0.8727	3.7414	0.2333
Single Bootstrap Confidence Intervals			
Fund Name	$\hat{S}h_i$	C. I.	Interval Width
Fidelity Magellan	0.2563	(0.1212, 0.4135)	0.2923
Neuberger/Berman Partners	0.2333	(0.0995, 0.3824)	0.2829
Studentized Bootstrap Confidence Intervals			
Fund Name	$\hat{S}h_i$	C.I.	Interval Width
Fidelity Magellan	0.2563	(0.1045, 0.3968)	0.2923
Neuberger/Berman Partners	0.2333	(0.0883, 0.3711)	0.2829
Double Bootstrap Confidence Intervals			
Fund Name	$\hat{S}h_i$	C.I.	Interval Width
Fidelity Magellan	0.2563	(0.2421,0.2654)	0.0233
Neuberger/Berman Partners	0.2333	(0.2174, 0.2454)	0.0280

3.3.2   The Treynor Measure

For the Treynor measure we run the following regression $R_{i,t} - R_{f,t} = \alpha_i + \beta_i (R_{m,t} - R_{f,t}) + \varepsilon_t$, where $R_{i,t}$ are the monthly returns of the mutual fund, $R_{f,t}$ are the 3-month T-Bill rates, and $R_{m,t}$ is the S&P 500 monthly returns. Table 2 lists the mean excess returns, standard deviations, results of the regressions, Treynor measures, $\hat{T}r_i$, and confidence intervals for the Putnam Vista and Elfun Trust Funds. The results show that the despite its slightly lower Treynor measure, the Elfun Trusts fund has a much narrower confidence interval width than the Putnam Vista Fund; the Putnam Vista interval width is 75 percent larger than the Elfun Trust fund. Such information, if available to the investor, can help them better determine the relative performances of various portfolios.[9]

3.4   Hypothesis Testing

The bootstrap approach on the Sharpe and Treynor measures can also, of course, be used for hypothesis testing. In this section of the paper we discuss JK's (1981) efforts

---

9. An analytic approach to generating confidence intervals has been developed by Morey and Morey (1999).

Table 3.2
Confidence Intervals (C.I.) for the Treynor Performance Measure

Descriptive Statistics		
Fund Name	$\bar{r}_i$	s_i
Putnam Vista	0.9095	4.9465
Elfun Trust	0.8224	4.1833
Regression Analysis		

Results from running $R_{i,t} - R_{f,t} = \alpha_i + \beta_i(R_{m,t} - R_{f,t}) + \varepsilon_t$. The standard errors are in parenthesis; a * indicates the variable is significantly different from zero at the 5 percent level of significance.

Fund Name	$\hat{\alpha}_i$	$\hat{\beta}_i$	R^2
Putnam Vista	0.1284	1.0329*	0.7937
	(0.1476)	(0.0341)	
Elfun Trust	0.1071	0.9460*	0.9307
	(0.0723)	(0.0167)	

Single Bootstrap Confidence Intervals			
Fund Name	$\hat{Tr}_i$	C.I.	Interval Width
Putnam Vista	0.8805	(0.6076, 1.1567)	0.5491
Elfun Trust	0.8693	(0.7266, 1.0264)	0.2998

Studentized Bootstrap Confidence Intervals			
Fund Name	$\hat{Tr}_i$	C.I.	Interval Width
Putnam Vista	0.8805	(0.5961, 1.1452)	0.5491
Elfun Trust	0.8693	(0.7193, 1.0191)	0.2998

Double Bootstrap Confidence Intervals			
Fund Name	$\hat{Tr}_i$	C.I.	Interval Width
Putnam Vista	0.8805	(0.8488, 0.8987)	0.0499
Elfun Trust	0.8693	(0.8573, 0.8858)	0.0285

to conduct hypothesis testing and then use the bootstrap to develop a hypothesis testing approach which improves upon their efforts.

JK (1981) developed hypothesis tests for whether one portfolio's performance measure is significantly different from another portfolio.[10] Their hypothesis test is not for the actual differences in the performance measures of the two portfolios, but for a certain transformation of the differences. The transformation is needed

---

10. Jobson and Korkie (1981) also develop a test statistic that examines multi-comparisons of one portfolio to many others. For the multiple comparison measure, a chi-square statistic is developed for a transformation of both performance measures. They found that the Sharpe multi-comparison measure was well behaved and that its power to detect differences increased as the number of portfolios increased. The Treynor multi-comparison measure, on the other hand, was not well behaved and, in general, Jobson and Korkie did not recommend its use. Moreover, Cadsby (1986) states that these have low power. Since the focus of our research is only on the single comparison method, we do not address multi-comparisons, although an extension from a comparison of two funds is quite feasible.

because of random denominators in the original performance measures. They then derive the asymptotic distribution and approximate bias of the estimators of the transformed difference using a Taylor series expansion. This method, known in the statistics literature the delta method, requires that the original random variable should be normally distributed.[11] It should be noted that to use the delta method on the transformed performance measures, JK (1981) implicitly assume Taylor series regularity conditions, which state that ignoring higher order terms is appropriate. These regularity conditions are not always satisfied. For example, when random denominators are close to zero, the ratios diverge, and the higher order Taylor series terms also diverge. We now summarize their approach.

For two portfolios, k and n, they examine the following hypotheses:

$$H_{OS} : Sh_k - Sh_n = 0, \tag{3.3}$$
$$H_{OT} : Tr_k - Tr_n = 0 \tag{3.4}$$

Since the sampling behavior of these differences is nonstandard, they use the transformed F(.) differences for the sample differences in the hope of finding better behaved statistics. The transformations used by JK (1981) are:

$$F(\hat{Sh}_{kn}) = s_n \bar{r}_k - s_k \bar{r}_k, \text{ and} \tag{3.5}$$
$$F(\hat{Tr}_{kn}) = \frac{s_{nm} \bar{r}_k}{s_m^2} - \frac{s_{km} \bar{r}_n}{s_m^2} \tag{3.6}$$

Note that (4a) is obtained from (3a) by multiplying through by $s_k s_n$. Also note that, when the null hypothesis is true, this multiplication makes no difference. However, when the alternative hypothesis is true, the difference in (3a) is a random variable and can assume any value. When we accept the null, we permit the random variable to assume all statistically insignificant values near zero. The power of the test depends on its performance for such departures from the null (e.g., 0.0001 instead of 0). The equivalence of (3a) and (3b) with (4a) and (4b), respectively, depends on the numerical magnitudes of variances and covariances and may be seriously compromised, especially in small samples. For example, zero times a large product of standard deviations $s_k s_n$ can be ignored, but 0.0001 times $s_k s_n$ may well be large. A truly equivalent test should maintain both the size and the power of the original test. Since the multiplication by $s_k s_n$ changes the value of the statistic under alternative hypothesis, we assert that JK's tests based on (4a) and (4b) are not truly equivalent to the tests for (3a) an (3b). Hence, it does change the

---

11. For more on the delta method see Greene (1997, p.278).

power. Clearly, one needs regularity conditions which do not permit the random denominators to become zero.

JK (1981) constructed the means and standard errors for their test statistics (4a) and (4b) by using Taylor series approximations to order $\frac{1}{T^2}$. The means (expectations) of the transformed differences in (4a) and (4b) are

$$E(F(\hat{Sh}_{kn})) \equiv (\sigma_n \mu_k - \sigma_k \mu_n)\left(1 - \frac{1}{4T} + \frac{1}{32T^2}\right) \text{ and} \tag{3.7}$$

$$E(F(\hat{Tr}_{kn})) = \left(\frac{\sigma_{nm}}{\sigma_m^2} - \frac{\sigma_{km}}{\sigma_m^2}\mu_n\right) \tag{3.8}$$

The mean and variance of asymptotic distributions of the transformed difference statistics are then defined. For the Sharpe transformed difference, the asymptotic distribution is approximately normal with the mean from (5a) and variance given by

$$\theta = \frac{1}{T}\left[2\sigma_l^2\sigma_n^2 - 2\sigma_k\sigma_n\sigma_{kn} + \frac{1}{2}\,mu_k^2\sigma_n^2 + \frac{1}{2}\mu_n^2 - \frac{\mu_k\mu_n}{2\sigma_k\sigma_n}(\sigma_{kn}^2 + \sigma_k^2\sigma_n^2)\right] \tag{3.9}$$

Since the expectation (5a) does not equal the population value, the sample statistic (4a) is biased. For the transformed Treynor difference, the asymptotic distribution is approximately normal with the mean equal to $F(Tr_{kn})$, i.e. (5b), and variance given by

$$\begin{aligned}\psi \;=\; & \frac{1}{T\sigma_m^2}\left[\sigma_k^2\sigma_{nm}^2 + \sigma_n^2\sigma_{km}^2 - 2\sigma_{km}\sigma_{kn} + \mu_k^2(\sigma_n^2\sigma_m^2 - \sigma_{nm}^2)\right.\\ & \left.+\mu_n^2(\sigma_l^2\sigma_m^2 - \sigma_{km}^2) - 2\mu_k\mu_n(\sigma_m^2 - \sigma_{km}\sigma_{nm})\right]\end{aligned} \tag{3.10}$$

Following Cadsby (1986) we have corrected an error in the original version of (7). Note that equations (6) and (7) involve unknown population means, variances and covariances. Estimators denoted by $\hat{\theta}$ and $\hat{\psi}$ are obtained by substituting sample estimators of means, variances and covariances.

Assuming asymptotic normality of $F(\hat{Sh})$ and $F(\hat{Tr})$ the test statistics on the null hypotheses: $H_{OS} = Sh_{kn} = 0$, and $H_{OT} = 0$ are then:

$$A_{Skn} = \frac{F(\hat{Sh}_{kn})}{\sqrt{\hat{\theta}}} \tag{3.11}$$

or

$$Z_{Tkn} = \frac{F(\hat{Tr}_{kn})}{\sqrt{\hat{\psi}}} \tag{3.12}$$

In examining the distributions of these Z statistics, JK (1981) found that the Sharpe Z statistic (8a) was well behaved at small sample sizes. However, the Treynor measure (8b), was not well behaved. Additionally, in both the Sharpe and Treynor cases, they found that the power in detecting differences between portfolios was small.

Our approach is as follows. Instead of using a Taylor series (delta method) approximation to compute the standard errors, we use the bootstrap to conduct hypothesis testing. The advantages of the bootstrap over the JK method are twofold. One, our methodology considers the sampling distribution of the actual difference between Sharpe and Treynor performance measures themselves. By contrast, JK provide the expected value and a standard error for a transformed quantity: $F(\hat{Sh}_{kn}) = s_n \bar{r}_k - s_k \bar{r}_k$. Again, the reason why these authors used the transformation was that sampling properties of the original difference are not tractable by the Taylor series methods and the results are unstable and unreliable. The second advantage of our methods is that the bootstraps are robust or distribution-free. In other words, the assumption of normality, which is clearly invalid in our small sample case with a random denominator, is avoided.

To illustrate the bootstrap approach for hypothesis testing we use the same two sets of funds used in the confidence interval approach plus a third set, the Fidelity Magellan Fund and the Rainbow Fund.[12] This additional set allows a clear illustration of two funds which have significantly different performance measures using the bootstrap yet are not considered to be significantly different under the JK (1981) approach.

Table 3 shows, for both fund sets 1 and 3, the Sharpe measures and the difference in the two fund's Sharpe measures. Also, the table presents the 95 percent confidence intervals of the Sharpe measure differences for the single, studentized and double bootstrap methods, and the transformed Sharpe difference and corresponding confidence intervals using the JK approach. If the confidence interval of the difference does not contain zero, it indicates that there is a significant difference in the performance measures of the two funds.

The two sets of funds in Table 3 show some interesting results. The difference between the Sharpe measures of the Fidelity Magellan/Neuberger Berman Partners is quite small and accordingly the JK (1981), single and studentized bootstrap show no significant difference. The double bootstrap on the other hand, with its increased precision (see Letson and McCullough (1998)), does show a significant difference

---

12. The data period for the Rainbow fund is the same as the other funds and the excess returns are calculated by subtracting the three-month T-Bill rates.

Table 3.3
Hypothesis Testing for the Sharpe Performance Measure

Two sets of funds presented: Set 1: Fidelity Magellan versus Neuberger/Berman Partners. Set 2: Fidelity Magellan versus Rainbow.

Data Period: January 1978 to December 1997. Frequency: Monthly.

Set 1: Fidelity Magellan against Neuberger/Berman Partners

Fund Name	Sharpe Measure
Fidelity Magellan	0.2563
Neuberger/Berman Partners	0.2333
Difference	0.0230

Bootstrap Method	Confidence Interval of the Difference in the Sharpe Measures
Single Bootstrap	(-0.1878, 0.2352)
Studentized Bootstrap	(-0.1878, 0.2351)
Double Bootstrap	(0.0008, 0.0422)*

Jobson and Korkie (1981)

Transformed Difference of the Sharpe Measures of the two funds: -0.4671
Confidence Interval of the Transformed Difference: $(-0.6334, 1.5675)$

Set 2: Fidelity Magellan against Rainbow

Fund Name	Sharpe Measure
Fidelity Magellan	0.2563
Rainbow	0.0404
Difference	0.2159

Bootstrap Method	Confidence Interval of the Difference in the Sharpe Measures
Single Bootstrap	(0.0240, 0.4189)*
Studentized Bootstrap	(0.0107, 0.4056)*
Double Bootstrap	(0.1911, 0.2296)*

Jobson and Korkie (1981)

Transformed Difference of the Sharpe Measures of the two funds: 5.6879
Confidence Interval of the Transformed Difference: (3.5283, 7.8475)*

* indicates the two funds are significantly different from each other

between the two funds. For the Fidelity Magellan/Rainbow set, which is located in the lower part of Table 3, the difference between the Sharpe measures is quite large. Correspondingly, there is a significant difference found in all of the forms of the bootstrap and in the JK (1981) approach as none of the confidence intervals contain zero.

Table 4 presents the 95 percent confidence intervals of the Treynor measure differences for JK (1981), single bootstrap, studentized bootstrap and double bootstrap methods. The results for the first set of funds—the set of funds which have similar Treynor measures—show that all 4 methods show no significant difference in the

Table 3.4
Hypothesis Testing for Treynor Performance Measure

Two sets of funds presented: Set 1: Putnam Vista versus Elfun Trust. Set 2: Fidelity Magellan versus Rainbow.

Data Period: January 1978 to December 1997. Frequency: Monthly.

Set 1: Putnam Vista and Elfun Trust

Fund Name	Treynor Measure
Putnam Vista	0.8805
Elfun Trust	0.8693
Difference	0.0112

Bootstrap Method	Confidence Interval of the Difference in the Treynor Measures
Single Bootstrap	$(-0.3166, 0.3511)$
Studentized Bootstrap	$(-0.3440, 0.3238)$
Double Bootstrap	$(-0.0297, 0.0253)$

Jobson and Korkie (1981)

Transformed Difference of the Treynor Measures of the two funds: -0.2631
Confidence Interval of the Transformed Difference: $(-14.162, 13.637)$

Set 2: Fidelity Magellan and Rainbow

Fund Name	Treynor Measure
Fidelity Magellan	1.2065
Rainbow	0.2212
Difference	0.9853

Method	Confidence Interval of the Difference in the Treynor Measures
Single Bootstrap	$(0.4861, 1.4709)$ [13]
Studentized Bootstrap	$(0.4929, 1.4779)$ [14]
Double Bootstrap	$(0.9267, 1.0462)$ [15]

Jobson and Korkie (1981)

Transformed Difference of the Treynor Measures of the two funds: 5.6820
Confidence Interval of the Transformed Difference: $(-17.967, 29.259)$

* indicates the two funds are significantly different from each other

Treynor values of the two funds. For the other set, Fidelity Magellan/Rainbow, all forms of the bootstrap method illustrate a significantly difference. The JK approach, however, indicates that there is no significant difference between the two funds; an extremely unsatisfactory result given the Fidelity Magellan Treynor measure is about 5 times the level of the Rainbow fund. The fact that bootstrap approach works relatively well for the Treynor performance measure is not surprising, since Jobson and Korkie's method is admittedly not well behaved for the Treynor measure.

3.5   Concluding Remarks

This paper has used the bootstrap methodology to construct confidence intervals and conduct hypothesis testing on the well-known Sharpe and Treynor portfolio performance measures. Due of the presence of random denominators in the definitions of the performance measures, and the difficulty in determining the sample size needed to achieve asymptotic normality, the Sharpe and Treynor performance measures have not allowed for the construction of confidence intervals. With this paper, however, we show that the bootstrap methodology can build confidence intervals around the point estimates of these measures, allowing investors further information on the performance of their portfolios. We have illustrated the use of the single, studentized and double bootstrap by constructing confidence intervals on the Sharpe and Treynor measures of several actual growth mutual funds.

The bootstrap methodology also allows for simple hypothesis testing for comparing one portfolio's Sharpe or Treynor measure against another portfolio. Since the bootstrap is largely distribution-free and requires no transformation of the difference of the performance measures of the two funds, the paper extends and improves upon the efforts of Jobson and Korkie (1981).

References

Cadsby, C. B., 1986, "Performance Hypothesis Testing with the Sharpe and Treynor Measures: A Comment," *Journal of Finance*, 41, no. 5, 1175–1176.

Davison, A. C. and D. V. Hinkley, 1997, *Bootstrap Methods and Their Applications*, New York: Cambridge University Press.

Greene, W. H., 1997, *Econometric Analysis*, 3rd ed., Upper Saddle River, NJ: Prentice Hall.

Jobson, J.D. and B.M. Korkie, 1981, "Performance Hypothesis Testing with the Sharpe and Treynor Measures," *Journal of Finance*, 36, no. 4, 889–908.

Judge, G. G., R.C. Hill, W. E. Griffiths, H. Lutkepohl and T-C Lee (1988) *Introduction to the Theory and Practice of Econometrics*. New York: Wiley.

Letson, David and B. D. McCullough, 1998, "Better Confidence Intervals: The Double Bootstrap with No Pivot," *American Journal of Agricultural Economics*, 80, 552–559.

McCullough B. D. and H. D. Vinod, 1998, "Implementing the Double Bootstrap," *Computational Economics*, 12, 79–95.

Morey, Matthew R. and Richard C. Morey, 1999, "An Analytical Confidence Interval for the Treynor Index: Formula, Conditions and Properties," *Journal of Business Finance and Accounting*, forthcoming.

Morningstar Principia Manual, Chicago, IL, 1998.

Roy S.N. and R.F. Potthoff, 1958, "Confidence Bounds on Vector Analogues of the 'Ratios of Means' and the 'Ratio of Variances' for Two Correlated Normal Variates and Some Associated Tests," *Annals of Mathematical Statistics*, vol. 29, 829–841.

Sharpe, W. F., 1966, "Mutual Fund Performance," *Journal of Business*, vol. 39, No. 1, Part 2, January, 119–138.

Treynor, J. L. , 1965, "How to Rate Management of Investment Funds," *Harvard Business Review*, vol. 43, January-February, 63–75.

Vinod, H. D., 1993, "Bootstrap, jackknife resampling and simulation: applications in econometrics," in G.S. Maddala, C.R. Rao, and H.D. Vinod (eds.), *Handbook of Statistics: Econometrics*, 11, 629–661, New York: North Holland.

Vinod, H. D., 1995, "Double bootstrap for shrinkage estimators", *Journal of Econometrics*, 68, 287–302.

Vinod, H. D., 1998, "Foundations of statistical inference based on numerical roots of robust pivot functions (Fellow's Corner)", *Journal of Econometrics*, 86, 387–396.

4   Conditional Value at Risk

Dirk Ormoneit and Ralph Neuneier

We suggest a new methodology to overcome several well-known deficiencies of Value at Risk computations. Our approach mainly addresses two aspects of Value at Risk: first, to avoid potentially disastrous clustering in predicted tail events we derive a new approach to accurately estimating the *conditional* distribution of asset returns using maximum entropy densities. Second, by the very nature of the maximum entropy model, we account for negative skewness and fat tails in asset returns. In particular, to obtain a robust and scalable estimate of the covariance matrix of the assets in the portfolio we extend an approach by Hull and White to the case of conditional distributions. In experiments with historical stock index data we compare the proposed methodology to alternative estimation approaches using a new, simulation-based statistical testing procedure for serial dependence in the predicted tail events.

4.1   Introduction

As value at risk ("VaR") has emerged as the dominant measure of market risk implied by a portfolio over the past years, extensive research both within academia and within the financial industry has recently focussed on effective and reliable algorithms to compute the VaR of complicated portfolios. Probably the most influential contribution in this field has been J.P. Morgan's RiskMetrics^{TM} methodology, within which a multivariate normal distribution is employed to model the joint distribution of the assets in a portfolio [Morgan 1996]. While this approach is doubtlessly appealing for its straightforwardness and computational simplicity, several authors have found that the observed frequency of extreme market movements is frequently higher than predicted by RiskMetrics (see, for example, [HullWhite 1998], Exhibit 3). Obvious explanations for this finding are negative skewness and excess kurtosis ("fat tails") in the true distribution of market returns, which cannot be accounted for using a normal density model as in RiskMetrics.

Hull and White suggest a robust and scalable approach to deal with the problem of non-normality by estimating the covariance matrix in a suitably transformed space within which the asset returns are jointly normal distributed [HullWhite 1998]. Within this work, we extend their approach to account for potentially disastrous serial dependency in the asset returns. The basic idea is that if Value at Risk is estimated based on the unconditional distribution of portfolio returns, such as in the case of historical simulations or in Hull and White's approach, the predicted tail

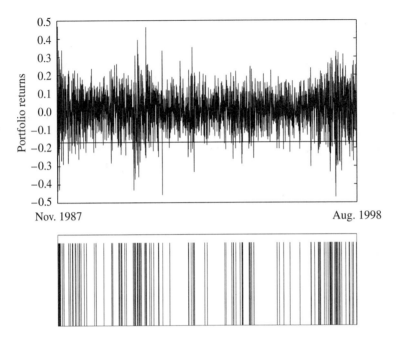

Figure 4.1
Daily unconditional VaR forecast for a sample portfolio consisting of the DAX, the DJIA, and the FTSE in the period from November 1987 to August 1998. The lower part shows an indicator variable that takes on the value one if the observed return is below the forecast.

events will typically reveal undesired serial dependency due to volatility clusters in the asset returns. An example of an unconditional VaR forecast for a sample portfolio consisting of several stock indices is shown in Figure 4.1. Note that the sequence of indicator variables for the predicted extreme events in the lower part of the figure is not independent but contains several clusters. These clusters are highly undesirable as they lead to larger reserve requirements than a sequence of independent events with equal probability. Put simply, extreme events should be equally surprising at each date because information on an increased risk level from previous observations should be reflected by a consequently lower VaR forecast. A straightforward way to avoid serial dependency in the predicted events is thus to base one's forecast on the *conditional* distribution of the portfolio returns given past information as it is shown in Figure 4.2. The conditional VaR forecast, indicated by the solid line, continually adapts in response to the prevailing market volatility in this case and consequently generates an indicator sequence with considerably less

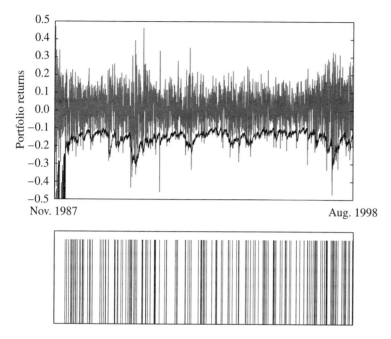

Figure 4.2
Daily conditional VaR forecast for the sample portfolio. The sequence of indicator variables in the lower part shows less serial dependency than in the case of the unconditional VaR forecast.

dependency. To obtain this forecast, we construct transformations of the individual asset returns to a normalized space within which the returns are jointly normal distributed *and serially independent* using an estimate of the conditional distribution of returns. As a consequence, the covariance matrix characterizing the interaction between the asset returns may be treated as stationary in the transformed space which greatly simplifies its estimation. In particular, to estimate the conditional distributions we use a mixture approach that separately accounts for short-term and long-term dependencies in the asset returns. By using a maximum entropy density to model the long-term dependencies, we explicitly account for negative skewness and excess kurtosis.

The organization of the remainder of this work is as follows. In Section 4.2 we introduce our notation as well as the mixture approach to estimating the conditional density of returns. In Section 4.3 we discuss our extension of Hull and White's forecasting method based on transformations. In Section 4.4 we apply the new method to evaluate the risk of a sample portfolio and present a new statistical test procedure to detect serial dependency in the predicted tail events. Section 4.5 summarizes our results and presents final remarks.

4.2   Conditional Density Filtration

Consider a portfolio Π consisting of the (possibly time-varying) positions $a_t = (a_{t,1}, \ldots, a_{t,N})'$ in N risky assets during the times $t = 0, \ldots, T$. Our focus is on assessing the risk associated with holding Π over some time period, say from $t-1$ to t. Formally, this risk is completely characterized by the probability distribution of the proportional price changes R_t of Π during this period, defined as

$$R_t = \sum_{i=1}^{n} a_{t,i} \frac{s_{t,i}}{s_{t-1,i}}. \tag{4.1}$$

Here $s_{t,i}$ denotes the price of asset i at time t and $s_{t,i}/s_{t-1,i}$ is the proportional price change of asset i. Value at risk is concerned with estimating the unknown probability distribution of R_t and evaluating that quantile of this distribution which corresponds to some specified probability α. In the simplest case it is assumed that the vector $(s_{t,1}/s_{t-1,1}, \ldots, s_{t,N}/s_{t-1,N})'$ is governed by a multivariate normal distribution $N(\mu_t, \Sigma_t)$, in which case also R_t is normally distributed with mean $a_t'\mu_t$ and variance $a_t'\Sigma_t a_t$. The problem is thus essentially reduced to the one of estimating μ_t and Σ_t as it is impressively illustrated by the RiskMetrics calculator.

While the assumption of normally distributed price changes is computationally convenient, there is significant empirical evidence that in reality the distribution of asset returns might be more complicated, involving nontrivial characteristics such as negative skewness and "fat tails".[1] As it was shown in the Introduction, additional bias may result from the serial dependence in asset returns when using an unconditional VaR forecast. As a consequence, VaR estimates based on normal distributions may systematically underestimate the risk exposure of a portfolio and have provoked justified criticism in the recent past (for an applied standpoint, see [Taleb 1997]). Below we model VaR based on an estimate of the distribution of the *returns* $r_{t,i} = \log(s_{t,i}/s_{t-1,i})$ rather than directly based on the proportional price

---

1. Another common source of non-normality are nonlinear dependencies among the components of r_t, e.g. due to derivative assets. For surveys on VaR calculations for derivative portfolios, see [DuffiePan 1997] or Chapter 15 of [Hull 1998].

changes.[2] In particular, we suggest a novel approach to estimating VaR within which a mixture density is used to model the distribution $p(r_{t,i}|I_{t,i})$ of the returns $r_{t,i}$ conditional on the information set $I_{t,i} = (r_{t-1,i}, \ldots, r_{1,i})$ of past returns. The basic idea underlying the mixture approach is to allow for the separate treatment of *short-term* effects such as volatility clusters and *long-term* events such as market crashes, which both seem highly relevant to predict market risk. However, using standard approaches involving a geometric decay of past information, such as in the case of exponentially weighted averages or GARCH [Bollerslev 1986], rare extreme events (market crashes) may be forgotten too quickly. On the other hand, using a very long memory as in the unconditional model in Section 4.1 or in IGARCH [Nelson 1990] prevents the identification of volatility clusters. By using separate short-term and long-term models, the mixture approach accounts for dependencies at different frequencies.

Formally, the proposed mixture is composed of a normal density f_1 to model the short-term dependencies and a *maximum entropy density* f_2 to capture negative skewness and excess kurtosis in the long-term dependencies of $r_{t,i}$:

$$p(x|I_{t,i}) = \kappa_1 f_1(x; \theta_1) + \kappa_2 f_2(x; \theta_2), \tag{4.2}$$

where

$$f_1(x; \theta_1) = N(x|\mu_{t,i}, \sigma_{t,i}^2),$$
$$f_2(x; \theta_2) = \exp\{-(\lambda_0 + \lambda_1 x + \lambda_2 x^2 + \lambda_3 x^3 + \lambda_4 x^4)\}.$$

κ_1 and κ_2 (satisfying $\kappa_1 \geq 0$, $\kappa_2 \geq 0$, and $\kappa_1 + \kappa_2 = 1$) are mixture weightings reflecting the prior probability of extreme market events. Note that a mixture of the suggested form is consistent with a jump-diffusion model of asset returns as suggested by Merton [Merton 1976] and Cox and Ross [CoxRoss 1976]. The mean and the variance parameters of the normal density $N(x|\mu_{t,i}, \sigma_{t,i}^2)$ are, like in RiskMetrics, computed as exponentially weighted averages:

$$\mu_{t,i} = \sum_{s=1}^{t} w_{t,s} r_{t,i}, \qquad \sigma_{t,i}^2 = \sum_{s=1}^{t} w_{t,s} r_{t,i}^2 - \mu_{t,i},$$

where

$$w_{t,s} = \frac{\exp\{-\delta(t-s)\}}{\sum_{s'=1}^{t} \exp\{-\delta(t-s')\}}.$$

---

2. In fact, also RiskMetrics uses the distribution of returns rather than of proportional price changes.

In our experiments, we tried several values for the decay parameter δ and for the mixture weighting κ_1 and found $\delta_1 = 0.05$ and $\kappa_1 = 0.9$ to be a suitable choice. The maximum entropy density $f_2(x; \theta_2)$ has the special property of being least presumptuous with regard to missing information when estimating the density of a random variable whose first four moments are known. Conveniently, the (non-standardized and unweighted) first four moments

$$\nu_{t,i,1} = \sum_{s=1}^{t} r_{s,i}, \qquad \nu_{t,i,2} = \sum_{s=1}^{t} r_{s,i}^2,$$

$$\nu_{t,i,3} = \sum_{s=1}^{t} r_{s,i}^3, \qquad \nu_{t,i,4} = \sum_{s=1}^{t} r_{s,i}^4$$

operate as sufficient statistics for maximum likelihood estimation using this density, and there exists a one-to-one correspondence between $\nu_{t,i,1}, \nu_{t,i,2}, \nu_{t,i,3}, \nu_{t,i,4}$ and the parameters $\lambda_1, \lambda_2, \lambda_3, \lambda_4$ in the specification of $f_2(x; \theta_2)$. Numerical algorithms for the evaluation of this correspondence have been suggested by Zellner [ZellnerHighfield 1988] and Ormoneit and White [OrmoneitWhite 1999]. A tabular description sufficient for the practical application of our approach is available on the World Wide Web [OrmoneitWhite 1997].

Below we use the mixture density (4.2) to construct a nonlinear transformation of the asset returns into a normalized space. Details of this transformation will be described next.

4.3   Conditional Transformation of Returns

Given an estimate of the conditional probability distribution of the return of each individual asset our main focus is on the construction of a transformation into a space within which the returns are jointly normal distributed and serially independent. Hull and White argue that the variance of an estimator of the covariance matrix characterizing multiple assets may be greatly reduced by transforming into a space with normally distributed returns as there are no outliers in this case.

In this work we argue that also serial dependence increases the variance of the estimate and should be removed by using a transformation based on the conditional distributions. Mathematically, the usual estimate of the covariance matrix is efficient in the transformed space as it coincides with the maximum likelihood estimate. It is well-known that a transformation with the desired properties may be constructed as

$$u_{t,i} = \Phi^{-1}\left[P_{t,i}(r_{t,i})\right], \qquad (4.3)$$

where $P_{t,i}(r) = \int_{-\infty}^{r} p(x|I_t)dx$ is the (conditional) distribution function of $r_{t,i}$ and Φ^{-1} is the inverse of the distribution function (the z-quantile) of the standard normal density [KendallStuart 1977, HullWhite 1998]. In a second step, the joint distribution of the random vector $u_t = (u_{t,1}, \ldots, u_{t,N})'$ is modeled by a multivariate normal distribution $N(u_t|0, \Sigma_t)$ using the usual covariance estimate

$$\Sigma_t = \frac{1}{t}\sum_{s=1}^{t} u_s u_s'. \qquad (4.4)$$

(Remember that the transformed returns u_t have zero mean.) In order to recover the VaR of the original portfolio from this approximation in principle we have to solve a multivariate integral involving the estimated normal density $N(u_t|0, \Sigma_t)$ and the inverses of the transformations (4.3). As the numerical evaluation of this integral is computationally extremely demanding, Hull and White suggest to use a stochastic approximation instead. In particular, we generate a large number of random vectors according to

$$\tilde{u}_t \sim N(0, \Sigma_{t-1})$$

and subsequently apply the *inverse transformation*

$$\tilde{r}_{t,i} = P_t^{-1}\left[\Phi(\tilde{u}_{t,i})\right] \qquad (4.5)$$

to obtain a sequence of *pseudo returns*. Here $P_{t,i}^{-1}(z)$ is the inverse of the distribution function (i.e. the z-quantile) of $p(r|I_t)$. Based on the sample price changes $\tilde{r}_{t,i}$ a sample realization of R_t may be computed in analogy to (4.1), and by repeating the last steps sufficiently often the VaR may be approximated by the appropriate quantile of the empirical distribution function.

4.4   Evaluating a Sample Portfolio

To assess the merit of our approach we evaluate a sample portfolio consisting of equal positions in three international stock market indices, namely the American DJIA, the German DAX, and the English FTSE index:

$$\Pi_t = a_1 \cdot DAX_t + a_2 \cdot DJ_t + a_3 \cdot FTSE_t. \qquad (4.6)$$

In our example, we chose constant portfolio weights $a_1 = a_2 = a_3 = 1/3$ for simplicity. However, also complicated time-dependent portfolios may easily be evaluated using our approach. To illustrate the effect of the normalization, we compare the raw returns of the DAX to its normalized returns in Figure 4.3. The histograms on the right show that the skewness and the fat tails of the raw returns were removed after the application of (4.3). Also, there is less evidence of volatility clusters in the normalized returns. The estimated covariance matrix in the transformed space at the last observation in the data set (July 28, 1998) is

$$\Sigma_{3802} = \begin{pmatrix} 1.0274 & 0.4464 & 0.2108 \\ 0.4464 & 1.0320 & 0.3643 \\ 0.2108 & 0.3643 & 1.0215 \end{pmatrix},$$

where the rows and returns are ordered as in (4.6).

A crucial issue for the comparison of VaR approaches is the identification of an appropriate performance measure. A discussion of amenable approaches may be found in [Lopez 1997]. A simple procedure which is commonly applied by both researchers and practitioners is to compare the specified probability of tail events, e.g. $\alpha = 5\%$ in our experiments, directly to their realized relative frequency. For this purpose, let δ_t denote a binary indicator variable taking the value one if the realized return R_t is below the predicted VaR boundary and taking the value zero otherwise. Let T be the number of samples in a test set and let $m = \sum_{t=1}^{T} \delta_t$ and $h = m/T$ denote the predicted number and relative frequency of tail events, respectively. As described in [Lopez 1997], a straightforward likelihood-ratio statistic to assess the difference between h and α is

$$LR = 2 \left[\log \left(h^m (1-h)^{T-m} \right) - \log \left(\alpha^m (1-\alpha)^{T-m} \right) \right]. \tag{4.7}$$

For independently and identically distributed (i.i.d.) δ_t, LR possesses an asymptotic $\chi^2(1)$ distribution which may easily be evaluated.[3] Below we use this asymptotic distribution to test the joint null-hypothesis of no significant difference between h and α and serial independence of δ_t.[4]

Besides obtaining the desired relative frequency h of tail events, the main focus of our experiments is on serial dependence in the indicator variable δ_t. As there exists no standard test statistic which is commonly used in the finance literature, we suggest a novel test procedure in this work which is based upon the discrete case analogue of the Ljung-Box test for continuous random variables [LjungBox

---

3. Under the i.i.d. assumption exact finite sample tests may of course be carried out using the Binomial distribution of h.

4. More precisely, the null-hypothesis is that the $\sum_t \delta_t$ has a Binomial distribution with parameter α.

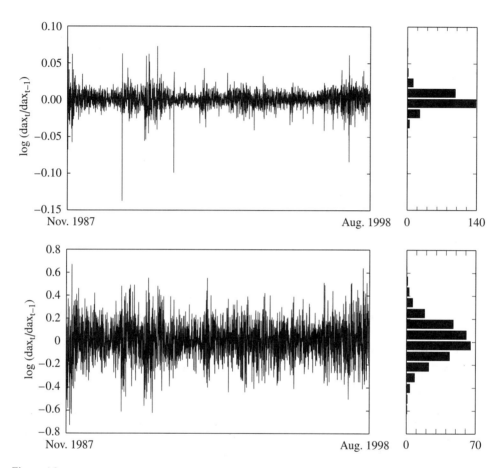

Figure 4.3
Raw and transformed daily returns of the DAX. The histograms on the right show the relative frequencies of the returns in the same scale.

1978]. The Ljung-Box statistic is a weighted average of squared autocorrelations at various lags. Formally, it may be written as

$$Q_l = T(T + 2) \sum_{k=1}^{l} \frac{\rho^2(k)}{T - k}, \tag{4.8}$$

where $\rho(k)$ denotes the estimated correlation coefficient of δ_t and δ_{t+k}. As δ_t is discrete in our application, the usual asymptotic properties of Q_l cannot be relied upon. Instead, a Monte-Carlo simulation approach to approximate the distribution

Table 4.1
Relative frequency and sample statistics of tail events as predicted by Conditional VaR and an
unconditional benchmark model. The VaR forecasts are based on a tail probability of $\alpha = 0.05$.
The numbers in columns four and six are the p-values of the statistics. To approximate the p-values
for the Q-statistics we used a Monte-Carlo simulation with 1000 samples.

	h	LR	p-value	Q_{20}	p-value
Conditional VaR	6.0%	5.5347	0.0186	0.0420	0.5174
Benchmark	4.998 %	0.00001879	0.9965	0.2908	0.000

of Q_l under the null-hypothesis of i.i.d. events may easily be derived. For this
purpose, we generate random sequences of binary variables with expectation α of
length T, which may subsequently be used to compute a sample realization of Q_l
according to (4.8). Repeating this procedure sufficiently often one may approximate
the true distribution of Q_l under the null-hypothesis using the empirical distribution
of the simulated Q-values.

In Table 4.1 we report h, the LR statistic, as well as Q_{20} for the VaR estimates
of the sample portfolio. To obtain these values, we split the available set of daily
prices ranging from January 2, 1984 to July 28, 1998 (3802 observations) into a
training and a test set ranging from January 2, 1984 to October 30, 1987 (1000
observations) and from November 2,1987 to July 28, 1998 (3801 observations), respectively. Here the training set was used to determine the optimal transformation
parameters $\delta = 0.05$ and $\kappa_1 = 0.9$, and the test set was used to compute the reported statistics. The first row of the table shows the results of Conditional VaR
and the second row shows the results of an ideal unconditional forecast computed
in hindsight, i.e. it corresponds to the 5% quantile of the returns in the test set.
The numbers in the fourth and sixth column denote the p-values for the rejection
of the null-hypothesis underlying LR and Q_{20} statistic, respectively.[5]

The results in Table 4.1 show that, with regard to the LR statistic, the benchmark
model performs exceptionally well, which is not surprising given that it is based on
information that would normally not be available to a risk manager. The p-value
of the LR statistic for Conditional VaR of 0.0186 is at the limit of rejection using
typical confidence levels, and thus indicates a possible systematic deviance of the
probability of tail events from the 5% level. Alternative explanations include serial
correlation in δ_t, which is also violating the null-hypothesis underlying the LR test,

---

5. The p-value is the probability that the statistic takes on a value of at least its observed realization
under the null-hypothesis. For example, a p-value of 3% means that the null-hypothesis must be
rejected in a test using a 95% confidence level.

as well as a significant deviation of the true finite sample distribution of LR from its asymptotic approximation. With regard to the Q_{20} statistic, the hypothesis of serial independence in δ_t must be rejected for any reasonable confidence level for the benchmark model, which is also not surprising given the evident serial dependence in the asset returns. For Conditional VaR, the hypothesis of serial independence cannot be rejected using the suggested test procedure.

4.5 Summary and Conclusion

We discussed a new method to overcome two important shortcomings of common VaR estimates. First, by using a mixture model of the individual asset returns, we allow for the separate treatment of long-term events such as market crashes and short-term events such as volatility clusters which are both essential to VaR. In particular, by using a maximum entropy density as one mixture component, we account for the presence of fat tails and non-zero skewness in asset returns. Second, by transforming the returns into a space within which they are jointly normal distributed and serially independent, we obtain a robust estimate of the covariances between different assets. In particular, as the transformations of the individual asset returns are carried out independently of each other, the danger of "overfitting" the data is drastically reduced in comparison to alternative approaches which aim at building a complete model of the conditional *joint* distribution of asset returns such as multivariate GARCH [BollerslevEngleWooldridge 1988, Christiansen 1998]. Our experiments confirm that Conditional VaR leads to serially independent predicted tail events while closely approximating the specified event probabilities.

4.6 Acknowledgments

The authors thank Alan Gous for his advice regarding the development of the correlation test in Section 4.4, as well as participants of the Computational Finance'99 conference in New York for helpful comments. The work of Dirk Ormoneit is supported by a grant of the Deutsche Forschungsgemeinschaft (DFG) in the framework of their postdoc program.

References

T. Bollerslev, Generalized autoregressive conditional heteroskedasticity, *Journal of Econometrics* **31** (1986), 307–327.

T. Bollerslev, R. Engle, and J. Wooldridge, A Capital Asset Pricing Model with time varying covariances, *Journal of Political Economy* **96** (1988), 116–131.

C. Christiansen, Value at Risk using the Factor-ARCH model, Tech. report, Department of Finance, Aarkus School of Business, 1998.

J. Cox and S. Ross, The valuation of options for alternative stochastic processes, *Journal of Financial Economics* **3** (1976), 145–166.

D. Duffie and J. Pan, An overview of value at risk, *Journal of Derivatives* **4** (1997), no. 3, 7–49.

J. C. Hull, *Introduction to futures and options markets*, third ed., Prentice Hall, 1998.

J. Hull and A. White, Value at risk when daily changes in market variables are not normally distributed, *Journal of Derivatives* **5** (1998), no. 3, 9–27.

M. Kendall and S. Stuart, *The advanced theory of statistics*, vol. 1, Charles Griffin & Cmopany, 1977.

G. M. Ljung and G. E. P. Box, On a measure of lack of fit in time series models, *Biometrica* **65** (1978), 297–303.

J. A. Lopez, Regulatory evaluation of Value-at-Risk models, *Staff Reports* 33, Federal Reserve Bank of New York, November 1997.

R. Merton, Option pricing when underlying stock returns are discontinuous, *Journal of Financial Economics* **3** (1976), 125–144.

J. P. Morgan, Statistics of financial market returns, 1996, `http://www.jpmorgan.com /RiskManagement/RiskMetrics/pubs.html`.

D. Nelson, Stationarity and persistence in the GARCH(1,1) model, *Econometric Theory* **6** (1990), 318–334.

D. Ormoneit and H. White, Table of the correspondence between moments and maximum entropy density parameters, 1997, `http://wwwbrauer.informatik.tu-muenchen.de/~ormoneit /lambda_table.txt`.

D. Ormoneit and H. White, An efficient algorithm to compute maximum entropy densities, *Econometric Reviews* (1999), forthcoming.

N. Taleb, The world according to Nassim Taleb, *Derivatives Strategy* (1997).

A. Zellner and R. A. Highfield, Calculation of maximum entropy distributions and approximation of marginal posterior distributions, *Journal of Econometrics* **37** (1988), 195–209.

5 Advances in Importance Sampling

Art Owen and Yi Zhou

Simulation is commonly used in finance to value options. Much recent work has considered ways to sample the input space more uniformly than Monte Carlo does. For spiky integrands, uniform sampling is wasteful and importance sampling can produce great increases in accuracy. Importance sampling can also cause devastating losses in accuracy, even when following the usual advice to sample nearly proportionally to a target function. This paper surveys recent techniques that protect against the worst outcomes of importance sampling without losing much when it works well.

5.1 Introduction

The value of a financial derivative is often expressed as an expectation

$$I = \int_{\mathcal{D}} f(x)q(x)dx, \tag{5.1}$$

with respect to a risk neutral density q on some state variables $x \in \mathcal{D} \subseteq R^d$. Equation (5.1) suggests that Monte Carlo sampling from q may be a good way to compute I, especially when d is not small. [Boyle et al 1996].

Under mild smoothness conditions on f and q, quasi-Monte Carlo (QMC) sampling [Niederreiter 1992] can improve the accuracy of the computation by sampling more uniformly. For applications of QMC to finance see [Paskov and Traub 1995, Joy et al 1996, Caflisch et al 1997]. With further mild smoothness assumptions, randomized QMC (RQMC) sampling gives even better accuracy [Owen 1997, Hickernell 1996] than QMC while providing data determined error estimates.

Direct simulation methods like Monte Carlo and quasi-Monte Carlo do not succeed well on spiky integration problems. We consider f to be spiky if an appreciable fraction of its variance under sampling from q may be attributed to a subset of $\mathcal{D}$ having relatively small probability under q. There is little to be gained from uniform sampling, whether by QMC or RQMC, of those parts of $\mathcal{D}$ that do not contribute much to the expectation of f.

In finance, spiky integrands may arise in the form of options that are far out of the money. There may be one or more very small regions in $\mathcal{D}$ containing all the x's for which $f(x) \neq 0$. Similar problems arise when one wants to estimate the expected loss or gain in a position given that it is unusually large. Examples include insurance deductables and the performance premiums charged by hedge funds.

Spiky integrands also arise implicitly in value at risk(VAR) problems, though the relevant q for VAR is not necessarily the risk neutral one. Suppose the future value in a portfolio is $v(x)$. We may be interested in a quantile like $Q_{0.01}$ for which $\Pr(v(X) \leq Q_{0.01} \mid X \sim q) = 0.01$. Such quantiles are commonly found by a simulation that estimates the probability of extreme losses $\Pr(v(X) \leq v_0)$. The estimate $\hat{Q}_{0.01}$ is that v_0 for which the estimated probability is 0.01. The extreme loss probability is of the form (5.1) where $f(x)$ is 1 when $v(x) \leq v_0$ and 0 otherwise. This f is 0 with high probability but has one or more spikes in which it is 1.

Spiky integrands are also encountered in insurance, high energy physics, Bayesian statistics, computer graphics, and reliability. The method of importance sampling is commonly used on spiky integrands. It can be combined with quasi-Monte Carlo sampling, but we will focus instead on its use with Monte Carlo sampling. Importance sampling works by sampling from some density p that provides more data from the important part of $\mathcal{D}$ containing the spikes. A recent and sophisticated example of importance sampling for financial valuation is [Glasserman et al 1999].

Importance sampling can achieve spectacular improvements in accuracy. It can also cause devastating losses in accuracy. Moreover, the usual advice on how to conduct importance sampling can lead to either outcome. Thus [Bratley et al 1983] conclude, as quoted in [Hesterberg 1995]: "Because there is no practical way to guard against gross misspecification of [p], multidimensional importance sampling is risky."

We survey recently developed ways of gaining the potentially large benefits from importance sampling while bounding the possible loss of efficiency. These methods are combinations of sampling from mixtures of densities and the use of control variates. The central result is that by sampling from a mixture of densities and using the mixture components as control variates, we can get an upper bound on the asymptotic variance. If any one of these densities would produce a small importance sampling variance, then the combined method will too.

We also describe some recent positivisation techniques for approaching zero variance in importance sampling of integrands f that take both positive and negative values. This technique can be combined effectively with a control variate h for which $f - h$ is usually zero, while h has known expectation under q. Examples in finance include f differing from h by a knockout condition, ceiling, floor, or combination thereof.

5.2   Importance sampling

Importance sampling begins by taking a sample X_i independently from a density p, where $p(x) > 0$ whenever $f(x)q(x) \neq 0$. Then the estimate of I is

$$\hat{I}_p = \frac{1}{n} \sum_{i=1}^{n} \frac{f(X_i)q(X_i)}{p(X_i)}. \tag{5.2}$$

The estimate (5.2) is unbiased because

$$E(\hat{I}_p) = \int_{\mathcal{D}} \frac{f(x)q(x)}{p(x)} p(x)dx = I.$$

There are two practical constraints on importance sampling: we must have an algorithm for sampling from p, and we must be able to compute fq/p. Assuming that we can compute f, we need to be able to compute the likelihood ratio q/p, and not necessarily p and q individually.

We can easily find that $\mathrm{Var}(\hat{I}_p) = \sigma_p^2/n$, where

$$\sigma_p^2 = \int \left(\frac{f(x)q(x)}{p(x)} - I \right)^2 p(x)dx = \int \frac{f^2(x)q^2(x)}{p(x)} dx - I^2 \tag{5.3}$$

is referred to as the asymptotic variance. The density p^* that minimizes (5.3) over p is known to be proportional to $|f(x)|q(x)$ [Kahn and Marshall 1953].

In many applications $f(x) \geq 0$ and $I > 0$, so that $p^*(x) = f(x)q(x)/I$. This density gives $\sigma_{p^*}^2 = 0$, but does not satisfy the practical constraints, because $fq/p^* = I$, and I is unknown.

The practical value of knowing that $p^* = fq/I$ is optimal, is that it suggests how one might construct an effective importance sampling density. A good importance sampling density should be nearly proportional to fq over $\mathcal{D}$. In particular a good density p should have spikes in nearly the same locations and of nearly the same shapes as fq. It is not necessary to arrange a perfect match between the spikes of p and fq. A crude qualitative match can bring great reductions in variance.

Even if matching the spikes of fq is necessary, it is not sufficient. Importance sampling can fail dramatically due to a mismatch between p and fq away from the spikes. In equation (5.3), suppose that p decreases to zero faster than does $(fq)^2$ as x moves away from the spiky region. It is possible to get $\sigma_p^2 = \infty$ in such cases. The irony is that a potentially effective importance sampling density p fails for lack of proportionality to fq in the region of $\mathcal{D}$ that is *unimportant* under the nominal distribution q.

5.3 Control variates

The use of control variates is a classical variance reduction technique, described in texts such as [Ripley 1987], [Bratley et al 1983], and [Hammersley and Handscomb

1964]. Here we review it, assuming that we are also using importance sampling. The idea is to use functions h_j $j = 1, \ldots, m$ with known integrals $\int h_j(x)dx$, or alternatively with known nominal expectations $\int h_j(x)q(x)dx$, to reduce the variance in the estimate of $\int f(x)q(x)dx$.

Suppose that the values $\int h_j(x)dx = \mu_j$, $j = 1, \ldots, m$ are known. Assume that $p(x) > 0$ if any $h_j(x) > 0$, or if $f(x)q(x) > 0$. Let $\beta = (\beta_1, \ldots, \beta_m)$ be a vector of real values. Under independent sampling of X_i from $p(x)$,

$$\hat{I}_{p,\beta} = \frac{1}{n}\sum_{i=1}^{n}\frac{f(X_i)q(X_i) - \sum_{j=1}^{m}\beta_j h_j(X_i)}{p(X_i)} + \sum_{j=1}^{m}\beta_j\mu_j \tag{5.4}$$

is an unbiased estimate of I.

The variance of $\hat{I}_{p,\beta}$ is $\sigma^2_{p,\beta}/n$, where

$$\sigma^2_{p,\beta} = \int\left(\frac{f(x)q(x) - \sum_j \beta_j h_j(x)}{p(x)} - I + \sum_j\beta_j\mu_j\right)^2 p(x)dx. \tag{5.5}$$

Let β^* minimize the integral in (5.5), over β, for the given functions f, p, and q. Equation (5.5) suggests that an estimate $\hat{\beta}$ of β^* can be found by a multiple regression (including an intercept term) of $f(X_i)q(X_i)/p(X_i)$ on predictors $h_j(X_i)/p(X_i)$ for data X_i sampled from p.

Because the regression includes an intercept coefficient $\hat{\beta}_0$, the residuals will sum to zero. It follows that equation (5.4) with $\beta = \hat{\beta}$ simplifies to $\hat{I}_{p,\hat{\beta}} = \hat{\beta}_0 + \sum_{j=1}^{m}\hat{\beta}_j\mu_j$. [Owen and Zhou 1998] prove:

Theorem 1 *Suppose that there is a unique vector β^* that minimizes $\sigma^2_{p,\beta}$, and let $\hat{\beta}$ be determined by least squares as described above. Suppose further that the expectations under sampling from p of the following quantities exist and are finite: $h_j^2 h_l^2/p^4$, and $h_j^2 f^2 q^2/p^4$, for $1 \le j \le l \le m$. Then $\hat{\beta}_j = \beta_j^* + O_p(n^{-1/2})$, for $j = 1, \ldots, m$, and $\hat{I}_{p,\hat{\beta}} = \hat{I}_{p,\beta^*} + O_p(n^{-1})$.*

Thus while $\hat{\beta}_j$ approaches β_j^* at the standard Monte Carlo rate, the effect of substituting $\hat{\beta}_j$ for unknown optimal β_j^* is asymptotically negligible. It is customary to analyze control variate methods as if the unknown optimal values were being used, while in practice one uses the estimated coefficients. This is reasonable if n is large, and in particular if $n \gg m$.

5.4   Defensive importance sampling

The idea behind defensive importance sampling [Hesterberg 1995] is to use a density that qualitatively matches the spiky part of fq and is not too small in the unimportant part of $\mathcal{D}$. Let $p(x)$ be a density that is thought to be a good approximation to fq/I, at least in the important part of $\mathcal{D}$. Now define the mixture density

$$p_\alpha(x) \equiv \alpha_1 q(x) + \alpha_2 p(x) \qquad (5.6)$$

where $\alpha_j > 0$ and $\alpha_1 + \alpha_2 = 1$.

Notice that $p_\alpha(x) \geq \alpha_1 q(x)$ for any $x \in \mathcal{D}$. As a result

$$\sigma^2_{p_\alpha} = \int \frac{f^2(x)q^2(x)}{p_\alpha(x)} dx - I^2 \leq \frac{1}{\alpha_1} \int f^2(x)q(x)dx - I^2 = \frac{1}{\alpha_1}\left(\sigma^2_q + I^2\alpha_2\right). \qquad (5.7)$$

Equation (5.7) provides a kind of insurance against the worst effects of importance sampling. If the nominal density provides a finite variance, then defensive importance sampling does too.

[Hesterberg 1995] recommends using α_1 between 0.1 and 0.5. It is not uncommon to find that $\sigma_q \gg I > 0$. In such cases this advice approximately bounds the importance sampling variance by between 2 and 10 times what it would be under the nominal density.

This simple version of defensive importance sampling can however bring about a great decrease in efficiency compared to sampling from p. The root of the problem is that if p is nearly proportional to fq then $\alpha_1 q + \alpha_2 p$ can not be, outside of trivial cases with q nearly proportional to fq.

[Owen and Zhou 1998] present the example below in which, as $\epsilon \to 0$, the density p differs from proportionality to fq by $O(\epsilon)$, and the asymptotic variance of defensive importance sampling is $O(\epsilon^{-2})$ times as large as ordinary importance sampling.

Example 1 *Let $\mathcal{D} = (0,1)$, with nominal density $q = U(0,1)$. The integrand is $f(x) = x^a$, for some $a > 1$ and $p(x) = (1 + a + \epsilon)x^{a+\epsilon}$, for $a + \epsilon > 1$.*

In Example 1 the integrand and the density both have a spike at 1. Easy calculations show that $\sigma^2_p = O(\epsilon^2)$ as $\epsilon \to 0$. But for $\alpha_1 > 0$, we find $\sigma^2_{p_\alpha}$ tends to a nonzero limit as $\epsilon \to 0$. Thus when importance sampling might have succeeded spectacularly, defensive importance sampling fails to reap the benefit. It increases the variance by $O(\epsilon^{-2})$.

5.5   Naive control variates

It is noteworthy that the bound (5.7) contains the integral I. For a fixed constant β, the function $f(x) - \beta$ has the same variance under sampling from q as has $f(x)$. But the unbiased estimate

$$\hat{I}_{\alpha,\beta} = \frac{1}{n} \sum_{i=1}^{n} \frac{(f(X_i) - \beta)q(X_i)}{p_\alpha(X_i)} + \beta$$

typically gives a different answer for each β. The variance bound in equation (5.7) becomes

$$\sigma_{\alpha,\beta}^2 \leq \frac{1}{\alpha_1} \left(\sigma_q^2 + (I - \beta)^2 \alpha_2 \right). \tag{5.8}$$

Equation (5.8) suggests that through judicious choice of β, we could reduce the upper bound in (5.7) to $\alpha_1^{-1}\sigma_q^2$, so that $\text{Var}(\hat{I}_{\alpha,c}) \leq \sigma_q^2/(n\alpha_1)$. The unknown value $\beta = I$ does this; the optimal β^* can be no worse. So we find that

$$\sigma_{\alpha,\beta^*}^2 \leq \frac{\sigma_q^2}{\alpha_1}. \tag{5.9}$$

In practice, we can expect to find a good value $\hat{\beta}$ by treating $q(x)$ as a control variate with known integral 1. This is equivalent to using likelihood ratio q/p as a control variate (having known expectation) as advocated by [Arsham et al 1989].

[Hesterberg 1995] obtained the bound σ_q^2/α_1 for the method using q as a control variate in combination with defensive importance sampling. He obtained it first for a method that uses the control variate in a ratio estimate. The asymptotic variance for the regression styled control variates described in Section 5.3 is no larger than that of the ratio estimate. The result also applies to several reweighting styled estimators described in [Hesterberg 1995].

It also holds that defensive importance sampling, with q as a control variate has an asymptotic variance no larger than σ_p^2/α_2. The simple use of a control variate not only provides the insurance (5.7), but it also cures the problem that arose because p_α was no longer proportional to fq. This was shown by [Owen and Zhou 1998].

The following reasoning shows why this should be true: The control variate coefficient is estimated by a regression of f/p_α on the predictors q/p_α. But p/p_α is collinear with q/p_α because $\alpha_1 q/p_\alpha + \alpha_2 p/p_\alpha = 1$. So the regression is equivalent to a regression on p/p_α. This allows us to interchange the roles of p and q thus turning (5.9) into

$$\sigma^2_{\alpha,\beta*} \leq \frac{\sigma^2_p}{\alpha_2}. \tag{5.10}$$

The proof in [Owen and Zhou 1998] is more detailed than the argument sketched above, but that argument captures the essence.

5.6   Mixture sampling

Defensive importance sampling uses a mixture of two densities, p and q. It can be advantageous to use more general mixtures. Suppose we have a list of density functions p_j, $j = 1, \ldots, m$. Let $\alpha_j > 0$ for $j = 1, \ldots, m$ with $\sum_{j=1}^m \alpha_j = 1$. Then the density

$$p_\alpha(x) = \sum_{j=1}^m \alpha_j p_j(x)$$

is an α mixture of the densities p_j. When multiple densities are being considered, one or more of them may be of the defensive type. These densities may be suggested by subject matter knowledge, or they may be found by a numerical search as in [Zhou 1998].

Here are some settings where mixture densities might be of value. We may have m different densities of which we hope at least one is suitable for f. There may be r different target functions f_k, $k = 1, \ldots, r$ to integrate over the same sample, where each density p_j is thought to be a good choice for a subset of them. There may equally well be r different nominal densities q_k, $k = 1, \ldots, r$ where each p_j is thought to be a good choice for a subset of them. In finance, multiple f_k might represent different portfolios, multiple q_k might represent different estimates of the nominal distribution, and multiple p_k could describe different stress testing scenarios.

We will sample from the mixture density $p_\alpha(x) = \sum_{j=1}^m \alpha_j p_j(x)$ where $\alpha_j > 0$ and $\sum_{j=1}^m \alpha_j = 1$. Because $\int p_j(x)dx = 1$, and $p_\alpha(x) > 0$ whenever $p_j(x) > 0$, we can use the p_j as control variates as described in Section 5.3. We write the resulting estimator as

$$\widetilde{I}_{\alpha,\beta} = \frac{1}{n} \sum_{i=1}^n \frac{f(X_i)q(X_i) - \sum_{j=1}^m \beta_j p_j(X_i)}{\sum_{j=1}^m \alpha_j p_j(X_i)} + \sum_{j=1}^m \beta_j. \tag{5.11}$$

The asymptotic variance $\sigma^2_{p_\alpha,\beta}$ of $\widetilde{I}_{\alpha,\beta}$ is given by (5.5) with $h_j = p_j$ and $\mu_j = 1$. The optimal β is not unique, because an α_j weighted sum of p_j/p_α is constant.

In practice this issue can be addressed by setting one of the β_j to zero, and using regression to estimate the others.

Theorem 2 below [Owen and Zhou 1998] shows thta $\widetilde{I}_{\alpha,\beta}$ is unbiased, and that for an optimal β, the variance is never larger than what one gets from an importance sample of size $n\alpha_j$ from p_j.

Theorem 2 *Let p_j, α_j and $\widetilde{I}_{\alpha,\beta}$ be as above. If at least one of $p_j(x) > 0$ whenever $f(x)q(x) > 0$, then for any β, we have $E(\widetilde{I}_{\alpha,\beta}) = I$.*

Let $\sigma^2_{p_\alpha,\beta}$ be the asymptotic variance of $\widetilde{I}_{\alpha,\beta}$ and let $\sigma^2_{p_j}$ be the asymptotic variance (5.3), under importance sampling from p_j. If β^* is any minimizer of $\sigma^2_{p_\alpha,\beta}$, then

$$\sigma^2_{p_\alpha,\beta^*} \leq \min_{1 \leq j \leq m} \alpha_j^{-1} \sigma^2_{p_j}. \tag{5.12}$$

This theorem means that the asymptotic variance, using an optimal β^* is never worse than what we would have gotten using $n_n = n\alpha_j$ observations in importance sampling from p_j. It is hard to expect much better than this in general. The reason is that we only expect to get $n\alpha_j$ observations from the density p_j and it is possible that p_j is the only density providing useful information. That is it may be that p_j is the only one of our mixture components with finite asymptotic variance.

The issue of convergence of $\hat{\beta}$ to β^* is addressed in [Owen and Zhou 1998]. To obtain the uniqueness described in Theorem 1, we need to drop one, or possibly more, control variates from the regression. To obtain the moment conditions there, it is sufficient to have at least one p_j for which the asymptotic variance $\sigma^2_{p_j}$ of (5.3) is finite.

Theorem 2 may be anticipated from the results in Section 5.5 for two component mixtures. For each j, we can view the mixture p_α as a mixture of p_j with the density $(1 - \alpha_j)^{-1} \sum_{k \neq j} \alpha_k p_k$.

5.7 Deterministic mixture sampling

A deterministic mixture sample has exactly $n_j = n\alpha_j$ observations (or an integer close to $n\alpha_j$) from the density p_j. Let $X_{ji} \sim p_j$ be independent, for $j = 1, \ldots, m$ and $i = 1, \ldots, n_j$. Incorporating control variates p_j the resulting estimate is,

$$\hat{I}_{\alpha,\beta} = \frac{1}{n} \left(\sum_{j=1}^{m} \sum_{i=1}^{n_j} \frac{f(X_{ji})q(X_{ji}) - \sum_{k=1}^{m} \beta_k p_k(X_{ji})}{p_\alpha(X_{ji})} \right) + \sum_{j=1}^{m} \beta_j, \tag{5.13}$$

where X_{ji} are independent and drawn from $p_j(x)$.

The estimate (5.13) is unbiased, and $\mathrm{Var}(\hat{I}_{\alpha,\beta}) \le \mathrm{Var}(\tilde{I}_{\alpha,\beta})$ [Hesterberg 1995].

The estimates $\hat{\beta}$ can be constructed using the same regressions as under ordinary mixture sampling. They provide an estimate of the vector β^* optimal for random mixture sampling. There remains the possibility of further improvement by devising an estimate of the possibly different vector β that would be optimal for deterministic sampling.

5.8   Multiple importance sampling

Multiple importance sampling is a method due to [Veach and Guibas 1995]. In graphical rendering, the image is an integral over a space of photon paths. The optimal importance sampling strategy from a list p_j, $j = 1, \ldots, m$ can vary greatly from pixel to pixel. Their idea is to reweight the integration problem to place more weight on the p_j that is "locally proportional" to fq.

Let $w_j(x)$, $j = 1, \ldots, m$ be a partition of unity: for every $x \in \mathcal{D}$, $0 \le w_j(x) \le \sum_{j=1}^m w_j(x) = 1$. Define

$$\hat{I}_{n,w} = \sum_{j=1}^m \frac{1}{n_j} \sum_{i=1}^{n_j} w_j(X_{ji}) \frac{f(X_{ji})q(X_{ji})}{p_j(X_{ji})}, \tag{5.14}$$

where X_{ji} are independent draws from p_j, and the subscripts on I denote the partition of unity and the sample sizes used. The estimate $\hat{I}_{n,w}$ is unbiased under the mild conditions that the p_j cover the whole of $\mathcal{D}$ and that w_j only weights the region that p_j samples.

[Veach and Guibas 1995] consider several ways of selecting w_j. Their balance heuristic takes weights

$$w_j(x) = \frac{n_j p_j(x)}{\sum_{k=1}^m n_k p_k(x)}, \tag{5.15}$$

matching deterministic mixture sampling (5.13) with $n_j = n\alpha_j$ and all $\beta_j = 0$.

Their cutoff heuristic takes

$$w_j(x) \propto n_j p_j(x) 1_{n_j p_j(x) \ge \gamma \max_k n_k p_k(x)}, \tag{5.16}$$

for some $0 \le \gamma \le 1$, and their power heuristic takes

$$w_j(x) \propto (n_j p_j(x))^\rho, \tag{5.17}$$

for $\rho \geq 0$. In both heuristics the weights are normalized to sum to unity. Sending $\rho \to \infty$ in the power heuristic or taking $\gamma = 1$ in the cutoff heuristic gives rise to the maximum heuristic

$$w_j(x) \propto 1_{n_j p_j(x) = \max_k n_k p_k(x)}. \tag{5.18}$$

Unless there are ties among the $n_j p_j$, equation (5.18) puts all of the weight on one of the j's.

They prove a central role for the balance heuristic. It is optimal under random mixture sampling, and nearly so under deterministic mixture sampling.

Theorem 3 *Let $\bar{w}_j$ be the weight functions from the balance heuristic (5.15) and let w_j be any other partition of unity. If $f(x) \geq 0$, then under deterministic mixture sampling*

$$Var(\hat{I}_{n,\bar{w}}) \leq Var(\hat{I}_{n,w}) + \left(\frac{1}{\min_j n_j} - \frac{1}{\sum_j n_j} \right) I^2. \tag{5.19}$$

Theorem 4 *Let $\bar{w}_j$ be the weight functions from the balance heuristic (5.15) and let w_j be any other partition of unity. Then under random mixture sampling*

$$Var(\hat{I}_{n,\bar{w}}) \leq Var(\hat{I}_{n,w}). \tag{5.20}$$

In simulated examples in [Owen and Zhou 1998], the various heuristics had comparable performance. They tended to be better than defensive importance sampling without control variates, but not as good as defensive importance sampling with control variates.

5.9   Positivisation

[Owen and Zhou 1998] show that (multiple) importance sampling can achieve zero variance for integrands of mixed sign, through a simple positivisation technique.

The simplest form of positivisation begins by writing $f = f_+ - f_-$ where $f_+(x) = \max(f(x), 0)$ and $f_-(x) = \max(-f(x), 0)$, so $I = \int f_+(x)q(x)dx - \int f_-(x)q(x)dx$. By sampling $n_\pm$ observations from $p_\pm \propto f_\pm q$ one can attain a zero variance estimate:

$$\hat{I}_\pm = \frac{1}{n_+} \sum_{i=1}^{n_+} \frac{f_+(X_{i,+})q(X_{i,+})}{p_+(X_{i,+})} - \frac{1}{n_-} \sum_{i=1}^{n_-} \frac{f_-(X_{i,-})q(X_{i,-})}{p_-(X_{i,-})}. \tag{5.21}$$

In practice of course, one finds densities $p_\pm$ thought to be nearly proportional to $f_\pm q$. As we have seen above it is prudent to employ defensive importance sampling with control variates to the two integrands.

Instead of positivising f, we can positivise the difference $f - h$ between f and a control variate h with known nominal expectation $\int h(x)q(x)dx = \mu$. Let $X_{i,\pm}$ be independent from $p_\pm$, $i = 1, \ldots, n_\pm$, and

$$\hat{I}_{h\pm} = \mu + \frac{1}{n_+} \sum_{i=1}^{n_+} \frac{[(f-h)_+ q](X_{i,+})}{p_+(X_{i,+})} - \frac{1}{n_-} \sum_{i=1}^{n_-} \frac{[(f-h)_- q](X_{i,-})}{p_-(X_{i,-})}. \tag{5.22}$$

The expression $[(f-h)_+ q](X)$ stands for $(f(X) - h(X))_+ q(X)$. The estimate (5.22) is unbiased if $p_\pm > 0$ when $(f - h)_\pm q > 0$ respectively. The ideal densities $p_\pm$ are now proportional to $(f - h)_\pm q$.

A good candidate for h would be a function that was close to f over most of $\mathcal{D}$ and for which one can guess where the greatest differences are likely to be, in order to target those regions with sampling densities. In a finance context, h might be a security that can be valued by the Black-Scholes formula, or by some other very fast method. Then f might be closely related to h, such as h subject to a floor and a cap, or h subject to some kind of knockout provision. The function $f - h$ is spiky, and financial intuition may be used to find densities $p_j(x)$ that concentrate in the region or regions where $f \neq h$.

[Owen and Zhou 1998] consider variations on this idea. Instead of working with $(f - h)_\pm$, it is possible to work with any set of functions $v_j(f - h)$, $j = 1, \ldots, r$ satisfying $\sum_{j=1}^r v_j(z) = z$ and for each j either $v_j(z) \geq 0$ for all z or $v_j(z) \leq 0$ for all z. These functions are called a "partition of identity". The functions v_j can be smooth unlike the positive and negative parts which are not differentiable.

5.10   Positivisation with mixture sampling

One can use deterministic mixture importance sampling with control variates for each function in the partition. If one uses the same sample for every integrand $v_j(f - h)$ then the partition recombines into $f - h$ and only one control variate coefficient is required for each mixture density, reducing the number of coefficients from mr to m.

With independent $X_i \sim p_\alpha$, the resulting estimator is

$$\tilde{I}_{h,\alpha,\beta} = \frac{1}{n} \sum_{i=1}^n \frac{[(f-h)q](X_i) - \sum_{k=1}^m \beta_k p_k(X_i)}{p_\alpha(X_i)} + \mu + \sum_{j=1}^m \beta_j, \tag{5.23}$$

while for deterministic mixtures it is

$$\hat{I}_{h,\alpha,\beta} = \frac{1}{n}\sum_{j=1}^{m}\sum_{i=1}^{n_j} \frac{[(f-h)q](X_{ji}) - \sum_{k=1}^{m}\beta_k p_k(X_{ji})}{p_\alpha(X_{ji})} + \mu + \sum_{j=1}^{m}\beta_j, \qquad (5.24)$$

where $X_{ji} \sim p_j$ are independent, for $i = 1, \dots, n_j$, and $j = 1, \dots, m$. The coefficients β_j are estimated by regression of $(f-h)q/p_\alpha$ on predictors p_k/p_α. It is also possible to estimate a coefficient for h here or to incorporate a linear combination of control variates h_j.

5.11 Positivisation example

Example 2 [Owen and Zhou 1998] is a simple case in which h can be integrated in closed form while f is h subject to a floor and a ceiling.

Example 2 *Take* $\mathcal{D} = (0,1)^5$, $q = U(0,1)^5$. *Let* $h(x) = 100(\sum_{j=1}^{5} x^j - 1)$ *and* $f(x) = \max(\min(h(x), 300), -25)$. *Under* p_1, *the components* X^j *are independent* $N(0, \sigma_1^2)$ *variables conditioned to lie in* $(0,1)$. *Under* p_2, *the components* X^j *are independent* $N(1, \sigma_2^2)$ *variables conditioned to lie in* $(0,1)$. *The third density is* $p_3 = q = U(0,1)^5$. *We take* $\sigma_2 = 0.2236$ *and* $\sigma_1 = 0.75 * \sigma_2 = 0.1677$.

We easily find that $\mu = 150$, and using a result on the volume of a simplex we find $I = 150 - 100/6! + (0.75)^5 * 75/6! = 149.8858$. Because h is monotone in its arguments and f is a clipped version of h it is easy to know qualitatively that $f - h$ has two spikes, one with all x components large and one with them all small. This sort of knowledge will often be available, but it may be hard in practice to find densities that match these spikes. The densities p_1 and p_2 are meant to mimic this qualitatively correct, but imperfect, knowledge. The given values for σ_1 and σ_2 produce some X's falling outside the spike regions and into the $f - h = 0$ region. But they fail to cover the certain corners of the spike regions. This should cause naive positivisation of $f - h$, without defensive sampling, to fail.

A simulation in [Owen and Zhou 1998] found that using h as a control variate reduces the variance by roughly a factor of 650. Mixture sampling with 45% probability in each spike and 10% from the nominal distribution produced a further variance reduction ranging from about 75 to about 230. This range accounts for small differences in the results depending on whether random or deterministic sampling was used and whether h was taken with coefficient 1 or with an estimated coefficient.

Acknowledgements

This work was supported by the National Science Foundation. We thank Bennett Fox, Paul Glasserman, Philip Heidelberger, Tim Hesterberg and Eric Veach for discussions. We thank Yaser Abu-Mostafa, Blake LeBaron, Andrew Lo, and Andreas Weigend for organizing CF99.

References

Arsham, H., A. Fuerverger, D. McLeish, J. Kreimer, and R. Rubinstein. 1989. Sensitivity analysis and the "what if" problem in simulation analysis. *Math. Comput. Modelling*, 12:193–219.

Boyle, P., M. Broadie, and P. Glasserman. 1996. Monte carlo methods for security pricing. *Journal of Economics, Dynamics and Control.* In press.

Bratley, P., B. L. Fox, and L. E. Schrage. 1983. *A Guide to Simulation.* Springer-Verlag.

Caflisch, R. E., W. Morokoff, and A. B. Owen. 1997. Valuation of mortgage backed securities using brownian bridges to reduce effective dimension. *Journal of Computational Finance*, 1:27–46.

Glasserman, P., P. Heidelberger, and P. Shahabuddin. 1999. Asymptotically optimal importance sampling and stratification for pricing path-dependent options. *Mathematical Finance.*

Hammersley, J. and D. Handscomb. 1964. *Monte Carlo Methods.* London: Methuen.

Hesterberg, T. 1995. Weighted average importance sampling and defensive mixture distributions. *Technometrics*, 37(2):185–194.

Hickernell, F. J. 1996. The mean square discrepancy of randomized nets. *ACM Trans. Model. Comput. Simul.*, 6:274–296.

Joy, C., P. Boyle, and K.-S. Tan. 1996. Quasi-Monte Carlo methods in numerical finance. *Management Science*, 42(6):926–938.

Kahn, H. and A. Marshall. 1953. Methods of reducing sample size in Monte Carlo computations. *Journal of the Operations Research Society of America*, 1:263–278.

Niederreiter, H. 1992. *Random Number Generation and Quasi-Monte Carlo Methods.* S.I.A.M., Philadelphia, PA.

Owen, A. B. 1997. Scrambled net variance for integrals of smooth functions. *Annals of Statistics*, 25(4):1541–1562.

Owen, A. B. and Y. Zhou. 1998. Safe and effective importance sampling. Technical report, Stanford University, Statistics Department.

Paskov, S. and J. Traub. 1995. Faster valuation of financial derivatives. *The Journal of Portfolio Management*, 22:113–120.

Ripley, B. D. 1987. *Stochastic Simulation.* John Wiley & Sons.

Veach, E. and L. Guibas. 1995. Optimally combining sampling techniques for Monte Carlo rendering. In *SIGGRAPH '95 Conference Proceedings*, pages 419–428. Addison-Wesley.

Zhou, Y. 1998. *Adaptive Importance Sampling for Integration.* PhD thesis, Stanford University.

6 Arbitrage and the APT—A Note

Manfred Steiner and Sebastian Schneider

Arbitrage pricing plays an important role in asset valuation. The most applications of arbitrage asset pricing theories are based on the law of one price or asymptotic arbitrage free markets. We provide some new results on arbitrage and especially the arbitrage pricing theory by distinguishing between the absence of arbitrage, the law of one price and the absence of riskless arbitrage. Then we find the implications of these conditions for arbitrage asset pricing. Since the three concepts of the absence of arbitrage imply that the linear functionals that give the mean and the cost of a portfolio are continuous, hence there exists unique portfolios that represent these functionals. We detect a positive distance between these portfolios and therefore between the functionals. Thus the law of one price and the absence of a riskless arbitrage opportunity lead to systematic mispricing if both the contingent claims and the assets are mispriced. The beta pricing literature usually makes strong assumptions to obtain exact asset pricing. This belongs to a debate over which factors have the best theoretical or empirical justification. In the light of our results it is more advisable to acknowledge that almost only approximate arbitrage asset pricing can be obtained. The introduction of risky arbitrage opportunities in the sense that there might be an arbitrage opportunity with positive probability but not with probability one requires the knowledge of the risk aversion of investors. Therefore exact asset pricing can only be obtained by equilibrium asset pricing models. Our results generalizes to other arbitrage asset pricing theories like the Black and Scholes option valuation model and even the Modigliani-Miller Theorem.

One of the most significant developments in financial economics has been the introduction of arbitrage by Modigliani and Miller and its later use for option pricing by Black and Scholes. Since the concept of arbitrage has generated an increased interest in the study of asset pricing it became one of the most popular concepts for evaluating risky cash flows. Beside the pricing of derivatives by arbitrage, Ross (1976, 1977) first derived the Arbitrage Pricing Theory (APT) for the evaluation of assets. The APT has the attractive feature that it requires a small number of assumptions about the nature of the economy, i. e. a factor structure for expected returns, frictionless trading, but unfortunately a large number of assets. Hence the minimal assumptions lead to some ambiguities like approximate pricing and unknown factors. However this theory has later been refined and discussed by Huberman (1982), Shanken (1982), Chamberlain and Rothschild (1983), Connor (1984), Franke (1984), Reisman (1988, 1992) and Connor and Korajczyk (1989).[1] Despite

---

1. The paper by Franke (1984) might be unknown to a larger community since it was published in English but in a German journal. However Franke (1984) anticipated most of the later APT discussion and derived some most important points first. For a recent discussion of the APT see also Shanken (1992).

the extensive research on arbitrage pricing done, paradoxically some issues concerning the definition and the implications of arbitrage and hence the conclusions of various arbitrage pricing theories remain. We show in our paper that almost all of this APT criticism is due to some confusion of what is exactly meant by the absence of arbitrage. Like Oh, Shanken and Ross (1997), we consider three different concepts of arbitrage which are used in the literature as synonymous for the absence of arbitrage and hence caused the mentioned confusion. The various concepts of the absence arbitrage are the law of one price, the absence of asymptotic or riskless arbitrage and finally the absence of arbitrage. We show that all concepts of the absence of arbitrage under certain conditions imply the existence of a single beta representation, that is a security market line. However, we show that the valuation functionals implied by the different concepts of arbitrage differ and hence the distance between their projections on returns or equivalently factors diverges from zero with positive probability. Hence, the law of one price and the no riskless arbitrage condition lead to systematically pricing errors. Hence the APT must be generalized to prohibit risky arbitrage opportunities which is not inconsistent with some factor structure for the return generation.

6.1   Arbitrage in Financial Markets

6.1.1   Law of One Price Arbitrage

The law of one price is implied by the statement that prices must be a linear function of the payoffs: $p(ax_1 + bx_2) = ap(x_1) + bp(x_2)$. Thus the law of one price basically says only that investors cannot make profits by repackaging portfolios. In infinite asset markets this implies that different assets offering the same payoffs must be quoted at the same price and different assets almost surely offering the same payoffs must sell for similar prices. Linearity for pricing means that the price functional $p(x)$ satisfies the linear condition of algebra. Applying $p(x)$ to the basic securities e_ω whose payoffs are one in a particular state and zero otherwise and considering assets as arbitrarily linear combinations of the basic securities the value of any payoff x can be written as:

$$p(x) = \sum_\omega q(\omega)e_\omega$$

where $q(\omega)$ denotes the state price. Crucial for the following is the assumption that the state price or equivalent risk neutral probabilities are known. This is a strong assumption, since asset markets are incomplete and options are not traded on every asset and at least not on continuous strike prices. Otherwise we could estimate risk neutral probabilities from option prices [see Rubinstein (1994) and Jackwerth and Rubinstein (1996)].

Overall the law of one price implies free portfolio formation. Under these circumstances the repackaging of portfolios does not lead to any riskless profits. Hence the law of one price implies two things: first, that the pricing rule needs to be linear, and, second, that there is one consistent discount factor m which correctly prices all assets. The existence of a continuous valuation functional under the absence of law of one price arbitrage was proven by Chamberlain and Rothschild (1983). The linearity follows from the Hahn-Banach extension theorem. The discount factor might be interpreted as a composition of contingent claim state prices because they represent discounted state dependent payoffs:[2]

$$p = E(mx).$$

As long as M is generated by a finite contingent claim payoff vector, i. e. the algebraic basis for the infinite set of feasible portfolios, then the linearity assumption holds by construction. From the Riesz representation theorem we know that for any continuous linear functional on M there exists a unique $x^* \in M$ such that $p = E(x^*x)$. Therefore the discount factor is in the payoff space. Because of the linearity it must be of the form: $x^* = \psi^T x$ with $\psi = E(x^T x)^{-1} p$. From the linearity assumption it also follows that $E(x^T x)^{-1}$ is not singular. Hence $x^* = E(x^T x)^{-1} p^T x$ is the discount factor in M and prices assets by construction [more generally Hansen and Richard (1987)]. Since the valuation is not affected by adding an arbitrary random variable ε orthogonal to all $x \in M$:

$$p = E\left[(x^* + \varepsilon)x\right],$$

there are an infinite number of random variables $m = x^* + \varepsilon$ satisfying $p = E(mx)$ [see Hansen and Jagannathan (1991) for details] unless markets are complete. However, the orthogonal random variables cannot be projected on M and hence x^* is unique. By construction it represents the market pricing kernel with the smallest second moment. Hence, the law of one price guarantees the existence of a consistent but unrestricted state price vector.

Clearly, law of one price arbitrage opportunities only occur if a riskless portfolio with a positive expected payoff, whose variance converges to zero, has a non positive price, i. e. if we have an infinite arbitrage opportunity without any net employment

---

2. Because of the state dependence of the discount factor it is usually called a stochastic discount factor or market pricing kernel.

of capital. In that context the law of one price represents the most popular notion of arbitrage and forms a substantial argument for the derivation of the some APT models and even option pricing models [Black and Scholes (1973)]. Nevertheless we will show in the subsequent sections that the law of one price is not sufficient to price assets by arbitrage since risky arbitrage opportunities might be present even if the law of one price holds. Thus the law of one price does not prohibit wrong fundamental valuations. It only guarantees that similar assets or the same assets in different markets are mispriced in the same degree.

6.1.2   Riskless Arbitrage

The absence of riskless or asymptotic arbitrage plays an important role in the derivation of the APT. This assumption states that if a sequence of portfolios $\{\phi\}$ with a positive net investment and a variance that converges to zero exists, then the limiting portfolio must earn the riskless rate or return. Like the law of one price, this assumption excludes some infinite arbitrage opportunities. The absence of asymptotic arbitrage is not necessarily stronger than the absence of law of one price arbitrage. However, the existence of a riskless asset guarantees that the former implies the latter [proof by Jarrow (1988)]. Whenever there is no riskless asset the absence of asymptotic arbitrage provides no constraints for the valuation of risky assets. Then all pricing implications in the light of infinite arbitrage opportunities with unconstrained Sharpe ratios come entirely from the law of one price. Furthermore a riskless investment opportunity is essential to guarantee that the absence of asymptotic arbitrage implies a continuous valuation functional. Otherwise the sequence of portfolios $\{\phi\}$ does not need to be cauchy. In that case the convergence of $\{\phi\}$ remains unrestricted. As long as riskless investment opportunities are feasible there exists a continuous linear valuation functional [Oh, Ross and Shanken (1997), Lemma 2].

A riskless asset requires the purchase of one contingent claim for each state. Since the concept of asymptotic arbitrage free markets means that we cannot earn the riskless rate of return with a zero investment, the sum of all state contingent claim prices must diverge from zero. Additionally no further restriction on the prices of contingent claims remains, which as will be shown later has important implications for the derivation of the security market line. However, like the law of one price arbitrage, no net capital expenditures are required so that infinite arbitrage opportunities result.

6.1.3   No Arbitrage

While the law of one price and the absence of riskless arbitrage focus on infinite arbitrage opportunities with an unconstrained Sharpe-ratio, the more general no-arbitrage condition includes risky and thus finite arbitrage opportunities with a constrained Sharpe-ratio. The introduction of risky arbitrage opportunities means that there might be an arbitrage opportunity η with positive probability but not with probability one. This condition is independent of the necessary condition that the price of portfolio η must be equal to the weighted sum of the prices of the basic securities. A risky arbitrage opportunity then can be characterized by a non-negative cash flow from purchasing portfolio η with probability one but a probability of less then one for a positive cash flow. Under this circumstances the finite arbitrage opportunity is caused by a non-positive price for this portfolio with probability one and hence a negative market value of η with a positive probability of less than one.

$$prob(x^T\eta \geq 0) = 1 \ prob(x^T\eta > 0) > 0 \ prob(x^T1 \leq 0) = 1 \ prob(x^T1 < 0) > 0 \ (6.1)$$

A payoff space M and a accompanying pricing functional $p(x)$ leave no arbitrage opportunities if every payoff that is almost surely positive and strictly positive with some positive probability has a strictly positive price. There is a striking difference to the common use of arbitrage since comprehensive mispricings where both the underlying asset and its duplication are mispriced are considered in our paper. In the light of the fundamental asset evaluation theorem the latter condition applies to contingent claims. Nevertheless it also relates to option pricing when some underlying and its riskless duplication portfolio are mispriced in the same degree such that no riskless arbitrage is possible. In contrast to a riskless arbitrage opportunity, risky arbitrage means an arbitrage opportunity by chance or probability. Hence there is a residual risk in probability and also in variance. This representation of the absence of arbitrage in a finite dimensional setting follows from the existence of a limited liability asset. In contrast, a riskless arbitrage opportunity requires $prob(x^T1 < 0) = 1$ and the existence of a riskless investment opportunity with a positive price in which the proceeds might be invested. Beyond that, risky arbitrage represents an intertemporal arbitrage strategy. Hence risky arbitrage corresponds to finite arbitrage opportunities with constrained Sharpe ratios. A riskless arbitrage portfolio cannot be formed because both the basic securities and the assets are mispriced to the same degree. The absence of risky arbitrage clearly implies the absence of riskless or law of one price arbitrage, since infinite arbitrage opportunities generally presume (6.1) with probability one.

The above definition of an arbitrage opportunity is constrained to finite asset markets. However its basic idea extends to infinite asset markets. The concept of the complete absence of arbitrage, which means that we cannot sell a portfolio for a positive current price which probably involves no future payoffs, can be defined in the familiar Hilbert space using the concept of 'no free lunches' [Kreps (1981)] or an even weaker axiom characterized by Clark (1993). More generally, an arbitrage opportunity still exists as long as future payoffs may be avoided by hedging the arbitrage position with a transaction at a price given the true valuation function [Garman (1976)]. In complete markets the no arbitrage condition implies that there exists a market pricing kernel $m > 0$ such that $E(mx) = p$ or equivalently $E(mr) = 1$. Since the completely absence of arbitrage entails the law of one price, there is a unique projection of the market pricing kernel on M with: $E(x^*x) = p$. The no arbitrage condition guarantees that the market pricing kernel is strictly positive. Formally consider the subspace L^{2+} of nonnegative random variables in L^2 and a strictly positive $l \in L^{2+}$. Also denote two sequences $\{x_i\}$ and $\{y_i\}$ with $x_i \geq y_i$ and $y_i \to l$ in $M \cap L^2$. The dominance of $\{x_i\}$ implies that x_i should sell at least at the price of y_i. Furthermore if we assume that x_i is a limited liability asset with:

$$prob_i(x \geq 0) = 1$$
$$prob_i(x > 0) > 0$$

for at least one not negligible investor then we have no arbitrage opportunities if and only if $\lim[\inf p(x_i)] > 0$. The most important implication of the absence of arbitrage is the existence of a positive continuous linear valuation functional which is the same as the existence of positive state prices that correctly price all assets by construction. Indeed this is the case whenever the state space is finite [proofs by Kreps (1981), Duffie and Huang (1986), Clark (1993)]. Furthermore, since arbitrage opportunities increase the budget of rational investors, the absence of arbitrage or even the existence of a positive continuous linear pricing rule is equivalent to an optimal demand for some risk averse agent. The equivalence between the absence of arbitrage, positive state prices and a linear valuation functional follows from Stiemke's lemma and was implicitly used by Ross (1977, 1978) to evaluate risky assets.[3] More generally the Hahn-Banach extension theorem implies that the valuation functional applies to all assets and not just those actually marketed.

---

3. Some authors only refer to the use of Farkas' Lemma. However the Farkas' Lemma does not guarantee the equivalent martingale properties which are satisfied by the Stiemke Lemma.

The above zero net profit condition from arbitrage trading also prohibits riskless arbitrage opportunities. As long as $\{x\} \to x^*$ prices must converge $p(x) \to p(x^*)$ in the limit whenever a positive state price vector is used as the valuation functional. Hence the latter is positive, linear and continuous [theorem 2, Clark (1993)].[4]

6.2 Single Factor Models and the APT

In this section we establish equivalencies between the three concepts of arbitrage and the market pricing kernel. By the market pricing kernel we mean a random variable that can be used to evaluate uncertain investments by discounting state by state the corresponding payoffs. We show that different arbitrage concepts imply different conditions on the market pricing kernel. Then we demonstrate some connections between the security market line and the arbitrage concepts. In contrast to the conventional use of the security market line (SML) in the context of the CAPM the SML is represented as a linear function of the covariances between returns and a benchmark variable. We employ the projection of the market pricing kernel on the return space as benchmark.

Market Pricing Kernel

Independently of the assumption of the absence of arbitrage or the weaker absence of the law of one price or riskless arbitrage, virtually all arbitrage asset pricing models imply that the gross return of any asset multiplied by a market pricing kernel has a constant conditional expectation:

$$E_t(m_{t+1}r_{t+1}) = 1.$$

Hence, observable implications of candidate arbitrage asset pricing models are summarized conveniently in terms of their implied market pricing kernels [Hansen and Richard (1987)].[5] Expected returns are then determined by the covariance of the market pricing kernel with the asset returns:

---

4. As reasoned above the absence of arbitrage is equivalent to utility maximization by some representative investor. The marginal utility of unsaturated consumers is always positive and hence the intertemporal marginal rate of substitution is likewise a positive random variable. From equilibrium asset pricing it is clear that the intertemporal marginal rate of substitution or analogously the intertemporal marginal rate of transformation is a valid market pricing kernel. Thus the state price vector should be positive such we cannot get a portfolio for free that probably pays off positively.

5. For the above reasons the market pricing kernel is a state dependent vector of discount factors. This vector multiplied with the matrix of state dependent asset returns has a constant expectation. In the subsequent sections we assume that the market pricing kernel m is a random variable

$$E_t(r_{t+1}) = E_t(m_{t+1})^{-1} \left[1 - \text{cov}_t(r_{t+1}, m_{t+1})\right].\tag{6.2}$$

Given the market pricing kernel as a benchmark variable, the conditional covariance of returns with m_{t+1} is a general measure of systematic risk. Thus, securities' expected returns should be ranked according to their conditional covariance with the benchmark variable. Since any valid benchmark should explain expected returns, the behavior of expected returns can be used to restrict the set of benchmark variables. This motivates the use of conditioning information for the estimation of expected returns and at least the application of conditional asset pricing models [e. g. see Ferson (1989), Harvey (1989), Ferson and Korajczyk (1995)]. If the conditional covariance is zero for a particular asset, the expected return equals the riskless rate of return, if available. Hence, the gross riskless rate of returns equals the recursive expectation of the market pricing kernel. Since the recursive gross riskless rate of return is determined by the sum of all state dependent contingent claim prices, this has substantial importance for the derivation of asset pricing models. An arbitrage-free valuation implies that all state dependent contingent claim prices are strictly positive. The weaker absence of riskless arbitrage only implies that the sum of the contingent claim prices diverges from zero. Indeed this implication follows entirely from the existence of a riskless investment opportunity. Otherwise the absence of asymptotic arbitrage has no further implications for the contingent claim prices. The law of one price guarantees that the state price vector represents a consistent pricing functional but nevertheless does not imply any restrictions on state dependent contingent claim prices. Clearly with the absence of only infinite arbitrage opportunities negative prices for contingent claims are possible and risky arbitrage opportunities remain. Beside that fundamental misleading pricing implications of the law of one price or the absence of asymptotic arbitrage, there is another major objection against the use of the law of one price and asymptotic arbitrage for asset valuation. Since the riskless rate of return, if available, is exogenously determined by the money or bond markets, the sum of the state contingent prices must sum up to the reverse gross riskless rate of return. Hence if some state contingent claim prices are negative, their undervaluation must be compensated by some overvaluation of the contingent claims which have positive prices. Thus the mispricing of some contingent claims necessarily implies the mispricing of other contingent claims. Since assets are linear combinations of the basic contingent claims with unknown weights, there is no need that both effects cancel out each other. Moreover since

---

represented by multiplying the payoff by the state dependent discount factors and weighted adding across states of nature using the underlying probabilities.

contingent claims and hence assets which provide some hedge against consumption
or income risks have higher prices and lower returns, the overvaluation of at least
one contingent claim and possibly of the corresponding assets with high loadings
on that particular contingent claim lead to a overestimation of the risk aversion of
investors. If markets do not permit any infinite arbitrage but provide some finite
arbitrage opportunities by probability a higher risk aversion is needed to explain
the risk premiums of asset returns due to the wrong valuation of at least one basic
security. Obviously some questions remain as to the extent of risk aversion that is
allowable for investors to still realize risky arbitrage.

The set of consistent market pricing kernels particularly with regard to the
different arbitrage scenarios might be described by:

$$M^{NA} = \left\{ m | m > 0, E(mr) = 1, E(m) = r_f^{-1} \right\} \tag{6.3}$$

$$M^{NRA} = \left\{ m | m \neq 0, E(mr) = 1, E(m) = r_f^{-1} \right\} \tag{6.4}$$

$$M^{LOOP} = \left\{ m | E(mr) = 1, E(m) = r_f^{-1} \right\} \tag{6.5}$$

where NA denotes the absence of arbitrage, NRA the no riskless arbitrage condition
and LOOP the law of one price. Clearly the no arbitrage condition is the most
restrictive assumption. However, since state contingent claim prices cannot be
inferred, reliable risky arbitrage opportunities are difficult to identify [for more
details see Ledoit (1995) and Ledoit and Bernado (1996)]. There are some equivalent
ways of representing a linear pricing rule. In one case, the price is the expected
value under risk-neutral probabilities discounted at the riskless return. Recently
some attempts were introduced to infer risk-neutral probabilities from option and
stock prices [Rubinstein (1994), Jackwerth and Rubinstein (1996)].

The security market line

By the Riesz representation theorem every bounded linear functional on a Hilbert
space has a unique representation in that space. Therefore every market pricing
kernel may be expressed as a portfolio of asset returns. Therefore Hansen and
Jagannathan (1991) run a regression of m on the asset returns:

$$m = E(m) + [r_{t+j} - E(r_{t+j})]^T \beta_m + \varepsilon$$

so that the projection of m on R follows from:

$$x^* = E(m) + [r_{t+j} - E(r_{t+j})]^T \beta_m.$$

The regression coefficients are subject to the requirement that the projection of the market pricing kernel correctly prices all assets:

$$E(rx^*) = 1. \tag{6.6}$$

Hence the weights are given by:

$$\beta_m = \Sigma^{-1} \left[1 - E(m) E_t(r_{i,t+j}) \right]$$

where Σ denotes the covariance-matrix of asset returns. By construction the regression residuals are uncorrelated with the returns. Thus the variance of the market pricing kernel is determined by the weighted variance of the returns and the variance of the regression residuals:

$$\text{var}(m) = \text{var}\left[(r_{t+1} - E(r_{t+1})) \beta_m \right] + \text{var}(\varepsilon)$$

The weights follow from the composition of the projection portfolio β_m. Clearly the projection of the market pricing kernel has the smallest second norm among all portfolios satisfying the pricing condition and hence represents a suitable benchmark variable.

From the variance decomposition of (9) it follows that all assets have an expected return equal to the riskless rate plus a risk adjustment due to covarying with the benchmark variable x^*:

$$E(r_i) = E(x^*)^{-1} - \text{cov}(r_i, x^*) E(x^*)^{-1} = r_f - \text{cov}(r_i, x^*) E(x^*)^{-1}.$$

This corresponds to the basic concept of the security market line, where expected security returns lie in the span of a riskless rate of return and the risk premia determined by the covariance between returns and a benchmark. Hence the security market line always exists if there is a random market pricing kernel in M satisfying the pricing condition. As long as we accept that the variance is a proxy for risk and the reward to variability is $-\text{var}(x^*) E(x^*)^{-1}$, we have:

$$E(r_i) = r_f + \left(\frac{\text{cov}(r_i, x^*)}{\text{var}(x^*)} \right) \left(-\frac{\text{var}(x^*)}{E(cx^*)} \right) = r_f + b_{i,x^*} \lambda_{x^*}. \tag{6.7}$$

In traditional analysis it is assumed that the security market line intercept is strictly non-zero. Clearly this is not necessarily the case. Implicitly it must be assumed that there are no infinite arbitrage opportunities and there is a riskless investment opportunity in M such that $E(m) \neq 0$ and hence, the security market line has a non-zero intercept.[6] Otherwise the market permits a simple covariance representation of the expected returns. Altogether the absence of riskless or law of one price arbitrage and the existence of a riskless asset provide sufficient conditions for a security market line with a non-zero intercept. Without a riskless asset, the no riskless arbitrage condition does not imply any relevant information for evaluating risky cash flows. Infinite arbitrage opportunities are then determined entirely by the law of one price. However, as reasoned above, the law of one price does not constrain the prices of state dependent contingent claims. Clearly negative prices for contingent claims are possible and due to the absence of a riskless rate of return the sum of the state contingent claim prices may equal zero. Hence, under and only under these assumptions the security market line (SML) can have a zero intercept without violating the law of one price. Gilles and LeRoy (1991) find in a different context that a zero-intercept of the security market line is not inconsistent with the law of one price. Regarding this issue they raise concern about the ability of the APT to price assets correctly. Gilles and LeRoy have gone further, arguing that alternative models could provide sufficient reasons for the conclusions of the APT. Unfortunately they miss the above arbitrage conditions. Clearly a zero intercept SML is not generally inconsistent with the absence of infinite arbitrage but under no circumstances is it compatible with the absence of infinite arbitrage opportunities whenever a riskless rate of return is in M. Furthermore a zero intercept SML is inconsistent with the absence of finite arbitrage opportunities. Even if there is a riskless investment opportunity and the market prohibits infinite arbitrage opportunities but permits finite arbitrage, the SML has a non-zero intercept. In that case the security market line does not reflect all the information needed to evaluate risky assets. As shown above, the complete absence of arbitrage implies that all state contingent claim prices are strictly positive. Hence the expected market pricing kernel needs to be positive, whether a riskless investment opportunity exists or not. Thus the intercept of the security market line is strictly positive whenever the market prohibits any arbitrage.

Generally the APT should assume the absence of arbitrage and consequently imply a security market line with a positive intercept. Unfortunately almost all APT models in practice only assume the absence of infinite arbitrage opportunities and hence miss substantial information for asset pricing. Among others this can be expressed by a non-positive intercept of the SML. This is also due to the single period characteristics of the traditional APT. Clearly, in a single period intertemporal ar-

---

6. In that case the absence of riskless arbitrage implies the absence of law of one price arbitrage.

bitrage explained by the mispricing of both contingent claims and traded securities may be impossible. Since the related arbitrage may be risky there is no need that this dual mispricing will disappear in one period. Accordingly the traditional APT is only referred to the absence of infinite arbitrage opportunities. As we have shown in the above sessions, the exclusion of finite arbitrage trades implies the no infinite arbitrage condition and forms a necessarily condition for arbitrage asset pricing. Hence, the absence of finite and thus of infinite arbitrage opportunities is essential for the derivation of a security market line that reflects necessary conditions for asset pricing. If the APT excludes risky arbitrage it provides a theoretical useful concept for asset pricing. Since trading in finite arbitrage opportunities is risky, the extent to which risky arbitrage is realized by investors depends on their risk aversion. Moreover, the traditional APT does not consider any finite arbitrage opportunities. Hence the failure of the traditional APT as well as the mispricing of the generalized APT must depend on the risk aversion of a representative investor. In some independent work, Dybvig (1983) and Grinblatt and Titman (1983) showed that the approximate pricing result of the traditional APT, e. g. the bound on individual assets' deviations from APT pricing, is restricted by the risk aversion of a representative investor. Under these circumstances the SML based criticism against the generalized APT altogether strictly fail, whereas the traditional APT obviously has some shortcomings. But clearly the criticism by Gilles and LeRoy (1991) do not affect the APT because a SML with a zero intercept is only possible when there is no riskless investment opportunity. Anyway, since finite arbitrage opportunities definitely represent some kind of intertemporal arbitrage whereby the traditional APT is a single period model, theoretical concepts and empirical studies of the APT should be based on the intertemporal APT by Connor and Korajczyk (1989) to entirely prohibit any arbitrage. Unfortunately the assumptions of this model, i. e., the factor structure for dividends, are restrictive, whereas the basic factor structure of returns and its empirical difficulties in the light of factor selection remain [i. e. the substantial criticism of Reisman (1992) and Nawalkha (1997)].[7]

---

7. However one major criticism by Gilles and LeRoy (1991) against the APT is still valid. Since the APT usually assumes that the returns form a Hilbert-Space there always exists an algebraic basis. Hence, there is always an equivalent factor representation of returns by construction. Therefore Gilles and LeRoy argue that exact and approximate factor pricing do not constitute substantive characterizations of asset pricing. Steiner and Wallmeier (1997) challenge this view. However, in the present paper we show that arbitrage considerations provide additional information compared to empirical factor pricing.

Arbitrage Pricing Theory

A valid market pricing kernel guarantees that there is a random variable in M such that the expected price of any payoff in L^2 can be presented as the inner product of the payoff and m. We have gone further by projecting the market pricing kernel on the payoff space to obtain a benchmark variable in terms of asset payoffs or returns. The benchmark variable indeed represents the market pricing kernel with a minimal second moment within a broader class of market pricing kernels. The market pricing kernel prices all assets by construction with respect to different arbitrage scenarios. Unfortunately it does not provide an easy to implement calculator for expected returns since we potentially use all N asset returns to price N assets. Thus we have no degrees of freedom. The basic concept of the APT developed by Ross (1976) is to substitute the projection of the market pricing kernel on returns or payoffs on all assets by a projection of the market pricing kernel of a limited set of K returns or payoffs which span the entire set of returns or payoffs, that means on the algebraic basis f of M.[8] Since the factors f generate M the pricing implications of both projections on asset returns and the algebraic basis are the same. Moreover we will have N—K degrees of freedom and can infer statistically reliable statements. Berberian (1976) proved that there always exist an algebraic basis in a Hilbert space. However a Hilbert space represents a sufficient but not a necessary condition for the existence of an algebraic basis. Friedman (1970) proved that an algebraic basis always exist for a set of traded assets whenever there are no arbitrage opportunities. Implicitly it must be asserted that all portfolios are traded. Hence the assumption of arbitrage free markets presents a sufficient condition for an algebraic basis.

The algebraic basis which spans the entire set of traded assets is represented by the smallest set of assets f, such that an arbitrary asset in M can be constructed as a finite unique linear combination of f. Therefore it is assumed that the factors are traded and linearly independent. However it is important to point out that, given the an algebraic basis, the linear combination weights are uniquely associated with the algebraic basis but the latter is not unique. The arbitrage pricing theory prices assets in M relative to the prices of the assets in the algebraic basis. The expected returns of the algebraic basis set are given exogenously and the expected returns of the other marketed assets in M are determined from these. That is, F is a finite-dimensional subspace of M, generated by the linear span of f under the covariance inner product. Since M is a subspace of L2 and represents a Hilbert space, F itself

---

8. We use the term algebraic basis in the sense of a common orthogonal basis in a Hilbert space. However mean variance spanning is not necessary for the derivation of the APT. Mean variance intersection provides a sufficient condition for exact factor pricing.

must be in accord with a Hilbert space. Hence F corresponds to a pseudofactor subspace, if for any return there exists some unique linear combination weights $b \in |^k$ such that:

$$r_i = \sum_{i \in K} b_i f_i + \varepsilon_i.$$

The definition of the factor space follows Gilles and LeRoy (1991) but is slightly different from Ross (1976, 1977). However no further assumptions are needed for the subsequent chapters and thus, our results apply to both strict and approximate factor structures. Given the pseudofactor space $F \subseteq M$ exact factor pricing holds with respect to a k-dimensional algebraic basis with a risk premia $\delta \in |^k$ such that:

$$E(r_i) = b_i \delta \forall i \in M. (11) \tag{6.8}$$

Exact factor pricing requires that expected returns are linear in the factor loadings and that residual risks ε do not influence expected returns, that is, only factor risks deserve nonzero current prices.

Since the factors in f in the ideal case span the entire set of returns, the market pricing kernel equivalently can be projected on the pseudofactor subspace F such that there exists one linear combination α of factors which correctly prices all assets:

$$E(f^* r) = E(x^* r) = 1.$$

According to the Riesz representation theorem and the generalized case when there is no riskless investment opportunity, one factor in the algebraic basis must represent the expectation functional [Chamberlain and Rothschild (1983)]. Clearly this is due to the continuous and linear characteristics of the expectation functional in M. Therefore we follow Chen and Knez (1994) in the sense that we choose the first factor f_1 in the algebraic basis to be the expectation-representing factor implied by the Riesz representation theorem. Without loss of generality the remaining factors are assumed to have zero mean, that is: $E(f_j) = 0$ for each $j \in [2, K]$. Clearly since the algebraic basis is constrained to include the expectation operator the algebraic basis cannot be chosen arbitrary. However under this assumptions the classical APT results:

$$r_i = E(r_i) + \sum_{j=2}^{K} b_{j,i} f_j + \varepsilon_i.$$

By the projection theorem we have:

$$1 = E(f^*r) = E(r)E(f^*f_1) + \sum_{j=2}^{k} b_j E(f_j f^*)$$

which asserts that the projected functional applies to all portfolios and hence traded factors.

If there are some residual returns that are not in the span of f they form a subspace $E \subset M$ which itself corresponds to a Hilbert space. Clearly, in this case $E \cup F$ spans the entire space of returns. Since an algebraic basis always exists in a Hilbert space, E is generated by a basis γ. Therefore the difference between the projection of the market pricing kernel on M and on F is represented by a linear combination a so that:

$$x^* - f^* = a^T \gamma.$$

All linear combinations of γ are by construction orthogonal to F. Since f^* prices all assets by the Riesz representation theorem, all linear combinations of (deserve zero current prices:

$$E(f^*\gamma) = 0.$$

Hence the systematic risk of e relative to the factors in the algebraic basis is zero such that a represents a $(N - K)$-dimensional vector of zeros.[9] Hence, the projections of the market pricing kernel on M and on F almost surely imply the same restrictions, that is: $f^* = x^*$, whenever we have exact factor pricing. Since we focus on differences in the evaluation of risky assets under different arbitrage concepts we assume exact factor pricing in the subsequent chapters. However our results generalize to approximate factor pricing but there would be additional errors aggravating our further analysis. Clearly we do not consider the central proposition of any factor pricing model, that is that the pricing functional can be precisely represented by some linear combination of factors. In particular the minimum distance between the projection x^* and at least one portfolio of factors should be zero.[10]

The basic valuation functional may be projected on the space of returns without a loss of generality. Since the inner product of the benchmark portfolio and any return

---

9. Since the price of all portfolios of (is assumed to be zero the product of the diagonal (N-K)((N-K) covariance matrix of basis residuals and the (N-K)-dimensional weight vector a must equal zero.

10. See Hansen and Jagannathan (1997) and Chen and Knez (1994) for more details on that problem.

has a constant conditional expectation the inner product of the benchmark portfolio and any excess return equals zero. Hence by the law of iterated expectations we have:

$$E(mr^E) = E(x^*r^E) = 0.$$

This implies by the covariance inner product:

$$\frac{\sigma(m)}{E(m)} = -\frac{E(r^E)}{\sigma(r)\rho(m, r^E)}. \tag{6.9}$$

where ρ denotes the correlation coefficient. Since the benchmark portfolio is maximum correlated with the market pricing kernel we have:

$$\left| \frac{\sigma(x^*)}{E(x^*)} \right| \leq \frac{E(r^E)}{\sigma(r^E)}. \tag{6.10}$$

The right hand side of the above formula represents the Sharpe ratio of a particular portfolio. Since the benchmark portfolio has the smallest second moment among all elements of the broader class of solutions for the market pricing kernel it represents an efficient portfolio due to the fact that the benchmark portfolio itself is traded. Clearly the moments of the benchmark portfolio as well as the moments of a class of market pricing kernels are restricted by the moments of asset returns.

Once we have assumed that some APT model permits exact factor pricing the projection of the valuation functional on M almost surely equals the projection on F. Hence exact factor pricing is equivalent to the demand for an efficient linear combination of the factors in f that span M. Indeed one efficient combination of factors is represented by the projection of the market pricing kernel f^* on F. This follows from (12) and in a different context from Roll (1977) where it is shown that at least one efficient portfolio of factors provides a sufficient condition for any linear factor pricing model exactly evaluating risky assets. Roll proved that any efficient portfolio guarantees an exact linear pricing model relative to that benchmark. The APT generates this benchmark variable using a linear factor model. Hence any efficient factor portfolio is sufficient to guarantee Roll's pricing equivalence [Grinblatt and Titman (1987) give a more general proof].

Interestingly, Kruschwitz and Löffler (1997) argue that the APT fails since the same pricing results follow from a single beta model without considering arbitrage as long as the benchmark is efficient. From the above analysis it is straightforward that indeed a single beta representation of an arbitrary K factor APT model is possible. However the single beta representation follows from the efficiency of the benchmark portfolio that is referred to be the projection of the valuation functional on F. Since this linear combination of factors in f is efficient by construction, there necessarily must be an equivalently efficient linear combination of returns due to the fact that almost surely $f^* = x^*$. Hence by equation (10) and by Roll's equivalence theorem there is always a single beta representation of any APT model relative to the benchmark that reflects not only a projection of the valuation functional on F but also on M. However, the benchmark always represents the projection of a valuation functional implied by a particular concept of arbitrage. Of course there are different efficient portfolios that allow exact factor pricing by construction but some of them miss additional information relevant for pricing which is implied by the absence of arbitrage. In the subsequent chapters we show that the different arbitrage concepts imply different benchmark portfolios and hence arbitrage matters for pricing. More precisely we will show that there is some distance between the market pricing kernels under the different arbitrage concepts. Since arbitrage matters, the critique of Kruschwitz and Löffler (1997) strictly fails because of the specification of the benchmark portfolio to be the projection of a valid valuation functional implied by the absence of arbitrage instead of an arbitrary efficient portfolio implied by empirical factor models. However in the context of the traditional APT, that is the exclusion of infinite arbitrage opportunities, the absence of riskless arbitrage implies the absence of law of one price arbitrage if there is a riskless investment opportunity. Then the law of one price provides a necessary condition for a single beta representation of the APT. If there is no riskless investment opportunity all pricing information comes from the law of one price. In this case the latter represents a sufficient condition for a single beta representation of the traditional APT. Hence there exist opportunities to present the results of the traditional APT without considering asymptotic arbitrage as a key concept of that APT. However this is also due to the existence of a continuous linear valuation functional which may be projected on the set of factors or equivalently on returns. Thus without considering all implications of arbitrage and dominance there is a single beta representation due to the Riesz representation theorem. If we go further to prohibit any arbitrage, that is the absence of both finite and infinite arbitrage, the key concept of no arbitrage provides additional information for the evaluation of risky cash flows. Clearly there are four categories of single beta representations. The first one is due to the equivalency theorem by Roll since every efficient portfolio enables a single beta representation relative to this efficient portfolio. Second the law of one price allows the projection of the associated functional on the space of returns and hence allows a unique single beta representation relative to this projection. If there is a riskless asset in M the absence of riskless arbitrage implies the law of one price and thus the existence of a third single beta representation. Finally the absence of arbitrage allows a unique single beta representation for the same reasons as the law of one price relative to the projection of the valuation functional on the space of returns. Altogether the single beta representations of the APT follow immediately from the efficient market pricing kernel representation of the APT functional and consequently, this does not mean that the APT is not valid.[11]

6.3   Conclusion

We show that different concepts of arbitrage under certain conditions imply the existence of a security market line. The existence of such a security market line follows from the Riesz representation theorem and hence by the equivalent presentation of arbitrage valuation functionals by certain efficient portfolios. From the Hansen-Jagannathan bounds it follows that the projection of the valuation functional on the set of returns is efficient. However as long as there is exact factor pricing, any arbitrage valuation functionals can equivalently be projected on an algebraic basis of factors. Because of the equality of both projections in the case of exact factor pricing, we have mean variance intersection in at least that efficient portfolio which reflects the projections of the valuation functional on both factors and returns. From Roll (1977) it is straightforward that any efficient portfolio then guarantees a single beta representation. However we establish that the valuation functionals implied by the different concepts of arbitrage differ and hence the distance between their projections on returns or equivalent factors diverges from zero with positive probability. This implies that the absence of arbitrage is independent of the existence of a security market line and eliminates the close connection between the absence of arbitrage and the existence of a security market line. Since a consistent valuation of assets requires the complete absence of arbitrage the law of one price and the no riskless arbitrage condition lead to systematic pricing errors. Hence the APT must be generalized to prohibit risky arbitrage opportunities. Clearly, this is not inconsistent with some factor structure for the return generation. Unfortunately this sufficient and necessary condition for asset pricing depends on the valuation of contingent claims. Generally contingent claim prices cannot be inferred reliably because markets are mostly incomplete and options are not traded at continuous strike prices. Hence we never can guarantee that any valuation functional prices assets without inducing risky arbitrage opportunities. Therefore we argue that the APT cannot be tested empirically or equivalently empirical tests of the APT must

---

11. Moreover a single factor presentation of a multifactor model is always possible [Sharpe (1977)].

be interpreted with caution. Moreover our analysis applies to almost all arbitrage pricing models like option pricing. Hence models based solely on the absence of infinite arbitrage like the APT but also a large number of option valuation models lead to systematic pricing errors and hence only approximate arbitrage pricing remains without specifying the range of the approximation. We also provide simulation evidence on our theoretical results. Indeed we find dramatically pricing errors induced by the law of one price compared to the absence of arbitrage. Finally we present an empirical investigation of a traditional APT model. Although the results do not allow the rejection the APT we discuss the shortcomings of the traditional APT and potential pricing errors. Since there might be enormous valuation errors the results should be interpreted with caution.

References

Berberian, S. K., 1976, *An introduction to Hilbert-Space,* Chelsea.

Bernado, A. and O. Ledoit, 1996, Gain, loss and asset pricing, Working paper, University of California at Los Angeles.

Black, F. and M. Scholes, 1973, Pricing of options and corporate liabilities, *Journal of Political Economy* 81, 637–654.

Chamberlain, G. and M. Rothschild, 1983, Arbitrage, factor structure, and mean-variance analysis on large financial markets, *Econometrica* 51, 1281–1304.

Chen, Z. and P. J. Knez, 1994, A pricing operator-based testing foundation for a class of factor models, *Mathematical Finance* 4, 121–141.

Clark, S. A., 1993, The valuation problem in arbitrage theory, *Journal of Mathematical Economics* 22, 463–478.

Connor, G. and R. A. Korajczyk, 1986, Performance measurement with the arbitrage pricing theory: A new framework for analysis, *Journal of Financial Economics* 15, 373–394.

Connor, G. and R. A. Korajczyk, 1989, An intertemporal equilibrium beta pricing model, *Review of Financial Studies* 2, 373–392.

Connor, G., 1984, A unified beta pricing theory, *Journal of Economic Theory* 34, 13–31.

Ferson, W. E. and R. A. Korajczyk, 1995, Do arbitrage pricing models explain the predictability of stock returns?, *Journal of Business* 68, 309–349.

Franke, G. , 1984, On tests of the arbitrage pricing theory, *OR Spektrum* 6, 109–117.

Friedman, A., 1970, *Foundations of modern analysis,* Holt, Rinehart & Winston, New York, 1970.

Gilles, C. and S. F. LeRoy, 1991, On the arbitrage pricing theory, *Economic Theory* 1, 213–229.

Hansen, L. P. and R. Jagannathan, 1991, Implications of security market data for models of dynamic economies, *Journal of Political Economy* 99, 225–262.

Hansen, L. P. and R. Jagannathan, 1997, Assessing Specification Errors in Stochastic Discount Factor Models, *Journal of Finance* 52, 557–590.

Hansen, L. P. and S. F. Richard, 1987, The role of conditioning information in deducing testable restrictions implied by dynamic asset pricing models, *Econometrica* 55, 587–613.

Harvey, C. R., 1989, Time-varying Conditional Covariances in Tests of Asset Pricing Models, *Journal of Financial Economics* 24, 289–318.

Huberman, G., 1982, A simple approach to arbitrage pricing theory, *Journal of Economic Theory* 28, 183–191.

Jackwerth, J. C. and M. Rubinstein, 1996, Recovering probability distributions from option prices, *Journal of Finance* 51, 1611–1631.

Jarrow, R. A., 1988, *Finance theory,* Prentice-Hall, Englewood Cliffs.

Kreps, D. M., 1981, Arbitrage and equilibrium in economies with infinitely many commodities, *Journal of Mathematical Economics* 10, 15–35.

Kruschwitz, L. and A. Löffler, 1997, Ross' APT ist gescheitert. Was nun?, *Zeitschrift für betriebswirtschaftliche Forschung* 49, 644–651.

Ledoit, O., 1995, Factor selection for beta pricing models, Working paper, University of California at Los Angeles.

Nawalkha, S. K., 1997, A Multibeta Representation Theorem for Linear Asset Pricing Theories, *Journal of Financial Economics* 46, 357–381.

Oh, G., S. A. Ross and J. Shanken, 1997, The absence of arbitrage: Some new results, Working paper.

Reisman, H., 1992, Reference variables, factor structure, and the approximate multibeta representation, *Journal of Finance* 47, 1303–1314.

Roll, R., 1977, Critique of the Asset Pricing Theory's Tests, *Journal of Financial Economics* 5, 1977, S. 129–176

Ross, S. A., 1976, The arbitrage pricing theory of capital asset pricing, *Journal of Economic Theory* 13, 341–360.

Ross, S. A., 1977, Return, risk, and arbitrage, In Friend, I., J. L. Blume (eds.): *Risk and Return in Finance* Volume I, Ballinger, Cambridge (Ma.), 189–218.

Ross, S. A., 1978, A simple approach to the valuation of risky streams, *Journal of Business* 51, 453–475.

Rubinstein, M., 1994, Implied binomial trees, *Journal of Finance* 49, 771–818.

Shanken, J, 1982, The arbitrage pricing theory: Is it testable?, it Journal of Finance 37, 1129–1140.

Shanken, J., 1992, The current state of the arbitrage pricing theory, *Journal of Finance* 47, 1569–1574.

7 Bayesian Network Models of Portfolio Risk and Return

Catherine Shenoy and Prakash P. Shenoy

A Bayesian network is a tool for modeling large multivariate probability models and for making inferences from such models. A Bayesian network combines traditional quantitative analysis with expert judgement in an intuitive, graphical representation. In this paper, we show how to use Bayesian networks to model portfolio risk and return.

Traditional financial models emphasize the historical relationship between portfolio return and market return. In practice, to forecast portfolio return, financial analysts include expert subjective judgement about other factors that may affect the portfolio. These judgmental factors include special knowledge about the stocks in the portfolio that is not captured in the historical quantitative analysis.

We show how a Bayesian network can be used to represent a traditional financial model of portfolio return. Then we show how expert subjective judgement can be included in the Bayesian network model. The output of the model is the posterior marginal probability distribution of the portfolio return. This posterior return distribution can be used to obtain expected return, return variance, and value-at-risk.

The main goal of this paper is to show how Bayesian networks can be used to model portfolio risk and return. Bayesian networks have been used as a tool for modeling large multivariate probability models and for making inferences from such models (Pearl 1986, Lauritzen and Spiegelhalter 1988, Shenoy and Shafer 1990). A Bayesian network combines traditional quantitative analysis with an analyst's judgement in an intuitive, graphical representation. It allows an analyst to visualize the relationships among the variables in the model.

Finance models focus on the historical, quantitative relationships between economic variables. However, financial analysts usually combine historical data with qualitative information and judge how this information affects stock returns, market return, interest rates, or any other input to a portfolio model. For example, the anti-trust lawsuit against Microsoft affects the stock returns of many companies, but this type of information is difficult to incorporate in traditional return models. Bayesian networks are especially well suited for situations that combine quantitative and qualitative information. In this paper we provide an overview of how to combine traditional financial models with judgments about qualitative information in a Bayesian network framework.

Traditional portfolio return models are static. There is no systematic way to update results in the light of new information. A Bayesian network representation of portfolio return allows analysts to incorporate new information, to see the effect of that information on the return distributions for the whole network, and to visualize the distribution of returns, not just the summary statistics. In a Bayesian network, an analyst first determines the qualitative structure of the model in an intuitive graphical way. A traditional portfolio model can easily be represented as a Bayesian network. From that basic structure, quantitative information is then added to the model. Any change to either the qualitative or quantitative structure of the model is immediately reflected as the model is updated. The output of the Bayesian network analysis is a distribution of portfolio returns based on the qualitative and quantitative structure of the model.

Most traditional financial models rely on strong implicit assumptions about the independence of various factors incorporated in the model. In a Bayesian network model, the analyst can explicitly model the dependence or independence of the factors. It is then possible to determine the sensitivity of the portfolio return to those simplifying assumptions by relaxing the assumptions.

Portfolio risk analysis is typically based on the assumption that the securities in the portfolio are well diversified. Portfolios that contain securities with several correlated risk factors do not meet the well-diversified criteria. Some portfolios by construction contain a predominant factor. Examples include sector or regional mutual funds. Other portfolios may be constrained in their ability to diversify. Examples include financial institutions' loan portfolios or an individual's personal portfolio. Using a Bayesian network model, we can examine the effect of risk concentration on portfolio risk. From the posterior return distribution, we calculate the portfolio variance and compare it to a non-diversifiable risk measure. Using this approach, we explore the dependence and independence assumptions used in traditional portfolio models.

Traditional financial analysis focuses on summary statistics—expected returns, beta, variance or standard deviation of returns. Recently, value-at-risk analysis has emphasized consideration of the whole distribution of returns, or at least, the left-hand tail of the distribution. Since the output of the Bayesian network model is a posterior portfolio return distribution, we can also calculate the cutoff return for a value-at-risk calculation. As information is added to the network, the return distribution in the network reflects those changes and the cutoff value-at-risk is updated as well.

The rest of the paper proceeds as follows. In section one, we briefly discuss some traditional portfolio return models. In section two, we define and describe the semantics of a Bayesian network. In section three, we model a simple gold stock portfolio using a Bayesian network. Finally, in section four we discuss some modeling issues and limitations of Bayesian networks.

7.1   Traditional Portfolio Return Models

In a traditional portfolio analysis, the hypothesized relationship assumes that the rate of return on an asset is a linear function of the market rate of return and an asset specific factor, as follows:

$$R_i = a_i + b_i R_M + E_i \qquad (7.1)$$

where R_i denotes return on asset i, a_i and b_i are constants, R_M denotes return on a market index, and E_i denotes an uncertain variable related to asset-specific factors.

Many studies have shown that some specific identifiable components of risk are not fully accounted for by just a market index. These studies have found that industry-specific risk, country-specific risk, and many other components account for correlation among individual securities. King (1966) finds that market factors explain 30% of return variation and industry factors explain an additional 10%. Goodman (1981) shows that in country-specific diversified portfolios, significant mis-measurement of risk occurs if the market proxy does not include global factors.

The arbitrage pricing theory (APT) (Ross 1976) and other multi-factor models (see Elton and Gruber 1997) extends the single factor model to account for these additional, identifiable factors. The multi-factor model can be represented as an expanded version of equation (7.1):

$$R_i = a_i + b_{i1} F_1 + b_{i2} F_2 + \cdots + b_{ik} F_k + E_i \qquad (7.2)$$

where $F_1, \ldots, F_k$ denote the k independent factors, and $b_{i1,\ldots,}b_{ik}$ are constants.

Portfolio return, denoted by R_p, is defined as the weighted average of the individual returns that comprise the portfolio, $R_p = \sum_{i=1}^{n} w_i R_i$, where w_i denotes the proportional amount invested in security i, and n denotes the number of securities in the portfolio. Portfolio variance, denoted by σ_p^2, is given by:

$$\sigma_p^2 = b_{1p}^2 \sigma_{F_i}^2 + \cdots + b_{kp}^2 \sigma_{F_k}^2 + w_1^2 \sigma_{E_1}^2 + \cdots + w_n^2 \sigma_{E_n}^2 + \sum_{j=1}^{n} \sum_{i=1}^{n} w_i w_j \mathrm{cov}(E_i, E_j) \ (7.3)$$

where b_{jp} denotes the portfolio beta for the jth independent factor, $\sigma_{F_j}^2$ denotes the variance of the jth independent factor, and $\sigma_{E_j}^2$ denotes the residual asset-specific variance of the jth asset.

It is often assumed that all asset-specific uncertain variables, $E_1, \ldots, E_n$, are mutually independent. So portfolio variance simplifies to:

$$\sigma_p^2 = b_{1p}^2 \sigma_{F_1}^2 + \cdots + b_{kp}^2 \sigma_{Fk}^2 + w_1^2 \sigma_{E_1}^2 + \cdots + w_n^2 \sigma_{E_n}^2 \qquad (7.4)$$

Portfolio risk is divided into two components—diversifiable risk, $w_1^2 \sigma_{E_1}^2 + \cdots + w_n^2 \sigma_{E_n}^2$, and non-diversifiable risk, $b_{1p}^2 \sigma_{F_1}^2 + \cdots + b_{kp}^2 \sigma_{F_k}^2$. It is normally assumed that diversifiable risk is small since each w_1^2 is small. However, in study of bank loan portfolios, Chirinko and Guill (1991) find that assuming the covariance terms are zero leads to portfolio variances being under-estimated from 24.6% to 45.75%. For an equally weighted loan portfolio with 46 industries, the variance was under-estimated by 36.36%.

7.2   Bayesian Networks

Bayesian networks have their roots in attempts to represent expert knowledge in domains where expert knowledge is uncertain, ambiguous, and/or incomplete. Bayesian networks are based on probability theory.

A Bayesian network model is represented at two levels, qualitative and quantitative. At the qualitative level, we have a directed acyclic graph in which nodes represent variables and directed arcs describe the conditional independence relations embedded in the model. Figure 7.1 shows a Bayesian network consisting of four discrete variables: Interest Rate (IR), Stock Market (SM), Oil Industry (OI), and Oil Company Stock Price (SP). At the quantitative level, we specify conditional probability distributions for each variable in the network. Each variable has a set of possible values called its *state space* that consists of mutually exclusive and exhaustive values of the variable. In Figure 7.1, e.g., Interest Rate has two states: 'high' and 'low;' Stock Market has two states: 'good' and 'bad;' Oil Industry has two states: 'good' and 'bad;' and Oil Company Stock Price has two states: 'high' and 'low.' If there is an arc pointing from X to Y, we say X is a *parent* of Y. For each variable, we need to specify a table of conditional probability distributions, one for each configuration of states of its parents. Figure 7.1 shows these tables of conditional distributions—P(IR), P(SM | IR), P(OI), and P(SP | SM, OI).

7.2.1   Semantics of Bayesian Networks

A fundamental assumption of a Bayesian network is that when we multiply the conditionals for each variable, we get the joint probability distribution for all variables in the network. In Figure 7.1, e.g., we are assuming that P(IR, SM, OI, SP) = P(IR) $\oplus$ P(SM | IR) $\oplus$ P(OI) $\oplus$ P(SP | SM, OI), where $\oplus$ denotes pointwise multiplication of tables. The rule of total probability tells us that

$$P(IR, SM, OI, SP) = P(IR) \oplus P(SM \mid IR) \oplus P(OI \mid IR, SM)$$
$$\oplus P(SP \mid IR, SM, OI).$$

Comparing the two, we notice that we are making the following assumptions: $P(OI\mid IR, SM) = P(OI)$, i.e., OI is independent of IR and SM; and $P(SP \mid IR, SM, OI) = P(SP \mid SM, OI)$, i.e., SP is conditionally independent of IR given SM and OI.

Notice that we can read these conditional independence assumptions directly from the graphical structure of the Bayesian network as follows. Suppose we pick a sequence of the variables in a Bayesian network such that for all directed arcs in the network, the variable at the tail of each arc precedes the variable at the head of the arc in the sequence. Since the directed graph is acyclic, there always exists one such sequence. In Figure 7.1 one such sequence is IR SM OI SP. The conditional independence assumptions in a Bayesian network can be stated as follows. For each variable in the sequence, we assume that it is conditionally independent of its predecessors in the sequence given its parents. The key point here is that missing arcs (from a node to its successors in the sequence) signify conditional independence assumptions. Thus the lack of an arc from IR to OI signifies that OI is independent of IR; the lack of an arc from SM to OI signifies that OI is independent of SM; and the lack of an arc from IR to SP signifies that SP is conditionally independent of IR given SM and OI.

In general, there may be several sequences consistent with the arcs in a Bayesian network. In such cases, the lists of conditional independence assumptions (associated with each sequence) are equivalent using the laws of conditional independence (Dawid 1979). There are other equivalent graphical methods for identifying conditional independence assumptions embedded in a Bayesian network graph (see Pearl (1988) and Lauritzen et al. (1990) for examples.).

7.2.2   Making Inferences in Bayesian Networks

Once a Bayesian network is constructed, it can be used to make inferences about the variables in the model. The conditionals given in Bayesian network representation specify the *prior* joint distribution of the variables. If we observe (or learn about) the values of some variables, then such observations can be represented by tables where we assign 1 for the observed values and 0 for the unobserved values. Then the product of all tables (conditionals and observations) gives the (unnormalized) *posterior* joint distribution of the variables. Thus the joint distribution of variables changes each time we learn new information about the variables.

In theory, the posterior marginal probability of a variable X, say $P(X)$, can be computed from the joint probability by summing out all other variables except X

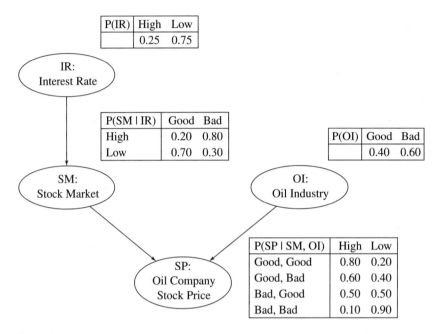

Figure 7.1
A Bayesian Network with Conditional Probability Tables

one by one. In practice, such a naive approach is not computationally tractable when we have a large number of variables because the joint distribution has an exponential number of states and values. The key to efficient inference lies in the concept of *local computation* where we compute the marginal of the joint without actually computing the joint distribution. A key feature of a Bayesian network is that it describes a joint distribution from the local relationships—such as a node and its parents. Instead of tackling the whole collection of variables simultaneously, Bayesian networks use the concept of factorization. Factorization involves breaking down the joint probability distributions into subgroups called factors in such a way that the naive computations described above need only be performed within each subgroup. Since the state space of a subgroup is much smaller than that of the joint probability distribution, the calculations become manageable.

Bayesian networks can be used for two types of inference.[1] Often we are interested in the values of some target variables. In this case, we make inferences by computing the marginal of the posterior joint distribution for the variables of interest. Consider the situation described by the Bayesian network in Figure 7.1. Suppose we are interested in the true state of Oil Company Stock Price (SP). Given the prior model (as per the probability tables shown in Figure 7.1), the marginal distribution of SP is 0.502 for high and 0.498 for low. Now suppose we learn that Interest Rate is low. The posterior marginal distribution of SP changes to 0.554 for high and 0.446 for low. Suppose we further learn that the state of Oil Industry is good. Then the marginal distribution of SP changes to 0.71 for high and 0.29 for low. This type of inference is referred to as *sum propagation*.

Sometimes we are more interested in the configuration of all variables ("the big picture") rather than the values of individual variables. In this case, we can make inferences by computing the mode of the posterior joint distribution, i.e., a configuration of variables that has the maximum probability. Consider again the situation described by the Bayesian network in Figure 7.1. Given the prior model (as per the probability tables shown in Figure 7.1), the mode of the prior joint distribution is (low interest rate, good stock market, bad oil industry, high oil company stock price). Now suppose we learn that Interest Rate is high. The mode of the posterior joint distribution changes to (high interest rate, bad stock market, bad oil industry, low oil company stock price). This type of inference is referred to as *max propagation*.

The results of inference are more sensitive to the qualitative structure of the Bayesian network than the numerical probabilities (Darwiche and Goldszmidt 1994). For decision making, the inference results are robust with respect to the numerical probabilities (Henrion et al. 1994).

There are several commercial software tools such as Hugin (www.hugin.com) and Netica (www.norsys.com) that automate the process of inference. These tools allow the user to enter the Bayesian network structure graphically, enter the numerical details, enter any additional information, and then do inference of either type. The results of the inference are then shown graphically using bar charts.

---

1. Lauritzen and Speigelhalter (1988), Jensen et al. (1990) and Shenoy and Shafer (1990) have devised propagation algorithms to perform efficient probabilistic inference.

7.3   A Bayesian Network Model of Multi-Factor Portfolio Return

In this section, we first describe a traditional security return model as a Bayesian network. Then we demonstrate how some of the independence assumptions in a traditional security return model can be relaxed using Bayesian networks.

7.3.1   Description of a Gold Stock Portfolio Network

A security return model is a conditional expectations model and is usually estimated using least squares regression, so that

$$E(R_i|F_1, F_2, \ldots, F_k) = a_i + b_{i1}F_1 + \cdots + b_{ik}F_k \qquad (7.5)$$

We can easily regard this as a Bayesian network model where the factors $F_1, \ldots, F_k$ are regarded as mutually independent variables.

The following Bayesian network model considers the return on an equally weighted portfolio of three stocks from the gold mining industry. Their ticker symbols are BGO, ABX, and AEM. In the representation shown in Figure 7.2, Market and Gold returns are parents of each stock's return. In addition, each stock return has an idiosyncratic component. The Portfolio Return is a function of each stock return and the weight of each stock in the portfolio. In the graph, each random variable is shown as a node. A variable that is conditionally deterministic given the values of its parents is shown as a double-bordered node.

The graphical model is supplemented by numeric information about the conditional probability distributions. For each variable in the model, we define the conditional probability distributions given each combination of states in the parent nodes. In Figure 7.2, Market, Gold, BGO Effects (e_{BGO}), ABX Effects (e_{ABX}), and AEM Effects (e_{AEM}) have no parents, so we specify a prior distribution for these nodes. BGO has Market, Gold and BGO Effects as its parents. Since BGO is a conditionally deterministic node, we specify a functional relation for its value as a function of the states of its parents. We also define a similar relation for ABX and AEM. Finally, Portfolio Return has BGO, ABX, and AEM. Since Portfolio Return is also a conditionally deterministic variable, it has a unique deterministic state given by some functional relation.

7.3.2   Inputs for the Bayesian Network

The conditional relationship for each of the stocks can be specified as an equation, such as the multi-factor model specified in equation (7.2); as a discrete conditional probability table; or as a continuous conditional probability distribution. Any com-

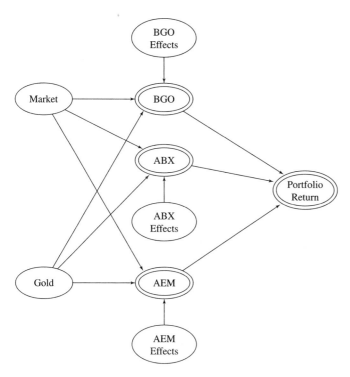

Figure 7.2
A Bayesian Network Model for a Portfolio

bination of historical data, forecasts, expert knowledge, or beliefs can be used to estimate the conditional relationships.

Initially for the primary inputs Market, Gold, and the individual stock effects we do not specify an explicit conditional relationship. We specify the a priori distribution for each of these as a normal distribution with parameters estimated over an arbitrary period from January 1996 through February 1998. We estimate weekly returns for these inputs. For example, using historical data over the estimation period, weekly market return has mean 0.55% and standard deviation 2.28%. These inputs are summarized in Table 7.1 below. For each stock effect, we assume a mean of zero and a standard deviation equal to the standard error of the regression equation.

For each of the stock returns, the distribution is conditioned on the Market and Gold returns and a stock-specific effect. The conditional distribution for each stock node is normal with mean based on equation (7.2) with factors of Market and Gold

Table 7.1
Parameter and Regression Estimates Used in Portfolio Network

Description	BGO Bema Gold Corp.	ABX Barrick Gold Gold Corp.	AEM Agnico Eagle Eagle Mines	Market S&P 500 Index	Gold London PM Gold Fix
Average monthly return (%)	0.68	−0.11	−0.42	0.55	−0.23
Standard deviation (%)	12.55	5.00	6.58	2.28	1.43
Regression estimates:					
Intercept	1.48	0.17	0.05		
Market coefficient	0.26	0.37	0.27		
Gold coefficient	3.96	2.26	2.76		
standard error	11.27	3.63	5.27		

returns. The mean stock return is the estimated regression for each stock node. The standard error of the regression is the standard deviation of the distribution.

The regression estimates are based on weekly returns from January 1996 through February 1998. The result of the equation using the state values of the inputs determines the stock return node. For ABX the conditional relationship is the estimated regression equation:

$$\text{ABX return} = 0.17 + 0.37 * \text{market} + 2.26 * \text{gold} + e_{\text{ABX}}, \tag{7.6}$$

A summary of all of the inputs and regression coefficients used for each of the nodes is presented in Table 7.1.

In order to generate the conditional return distributions for BGO, ABX, AEM, and the portfolio, we use Monte Carlo simulation. In the simulation, we specify the functional relationships between the nodes to generate the estimated return distributions. The portfolio return distribution is a simple average of the stock returns; that is, an equally weighted portfolio.

Table 7.2 reports additional statistics for each of the conditional probability return distributions based on the simulation results. The average weekly portfolio return is 0.06% with a standard deviation of 6.15%.

Figure 7.3 shows the simulated distribution of portfolio returns from the Bayesian network based on 10,000 iterations. Because we modeled the inputs to the network as normal distributions, the portfolio return distribution is also approximately normal. From the confidence interval for the mean and the median, we see that the mean return on this portfolio is not significantly different from zero. In Section 7.3.4 we compare this model and several other Bayesian network models to the actual portfolio return.

Table 7.2
Conditional Probability Distributions for Bayesian Network

	Market	Gold	BGO	ABX	AEM	Portfolio
Mean	0.55	−0.23	0.72	−0.43	−0.15	0.06
standard deviation	2.28	1.43	12.73	6.60	4.95	6.15
Minimum	−6.94	−5.10	−48.86	−24.84	−17.46	−19.39
Maximum	8.69	4.48	49.73	20.15	18.64	18.52
5th percentile	−3.19	−2.57	−20.00	−11.34	−8.09	−10.32
50th percentile	0.55	−0.23	0.82	−0.54	−0.26	0.18
95th percentile	4.30	2.12	20.61	10.13	8.15	9.85

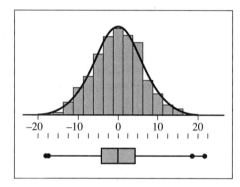

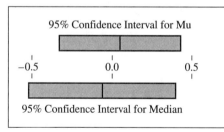

Variable: PortRet

Anderson-Darling Normality Test

A-Squared	0.25
p-value	0.74

Mean	0.05
Std Dev	6.17
Variance	38.10
Skewness	0.09
Kurtosis	−0.06
n of data	1000.00

Minimum	−18.07
1st Quartile	−4.20
Median	−0.10
3rd Quartile	4.34
Maximum	21.74

95% Confidence Interval for Mu
−0.33   0.43

95% Confidence Interval for Sigma
5.91   6.46

95% Confidence Interval for Median
−0.52   0.40

Figure 7.3
Portfolio Return Statistics from Bayesian Network Model

7.3.3   Bayesian Network as a Management Tool

A principal advantage of a Bayesian network representation of portfolio risk is in its flexibility as a management tool. In this section we show how new evidence can be entered into a network and how new information can be added to a network. Studies (see Henrion et al. (1994, 1996), and Pradhan et al. (1996)) have shown that the graphical representation of the conditional probabilities is the most important step

Table 7.3
Evidence for BGO

State for BGO	Likelihoods
Return of 0	0.20
Return of 10	0.80

Table 7.4
Revised Conditional Return Distributions

	BGO	Portfolio Return
Mean	4.30	1.25
standard deviation	4.95	3.69
Minimum	0.00	−12.06
Maximum	10.00	12.66
5th percentile	0.00	−4.73
50th percentile	0.00	1.09
95th percentile	10.00	7.27

in modeling. The exact numerical form is of secondary importance. Most decisions will be robust as long as the conditional independence relationships as encoded in the network are specified correctly. Managers usually have a good idea of the influences on a portfolio, but not their exact numerical form.

New information can be easily incorporated in the model. For example, suppose we learn that BGO will perform well in the next period if a new product is launched, but BGO will remain flat if the product is not launched on time. We also believe that it is very likely that the product launch will be on time. Specifically we model the evidence as a table of likelihoods as shown in Table 7.3 where a return of 10 is four times more likely than a return of 0. We incorporate this new evidence in the model, and recompute the marginals of the posterior distributions (as shown in Table 7.4) to reflect the new information.

A Bayesian network can also accommodate some types of information that is not easily incorporated in other types of models. Suppose an analyst learns that AEM and ABX have a common supplier whose favorable actions will affect both AEM and ABX. This new information can be added to the network using subjective probabilities. Figure 7.4 shows the addition of a new node that directly affects the nodes ABX effects (e_{ABX}) and AEM effects (e_{AEM}).

7.3.4 Additional Conditions in the Portfolio Return Model

The model we specify in Figure 7.2 is based on the traditional finance model that assumes the residual correlations are independent. We use the original return data to calculate the regression residuals and find the residual correlations among the

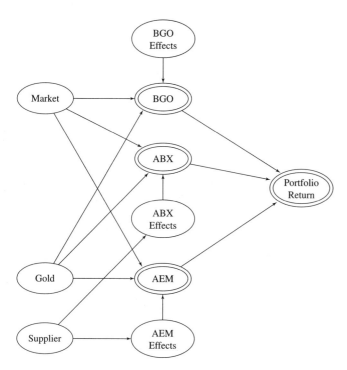

Figure 7.4
Revised Bayesian Network with Supplier Information

Table 7.5
Residual Correlations

	BGO Effects	ABX Effects	AEM Effects
BGO Effects	1		
ABX Effects	0.1814	1	
AEM Effects	0.3367	0.4427	1

stocks. The residual correlation is reported in Table 7.5. We find relatively large residual correlation between e_{ABX} and e_{AEM} and between e_{BGO} and e_{AEM}. We use this correlation data to specify three additional Bayesian network models that take into account these dependencies.

This high correlation indicates that there are still unmodeled factors which affect these stocks. If these factors are unknown, it is still possible to model the dependencies among the residuals. For any ordering of e_{BGO}, e_{AEM}, and e_{ABX}, using the multiplication rule, we have

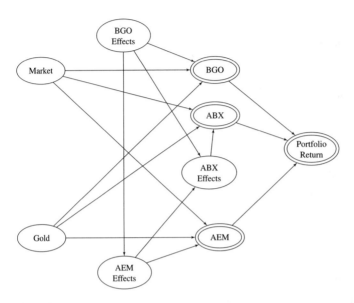

Figure 7.5
A Bayesian Network Model with Correlated Residuals

$$f(e_{\text{BGO}}, e_{\text{AEM}}, e_{\text{ABX}}) = f(e_{\text{BGO}})f(e_{\text{AEM}}|e_{\text{BGO}})f(e_{\text{ABX}}|e_{\text{BGO}}, e_{\text{AEM}}). \qquad (7.7)$$

Any other ordering of the residuals are equivalent to this ordering. This fact implies that a Bayesian network that captures all residual correlation can be specified with the following representation:

If X and Y are bivariate normal, the conditional distribution f(y | x) is given as:

$$f(y|x) \sim N\left(\frac{\rho\sigma_y}{\sigma_x}(x - \mu_x), (1 - \rho^2)\sigma_y^2\right). \qquad (7.8)$$

So if we assume that e_{BGO}, e_{ABX}, and e_{AEM} are multivariate normal, we specify three additional models with the following independence conditions:[2]

1. Model 2: $e_{\text{BGO}} \rightarrow e_{\text{AEM}}$, i.e., e_{BGO} is independent of e_{ABX}, and e_{AEM} is conditionally independent of e_{ABX} given e_{BGO};

2. Model 3: $e_{\text{AEM}} \rightarrow e_{\text{ABX}}$, i.e, e_{AEM} is independent of e_{BGO}, and e_{ABX} is conditionally independent of e_{BGO} given e_{AEM}; and

---

2. Model 1 is the Bayesian network shown in Figure 7.2 where we are assuming that the three effects are mutually independent.

Table 7.6
Comparison of Actual Portfolio Return and Portfolio Return Models

Portfolio	Mean	Std(Risk)	% difference from actual	
			Mean	Std
Actual portfolio return	0.050	6.8		
Finance Model–Non-diversifiable risk	0.053	4.3	5.4	−35.9
1. Simple Bayes Net (BN)	0.049	6.2	−1.8	−8.8
2. BN with $e_{BGO} \rightarrow e_{AEM}$	0.053	6.6	5.1	−2.9
3. BN with $e_{AEM} \rightarrow e_{ABX}$	0.052	6.2	4.1	−8.8
4. BN with $e_{BGO} \rightarrow e_{AEM} \rightarrow e_{ABX}$	0.054	6.7	7.3	−0.4

3. Model 4: $e_{BGO} \rightarrow e_{AEM} \rightarrow e_{ABX}$, i.e., e_{BGO} and e_{ABX} are conditionally independent given e_{AEM}.

To see the effect of adding these conditional probabilities we compare the actual returns over the three year period to each of the Bayesian network models and to the finance model. In Table 7.6, we find that each model slightly overestimates the mean and underestimates the standard deviation.

Actual portfolio return is measured assuming weekly portfolio rebalancing. The mean of the actual portfolio return is the arithematic average of the weekly portfolio returns. For the finance model we measure non-diversifiable risk as

$$\sqrt{b_{p,m}^2 \sigma_m^2 + b_{p,g}^2 \sigma_g^2},$$

where $b_{p,m}^2$ is the market portfolio beta squared, and $b_{p,g}^2$ is the gold portfolio beta squared. The portfolio beta is the weighted average of the appropriate gold or market return coefficients from the three regression equations. We see that modeling the effects with the largest residual correlations, $\rho_{BGO,AEM}$ and $\rho_{ABX,AEM}$ provides improvements in the risk and return estimation

Table 7.7 reports confidence intervals for the mean and standard deviation for the four Bayesian network models and the actual return. There are 115 weekly observations for the actual returns. The Bayesian network models are based on simulations of 10,000 iterations.

7.4 Modeling Issues and Limitations

Bayesian networks are able to incorporate different types of information. In this section we address the issues of how to find inputs to the network, discrete vs. continuous probability distributions, and some model limitations.

Table 7.7
95% Confidence Intervals for μ and σ

	Conf. Interval for μ			Conf. Interval for σ		
	$\overline{x}$	Lower	Upper	s	Lower	Upper
Actual	0.050	−1.200	1.300	6.8	6.1	7.6
Model 1	0.049	−0.334	0.432	6.2	6.0	6.4
Model 2	0.053	−0.355	0.460	6.6	6.3	6.8
Model 3	0.052	−0.331	0.435	6.2	6.0	6.4
Model 4	0.054	−0.365	0.472	6.7	6.1	7.6

7.4.1   Inputs to the network

Two types of inputs are needed for the network. First, factors that affect each asset return in the portfolio have to be identified. Then the conditional probability distributions for the asset returns have to be specified. Both types of inputs can be any combination of empirical data, expectations, judgment, or forecasts.

Many empirical studies have attempted to identify the factors that cause variation in security returns. Roll and Ross (1980), Dhrymes et al. (1984), Chen et al. (1986), Elton and Gruber (1997) identify factors such changes in inflation, industrial production, and yield spreads. Other portfolio specific factors may also be important. For example, a geographically limited portfolio would have a factor relating regional economic conditions to the stock returns. Common production inputs, customers, and other special circumstances can also be included.

Empirical analysis tools such as linear regression, factor analysis, time series analysis, neural nets and data mining techniques can all be used to generate the conditional probabilities for the dependent nodes. These tools examine the historical relationship among the nodes. Using these analytical tools may be equivalent to using current financial models, if the independence assumptions are the same. For example, Model 1 is equivalent to a traditional multi-factor model because each specific stock effect is assumed to be mutually independent, and all inputs are based on historical data.

Judgment and forecasts can be added to the model by revising the conditional probability tables for the nodes, by revising the priors for nodes with no parents, or by adding new nodes. Studies (see Henrion et al. (1994, 1996), and Pradhan et al. (1996)) have shown that the graphical representation of the probability model is the most important step in modeling. The numerical details of the probability model are of secondary importance. Most decisions will be robust as long as the conditional independence relationships as encoded in the network are specified correctly. Managers usually have a good idea of the influences on a portfolio, but not their exact numerical form. Discrete conditional distributions can be used as approximations of the exact form of the distribution.

The Bayesian network representation forces the modeler to make explicit judgments of the causal structure of the model. Traditional statistical models have an implicit causal structure that is not always appropriate. The decision-maker can examine the effect of assuming independent residuals and other factors in the model. For example, a model may have a geographic factor and a market factor. In a multi-factor model it is usually assumed the factors are independent; however, the market and geographic factor may not be independent. In a Bayesian network the dependence between the two factors can also be modeled.

7.4.2 Value-at-Risk

The value at risk (VAR) for a portfolio is the expected maximum loss over a target horizon within a given confidence interval. Recent, large corporate losses in Orange County, Barings Bank, Daiwa and others have received media and regulatory attention. Academicians, regulators, and financial managers have asserted to the need for a better method of summarizing risk. The value at risk metric is one way to quantify portfolio risk. This measure is easily incorporated into a Bayesian network model. The VAR measure is a linear function of the portfolio return defined as:

$$\text{VAR} = W_0 R^*, \tag{7.9}$$

where W_0 is initial investment and R^* is the cutoff portfolio return for the ith percentile. Using Model 1 at a cutoff percentile of 5, R^* and is equal to -10.32 percent, and $\text{VAR} = W_0(-0.1032)$ for a period of one week. An important consideration for VAR measures is the time over which risk is measured.

7.4.3 Limitations of Bayesian Network Models

A major limitation in using Bayesian networks to model portfolio returns is determining the graphical structure of the Bayesian network model. A graphical structure can either be obtained subjectively from an expert or one can be induced from data. The latter technique is the subject of current research in the uncertain reasoning literature (see (Heckerman 1997) for a recent survey). Once a graphical structure is obtained, determining the numerical parameters of the model is straightforward when securities are publicly traded and when data is often readily available.

If all variables in a Bayesian network are discrete, then the marginal distribution of any variable can be computed exactly using the local computational algorithms proposed, e.g., by Pearl (1988), Lauritzen and Spiegelhalter (1988), and Shenoy

and Shafer (1990). These algorithms are encoded in commercial software such
as Netica (www.norsys.com) and Hugin (www.hugin.com). Since security returns
are usually modeled as continuous variables, exact computation of the Bayesian
network is not always possible. We can either discretize the distributions or use
simulation methods. We can compute the posterior marginals approximately using
Monte Carlo methods (see, e.g., Henrion 1988). As the number of variables grows,
even Monte Carlo methods require an inordinate amount of sampling for a decent
approximation. In such cases, Markov Chain Monte Carlo methods have been
proposed for faster convergence (see, e.g., Gilks et al. 1996).

In our example, we assumed an equally weighted portfolio. If a manager is
evaluating a currently held portfolio, the weights will change as the stock prices
of the component returns change. Therefore assuming constant weights implies
constant rebalancing of the portfolio (to maintain the constant weights) as the
stock prices change. Of course, it is not possible to rebalance a portfolio without
incurring transaction costs, so the actual return from this type of a portfolio would
be lower. It is possible to construct a Bayesian network that calculates portfolio
return based on share prices and constant number of shares held. However, such
a model is quite different from a traditional finance model, and is the subject of
future research.

7.5 Conclusions

The main goal of this paper is to propose Bayesian networks as a tool for modeling
portfolio returns. Bayesian networks allow us to explicitly model the dependence
between the various factors that affect portfolio return. Also, recent advances in
the uncertain reasoning literature allow one to compute the marginal posterior
distribution of the portfolio return even when we have a multivariate probability
model with many variables. The marginal distribution of portfolio return can be
dynamically updated (using Bayes rule) as we observe the values of some of the
variables.

References

Chen, N., R. Roll and S. A. Ross (1986), "Economic Forces and the Stock Market," *Journal of Business*, 59, 386–403.

Chirinko, R. S. and G. D. Guill (1991), "A framework for assessing credit risk in depository institutions: Toward regulatory reform," *Journal of Banking and Finance*, 15, 785–804.

Darwiche, A. and M. Goldszmidt (1994), "On the relation between kappa calculus and probabilistic reasoning," in R. L. Mantaras and D. Poole (eds.), *Uncertainty in Artificial Intelligence: Proceedings of the Tenth Conference*, 145–153, Morgan Kaufmann, San Francisco, CA.

Dawid, A. P. (1979), "Conditional independence in statistical theory (with discussion)," *Journal of the Royal Statistical Society*, Series B, 41(1), 1–31.

Dhrymes, P. J., I. Friend, and N. B. Gultekin (1984), "A Critical Reexamination of the Empirical Evidence on the Arbitrage Pricing Theory," *Journal of Finance*, 39(2), 323–346.

Elton, E. J., M. J. Gruber and C. R. Blake (1997), "Common factors in mutual fund returns," Working Paper S-97-42, The NYU Salomon Center for Research in Financial Institutions and Markets, New York University, NY.

Elton, E. J., and M. J. Gruber (1997), *Modern Portfolio Theory and Investment Analysis*, 4th Ed., John Wiley & Sons, New York.

Gilks, W. R., S. Richardson, and D. J. Spiegelhalter (1996), *Markov Chain Monte Carlo in Practice*, Chapman & Hall, London.

Goodman, L. S. (1981), "Bank Lending to Non-OPEC LDCs: Are Risks Diversifiable?," *FRBNY Quarterly Review*, 10–20.

Heckerman, D. (1997), "Bayesian networks for data mining," *Data Mining and Knowledge Discovery*, 1, 79–119.

Henrion, M. (1988), "Propagating uncertainty in Bayesian networks by probabilistic logic sampling," in J. F. Lemmer and L. Kanal, N. (eds.), *Uncertainty in Artificial Intelligence*, 2, 149–164, North-Holland, Amsterdam.

Henrion, M., A. Darwiche, M. Goldszmidt, G. Provan, and B. Del Favero (1994), "An experimental comparison of infinitesimal and numerical probabilities for diagnostic reasoning," *Proceedings of the Fifth Workshop on the Principles of Diagnosis*, 131–139.

Henrion, M., M. Pradhan, B. Del Favero, K. Huang, G. Provan and P. O'Rorke (1996), "Why is diagnosis using belief networks insensitive to imprecision in probabilities," in E. Horvitz and F. Jensen (eds.), *Uncertainty in Artificial Intelligence: Proceedings of the Twelfth Conference*, 307–314, Morgan Kaufmann, San Francisco.

Jensen, F. V., S. L. Lauritzen and K. G. Olesen (1990), "Bayesian updating in causal probabilistic networks by local computation," *Computational Statistics Quarterly*, 4, 269–282.

Jorion, P. (1997), *Value at Risk: The New Benchmark for Controlling Market Risk,* McGraw Hill, NY.

Kao, D. (1993), "Illiquid securities: Pricing and performance measurement," *Financial Analysts Journal*, 28–35.

Keefer, D. L. (1994), "Certainty equivalents for three-point discrete-distribution approximations," *Management Science*, 40, 760–772.

King, B. (1966), "Market and industry factors in stock price behavior," *Journal of Business*, 39, 139–140.

Lauritzen, S. L. and D. J. Spiegelhalter (1988), "Local computations with probabilities on graphical structures and their application to expert systems (with discussion)," *Journal of Royal Statistical Society*, Series B, 50(2), 157–224.

Lauritzen, S. L., A. P. Dawid, B. N. Larsen and H.-G. Leimer (1990), "Independence properties of directed Markov fields," *Networks*, 20(5), 491–505.

Pearl, J. (1986), "Fusion, propagation and structuring in belief networks," *Artificial Intelligence*, 29, 241–288.

Pearl, J. (1988), *Probabilistic Reasoning in Intelligent Systems: Networks of Plausible Inference*, Morgan Kaufmann, San Mateo, CA.

Pradhan, M., M. Henrion, G. Provan, B. Del Favero, and K. Huang. (1996), The sensitivity of belief networks to imprecise probabilities: An experimental investigation, *Artificial Intelligence*, 85(1-2), 363–397.

Roll, R., and Ross, S. A. (1980), "An Empirical Investigation of the Arbitrage Pricing Theory," *Journal of Finance*, 35(5), 1073–1103.

Ross, S. A. (1976), "The Arbitrage Theory of Capital Asset Pricing," *Journal of Economic Theory*, 13, 341–360.

Shenoy, P. P. and G. Shafer (1990), "Axioms for probability and belief-function propagation," in Shachter, R. D., T. S. Levitt, J. F. Lemmer and L. N. Kanal (eds.), *Uncertainty in Artificial Intelligence*, 4, 169–198, North-Holland, Amsterdam. Reprinted in: Shafer, G. and J. Pearl (eds.), *Readings in Uncertain Reasoning*, 575–610, 1990, Morgan Kaufmann, San Mateo, CA.

Smith, J. E. (1993), "Moment methods for decision analysis," *Management Science*, 39, 340–358.

II Volatility

8 Change of Measure in Monte Carlo Integration via Gibbs Sampling with an Application to Stochastic Volatility Models

Filippo Altissimo

In this work the idea of change of measure in performing Markov chain Monte Carlo integration is investigated. The focus is posed on the Gibbs sampling and on how the change of measure modifies the Gibbs sampling algorithm to simulate from a target density. In Markov chain Monte Carlo the change of measure has a twofold importance. On one side, as in the independent Monte Carlo, it can induce a lower contemporaneous variance of the estimates if there is a proper choice of the augmenting function. On the other side, the modification of the target density can improve the mixing properties of the Markov chain with respect to the chain built up under the original measure. The idea has been specialized to the cases of smoothing the unobservable volatility in a stochastic volatility model, which illustrates the gain of performing the change of measure.

In finance and econometrics applications, it is not uncommon to work with models having latent factors (or missing observations) which have to be integrated out in the joint distribution of the observable and unobservable variables. Except for the linear case, this step of marginalization relies upon numerical integration of the joint density, given the dimension and the analytical intractability of those integrals. Among the various methods, the Monte Carlo integration has been increasingly used for its simplicity and for its accuracy compared with deterministic methods of integration in the case of large dimensional integral, as often occurs in economic model when the unobservable variables have dynamic.

Independent Monte Carlo method of integration relays upon *iid* samples from the objective distribution to average over; Markov chain Monte Carlo[1] draws those samples by running a properly constructed Markov chain that has the distribution to sample from as the invariant one. Initially, Markov chain techniques were extremely attractive in Bayesian inference since that some problems of interest in that framework can be solved by properly simulating the posterior distribution, and the MCMC proved to be a powerful tool in doing it. Lately, no Bayesian application of Monte Carlo Markov chain methods are becoming largely popular; in the generality of cases they are based on the possibility of using MCMC to calculate probabilities or expectations that otherwise cannot be computed analytically. Some applications of those techniques have been presented in the literature to likelihood maximization, by [Geyer and Thompson 1992], to simulated EM, by [Shephard 1994], and to filtration in nonlinear state space models by [Carter and Kohn 1994], [Dejong and Shephard 1995] and [Kim et al 1996].

---

1. Markov Chain Monte Carlo will be referred as MCMC, here on.

There are several ways of constructing those Markov chains and in many cases "plain vanilla" applications, in particular of the Gibbs sampler, worked surprising well; however, as the complexity of the applications increases the performance in term of speed and accuracy of those methods is likely to be affected. A large literature has developed refining and improving the performance of independent Monte Carlo integration through variance reduction technique and in particular through important sampling methods. However the use of the realizations from a MCMC chain to perform Monte Carlo integration adds the problem of how to extend those techniques to this new framework and how the problem of the dependence of the realizations induced by the chain can affect the results of the computation.

Here we will focus on the Gibbs sampler and we will show how to combine the important sampling within the Gibbs sampler, employing an augmenting function to modify the target distribution of the sampler. Similar to those of [Geweke 1989], results will be provided in which the important sampling function is used to define a change of measure with respect to which the variance of the Monte Carlo integration can be reduced. More interestingly the change of measure will induce a modification of the Markov chain associated with the Gibbs sampler and for a proper choice of the important sampling function the new chain will show better mixing properties than the original one.

The work is organized as follows. Section 1 is devoted to introduce Monte Carlo integration, important sampling and the Gibbs sampler. Section 2 presents how to perform the change of measure in the construction of the Gibbs sampler. Section 3 specializes this method to the smoothing of the unobservable volatility in a stochastic volatility model.

8.1   Monte Carlo integration, important sampling and the Gibbs sampler

Suppose that we are trying to evaluate the following integral

$$I = \int g(x) p(x) dx \tag{8.1}$$

where $p(x)$ is the probability density of the random vector $x \in \Re^m$. The problem is clearly a standard one in econometric analysis which regularly arises in computing the likelihood function in presence of latent variables or in filtering some unobservable variables. Using a brute force approach, let $\{x_i\}_{i=1}^{N}$ be an *i.i.d.* sample from the *pdf* $p(x)$, then the Monte Carlo estimator of I is

$$\tilde{I} = \frac{1}{N} \sum_{i=1}^{N} g(x_i) \tag{8.2}$$

and by a standard strong law of large number it will converge almost surely to I if some regularity conditions are satisfied. The asymptotic variance of the estimator $\sqrt{N}\left(\tilde{I} - I\right)$ is given by

$$\int \left[g(x) - I\right]^2 p(x)\, dx; \tag{8.3}$$

in most cases the value of (8.3) can be sizable, resulting in an inefficient numerical evaluation of the integral of interest. The precision of the Monte Carlo methods of integration can be improved by the choice of the proper weighting function, used to select and weight the points at which the function of interest has to be evaluated. A way of reducing the variance of the Monte Carlo integral is to properly define a change of measure through an important sampling function $w(x)$ such that

$$I = \int g(x) \frac{p(x)}{w(x)} w(x)\, dx \tag{8.4}$$

and the important sampling estimator of the integral is given by

$$\hat{I} = \frac{1}{N} \sum_{i=1}^{N} g(x_i) \frac{p(x_i)}{w(x_i)}, \tag{8.5}$$

where $\{x_i\}$ be an *i.i.d.* sample from the density $w(x)$. $\hat{I}$ is an unbiased estimator of I and it will converge to it by a standard *SLLN* result. The asymptotic variance of the important sampling estimator of I is

$$\int \left[g(x) \frac{p(x)}{w(x)} - I\right]^2 w(x)\, dx. \tag{8.6}$$

The important sampling scheme has two advantages: first it can be helpful in cases in which there are no simple methods for constructing draws from the known distribution p and, more relevant, it is possible that a proper choice of the weight function w will induce a reduction in the variance of the estimator of the integral, i.e. (8.6) is smaller than (8.3).

Sometimes the independent Monte Carlo method, just described, cannot be implemented due to the incomplete knowledge and/or non tractability of the density p; in those cases a generalization of the independent Monte Carlo, that has become known as Markov chain Monte Carlo, can be a useful alternative.

Markov chain Monte Carlo methods are simulation techniques that generate a sample from a target distribution through the specification of a Markov process whose invariant distribution is the target distribution itself. Among the various MCMC algorithms proposed in the literature,[2] we focus on the Gibbs sampler that allows to draw a random vector fro the joint distribution without its full knowledge but knowing the sequence of conditional distributions. The subsequent elements of the Markov chain are obtained by sampling elements of the random vector one at the time from the conditional distributions. Only requiring the knowledge of conditional distributions, the Gibbs sampler is now increasingly used as a tool to fit non-Gaussian state space models as in [Carter and Kohn 1994] and [Shephard 1994].

Consider again a random vector x with density $p(x)$ and consider a blocking scheme of the vector $(x_{(1)}, ..., x_{(k)})$ such that $x_{(i)} = (x_{i1}, ..., x_{im(i)})$ and $\sum m(i) = m$. The goal is to perform a draw of x from $p(x)$ but the function is not known or it is unfeasible to draw from it. Instead the conditional distribution of the i block respect to the rest of the variables, $p(x_{(i)}|x_{(-i)})$, is available and it is easy to handle.

The sampler works in a sequential way as follows:[3]

1) Specify a starting value x^0 of the chain and set $x^i = x^0$ and $i = 1$;

2) draw $x_{(1)}^{i+1}$ from $p(x_{(1)}^{i+1}|x_{(j>1)}^i)$,

...

draw $x_{(i)}^{i+1}$ from $p(x_{(i)}^{i+1}|x_{(j<i)}^{i+1}, x_{(j>i)}^i)$,

...

draw $x_{(k)}^{i+1}$ from $p(x_{(k)}^{i+1}|x_{(-k)}^{i+1})$;

3) set $i = i + 1$ and $x^i = x^{i+1}$ and goto step 2.

The iteration of this algorithm thus provides a Markov chain whose transition probability from x to $\widetilde{x}$ is given by

$$K_{GS}(x, \widetilde{x}) = \prod_{i=1}^{k} p(\widetilde{x}_{(i)}|\widetilde{x}_{(j<i)}, x_{(j>i)}), \tag{8.7}$$

---

2. A comprehensive reference for MCMC methods is in the booklength review by [Gilks et al 1996].

3. Under-scores will mean blocks of the random vector, while upper-scores will indicate iterations of the sampler. The notation $x_{(-i)}$ will indicate all the elements of the vector but the $i-th$. $x_{(i<j)}$ will refer to all the elements of the vector before the $i-th$; similarly for $x_{(i>j)}$.

and it is easy to see that if x^0 is drawn from $p(x)$ then also x^i for $i > 0$ is a draw from $p(x)$. If instead x^0 is not a draw from $p(x)$ then, as $i \to \infty$, and if some regularity conditions are satisfied the distribution of x^i converges to p.

In operating the Gibbs sampler two aspects of its implementation are crucial: the blocking scheme and the length of the simulation path. First, the choice of the blocking scheme is in part constrained by the knowledge of the conditional distributions, but a proper choice of the blocking can be crucial for the performance of the sampler; in fact if some components of the random vector are highly dependent, grouping them together can increase the speed of convergence and reduce the dependence of the Markov chain itself ([Lui et al 1994]). Second, both in the single and the multiple paths sampler, there is the problem of choosing the length of the simulation and determining how long the warming-up phase has to be, before it is possible to consider that the sampler has reached its invariant distribution. The length of the simulation relates to the degree of precision desired in the computation of the object of interest, while the length of the warming-up is related to the dependence on the initial condition.

The Gibbs proved to be a powerful tool for cases in which we need to make draws from a distribution of which we have limited knowledge or it is difficult to handle, but whose conditional distributions are easy to work with. However similar to the case of the independent Monte Carlo, the possibility of simulating from p via MCMC does not mean that we can make an efficient draw from the target distribution in term of variance of the estimated and, more relevant, in term of the dependence of the Markov chain generating the draws.

8.2   Change of measure and the modification of Gibbs sampler

In this work, we exploit the idea that, instead of constructing the Markov chain respect to the original measure p, an "useful" change of measure by an augmenting density function f can be performed such that

$$I = \int \frac{g(x)}{f(x)} f(x) p(x) \, dx, \tag{8.8}$$

where the new measure is given by $f(x) p(x)$ and the function f is the Radon-Nykodym derivative of the new measure with respect to the original one, and the Gibbs sampler can be designed to have the new measure $f(x) p(x)$ has invariant distribution. The term "useful" means that the variance of the sample estimates (8.8) can be lower than the one obtained constructing the Gibbs sampler under the original measure and also that the chain having $f(x)p(x)$ as invariant distribution can have better mixing properties respect to the chain define under the measure p.

Note that the new measure is the product of the augmenting and the original density and so three things needs to be verified in order to perform the change of variable: first that the function $f(x)p(x)$ is itself a density function (or proportional to it), second that we are able to make draws from the new invariant distribution modifying properly the transition kernel of the chain and finally that the estimate of I under the new measure actually converges to the desired value.

If both f and p are densities, the necessity of ensuring that $f(x)p(x)$ is actually the kernel of a density, mainly reduces to check the fact that the functions have a common domain with positive measure in which they are both strictly positive. It means that $D \equiv D_f \cap D_p \neq \emptyset$ where $D_f = \{x|f(x) > 0\}$ and $D_p = \{x|p(x) > 0\}$. However the presence of a common domain of f and p will not be sufficient to guarantee the convergence of the sample estimates under the new measure to I so the requirement will be strengthened by assuming that $D_p \subset D_f$. This assumption is a regularity condition which is intended to ensure that the new measure has positive mass on the same domain as the original one.

The change of measure induces a modification of the target distribution from which it is aimed to sample from and, consequently, it is necessary a modification of the transition kernel generating the chain; in the following, it is proposed an algorithm which samples from the new measure $p(x)f(x)$. Consider the same blocking structure as before and iterate the following algorithm:

1) Specify a starting value x^0 of the chain and set $x^i = x^0$ and $i = 1$;

2) draw $x_{(1)}^{i+1}$ from $p(x_{(1)}^{i+1}|x_{(j>1)}^i)f(x_{(1)}^i|x_{(j>1)}^i)$,

...

draw $x_{(i)}^{i+1}$ from $p(x_{(i)}^{i+1}|x_{(j<i)}^{i+1}, x_{(j>i)}^i)f(x_{(i)}^i|x_{(j<i)}^{i+1}, x_{(j>i)}^i)$,

...

draw $x_{(k)}^{i+1}$ from $p(x_{(k)}^{i+1}|x_{(-k)}^{i+1})f(x_{(k)}^{i+1}|x_{(-k)}^{i+1})$;

3) set $i = i + 1$ and $x^i = x^{i+1}$ and goto step 2.

The densities in step (2) of the algorithm are actually kernels of densities and they are the result of the product of two conditionals $p(\cdot|\cdot)$ and $f(\cdot|\cdot)$. It is possible that in a variety of cases the product of those density has known form that can be sampled directly; but generally this is not the case and other methods have to be applied.

Three different strategies can be implemented in performing random draws from the kernel densities in step (2). The first one is a straight acceptance/rejection method based on finding an auxiliary function $h(\cdot)$ and a constant M such that $\frac{p(\cdot|\cdot)f(\cdot|\cdot)}{h(\cdot)} \leq M < \infty$. The goodness of the methods is based on the ability of the auxiliary function h to mimic $p(\cdot|\cdot)f(\cdot|\cdot)$; operatively, the algorithm should work as follows:

i) make a draw $x_{(i)}$ form $h(x_{(i)})$;

ii) draw u from a uniform distribution defined on the interval zero-one;

iii) accept $x_{(i)}$ if u is less then $\frac{p(x_{(i)}|x_{(-i)})f(x_{(i)}|x_{(-i)})}{Mh(x_{(i)})}$, otherwise goto (i).

The choice of the function h becomes critical, however a sensible and easy choice for h is given by f so that the acceptance probability reduces to $\frac{p}{M}$.

Second alternative strategy is to make use of the adaptive/rejection method proposed by [Gilks and Wild 1994] for log-concave density function. The method is similar to the acceptance/rejection one with the difference that the function h is properly constructed using tangent method so to form a tight envelope of the original function. The method applies to log-concave densities and if both p and f are log-concave, then their product is log-concave too and the adaptive/rejection procedure can be applied to the new measure.

The third method consists in combining the original Gibbs sampler with a Metropolis-Hastings independent step, in which the transition probability of the block j does not depend on its previous realization. This can be performed at each step of (2) by drawing from a transitional kernel $q(x_{(j)}^{i+1}|x_{(-j)})$ and then accept $x_{(j)}^{i+1}$ with probability $\alpha\left(x_{(j)}^{i+1}, x_{(j)}^{i}|x_{(-j)}\right)$ where

$$\alpha\left(x_{(j)}^{i+1}, x_{(j)}^{i}|x_{(-j)}\right) = \min\left\{\frac{p(x_{(j)}^{i+1}|x_{(-j)})f(x_{(j)}^{i+1}|x_{(-j)})q(x_{(j)}^{i}|x_{(-j)})}{p(x_{(j)}^{i}|x_{(-j)})f(x_{(j)}^{i}|x_{(-j)})q(x_{(j)}^{i+1}|x_{(-j)})}, 1\right\},$$

if the $x_{(j)}^{i+1}$ element is accepted then the chain moves to draw the block $(j+1)$ having in block (j) the element $x_{(j)}^{i+1}$, on the contrary having in (j) the element $x_{(j)}^{i}$; so at each loop of the Gibbs sampler, it is possible that some elements of x are updated while others are not.

The iteration of steps (1-3) of the Gibbs algorithm under the modified measure generates a sample $\left\{x^i\right\}_{i=1}^{N}$ of a stochastic process which has transition kernel from x to $\tilde{x}$ equal to

$$K_{IGS}(x, \tilde{x}) = \prod_{i=1}^{k} \frac{1}{c_i}p(\tilde{x}_{(i)}|\tilde{x}_{(j<i)}, x_{(j>i)})f(\tilde{x}_{(i)}|\tilde{x}_{(j<i)}, x_{(j>i)})$$

where $c_i \equiv \int p(x_{(i)}|x_{(j<i)}^{i+1}, \; x_{(j>i)}^i)f(x_j|x_{(j<i)}^{i+1}, \; x_{(j>i)}^i)dx_{(i)}$, if the draw in step (2) are performed without using the Metropolis steps; in the presence of the Metropolis step, the transition kernel has to be modified accordingly and it is equal to

$$K_{IGSM}(x, d\widetilde{x}) = \prod_{i=1}^{k} \{ q(\widetilde{x}_{(i)}|\widetilde{x}_{(j<i)}, \; x_{(j>i)})\alpha\left(\widetilde{x}_{(i)}, x_{(i)}|\widetilde{x}_{(j<i)}, \; x_{(j>i)}\right))d\widetilde{x}_i$$

$$+(1-\int q(\widetilde{x}_{(i)}|\cdot)\alpha(\widetilde{x}_{(i)}, x_{(i)}|\cdot)d\widetilde{x}_i)\delta_x(d\widetilde{x})\}$$

where δ_x is an impulse function to account the case when the element of the chain does not move.

It is clear from the above description, that the modification of the target density does not imply an increase in the difficulties and computational time of running the sampler given that all described strategies to sample from the conditionals can be quickly implemented. In particular, when standard auxiliary functions are utilized in the acceptance/rejection method and in the Metropolis step, then the algorithm simply consists in sampling from $h(\cdot)$ or $q(\cdot)$ and then the draw must be accepted or rejected in function of a proper weighting.

The prove that the algorithm described in (1-3) delivers the desired result, is given in the following corollaries. First, it is shown that the two transition kernels of the two algorithms have the new measure $f(x)p(x)$ as invariant distribution.

Corollary 1

The $f(x)p(x)$ is proportional to an invariant distribution of the transition kernels $K_{IGS}(\widetilde{x}, x)$ and $K_{IGSM}(\widetilde{x}, x)$.

Second, if the augmenting function is sufficiently well behaving, the modification of the chain will not prevent the convergence of the estimates under mild regularity conditions and, given a sample $\{x_i\}_{i=1}^{N}$, it is now possible to state the following strong law of large number result.

Corollary 2

If $D_p \subset D_f$, $E_p|g| < \infty$ and if $\{x^i\}_{i=1}^{N}$ is a sample from an $pf-$irreducible Markov chain with transition kernels K_{IGS} or K_{IGSM} then

$$\widehat{I} = \frac{\sum_{i=1}^{N} \frac{g(x^i)}{f(x^i,\theta)}}{\sum_{i=1}^{N} \frac{1}{f(x^i,\theta)}} \xrightarrow{a.s.} I$$

and

$$\frac{1}{N} \sum_{i=1}^{N} \frac{1}{f(x^i, \theta)} \xrightarrow{a.s.} \frac{1}{c}$$

as $N \to \infty$, where $c \equiv \int f(x)p(x)dx$.

The proof of the corollaries and a set of primitive conditions ensuring the pf-irreducibility are provided in [Altissimo 1997]. Two things deserve to be noted. First, there is the necessity of computing the constant of integration of the new measure that is unknown, due to the fact that it is constructed in a multiplicative way. Second, the primitive conditions for the pf-irreducibility are indeed extremely weak and are mainly meant to rule out particular anomalies, such as the case of densities having positive mass on separate regions of their domain.

The results of the above corollaries show that under the new measure the estimates satisfy a strong law of large number, however those results do not provide a rule for the choice of the augmenting function f. The problem of the optimal choice of the important sampling function in the case of the MCMC is still open; however two main criterions can be used as guideline. First, the function f has to have sufficient mass on the domain of interest, otherwise this will affect the variance of the estimates. Second, the function f has to be tailored to the function p to undo the correlation among the block of the chain.

8.3 Smoothing underlying stochastic volatility via simulation

Stochastic volatility (SV here on) models arise naturally as discrete approximation of various diffusion processes in the continuous asset pricing literature. They found limited application mainly due to the difficulties in handling them with respect to alternative ways of modeling the conditional volatility (see [Ghysels et al 1996] for a survey). However standard $GARCH$ models do not have some of the interesting features that are present in the SV models, such as: better matching of the second moment properties of data on returns, the higher degree of excess kurtosis and the possibility of leverage effect.

Recently the issue of prediction and inference in these models has found large attention as a natural application of Markov chain methods. The stochastic volatility models have become a battleground for the application of different MCMC techniques; among the others [Jacquier et al 1994, Shephard 1994, Kim et al 1996]. Let us consider the same simple stochastic volatility model of Jacquier, Polson and Rossi, which is given by

$$\varepsilon_t \;=\; h_t^{1/2} u_t \tag{8.9}$$

$$\ln h_t = \alpha + \delta \ln h_{t-1} + \sigma_v v_t$$

the sample is of dimension T, h_T indicates the whole vector of unobservable volatility and $\theta = \{\alpha, \delta, \sigma_v\}$ are the parameters that are considered given for the purpose of the exercise or previously estimated. The two innovations are independent standard normal. Consider the problem of smoothing the unobservable volatility given the observed innovation ε_T, so the problem consists in computing the following integral

$$E(h_T|\varepsilon_T, \theta) = \int h_T p(h_T|\varepsilon_T, \theta) dh. \tag{8.10}$$

The difficulties arise by the fact that the density $p(h_T|\varepsilon_T, \theta)$ is known only up to a constant and there are no obvious methods to sample directly from it; the density $p(h_T|\varepsilon_T, \theta)$ is equal to

$$p(h_T|\varepsilon_T, \theta) = \frac{p(h_T, \varepsilon_T|\theta)}{p(\varepsilon_T|\theta)} = \frac{p(\varepsilon_T|h_T, \theta)p(h_T|\theta)}{p(\varepsilon_T|\theta)} \tag{8.11}$$

$$\propto p(\varepsilon_T|h_T, \theta)p(h_T|\theta)$$

$$\propto \prod_{t=1}^{T} h_t^{-3/2} \exp(-\frac{\sum_{t=1}^{T} \varepsilon_t^2}{2h_t}) \exp(-\frac{\sum_{t=1}^{T} (\ln h_t - \alpha - \delta \ln h_{t-1})^2}{2\sigma_v^2}).$$

A solution proposed by [Jacquier et al 1994] and [Geweke 1995] consists in building a Markov chain that draws each element of h_T one at the time (multi steps sampler) and so it constructs a sequence of $\{h_T^i\}_{i=1}^{N}$ where N is the number of iteration of the sampler. To implement this strategy, the starting point is the conditional density of the individual elements of the vector h_T which, for $t = 2, ..., T-1$, is equal to

$$p(h_t|h_{(-t)}, \varepsilon_T, \theta) \propto h_t^{-3/2} \exp(-\frac{\varepsilon_t^2}{2h_t}) \exp(-\frac{(\ln h_t - \mu_t)^2}{2\sigma^2}) \tag{8.12}$$

where $\mu_t = \frac{\alpha(1-\delta) + \delta(\ln h_{t-1} + \ln h_{t+1})}{1+\delta^2}$ and $\sigma^2 = \frac{\sigma_v^2}{1+\delta^2}$.

To draw from the above density kernel two alternatives are feasible. The first one, pursued by [Geweke 1995], is to use a transformation of variables and to work directly with the conditional distribution of $H_t = \ln(h_t)$, as

$$p(H_t|H_{(-t)}, \varepsilon_T, \theta) \propto \exp(-\frac{\varepsilon_t^2}{2} \exp(-H_t)) \exp(-\frac{(H_t - \mu_t^*)^2}{2\sigma^2}) \tag{8.13}$$

where $\mu_t^* = \mu_t - .5\sigma^2$, and to sample H_t either by acceptance/rejection or by the adaptive/rejection methods of [Gilks and Wild 1994]. Alternatively, it is possible to apply the Jacquier, Polson and Rossi algorithm by introducing a Metropolis independence step into the multi move Gibbs sampler. All these different methods of sampling will produce a multi steps sampler whose iteration will generate a chain having as invariant the distribution of interest (8.11).

Following the result of [Lui et al 1994], Shephard, in a sequance of papers [Shephard 1994, Kim et al 1996], argued that due to the high correlation of the elements of h_T, it is likely that sampling the elements of h_T separately will induce a slow mixing of the chain and it will affect the computation of the smoothed value. To avoid this, they introduced the mixture approximation for the distribution of $ln(\varepsilon_t^2)$ which allows to speed up the sampler by drawing all the elements of h_T vector all at once. The drawbacks of their method is twofold; on one side it is an approximation and it is likely that the mixture of normal is not a good proxy, in particular in term of tail behavior, and, on the other side, the proposed method increases the dimensionality of the integral and it is clearly necessary that all the states of the mixture are visited a sufficient number of time by the sampler to assure a good performance of the algorithm.

However it is a fact that the high dependence of the blocks can jeopardize the performance of the sampler. In the SV models, high dependence of the blocks is associated with values of δ close to unity and σ_v close to zero and in many applications to financial assets the estimated values of the parameters end up in those regions. To reach a better understanding of the effect of slow convergence on the properties of the estimates of the unobservable volatility, we perform an experiments with $T = 200$ and $\theta = \{-0.368, 0.95, 0.26\}$, which is one of parametrizations analyzed by [Jacquier et al 1994], by running the multi steps sampler using an acceptance/rejection algorithm to draw from the conditional distributions in (8.13) with a normal density as envelope density with mean and variance set to maximize the acceptance probability.[4] The result in the first figure reports the average of the estimated smoothed volatility, $\widehat{h}_T = \frac{1}{N} \sum_{i=1}^{N} h_T^i$, in 1000 independent samplers each with initial condition $h_T^0 = \exp(-5)$ for $N = 100, 200, 500$ and 1000 iterations of the sampler and its aim is to assess the last of the initial conditions in the sampler. The second figure reports the autocorrelation function computed for the draws of H_{100} (10.000 replication are used, after discarding the first 5.000 as warming up).

As pointed by Shephard and as it is clearly evident from these figures, the dependence in the sampler is sizable as the last of the initial conditions and the autocorrelation function show; this affects the performance of the sampler in various

---

4. The algorithm is similar to the one given by [Geweke 1995] and by [Kim et al 1996], in which mean and variance of the normal envelope have been setted to maximize the acceptance rate.

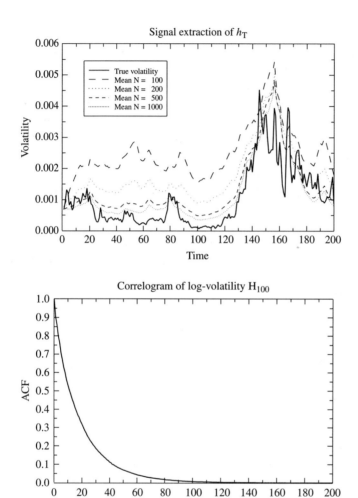

Figure 8.1
Multi steps Gibbs Sampler with respect to the original measure

directions, among the others, the standard deviation of the sample estimates and
the applicability in the parameters estimation.

To improve upon the performance of the sampler without resort to approximation, the described change of measure method is applied to the example. Consider

the expectation in (8.10) respect to $H_T = \ln(h_T)$ and give an augmenting function $f(H_T|\theta_0)$, the expression under the change of measure can be written as

$$E(h_T|\varepsilon_T, \theta) = \int \frac{\exp(H_T)}{f(H_T|\theta_0)} p(H_T|\varepsilon_T, \theta) f(H_T|\theta_0) dH. \tag{8.14}$$

An augmenting function, we look for a density with sufficient mass on the domain of p and such that the conditional of the f would be useful in undoing the dependence present in the conditional distributions under the original measure. For this reason, a multivariate student t with degree of freedom ν_0 has been chosen as augmenting function with parameters $\theta_0 = (\alpha_0, \delta_0, \sigma_0^2)$

$$f(H_T|\nu_0, \theta_0) \propto (1 + \frac{(H_T - \alpha_0)' V (H_T - \alpha_0)}{\nu_0})^{-\frac{T+\nu_0}{2}} \tag{8.15}$$

where $V = \frac{1}{\sigma_0^2} RR'$ and R is a $T \times T$ matrix as having ones on the main diagonal but the $(1,1)$ element equal to $\sqrt{1 - \delta_0^2}$, $-\delta_0$ on the first lower diagonal and zeros elsewhere.

The nice property of the multivariate t is that the conditional distribution $f(H_t|H_{(-t)}, \nu_0, \theta_0)$ is univariate student t with $(T + \nu_0 - 1)$ degrees of freedom and mean equal to $m_t = \frac{\alpha_0(1-\delta_0) + \delta_0(H_{t+1} + H_{t-1})}{1 + \delta_0^2}$ and variance $s^2 = \frac{\nu_0}{T + \nu_0 - 3} \frac{(1+q)\sigma_0^2}{1 + \delta_0^2}$ where $q = H_T' V H_T - \frac{\sigma_0^2}{1 + \delta_0^2}(H_t - m_t)^2$. The fact that the conditional mean of the function f is of the same form of the mean of the conditional density under the original measure, is the reason why this specification has been chosen. Under the new measure, the sampler will have invariant distribution pf and it will be run by drawing from the distribution of H_t conditional $H_{(-t)}$ on respect to the new measure,

$$p(H_t|H_{(-t)}, \varepsilon_T, \theta) f(H_t|H_{(-t)}, \theta_0) \propto$$
$$\exp(-\frac{\varepsilon_t^2}{2} \exp(-H_t)) \exp(-\frac{(H_t - \mu^*)^2}{2\sigma^2})(1 + \frac{1}{(T+\nu_0-1)s^2}(H_t - m_t)^2)^{-\frac{T+\nu_0}{2}}. \tag{8.16}$$

The draws from the above distribution can be performed by a Metropolis independence step using as auxiliary function a student t distribution with degrees of freedom ν_q, fixed mean μ_q and variance σ_q.

The experiments performed before are repeated with the following parameters specification: $\alpha_0 = -7.36$, $\delta_0 = 0$, $\sigma_0 = 2$, $\nu_0 = 2$, $\nu_q = 5$, $\mu_q = -7.36$ and $\sigma_q = 2$. The parameters value of the augmenting function has been chosen to partially undo the dependence present under the original measure between the elements of the chain and the mean have been setted equal to the unconditional one of the volatility process. The mean and variance of the auxiliary distribution are be chosen

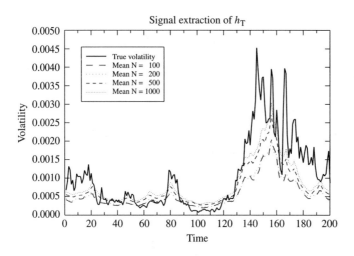

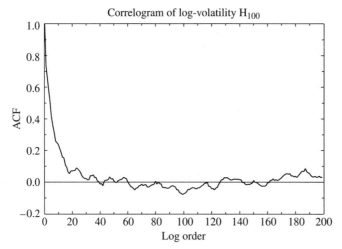

Figure 8.2
Multi steps Gibbs Sampler with change of measure

so to have a proper envelope of the product of the two conditional distributions in
(8.16). The result of the experiment are reported in the following figures.

By comparing these results with the previous ones, it is evident the gain by
running the sampler under the new measure; the initial condition of the sampler
washes out quickly and the correlation is reduced, even if there is some minor
dynamic at long lags. The better mixing properties of the sampler also improves the

smoothing performance of the algorithm. To evaluate it, we computed the $RMSE$, $(1/T \sum_{t=1}^{T}(h_t - \widehat{h}_t)^2)^{.5}$, by running the multistep sampler for 5000 iterations and, after discarding the first 1500, we used the remaining to compute $\widehat{h}_t$ both in the case of the original measure and in the case of the change of measure; the $RMSE$ results equal to 0.0012 and 0.00045 respectively. These findings highlights that the combination of the important sampling and the Gibbs sampling allows to compute the integral in (8.14) with higher precision and lower degree of dependence of the sample than performing the integral under the original measure and without resorting to approximation.

References

Altissimo, F. 1997. *Essays in Macroeconometrics*. PhD thesis, University of Pennsylvania.

Carter, C. and A. Kohn. 1994. On gibbs sampling state space models. *Biometrika*, 81:541–553.

Dejong, P. and N. Shephard. 1995. The simulation smoother for time series models. *Biometrika*, 82:339–350.

Geweke, J. 1989. Bayesian inference in econometrics models using monte carlo integration. *Econometrica*, 57:1240–1317.

Geweke, J. 1995. Monte carlo simulation and numerical integration. Technical Report 192, Federal Reserve Bank of Minneapolis.

Geyer, C. and E. Thompson. 1992. Constrained monte carlo maximum likelihood for dependent data. *Journal of the Royal Statistical Society, series B*, 54:657–699.

Ghysels, E., A. C. Harvey, and E. Renault. 1996. *Stochastic Volatility*, chapter in Statistical Methods in Finance, pages 119–191. North Holland.

Gilks, W., S. Richardson, and D. Spiegelhalter. 1996. *Markov Chain Montecarlo in Practice*. Chapman and Hall.

Gilks, W. and P. Wild. 1994. Adaptive rejection sampling for gibbs sampling. *Appl. Statistics*, 41:337–348.

Jacquier, E., N. Polson, and P. Rossi. 1994. Bayesisn analysis of stochastic volatility models. *Journal of Business and Economic Statistics*, 12:371–417.

Kim, S., N. Shephard, and S. Chib. 1996. Stochastic volatility: Likelihood inference and comparison with arch models. mimeo, Nuffield College, Oxford.

Lui, J., W. Wong, and A. Kong. 1994. Covariance structure of the gibbs sampler with application to the comparison of estimators and augmenting schemes. *Biometrika*, 81:27–40.

Shephard, N. 1994. Partial non-gaussian state space. *Biometrika*, 81:115–131.

9 Comparing Models of Intra-day Seasonal Volatility in the Foreign Exchange Market

Claudio Morana and Andrea Beltratti

9.1 Introduction

The recent availability of high frequency data is useful to applied researchers and practitioners for a number of reasons. First is the possibility of determining the parameters of the stochastic process followed by the price of a certain asset with great accuracy. This has been pursued in the literature especially with regard to estimation of volatility, even though Dacorogna et al. [1996] also look at expected returns. Second is the possibility of frequent evaluation of options on the basis of improved estimates of volatility. This can be obtained rather precisely with high frequency data without the need to use a long low-frequency time series of data, which could be subject to structural breaks. Third is the possibility of frequent measurement of risk, which is of interest to those advocating the evaluation of financial portfolios on the basis of an intra-day value at risk.

The empirical applications have to recognize the existence of intra-day components of volatility which, if ignored, may bias econometric estimates. For example Andersen and Bollerslev [1997b] show that it is necessary to correct for seasonality when retrieving an estimate of the coefficient of fractional differencing with time series methods. Andersen and Bollerslev [1997a] moreover show that the use of raw data produces GARCH estimates over various frequencies which are not in line with the theoretical aggregation properties described by Drost and Nijman [1993]. The estimates obtained by eliminating intra-day seasonality are more in line with such theoretical aggregation properties.

The treatment of intra-day seasonals has found various solutions in the literature. Andersen and Bollerslev [1997a], [1997b], [1997c] and [1996] propose a deterministic model for capturing intra-day seasonals. Dacorogna et al. [1993] use time deformation methods to obtain a well-behaved volatility process when measured in the new scale, called theta-time. Beltratti and Morana [1998] propose a stochastic volatility model and analyze its properties in terms of consistency with the theoretical aggregation properties of GARCH and flexibility to describe the reactions to announcements.

In this paper we propose a more extensive analysis of the stochastic volatility model with certain innovations on the empirical analysis. First we thoroughly compare our model with those proposed by the other researchers on a number of dimensions like ability to produce standardized returns whose unconditional distribution is close to normality and conformity with the theoretical aggregation properties of GARCH models. Second we estimate various models using a new data set of high frequency data which extends from 1992 to 1997, considerably larger than most of the data sets used in the existing empirical studies. The plan of the paper is as follows: after this introduction, the second section describes the stochastic volatility model, the third section reports the empirical results and the fourth section concludes.

9.2   Models of cyclical volatility

There is no reason to believe that the daily or weekly seasonal patterns in foreign exchange volatility repeat themselves exactly. The geographical model of Dacorogna et al. [1993] interprets volatility in terms of the level of activity in the market. According to the evidence reported in that paper the level of activity may be proxied by the number of traders who are active in the market, for example it is highest when there is an overlap between two important markets belonging to different time zones. The level of activity is presumably stochastic, depending on how many traders actually participate in the market, a factor which may well change from one day to the other. Under this interpretation it cannot be ruled out a priori that the intra-day seasonal component is stochastic.

We propose a model including stochastic volatility terms. This idea is not new to the analysis of financial markets. Harvey, Ruiz and Shephard [1994] have applied a stochastic volatility model based on the structural time series approach to the analysis of daily exchange rate returns. Payne [1996] has extended this methodology to incorporate an intra-day fixed seasonal component. In this paper we further extend the model to account for stochastic intra-daily cyclical components. We consider the following model for exchange rate returns:

$$r_{t,n} = \bar{r}_{t,n} + \sigma_{t,n}\varepsilon_{t,n} = \bar{r}_{t,n} + \sigma\varepsilon_{t,n}\exp\left(\frac{\mu_{t,n} + h_{t,n} + c_{t,n}}{2}\right) \tag{9.1}$$

where $t = 1, ..., T$ is the number of trading days, $n = 1, ..., N$ is the number of intra-day periods, $\bar{r}_{t,n} = E[r_{t,n}]$ is the expected intra-daily return, $\sigma_{t,n}$ is the intra-daily conditional standard deviation, σ is a scale factor, $\varepsilon_{t,n} \sim IID(0,1)$, $\mu_{t,n}$ is the non-stationary volatility component:

$$\mu_{t,n} = \mu_{t,n-1} + \xi_{t,n}, \qquad \xi_{t,n} \sim NID\left(0, \sigma_\xi^2\right), \tag{9.2}$$

$h_{t,n}$ is the stochastic stationary volatility component:

$$h_{t,n} = \phi h_{t,n-1} + \eta_{t,n}, \quad \eta_{t,n} \sim NID\left(0, \sigma_\eta^2\right) \quad |\phi| < 1, \tag{9.3}$$

c_t is the cyclical volatility component. Squaring both sides and taking logs, the model may be rewritten as:

$$\ln\left(|r_{t,n} - \bar{r}_{t,n}|\right)^2 = \ln\left[\sigma\varepsilon_{t,n}\exp\left(\frac{\mu_{t,n} + h_{t,n} + c_{t,n}}{2}\right)\right]^2 \tag{9.4}$$

that is:

$$2\ln|r_{t,n} - \bar{r}_{t,n}| = \varphi + \mu_{t,n} + h_{t,n} + c_{t,n} + w_{t,n} \tag{9.5}$$

where $\varphi = \ln\sigma^2 + E\left[\ln\varepsilon_{t,n}^2\right]$ and $w_{t,n} = \ln\varepsilon_{t,n}^2 - E\left[\ln\varepsilon_{t,n}^2\right]$.

The $c_{t,n}$ component is broken into a number of cycles corresponding to the fundamental daily frequency and its intra-daily harmonics $c_{t,n} = \sum_{i=1}^2 c_{i,t,n}$. We model $c_{1,t,n}$, the fundamental daily frequency, as stochastic while its harmonics are modelled as deterministic as in Anderson and Bollerslev [1996]. Following Harvey [1989], the stochastic cyclical component can be rewritten in state space form as

$$c_{1,t,n} = \begin{bmatrix} \psi_{1,t,n} \\ \psi_{1,t,n}^* \end{bmatrix} = \rho \begin{bmatrix} \cos\lambda & \sin\lambda \\ -\sin\lambda & \cos\lambda \end{bmatrix} \begin{bmatrix} \psi_{1,t,n-1} \\ \psi_{1,t,n-1}^* \end{bmatrix} + \begin{bmatrix} \kappa_{1,t,n} \\ \kappa_{1,t,n}^* \end{bmatrix} \tag{9.6}$$

where $0 \leq \rho \leq 1$ is a damping factor, $\psi_{1,1,0} = \delta_c$, $\psi_{1,1,0}^* = \delta_s$, and $\kappa_{1,t,n} \sim NID\left(0, \sigma_{1,\kappa}^2\right)$ and $\kappa_{1,t,n}^* \sim NID\left(0, \sigma_{1,\kappa}^{*2}\right)$, are white noise disturbances with $Cov\left(\kappa_{1,t,n}, \kappa_{1,t,n}^*\right) = 0$. Assuming that $\kappa_{1,t,n}$ and $\kappa_{1,t,n}^*$ are not correlated is sufficient to achieve identification of the two components $\psi_{1,t,n}$ and $\psi_{1,t,n}^*$. In addition, the restriction of equal variances of the noise components, $\sigma_{1,\kappa}^2 = \sigma_{1,\kappa}^{*2}$, is imposed for parsimony reasons. This allows the cyclical component, while maintaining constant its period, to evolve over time with respect to both the vertical (amplitude) and horizontal axes (phase). We model $c_{2,t,n}$ as a deterministic flexible Fourier form originally proposed by Gallant [1981]:

$$c_{2,t,n} = \mu_1 n_1 + \mu_2 n_2 + \sum_{p=2}^{P}(\delta_{cp}\cos p\lambda n + \delta_{sp}\sin p\lambda n)$$

where $n_1 = 2n/(N+1)$ and $n_2 = 6n^2/(N+1)(N+2)$ are scaling variables. The model of Andersen and Bollerslev [1997a] and Payne [1996] can be considered special cases of ours when $\rho = 1$ and $\sigma_{1,\kappa}^2 = \sigma_{1,\kappa}^{*2} = 0$. Moreover Andersen and Bollerslev [1997a] estimate their model in two steps, first retrieving σ_t^2 from a GARCH model computed on daily returns and then modeling the cyclical component in terms of the Fourier flexible functional form while we estimate simultaneously all the components. The full stochastic volatility model in state space form reads as follows:

$$y_{t,n} = z'\alpha_{t,n} + \omega_{t,n} \tag{9.7}$$
$$\alpha_{t,n} = R\alpha_{t,n-1} + m'\nu_{t,n} \tag{9.8}$$

where:

$$y_{t,n} = 2\ln\left(|r_{t,n} - \bar{r}_{t,n}|\right)$$

$$\alpha'_{t,n} = \left[\begin{array}{cccccccccc} \mu_{t,n} & h_{t,n} & \psi_{1,t,n} & \psi^*_{1,t,n} & \cos 2\lambda n & \sin 2\lambda n & .. & \sin P\lambda n & I_1 & .. & I_k \end{array}\right]$$

$$z' = \left[\begin{array}{cccccccccc} 1 & 1 & 1 & 0 & \delta_{c2} & \delta_{s2} & ... & \delta_{sP} & \theta_1 & ... & \theta_k \end{array}\right]$$

$$\nu'_{t,n} = \left[\begin{array}{cccccc} \xi_{t,n} & \eta_{t,n} & \kappa_{1,t,n} & \kappa^*_{1,t,n} & 0 & ... & 0 \end{array}\right]$$

and where I_i $i = 1, ..., k$ are the scaling variables, n_1 and n_2, and a number of dummy variables that take into account day-of-the-week effect, outliers and Tokyo opening, $\omega_{t,n} \sim IID\left(0, \sigma^2_\omega\right)$, m is a $(4 + (P-1) + k \times 1)$ selection vector and R is a $(4 + (P-1) + k \times 4 + (P-1) + k)$ sparse selection matrix. The stochastic disturbances of the measurement and transition equations are assumed to be uncorrelated with each other in each time period. As suggested in Ruiz [1994] a quasi-maximum likelihood method (QML), computed using the Kalman filter, yields reasonably efficient estimates. QML estimators are asymptotically normal with covariance matrix computed as in Dunsmuir [1979].

9.3 Empirical results

We estimate the various models for the time series of the exchange rate between the Deutsche mark and the US dollar. The daily data cover the period 12:31:1972-31:12:1997, corresponding to 6784 observations; the source is Datastream. The high-frequency data are measured every half hour for the period 01:01:1992-31:12:1997, corresponding to 75168 observations; the source is Olsen and Associates. We follow the other researchers in the high frequency field and define the rate of return as the difference between two averages between the log of the bid and ask prices measured at different times, see e.g. Dacorogna et al. [1993]. We have cut the week-ends from the series, as done by Andersen and Bollerslev. Moreover, as in Andersen and Bollerslev [1996], a number of dummies were considered in the specification, to account for market closure effects, Tokyo opening and lunch effects, and to allow for heterogeneity in the days of the week.

In this section we compare the competing specifications by means of various tests and analyze to what extent the filters yield filtered returns with empirical distributions closer to normality. Finally, we will estimate GARCH models to the filtered returns to evaluate compatibility with theoretical aggregation properties of GARCH models.

An additional important issue for the specification of the model concerns the inclusion of dummy variables. Ideally, we would like a specification to be as parsimonious as possible for the volatility process. Modelling the intradaily volatility component as stochastic may give to the model the additional flexibility necessary to account for these one-off effects onto the volatility process, without the need of including additional dummies in the specification. Moreover, in many cases it is not clear whether an autoregressive component really needs to be considered in the specification. For this reason we will consider each specification in four versions, that is with and without dummy variables and with and without autoregressive components.

In the tables below, D(I) refers to the deterministic seasonal model of Andersen and Bollerslev with dummies included; D refers to the deterministic seasonal model of Andersen and Bollerslev without dummies; S(d,A,I) refers to the deterministic seasonal version of the stochastic volatility model with the autoregressive component and the dummies included. The version is seasonal deterministic because the stochastic volatility model is restricted to have a deterministic intra-day seasonal similar to that of Andersen and Bollerslev. S(d,A) refers to the deterministic seasonal version of the stochastic volatility model without dummies but with the autoregressive component included; S(d,I) refers to the deterministic seasonal version of the stochastic volatility model with dummies but without autoregressive component. S(d) refers to the deterministic seasonal version of the stochastic volatility model without both the autoregressive component and the dummy variables; S(A,I) refers to the stochastic volatility model with the autoregressive component and the dummies included; S(A) refers to the stochastic volatility model without dummies but with the autoregressive component included; S(I) refers to stochastic volatility model with dummies but without autoregressive component; S refers to the stochastic volatility model without both the autoregressive component and the dummy variables.

Table 9.1 reports specification tests for volatility models. BL is the Box-Ljung test for autocorrelated residuals; R^2 is the coefficient of determination; AIC is the Akaike information criterion; pm is the square of the ratio between the prediction error variance and the mean deviation.

Table 9.1
Specification tests for volatility models

	S(d,A,I)	S(d,A)	S(d,I)	S(d)	S(A,I)	S(A)	S(I)	S
BL	118.1	119.4	666.3	674.1	100.9	108.9	118.7	133.5
R^2	.153	.151	.142	.134	.151	.147	.151	.147
AIC	1.935	1.937	1.949	1.951	1.938	1.942	1.938	1.942
pm	1.210	1.211	1.213	1.213	1.212	1.212	1.211	1.212

Table 9.2
Standard deviations of various components

	S(d,A,I)	S(d,A)	S(d,I)	S(d)	S(A,I)	S(A)	S(I)	S
σ_ω	2.488	2.489	2.581	2.583	.975	1.445	2.466	2.472
σ_μ	.029	.030	.134	.135	.059	.059	.057	.056
σ_ψ	-	-	-	-	.417	.401	.537	.536
σ_h	.456	.461	-	-	2.305	2.055		

Table 9.2 reports the standard deviations of the components of the various volatility models. In particular σ_ω is the standard deviation of the residual, σ_μ is the standard deviation of the innovation to the permanent component, σ_ψ is the standard deviation of the innovation to the stochastic cyclical component, σ_h is the standard deviation of the innovation to the autoregressive component.

Table 9.3 reports the correlation coefficients between the various filters.

Several considerations emerge from these Tables. Firstly, the AIC criterion indicates that the most parsimonious specifications in both categories of model should be selected, with a preference for the simple deterministic specification with no dummies and no autoregressive components. On the other hand the stochastic cycle version is preferred to its deterministic version in terms of coefficient of determination, Box-Ljung statistics and the ratio between prediction error variance and mean deviation. The evidence is therefore partly conflicting.

Secondly, both classes of models would seem to be little affected by the exclusion of the dummy variables in terms of Box-Ljung statistics and the ratio between prediction error variance and mean deviation. Thirdly, the deterministic cycle version of the model would appear to be much more sensitive to the exclusion of the autoregressive component in terms of Box-Ljung statistics than its stochastic cycle counterpart. The autoregressive component could be eliminated from the models which include a stochastic intradaily component, but not from the models which include a deterministic intradaily component.

As shown in Table 9.2, the main implication of eliminating the autoregressive component is that the stationary dynamics results to be almost entirely absorbed in the irregular component, while the estimated standard deviation of the residuals

Table 9.3
Correlation coefficients

Panel A: correlations between deterministic filters

	D(I)	D	S(d,A,I)	S(d,A)	S(d,I)	S(d)
D(I)	1					
D	.9830	1				
S(d,A,I)	.9916	.9887	1			
S(d,A)	.9807	.9981	.9909	1		
S(d,I)	.9793	.9850	.9955	.9864	1	
S(d)	.9807	.9982	.9901	1	.9864	1

Panel B: correlations between stochastic filters

	S(A,I)	S(A)	S(I)	S
S(A,I)	1			
S(A)	.9858	1		
S(I)	.9956	.9795	1	
S	.9828	.9911	.9883	1

Panel C: correlations between deterministic and stochastic filters

	D(I)	D	S(d,A,I)	S(d,A)	S(d,I)	S(d)
S(A,I)	.8541	.8504	.8602	.8512	.8587	.8513
S(A)	.8515	.8613	.8565	.8622	.8532	.8624
S(I)	.8202	.8160	.8255	.8168	.8239	.8168
S	.8021	.8096	.8060	.8105	.8027	.8107

of the level (σ_μ) and stochastic cyclical (σ_ψ) components are virtually unchanged. In addition, from Table 9.3 it can be noticed that there is high correlation inside each category of filters but less across the two categories. It is interesting to notice that the deterministic filter estimated by the structural time series approach is very similar to the one estimated via the Andersen and Bollerslev approach as the correlation coefficient is very close to one. This suggests that the two-step estimation methodology is not a relevant disadvantage in this context.

The better performance of the stochastic model over the deterministic one is also suggested by the distributional properties of the filtered returns reported in Table 9.4.

Several facts are noticeable from the tables. First, the stochastic filter outperforms the deterministic filter in terms of both kurtosis and skewness. Clearly some excess kurtosis still characterizes the unconditional distribution but this is entirely consistent with the existence of conditional heteroskedasticity shown by the results in table 9.5. Secondly, the results appear to be very sensitive to the inclusion of the deterministic dummies, in that excluding the dummies dramatically increases both skewness and kurtosis . Finally, excluding the autoregressive component from the SV models improves the results only for the stochastic version of the model, supporting therefore the selection of a more parsimonious model.

Table 9.4
Distributional properties of actual and filtered returns

Panel A: raw and deterministically filtered returns

	raw	D(I)	D	S(d,A,I)	S(d,A)	S(d,I)	S(d)
Maximum	.032	.033	.046	.034	.045	.035	.045
Minimum	-.02	-.015	-.019	-.017	-.019	-.017	-.019
100,000×Mean	2.27	4.45	4.44	4.64	4.64	4.50	4.64
1,000×S. Dev.	9.73	9.51	9.67	9.70	9.83	9.73	9.83
Skewness	.49	.44	1.19	.48	1.09	.51	1.10
Kurtosis	38.48	35.25	87.06	39.36	81.78	41.34	82.08

Panel B: stochastically filtered returns

	S(A,I)	S(A)	S(I)	S
Maximum	.029	.041	.027	.036
Minimum	-.015	-.016	-.014	-0.15
100,000×Mean	.40E-5	.43E-5	.40E-5	.44E-5
1,000×S. Dev.	.85E-3	.87E-3	.83E-3	.84E-3
Skewness	.473	1.141	.404	.927
Kurtosis	29.26	75.67	24.48	58.31

Table 9.5
Estimated parameters of MA(1)-GARCH(1,1)

Panel A: raw and deterministically filtered returns

	raw	D(I)	D	S(d,A,I)	S(d,A)	S(d,I)	S(I)
α	0.27	0.11	0.11	0.13	0.12	0.13	0.11
β	0.73	0.87	0.87	0.84	0.86	0.85	0.86
Skewness	0.32	0.20	0.50	0.22	0.51	0.22	0.51
Kurtosis	27.72	21.48	35.57	21.11	35.39	21.37	35.46

Panel B: stochastically filtered returns

	S(A,I)	S(A)	S(I)	S
α	0.02	0.02	0.02	0.01
β	0.98	0.97	0.98	0.98
Skewness	0.08	0.18	0.06	0.15
Kurtosis	11.59	18.84	10.15	16.10

To complete the assessment of the filtering procedures, the actual returns and the filtered returns produced by the various models have been fitted by an MA(1)-GARCH(1,1) model to provide a common reference. Table 9.5 collects the results. While the table contains only the parameters relative to the lagged squared residuals and conditional variance , a full set of results is available upon request from the authors.

First, as also reported in Andersen and Bollerslev [1997a], the deterministic filter fails to solve the aggregation problem for the data sampled below the half hour frequency, as the coefficient α is significantly different from zero. Second, from a comparison of the second (two-step approach) and the third (simultaneous estimation) column one sees that constraining the cyclical component in the SV model to be fully deterministic does not yield different results from the Andersen and Bollerslev methodology. Third and more important, the GARCH estimated using the stochastically filtered data yields results which are much closer to the expected theoretical values, in that α is very close to zero and β is close to one. This is evidence that the randomness of the intra-daily periodic component matters, and, therefore, should be taken into account at the filtering stage.

9.4 Conclusions

We have performed a statistical comparison of several models of intra-day volatility in the foreign exchange markets. Such models are useful for various applications to financial markets like option pricing and risk measurement. The basic distinction is between models that assume a deterministic pattern of intra-day volatility and models that allow for stochastic components. Each class of models can then be implemented with various modifications, like inclusion of dummy variables forcing the model to take into account of institutional market characteristics known to the econometrician. We have evaluated the competing models from two points of view. The first is the ability to produce unconditional distribution of filtered returns which is close to normality. The second is the possibility of fitting the filtered returns with GARCH models which are not far from the theoretical time aggregation properties.

We have found that stochastic models are in general superior to deterministic models for seasonality. They are characterized by filtered returns with less skewness and kurtosis and most of all are much closer to producing filtered returns which satisfy the temporal aggregation properties. This is particularly relevant for multi-period forecasting of the variance. We have also found that including dummies for specific and recurring events like closure of certain markets and holidays is important towards producing filtered returns with less skewness and excess kurtosis.

Two areas of research are in our opinion particularly promising. The first has to do with application of the stochastic volatility model to study events like the reaction of markets to announcements. In Morana and Beltratti [1998] we apply the model to the study of the effects of central banks interventions in the foreign exchange market and find that the flexibility allowed by the stochastic volatility model is important. The second has to do with the evaluation of the various models in the context of out of sample forecasting of the variance. The forecasting ability must be evaluated over several time horizons, given that often the practical applications of volatility models are connected to problems with a multi-period extension, like option pricing and risk measurement.

Of course this paper does not prove that stochastic volatility models are better suited than deterministic intra-day volatility models to the use of practitioners. Very often practitioners need to assess quickly the risk of financial portfolios in light of new information. From this point of view the easy applicability of deterministic intra-day volatility models seems to be a relevant advantage. It remains to be seen whether the statistical advantages of stochastic volatility models are superior to the extra-costs connected with more time-consuming computations.

Acknowledgments

In this paper we have used a data set which was kindly provided to us by Olsen and Associates, Zurich. We thank Michel Dacorogna for helpful comments and assistance with the data and Olsen and Associates for fantastic hospitality during a visit in the Summer of 1998. We are grateful to Bocconi University for its support with the Contributi per la ricerca di base anno 1999.

References

Andersen, T.G. and T. Bollerslev, 1997a, Intraday periodicity and volatility persistence in financial markets, *Journal of Empirical Finance*, 4, 115–158.

Andersen, T.G. and T. Bollerslev, 1997b, Heterogeneous information arrivals and return volatility dynamics: uncovering the long-run in high frequency returns, *Journal of Finance*, 52, 975–1005.

Andersen, T.G. and T. Bollerslev, 1997c, Answering the skeptics: Yes, standard volatility models do provide accurate forecasts, *International Economic Review*, 39, 885–905.

Andersen, T.G. and T. Bollerslev, 1996, Deutsche mark-dollar volatility: Intraday activity patterns, macroeconomic announcements, and longer run dependencies, *Journal of Finance*, 53, 219–265

Beltratti, A. and C. Morana, 1998, Computing value at risk with high frequency data, Centro di Economia Monetaria e Finanziaria Paolo Baffi, Bocconi University, Milan.

Dacorogna, M.M., U.A. Muller, R.J. Nagler, R.B. Olsen and O.V. Pictet, 1993, A geographical model for the daily and weekly seasonal volatility in the foreign exchange market, *Journal of International Money and Finance*, 12, 413–438.

Dacorogna, M.M., C.L. Gauvreau, U.A. Muller, R.B. Olsen and O.V. Pictet, 1996, Changing time scale for short-term forecasting in financial markets, *Journal of Forecasting*, 15, 203–227

Drost, F.C. and T.E. Nijman, 1993, Temporal aggregation of GARCH processes, *Econometrica*, 61, 909–927

Dunsmuir, W., 1979, A central limit theorem for parameter estimation in stationary vector time series and its application to models for a signal observed with noise, *Annals of Statistics*, 7, 490–506.

Engle, R.F. and Ng, V.K., 1991, Measuring and testing the impact of news on volatility, mimeo, University of California, San Diego.

Gallant, A.R., 1981, On the bias in flexible functional forms and an essentially unbiased form: The Fourier flexible form, *Journal of Econometrics*, 15, 211–245.

Harvey, A.C., 1989, *Forecasting, structural time series models and the Kalman filter*, Cambridge University Press, Cambridge.

Harvey, A.C., E. Ruiz and N. Shephard, 1994, Multivariate stochastic variance models, *Review of Economic Studies*, 61, 247–64.

JPMorgan, 1995, *Introduction to riskmetrics*, fourth edition.

Morana, C. and A. Beltratti, 1998, Interventions and exchange rates: An analysis with high frequency data, Centro di Economia Monetaria and Finanziaria Paolo Baffi, Bocconi University, Milan.

Payne, R., 1996, Announcements effects and seasonality in the intra-day foreign exchange market, LSE Financial Market Group Discussion Paper, no. 238.

Ruiz, E., 1994, Quasi-maximum likelihood estimation of stochastic volatility models, *Journal of Econometrics*, 63, 289–306.

10 A Symbolic Dynamics Approach to Volatility Prediction

Peter Tiňo, Christian Schittenkopf, Georg Dorffner, and Engelbert J. Dockner

We consider the problem of predicting the direction of daily volatility changes in the Dow Jones Industrial Average (DJIA). This is accomplished by quantizing a series of historic volatility changes into a symbolic stream over 2 or 4 symbols. We compare predictive performance of the classical fixed-order Markov models with that of a novel approach to variable memory length prediction (called prediction fractal machine, or PFM) which is able to select very specific deep prediction contexts (whenever there is a sufficient support for such contexts in the training data). We learn that daily volatility changes of the DJIA only exhibit rather shallow finite memory structure. On the other hand, a careful selection of quantization cut values can strongly enhance predictive power of symbolic schemes. Results on 12 non-overlapping epochs of the DJIA strongly suggest that PFMs can outperform both traditional Markov models and (continuous-valued) GARCH models in the task of predicting volatility one time-step ahead.

10.1 Introduction

Traditionally, option price forecasts are based on implied volatilities derived from an observed series of option prices. The basic assumption behind this approach is that in efficient capital markets with constant volatility of asset returns, the volatility must be reflected in option prices. Taking a different route, Noh, Engle and Kane [Noh et al 1994] used a GARCH model [Bollerslev 1986] to predict the volatility of the rate of return of an asset and then based their predictions of option prices on the GARCH-predicted volatilities. In addition, the volatility change forecasts (volatility is going to increase or decrease) based on historical returns can be interpreted as a buying or selling signal for a straddle. This enables one to implement simple trading strategies to test the efficiency of option markets (e.g. S&P 500 index [Noh et al 1994], or German Bund Future Options [Dockner et al 1988]). If the volatility decreases we go short (straddle is sold), if it increases we take a long position (straddle is bought). In this respect, the quality of a volatility model can be measured by the percentage of correctly predicted directions of volatility change from this period to the next.

In our previous work on predicting the daily volatility of the Austrian stock market index ATX [Schittenkopf et al 1998], real-valued volatility models were evaluated by considering the squared daily returns the "true" volatilities and comparing them with the model forecasts. In this paper, we take a symbolic dynamics route. The time series of historic volatility changes is quantized into a symbolic sequence characterizing the original real-valued sequence only through a few distinct events (symbols) such as *sharp increase, small decrease*, etc... Instead of modeling the original real valued trajectory, we look for a set of grammatical and probabilistic constraints characterizing its symbolic counterpart.

There have not been many applications of symbolic methods to modeling financial time series. Papageorgiou built predictive models to determine the direction of change in high frequency Swiss franc/U.S. dollar exchange rate (XR) tick data [Papageorgiou 1997] and studied the correlational structure of coupled time series of daily XRs for five major currencies measured against the U.S. dollar [Papageorgiou 1998]. In both cases the real-valued XR returns were quantized into 9 symbols. Papageorgiou predicts the directions of changes in Swiss franc/U.S. dollar XRs using a second order Markov model (MM) and analyses the correlational structure in the five major XRs through a mixed memory MM [Saul and Jordan 1998]. Giles, Lawrence and Tsoi [Giles et al 1997] considered the same set of five major XRs and predicted the XR directional changes by applying recurrent neural networks to symbolic streams obtained by quantizing the historic real-valued directional change values using the self-organizing map [Kohonen 1990].

Generally, it was found that discretization of financial time series can potentially effectively filter the data and reduce the noise. Even more importantly, the symbolic nature of the pre-processed data enables one to interpret the predictive models as lists of clear (and often intuitively appealing) rules. Yet, there are serious shortcomings in using such techniques:

• The determination of the number of quantization intervals (symbols) and their cut values is ad hoc. No strongly supported explanation is given in [Papageorgiou 1997, Papageorgiou 1998] why 9 symbols with their particular quantization intervals were used. The authors of [Giles et al 1997] use up to eight symbols with the cut values determined by the self-organizing map without any attempt to set the quantization intervals to an "optimal"[1] configuration. Kohavi and Sahami [Kohavi and Sahami 1996] warn that naive discretization of continuous data can be potentially disastrous as critical information may be lost due to the formation of inappropriate quantization boundaries. Indeed, discretization should be viewed as a form of knowledge discovery revealing the critical values in the continuous domain.

• Due to (non)stationarity issues, it is a common practice to slide a window containing both training and test sets through the available data thus substantially reducing the amount of training data for model fitting. In such situations using many symbols can be potentially hazardous as the subsequence statistics is poorly de-

---

1. with respect to the performance measure

termined. In fact, the results in [Giles et al 1997] indicate that the predictive model achieved the best performance with binary input streams.

• Due to training sequence length constraints and the size of used alphabets, the order of MMs is usually set to 2 or 3, whereas only a small set of deeper prediction contexts may really be needed to achieve a satisfactory performance. In case of recurrent neural networks one runs across the well-known vanishing gradient effect [Bengio et al 1994] reducing the network memory capacity.

We address these issues by

• transforming real-valued time series into symbolic sequences over 2 or 4 symbols. Quantization into 4 symbols is done in an intuitively appealing parametric way.

• using variable memory length Markov models (VLMM) [Ron et al 1994] instead of classical fixed-order MMs. VLMMs deal with the familiar explosive increase in the number of MM free parameters (when increasing the model order) by including predictive contexts of variable length with a deep memory *just where it is really needed.*

Apte and Hong [Apte and Hong 1994] address the issue of optimal alphabet size and cut values. They applied a minimal rule generation system R-MINI to monthly S&P 500 data quantized by a special feature discretization subsystem. However, the features were quantized prior to the rule generation process without any reference to the final model's predictive behavior. The R-MINI rules are in disjunctive normal form.

Bühlmann [Buhlmann 1998] models the extreme events of return of the Dow Jones and volume of the NYSE given their previous histories. The original return and volume series are quantized into streams over 3 ordinal categories (*lower extreme, usual, upper extreme*) that are used to fit a hierarchy of generalized linear models viewed as sieve approximations to a finite state Markov chain. The cut values for the 3 categories correspond to the 2.5% and 97.5% sample quantiles, so that the *lower* and *upper extreme* categories describe extreme events with expected overall occurrence of about 5%. We adopt this quantization strategy (in a slightly modified form) in our experiments.

10.2 Prediction system

The main idea in building a variable memory length (VLMM) Markov model on a given input stream S over an alphabet $\mathcal{A} = \{1, 2, ..., A\}$ is to consider all predictive contexts[2] $w \in \mathcal{A}^l$, $1 \le l \le L$, up to a certain pre-specified depth L and select only contexts v the predictive (empirical) distributions $P(s|v)$, $s \in \mathcal{A}$, of which differ significantly from those of their suffices, e.g. include an extended context au, $a \in \mathcal{A}$, $u \in \mathcal{A}^l$, $1 \le l \le L-1$, if the Kullback-Leibler divergence between the next-symbol distributions for the candidate prediction contexts u and au, weighted by the prior (empirical) distribution of the extended context au, exceeds a given threshold ϵ [Ron et al 1994]

$$P(au) \sum_{s \in \mathcal{A}} P(s|au) \log \frac{P(s|au)}{P(s|u)} \ge \epsilon. \tag{10.1}$$

The parameters ϵ and L are supplied by the modeler. We have shown [Tino and Dorffner 1998] that constructing VLMMs in this manner can be very troublesome. The construction parameters determine the VLMM size only implicitly without any intuitive specific relation and often one has to spend a fair amount of time when constructing a series of VLMMs of increasing size.

In an attempt to deal with this problem we introduced a novel class of predictive models, called prediction fractal machines (PFMs) [Tino and Dorffner 1998], similar in spirit to VLMMs, the construction of which is fast and intuitive in the model size. Construction of PFMs starts by transforming the n-block structure of the training sequence $S = s_1 s_2 ...$ over $\mathcal{A}$ into a spatial structure of points in a unit hypercube, called the chaos n-block representation of S. The n-blocks $u = u_1 u_2 ... u_n \in \mathcal{A}^n$ are represented as points

$$u(x) = u_n(u_{n-1}(...(u_2(u_1(x)))...)) = (u_n \circ u_{n-1} \circ ... \circ u_2 \circ u_1)(x), \quad x \in X, \tag{10.2}$$

where $X = [0, 1]^N$, $N = \lceil \log_2 A \rceil$, and the maps $1, 2, ..., A$,

$$i(x) = kx + (1-k)t_i, \quad t_i \in \{0, 1\}^N, \quad t_i \ne t_j \text{ for } i \ne j, \tag{10.3}$$

act on X with a contraction coefficient $k \in (0, \frac{1}{2}]$. For $Y \subseteq X$, $u(Y) = \{u(x)| \ x \in Y\}$.

---

2. To keep the construction procedure feasible it is common to consider only contexts with probability of occurrence greater than some pre-determined threshold θ.

Denote the center $\{\frac{1}{2}\}^N$ of X by x_*. The chaos n-block representation of S is a sequence of points

$$CBR_{n,k}(S) = \left\{ S_i^{i+n-1}(x_*) \right\}_{i \geq 1}, \tag{10.4}$$

containing a point $w(x_*)$ for each n-block $S_i^{i+n-1} = s_i s_{i+1}...s_{i+n-1} = w$ in S. The map $w \to w(x_*)$ is one-to-one.

The chaos n-block representation of symbolic sequences is related to the chaos game representation of DNA sequences introduced by Jeffrey [Jeffrey 1990] and has many useful properties. We proved [Tino 1999] that the estimates of generalized Rényi dimension spectra, quantifying the multifractal scaling properties of $CBR_{n,k}(S)$, directly correspond to the estimates of the Rényi entropy rate spectra measuring the statistical structure in the sequence S. In particular, for infinite sequences S, as the block length n grows, the box-counting fractal dimension and the information dimension estimates on $CBR_{n,k}(S)$, tend to the sequences' topological and metric entropies, respectively, scaled by $(\log \frac{1}{k})^{-1}$.

The chaos n-block representation codes the n-block suffix structure in the following sense [Tino 1999](see also [Tino and Koteles 1999]: if $v \in \mathcal{A}^+$ is a suffix of length $|v|$ of a string $u = rv$, $r, u \in \mathcal{A}^+$, then $u(X) \subset v(X)$, where $v(X)$ is an N-dimensional hypercube of side length $k^{|v|}$. Hence, the longer is the common suffix shared by two n-blocks, the closer the n-blocks are mapped in the chaos n-block representation $CBR_{n,k}(S)$. On the other hand, the Euclidean distance between points representing two n-blocks u, v, that have the same prefix of length $n-1$ and differ in the last symbol, is at least $1 - k$.

Suppose our model cannot have more than M prediction contexts. A natural smoothness constraint that L-blocks with long common suffices are likely to produce similar continuations, whereas L-blocks with different suffices may lead to different future scenarios leads us to the idea that L-blocks (potential predictive contexts of maximal depth) should factorize the set $[S]_L$ of allowed L-blocks in the training sequence S into a set of M equivalence classes, such that blocks within each equivalence class share as long a common suffix as possible. Recalling the suffix structure coding properties of the chaos L-block representation $CBR_{L,k}(S)$ of the training sequence S, this corresponds to partitioning the $CBR_{L,k}(S)$ into M subsets, each of diameter as small as possible. In practical terms, this means allocation of points from $CBR_{L,k}(S)$ to M codebook vectors $b_1, ..., b_M \in X$, such that the loss

$$E(S) = \sum_{w \in [S]_L} P(w) \, d_E^2(w(x_*), c(w)) \tag{10.5}$$

is minimal, where $c(w) \in \{b_1, ..., b_M\}$ is the codebook vector to which the point $w(x_*)$ is allocated, and d_E is the Euclidean distance.

The prediction probabilities in PFMs are determined by

$$\mathcal{P}(s|b_i) = \frac{N(i,s)}{\sum_{a \in \mathcal{A}} N(i,a)}, \quad s \in \mathcal{A}, \tag{10.6}$$

where $N(i,a)$ is the number of $(L+1)$-blocks wa, $w \in \mathcal{A}^L$, $a \in \mathcal{A}$, in the training sequence, such that the point $w(x_*)$ is allocated to the codebook vector b_i.

Given a history $w \in \mathcal{A}^L$ of L symbols, the next symbol distribution provided by the PFM is $\mathcal{P}(s|c(w))$, with $c(w)$ defined in (10.5).

10.3 Experiments

The time series $\{x_t\}$ of the Dow Jones Industrial Average (DJIA) from Feb. 1 1918 until Dec. 31 1997 (21620 measurements) was transformed into a time series of returns $r_t = \log x_{t+1} - \log x_t$ and divided into 13 epochs (as shown in figure 10.1) each containing 1663 values (spanning approximately 6 years). The series $\{r_{t+1}^2 - r_t^2\}$ of differences between the successive squared returns is quantized with respect to the direction of daily volatility change into a binary sequence $\{C_t\}$

$$C_t = \begin{cases} 1 \text{ (down)}, & \text{if } r_{t+1}^2 - r_t^2 < 0 \\ 2 \text{ (up)}, & \text{otherwise.} \end{cases} \tag{10.7}$$

Since within each epoch, *downs* (1s) and *ups* (2s) occur with approximately the same frequency, sequences $\{D_t\}$ over 4 symbols are obtained by quantizing the series $\{r_{t+1}^2 - r_t^2\}$ as follows:

$$D_t = \begin{cases} 1 \text{ (extreme down)}, & \text{if } r_{t+1}^2 - r_t^2 < \theta_1 < 0 \\ 2 \text{ (normal down)}, & \text{if } \theta_1 \le r_{t+1}^2 - r_t^2 < 0 \\ 3 \text{ (normal up)}, & \text{if } 0 \le r_{t+1}^2 - r_t^2 < \theta_2 \\ 4 \text{ (extreme up)}, & \text{if } \theta_2 \le r_{t+1}^2 - r_t^2, \end{cases} \tag{10.8}$$

where the parameters θ_1 and θ_2 correspond to $\mathcal{Q}$ percent and $(100 - \mathcal{Q})$ percent sample quantiles, respectively. So, the upper (lower) $\mathcal{Q}\%$ of all daily volatility increases (decreases) in the sample are considered extremal, and the lower (upper) $(50 - \mathcal{Q})\%$ of daily volatility increases (decreases) are viewed as normal. In our experiments $\mathcal{Q} \in \{5, 10, 15, ..., 45\}$.

We performed two experiments. The first experiment identifies the amount of detectable memory in the daily volatility change process. In the second experiment

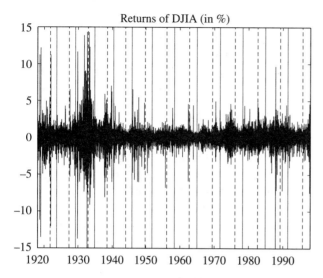

Figure 10.1
Returns of the DJIA form Feb.1 1918 until Dec. 31 1997. The data is divided into 13 epochs (dotted vertical lines). Each epoch is split into a training sequence and a test sequence (dashed vertical lines).

we simulate a realistic setting, where one is forced to split the available data into separate training and validation sets, the latter used for selection of the most appropriate model size M and quantization quantile Q for the models trained on the training set.

In [Tino and Dorffner 1998] we have shown that our prediction fractal machines (PFMs) and variable memory length Markov models (VLMM) outperform the classical fixed-order Markov models (MMs) on chaotic sequences with deep memory structure. In such cases it is beneficial, instead of simply considering all prediction contexts of certain length, to accept only a limited set of carefully selected long contexts. On the other hand, a shallow memory structure in sequences reduces the advantage of using VLMMs (or PFMs) instead of the classical MMs. In the experiments reported here, the length of the window in constructing the chaos block representations of the training sequences was set to $L = 20$ and the contraction factor is $k = \frac{1}{2}$.

In the first experiment, for each epoch, we split the data into a training sequence (the first 1100 symbols) and a test sequence (the rest of the epoch). The two sequences are quantized according to the extremal event quantile Q (see (10.8)).

Then, PFMs and MMs of increasing size are trained on the training set and tested on the test set with respect to the percentage of correct guesses of the volatility change direction for the next day[3]. If the next symbol in the test set is 1 or 2 (3 or 4) and the sum of conditional next symbol probabilities for 1 and 2 (3 and 4) given by a model is greater than 0.5, the model guess is considered correct. Figures 10.2 and 10.3 show the performance of PFMs and MMs, respectively, on the out-of-sample data in the first epoch. The 35% quantile Q for the extremal events seems to work best for both models. PFMs achieve the best performance with very few prediction contexts (up to 10). Further increase in the model size does not give any improvement in the prediction performance. The performance of MMs improves up to a memory of order 3 and then the MMs clearly overfit the training set (the performance on the test set deteriorates). Figure 10.4 suggests that similar observations can be made for the remaining epochs. Shown are the results for epochs 2–7. Results for epochs 8–13 were analogical to those shown in figures 10.2, 10.3 and 10.4. Depending on the epoch, the optimal value for the quantile Q ranges from 15 to 40, and the best-performing MM order varies from 1 to 3. In general, in accordance with intuition, more volatile epochs need deeper memory and larger extreme events quantile Q.

It is interesting that PFMs do not identify deep dominant prediction contexts that would lead to a highly superior performance (compared to MMs) as is, for example, the case with the chaotic Feigenbaum sequence [Tino and Dorffner 1998]. This supports the widely held belief [Jaditz and Sayers 1993] that noise is a dominant component in financial data and that a direct use of techniques known from chaotic dynamics[4] does not bring any dramatic improvement in data description and predictability.

In the second experiment we take a more realistic view. If we were to use our models in a day-to-day trading, we would need to decide (based on the historic data) what extreme event quantile Q and model size to use for future predictions. The experimental setting from the first experiment is slightly modified in that the test sets from the first experiment are now validation sets on which we select, using the models fitted on the training sets[5], the optimal (model size,quantile Q)

---

3. Reported results for PFMs are average values across 10 vector quantization runs (K-means clustering) in the PFM construction

4. based on the assumption that there is no (or very little) noise affecting the dynamics of the system

5. the training sets remain unchanged

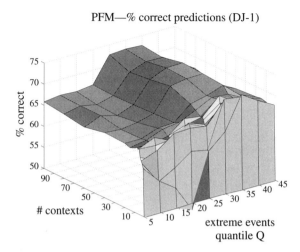

PFM—% correct predictions (DJ-1)

Figure 10.2
Performance of PFMs on the first DJIA data epoch measured by the percentage of correct volatility direction predictions on out-of-sample data.

combination. The selected models are then tested on test sets, which are in this case the first 600 symbols from the next epoch.

The results are summarized in figure 10.5. We also plot the performance of a simple 2 symbol (first-order) reversal strategy (dotted line) predicting *up* whenever the previous move was *down* and vice-versa. 4 symbol quantization schemes (solid line) yield consistently better performance than their 2 symbol counterparts (dashed line). Moreover, PFMs (squares) working under 4 symbol schemes tend to have better performance than classical MMs (stars). The situation is reversed in the 2 symbol case, where the validation strategy does not prevent PFMs from including a few over-specialized contexts. PFMs rarely perform better than the reversal strategy. This is partially caused by the sample distribution that varies from epoch to epoch. Regime shifts in data distribution can be dangerous for potentially highly specialized models like PFMs or VLMMs. In real trading, the best strategy would be to often re-estimate the predictive model as the new samples arrive.

We also tested the approaches presented in [Noh et al 1994, Dockner et al 1988] that use GARCH-based methods to model the volatility of the returns and then plug the volatility change forecasts into trading strategies. GARCH [Bollerslev 1986] and GJR [Glosten et al 1993] are among the most widely used (real-valued) models of volatility. Basic to these models is the notion that the financial time series $\{x_t\}$ under study can be decomposed into a predictable component μ_t and

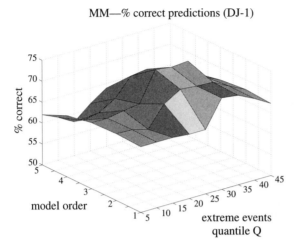

MM—% correct predictions (DJ-1)

Figure 10.3
Performance of the classical MMs on the first DJIA data epoch measured by the percentage of
correct volatility direction predictions on out-of-sample data.

an unpredictable component e_t, which is assumed to be zero mean Gaussian noise of
finite variance σ_t^2: $x_t = \mu_t + e_t$. The models are thus characterized by time-varying
conditional variances σ_t^2 and are therefore well suited to explain volatility clusters.
The conditional mean is often modelled as a linear function of the previous value:
$\mu_t = ax_{t-1}$. For a GARCH(p,q) model the conditional variance σ_t^2 is given by

$$\sigma_t^2 = \alpha_0 + \sum_{i=1}^{q} \alpha_i e_{t-i}^2 + \sum_{i=1}^{p} \beta_i \sigma_{t-i}^2. \tag{10.9}$$

The GJR model is an extension of the GARCH(1,1) model, and it incorporates also
asymmetric effects:

$$\sigma_t^2 = \alpha_0 + \alpha_1 e_{t-1}^2 + \alpha_2 \phi_{t-1} e_{t-1}^2 + \beta_1 \sigma_{t-1}^2 \tag{10.10}$$

where $\phi_{t-1} = 1$ if $e_{t-1} < 0$ and $\phi_{t-1} = 0$ otherwise. GJR models are motivated
by the fact that stock returns are characterized by a leverage effect, i.e. volatility increases as returns for stocks decrease. In each epoch, the GARCH(1,1),
GARCH(2,2) and GJR models were fit to the training set in the maximum likelihood framework. Following [Schittenkopf et al 1998], the fitted models were
evaluated by considering the squared returns r_t^2 the "true" volatility and comparing them with the forecasted volatility σ_t^2. A prediction is classified correct if

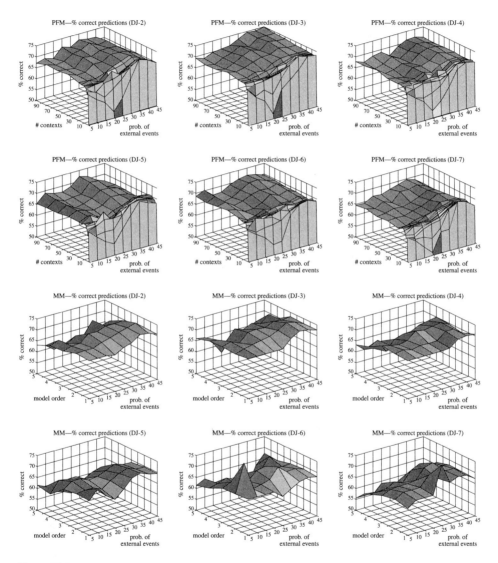

Figure 10.4
Performance of PFMs and classical MMs on the DJIA data epochs 2–7. (upper-left to lower-right, upper half - PFMs, lower half - MMs).

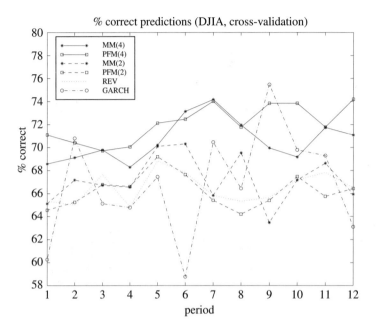

Figure 10.5
Prediction performance of the PFM (squares) and MM (stars) validation set candidates. The performance is evaluated on the test set containing the first 600 points of the next epoch. Results corresponding to 4 and 2 symbol quantization schemes are shown as solid and dashed lines, respectively. The dotted line corresponds to the simple reversal strategy. Also shown is the performance of the GARCH-based candidates (dashed-dotted line with circles).

$(\sigma_t^2 - r_{t-1}^2)(r_t^2 - r_{t-1}^2) > 0$. As with the symbolic models, based on the validation set performance, we select a GARCH-based candidate and test it on the first 600 points from the following epoch. The results (dashed-dotted line with circles in figure 10.5) indicate that, compared with symbolic models, the GARCH-based models are more sensitive to shifts in probability regimes of returns. The worst performances of these models (epochs 1, 6 and 12) correspond to cases where the training set distribution seem to differ from that of the test set (the first 600 points in the next period). We stress, however, that the GARCH-based models were evaluated with respect to volatility change direction predictions, whereas they were trained with a different perspective in mind - to model the conditional distribution of returns, so that the training data are likely to be generated from the model distribution. We included the GARCH experiment for a comparison with the previous approaches to volatility change direction prediction using real-valued models.

In order to test the differences between the three major methods, we performed several significance tests. A t-test over the twelve percentage values indicated that the PFM is significantly better than both the MM ($p < 0.05$) and GARCH ($p < 0.005$). A Wilcoxon matched-pairs signed-ranks test also revealed significant differences between the PFM and MM ($p < 0.05$) and GARCH ($p < 0.005$), respectively. Finally, we performed a McNemar test on the two pairs of classifiers over the twelve independent test sets separately. In eight of the ten test sets where PFM showed better classification performance than the GARCH models, the test indicated significance. For the PFM vs. the MM, this was the case in 4 out of 8 cases. For none of the test sets, either MM or GARCH was ever significantly better than the PFM. One must add, however, that for all three tests, some assumptions appear to be at least mildly violated (non-Gaussian distributions, skewness of differences, possible dependencies between observations).

10.4   Conclusion

We have investigated potential benefits of using ideas from symbolic dynamics in prediction of daily volatility changes. The two key points of this contribution are

1. the use of a simple parametric scheme to find the best quantization cut values in a data-driven fashion

2. the use of Markov models with variable length contexts to test the amount of detectable memory in the process.

Although the results from the significance tests have to be taken with caution, the results strongly suggest

• that there appears to indeed lie some potential in using a symbolic dynamics approach to volatility forecasting, in which continuous values are replaced by symbols through quantization, and

• that our novel prediction fractal machine can outperform more traditional Markov models in the prediction task.

In addition, the results suggest that daily volatility changes of the DJIA only show rather shallow finite memory structure (both MM and PFM tended to be of depth 2 or 3). 4 symbol quantization schemes, *when the cut values are carefully selected*, yield better performance than the 2 symbol schemes. This (together with the fact that in 4 symbol schemes variable memory length models tend to slightly outperform the classical MMs) suggests that there is a grammatical structure in the data to be grasped, but one cannot use ad hoc quantization techniques.

Of course, implementation and evaluation of different trading strategies using predictions of volatility changes given by various models would be highly desirable (this work has already been started). We did not investigate quantization schemes using more than 4 symbols, since the space of possible quantization parametrizations would rapidly grow. It may be an interesting topic for the future research, though. Also, in this study, we did not discard the rules with little predictive power, i.e. rules that predict *ups* with only slightly higher probability than *downs* and viceversa. Discarding such rules would lead to no-trading situations as in [Papageorgiou 1997]. We plan to continue our research in this direction. Rules will be discarded according to a special discard parameter. The value of the discard parameter should reflect a balance between the number of rules we are willing to get rid of and the number of trading steps we should perform in order to accumulate a profit. Trading strategies using our predictive models will play a prominent role in this study.

Acknowledgments

This work was supported by the Austrian Science Fund (FWF) within the research project "Adaptive Information Systems and Modeling in Economics and Management Science" (SFB 010). The Austrian Research Institute for Artificial Intelligence is supported by the Austrian Federal Ministry of Science and Transport.

We thank our colleagues Arthur Flexer and Peter Sykacek for providing help with the significance tests. Furthermore we are grateful to Fritz Leisch and Andreas Weingessel for valuable discussions.

References

Apte, C. and S. Hong. 1994. Predicting equity returns from securities data. In Fayyad, U., G. Piatetsky-Shapiro, P. Smyth, and R. Uthurusamy, editors, *Advances in Knowledge Discovery and Data Mining*, pages 541–560. AAAI/MIT Press.

Bengio, Y., P. Simard, and P. Frasconi. 1994. Learning long-term dependencies with gradient descent is difficult. *IEEE Transactions on Neural Networks*, 5(2):157–166.

Bollerslev, T. 1986. A generalized autoregressive conditional heteroscedasticity. *Journal of Econometrics*, 31:307–327.

Buhlmann, P. 1998. Extreme events from return-volume process: adiscretization approach for complexity reduction. *Applied Financial Economics, to appear.*

Dockner, E., G. Strobl, and A. Lessing. 1988. Volatility forecasts and the profitability of option trading strategies. Technical report, University of Vienna, Austria.

Giles, C., S. Lawrence, and A. Tsoi. 1997. Rule inference for financial prediction using recurrent neural networks. In *Proceedings of the Conference on Computational Intelligence for Financial Engineering, New York City, NY*, pages 253–259.

Glosten, L., R. Jagannathan, and D. Runkle. 1993. On the relation between the expected value and the volatility of the nominal excess return on stocks. *Journal of Finance*, 48:1779–1801.

Jaditz, T. and C. Sayers. 1993. Is chaos generic in economic data? *Int. Journal of Biffurcation and Chaos*, 3(3):745–755.

Jeffrey, J. 1990. Chaos game representation of gene structure. *Nucleic Acids Research*, 18(8):2163–2170.

Kohavi, R. and M. Sahami. 1996. Error-based and entropy-based discretization of continuous features. In Simondis, E., J. Han, and U. Fayyad, editors, *Proceedings of the Second International Conference on Knowledge Discovery in Databases*, pages 114–119. AAAI Press.

Kohonen, T. 1990. The self–organizing map. *Proceedings of the IEEE*, 78(9):1464–1479.

Noh, J., R. Engle, and A. Kane. 1994. Forecasting volatility and option prices of the s&p 500 index. *Journal of Derivatives*, pages 17–30.

Papageorgiou, C. 1997. High frequency time series analysis and prediction using markov models. In *Proceedings of the conference on Computational Intelligence for Financial Engineering, New York City, NY*, pages 182–185.

Papageorgiou, C. 1998. Mixed memory markov models for time series analysis. In *Proceedings of the conference on Computational Intelligence for Financial Engineering, New York City, NY*, pages 165–170.

Ron, D., Y. Singer, and N. Tishby. 1994. The power of amnesia. In *Advances in Neural Information Processing Systems 6*, pages 176–183. Morgan Kaufmann.

Saul, L. and M. Jordan. 1998. Mixed memory markov models. In *Proceedings of the 6th International Workshop on Artificial Intelligence and Statistics, Fort Lauderdale, Florida*.

Schittenkopf, C., G. Dorffner, and E. Dockner. 1998. Volatility prediction with mixture density networks. In *Proceedings of the 8th International Conference on Artificial Neural Networks*, pages 929–934. Springer, Berlin.

Tino, P. 1999. Spatial representation of symbolic sequences through iterative function systems. *IEEE Transactions on Systems Man and Cybernetics, part B: Cybernetics*, in press.

Tino, P. and G. Dorffner. 1998. Constructing finite-context sources from fractal representations of symbolic sequences. Technical Report TR-98-18, Austrian Research Institute for Artificial Intelligence, Austria.

Tino, P. and M. Koteles. 1999. Extracting finite state representations from recurrent neural networks trained on chaotic symbolic sequences. *IEEE Transactions on Neural Networks*, in press.

11 Does Volatility Timing Matter?

Jeff Fleming, Chris Kirby, and Barbara Ostdiek

This chapter examines the performance of volatility-timing strategies. We consider a short-horizon investor who uses mean-variance optimization to allocate funds between stocks, bonds, gold, and cash. Specifically, the investor rebalances his portfolio daily based on the current estimate of the conditional covariance matrix of returns. Our results indicate that volatility timing can yield substantial benefits. Moreover, the benefits are robust to practical considerations such as estimation risk and transaction costs.

A great deal of evidence suggests that volatility in financial markets is predictable.[1] This is reflected in products such as Barra's *Short Term Risk Model* and J.P. Morgan's *RiskMetrics* that promise to use volatility modeling to enhance the performance of standard portfolio optimization and risk management techniques. In addition, Busse (1998) finds that many portfolio managers behave like volatility timers, reducing their market exposure during periods of high expected volatility. Despite this anecdotal evidence that volatility timing matters, researchers have yet to establish whether these strategies yield any real economic benefits. We examine this issue by measuring the value of volatility forecasts to investors who engage in short-horizon asset allocation strategies.

We consider a short-horizon investor who uses mean-variance optimization to allocate funds between stocks, bonds, gold, and cash. The investor's objective is to maximize expected return (or minimize volatility) while matching the volatility (or expected return) of a fixed-weight benchmark portfolio. To solve the portfolio problem, we need inputs for the conditional expected asset returns and the conditional covariance matrix. There is little evidence, however, that we can detect short-term variation in expected returns. Therefore, we treat the expected returns as constant, and let the variation in the optimal portfolio weights be driven purely by changes in the conditional covariance matrix.

To estimate this matrix, we use a general nonparametric approach developed by Foster and Nelson (1996). The estimator is a rolling weighted average of the squares and cross products of past return innovations, constructed to be asymptotically optimal. This approach accommodates a variety of return generating processes and nests most ARCH, GARCH, and stochastic volatility models as special cases. We use the time-series of these covariance matrix estimates to construct the investor's optimal portfolio weights. This yields a dynamic trading strategy that specifies the proportion of funds invested in each asset class as a function of time. The

---

1. See Bollerslev, Chou, and Kroner (1992) for a review of this literature.

performance differential between the dynamic strategy and an appropriate fixed-weight benchmark portfolio reveals the economic value of the volatility forecasts.

Our analysis is based on a 15-year sample of daily returns for stock, bond, and gold futures.[2] The results indicate that volatility timing can have substantial benefits. Ignoring the uncertainty in estimating expected returns, the dynamic strategy that minimizes conditional volatility reduces the portfolio's realized volatility from 11.3% to 8.8% relative to a traditional benchmark portfolio (a 60/40 split between stocks and bonds for 95% of the portfolio and 5% invested in gold). The maximum expected return strategy increases the realized return from 8.1% to 11.6%. The benefits are smaller, but still positive, after we control for estimation risk and the uncertainty in selecting an appropriate benchmark portfolio. Moreover, although these benefits are achieved by active trading, they are still apparent after we account for transaction costs.

11.1 Data

Our data consist of daily returns for stock, bond, and gold futures for January 3, 1983 to December 31, 1997. The specific contracts are the S&P 500 index futures traded at the Chicago Mercantile Exchange, the Treasury bond futures traded at the Chicago Board of Trade, and the gold futures traded at the New York Mercantile Exchange. The gold futures contract closes at 1:30 CST each day while the bond and stock contracts close at 2:00 CST and 3:15 CST, respectively. To align the price observations across contracts, we use daily closing prices for gold futures and the last transaction prices before 1:30 CST for the bond and stock contracts. The source for the gold futures data is Datastream International and the source for the bond and stock futures data is the Futures Industry Institute's intraday transactions data. To maintain a uniform measurement interval across contracts, we exclude all days when any of the three markets is closed.

We compute the daily returns using the day-to-day price relatives for the nearest to maturity contract. As the nearby contract approaches maturity, we switch to a new contract, timing the switch to capture the contract month with the greatest trading volume. This results in switching contracts for S&P 500 futures once the nearby contract enters its final week and for bond and gold futures once the nearby contract enters the delivery month. This procedure yields a continuous series of

---

2. We use futures data to avoid problems induced by infrequent trading, but our analysis generalizes to the underlying spot assets via the no-arbitrage relation between futures and spot prices.

3,763 daily returns for each market. The summary statistics indicate that the average return is highest for stock index futures (10.82%) followed by bonds (6.53%) and then gold (−7.76%). Stocks also have a greater volatility (16.2%) than bonds (10.5%) and gold (14.7%). Finally, the correlation between stock and bond returns is positive (0.397), while the correlations between stock and gold returns (−0.105) and bond and gold returns (−0.157) are negative.

11.2   Conditional covariance matrix estimation

Numerous techniques for estimating conditional covariance matrices have been developed in the literature.[3] We rely on a simple nonparametric approach that uses rolling estimators constructed in an asymptotically optimal manner. This approach nests a broad range of ARCH and GARCH models as special cases and has some distinct advantages in our application. Unlike multivariate ARCH and GARCH models, the computational demands of rolling estimators are modest and it is easy to ensure that the covariance matrix estimate is invertible. In addition, the general nature of the approach allows us to provide baseline evidence — without searching for the "best" volatility model — on the economic significance of volatility timing.

To develop the rolling estimator, let $\mathbf{r}_{t+1}$, $\mu_t \equiv \mathrm{E}_t[\mathbf{r}_{t+1}]$, and $\Sigma_t \equiv \mathrm{E}_t[(\mathbf{r}_{t+1} - \mu_t)(\mathbf{r}_{t+1} - \mu_t)']$ denote, respectively, a 3×1 vector of returns on stock, bond, and gold futures, the conditional expected value of $\mathbf{r}_{t+1}$, and the conditional covariance matrix of $\mathbf{r}_{t+1}$. The rolling estimator can be written as

$$\hat{\Sigma}_t = \sum_{l=-t+1}^{T-t} \omega_{t+l}(\mathbf{r}_{t+l} - \mu_{t+l})(\mathbf{r}_{t+l} - \mu_{t+l})' \tag{11.1}$$

where ω_{t+l} is the weight placed on the product of the return innovations for date $t + l$ and T is the number of observations in the sample. Foster and Nelson (1996) demonstrate that the optimal weights depend on the characteristics of the process. If volatility is stochastic, the optimal weights for the two-sided rolling estimator are given by

$$\omega_{t+l} = (\alpha/2)e^{-\alpha|l|}, \tag{11.2}$$

---

3. Officer (1973) and Fama and MacBeth (1973) employ *ad hoc* rolling estimators. Merton (1980), Poterba and Summers (1986), and French, Schwert, and Stambaugh (1987) divide the data into nonoverlapping blocks and treat the variances and covariances as constant within each block. More recently, ARCH models [e.g., Engle (1982) and Bollerslev (1986)] have gained popularity.

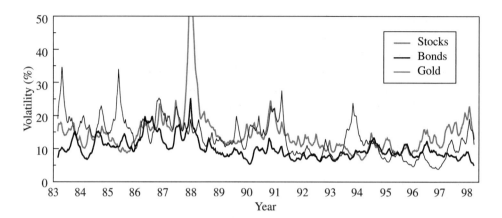

Figure 11.1
Daily volatility estimates for S&P 500, T-bond, and gold futures returns.

where α is the decay rate. This is called a two-sided estimator because it uses both leads and lags of returns to estimate Σ_t. To construct the corresponding one-sided estimator, we set $\omega_{t+l} = 0$ for $l > 0$ and double each of the weights for $l \leq 0$.

We estimate the optimal decay rate using the procedure developed by Fleming, Kirby, and Ostdiek (1999). This yields $\alpha = 0.0679$. The resulting two-sided estimates of the conditional volatilities are plotted in Figure 11.1.[4] The average estimates are consistent with the unconditional volatilities reported earlier with stocks the most volatile, followed by gold and then bonds. Moreover, the variability in these estimates suggests that volatility changes over time.

Figure 11.2 shows the two-sided estimates of the conditional return correlations. As with the volatilities, the average estimates are generally consistent with the

---

4. As is common practice, we use seasonally-adjusted data to generate these estimates. We begin by regressing the raw returns on a set of six variables: a dummy variable for each weekday and a variable (NTDYS) that counts the number of nontrading days covered by each return. The residual in this regression, r_{it}^*, is the unexpected component of the day t return in market i. To remove the daily seasonal in volatility, we estimate the regression,

$$[(r_{it}^*)^2/var(r_{it}^*)] - 1 = \beta_{1i}\text{MON}_t + \beta_{2i}\text{TUE}_t + \cdots + \beta_{5i}\text{FRI}_t + \beta_{6i}\text{NTDYS}_t + e_t$$

where $var(r_{it}^*)$ is the sample variance of r_{it}^*. The resulting coefficient estimates are used to construct the seasonally-adjusted returns,

$$r_{it} = r_{it}^*/\sqrt{1 + \beta_{1i}\text{MON}_t + \beta_{2i}\text{TUE}_t + \cdots + \beta_{5i}\text{FRI}_t + \beta_{6i}\text{NTDYS}_t},$$

that we use to construct the covariance matrix estimates.

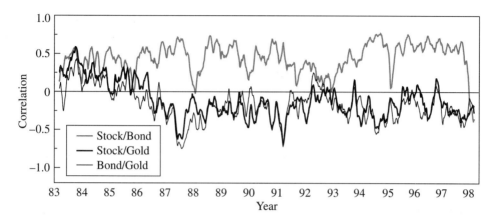

Figure 11.2
Daily correlation estimates between S&P 500, T-bond, and gold futures returns.

unconditional correlations and there is considerable evidence that the correlations change over time. In particular, the estimated stock/gold and bond/gold correlations sharply decrease after 1986 and the stock/bond estimates widely fluctuate throughout the sample.

11.3 Volatility timing in a mean-variance framework

To determine whether the variation in the conditional covariance matrix can be exploited to improve asset allocation decisions, we consider a hypothetical investor who uses conditional mean-variance analysis to allocate funds.[5] The investor wants to minimize his portfolio's conditional variance subject to achieving a particular conditional expected rate of return. For each date t, he solves the quadratic program

$$\min_{\mathbf{w}_t} \quad \mathbf{w}_t' \Sigma_t \mathbf{w}_t$$
$$\text{s.t.} \quad \mathbf{w}_t' \mu_t = \mu_{pt}, \tag{11.3}$$

where $\mathbf{w}_t$ is a 3×1 vector of portfolio weights on stock, bond, and gold futures. Note that we omit the riskless interest rate from this specification because we are

5. Sufficient conditions for an investor to demand a conditionally mean-variance efficient portfolio are (i) returns are conditionally multivariate normal, which is consistent with an important class of trading models [see, e.g., Clark (1973) and Tauchen and Pitts (1983)]; and (ii) the investor has lognormal utility of wealth.

dealing with futures returns. Under the cost-of-carry model, the return on a futures contract equals the total return on the spot asset minus the riskless rate. $1 - \mathbf{w}_t'\mathbf{1}$ represents the weight held in "cash equivalent" securities which earn an excess return equal to zero. The solution to our optimization problem,

$$\mathbf{w}_{pt} = \frac{\mu_{pt}\Sigma_t^{-1}\mu_t}{\mu_t'\Sigma_t^{-1}\mu_t}, \tag{11.4}$$

delivers the weights on the risky assets.[6]

To construct the optimal dynamic portfolio weights, we use the one-step-ahead forecasts of the conditional covariance matrix from Section 11.2. We also, in general, need one-step-ahead forecasts of the expected returns. However, there is little evidence to suggest that we can detect daily variation in expected returns. Therefore, we treat the expected returns as constant and let the trading decisions depend only on changes in our estimates of the conditional covariance matrix.

We could conduct a similar analysis where the investor's objective is to maximize conditional expected return subject to achieving a particular conditional variance. Therefore, our optimal portfolio analysis suggests two candidate volatility-timing strategies. First, we solve for the weights that set the expected return equal to some fixed target and minimize volatility (the "minimum volatility strategy"). Second, we solve for the weights that set volatility equal to some fixed target and maximize expected return (the "maximum expected return strategy").

Implementing the dynamic strategies To implement our methodology, two remaining issues must be resolved. The first is that we must estimate the expected returns for the assets. One possible approach is to use data available at the beginning of our sample period. Unfortunately, this produces unreliable estimates for bonds and gold due to dramatic changes in the 1970s caused by the shift in Federal Reserve interest rate policy and the elimination of the gold standard. Alternatively, we could use the first few years of our sample to estimate the expected returns and use the remaining period to evaluate the dynamic strategies. This is also problematic, however, because the expected return estimates would be very imprecise.

We address this issue by adopting a bootstrap approach [Efron (1979)]. First, we randomly sample with replacement from the actual data to generate a series of artificial returns. We then compute the mean returns in this artificial sample and use them, along with our conditional covariance matrix estimates, to compute the

---

6. Fleming, Kirby, and Ostdiek (1999) show that under standard no-arbitrage arguments we would obtain the same weights by formulating the optimization in terms of spot assets.

optimal portfolio weights. Finally, we apply the weights to the actual returns and evaluate the performance of the dynamic strategies. This approach ensures that our analysis is based on a representative sample and allows us to directly assess the impact of estimation risk.

The second unresolved issue is how to measure the performance gains attributable to volatility timing. The most straightforward approach is to compare the performance of the dynamic strategies to that of a fixed-weight benchmark portfolio. But then we must choose an appropriate benchmark. To control for the uncertainty regarding this choice, we adopt the following approach. Initially, we use a traditional benchmark portfolio, defined as a 57/38/5 split between stocks, bonds, and gold. This reflects the general guideline among asset allocation managers of a 60/40 split between stocks and bonds, with five percent of the portfolio invested in gold to provide a hedge against inflation. After providing this evidence, we evaluate the performance of the dynamic strategies relative to the ex-post efficient frontier.

Results of the optimal portfolio analysis   We now examine the optimization results for the limiting case in which the true expected returns are known. These results are obtained by solving for the optimal portfolio weights in Equation (11.4) where the inputs are (i) the sample mean returns for each asset, and (ii) our estimates of the conditional covariance matrix. We refer to this as the case of no estimation risk.[7]

Figure 11.3 plots the optimal weights for the minimum volatility strategy. The sign and magnitude of each weight depends on the estimated expected returns and the forecasted volatilities and correlations. For example, the average return on gold futures is negative in our sample and, in general, the weight in gold is negative. But the size of this short position decreases when the forecasted gold volatility increases, as in 1985 and 1993 (Figure 11.1), and also when gold's forecasted correlation with stocks and bonds becomes more negative, as in early- to mid-1987 and the beginning of 1991 (Figure 11.2). Similarly, the split between stocks and bonds is sensitive to their relative volatilities. Stock volatility decreases steadily from 1991 to 1994 while bond volatility remains relatively constant. As a result, the weight in stocks steadily increases over this period while the weight in bonds decreases. The opposite occurs from 1996 to 1998 as stock volatility rises and bond volatility falls.

Figure 11.4 shows the anticipated reduction in volatility according to our optimization results. The unconditional return on the benchmark portfolio is 8.26%,

---

7. We use this terminology loosely because we still face the risk associated with estimating the conditional covariance matrix. However, Merton (1980) implies that this risk is likely small in comparison to that associated with estimating expected returns.

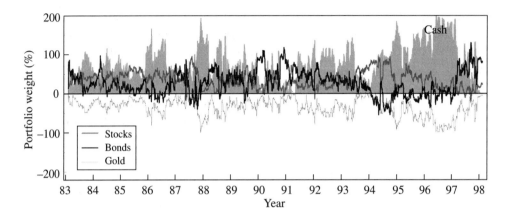

Figure 11.3
Optimal dynamic portfolio weights with minimum volatility.

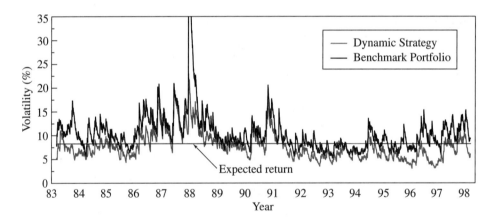

Figure 11.4
Ex-ante comparison of the minimum volatility dynamic strategy to the static benchmark portfolio.

but its forecasted volatility changes as a function of our daily covariance matrix. The average volatilities for the benchmark and dynamic portfolios are, respectively, 10.6% and 7.7%. Not surprisingly, the anticipated volatility reduction is greatest during periods of high stock market volatility such as 1986, the 1987 crash, the 1989 mini-crash, and near the end of the sample. During these periods, the minimum volatility strategy has a much lower weight in stocks than the benchmark portfolio.

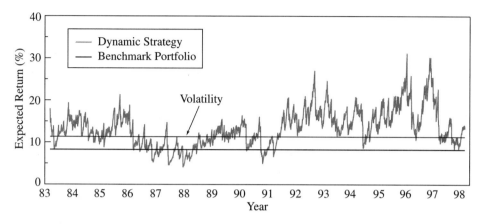

Figure 11.5
Ex-ante comparison of the maximum return dynamic strategy to the static benchmark portfolio.

Turning to the maximum expected return strategy, the optimal weights (not shown) are similar to those for the minimum volatility strategy. The main difference is that the changes tend to be more pronounced because a greater risk exposure is generally needed to match the benchmark's volatility. Figure 11.5 shows the anticipated improvement using this strategy, measured with the estimated expected returns. The strategy's average expected return is 13.42%, a gain of more than five percentage points over the benchmark portfolio (8.26%), although gains of more than ten points are apparent during much of the second half of the sample.

11.4   Evaluating the performance of the dynamic strategies

Our portfolio optimization results suggest that the anticipated benefits to volatility timing are substantial. In practice, however, the realized benefits may be smaller than anticipated (Figures 11.4 and 11.5) because the portfolio weights are based on estimates of the expected returns and conditional covariance matrix. To assess the realized benefits, we need to form the portfolios implied by the dynamic weights and compute their realized returns and volatilities.

We compute the ex-post return for each strategy by multiplying the portfolio weights on a given day by the observed next-day returns on stock, bond, and gold futures. Table 11.1 summarizes the results. For the minimum volatility strategy, the average return is comparable to that of the benchmark portfolio, but its sample volatility (8.8%) is considerably lower than the benchmark's (11.3%). As a result,

Table 11.1
Ex-post performance of the static and dynamic asset allocation strategies.

| | Static: Benchmark Portfolio | | | Dynamic: Minimum Volatility | | | Dynamic: Maximum Return | | |
Period	μ	σ	SR	μ	σ	SR	μ	σ	SR
Entire Sample	8.13	11.30	0.719	8.01	8.84	0.906	11.62	12.65	0.919
1983−1985	6.35	10.03	0.633	6.77	7.46	0.907	10.47	12.38	0.846
1986−1988	7.64	16.73	0.457	8.46	12.59	0.672	6.54	13.27	0.493
1989−1991	8.15	10.05	0.811	8.31	9.33	0.891	9.69	12.85	0.754
1992−1994	2.77	7.71	0.358	3.37	6.33	0.533	5.07	12.07	0.420
1995−1997	15.67	9.70	1.615	13.09	6.86	1.909	26.50	12.61	2.102
Excluding:									
Oct 19-30, 1987	8.12	10.43	0.778	7.49	8.66	0.865	11.15	12.56	0.888
1986−1988	8.25	9.41	0.877	7.89	7.59	1.040	12.93	12.49	1.035

the Sharpe ratio for this strategy (0.91) is substantially higher than the Sharpe ratio for the benchmark (0.72), indicating greater ex-post efficiency. The maximum expected return strategy achieves similar results. Ex-post, the strategy has a slightly higher sample volatility (12.7%) than the benchmark, but a substantially greater average return (11.6%). Therefore, its Sharpe ratio (0.92) also indicates improvement.

Table 11.1 also breaks down the ex-post returns by three-year subperiods. These subperiod results indicate that our general findings are robust across the sample. Although there is substantial variation in the average returns and sample volatilities, both of the dynamic strategies outperform the benchmark portfolio in every three-year subperiod except 1989−1991. Even in this subperiod, the minimum volatility strategy outperforms the benchmark and the maximum expected return strategy achieves a Sharpe ratio (0.75) that is comparable to that of the benchmark (0.81).

The final two lines of Table 11.1 show the impact of the 1987 crash. Excluding the crash has a greater impact on the benchmark than on either of the dynamic strategies. At the time of the crash, the conditional volatilities for both stocks and bonds are relatively high (Figure 11.1). Therefore, the dynamic strategies are predominately invested in cash, with relatively low weights in stocks and bonds (Figure 11.3), causing them to outperform the benchmark. It is unclear, however, how much we should credit this to "timing" ability. The large cash positions persist before and after the crash, making it difficult to evaluate the strategies over a noncrash sample. If we exclude the period when the strategies did well because they were holding cash, we should also exclude the surrounding period when, for the same reason, they did poorly. One alternative is to simply exclude the entire 1986−1988 subperiod. As shown in Table 11.1, the relative performance of the static and dynamic strategies over this sample is similar to that over the full sample.

Significance tests   We assess the statistical significance of the performance gains for the dynamic strategies by comparing the results in Table 11.1 to those obtained when the asset returns are generated independently of the portfolio weights. This is accomplished using a simple randomization scheme. First, we form a permutation of the actual data series by randomly sampling without replacement from the joint distribution of returns. Next, we apply the actual weights for the dynamic strategies to the randomized returns to get a time-series of daily portfolio returns.[8] We repeat this process 10,000 times. Note that the mean return and volatility of the benchmark portfolio are the same as in the actual data because we sample without replacement.

If the performance gains of the dynamic strategies are significant, then these strategies should perform substantially worse in the artificial samples than they do using the actual data. We find this to be the case. For the minimum volatility strategy, the mean return for the 10,000 trials is 8.0% with a standard error of 1.3%. The mean volatility is 10.6% with a standard error of 0.3%. None of the 10,000 trials produce an ex-post volatility as low as that observed using the actual return series (8.8%), and only 11.2% of the trials yield a higher Sharpe ratio. For the maximum expected return strategy, the mean return is 13.0% with a standard error of 2.6%, and the mean volatility is 18.3% with a standard error of 0.6%. Only 7.3% of the trials produce a Sharpe ratio that is higher than that observed for the actual returns. These findings indicate it is unlikely that the superior performance of the dynamic strategies is due to chance.

The impact of estimation risk   We evaluate the impact of estimation risk on our results using the bootstrap approach described earlier. First, we randomly sample with replacement from the actual returns to generate a series of 3,763 artificial returns. We then compute the average return for each asset in this artificial sample and use these averages (instead of the true sample means) to determine the optimal portfolio weights. Finally, we apply these weights to the actual returns and evaluate the performance of the dynamic strategies as before. Relying on the artificial sample to estimate the expected returns mimics the uncertainty about

---

8. This procedure is asymptotically equivalent to using the actual returns series and randomizing the portfolio weights. Either way, the portfolio weights are independent of the realized returns on the assets.

expected returns that an investor would face in practice.[9] Therefore, if the dynamic strategies still outperform the benchmark portfolio, we can conclude that estimation risk does not offset their superior performance.

In this set of experiments, the mean return for the minimum volatility strategy is 7.2% and the mean volatility is 8.5%, with an average Sharpe ratio of 0.84. This is lower than the value obtained using the true sample means (0.91), but higher than that for the benchmark (0.72). In 94.4% of the trials, this strategy produces a higher Sharpe ratio than the benchmark portfolio. This indicates that the benefits of the dynamic strategy are apparent even after we account for the uncertainty about expected returns. The results for the maximum expected return strategy are similar — the mean return is 10.8% and the mean volatility is 12.6%. The average Sharpe ratio for this strategy is 0.85 and 96.6% of the trials produce a higher Sharpe ratio than the benchmark portfolio. Based on these results, it does not appear that the superior performance of the dynamic strategies is eliminated when we account for estimation risk.

11.5   Robustness Tests

The evidence reported in Section 11.4 is consistent with the view that volatility timing can improve the performance of asset allocation decisions. However, our analysis to this point assumes a specific benchmark portfolio, a given target expected return or volatility, no transaction costs, and infinitely divisible contract sizes. In this section, we assess the impact of these issues on our results.

Alternative benchmark portfolios   To control for the uncertainty about the appropriate benchmark portfolio, we consider *all* possible combinations of static weights in stocks, bonds, and gold. For each combination, we compute the realized return and volatility during our sample. This set of benchmarks, plotted in Figure 11.6, defines a region in expected return/standard deviation space whose boundary is the ex-post minimum variance frontier. To allow a positive weight in cash, we would draw a line from the origin through the tangency portfolio. The slope of this line represents the highest Sharpe ratio we could have attained using

---

9. Most investors would also weigh the expected returns obtained from sampling against their prior expectations. Specifically, asset pricing theory suggests that the unconditional expected returns for stock and bond futures should be positive, and that returns should be highest for stocks, followed by bonds and then gold. We incorporate these priors into our bootstrap experiment by requiring that the average returns in each of our artificial samples satisfy these conditions.

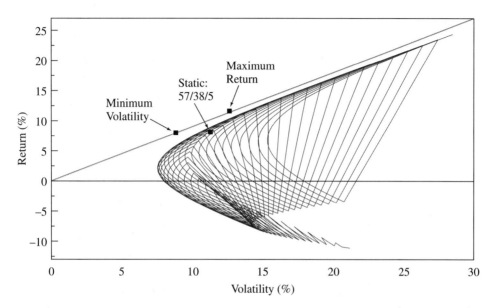

Figure 11.6
Ex-post performance of the static portfolio using different combinations of weights.

the most efficient (ex-post) set of static portfolio weights. Note that the Sharpe ratios for the two dynamic strategies are even greater.

The implication of this finding is clear. It is unlikely that we would have chosen ex-ante the portfolio that turns out to be most efficient; but, even if we had, the dynamic strategies still would have outperformed it. This indicates that our earlier findings are robust to alternative benchmarks.

Varying the target expected returns and volatilities   Table 11.2 shows how the performance of the dynamic strategies varies with the target expected return or volatility used in solving our daily portfolio optimizations. For comparison, the middle line of the table contains the results from Section 11.4 where the target is based on the benchmark portfolio's mean return or volatility. As expected, lowering the target return or volatility reduces both the realized return and volatility, however, the effects on the Sharpe ratios are ambiguous. Moreover, across the entire range of target parameter values, there is little variation in the realized performance. This indicates that the dynamic strategies are relatively insensitive to variation in the target return or target volatility.

Table 11.2
Ex-post performance of the dynamic strategies under different target returns and volatilities.

Minimum Volatility Strategy				Maximum Return Strategy			
Target Return	Realized returns μ	σ	SR	Target Volatility	Realized returns μ	σ	SR
6.00	5.77	6.43	0.898	9.00	9.31	10.10	0.921
6.50	6.27	6.96	0.900	9.50	9.84	10.66	0.923
7.00	6.77	7.50	0.902	10.00	10.35	11.21	0.923
7.50	7.26	8.03	0.904	10.50	10.85	11.76	0.923
8.00	7.75	8.56	0.905	11.00	11.33	12.31	0.921
8.26	8.01	8.84	0.906	11.31	11.62	12.65	0.919
8.50	8.24	9.09	0.906	11.50	11.80	12.86	0.918
9.00	8.74	9.62	0.908	12.00	12.27	13.41	0.915
9.50	9.23	10.15	0.909	12.50	12.75	13.95	0.914
10.00	9.72	10.68	0.910	13.00	13.22	14.50	0.912
10.50	10.21	11.21	0.910	13.50	13.69	15.05	0.910

Transaction costs We evaluate the effect of transaction costs by first estimating the transaction costs for S&P 500 futures. We estimate the bid/ask spread using the Smith and Whaley (1994) approach based on intraday transaction prices. This yields an average spread of 0.0593, or $29.65 per contract.[10] In addition, roundtrip commissions and fees for large institutions are about $6.00 per contract.[11] Combining these estimates with the average index level during our sample period (384.51) indicates that the average one-way transaction cost is $17.825 on a contract size of $384.51×500, or 2.34% annualized. In other words, if we traded one contract every day for a year (buy or sell), transaction costs would reduce the realized return by 234 basis points. We assume that the transaction costs for T-bond and gold futures are comparable to those for S&P 500 futures.

Table 11.3 shows the effect of various levels of transaction costs, centered around our estimate of 2.34%. We impose the transaction costs on every trade, including those required for establishing the initial position, daily rebalancing, rolling into each subsequent contract month, and liquidating the position at the end of the sample. For the dynamic strategies, the daily rebalancing represents the trading required to track time-variation in the optimal portfolio weights and, for the benchmark portfolio, it represents the trading needed to maintain a constant weight

10. This slightly exceeds the estimate of 0.0508 reported in Smith and Whaley (1994) because their sample ends in 1987 while ours extends through 1997.

11. This estimate is the same as that used in Fleming, Ostdiek, and Whaley (1996).

Table 11.3
Performance of the static and dynamic asset allocation strategies after imposing transaction costs.

Pct. Costs	Static: Benchmark Portfolio			Dynamic: Minimum Volatility			Dynamic: Maximum Return		
	μ	σ	SR	μ	σ	SR	μ	σ	SR
0.0%	8.13	11.30	0.719	8.01	8.84	0.906	11.62	12.65	0.919
0.5%	8.11	11.30	0.717	7.95	8.84	0.899	11.52	12.65	0.911
1.0%	8.09	11.30	0.716	7.89	8.84	0.892	11.42	12.65	0.903
1.5%	8.07	11.30	0.714	7.83	8.84	0.886	11.32	12.65	0.895
2.0%	8.05	11.30	0.712	7.77	8.84	0.879	11.22	12.65	0.887
2.5%	8.03	11.30	0.711	7.71	8.84	0.872	11.12	12.65	0.879
3.0%	8.01	11.30	0.709	7.65	8.84	0.866	11.02	12.65	0.871
3.5%	7.99	11.30	0.707	7.59	8.84	0.859	10.92	12.65	0.863
4.0%	7.97	11.30	0.706	7.53	8.84	0.852	10.81	12.65	0.855
4.5%	7.95	11.30	0.704	7.47	8.84	0.846	10.71	12.65	0.847
5.0%	7.93	11.30	0.702	7.41	8.84	0.839	10.61	12.65	0.839

in each asset. The transaction costs are imposed each day by subtracting the percentage cost from that day's realized return.

As the table indicates, transaction costs have the greatest effect on the maximum expected return strategy. This is not surprising because, as noted earlier, the weights for this strategy exhibit the most time-variation. Imposing transaction costs of, say, 2.5% reduces the strategy's realized return from 11.6% to 11.1% with just a trivial effect on its volatility. As a result, the strategy still earns a greater Sharpe ratio (0.88) than the benchmark portfolio (0.71). In order to equate the Sharpe ratios for the two strategies, transaction costs would need to be 15.9% (not shown in the table) — an amount that is almost seven times our previous estimate.

A related issue is whether the strategies require so much trading that they impact market prices. To examine this, we need to consider a specific value for the underlying portfolio. Suppose we begin with $100 million, which by the end of our sample grows to over $300 million. The contract sizes for the stock, bond, and gold futures contracts are, respectively, 500, 1000, and 100 times price.[12] Given these parameters, the maximum return strategy requires, on average, daily trade sizes of 23, 67, and 116 contracts (in absolute value), respectively, for stock, bond, and gold futures. For comparison, the average daily volumes in these markets during our sample period are 59,000 for stocks, 267,000 for bonds, and 30,000 for gold. Based

---

12. The contract size for S&P 500 futures changed to 250 times price after October 31, 1997.

Table 11.4
The effect of trading discrete contract sizes on the ex-post performance of the static and dynamic asset allocation strategies.

	Static: Benchmark Portfolio			Dynamic: Minimum Volatility			Dynamic: Maximum Return		
Initial Wealth	μ	σ	SR	μ	σ	SR	μ	σ	SR
$ 100,000	12.46	17.30	0.720	8.21	9.18	0.894	11.29	12.84	0.880
500,000	7.94	11.58	0.686	8.46	8.95	0.945	11.94	12.71	0.939
1,000,000	8.18	11.17	0.733	8.01	8.88	0.903	11.66	12.65	0.922
5,000,000	8.12	11.29	0.719	8.03	8.84	0.908	11.67	12.65	0.922
10,000,000	8.12	11.30	0.718	8.02	8.84	0.907	11.60	12.65	0.917
50,000,000	8.13	11.30	0.719	8.01	8.84	0.906	11.62	12.65	0.919
100,000,000	8.12	11.30	0.719	8.01	8.84	0.906	11.63	12.65	0.919
500,000,000	8.13	11.30	0.719	8.01	8.84	0.906	11.62	12.65	0.919

on this evidence, it seems unlikely that the dynamic strategies entail market-impact costs large enough to materially affect their performance.

Trading discrete quantities of contracts   Our analysis to this point assumes that we can trade fractional contracts, i.e., if we have $100 to invest, and the optimal weight is 0.50 for a contract worth $100, we can buy only half a contract. If instead we require each trade to be a discrete number of contracts, then we incur rounding error in the sense that our portfolio weight is suboptimal. This error has the greatest effect when the portfolio value (i.e., the number of contracts traded) is small.

We examine the impact of this rounding error using the following procedure. For a given level of initial wealth, we compute the number of contracts implied by our optimal weights and we round to the nearest integer. Any residual funds created by the rounding procedure are held in cash.[13] After each day, we compute our new portfolio value, and we apply the same rounding procedure to the optimal weights for the following day to determine the new number of contracts. Table 11.4 reports the results.

Imposing discrete trade sizes has an unpredictable effect on the mean returns, but generally increases volatility. As expected, the effects are greatest for smaller initial portfolio values. Beginning with $100,000, for example, the volatilities for each trading strategy sharply increase relative to those using continuous trade sizes. The mean returns are higher for the benchmark and minimum volatility strategy

---

13. A more precise procedure for determining the number of contracts would be to include the quantity discreteness in our daily portfolio optimization. This approach, however, is more complex and seems unnecessary given the small effects we report below using the simpler approach.

but lower for the maximum return strategy. These effects cause the Sharpe ratios to increase for the benchmark portfolio and decrease for the dynamic strategies. This result seems random, however, when compared to the results using other levels of initial wealth. In any case, the effect of discrete trade sizes disappears quickly. For an initial wealth as low as $5,000,000, the performance of each of the strategies is comparable to that using continuous trade sizes. This suggests that rounding error does not have much of an effect for even moderately-sized portfolios.

11.6 Conclusions

Our results indicate that volatility timing can improve the performance of short-horizon investment strategies. In particular, an investor trading stock, bond, and gold futures can use daily forecasts of the conditional covariance matrix to form a dynamic trading strategy that outperforms any fixed-weight benchmark portfolio. For the limiting case with no estimation risk, the dynamic strategies that minimize volatility and maximize return realize Sharpe ratios of 0.91 and 0.92, respectively. By comparison, the Sharpe ratio for a traditional benchmark portfolio is 0.72. The benefits of volatility timing are smaller, but still positive, after we account for estimation risk and the optimal choice of benchmark portfolio.

Additional tests indicate that the performance differential is robust to several practical considerations. First, accounting for the transaction costs of active trading and for discrete contract sizes does not eliminate the advantage of the dynamic strategies. Second, the results are insensitive to the target level of expected return or volatility. Finally, our results may be conservative in that they rely on a simple volatility specification rather than on a more complex parametric model.

References

Bollerslev, T. 1986. Generalized autoregressive conditional heteroskedasticity. *Journal of Econometrics*, 31:307–328.

Bollerslev, T., R. Y. Chou, and K. F. Kroner. 1992. ARCH modeling in finance: A review of the theory and empirical evidence. *Journal of Econometrics*, 52:5–60.

Busse, J. 1998. Volatility timing in mutual funds: Evidence from daily returns. Unpublished (Stern School of Business, New York University).

Clark, P. K. 1973. A subordinated stochastic process model with finite variance for speculative prices. *Econometrica*, 41:135–156.

Efron, B. 1979. Bootstrap methods: Another look at the jacknife. *Annals of Statistics*, 7:1–26.

Engle, R. F. 1982. Autoregressive conditional heteroskedasticity with estimates of the variance of United Kingdom inflation. *Econometrica*, 50:987–1008.

Fama, E. F. and J. D. MacBeth. 1973. Risk, return, and equilibrium: Empirical tests. *Journal of Political Economy*, 81:607–636.

Fleming, J., C. Kirby, and B. Ostdiek. 1999. The economic value of volatility timing. Unpublished (Jones Graduate School of Management, Rice University).

Fleming, J., B. Ostdiek, and R. E. Whaley. 1996. Trading costs and the relative rates of price discovery in stock, futures, and option markets. *Journal of Futures Markets*, 16:353–387.

Foster, D. P. and D. B. Nelson. 1996. Continuous record asymptotics for rolling sample variance estimators. *Econometrica*, 64:139–174.

French, K. R., G. W. Schwert, and R. F. Stambaugh. 1987. Expected stock returns and volatility. *Journal of Financial Economics*, 19:3–30.

Merton, R. C. 1980. On estimating the expected return on the market: An exploratory investigation. *Journal of Financial Economics*, 8:323–361.

Officer, R. R. 1973. The variability of the market factor of the New York Stock Exchange. *Journal of Business*, 46:434–453.

Poterba, J. M. and L. H. Summers. 1986. The persistence of volatility and stock market fluctuations. *American Economic Review*, 76:1142–1151.

Smith, T. and R. E. Whaley. 1994. Estimating the effective bid/ask spread using time and sales data. *Journal of Futures Markets*, 14:437–455.

Tauchen, G. E. and M. Pitts. 1983. The price variability-volume relationship on speculative markets. *Econometrica*, 51:485–505.

III Time Series Methods

12 Goodness of Fit, Stability and Data Mining

Juan del Hoyo and J.-Guillermo Llorente

Most specification search processes select models based on some goodness of fit statistic (i.e. R^2 or related F). Sequential search should be taken into account when looking for the maximum goodness of fit. To avoid misspecified models it is convenient to study the selected models not only based on the full sample, but also along the sample. Testing for stability of the estimated coefficients along the sample reduces the likelihood of accepting spurious models. This paper presents a conditional sequential procedure to be used in the specification search process of linear regression models, as a way to minimize data snooping or data mining. It is a combined test, first it considers the search for the "best" set of regressors, and conditional on this set, it studies the stability. The characteristics of the conditional test are presented. Its usefulness is considered with one application.

12.1 Introduction

This paper presents a framework for model specification search and its use in linear regression models. The diversity in modeling situations leads to the need for flexibility as an essential feature of any specification search process. The first issue to be faced in any specification search is the following, given a dependent (endogenous) variable and a set of m possible explanatory (independent, regressor or predictor) variables proposed by the relevant theory or previous studies, the problem becomes to choose the optimal subset of k ($k \leq m$) predictor variables. The number k is fixed a priori by the researcher. This search is often called *discrimination procedure*, its aim is to select the best model (group of k variables) in terms of a previously chosen measure. The usual measure in finance is maximizing the goodness of fit or R^2. This measure is related to minimizing the residual variance under the null of a correctly specified model. The common strategy is to compare the R^2 among candidate models and choose that one with the highest R^2. This criteria is *optimistic*, because maximizing the R^2 only ensures that the pertinent independent variables will not be removed. One important issue in this sequential search process is that conducting inference without properly considering the sequential selection process, commonly referred as data mining or data snooping, can be extremely misleading.

Foster *et al.* (1997) study the sequential model selection process using the criterion of maximal R^2 in obtaining the best regression model. The considered model has a fixed dependent variable and k regressors chosen among a set of m potential explanatory variables. They propose to use Bonferroni's and Rencher and Pun's approximations, as a way to avoid Monte Carlo simulations to numerically compute the distribution for the maximal R^2 (hereafter R^2_{max}).

The above mentioned discrimination approach is useful and covers one of the most important steps in any model validation or specification search process. Discrimination procedures select the best model in terms of the chosen measure, but do not provide any indication about possible misspecification errors of the entertained model. They do not consider some other characteristics related to the specification analysis, as the statistical significativeness and stability of the selected model along the sample.

White (1997) proposes to use what he calls "Reality Check" for studying model selection procedures. This method compares the forecasting performance of candidate models against a given benchmark model. Though out of the sample prediction accuracy is one of the best tests for any model, the choice of the right benchmark could be a difficult task. We would like to know a priori how is the benchmark insample. It is possible to have models that comply with the usual tests when considering the full sample, while being spurious. Hoyo and Llorente (1998, 1999) consider the information from the recursive estimations to detect this situation[1].

This paper adds to the debate about model selection and data mining, the idea of recognizing that the coefficients in spurious models are likely to either change and/or not be significant along the sample. This fact should help to avoid the choice of a wrong benchmark model in the specification search process. It is somehow surprising that the information embodied in the sample is generally not fully exploited in applied work. The problem of data mining should be reduced when the "best" selected model is tested using both the full sample as well as the recursive estimations along the sample. In particular, if under the null hypothesis the coefficients of the "true model" are constant along the sample, then before accepting any "approximation" with highly significant full sample R^2, it is convenient to test whether the hypotheses of statistical significance and constant coefficients of the chosen model remain valid along the sample.

The main feature of this paper is to propose a specification search procedure based on a combination of two existing search processes in the literature. We propose and study the characteristics of a combined sequential test. This test first considers the discrimination process, and conditional on it, the significance and stability of the relationship by means of recursive statistics. We study the distributions of the conditional test and how they are related to the unconditional ones. Given the complexity of the conditional distributions they are studied by Monte Carlo simulations. The main result of the paper is the "almost" independence

---

1. The tests can be applied to simple linear models as well as to more general ones with dynamic structures (Hoyo and Llorente, 1999).

between both steps (i.e. discrimination and recursive). Thus, it does not matter which distributions associated to the recursive estimations are used: conditional or unconditional.

The paper proceeds as follows. Section 12.2 reviews and studies the main properties of the R^2_{max} and the recursive statistics. Section 12.3 proposes the sequential procedure for the specification search process and studies the characteristics of the associated distributions. Section 12.4 presents an empirical application. Finally, Section 12.5 concludes.

12.2   Discrimination and Recursive Tests

This section reviews the discrimination tests (variable selection statistics), in particular the R^2_{max}, and the recursive tests.

Assume the model under consideration is an asset pricing model, where y is a $T \times 1$ vector of security returns. The potential predictor variables of these returns are m variables, and the researcher chooses k out of m ($k \leq m$). The number of potential regressors (m) does not have any limit a priori. The number of regressors (k) depends on the problem at hand (it can even include lagged returns), but it is often less than ten.

To emphasize the predictive nature of the considered model, and for easy exposition motives, the observations on y_t are assumed to be generated by a model of the following type[2]

$$y_t = X_{t-1}\beta_t + \epsilon_t , \quad t = 2, 3, \ldots, T. \tag{12.1}$$

Under the null hypothesis $\beta_t = \beta$ is a $(k+1) \times 1$ vector of k constant slope parameters plus the intercept, the errors (ϵ_t) are assumed to be a martingale difference sequence with respect to the σ-fields generated by $\{\epsilon_{t-1}, X_{t-1}, \epsilon_{t-2}, X_{t-2}, \ldots\}$, and X_t is a $1 \times (k+1)$ vector of regressors. The regressors are assumed to be constant and/or $I(0)$ with $E(X'_t X_t) = \Sigma_X$. Denote $\lambda = \frac{t}{T}$, $\Rightarrow$ weak convergence on $D[0,1]$, and $[\bullet]$ the integer part of the value inside brackets. Also assume that $T^{-1}\sum_{i=1}^{[T\lambda]} X'_i X_i \overset{P}{\to} \lambda\Sigma_X$ uniformly in λ for $\lambda \in [0,1]$; $E(\epsilon_t^2) = \sigma^2 \; \forall \; t$, and $T^{-1}\sum_{i=2}^{[T\lambda]} X'_i \epsilon_i \Rightarrow \sigma\Sigma^{1/2}W_k(\lambda)$, with $W_k(\lambda)$ a k-dimensional vector of independent Wiener or Brownian motion processes[3]. X_{t-1} can include lags of the dependent variable as long as they are $I(0)$ under the null (see Stock 1994). Given the

---

2. Boldface is used for vectors and matrices.

3. ϵ_t can be conditionally (on lagged ϵ_t and X_t) heteroskedastic and the results do not change.

m candidates explanatory variables, there are $N = \binom{m}{k}$ possible model regression specifications with k explanatory variables.

12.2.1   Distribution of the Maximal R^2

Under the classical assumptions, the R^2 of the regression, representing the proportion of variation in the dependent variable explained by the regressors, is distributed as Beta $\left(\frac{k}{2}, \frac{T-(k+1)}{2}\right)$, under the null hypothesis that $\beta_{k \times 1} = 0$ (all the slope coefficients of the linear regression are equal to zero, against the alternative that at least one of the coefficients is different from zero)[4] [5]. This distribution does not take into consideration the selection process among the potential explanatory variables. Thus, the cutoff values of the distribution for the R^2 statistics need to be adjusted for this process, assuming the "best" k regressors have been chosen by maximizing the R^2.

The distribution function for the R^2_{max} may be derived applying the standard order statistic argument. Nevertheless, for the considered model, where y does not change among regressions, the selection process induces overlapping elements in the matrices, and there may exist correlation among regressors, this is a difficult task. This induces the use of some approximation[6] for the joint distribution function of the R^2_{max}. In particular, the Bonferroni bound is $U_{R^2}(r) \geq 1 - \{[1 - \text{Beta}(r)]\,N\}$, and the Rencher and Pun (1980) approximation to the cutoff levels is given by $R^2_\gamma \approx F^{-1}\left[1 + (\ln(\gamma)/\ln(N)^{1.8N^{0.04}})\right]$, where γ is the percent cutoff level, and F^{-1} is the inverse of the beta cumulative distribution function.

The distribution for the R^2_{max} can also be computed numerically using Monte Carlo simulations. In this paper this distribution as well as the distributions related to other statistics will be numerically computed. Table 12.1 illustrates the differences between the cutoff levels computed with the approximated bounds (values taken from Foster *et al.* 1997), and those calculated numerically by simulations. Comparing these values it can be seen that the Bonferroni bound is very conservative, and that the Rencher and Pun approximation is close to the numerical results.

---

4. The intercept is excluded from the hypothesis.

5. The significance of the regression can also be tested using the $F-$statistics.

6. See Foster *et al.*, 1997.

Table 12.1
Maximal R^2 cutoff levels: comparisons between methods

Number of Potential	Number of Regressors Selected (k)				
Regressors (m)	1	2	3	4	5
Panel A: Bonferroni Bound					
10	0.036	0.055	0.071	0.084	0.094
25	0.040	0.068	0.094	0.116	0.136
50	0.044	0.079	0.110	0.138	0.164
100	0.048	0.089	0.126	0.159	0.189
Panel B: Rencher/Pun Rule-of-Thumb					
10	0.027	0.046	0.060	0.071	0.079
25	0.032	0.054	0.072	0.088	0.103
50	0.035	0.060	0.081	0.100	0.119
100	0.038	0.066	0.090	0.113	0.135
Panel C: Numerical Calculations					
10	0.031	0.045	0.056	0.062	0.066
25	0.037	0.058	0.073	0.085	0.095
50	0.042	0.065	0.084	0.100	0.114
100	0.043	0.067	0.088	0.106	0.121

NOTE: Entries are the 95 percent cutoff values for the "best" k-variable regressions R^2 given different number of potential regressors (m) and a fixed sample size of 250 observations. The table reports the 95 percent confidence limits for R^2 for the null hypothesis that all of the slope coefficientes of and OLS regression are equal to zero, where (a) only k of m potential regressors are used, (b) all possible regression combinations are tried, and (c) only the regression with the highest R^2 is reported. The alternative hypothesis is that at least one of the OLS slope coefficients is not equal to zero. The Bonferroni inequality is a bound and therefore represents a conservative test. The Rencher/Pun rule-of-thumb is an approximation of the exact distribution. The Numerical Calculations are computed by Monte Carlo simulations based on 5000 replications. The values in Panel A and B are from Foster *et al.* (1997) Table II, pp. 599.

12.2.2   Recursive Tests

This section presents the asymptotic distributions for the recursive statistics that consider the possibility of at least one change in the parameters along the sample with unknown a priori break date. Recursive tests can be considered as a tool to detect misspecifications, in particular, spurious models. It is assumed that the optimal set of regressors (k) is already chosen. Recursive statistics are computed using subsamples of increasing size $t = [\lambda_{min}T], [\lambda_{min}T] + 1, \ldots, T$, which are equivalent to $t = t_{min}, \ldots, T$, with $\lambda_{min} = \frac{t_{min}}{T}$ a startup value, and $[T\lambda] = t$.

The recursive OLS coefficients can be written as random elements on $D[0,1]$ as

$$\hat{\beta}(\lambda) = \left(\sum_{t_{min}}^{[T\lambda]} X'_{t-1} X_{t-1} \right)^{-1} \left(\sum_{t_{min}}^{[T\lambda]} X'_{t-1} y_t \right) \qquad 0 \leq \lambda_{min} \leq \lambda \leq 1. \tag{12.2}$$

The Wald type statistics used in this paper to test $q \leq (k+1)$ linear restrictions on β ($H_0 : R\hat{\beta}(\lambda) = r$, where R is a $q \times (k+1)$ nonstochastic matrix, and r is a $q \times 1$ vector) have as general form

$$\hat{F}_T(\lambda) = \frac{\left(R\hat{\beta}(\lambda) - r \right)' \left[R \left(\sum_{t_{min}}^{[T\lambda]} X'_{t-1} X_{t-1} \right)^{-1} R' \right]^{-1} \left(R\hat{\beta}(\lambda) - r \right)}{q\hat{\sigma}^2(\lambda)}, \tag{12.3}$$

where $\hat{\sigma}^2(\lambda)$ is the recursive estimation of the variance, and t_{min} the corresponding beginning of the recursive computations.

The asymptotic behavior of this statistic is derived by applying the Functional Central Limit Theorem (FCLT) and the Continuous Mapping Theorem (CMT). Therefore, $\hat{F}_T(\lambda) \Rightarrow \hat{F}(\lambda)$. The form of the final distributions depends on R and r as determined by the null hypothesis.

In what follows, the subscripts refer to the null hypothesis to be tested, and the superscripts to the number of parameters involved. For example, $\hat{F}(\lambda)_0^k$ represents the particularization of the statistic to test the null hypothesis that all the slope parameters of the model recursively estimated are equal to zero.

Following Stock (1994), the Wald type statistic to test for the significance of q coefficients along the sample ($H_0 : R\hat{\beta}(\lambda) = 0$), has the following asymptotic distribution

$$\hat{F}(\lambda)_0^q \equiv \max_{\lambda_{min} \leq \lambda \leq 1} \left[\lambda q * \hat{F}(\lambda) \right] \Rightarrow \sup_{\lambda_{min} \leq \lambda \leq 1} W_q(\lambda)' W_q(\lambda). \tag{12.4}$$

The statistic to test for the stability of the model along the sample, comparing the recursive estimations with those from the full sample, has the following expression ($H_0 : R(\hat{\beta}(\lambda) - \hat{\beta}(1))$ $\lambda \in [\lambda_{min}, 1]$)

$$\hat{F}(\lambda)_{\hat{\beta}(1)}^q \equiv \max_{\lambda_{min} \leq \lambda \leq 1} \left[\lambda q * \hat{F}(\lambda) \right] \Rightarrow \sup_{\lambda_{min} \leq \lambda \leq 1} B_q(\lambda)' B_q(\lambda), \tag{12.5}$$

where $B_q(\lambda) = W_q(\lambda) - \lambda W_q(1)$ is a q dimensional Brownian Bridge[7].

---

7. This expression conveniently scaled is similar to the *supW* in Andrews (1993).

Table 12.2
R^2_{max} cutoff levels

Percentile	Number of Regressors Selected (k)									
	1	2	3	4	5	6	7	8	9	10
Panel A: 150 observations										
0.100	0.043	0.065	0.079	0.089	0.096	0.101	0.103	0.105	0.106	0.106
0.050	0.052	0.076	0.092	0.102	0.109	0.114	0.117	0.118	0.119	0.119
0.001	0.071	0.096	0.114	0.126	0.136	0.141	0.146	0.148	0.149	0.150
Panel A: 500 observations										
0.100	0.013	0.019	0.024	0.027	0.029	0.030	0.031	0.031	0.032	0.032
0.050	0.015	0.023	0.027	0.031	0.033	0.034	0.035	0.036	0.036	0.037
0.001	0.022	0.030	0.035	0.039	0.041	0.043	0.044	0.045	0.045	0.046
Panel A: 1000 observations										
0.100	0.006	0.010	0.012	0.014	0.015	0.015	0.016	0.016	0.016	0.016
0.050	0.008	0.012	0.014	0.016	0.017	0.017	0.017	0.018	0.018	0.018
0.001	0.011	0.016	0.018	0.019	0.021	0.022	0.022	0.023	0.023	0.023

NOTE: Entries are the 90,95 and 99 percent cutoff values for the "best" k-variable regressions R^2 given $m = 10$ potential regressors (m) and three sample sizes 150, 500 and 1000 observations. The table reports the confidence limits for R^2 for the null hypothesis that all of the slope coefficients of and OLS regression are equal to zero where (a) only k of $m = 10$ potential regressors are used, (b) all possible regression combinations are tried, and (c) only the regression with the highest R^2 is reported. The alternative hypothesis is that at least one of the OLS slope coefficients is not equal to zero. The numerical calculations are computed by Monte Carlo simulations based on 10000 replications.

12.2.3   Monte Carlo Results

Critical values for the R^2_{max} and the two recursive statistics are reported in this section, size and nominal power are also obtained. The basic model is of the type presented in Equation (12.1) corresponding to several possible choices of k.

Following the convention established before, the two recursive statistics are denoted by $\hat{F}(\lambda)^k_0$, and $\hat{F}(\lambda)^k_{\hat{\beta}(1)}$, to test the statistical significance of all parameters except the intercept, and the deviation of the recursive estimations from their full sample estimates, respectively. The intercept is not considered in the statistics to keep in line with the usual tests, and with the R^2_{max}.

Table 12.2 presents the tabulation for the R^2_{max}. The cutoff levels are 90, 95 and 99 percent and $T = 250, 500$ and 1000 observations. The regressions depend on the number of regressors chosen (k) between the potential independent variables ($m = 10$). The numerical distributions where calculated using 10000 replications, and the m regressors where simulated as independent $N(0,1)$ variables.

The recursive statistics were tabulated using a symmetric 15 percent trimming, as it is usual in this kind of work[8]. Approximate critical values for these recursive

---

8. $\lambda_{min} \leq \lambda \leq \lambda_{max}$, with $\lambda_{min} = 0.15$, and $\lambda_{max} = 0.85$.

Table 12.3
Critical Values Recursive Tests

Percentile	Number of Regressors k									
	1	2	3	4	5	6	7	8	9	10
	$F(\lambda)_0^k$									
0.100	6.109	4.324	3.654	3.226	2.958	2.764	2.634	2.489	2.382	2.303
0.050	7.527	5.206	4.244	3.718	3.343	3.156	2.939	2.773	2.627	2.537
0.001	10.701	7.164	5.759	4.873	4.321	3.919	3.636	3.379	3.198	3.112
	$F(\lambda)_{\hat{\beta}(1)}^k$									
0.100	4.462	3.158	2.597	2.327	2.165	2.016	1.907	1.849	1.761	1.704
0.050	5.504	3.707	3.077	2.709	2.535	2.314	2.178	2.057	1.999	1.923
0.001	7.741	5.223	4.188	3.658	3.309	3.018	2.729	2.599	2.464	2.324

NOTE: Entries are the *sup* values of the functionals of Brownian motion. All critical values were computed by Monte Carlo simulation of the limiting functionals of Brownian motion as described in the main text. They are based on 10000 Monte Carlo replications and T=3600 observations. k is the number of parameters in the regression excluding the intercept. $\hat{F}(\lambda)_0^k$ statistic tests for the null hypothesis that all coefficients in the regression but the intercept are equal to zero, and $\hat{F}(\lambda)_{\hat{\beta}(1)}^k$ is the Wald type statistic to test the recursive estimations against the full sample estimations, considering all the parameters in the regression but the intercept. Each recursive statistic was computed with symmetric 15 percent trimming.

statistics are reported in Table 12.3. Entries are the *sup* values of the functionals of Brownian motions. The critical values were computed performing Monte Carlo simulations of the limiting functionals of Brownian Motion processes involved in the statistics. All critical values were computed using 10000 replications and $T = 3600$ in each replication.

Size and nominal power (not adjusted by size) of the statistics are summarized in Tables 12.4 and 12.5 respectively. Entries are percent rejections at 10% critical values from Tables 12.2 and 12.3. Power was simulated under the hypothesis that the coefficients follow a random walk. All pseudodata were generated including T startup values (initial observations not used in computing the statistics). The simulations are based on 1000 replications.

All the statistics have sizes near their levels when considering $T = 500$ or more observations in the sample. The nominal power of the considered statistics is really good when testing against a random walk process to describe the changing parameters. These results suggest that these statistics could be powerful and reliable diagnostic tools for the considered null hypotheses.

12.3 Sequential Specification Procedure

The methodologies presented in the last section have been used in previous papers as useful tools in specification search processes. Nevertheless, they have not been

Table 12.4
Size of the Recursive Tests

150 observ.				500 observ.				1000 observ.			
k=1	k=3	k=5	k=7	k=1	k=3	k=5	k=7	k=1	k=3	k=5	k=7
$F(\lambda)_0^k$											
11.10	13.60	15.90	18.00	9.50	8.10	8.80	8.50	9.00	7.30	7.70	7.00
$F(\lambda)_{\hat{\beta}(1)}^k$											
9.90	13.50	14.40	18.60	9.70	11.20	11.80	11.70	10.50	9.20	10.20	10.80

NOTE: Entries are percent rejections at 10% critical values; for the selected sample sizes and number of independent variables. The reported values are the percent rejections by the various statistics based on 10% critical values from Table 12.3. They were computed as described in the text. All pseudodata were generated including T startup values (initial observations not used in computing the statistics). k is the number of independent variables included in the regression except the intercept. Based on 1000 replications.

Table 12.5
Power of the Tests

150 observ.				500 observ.				1000 observ.			
k=1	k=3	k=5	k=7	k=1	k=3	k=5	k=7	k=1	k=3	k=5	k=7
R_{max}^2											
92.90	99.80	100	100	93.20	99.70	100	100	95.10	99.90	100	100
$F(\lambda)_0^k$											
100	100	100	100	100	100	100	100	100	100	100	100
$F(\lambda)_{\hat{\beta}(1)}^k$											
99.70	100	100	100	100	100	100	100	100	100	100	100

NOTE: Entries are percent rejections at 10% critical values, for different sample sizes. k refers to the number of independent variables in the regression excluding the intercept. The reported values are the percent rejections by the various statistics based on 10% critical values from Tables 12.2 and 12.3. The coefficients were assumed to follow a random walk process with $N(0,1)$ noise. All pseudodata were generated including T startup values (initial observations not used in computing the statistics). Based on 1000 replications.

studied when applied sequentially. It seems natural to consider both tests to reduce the likelihood of data snooping or data mining. We could find models that satisfy the R_{max}^2 criterion but are unstable. This could be due to the fact that the R^2 concentrates on the residual sum of squares calculated from the full sample, but it does not take into consideration possible misspecifications. If the misspecification shows up as time varying parameters, they can be detected with tests based on recursive estimators.

This paper proposes a sequential specification procedure in two steps. First, the procedure selects one model based on either the R^2 or the R_{max}^2 (if there has been selection process among regressors). Once the model is accepted, the second step is to apply the recursive statistics. Recursive statistics can test the significativeness of the coefficients along the sample, and/or test the statistical discrepancy between the recursive and the full sample estimates. The nature of the sequential specification procedure makes it necessary to calculate the conditional distributions of the recursive statistics conditional to the first step.

Before studying the conditional distributions we would like to clarify two points. First, the R^2 has to be used in those ideal situations where the researcher has not done sequential selection among variables. Second, the recursive statistics to test for the significativeness of the relationship along the sample $(F(\lambda)_0^k)$, does not add information if the model complies with the R^2 or R_{max}^2 criterion. The consideration of the *sup* in the derivation of the recursive test should induce the rejection of the null of parameters different from zero, at least towards the end of the sample[9]. Thus, we will concentrate mainly on the conditional distribution to test for recursive stability. The distribution that conditions will be either the R^2 or the R_{max}^2 $(F(\lambda)_{\hat{\beta}(1)}^k | R^2$, or $F(\lambda)_{\hat{\beta}(1)}^k | R_{max}^2)$. Given the analytical difficulties, the recursive conditional distributions presented in this paper were simulated by Monte Carlo methods. The simulation experiment is described below.

The objective is to derive the conditional probability function for the recursive statistics depending on the $(1 - \alpha_1)$ probability chosen for the R^2 or R_{max}^2. To achieve this objective we simulated 10000 models under the null hypothesis for the R^2 or R_{max}^2 (the null is that all slope parameters are zero), the corresponding R^2 or R_{max}^2 were calculated to obtain its distribution later. For each of these models the $F(\lambda)_{\hat{\beta}(1)}^k$ statistic was also calculated. The next step was to select only the $F(\lambda)_{\hat{\beta}(1)}^k$ values corresponding to those models that comply with the chosen $(1 - \alpha_1)$ probability for the R^2 or R_{max}^2. These $F(\lambda)_{\hat{\beta}(1)}^k$ values form the conditional distribution. The result can be presented in a three dimensional graph. It is a probability surface. The roughness or smoothness of the surface gives an idea about the characteristics of the conditional distributions. The experiment was done for $m = 10$ and $k = 1, 3, 5$, and 7, and sample sizes $T = 150, 500$, and 1000 observations respectively. We think these situations are representative enough to ascertain the characteristics of the conditional distributions.

Figure 12.1 presents the probability surface for the combined test $F(\lambda)_{\hat{\beta}(1)}^k | R_{max}^2$ for $k = 3$ and $T = 1000$ observations. The x-axis presents the $(1 - \alpha_2)$ probability for the F statistic that will be used for the conditional distribution, the y-axis shows the $(1 - \alpha_1)$ probability for the R_{max}^2 statistics, and the z-axis gives the

---

9. It will depend on the amount of trimming, and on the sample size.

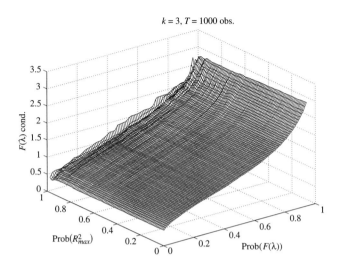

$k = 3$, $T = 1000$ obs.

Figure 12.1
Conditional distribution $F(\lambda)^k_{\hat{\beta}(1)}|R^2_{max}$

values for $F(\lambda)^k_{\hat{\beta}(1)}|R^2_{max}$. The way to interpret the graph is the following. Choose a $(1 - \alpha_1)$ probability for the R^2_{max}, the corresponding F-curve for the conditional distribution is determined by the intersection between the probability surface and the $y = (1 - \alpha_1)$ plane. The curve for a $Prob(R^2_{max}) = 0$ (i.e. when H_0 is rejected in all the models) corresponds to the unconditional $F(\lambda)^k_{\hat{\beta}(1)}$.

The probability surface is quite smooth but at the extremes, particularly along the y-direction. The roughness of the surface is related to the degree of independence between both tests. Figure 12.2 presents the same surface but from a different view point. Now the graph is viewed from the x-axis side (it is represented in two dimensions), the result is an envelop of curves. The higher the dependence between both tests the wider the envelop. The "almost" independence between both tests is evident when observing the graph. Most of the curves are concentrated around the same values, except some minor variations corresponding to the extremes[10].

The main conclusion from the combined conditional test is the "almost" independence between both tests, thus, there is not much loss of efficiency by using the unconditional distributions instead of the conditional ones.

---

10. The graphs not presented, corresponding to the other studied combinations, have similar characteristics.

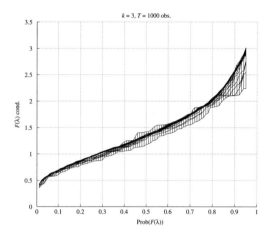

Figure 12.2
Conditional distribution $F(\lambda)^k_{\hat{\beta}(1)} | R^2_{max}$

12.4   Empirical Application

This section presents one example using the previously proposed sequential procedure. The model is postulated in Campbell, Grossman and Wang (1993). The
stability of the example is studied in Hoyo and Llorente (1998). The application is
done for the USA and Spanish stock markets. The data is composed by daily observations, with sample periods 7/3/62–12/31/93 for USA, and 1/4/92–12/31/95
for Spain. The working expression is the following equation

$$R_{t+1} = \beta_0 + (\sum_{i=1}^{5} \beta_i D_i + \gamma V_t) R_t + \epsilon_t, \tag{12.6}$$

where R_t is the return of the market on day t, V_t is the volume traded on the
market on day t, and D_i is a dummy variable corresponding to the $i-th$ day of the
week. The consideration of dummy variables, one for each day of the week, tries
to account for the accepted different behavior of the relationship between returns
depending on the day of the week. The characteristics of small market, and heavy
external influence on the Spanish market, leads us to consider the foreign influence
in the form of two additional variables representing the USA stock market behavior.
The first one is called *dowov* and represents the overnight return of the Dow Jones
Index; the second one called *dowin* reports the intraday return on the Dow Jones

Table 12.6
Maximal R^2 cutoff levels

Percentile	$m = 14, k = 7$	$m = 16, k = 9$
0.100	0.0024	0.0219
0.050	0.0027	0.0244
0.001	0.0037	0.0289

Index. Both variables are included in the equation corresponding to the Spanish market.

Campbell *et al.* (1993) [11] try 14 potential explanatory variables, and conclude that the best regression is the one presented in Equation 12.6, with 7 predictor variables for the USA data, for the Spanish data two more variables where added as explained above. Thus, the R^2_{max} should be tabulated for $m = 14, k = 7, T = 8000$ for the USA, and for $m = 16, k = 9, T = 1000$ for the Spanish example. The cutoff levels for the R^2_{max} are presented in Table 12.6. In Hoyo and Llorente (1998) the estimated R^2 were 0.055 and 0.17 for USA and Spain respectively. Therefore, comparing these values with those in Table 12.6 we reject the null hypothesis in favor of the alternative about the existence of at least one slope parameter different from zero.

Thus, the model is accepted according to the R^2_{max} statistic. The next step is to validate its singnificativeness and stability using the conditional distributions of the recursive statistic.

Recursive estimations were calculated to test the hypotheses of significance and stability. The first test studies the validity of the relationship through time (all the parameters but the intercept equal to zero)[12]. The second tests the stability of the recursive estimates when compared with the estimations with the full sample. The results are summarized in Table 12.7, entries are test statistics. Tests are significant at the ** 5 percent and *** 1 percent levels, using the tabulation from Table 12.3, because of the "almost" independence between the steps in the sequential procedure.

The $\hat{F}(\lambda)^k_0$ statistic provides evidence that the relation is significative at the 1% level for both countries, as was expected. The statistic $\hat{F}(\lambda)^k_{\hat{\beta}(1)}$ rejects the null hypothesis that the slope coefficients are constant and equal to the full sample

---

11. The example differs slightly from Campbell *et al.* (1993). We assume they have fixed a priori k and m.

12. As it was already commented, a priori we expect this test to reject the null hypothesis, because of the acceptance of the model using the R^2_{max}.

Table 12.7
Empirical Results: Evidence on Recursive Tests

$\hat{F}(\lambda)^k_0$		$\hat{F}(\lambda)^k_{\hat{\beta}(1)}$	
$k = 7$	$k = 9$	$k = 7$	$k = 9$
84.92***	27.09***	8.39***	2.26**

estimation at the 1% level for USA ($k = 7$) and at the 5% percent level for Spain ($k = 9$). Thus, we conclude accepting the model with the number of included variables among the potential ones, though the relation is not stable.

12.5   Conclusions

Specification search is an important process in any applied work. It is closely connected to data mining or data snooping. This paper proposes a combined test to reduce the likelihood of accepting spurious models. The combined test consists of two statistics. First, a goodness of fit measure (R^2 or R^2_{max}) that considers the sequential search for the best set of explanatory variables. The second is a recursive statistic to test for the stability of the considered model. The unconditional distributions of both tests are studied, as well as the conditional distribution for the combined test. The main result of the paper shows the "almost" independence in the steps of the conditional procedure. Thus, there is a small loss of efficiency in using the unconditional instead of the conditional distributions. An example illustrates the applicability of the proposed procedure.

Acknowledgements

We are grateful for helpful comments to Blake LeBaron, Richard Watt, and seminar participants at Dept. de Economía Cuantitativa, Universidad Autónoma de Madrid. Partial financial support from the DGICYT under grant PB94-018 is acknowledged.

References

ANDREWS, D.W.K. 1993. "Tests for Parameter Instability and Structural Change with Unknown Change Point". *Econometrica*, 61:821–856.

CAMPBELL, J., S. GROSSMAN, AND J. WANG. 1993. "Trading Volume and Serial Correlation in Stock Returns". *Quarterly Journal of Economics*, pages 905–940.

FOSTER, F.D., T. SMITH, AND R.E. WHALEY. 1997. "Assessing Goodness-of-Fit of Asset Pricing Models: The Distribution of the Maximal R^2". *Journal of Finance*, 52, 2:591–607.

HOYO, J. DEL, AND J.G. LLORENTE. 1998. "Stability Analysis and Forecasting Implications". In A.-P. N. Refenes, A.N. Burgess, and J.E. Moody, editor, *Decision Technologies for Computational Management Science*. Kluwer Academic, London.

HOYO, J. DEL, AND J.G. LLORENTE. 1999. "Recursive Estimation and Testing of Dynamic Models". *Computational Economics*. forthcoming.

STOCK J.H. 1994. "Unit Roots Structural Breaks and Trends". In R.F. Engle, and D.L. Mac-Fadden, editor, *Handbook of Econometrics*, chapter 46, pages 2739–2839. Elsevier Science.

WHITE, H. 1997. "A Reality Check for Data Snooping". Working paper, UCSD, Dept of Economics.

13 A Bayesian Approach to Estimating Mutual Fund Returns

Amir F. Atiya and Malik Magdon-Ismail

Accurate estimation of mutual fund statistics, such as mean return and standard deviation, can help shedding some light onto whether some mutual funds can consistently outperform the general market. In addition, it can help investors make more sound investment decisions. Because the available sample of returns is often not enough to give sufficient confidence in the estimates, we propose a novel Bayesian estimation approach, whereby the priors are obtained from the general market returns (by general market we mean the collection of thousands of available mutual funds). The justification for this is that any mutual fund is a subset of the general market, and it will therefore inherit some of its statistical properties. The advantages we gain is that we make use of the extensive sample size of the general market returns to fine tune our fund return estimates. The problem we face, however, is that the *a priori* density of the mean and standard deviation of the general market returns are unknown. The reason is that for an individual fund, the mean and standard deviation of the return can not be obtained exactly, as we can only estimate them from the finite sample available from historical data. In this paper we develop a new algorithm to tackle this estimation problem. We develop an EM-like algorithm that iteratively obtains the desired estimates. In addition, we present an approximate analytical solution to this problem. We use our approach to produce novel rankings of some available mutual funds. Our approach is not limited to mutual fund estimation and can be applied whenever parameters from a group of populations have to be estimated.

13.1 Introduction

There has been a raging debate about whether there are trading strategies or money managers that can consistently beat the general stock market. Although the dominant belief now is that the stock market exhibits some predictability, it is not clear whether this predictability offsets the associated risk. Researchers have looked at the performance of mutual funds for evidence. There are funds that consistently produce risk adjusted returns higher than the overall market. However, taking into account that there are over 4000 mutual funds, one cannot rule out the possibility that this is merely due to chance, by sheer number of funds. The topic of data snooping presents an analytical framework for assessing the effect and bias due to "model search" (see the studies in [White 1996, Lo and Mackinlay 1990]). Another approach to testing whether the differences in the returns of the funds is significant would be to perform an ANOVA analysis testing the hypothesis that the mean returns are different, [Casella and Berger 1990].

In this paper, we propose a new idea to estimate the mutual fund returns. The method we develop will shed some light into whether some funds can significantly and consistently beat the overall market. In addition, it will help investors have more accurate estimates of the mean and standard deviation of the funds' returns, and therefore help them make more sound investment decisions. We will also produce a ranking of mutual funds according to several performance criteria using our approach.

13.2   Bayesian Estimation of Return Statistics

The Bayesian approach is widely studied by researchers in computational fields such as artificial intelligence, inference, pattern recognition, and neural networks (see [Bishop 1995] for example), but also has been applied in several finance problems. The usual criticism of most Bayesian approaches is that the choice of the prior tends to be arbitrary. In this study, however, we propose a more principled approach to obtaining the prior by using the density of the general market returns as our prior. The approach is suitable for our particular problem for several reasons. In the absence of compelling reasons, no funds will behave much better than the overall market, hence using the density of the overall market returns as our prior, acts as a suitable regularization factor, that will pull the return estimates justifiably towards those of the general market. Also, the general market is a superset of all mutual funds, and hence the individual funds will inherit some of the statistical properties of the general market, and this can be taken into account by using the Bayesian formulation we propose. Essentially, we view the funds as having been drawn from some distribution, i.e., there is some joint distribution for μ and σ^2 from which a particular fund's mean and variance are drawn. We use the observed means and variances in the universe of funds to estimate this distribution. As an extreme example, consider a fund that has a very short track record of only a few months of very high returns. Although the sample mean and variance will give some indication of the fund's return statistics, it will not be of a high confidence, and one would tend to assume the fund performance is closer to the market index performance than is apparent from simply looking at the sample mean.

Before we proceed to the details of our approach, we summarize the main difficulty in applying our Bayesian technique. As already mentioned, it is the *a priori* density of the mean and standard deviation of the general market returns that is not known. If we consider estimating this density from the data, we face the problem that the data are noisy, the reason being that for the available funds, the sample means and standard deviations of the returns are not accurate, since they are only finite sample estimates from historical data. Thus, information about the *a priori* density that will be used to estimate the means and variances of the funds needs to be extracted from these noisy estimates of the means and variances. We are faced with an apparent dilemma: in order to estimate the mean and variance of a given mutual fund, we need the *a priori* density for the means and variances, and in order to estimate this density, we need estimates of the means and variances themselves. We propose an approach that overcomes this dilemma.

13.2.1   The Proposed Method

Let $M_1, ..., M_K$ denote the universe of mutual funds, and let μ_i and σ_i denote respectively the expectation and the standard deviation of the percentage returns of fund M_i. Assume we have available the historical returns of each fund (say the monthly returns): $x_i(t)$, $t = 1, ..., N_i$ where N_i is the number of observations we have for fund i. Assume that the realizations $x_i(t)$ are independent over time and across funds[1], and let $X_i = \{x_i(1), ..., x_i(N_i)\}$. Let us combine μ_i and σ_i into a single "parameter vector" $\alpha_i = (\mu_i, \ \sigma_i)^T$.

By Bayes rule,

$$p(\alpha_i | X_i) = \frac{p(X_i | \alpha_i) p(\alpha_i)}{p(X_i)} \qquad (13.1)$$

where $p(\alpha_i)$ is the *a priori* probability density, meaning the density of the α parameter from which the α_i's were drawn. It is this density that is to be estimated from the overall market. Having obtained $p(\alpha_i)$ and $p(X_i | \alpha_i)$, we are in principle done, because we can obtain $p(\alpha_i | X_i)$ using Bayes rule. We can now use $p(\alpha_i | X_i)$ to obtain our estimate of α_i according to any loss criterion we choose. We postpone the development of this more general method to a future presentation. Here, we will be satisfied with the mode of the density $p(\alpha_i | X_i)$, which can be obtained by finding the parameter estimate $\hat{\alpha}_i$ which maximizes the log of expression (13.1):

$$L_i = \ln\big(p(X_i | \alpha_i)\big) + \ln\big(p(\alpha_i)\big) - \ln\big(p(X_i)\big) \qquad (13.2)$$

This is commonly known as the maximum *a posteriori* probability (MAP) estimate. We now consider each term in expression (13.2). One can write

$$p(X_i | \alpha_i) = \prod_{t=1}^{N_i} p(x_i(t) | \alpha_i) \qquad (13.3)$$

---

1. The independence assumption across funds can be relaxed considerably for the purposes of the algorithm we propose. This more general case will be discussed in a later presentation.

which follows from our independence assumption for the daily returns. The term $p(x_i(t)|\alpha_i)$ can be considered Gaussian, because although it is well-known that the individual stock percentage returns are log-normal [Ritchken 1987], the overall average percentage return for a portfolio of several stocks can be approximated as Gaussian by virtue of the central limit theorem (for the case of continuous compounding, the individual stock returns themselves are Gaussian and so the Gaussian assumption would still be valid). Hence, we are justified in writing

$$p(x_i(t)|\alpha_i) = \frac{1}{\sqrt{2\pi}\sigma_i}e^{-\frac{(x_i(t)-\mu_i)^2}{2\sigma_i^2}} \tag{13.4}$$

Now, consider $p(\alpha)$. The most self-evident approach would suggest estimating this density from the data, i.e. in terms of the μ_i's and σ_i's of the individual funds. Although we have plenty of data (up to 4000 mutual funds are available) to estimate $p(\alpha)$, these data are noisy since they give only estimates of each fund's μ_i and σ_i, rather than the true values. To alleviate this problem, we suggest the following: Assume that $p(\alpha)$ is determined with respect to the true α_j's of the individual funds (which are unknown and not available), by a kernel density estimate:

$$p(\alpha) = \frac{1}{Kh^2}\sum_{j=1}^{K}\phi\left(\frac{\|\alpha - \alpha_j\|}{h}\right) \tag{13.5}$$

where h is the kernel bandwidth, and ϕ is the kernel, which is typically chosen as a Gaussian function[2]. For the two-dimensional case, the Gaussian kernel is given by

$$\phi(x) = \frac{1}{2\pi}e^{-\frac{1}{2}x^2} \tag{13.6}$$

Note that the density function $p(\alpha)$ is a function of the parameters α_j, that are exactly the quantities we are trying to estimate. This is one of the sources of difficulty that needs to be overcome. The term $p(X_i)$ can be obtained by integrating out the α_i parameter vector:

$$p(X_i) = \int p(X_i|\alpha_i)p(\alpha_i)d\alpha_i \tag{13.7}$$

Substituting from (13.3),(13.4),(13.5),(13.7) into (13.2), we get the following somewhat complicated expression for L_i

---

2. Note that in the asymptotic limit ($K \to \infty$), there is no loss of generality in the assumption that $p(\alpha)$ is given by (13.5) as long as $h \to 0$ and $Kh \to \infty$. This is because in this limit, $p(\alpha)$ in (13.5) will converge to the true prior [Silverman 1993].

$$L_i = -\ln\left(2\pi^{N_i/2}\sigma_i{}^{N_i}Kh^2\right) - \sum_{t=1}^{N_i}\frac{(x_i(t)-\mu_i)^2}{2\sigma_i^2}$$

$$+\ln\left(\sum_{j=1}^{K}\phi\left(\frac{\sqrt{(\mu_i-\mu_j)^2+(\sigma_i-\sigma_j)^2}}{h}\right)\right)$$

$$-\ln\left(\int d\mu_i d\sigma_i \left[\prod_{t=1}^{N_i}\frac{1}{\sqrt{2\pi}\sigma_i}e^{-\frac{(x_i(t)-\mu_i)^2}{2\sigma_i^2}}\right]\right.$$

$$\left.\frac{1}{Kh^2}\left[\sum_{j=1}^{K}\phi\left(\frac{\sqrt{(\mu_i-\mu_j)^2+(\sigma_i-\sigma_j)^2}}{h}\right)\right]\right) \qquad (13.8)$$

Note that taking the exponential of (13.8), one obtains the posterior density $p(\alpha_i|X_i)$ We propose obtaining the estimates of the α_i's as those that maximize the sum of the likelihood functions $L_1, \cdots, L_K$, which corresponds to the MAP estimate for the $\alpha_1 \ldots \alpha_K$ under the independence assumption across funds. The problem is that all the L_i are coupled together, thus we have an optimization problem in all the parameters $\alpha_1 \ldots \alpha_K$. In principle, this is the optimization problem that we need to solve. In practice, however, we have 2 parameters for each fund, and, in all, about 4000 funds, giving a total of 8000 parameters. Thus, we are faced with a massive optimization problem, that is from the practical point of view intractable, even using some of the most sophisticated optimization procedures. To overcome this problem, we propose two approaches. The first one is an iterative procedure, while the second one is an analytic technique which attempts to undo the effect of the α_i's being random rather than deterministic. The following are the two approaches:

13.2.2   An Iterative Estimation Procedure

In this procedure, we assume that we have a fairly reasonable starting choice of the parameters, say for the example the fund's sample mean and standard deviation, and hence we have a fairly reasonable estimate of $p(\alpha)$. Fixing $p(\alpha)$, we find the optimal α_i's. The L_i's are coupled together only through $p(\alpha)$, thus, fixing $p(\alpha)$, we convert the coupled optimization problem into K two parameter optimization problems. Since the parameters have changed in the course of this iteration, an update for $p(\alpha)$ now needs to be performed, yielding a more accurate estimate of the *a priori* density. With the new $p(\alpha)$, we iterate again for the optimal α_i's. We continue these iterations till convergence. We can see that the algorithm bears certain similarities to the EM algorithm [Dempster et al 1977]. The following are the details of the algorithm (we assume here Gaussian kernels for simplicity):

1 Initialize $\hat{\mu}_i$ and $\hat{\sigma}_i^2$ to their sample values:

$$\hat{\mu}_i = \bar{x}_i \equiv \frac{1}{N_i} \sum_{t=1}^{N_i} x_i(t) \tag{13.9}$$

$$\hat{\sigma}_i^2 = s_i^2 \equiv \frac{1}{N_i} \sum_{t=1}^{N_i} (x_i(t) - \hat{\mu}_i)^2 \tag{13.10}$$

2 Calculate so-called β parameters:

$$\beta_{ij} = \frac{e^{-[(\hat{\mu}_i - \hat{\mu}_j)^2 + (\hat{\sigma}_i - \hat{\sigma}_j)^2]/2h^2}}{\sum_{k=1}^{K} e^{-[(\hat{\mu}_i - \hat{\mu}_k)^2 + (\hat{\sigma}_i - \hat{\sigma}_k)^2]/2h^2}} \tag{13.11}$$

Note that the matrix $\beta \equiv [\beta_{ij}]$ is a Markov matrix, meaning that it has nonnegative entries, and each row sums to 1. This property is useful in understanding the convergence properties of the algorithm.

3 For $i = 1$ to K, update the parameters as follows

$$\hat{\mu}_i(\text{new}) = \bar{x}_i + \text{bias}_i \tag{13.12}$$

where

$$\text{bias}_i = \hat{\mu}_i(\text{new}) - \bar{x}_i = \frac{1}{1 + \frac{N_i h^2}{\hat{\sigma}_i^2}} \sum_{j=1}^{K} \beta_{ij}(\hat{\mu}_j - \bar{x}_i) \tag{13.13}$$

where $\bar{x}_i$ is the sample average, defined in Step 1. To obtain the update for $\hat{\sigma}_i$, first, solve the following one-dimensional polynomial equation by some search method:

$$\frac{y^4}{h^2} - \frac{y^3}{h^2} \sum_{j=1}^{K} \beta_{ij}\hat{\sigma}_j + N_i y^2 - N_i \left(s_i^2 + \text{bias}_i^2\right) = 0 \tag{13.14}$$

Suppose the solution to this equation occurs at y^*, then set

$$\hat{\sigma}_i(\text{new}) = y^* \tag{13.15}$$

(s_i^2 denotes the sample variance as defined in Step 1).

4 Repeat Steps 2 and 3 till convergence.

We briefly describe how we obtain the updates in step 3. Fixing $\hat{\mu}_j$ and $\hat{\sigma}_j$, the kernel centers in $p(\alpha_i)$, L_i becomes a function of μ_i and σ_i only:

$$L_i = -\ln \sigma_i^{N_i} - \sum_{t=1}^{N_i} \frac{(x_i(t) - \mu_i)^2}{2\sigma_i^2} + \ln \left(\sum_{j=1}^{K} e^{-\frac{(\mu_i - \hat{\mu}_i)^2 + (\sigma_i - \hat{\sigma}_i)^2}{2h^2}} \right) + \text{const.} \qquad (13.16)$$

We now set

$$\frac{\partial L_i}{\partial \mu_i} = 0 \quad \text{and} \quad \frac{\partial L_i}{\partial \sigma_i} = 0,$$

Thus we have to solve a non-linear system of two equations in two unknowns. It is then easily seen that any fixed point of the iterative updates given by (13.13) and (13.14) represent a solution to this system. The interpretation of the mean update step of the algorithm is as follows. The new mean represents the weighted average of the sample mean and the weighted average of the mean returns of the other mutual funds (weighted according to how close the parameters are to the considered fund). This tells us an interesting fact that the funds having similar means and standard deviation have a more significant effect on the fund's return estimates. Such an interpretation for the standard deviation update is not as clear as that of the mean. We have proven that for the case of estimating the mean alone, the algorithm converges to a solution. We are still considering the general case of estimating both the mean and the standard deviation. In our experimental simulations, convergence always occurred.

13.2.3   An Approximate Analytic Solution

We present here an approximate analytic form for the solution which can either be used as a solution itself, as starting input to the initialization stage of the iterative algorithm above or as starting input to the full optimization problem. Suppose once again that

$$p(x_i(t)|\alpha_i) = \frac{1}{\sqrt{2\pi}\sigma_i} e^{-\frac{(x_i(t) - \mu_i)^2}{2\sigma_i^2}} \qquad (13.17)$$

Let $\bar{x}_i$, and s_i^2 denote the sample estimates for the mean and the variance. Then, it is well known that these two quantities are independent random variables and further that the distribution for the mean is normal and the distribution for the variance is $\chi^2_{N_i-1}$, which for large N_i is approximately normal [DeGroot 1989]. Thus we can write

$$\mu_i = \bar{x}_i + Z_i \qquad \sigma_i^2 = \frac{N}{N-1}s_i^2 + Y_i \tag{13.18}$$

where Z_i and Y_i are independent normal random variables[3] with $Z_i \sim N(0, \sigma_i^2/N_i)$ and $Y_i \sim N(0, \sigma_i^4/(N_i - 1))$. We compute $p(\alpha)$ as follows:

$$p(\alpha) = \int dZ_i dY_i \; p(\alpha, Z_i, Y_i) = \int dZ_i dY_i \; p(\alpha|Z_i, Y_i)p(Z_i, Y_i) \tag{13.19}$$

Given Z_i, Y_i we know α_i from (13.18) because both $\bar{x}_i$ and s_i^2 are computable from the data. Therefore using (13.5), we can obtain $p(\alpha|Z_i, Y_i)$ as follows[4]:

$$p(\alpha|Z_i, Y_i) = p(\mu, \sigma^2|Z_i, Y_i) = \frac{1}{Kh^2}\sum_{i=1}^{K}\frac{1}{2\pi^2}e^{-\frac{[(\mu-\bar{x}_i-Z_i)^2+(\sigma^2-\frac{N}{N-1}s_i^2-Y_i)^2]}{2h^2}} \tag{13.20}$$

where we are assuming a Gaussian kernel estimator. We use the fact that Z_i and Y_i are independent Normals to obtain $p(Z_i, Y_i)$ as follows:

$$p(Z_i, Y_i) = \frac{1}{\sqrt{2\pi\sigma_i^2/N_i}}e^{-\frac{Z_i^2}{2\sigma_i^2/N_i}}\frac{1}{\sqrt{2\pi\sigma_i^4/(N_i-1)}}e^{-\frac{Y_i^2}{2\sigma_i^4/(N_i-1)}} \tag{13.21}$$

Note that $p(Z_i, Y_i)$ depends on σ_i^2. As we will be interested in an asymptotic expansion, we will eventually replace σ_i^2 by s_i^2. Finally, we can use (13.20) and (13.21) in (13.19) and doing the integration, we find:

$$p(\mu, \sigma^2) = \frac{1}{K}\sum_{i=1}^{K}\frac{1}{h_{\bar{x}_i}}\tilde{\phi}\left(\frac{\|\mu - \bar{x}_i\|}{h_{\hat{\mu}_i}}\right)\frac{1}{h_{\hat{\sigma}_i^2}}\tilde{\phi}\left(\frac{\|\sigma^2 - s_i^2\|}{h_{\hat{\sigma}_i^2}}\right) \tag{13.22}$$

where $h_{\hat{\mu}_i}^2 \approx h^2 + s_i^2/(N_i - 1)$ and $h_{\hat{\sigma}_i^2}^2 \approx h^2 + s_i^4/(N_i - 1)$ and $\tilde{\phi}(x) = e^{-x^2/2}/\sqrt{2\pi}$. We see that this is formally identical to (13.5) with two (different) larger kernel widths corresponding to the mean and variance estimation. Thus we see that as far as the density estimation is concerned, the fact that $\bar{x}_i$ and s_i^2 are noisy versions of μ_i and σ_i^2 appears as increased regularization for the kernel estimate. To complete the analysis, we use (13.22) to obtain $p(\alpha_i)$ for the purposes of maximizing (13.2). From (13.2) we see that the prior introduces a correction to the maximum likelihood estimator that is $O(1/N_i)$. We thus compute the estimates of μ_i, σ_i^2 that maximize (13.2) as a series in $1/N_i$. This leads to the following expressions for $\hat{\mu}_i$, $\hat{\sigma}_i^2$, our estimates of μ_i, σ_i^2:

---

3. We use the notation $X \sim N(a, b)$ to mean that X is a Normal random variable with mean a and variance b.

4. For the purposes of the present discussion, we consider the parameter vector as $\alpha_i = [\mu_i, \sigma_i^2]^T$.

$$\hat{\mu}_i = \bar{x}_i + \frac{a_i}{N_i} + O\left(\frac{1}{N_i^2}\right) \tag{13.23}$$

$$\hat{\sigma}_i^2 = s_i^2 + \frac{b_i}{N_i} + O\left(\frac{1}{N_i^2}\right) \tag{13.24}$$

where

$$a_i = s_i^2 \sum_{j=1}^{K} \beta_{ji} \frac{\bar{x}_j - \bar{x}_i}{h_{\hat{\mu}_j}^2} \tag{13.25}$$

$$b_i = s_i^4 \sum_{j=1}^{K} \beta_{ji} \frac{s_j^2 - s_i^2}{h_{\hat{\sigma}_j^2}^2} \tag{13.26}$$

where

$$\beta_{ij} = \frac{\lambda_{ij}}{\displaystyle\sum_{k=1}^{K} \lambda_{ki}} \quad , \quad \lambda_{ij} = \frac{1}{h_{\hat{\mu}_i}} \tilde{\phi}\left(\frac{\|\bar{x}_j - \bar{x}_i\|}{h_{\hat{\mu}_i}}\right) \frac{1}{h_{\hat{\sigma}_i^2}} \tilde{\phi}\left(\frac{\|s_j^2 - s_i^2\|}{h_{\hat{\sigma}_i^2}}\right) \tag{13.27}$$

β_{ij} is analogous to the β−matrix of the previous section where h was used in place of $h_{\hat{\mu}_i}$, $h_{\hat{\sigma}^2}$. β_{ij} represents the interaction between the mutual funds represented by the prior. β_{ij} is significant only for mutual funds with $\hat{\alpha}_i \approx \hat{\alpha}_j$. We see that the prior affects our estimates for α_i only through this interaction term.

13.3   Simulations

We have applied both the iterative and analytical methods to a collection of 1527 mutual funds using up to five years of data (ending June 1998) for each fund. The purpose is to obtain a novel ranking of mutual funds, and compare this ranking with the conventional ranking. We rank the mutual funds according to their mean return, μ, and their Sharpe ratio, μ/σ.

Tables 13.1, 13.2 and 13.3 show such rankings according to the sample values, the iterative updates and analytical solution respectively. One can see that for both proposed methods, as well as for the standard method of using the sample mean and the sample Sharpe ratio, the top ten funds are mostly the same. What is different is the relative positions of these top ten funds. We point out here that there is perhaps a slight bias in the Bayesian updating because in estimating the prior, one really wants to have access to all the funds that appeared, their means and variances. However, in the market, there is a selection bias that favors the survival of funds with higher μ's and lower σ's. To the extent that this is so, our prior

Table 13.1
Ranking of the funds according to sample annualized mean return and Sharpe ratio.

Ranking using $\bar{x}_i$			Ranking using $\bar{x}_i/s_i$		
Fund	$\mu(\%)$	σ	Fund	$\mu(\%)$	μ/σ
TrnsAm Sml Co	69.67	0.054	State Str Glbl Adv Yld	4.91	2.56
State Str Aurora Fnd	62.54	0.047	Str Muni Adv Fnd	4.81	2.45
Frnkln Fin Svcs A	61.19	0.028	Str Adv Fnd	6.16	2.37
Frnkln Fin Svcs B	61.19	0.027	DFA One Yr Fxd Inc	5.31	1.83
PBHG Mid Cap	59.73	0.040	Frnkln Fin Svcs B	61.19	1.49
Oakmark Sel	57.12	0.046	Frnkln Fin Svcs A	61.19	1.47
Warburg Pncs Hlth	55.04	0.029	Str Sh Trm Glbl Bnd	8.32	1.36
TrnsAm Aggr Gr	54.52	0.055	Harbor Shrt Dur	5.43	1.29
Janus Sp Sit	53.33	0.037	Htckis & Wiley low Dur	8.46	1.28
Vista Grp Sml Cap B	53.33	0.050	UAM Trst/FPA Cresc	26.42	1.27

Table 13.2
Ranking of the funds according to annualized mean return and Sharpe ratio from the iterative procedure

Ranking using $\hat{\mu}_i$ from Iter Proc			Ranking using $\hat{\mu}_i/\hat{\sigma}_i$ from Iter Proc		
Fund	$\mu(\%)$	σ	Fund	$\mu(\%)$	μ/σ
TrnsAm Sml Co	69.67	0.049	State Str Glbl Adv Yld	4.91	3.02
State Str Aurora Fnd	59.72	0.042	Str Muni Adv Fnd	4.81	2.61
Oakmark Select	59.66	0.042	Str Adv Fnd	6.11	2.44
PBHG Mid Cap	59.64	0.036	DFA One Yr Fxd Inc	5.28	1.95
Frnkln Fin Svcs A	59.36	0.025	Frnkln Fin Svcs A	59.36	1.56
Frnkln Fin Svcs B	59.36	0.025	Frnkln Fin Svcs B	59.36	1.56
Warburg Pncs Health	59.22	0.026	Warburg Pncs Health	59.22	1.55
TrnsAm Aggr Gr	51.00	0.049	Harbor Shrt Dur	4.49	1.43
Warburg Pncs Sml Co	51.00	0.049	Icon Shrt Trm Fxd Inc	3.70	1.38
Vista Grp Sml Cap B	51.00	0.049	Htckis & Wiler Low Dur	5.38	1.34

will be biased in those directions with respect to the true prior. Thus even these Bayesian estimates will be slightly optimistic - this, however, is not a flaw with the Bayesian estimate itself, because in principle we could have access to all the funds that ever traded. We merely note it here as a practical point to be kept in mind when applying the Bayesian method.

Figure 13.1 displays the effect that the Bayesian update of the parameter estimation has on the distribution of the μ's and σ's. Notice that the distributions after Bayesian update are more concentrated indicating that the outliers have been brought closer to the general market (in a principled way).

Table 13.3
Ranking of the funds according to annualized mean return and Sharpe ratio from the analytic solution.

Ranking using $\hat{\mu}_i$ from Anal Sol			Ranking using $\hat{\mu}_i/\hat{\sigma}_i$ from Anal Sol		
Fund	$\mu(\%)$	σ	Fund	$\mu(\%)$	μ/σ
Frnkln Fin Svcs B	59.31	0.028	State Str Glbl Adv Yld	4.91	2.56
Frnkln Fin Svcs A	59.12	0.028	Str Muni Adv Fnd	4.82	2.45
Warburg Pncs Health	54.53	0.030	Str Adv Fnd	6.15	2.37
PBHG Mid Cap	52.52	0.040	DFA One Yr Fxd Inc	5.31	1.84
State Str Aurora Fnd	50.62	0.048	Frnkln Fin Svcs B	59.31	1.41
TrnsAm Sml Co	50.39	0.053	Frnkln Fin Svcs A	59.12	1.39
Oakmark Select	49.57	0.046	Str Sh Trm Glbl Bnd	4.49	1.35
Janus Sp Sit	49.34	0.037	Icon Shrt Trm Fxd Inc	8.82	1.34
FBR Sml Cap Fin	48.22	0.035	Harbor Shrt Dur	3.62	1.32
PBHG Sml Cap Val	45.88	0.040	Htckis & Wiley low Dur	5.42	1.29

13.4 Conclusions

We have developed a method for understanding the small sample effects that could lead to misleading estimates of a funds performance using a Bayesian approach. The Bayesian approach requires a prior and we have provided a natural prior that is available in the case where a large population of groups is available (in our case, each group consisted of a particular fund's returns). The general effect of using this prior is to pull the parameters of a particular group for which only a few observations are available toward the statistics of the overall population. Intuitively this seems like the correct thing to do and what we have presented is a quantitative way of doing so.

13.5 Acknowledgments

We would like to acknowledge the generous support of the National Science Foundation under NSF Cooperative Agreement EEC 9402726 to the Center for Neuromorphic Systems Engineering.

References

Bishop, C. M. 1995. *Neural Networks for Pattern Recognition.* Clarendon Press, Oxford.

Casella, G. and R. L. Berger. 1990. *Statistical Inference.* Duxbury, Belmont, CA.

DeGroot, M. H. 1989. *Probability and Statistics.* Addison–Wesley, Reading, Massachusetts.

Dempster, A. P., N. M. Laird, and D. B. Rubin. 1977. Maximum likelihood from incomplete data via the E-M algorithm. *Journal of the Royal Statistical Society B,* 39:1–38.

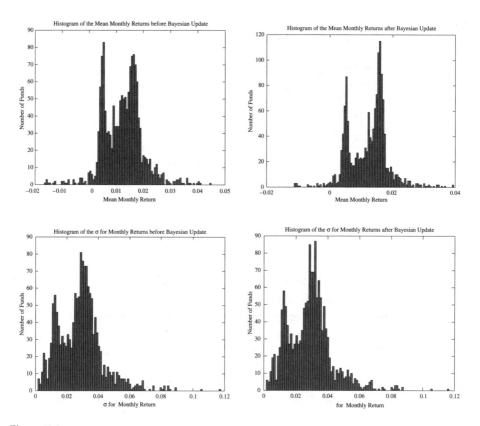

Figure 13.1
Histograms of the distributions of μ and σ before and after Bayesian update (using the analytical solution). The top two are for μ and the lower two are for σ. The graphs on the right show the histograms after update and the ones on the left are before update.

Lo, A. and A. Mackinlay. 1990. Data snooping biases in tests of financial asset pricing models. *Review of Financial Studies*, 3(3):431–467.

Ritchken, P. 1987. *Options: Theory, Strategy and Applications.* Harper-Collins.

Silverman, B. 1993. *Density Estimation for Statistics and Data Analysis.* Chapman and Hall, London, UK.

White, H. 1996. Data snooping with confidence. In *Neural Networks in the Capital Markets*, Pasadena, CA.

14 Independent Component Ordering in ICA Analysis of Financial Data

Zhi-bin Lai, Yiu-ming Cheung, and Lei Xu

Back and Weigend (1997) have shown that the so-called dominant independent components obtained by independent component analysis (ICA) can reveal more underlying structure of the observed financial series than principal component analysis. With the independent components ordered in list based on the L_∞ norm of each individual component, they select a subset from the list as the dominant components. However, this simple ordering method considers no interaction among components in their contribution to the observed series. In this paper, we propose an alternative ordering approach to sort the components according to their joint contribution to the trend reservation of the observed series, which leads to a typical combinational optimization problem. To avoid exhaustive search, we present a sub-optimum ordering algorithm called *testing-and-acceptance* (TnA). The experiments on foreign exchange rates have demonstrated that the TnA outperforms the L_∞ norm method.

14.1 Introduction

Analysis of financial time series such as stock price, foreign exchange rate is an important procedure in financial investment and decision. The purposes of time series analysis are generally two-fold.

1. Find out the regularity in time series so that more efficient financial models can be built to predict the future values of a series according to the past data, which is much helpful in making investment strategy, portfolio management and so on.

2. Understand the stochastic mechanism that gives rise to the variation of a financial series, which can provide financial authority with useful information to monitor the market.

In the past, principal component analysis (PCA) [Johnson and Wichern 1992, Utans et al 1996] has been a major analysis tool in literature because:

- a set of de-correlated principal components can be easily obtained.

- the underlying structure of financial series can be revealed in using the first few principal components.

However, the PCA technique uses only second-order statistics information. As a result, the obtained components are only de-correlated but not really independent from each other.

Recently, *independent component analysis* (ICA) has been widely studied in signal processing with success on blind signal separation [Bell and Sejnowski 1995,

Amari et al 1996, Xu et al 1997, Xu et al 1998]. In ICA, the component extraction involves higher-order statistics, which makes the dominant independent components reveal more underlying structure of the series than principal components. Hence, it has been realized that ICA, rather than PCA, is more appropriate for use in financial series analysis as shown in paper [Back and Weigend 1997], where ICA has been applied to analyze the stock in Japan market [Back and Weigend 1997].

To find those dominant components, Back and Weigend (1997) list the independent components in an order, and then select a subset from the ordered components as dominant ones. They determine the order according to L_∞ norm of each individual component. However, that ordering method does not consider the interactive contribution of these components to the observed series, and has no guidance on how to control the reconstruction performance from the selected dominant components.

We have noticed that the reconstruction from dominant independent components should have a similar variation of the observed time series because they reveal the underlying structure of the series. Hence, in this paper, we propose to order the independent components according to their joint contribution to the trend reservation of the observed series, which can be measured by the *relative hamming distance* (RHD) error between the observed series and the reconstruction from these components. In this ordering approach, the component order is controlled by minimizing the RHD error, which naturally leads to a typical combinational optimization problem. To avoid exhaustive search, we present a sub-optimum algorithm called *Testing-and-Acceptance* (TnA) for ordering. The experiments on foreign exchange rates have demonstrated that the TnA approach outperforms the L_∞ norm method in [Back and Weigend 1997].

This paper is organized as follows: Section 14.2 briefly introduces ICA model, and the algorithm used in this paper. Section 14.3 shows our approach for independent component ordering, where the TnA approach is also given explicitly. Section 14.4 shows the experimental results and Section 14.5 draws a conclusion.

14.2 ICA in Analysis of Financial Data

14.2.1 ICA Model

In ICA financial series analysis, we suppose that the observed k financial time series denoted by $\{x(t)\}_{t=1}^N$ with $x(t) = [x_1(t), \ldots, x_k(t)]^T$ are the instantaneous linear mixture of k unknown statistically independent time series $\{y(t)\}_{t=1}^N$ with

$y(t) = [y_1(t), \ldots, y_k(t)]^T$. Here, each series $\{y_j(t)\}_{t=1}^N$ is called an *independent component*. Hence, the data $x(t)$ can be modeled by:

$$x(t) = Ay(t), \quad \text{with} \quad 1 \leq t \leq N, \tag{14.1}$$

where A is an unknown $k \times k$ mixing matrix. As depicted in Figure 14.1, the use of ICA on the observed series x can recover the independent components up to an unknown constant and a permutation of indices through a de-mixing process W with:

$$\hat{y}(t) = Wx(t) = WAy(t) = P\Lambda y(t), \quad 1 \leq t \leq N, \tag{14.2}$$

where P is a permutation matrix and Λ is a diagonal matrix. The W can be tuned by existing ICA algorithms. In this paper, we use an ICA approach called *Learned Parametric Mixture Based ICA algorithm* (LPM) [Xu et al 1997, Xu et al 1998] to learn W on line. The advantage of LPM is that it can separate any combinations of sub-Gaussian and super-Gaussian signals [1] due to adaptive-learned nonlinearity, whereas other existing ICA algorithms such as Maximization Entropy approach [Bell and Sejnowski 1995] and Minimum Mutual Information approach [Amari et al 1996] can only separate either super-Gaussian signal or sub-Gaussian signal because of using fixed nonlinearity.

14.2.2   LPM Algorithm

The LPM algorithm has been proposed in [Xu et al 1997, Xu et al 1998]. To save space, here we briefly introduce its main steps only. For details, please refer to the relevant papers.

For each data point $x(t)$, the LPM algorithm learns the de-mixing matrix W by

$$W(t+1) = W(t) + \eta \Delta W(t), \tag{14.3}$$

with

$$\Delta W(t) = (I + \phi(\hat{y}(t))\hat{y}(t)^T)W(t), \tag{14.4}$$

$$\hat{y}(t) = W(t)x(t), \tag{14.5}$$

where η is a small positive learning rate, and the nonlinearity $\phi(\hat{y}) = [\phi_1(\hat{y}_1), \phi_2(\hat{y}_2), \ldots, \phi_k(\hat{y}_k)]^T$ with $\phi_j(\hat{y}_j) = \frac{\partial \ln g_j(\hat{y}_j)}{\partial \hat{y}_j}$. The $g_j(\hat{y}_j)$ is a certain probability density function (pdf) of $\hat{y}_j$, which is represented by a mixture of densities:

---

1. We call the time series z is super-Gaussian if $kurt(z) = E(z^4) - 3E(z^2)^2 > 0$; If $kurt(z) < 0$, z is called sub-Gaussian time series.

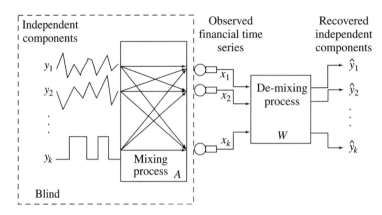

Figure 14.1
ICA in analysis of financial time series, where the observed financial series are regarded as the linear mixture of k independent components, which may be interpreted as certain factors influencing the investment environment. From the observed series x, ICA can find out the independent components up to an unknown constant and a permutation of indices through a de-mixing process W.

$$g_j(\hat{y}_j) = \sum_{i=1}^{n_j} \alpha_{ji} q(\kappa_{ji}), \tag{14.6}$$

$$\kappa_{ji} = b_{ji}(\hat{y}_j - a_{ji}) \tag{14.7}$$

with

$$\sum_{i=1}^{n_j} \alpha_{ji} = 1, \quad \alpha_{ji} = \frac{\exp(\gamma_{ji})}{\sum_{m=1}^{n_j} \exp(\gamma_{jm})}. \tag{14.8}$$

In particular, if $q(\kappa_{ji}) = b_{ji} h'(\kappa_{ji})$ with $h'(\kappa_{ji}) = \frac{\exp(-\kappa_{ji})}{[1+\exp(-\kappa_{ji})]^2}$, we have

$$\phi_j(\hat{y}_j) = \frac{1}{g_j(\hat{y}_j)} \sum_{i=1}^{n_j} \alpha_{ji} b_{ji} q'(\kappa_{ji}) \tag{14.9}$$

with

$$q'(\kappa_{ji}) = h''(\kappa_{ji}) b_{ji} \tag{14.10}$$

$$h''(\kappa_{ji}) = \frac{\exp(-2\kappa_{ji}) - \exp(-\kappa_{ji})}{[1 + \exp(-\kappa_{ji})]^3}. \tag{14.11}$$

As shown in [Xu et al 1997, Xu et al 1998], the parameters $\{\{\gamma_{ji}, b_{ji}, a_{ji}\}_{i=1}^{n_j}\}_{j=1}^{k}$ can be learned by the gradient descent method:

$$\Delta \gamma_{ji} = \frac{1}{g_j(\hat{y}_j))} \sum_{m=1}^{n_j} b_{jm} h'(\kappa_{jm}) \alpha_{jm}(\delta_{im} - \alpha_{ji}) \tag{14.12}$$

$$\Delta b_{ji} = \frac{\alpha_{ji}}{g_j(\hat{y}_j)} \{h'(\kappa_{ji}) + h''(\kappa_{ji})\kappa_{ji}\} \tag{14.13}$$

$$\Delta a_{ji} = -\frac{1}{g_j(\hat{y}_j)} \alpha_{ji} b_{ji}^2 h''(\kappa_{ji}), \tag{14.14}$$

where δ_{im} is the Kronecker delta function.

14.3   Determination of Independent Component Order

Given a set of independent components obtained by LPM, we decide a list L_i, whose elements are the component subscripts, to show their order according to the RHD error between the observed series and the reconstruction from these components.

14.3.1   Independent Component Ordering

On the ith financial series $\{x_i(t)\}_{t=1}^N$, we denote the estimate of the jth weighted independent components u_{ij} by

$$\hat{u}_{ij}(t) = W_{ij}^{-1} \hat{y}_j(t), \quad 1 \leq j \leq k. \tag{14.15}$$

Also, we denote the returns of both x_i and its reconstruction $\hat{x}_{L_i}^m$ under any specific order list L_i as R_i and $\hat{R}_{L_i}^m$ respectively, defined by

$$R_i(t) = \text{sign}[x_i(t+1) - x_i(t)], \quad \text{and} \quad \hat{R}_{L_i}^m(t) = \text{sign}[\hat{x}_{L_i}^m(t+1) - \hat{x}_{L_i}^m(t)], \tag{14.16}$$

with

$$\text{sign}(r) = \begin{cases} 1 & \text{if } r > 0 \\ 0 & \text{if } r = 0 \\ -1 & \text{otherwise}, \end{cases} \quad \hat{x}_{L_i}^m(t) = \sum_{r=1}^{m} \hat{u}_{iq(r)}(t), \tag{14.17}$$

where $q(r)$ is the rth element of L_i.

Based on $\{\hat{u}_{ij}(.)\}_{j=1}^k$, the optimum order L_i^* under RHD reconstruction criterion should satisfy:

$$L_i^* = argmin_{L_i} J_{L_i}, \tag{14.18}$$

where the function J_{L_i} is the cumulative RHD reconstruction error under L_i, defined by

$$J_{L_i} = \sum_{m=1}^{k} RHD(x_i, \hat{x}_{L_i}^m), \tag{14.19}$$

with

$$RHD(x_i, \hat{x}_{L_i}^m) = \frac{1}{N-1} \sum_{t=1}^{N-1} \text{sign}\{[R_i(t) - \hat{R}_{L_i}^m(t)]^2\}. \tag{14.20}$$

14.3.2   Testing-and-Acceptance (TnA) Approach

Since the exhaustive search for L_i^* out of all $k!$ possible order is quite time consuming, we use a sub-optimum algorithm called Testing-and-Acceptance (TnA) to decide the order of the independent components. First, we pick up an independent component $\hat{y}_r$ as the last one, which makes the RHD reconstruction error minimized when those $\{\hat{y}_j\}_{j=1, j \neq r}^k$ are used to reconstruct the data. Removing this independent component, then in the next step, we repeat the first step under the remaining $\{\hat{y}_j\}_{j=1, j \neq r}^k$, and denote the independent component we have selected out as the second last one. In this way, lastly we can arrange the k independent components in an order. The following is the specific TnA algorithm:

Step 1   Let the set of independent component subscripts $Z = \{j | 1 \leq j \leq k\}$, $n = 0$, and the order list $L_i = ()$.

Step 2   For each $j \in Z$, let

$$v_{ij}(t) = \sum_{m \neq j, m \in Z} \hat{u}_{im}(t), \quad 1 \leq t \leq N. \tag{14.21}$$

We pick up the β with

$$\beta = argmin_{j \in Z} RHD(x_i, v_{ij})$$
$$n^{new} = n^{old} + 1, \tag{14.22}$$

as the nth element of L_i. Let

$$L_i^{new} = L_i^{old} + \beta,$$
$$Z^{new} = Z^{old} - \{\beta\}. \tag{14.23}$$

Step 3.   If $Z \neq \{\}$, goto Step 2; otherwise let the L_i^*'s estimate $\hat{L}_i^* = L_i^{-1}$, and stop, where L^{-1} denotes the inverse order of L, e.g. $L^{-1} = (3, 2, 4, 1)^{-1} = (1, 4, 2, 3)$.

Table 14.1
The RHD data reconstruction error by using the first m independent components, respectively shown in $\hat{L}_1^*$ and L_1, where $\hat{L}_1^*$ is given by the TnA approach, whereas L_1 is obtained by the L_∞ norm method.

Values of m	1	2	3	4	5	6
TnA	0.3735	0.3483	0.2565	0.1350	0.0963	0
L_∞ norm	0.5221	0.3852	0.2565	0.1350	0.0963	0

14.4 Experiments

We demonstrate the TnA performance on foreign exchange rates with some comparisons to the L_∞ *norm* method.

14.4.1 Experimental Data

In the experiments, we use six foreign exchange rates from November 26, 1991 to August 30, 1995, which are *US Dollar* (USD) versus *Australian Dollar* (AUD), *French Franc* (FRN), *Swiss Franc* (SWF), *German Mark* (DEM), *British Pound* (GRP), and *Japanese Yen* (JAP) respectively as shown in Figure 14.2.

14.4.2 Experimental Results

Figure 14.3 shows the independent components obtained by using LPM algorithm. To save space, we select a rate series of USD versus AUD (USD-AUD) as an example. The order of independent components obtained from the TnA approach and the L_∞ *norm* method respectively are:

TnA: $\hat{L}_1^* = (5, 3, 1, 6, 4, 2)$
L_∞ norm : $L_1 = (1, 5, 3, 6, 4, 2)$

Table 14.1 listed the RHD reconstruction error between the USD-AUD series and the reconstructions by using the first several independent components, respectively shown in $\hat{L}_1^*$ and L_1.

Figure 14.4 showed the reconstructed series by using $\hat{y}_5$ and $\hat{y}_1$ respectively, where we noticed that the reconstruction from the component $\hat{y}_5$ has the similar variation of the USD-AUD series, but that from $\hat{y}_1$ has totally lost the trend of the observed series. That is, the independent component $\hat{y}_5$ can dominate the trend of USD-versus-AUD series, but $\hat{y}_1$ cannot.

Furthermore, we also showed the reconstruction results in Figure 14.5 by using the first two independent components as shown in $\hat{L}_1^*$, and L_1 respectively. We

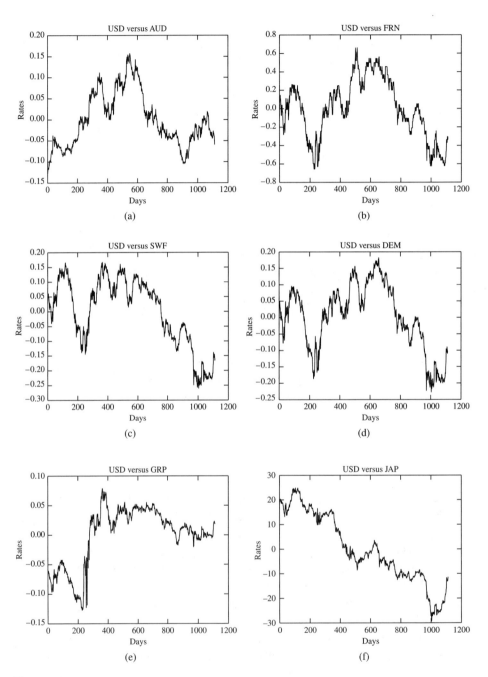

Figure 14.2
Six foreign exchange rates: USD versus AUD, FRN, SWF, DEM, GRP, and JAP respectively, from November 26, 1991 to August 30, 1995, each of which has been normalized to zero mean to conform to the requirement of LPM algorithm.

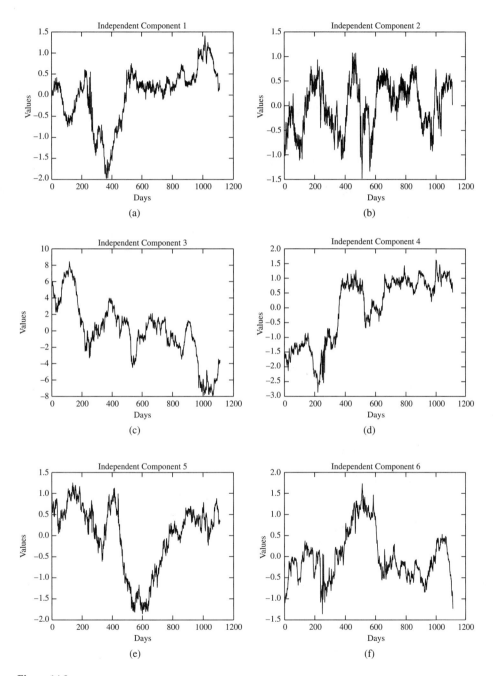

Figure 14.3
From the foreign exchange rates in Figure 14.2, six independent components obtained by LPM algorithm, where we let the number of density mixtures be $n_j = 5$ with $1 \leq j \leq 6$, and the learning rate set at $\eta = 0.0001$.

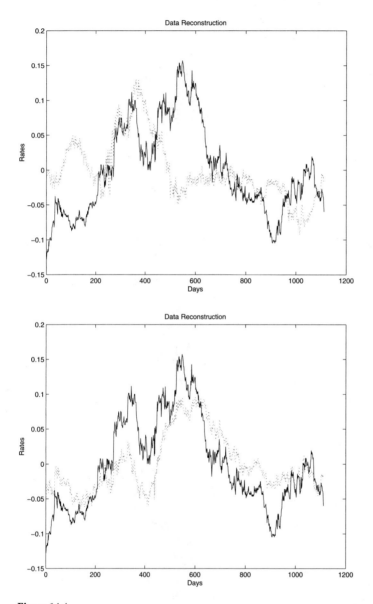

Figure 14.4
The observed series of USD versus AUD (the solid line) and the reconstructed series (the dotted line) by only using (a) $\{\hat{y}_1(t)\}_{t=1}^{N}$; (b) $\{\hat{y}_5(t)\}_{t=1}^{N}$.

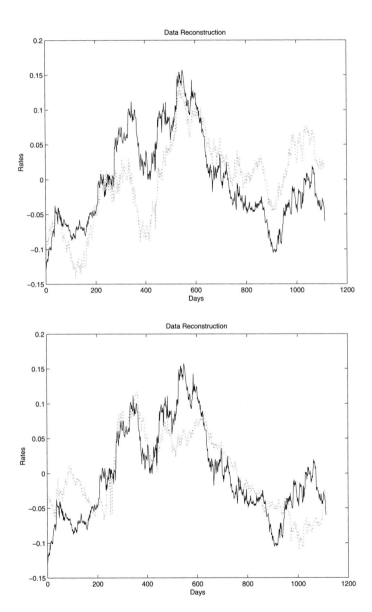

Figure 14.5
The reconstruction by using (a) the first two independent components shown in $\hat{L}_1^*$; (b) the first two independent components shown in L_1, where the solid line is the rate series of USD versus AUD, whereas the dotted line is the reconstruction series.

found that the joint contribution of $\hat{y}_5$ and $\hat{y}_3$ can dominate the trend of USD-AUD series almost all. However, $\hat{y}_1$ and $\hat{y}_5$ cannot, whose reconstructed series can keep the trend of USD-AUD series only in partial region as shown in Figure 14.5(b). Hence, the order list $\hat{L}_1^*$ is better than L_1.

14.5   Conclusion

We have proposed an alternative ordering approach to sort independent components according to their interactive contribution to the trend reservation of the observed series. To avoid exhaustive search, we have presented a sub-optimum ordering algorithm called *Testing-and-Acceptance* (TnA). Although some artificial ordering is implied in the TnA, the experiments on foreign exchange rates have demonstrated that this algorithm outperforms the L_∞ norm method as shown in Figure 14.4 and Figure 14.5.

References

Amari, S. I., A. Cichocki, and H. Yang. 1996. "A new learning algorithm for blind signal separation". *Advances in Neural Information Processing 8*, pages 757–763.

Back, A. D. and A. S. Weigend. 1997. "A first application of independent component analysis to extracting structure from stock returns". *International Journal of Neural Systems*, 8(4):473–484.

Bell, A. J. and T. J. Sejnowski. 1995. "An information-maximization approach to blind separation and blind deconvolution". *Neural Computation*, 7:1129–1159.

Johnson, R. A. and D. W. Wichern. 1992. *Applied Multivariate Statistical Analysis*. Prentice Hall International Editions, third edition.

Utans, J., W. T. Holt, and A. N. Refenes. 1996. "Principal Components Analysis for Modelling Multi-currency Portfolios". *Proceedings of the Fourth International Conference on Neural Networks in the Capital Markets (NNCM'96)*, pages 359–368.

Xu, L., C. C. Cheung, and S. I. Amari. 1998. "Learned Parametric Mixture Based ICA Algorithm". *Neurocomputing*, 22:69–80.

Xu, L., C. C. Cheung, J. Ruan, and S. I. Amari. 1997. "Nonlinearity and Separation Capability: Further Justification for the ICA Algorithm with A Learned Mixture of Parametric Densities". *Proceedings of 1997 European Symposium on Artificial Neural Networks*, pages 291–296.

15 Curved Gaussian Models with Application to Modeling Foreign Exchange Rates

Juan K. Lin and Peter Dayan

Gaussian distributions lie at the heart of popular tools for capturing structure in high dimensional data. Standard techniques employ as models arbitrary *linear* transformations of spherical Gaussians. In this paper, we present a simple extension to a class of non–linear, volume preserving transformations which provides an efficient local description of curvature. The resulting generalized Gaussian models give a simple statistical tool for measuring deviations from multivariate Gaussian distributions. Remarkably, there is a computationally efficient, analytic solution for fitting the parameters of the non–linear models. The power of this approach is demonstrated in a curvature analysis of the Asian foreign exchange market.

15.1 Introduction

In many strategies for risk management and asset allocation amongst multiple investments, the expected values and covariance structure of the returns are the fundamental statistical quantities of interest (*eg* [Burmeister et al 1994]). These quantities emerge exactly as a result of fitting Gaussian probability distributions to the data – making critical the task of understanding and broadening the nature of Gaussian fits.

Principal component analysis (PCA) is one of the main tools used in fitting Gaussian distributions. The idea underlying PCA is that high dimensional data often have lower dimensional structure, and that this structure can be described in a computationally efficient manner by finding the eigenvectors associated with the largest eigenvalues of the covariance matrix of the data. PCA is a well established multivariate modeling and signal processing tool, favored for its simplicity and ease of interpretation. Recently, for example, researchers in computational finance investigated the use of PCA for isolating the driving factors in the market (*eg* [Utans et al 1997]).

From a statistical perspective, PCA can be seen as having two linked aspects – one which models the data with a multivariate Gaussian distribution, and the other which finds the coordinate directions that optimizes the reconstruction of the data by minimizing the variance of the data components that are not modeled. Many researchers have worked to extend the applicability of PCA to more general situations. This includes work on neural network extensions of PCA (*eg* [Karhunen and Joutsensalo 1995], [Oja 1995]), local versions of PCA (*eg* [Tipping 1997], [Kambhatla and Leen 1997]), work on Principal Curves [Hastie and Stuetzle 1989] and the support vector machine based kernel PCA [Schölkopf et al 1998]. Many of these

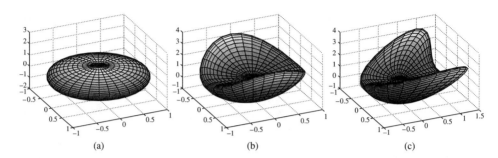

Figure 15.1
Contrasting flat and curved multivariate Gaussian models. (A) Flat Gaussian model, as defined by Principal Component Analysis and represented with an iso–density surface. (B) Curved Gaussian model, with one curved coordinate φ_3; $k_{31} = 3$, $k_{32} = 1$, all other $k_{ij} = 0$. (C) Curved Gaussian model with two curved coordinates φ_2 and φ_3; $k_{21} = 1, k_{31} = 3$, $k_{32} = 1$.

extensions have lost the simple analytic nature of the PCA solution, relying instead on non–linear optimization algorithms. Furthermore, none have retained the dimension reduction, least squares reconstruction, and maximum likelihood density estimation aspects of PCA. Our new generalization of PCA extends the multivariate linear Gaussian models to non–linear Gaussian models with curvature parameters, while successfully retaining the desirable analytical parameter estimation, least squares reconstruction and maximum likelihood density modeling properties.

Section 15.2 discusses the basic Curved Gaussian model; section 15.3 presents the curvature analysis of the Asian foreign exchange market; and section 15.4 considers natural extensions of the model.

15.2   Curved Gaussian Model

15.2.1   Non–Linear Transformation

In PCA, data are linearly projected onto a lower dimensional hyperplane, and the resulting reduced dimensional data modeled with a multivariate Gaussian distribution. Since all such models can be described by a symmetric covariance matrix which can be diagonalized through an orthogonal transformation, PCA can be considered as a model of the reduced dimensional data with a dilated then rotated spherical multivariate Gaussian distribution. To extend the linearly transformed multivariate Gaussian models, we consider subsequent compositions with non–linear volume preserving transformations, as seen in Figure 15.1.

Consider a volume preserving non–linear transformation $\mathcal{T} : \Re^n \mapsto \Re^n$ with $\mathcal{T}(\mathbf{x}) = \varphi = (\varphi_1, \varphi_2, ..., \varphi_n)$ of the form:

$$
\begin{aligned}
\varphi_1 &= x_1 + k_1 \\
\varphi_2 &= x_2 + \sum_i k_{2i} m_{2i}(x_1) \\
\varphi_3 &= x_3 + \sum_i k_{3i} m_{3i}(x_1, x_2) \\
&\ \ \vdots \\
\varphi_n &= x_n + \sum_i k_{ni} m_{ni}(x_1, x_2, \ldots, x_{n-1}) \,,
\end{aligned}
$$

where the non–linear functions $m_{ij}(x_1, ..., x_{i-1})$ are suitably well-behaved and *fixed* basis functions of $x_1, ..., x_{i-1}$. In particular, we require that the functions $m_{ij}(x_1, ..., x_{i-1})$ and their inverses have continuous partial derivatives. The Jacobian of the transformation is lower diagonal everywhere with 1's along the diagonal, so the determinant is 1, and the transformation is volume preserving. Note that an ordering of the coordinates is assumed, with different orderings leading to different transformations.

15.2.2   Transformation Model

Since the non–linear transformation defined above and its partial derivatives are continuous by our constraint on the m_{ij}'s, a simple induction proof shows that the inverse transformation $\mathcal{T}^{-1}$ exists and also has continuous partial derivatives. By the change of variables theorem, the non–linear transformation of a multivariate Gaussian probability density function will already be normalized since the transformation considered is volume-preserving.

We are now able to define a "curved" multivariate Gaussian likelihood model of the form

$$
P(\mathbf{x}; \mathbf{w}, \mathbf{k_{ij}}) \propto (w_1 ... w_n)^{1/2} \exp[-w_1 \varphi_1^2 ... - w_{n-1} \varphi_{n-1}^2 - w_n \varphi_n^2], \tag{15.1}
$$

where $\mathbf{x} = (x_1, x_2, ..., x_n)$ is the principal component coordinate system of the dataset. In essence, the data is modeled by the non–linear transformation $\mathcal{T}^{-1}$ of a multivariate Gaussian as defined in Eqn. 15.1 in the $\{\varphi\}$ coordinate system. A few non–linear transformations of Gaussians are shown in Figure 15.1. These curved Gaussian models provide a much larger class of parametric models for density estimation. Remarkably, it is easy to fit these models to data.

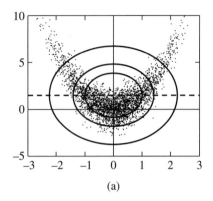
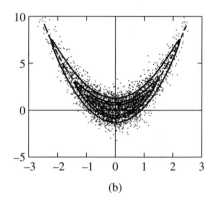

(a)   (b)

Figure 15.2
Data with a naturally curved distribution in x_1, x_2 is modeled with both a conventional two-dimensional Gaussian and a more flexible curved Gaussian model. The solid contours correspond to the σ, $\sqrt{2}\sigma$ and $\sqrt{5}\sigma$ density contours. (A) Conventional two-dimensional Gaussian model. The dashed line is the line $x_2 = 1.5$. (B) Curved two-dimensional Gaussian with $w_1 = 1$, $w_2 = 3$ and $k_{21} = 1.5$. The dashed line is the image of the line $\varphi_2 = x_2 + k_{21}x_1^2 = 0$; 3000 points were drawn from the distribution.

15.2.3   Analytic Parameter Estimation

Consider fitting a model of the form Eqn. 15.1 to data $\mathcal{D} = \{\mathbf{x}^l\}$. Maximizing the log likelihood with respect to the coefficients of m_{ij} gives optimizing equations

$$\frac{\partial}{\partial k_{ij}}\langle \varphi_i^2 \rangle = 0. \tag{15.2}$$

To make the notation more compact, let $\mathbf{k_i} = (k_{i1}, k_{i2}, ..., k_{i\hat{i}})^T$ denote the coefficients in the transformation for the φ_i component. Using the expansion for φ_i given above, this implies $\langle \varphi_i m_{ij} \rangle = 0$ for $j = 1, ..., \hat{i}$. Define $\mathbf{l_i} \in \Re^{\hat{i}}$, and $\mathbf{\Gamma(i)} \in \Re^{\hat{i}} \times \Re^{\hat{i}}$ as follows

$$\mathbf{l_i} = -(\langle x_i m_{i1} \rangle, \langle x_i m_{i2} \rangle, ..., \langle x_i m_{i\hat{i}} \rangle)^T, \tag{15.3}$$

$$\mathbf{\Gamma(i)}_{jk} = \langle m_{ij} m_{ik} \rangle. \tag{15.4}$$

The maximum likelihood condition can be expressed as $\mathbf{\Gamma(i)}\mathbf{k_i} = \mathbf{l_i}$, with solution $\mathbf{k_i} = \mathbf{\Gamma(i)}^{-1}\mathbf{l_i}$. Or more compactly

$$k_{ij} = \left[\mathbf{\Gamma(i)}^{-1}\mathbf{l_i}\right]_j. \tag{15.5}$$

This solution, if it exists, is the unique global maximum of the log likelihood.

The maximum likelihood solution with respect to the inverse variance parameters are

$$w_i = \frac{1}{2\langle \varphi_i^2 \rangle}. \tag{15.6}$$

Surprisingly, just like in Principal Component Analysis, we have analytic solutions for all of the model parameters. Furthermore, the determination of these parameters only involve simple linear algebra – this is a significant advantage over the numerous extensions of PCA which rely on non–linear optimization algorithms. Figure 15.2 compares a two dimensional curved Gaussian model to a flat Gaussian model of data drawn from a naturally curved distribution.

In selecting the non–linear functions $m_{ij}(x_1, ..., x_{i-1})$, it is simplest to consider the case where they are products of non-negative powers of the variables $\{x_1, ..., x_{i-1}\}$. More specifically, let m_{ij}'s be multinomials

$$m_{ij} = \prod_{k=1}^{i-1} x_k^{c_k}, \tag{15.7}$$

with $c_k \geq 0$ for all k. The restriction to positive powers in the polynomial ensures that there are no singularities in the transformation. In the numerics presented in this paper, we considered quadratic non–linear transformations where $m_{ij} = x_j^2$ for $0 < j < i$ and $m_{i0} = 1$. The parameters k_{ij} in this case have an intuitive interpretation as curvatures.

15.2.4   Least Squares Reconstruction

The optimizing Eqns. 15.5–15.6 reveal a direct connection with least squares. From Eqn. 15.2, the maximum likelihood solution coincides with an extremum for $\langle \varphi_i^2 \rangle$, viewed as a function of the multinomial coefficients $\mathbf{k_i}$. Only minima exist since $\langle \varphi_i^2 \rangle$ is unbounded above, so the maximum likelihood solution is the least squares solution. Parameter estimation for the model thus corresponds to a set of n uncoupled least squares fits.

By specifying that $m_{i0} = 1$, we impose the condition $\langle \varphi_i \rangle = 0$. Because the coefficients $\mathbf{k_i}$ minimize $\langle \varphi_i^2 \rangle$, this implies $\langle \varphi_i^2 \rangle \leq \langle x_i^2 \rangle$, and hence $Var(\varphi_i) \leq Var(x_i)$ since $\langle \varphi_i \rangle = \langle x_i \rangle = 0$. Applying the curved Gaussian model to dimension reduction therefore guarantees an improved least squares reconstruction of the data over conventional PCA approaches.

15.2.5   Sequential Flattening

Finally, because $\mathbf{k_i}$ and $\mathbf{k_{i'}}$ are uncoupled for $i \neq i'$, the multinomial coefficients $\mathbf{k_i}$ can be computed in parallel, completely independently of each other. Alternatively, consider single coordinate non–linear transformations $T^j : \Re^n \mapsto \Re^n$, $T^j(\mathbf{x}) = \rho = (\rho_1, \rho_2, ..., \rho_n)$ defined as follows:

$$\rho_j = x_j + \sum_i k_{ji} m_{ji}(x_1, x_2, \ldots, x_{j-1}),$$

$$\rho_i = x_i, \quad i \neq j.$$

The composition $T^n \circ T^{n-1} \circ \ldots \circ T^1$ of single coordinate transformations couples the $\mathbf{k_j}$'s and sequentially transforms the data starting with the x_1 component. After a simple rewriting of the equations, the resulting composite transformation is given by $\varphi = T^n \circ T^{n-1} \circ \ldots \circ T^1(\mathbf{x})$ with

$$x_1 = \varphi_1 - k_1$$
$$x_2 = \varphi_2 - \sum_i k_{2i} m_{2i}(\varphi_1)$$
$$\vdots$$
$$x_n = \varphi_n - \sum_i k_{ni} m_{ni}(\varphi_1, \varphi_2, \ldots, \varphi_{n-1}) \ .$$

It is now clear that we are in fact directly parameterizing the transformation of the multivariate Gaussian instead of its inverse, and that we can model data with this direct parameterization of the transformation of a multivariate Gaussian distribution by solving for $\mathbf{k_1}, \mathbf{k_2}, ..., \mathbf{k_n}$ in sequence. Intuitively, this analysis "sequentially flattens" the data one coordinate at a time, in the given ordering of the coordinates.

15.3   Curvature Analysis of Asian Foreign Exchange Rates

15.3.1   Data Preprocessing

We investigated the Asian foreign exchange market consisting of the Indonesian Rupiah, Japanese Yen, Korean Won, Malaysian Ringgit, Taiwan Dollar, Philippine Peso, Singapore Dollar, and the Thai Baht. Daily price values of the various currencies as measured in U.S. Dollar were taken from October 23, 1993 to August 27, 1998, corresponding to a dataset of 1769 eight-dimensional datapoints. They were

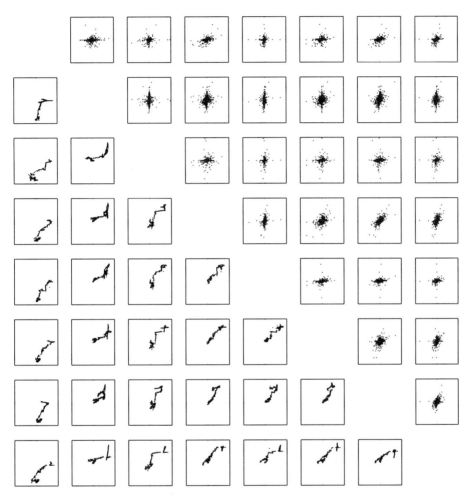

Figure 15.3
Pairwise plots of the value in U.S. Dollar of various Asian currencies. Lower diagonal and upper diagonal plots correspond to price and return data respectively. Beginning with the first column/row from the top left corner, the currencies are the Indonesian Rupiah, Japanese Yen, Korean Won, Malaysian Ringgit, Taiwan Dollar, Philippine Peso, Singapore Dollar, and the Thai Baht. The corresponding column identification is plotted as a function of the row identification.

first normalized relative to their values on August 27, 1998, resulting in a multi–currency portfolio with components weighted equally according to the exchange rates of that date. The relative return data was calculated by taking differences of

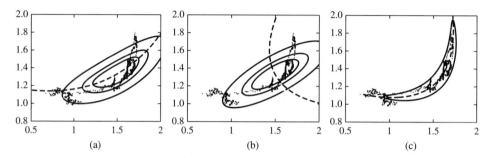

Figure 15.4
Analysis of Japanese Yen vs. Korean Won price data. Plotted are curved Gaussian models starting
from the principal component coordinate system with (A) the smallest variance principal component taken as the curvature direction, (B) the largest variance component as the curvature
direction. In units of inverse U.S. Dollar, the curvature constants are $k = .35$ in A, and 1.03 in B,
corresponding to dimensionless curvatures of $.30$ and $.03$ respectively. The dimensionless curvature gives a much better handle on the significance of the curvatures because of the normalization
relative to the σ_i length scales. The solid lines are the σ, $\sqrt{2}\sigma$ and $\sqrt{5}\sigma$ contours of the model,
while the dashed line shows the transformation of the $\varphi_2 = 0$ line. The analytic fit in (A) captures
some of the curvature, though qualitatively there appears to be more curvature. This is partly due
to the asymmetric concentration of the data. (C) Additional parameterization of the coordinate
system, as described in section 15.4, results in a better curvature fit of the data.

the logarithms of the normalized price data. Two–dimensional projections of both
the price and return data are shown in Figure 15.3.

15.3.2 Japanese Yen vs. Korean Won

From Figure 15.3, curvature is clearly present is some pairwise price data. A simple
curved Gaussian model of the Japanese Yen vs. Korean Won data is presented
in Figure 15.4, with significant curvature fits of $k = 0.35$ and 1.03 in units of
inverse U.S. Dollar for the two possible choices of the curved coordinate (*ie* the
two possible orderings of the principal components). From the plot, we see that
the magnitude of k is not directly indicative of its importance in the model fit. In
Figure 15.4A the curvature in the fitted model describes a significant non–linear
warping in the data of the curved coordinate relative to the standard deviation of
the curved coordinate. In comparison, for the model in Figure 15.4B, the large value
of k is due to the small variance in the non–curved coordinate. Clearly the $\{k_{ij}\}$
parameters need to be considered relative to the standard deviation length scales, as
determined by the $\{\mathbf{w}\}$ parameters. In order to better represent the magnitudes of
the curvature coefficients, we define the dimensionless curvature as $k_{ij}^* = k_{ij}\sigma_j^2/\sigma_i$,
where the standard deviation is related to the $\{\mathbf{w}\}$ parameters by $w_i = \frac{1}{2\sigma_i^2}$. The

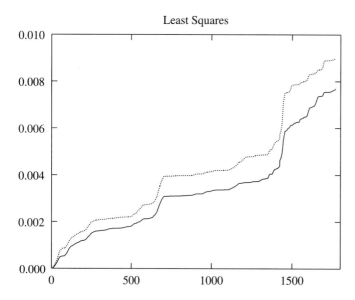

Figure 15.5
Cumulative least squares reconstruction error of the Japanese Yen price data. The minimal variance coordinate was chosen as the curved coordinate x_8 and thrown away to reduce the dimensionality of the data to 7. The dotted line corresponds to the cumulative square error of the conventional PCA reconstruction, and the solid line the lower reconstruction error achieved with the curved Gaussian reconstruction.

numerator $k_{ij}\sigma_j^2$ is a length scale along the i-th coordinate due to the curvature parameter k_{ij}. The dimensionless curvature measures this length scale relative to the standard deviation of the i-th coordinate σ_i. Justifying our intuitive definition, the dimensionless curvature in the model depicted in Figure 15.4A is 30% while it is only 3% for the model in Figure 15.4B.

To demonstrate an application of the curved Gaussian model to dimension reduction, after principal component analysis and curved Gaussian analysis of the data, we discarded the minimal variance principal component, and reduced the dimensionality of the data to seven. The PCA and curved Gaussian reconstructions of the Japanese Yen price data are then compared. The cumulative least squares reconstruction errors for the two reconstructions are shown in Figure 15.5. As expected, the least squares reconstruction error over the entire dataset of the curved Gaussian reconstruction is lower than the PCA reconstruction error.

15.3.3   Single Component Curved Gaussian Model

In addition to the curvature analysis of a two dimensional projection of the price data, we also performed a multidimensional curvature analysis on the relative return data. Here we first performed PCA on the full eight dimensional data, then successively chose each of the eight PCA directions as the direction in which to fit a single component curved Gaussian model. Each curved model has seven parameters, one for each of the other PCA directions. Out of the total of 56 curvature parameters, dimensionless curvature values with magnitudes as high as four and five percent were found.

For the eight separate curved Gaussian models, we found the standard deviation of the curved coordinate φ_8 relative to the flat coordinate x_8 to be .916, .948, .977, .979, .989, .993, .996 and .999 respectively. As discussed in section 15.2, this resulting variance reduction from the volume preserving non–linear transformations is indicative of the better fits achievable with the introduction of curvature parameters.

15.3.4   Sequential Flattening

Finally, we proceeded with the full multi–dimensional curved Gaussian model of the price data with a direct parameterization of the non–linear transformation of the Gaussian. Since ordering of the principal components matters, there is a total of 8! models — one for each order in which the components are flattened. A compilation of the dimensionless curvatures of all 8! models of the foreign exchange data are shown in Figure 15.6AB for the price and return data. Because the dataset consists of less than two thousand datapoints, it is important to perform the same analysis on data sets of the same size sampled from the Gaussian distribution. The resulting curvature distribution of the normally distributed data is shown in Figure 15.6C. The curvatures in the price data are an order of magnitude larger than what is expected of a Gaussian dataset of the same size. In contrast, curvatures in the return data are comparatively smaller, indicative of the sparse nature of the return data.

15.4   Extensions

15.4.1   Linear Coordinate Transformations

The lesson from Figure 15.4B and the lack of a principled approach to ordering the flat coordinates is that the coordinate system itself should be parameterized and optimized.

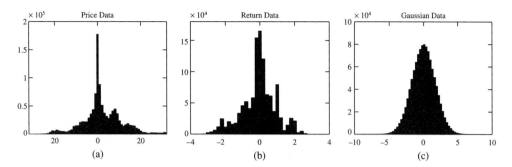

Figure 15.6
Histogram of the dimensionless curvature parameters (quoted in percentage values) in the curved Gaussian models of the price and return data. (A) Dimensionless curvatures for models corresponding to all 8! coordinate permutations of the price data. (B) Similar plot for the return data. (C) Curvature histogram for 5040 datasets of 1768 data points sampled from eight dimensional Gaussian distributions with unit variance. Eight random coordinate permutations are considered for each dataset.

Drawing inspiration from Independent Component Analysis (*eg* [Bell and Sejnowski 1995, Amari et al 1996, Cardoso and Laheld 1996, Lin et al 1997, Lin 1998]), one way to do this is to consider a curved, source datapoint $\mathbf{x}$ being used to generate an observed datapoint $\mathbf{y}$ through a linear transformation:

$$\mathbf{y} = \mathbf{W}^{-1}\mathbf{x} - \mathbf{b} \tag{15.8}$$

where $\mathbf{b}$ is a translation, and $\mathbf{W}^{-1}$ is an invertible 'mixing' transformation. Given a dataset $\mathcal{D} = \{\mathbf{y}^l\}$, the task is to find the unmixing linear transformation parameters $\mathbf{b}$ and $\mathbf{W}$, together with the parameters $\mathbf{w}$ and $\mathbf{k_j}$ of the curved source model so as to fit the data as tightly as possible. The contribution to the log likelihood from the datapoint $\mathbf{y}^l$ is

$$\log |\mathbf{W}| + \log p(\mathbf{W}(\mathbf{y}^l + \mathbf{b}), \mathbf{w}, \mathbf{k_{ij}}).$$

It does not seem possible, in general, to derive closed–form optima for the likelihood as a function of all the parameters. Instead, we consider an iterative stochastic gradient ascent of the likelihood. In each step, first the global maximum of the likelihood in $\mathbf{w}$ and $\mathbf{k_{ij}}$ for the current values of $\mathbf{W}$ and $\mathbf{b}$ is calculated, then the latter variables are changed by stochastic gradient ascent. The partial derivatives of the log likelihood with respect to the mixing parameters are straightforward to calculate.

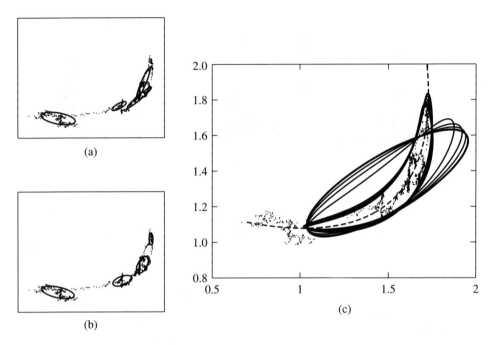

Figure 15.7
Mixture of Gaussians models for modeling the Japanese Yen *versus* the Korean Won data. (A;B) Two different mixtures of Gaussian fits to these data using four full covariance two-dimensional Gaussians. The centers of the Gaussians are marked by a cross, $\sqrt{2}\sigma$ values by the ellipses, and the mixing proportions by the widths of the outlines of the ellipses. (C) Curved model fit with coordinate system parameterization. The dashed line is the quadratic 'skeleton' of the final curved model and the thick solid line the final $\sqrt{2}\sigma$ contour for the model.

Note that there is substantial redundancy in the model. For example, the linear transformation $\mathbf{W}$ can be restricted to an arbitrary orthogonal transformation. However, the learning rule is considerably simpler with the model parameterization given above. Just as for ICA, we can use the natural gradient ascent algorithm [Amari et al 1996, Cardoso and Laheld 1996] to update the mixing transformation along the direction of steepest ascent by right multiplying the update rule for $\mathbf{W}$ by the matrix $\mathbf{W}^T\mathbf{W}$.

An example of the dynamics of the iterative curved Gaussian model fit to the Japanese Yen vs. Korean Won data is shown in Figure 15.7C. Initialized according to a linear Gaussian model, the algorithm quickly settles into an optimal curved Gaussian fit of the data. However, as can be expected with adaptive optimization approaches, the algorithm sometimes falls into local maxima.

15.4.2   Mixture Models

Another natural extension is to consider mixtures of curved Gaussians. One of the most popular extensions of standard Gaussian models is to *mixture* models such as the mixture of Gaussians [Nowlan 1991], and in more recent work, mixtures of principal component or factor analyzers [Bregler and Omohundro 1995, Kambhatla and Leen 1997, Hinton et al 1997, Roweis and Ghahramani 1999, Tipping 1997]. Such mixture models are attractive because the expectation maximization algorithm (EM; [Dempster et al 1977]) allows them to be fit to data in a computationally efficient manner.

The curved Gaussian model can substitute exactly for flat Gaussian model in mixtures. As seen in Figure 15.7, few curved Gaussians can often capture the information contained in many linear Gaussians. The E phase of EM, in which the responsibility of each element of the mixture for each data point is assigned is straightforward because the non–linear transformation is volume preserving. The M phase of EM, in which the parameters of each element are changed to reflect their responsibilities is straightforward because of the analytical solution for the curved models presented in section 15.2.3.

15.5   Discussion

We have presented an analytic generalization of the linear Gaussian models that captures weak non–linear correlations in the data. There are various natural extensions of the work. Particularly important is the adoption of ideas from independent component analysis to infer the appropriate coordinate system in which to fit the curved model, and the notion of using *mixtures* of the curved Gaussian distributions, in the same way that one uses mixtures of standard Gaussian distributions. This presents no conceptual or computational hurdle, and can be done simply using the expectation–maximization algorithm. Another extension is that of using the curvature information for things other than fitting a Gaussian model. For instance, the information could be used to enhance local kernel methods in a curved form of tangent distance [Simard et al 1993]. Also, more general non–linear models could be used in place of the simple quadratic form used in our analysis of the foreign exchange data. To manage the trade–offs of bias for variance in assuming more flexible parameterizations, more sophisticated cross–validation or Bayesian methods could be considered for choosing the orders of the polynomials or the forms of the non–linearities.

There is great interest in multivariate statistical analysis tools beyond linear Gaussian models. The curved Gaussian models presented in this paper provide a simple way of looking at non–linearities in the data. Since the curvature parameter fit is still analytic, all current applications of PCA will benefit from the added flexibility. Although the subsequent non–linear transformation might be very close to the identity for some datasets, the existence of a computationally inexpensive analytic solution strongly motivates the consideration of these curvature parameters. In conclusion, the curved Gaussian models provide an extremely simple tool for probing and characterizing deviations of the data from a multivariate Gaussian distribution. The alternative of considering higher order multivariate moments, which are higher order tensors, quickly runs into the curse of dimensionality. Finally, with respect to computational finance, this curvature modeling provides the fundamental basis for non–linear asset allocation strategies and new non–linear financial products. We believe curved Gaussian models will be a very useful multivariate statistical modeling and signal processing tool.

References

Amari, S., A. Cichocki, and H. Yang. 1996. A new learning algorithm for blind signal separation. In Touretzky, D. S., M. C. Mozer, and M. E. Hasselmo, editors, *Advances in Neural and Information Processing Systems, 8*, pages 757–763, Cambridge, MA. MIT Press.

Bell, A. J. and T. J. Sejnowski. 1995. An information–maximizatin approach to blind separation and blind deconvolution. *Neural Computation*, 7:1129–1159.

Bregler, C. and S. M. Omohundro. 1995. Nonlinear image interpolation using manifold learning. In Tesauro, G., D. S. Touretzky, and T. K. Leen, editors, *Advances in Neural and Information Processing Systems, 7*, pages 971–980, Cambridge, MA. MIT Press.

Burmeister, E., R. Roll, and S. A. Ross. 1994. A practitioner's guide to arbitrage pricing theory. *Finanzmarkt und Portfolio Management*, 8 Jahrgand Nr. 3:312–331.

Cardoso, J.-f. and B. Laheld. 1996. Equivariant adaptive source separation. *IEEE Transactions on Signal Processing*, 45:2:434–444.

Dempster, A. P., N. M. Laird, and D. B. Rubin. 1977. Maximum likelihood from incomplete data via the em algorithm. *Journal of the Royal Statistical Society*, series B 39:1–38.

Hastie, T. and W. Stuetzle. 1989. Principal curves. *Journal of the American Statistical Association*, 84 no. 406:502–516.

Hinton, G. E., P. Dayan, and M. Revow. 1997. Modeling the manifolds of images of handwritten digits. *IEEE Transactions on Neural Networks*, 8:65–74.

Kambhatla, N. and T. K. Leen. 1997. Dimension reduction by local principal component analysis. *Neural Computation*, 9:1493–1516.

Karhunen, J. and J. Joutsensalo. 1995. Generalizations of principal component analysis, optimization problems and neural networks. *Neural Networks*, vol 8 no 4:549–562.

Lin, J. K. 1998. Factorizing multivariate function classes. In Jordan, M. I., M. J. Kearns, and S. A. Solla, editors, *Advances in Neural and Information Processing Systems, 10*, pages 563–569, Cambridge, MA. MIT Press.

Lin, J. K., D. G. Grier, and J. D. Cowan. 1997. Faithful representation of separable distributions. *Neural Computation*, 9:1303–1318.

Nowlan, S. J. 1991. Soft competitive adaptation: neural network learning algorithms based on fitting statistical mixtures. Technical Report PhD Thesis, Department of Computer Science, Carnegie–Mellon University.

Oja, E. 1995. The nonlinear pca learning rule and signal separation - mathematical analysis. Technical Report Report A26, Helsinki University of Technology, Laboratory of Computer and Information Science, Helsinki.

Roweis, S. and Z. Ghahramani. 1999. A unifying review of linear gaussian models. *Neural Computation*, 11:305–345.

Schölkopf, B., A. Smola, and K. Müller. 1998. Nonlinear component analysis as a kernel eigenvalue problem. *Neural Computation*, 10:1299–1319.

Simard, P., Y. LeCun, and J. Denker. 1993. Efficient pattern recognition using a new transformation distance. In Cowan, J. D., S. J. Hanson, and C. L. Giles, editors, *Advances in Neural and Information Processing Systems, 5*, pages 50–58, San Mateo, CA. Morgan Kaufmann.

Tipping, ME & Bishop, C. 1997. Mixtures of principal component analyzers. *Fifth International Conference on Artificial Neural Networks*.

Utans, J., W. T. Holt, and A. N. Refenes. 1997. Principal component analysis for modeling multi–currenty portfolios. In Weigend, A. S., Y. S. Abu-Mostafa, and A.-P. N. Refenes, editors, *Proceedings of the fourth international conference on neural networks in the capital markets*, pages 359–369, Singapore. World Scientific.

16 Nonparametric Efficiency Testing of Asian Foreign Exchange Markets

Cornelis A. Los

16.1 Introduction

In the second half of 1997, after the devaluation of the Thai baht on July 2, 1997, the foreign exchange markets in Asia were severely shocked and their volatility increased dramatically. Questions were raised about their efficiency. This chapter tests the informational efficiency of the Asian FX markets before and after the July 2, 1997, using high frequency (HF) - minute-to-minute - FX quotations from January 1 1997 - December 31, 1997.

16.1.1 Definitions

Financial markets are considered efficient when their prices follow random walks = their price changes are innovations = their price changes are *stationary* and *independent*. The FX markets are fair games and can be described by martingales. A closely related definition is that their prices follow geometric Brownian motions.

16.1.2 Questions

Focusing on weak market efficiency, this chapter attempts to answer three questions:

1. Which Asian FX markets operated efficiently in 1997 and continued to operate efficiently after July 2nd, 1997?

2. Which Asian FX markets operated inefficiently in 1997, or broke down after July 2nd, 1997?

3. When an FX market is found to be inefficient, how should such an efficiency be modeled?

16.1.3 Methodology

Nonparametric tests are applied, since non-stationarities in the FX quotation series were expected, based on earlier research reported in the literature.

16.1.4 Data

The data are high-frequency, minute-by-minute FX quotations from eight Asian FX markets, with the Deutschemark as efficient benchmark currency.

16.1.5 Some Conclusions

1. The low-power nonparametric tests show that there was a clear Asian FX market regime discontinuity in the middle of 1997, in particular in Indonesia, Malaysia, Singapore and Thailand.

2. All Asian FX markets traded stationarily, (i.e., consistently) before and after the mid-year discontinuity, with the exception of Malaysia (and, perhaps, Indonesia and Taiwan), which showed significant non-stationary behavior after the discontinuity. Thus, after the market break, FX traders of the Malaysian Ringgit were exposed to maximum uncertainty, because the Malaysian market regime was inconsistent

3. Hong Kong, the Philippines and Japan did not experience any FX nonstationarity in 1997.

4. None of the Asian FX markets was efficient in 1997, either before or after the devaluation of the Thai baht, due to dependent price changes. Supra-normal profits and losses were possible.

5. Even the Philippines and Taiwan, which showed less of such dependencies in the first half of 1997, showed more dependent price changes in the second half year.

6. Significant temporal trading windows of up to twenty minutes existed throughout 1997.

7. The price changes can be modeled by order-1 or order-2 (two to three minutes) Markov processes in the first half of 1997 and by order-2, order-3 (three to four minutes), or even higher-order Markov processes in the second half of the year.

16.2 Literature Review

The literature on the efficiency of speculative markets currently involves four areas of interdisciplinary research: Markov and martingale theory, microstructure of FX markets, nonparametric tests and time-frequency analysis.

16.2.1 Markow and Martingale Theory

Bachelier and Poincaré formulated around 1900 a theory of speculation, in which efficient market prices follow Brownian motion, so that no supra-normal profits are possible. At the same time Markov studied stochastic processes with complete mathematical dependencies in discrete time. In 1923 Wiener formulated his continuous time counterparts and in 1927 Kolmogorov axiomatized conventional probability theory. In the 1950s and 1960s the mathematical theory of both discrete Markov and continuous Wiener processes was generalized further as state space theory [Kalman 1960]. In finance, using conditional probability theory, [Fama 1970] formulated the Efficient Market Hypothesis, in which market pricing processes are fair games, i.e., martingales, so that price innovations = efficient price changes = martingale differences. In the 1970s-1980s the focus of the theoreticians was on discrete-time martingale convergence results and estimation of the nonlinear development structures of time series using Kalman Filters [Los 1982]. In the 1970s - 1990s stochastic calculus and Markow methods were incorporated in derivatives valuation [Rogers 1997].

16.2.2   Microstructure of FX Markets

[Follod 1991] focused on the problem that quotations are not directly related to transactions. But [Bollerslev and Domowitz 1993] asserted that reputation effects would ensure the quality of such quotations data and [Goodhart and Payne 1997] showed how transactions data could be filtered from them. Laconically, [Evans 1997] suggested to use transactions data directly, where available.

16.2.3   Nonparametric Tests

[Boothe and Glassman 1987] found that FX distributions are Student-t or mixtures of normals, and that their parameters evolve over time, which induced [Loretan and Phillips 1994] to test the covariance stationarity. They found that FX (and stock market) distributions are heavy-tailed and that their unconditional covariances evolve over time, negating the legitimacy of (G)ARCH modeling, which was popularized in the FX markets by Salomon Brothers, Inc.. In addition, [Antoniou and Holmes 1997] found that, because of feedback processes, non-linearity of the dynamic pricing processes renders conventional (econometric) parametric correlation analysis very questionable. Thus [Hinich 1995] focuses on the non-linear time dependencies and [Sherry 1992] to apply the kind of non-parametric statistical testing developed to test information processing in nervous systems, on stock market price series. It is Sherry's relatively agnostic, non-parametric approach to test for the stationarity of the distributions and for serial independence of the price changes, which this paper applies to the Asian FX series.

16.2.4   Time-Frequency Analysis

Recently, [Ramsey and Zhang 1997] showed in time-frequency plots - by Gabor's windowed Fourier-transform spectrograms and by multiresolution wavelet analysis in scalograms - the hypothesized nonstationarities of FX series, in particular the changing third (skewness) and fourth (kurtosis) moments. In addition, they find transitory frequencies of limited duration (transients), bunched transactions and discontinuities (Dirac deltas). In other words, price data from speculative pricing markets, like FX or stock markets, are like speech data, as Sherry had conjectured. They contain very structured and interpretable signals, which are almost, but not quite unpredictable. They are, perhaps, predictable only in a very short-term and nonlinear filtering sense.

16.3   Methodology

16.3.1   Efficient Market Model: Martingale Differences

An efficient market is represented by the following martingale difference model:[1]

$$E(\varepsilon_{j,t+1}|\Phi_t) = E(P_{j,t+1} - P_{j,t}) = E(P_{j,t+1}) - P_{j,t} = 0, \qquad (16.1)$$

where $\varepsilon_{j,t+1}$ = price change, i.e., the difference between actual price P at time t and the expected price at time $t+1$ for instrument j; and Φ_t = the set of information assumed to have been reflected into the price $P_{j,t}$ of instrument j at time t. When this simple model holds true, the price process $P_{j,t}$ is a martingale and the market pricing process represents a "fair game."

The important assumptions to be tested are then:

1. Φ_t = the information set = the *complete* accumulated distribution of $\varepsilon_{j,t+1}$. Unfortunately, in a finite universe we can make only a finite number of observations and the theoretical completeness, or "randomness," of a Kolmogorovian probability distribution can never be ascertained. Thus, the two remaining researchable questions are:

2. Φ_t = a *stationary* distribution of price changes?

3. $\varepsilon_{j,t+1}$ is *independent* of $\varepsilon_{j,t}$? Elementary statistics demonstrates that independence is a much broader requirement and much harder to satisfy than (parametric) uncorrelatedness.

16.3.2   Nonparametric Tests

1. [Sherry 1992] suggested to look at the whole distribution of historically observed price changes $e_{j,t+1} = P_{t+1} - P_t$ and test for stationarity of distribution and for independence of $e_{j,t+1}$ using *informational pattern analysis*, in particular price change transition arrays. This paper uses his array of tests, as in Table 16.1.

---

1. A fair pricing game is, mathematically speaking, a martingale, since the discrete price innovations $\varepsilon_{j,t+1}$ are martingale-differences. Cf. Los, 1982, pp 32 - 40 and Rogers, 1997, pp. 18 - 23.

Table 16.1
Random Walk Tests

1. Stationarity	2. Independence
(i) Cumulative Distributions	(i) Differential Spectra
(ii) Percentile Graphs	(ii) Relative Price Change Transition Arrays
	(iii) Category Price Change Transition Arrays
	(iv) Markow Analysis of the CPCT Arrays

Table 16.2
Theoretical Probabilities of Tetragrams

Tetragram	Probability
1111 or 2222	1/120
1112, 1222, 2111, or 2221	1/30
1121, 1211, 2122, or 2212	3/40
1122 or 2211	1/20
1212 or 2121	4/30
1221 or 2112	11/120

2. The only statistical tests used in this chapter are Chi-Square distributed, comparing observed and expected frequency of patterns

$$\chi^2 = \sum_1^n \frac{(\text{Observed frequency-Expected frequency})^2}{\text{Expected frequency}},$$

3. Two types of transition arrays are used:

(i) *Relative Price Change Transition* (RPCT) arrays consist of two states only: simple strings of "1" (= "down") and "2" (= "up") assigned to the price changes $e_{j,t+1}$. E.g., what is the expected probability of finding the following tetragrams = patterns of four transitions, when the observed $e_{j,t+1}$ are truly independent innovations? The theoretical probabilities for such tetragrams are in Table 16.2.

(ii) *Category Price Change Transition* (CPCT) arrays consist of more than two states, because they take also account of the size of the price changes.

Markov analysis tries to determine the required number of states (= order) of the various CPCT arrays: digrams, trigrams, tetragrams, etc. The identified order represents the time dependencies, respectively the frequencies of the FX price changes.

16.4   Currency Data

The tested data have the following characteristics:

1. Indicative quotes of one minute intervals were collected from Dow Jones Telerate in the Simulated Trading Room on campus of the Nanyang Technological University in Singapore.

2. The data cover the following eight Asian currencies for a one-year period starting from 1 January 1997 and ending on 30 December 1997: Hong Kong dollar (HKD), Indonesian rupiah (IDR), Malaysian ringgit (MYR), Philippines peso (PHP), Singapore dollar (SGD), Taiwan dollar (TWD), Thai baht (THB) and the Japanese Yen (JPY).

3. Besides the eight Asian currencies, as developed economy benchmark is used: German Deutschemark (DEM)

4. The base currency is the US dollar (USD).

5. There is round-the-clock trading in the FX markets and the total number of available minute-by-minute observations on each series is $T = 360 \times 24 \times 60 = 518\,400$, thus $t = 1, ..., 518400$ for $j = 1, ..., 9$ Asian FX series.[2]

16.5   Stationarity Tests

According to Sherry's methodology ([Sherry 1992], pp. 12 - 20), each data series is first divided into two equal halves (the earlier chronological half is addressed as half 1 and the successive half as half 2. The data in the two halves are then separated into bins of equal interval size. A cumulative graph of both halves is constructed. Insert charts with differential spectra include data points in both halves corresponding to percentile increments of 10%, that is, the $10\%, 20\%, 30\%, ...$ data values for half 2 are plotted against those in half 1. The deviation from the 45^0 line is tested against both halves. Formal quantitative Chi-square tests are conducted on these differential spectra.

16.5.1   Stationarity: Regime Break Tests

Cumulative Distributions and Percentile Graphs   The cumulative distributions and percentile charts are plotted in Figures 16.1–16.9. The insert charts in the figures show that the HKD, PHP, DEM and JPY markets were overall stationary in their price changes. The price changes of the first half of the year are of about the same magnitude as those in the second half: the data points are either extremely

---

2. Due to a technical disruption in our NTU on-campus Simulated Trading Room, there was an unfortunate lapse of data availability from the 25th till the 31st of October 1997, missing five days of trading. Thus the data points from November 1st, 1997, onwards are adjoined to the previous data stream ended on October 24th 1997.

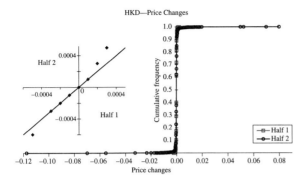

Figure 16.1
HKD—Price Changes, Jan-Dec 1997

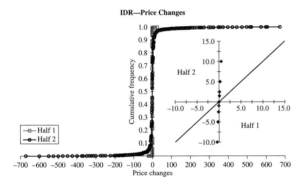

Figure 16.2
IDR—Price Changes, Jan-Dec 1997

close to, or on the 45^0 lines. The DEM and JPY were apparently not affected by the Asian currency crisis in 1997. All the other currencies show clearly non-stationary differences.[3]

Chi-square Test Results   The Chi-square tests for the price changes of HKD, PHP, DEM and JPY are insignificant (Cf. Table 2 in [Los 1998]). Thus for these four currencies, the null hypothesis of stationarity is not rejected with 99% confidence.

---

3. All figures and tables are available in [Los 1998], which can be downloaded as PDF file from the web page of NTU's Centre for Research in Financial Services (CREFS): http://www.ntu.edu.sg/nbs/crefs/working_papers.htm

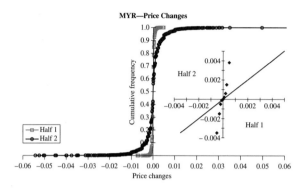

Figure 16.3
MYR—Price Changes, Jan-Dec 1997

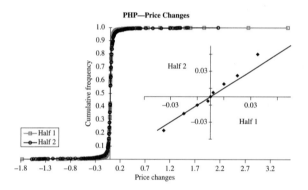

Figure 16.4
PHP—Price Changes, Jan-Dec 1997

The Chi-square result for TWD surprisingly shows it to be marginally insignificant too, despite the fact that its chart looks similar to the SGD's. The Chi-square results for the IDR, MYR, SGD and THB confirm the conclusions obtained by visual inspection.

16.5.2   Stationarity: Intra-Regime Tests

Cumulative Distributions and Percentile Graphs   The second half of 1997 shows some interesting changes in FX trading behavior and it clearly separates the sheep from the goats, i.e., the markets which remained predictably stationary and which became non-stationary and possibly chaotic. For example, the insert

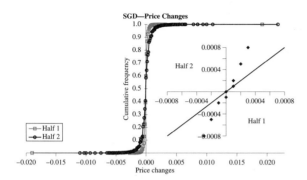

Figure 16.5
SGD—Price Changes, Jan-Dec 1997

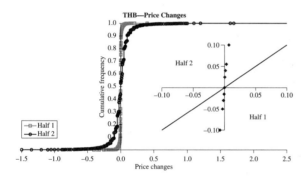

Figure 16.6
THB—Price Changes, Jan-Dec 1997

percentile chart for the IDR shows that the price differences lie somewhat between the 45^0 line and the y-axis, though it is still comparatively closer to the 45^0 line, but the magnitude of price changes increased dramatically. Whereas most of the price differences fell within the -5.0 to 5.0 range in the January to June 1997 period, the price differences increased 120 times to fall within a -600 to 600 range in the later half of 1997.

Chi-square Test Results The Chi-square test values increased from the first half to the second half of 1997, but all tests remained insignificant with the exception of the 99% confidence test for MYR in the July - December period (Cf. Table 3 in [Los 1998]). This seems to suggest that the markets remained overall stationary and that there was not much structural change, with the exception of the MYR.

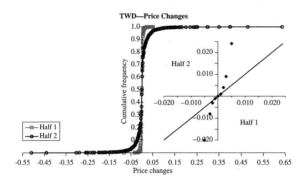

Figure 16.7
TWD—Price Changes, Jan-Dec 1997

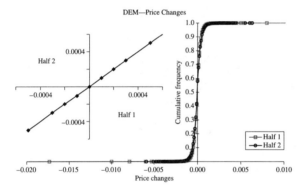

Figure 16.8
DEM—Price Changes, Jan-Dec 1997

16.6 Independence Tests

The independence tests attempt to determine if the price changes $\varepsilon_{j,t+1}$ are independent of one another. We look at the differential spectra, the relative price changes, compute category price change transition (CPTC) arrays and conduct a Markov analysis of these CPTC arrays.

16.6.1 Differential Spectra

Following again the example of [Sherry 1992], pp. 86 - 91, the following recipe to form differential spectra is used to test for independence. The price changes $\varepsilon_{j,t+1}$

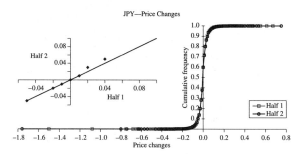

Figure 16.9
JPY—Price Changes, Jan-Dec 1997

are allocated to pre-specified bins. The positive price change bins, which are the "observed" data are paired with the "negative" bins, which are the expected data, to ensure a symmetric matching of bins. Here $n =$ (number of bins in the histogram/2). The critical value of the test depends on the number of symmetrical bins used. If the price changes $\varepsilon_{j,t+1}$ are independent, the distribution of the price changes around the zero point is symmetrical. But if this distribution is asymmetrical, the price changes are not independent.

Chi-square Test Results   Based on the Chi-square tests, all FX price changes were significantly dependent in 1997, except HKD, SGD and DEM (Cf. Table 4 in [Los 1998]). Surprisingly, even JPY exhibits significant dependency according to this test.

16.6.2   Relative Price Change Transition Arrays

One shortcoming of the differential spectrum is that it only decides whether price changes are independent. It fails to identify the type of serial dependence that may be present. The relative price change method assists in determining the type of serial dependence and the duration of the temporal window during which the dependency exists. Relative price change transition (RPCT) arrays are used to test for independence, following Sherry, who also computed all the theoretical relative frequencies or probabilities ([Sherry 1992], pp. 93 - 112; also available as Tables 7, 8 and 9 in [Los 1998]).

Chi-square Test Results   The Chi-square tests show that in 1997 the price changes of all nine currencies were not independent, with 99% confidence, up to and including temporal windows of at least four minutes (Cf. Table 10 in [Los

1998]). This means that, according to this non-parametric test, all nine FX markets - including the DEM and JPY markets - were inefficient in 1997. The sequential strings of up to four symbols (i.e., five price changes) have been used to detect invariant trading patterns, that could have been used for profitable FX trading strategies.

Interestingly, when we proceed to test for independence in each of the two half years, we find, first, that in the first half of 1997 the price changes of the PHP and TWD were independent, with 99% confidence and that these FX markets operated efficiently (Cf. Table 11 in [Los 1998]). However, in the second half of 1997 these two currencies also lost their independence of price changes and that thus none of the Asian FX rates showed serial independence (Cf. Table 12 in [Los 1998]). Thus profitable trading strategies could have been developed in the second half of 1997, most likely because of the general depreciation of all currencies versus the US dollar (like "an unstoppable train rolling down hill").

16.6.3   Length of Temporal Trading Windows

The relative price change transition arrays can be used to determine the existence as well as the duration of a temporal trading window during which the price changes exhibit serial dependencies. A lag$-n$ window examines the existence of serial dependencies between a price change with the nth price change. This means that, if a temporal window is identified, a technical trading strategy can be devised within the limits of this window. Technical analysis is without merit, if no such window can be identified,

Chi-square Test Results   All nine currencies exhibit significant serial dependencies in their price changes for up to the lag-20 temporal window at the 99% confidence level (Cf. Tables 13, 14 and 15 in [Los 1998]). There is no difference between the first or second half of 1997. Since a lag-20 temporal window represents only 20 minutes of trading, this kind of analysis should be extended to larger intra-day windows or even to intra-week windows.

16.6.4   Category Price Change Transition Arrays

Using CPCT arrays, the underlying FX time series can be examined in greater detail than with the relative price change transition arrays of Section 6.2. By categorizing these time series according to a set of predetermined criteria, one determines if relatively large or small price changes deviate from independence. There can be as many categories as desired, as long as some non-varying rule for categorization is used. It is important to emphasize that if a series categorized by one set of criteria is independent, this does not imply that a categorization by different criteria also leads to independence. Thus, in principle, there is an infinite number of ways of categorizing FX time series to test for independence.

The recipe to form category price *change* transition matrices to test for independence is again adapted from [Sherry 1992], pp. 131 - 140. The cumulative frequency distribution of the price changes $\varepsilon_{j,t+1}$ of Section 2. is divided into three parts: the lowest 10% of the series, the next 80% and the highest 10%. Determine in which third each price change $\varepsilon_{j,t+1}$ belongs. If a price change belongs to the "ith" portion, we encode it with symbol "i"=1,2, or 3, i.e. "1" represents the lowest 10% portion, "2" represents the 80% portion, and "3" the highest 10% portion of the cumulative frequency distribution of the FX series. The CPCT array is generated by specifying how often a "1", "2" or "3" is followed by "1", "2" or "3". The frequency of occurrence of a symbol "i" is the number of price changes in the "i" portion. For example, the expected frequency for the digram "13" is determined by:

$$
\begin{aligned}
\text{expected frequency} \; &= \; (\text{theoretical probability of 1}) \\
&\times (\text{theoretical probability of 3}) \\
&\times (\text{total number of price changes})
\end{aligned}
\tag{16.2}
$$

Chi-square Test Results   Again, all nine currencies exhibit significant serial dependencies in their price changes for the $10\% - 80\% - 10\%$ categorization (Cf. Tables 16, 17 and 18 in [Los 1998]). This means that relatively small and large price changes of the nine FX series diverge significantly from independence at the 99% confidence level. Furthermore, there is no discernible difference between the test results for the first or for the second half of 1997.

16.6.5   Markov Analysis of CPCT Arrays

Following the Markov analysis of the CPCT matrices of [Sherry 1992], pp. 140 - 160, we start with the test for a zero-order Markov process, as in the preceding section. The degrees of freedom for a zero-order Markov process is $(C-1)^2$, where C is the number of Markovian "states". For example, digrams have two states so that the degrees of freedom is $(C-1)^2 = 1$, while trigrams have three states and the degrees of freedom is $(C-1)^2 = 4$. For an order-1 Markov process, the Chi-square test statistic is calculated as follows:

$$
\chi^2 = \sum_{ijk} \frac{(O_{ijk} - E_{ijk})^2}{E_{ijk}},
\tag{16.3}
$$

where O_{ijk} is the observed number of occurrences of trigram "ijk". E_{ijk} is the expected number of occurrences of the trigram "ijk", defined as follows:

$$E_{ijk} = \frac{O_{.jk}O_{ij.}}{O_{.j.}}. \tag{16.4}$$

In case of $O_{.jk}$ the trigram will begin with any "symbol" (that is 1, 2 or 3), but will end with a specific digram jk. In case of $O_{ij.}$ the trigram begins with a specific digram "ij", but ends with any symbol. Finally, in case of $O_{.j.}$ the trigram begins and ends with any symbol, but has a specific symbol in the middle. The degrees of freedom for this order-1 Markov process test is $C(C-1)^2 = 3(3-1)^2 = 12$. If the calculated Chi-square value is still significant, we perform an order-2 Markov analysis. For an order-2 Markov process, the Chi-square test statistic is as follows:

$$\chi^2 = \sum_{ijk} \frac{(O_{ijkl} - E_{ijkl})^2}{E_{ijkl}}, \tag{16.5}$$

where E_{ijkl}, the expected number of occurrences of the tetragram "$ijkl$" is defined as:

$$E_{ijkl} = \frac{O_{.jkl}O_{ijk.}}{O_{.jk.}}. \tag{16.6}$$

The degrees of freedom for this order-2 Markov process Chi-square test on trigrams is $C^2(C-1)^2 = 3^2(3-1)^2 = 36$. If the calculated Chi-square value is statistically significant, an order-3 Markov process is performed, etc.

Chi-square Test Results   All results for the whole of 1997 for order-0, -1 and -2 Markov processes are significant at the 99% confidence level Cf. Table 19 in [Los 1998]). For the first half of 1997, the price changes of PHP and TWD exhibit independence at order-2 processes: the price changes were thus order-1 Markov and not independent innovations (Cf. Table 20 in [Los 1998]). The price changes could have been filtered and predicted supra-normal profitably by an order-1 Kalman filter. In addition, the price changes of HKD, MYR and SGD exhibit independence at order-3 Markov (Cf. Table 20 in [Los 1998]). The price changes of the PHP and, perhaps surprisingly, of the THB, show order-2 Markov behavior, while those of all other currencies show order-3 or higher Markov behavior (Cf. Table 21 in [Los 1998]).

Currency	HKD	IDR	MYR	PHP	SGD	THB	TWD	DEM	JPY
Stationarity Test									
—1997: Visual Inspection	✔	•	•	✔	•	•	•	✔	✔
Chi-Square	✔	•	•	✔	•	•	✔	✔	✔
—Jan to Jun 97: Visual Insp	✔	✔	✔	✔	✔	✔	✔	✔	✔
Chi-Square	✔	✔	✔	✔	✔	✔	✔	✔	✔
—Jul to Dec 97: Visual Insp	✔	•	•	✔	✔	✔	•	✔	✔
Chi-Square	✔	✔	•	✔	✔	✔	✔	✔	✔
Differential Spectrum									
—1997	✔	•	•	•	✔	•	•	✔	•
—Jan to Jun 97	•	✔	✔	•	✔	•	•	✔	•
—Jul to Dec 97	✔	•	•	✔	✔	•	•	•	•
Relative Price Change									
—1997: Digram	•	•	•	•	•	•	•	•	•
Trigram	•	•	•	•	•	•	•	•	•
Tetragram	•	•	•	•	•	•	•	•	•
—Jan to Jun 97: Digram	•	•	•	✔	•	•	✔	•	•
Trigram	•	•	•	—	•	•	—	•	•
Tetragram	•	•	•	—	•	•	—	•	•
—Jul to Dec 97: Digram	•	•	•	•	•	•	•	•	•
Trigram	•	•	•	•	•	•	•	•	•
Tetragram	•	•	•	•	•	•	•	•	•
Temporal Windows									
—1997: Lag-5	•	•	•	•	•	•	•	•	•
Lag-10	•	•	•	•	•	•	•	•	•
Lag-15	•	•	•	•	•	•	•	•	•
Lag-20	•	•	•	•	•	•	•	•	•
—Jan to Jun 97: Lag-5	•	•	•	•	•	•	•	•	•
Lag-10	•	•	•	•	•	•	•	•	•
Lag-15	•	•	•	•	•	•	•	•	•
Lag-20	•	•	•	•	•	•	•	•	•
—Jul to Dec 97: Lag-5	•	•	•	•	•	•	•	•	•
Lag-10	•	•	•	•	•	•	•	•	•
Lag-15	•	•	•	•	•	•	•	•	•
Lag-20	•	•	•	•	•	•	•	•	•
Category Price Transition									
—1997: Digram	•	•	•	•	•	•	•	•	•
Trigram	•	•	•	•	•	•	•	•	•
Tetragram	•	•	•	•	•	•	•	•	•
—Jan to Dec 97: Digram	•	•	•	•	•	•	•	•	•
Trigram	•	•	•	•	•	•	•	•	•
Tetragram	•	•	•	•	•	•	•	•	•
—Jul to Dec 97: Digram	•	•	•	•	•	•	•	•	•
Trigram	•	•	•	•	•	•	•	•	•
Tetragram	•	•	•	•	•	•	•	•	•
Markov Analysis									
—1997: Order-0	•	•	•	•	•	•	•	•	•
Order-1	•	•	•	•	•	•	•	•	•
Order-2	•	•	•	•	•	•	•	•	•
—Jan to Jun 97: Order-0	•	•	•	•	•	•	•	•	•
Order-1	•	•	•	•	•	•	•	•	•
Order-2	•	•	•	✔	•	•	✔	•	•
Order-3	✔	•	✔	—	✔	•	—	•	•
—Jul to Dec 97: Order-0	•	•	•	•	•	•	•	•	•
Order-1	•	•	•	•	•	•	•	•	•
Order-2	•	•	•	•	•	•	•	•	•
Order-3	•	•	•	✔	•	✔	•	•	•

• Significant Result (does not exhibit stationarity or serial independence)

Table 16.3
Summary of Nonparametric Efficiency tests for Asian FX Rates

16.7   Conclusions

All results are summarized in Table 16.3 (= Table 22 in [Los 1998]).

The main conclusions are:

1. All nine currencies - the eight Asian currencies (Hong Kong dollar, Indonesian rupiah, Malaysian ringgit, Philippines peso, Singapore dollar, Thai baht, Taiwan dollar and Japanese Yen), plus the benchmark currency of the Deutschemark - reveal stationarity before the currency turmoil started (i.e. before the 2nd of July, 1997). The Malaysian ringgit (MYR) was the only non-stationary currency in the second half of 1997. However, when all the 1997 data are tested, only the Hong Kong dollar (HKD), the Philippines peso (PHP) and the Taiwan dollar (TWD) and the two benchmark currencies (DEM and JPY) show stationarity.

2. All nine currencies exhibited significant dependencies in both the whole 1997 data set and in each of the half year data sets, in particular, when they were tested for category price change transition matrices and temporal windows. Using the relative price change approach, the price changes of all nine currencies exhibited significant serial dependencies in the whole year data set.

3. Significant trading windows of up to 20 minutes were identifiable throughout 1997. Using Markov analysis, the price changes of all currencies showed significant higher order Markov behavior in both the whole year and half year subset data sets. While the Markov processes were mostly of order-1 and order-2 in the first half of the year, their orders increased to order-2 and order-3 or higher in the second half of the year, exhibiting more complex persistence behavior.

References

Antoniou, A., N. E. and P. Holmes. 1997. Market efficiency, thin trading and nonlinear behavior: Evidence from an emerging market. *European Financial Management*, 3:175–190.

Bollerslev, T. and I. Domowitz. 1993. Trading patterns and prices in the interbank foreign exchange market. *Journal of Finance*, 48:1421–1443.

Boothe, P. and D. Glassman. 1987. The statistical distribution of exchange rates. *Journal of International Economics*, 22:297–319.

Evans, M. 1997. The microstructure of foreign exchange dynamics. Working paper, Georgetown University, Wahington, DC.

Fama, E. 1970. Efficient capital markets: A review of theory and empirical work. *Journal of Finance*, 25:383–417.

Follod, M. 1991. Microstructure theory and the foreign exchange market. *Federal Reserve Bank of St. Louis Review*, 73:52–70.

Goodhart, C.Y., Y. C. and R. Payne. 1997. Calibrating an algorithm for estimating transactions from FX exchange rates. *Journal of International Money and Finance*, 16:921–930.

Hinich, J. 1995. Testing for dependence in the input to a linear times series model. *Journal of Nonparametric Statistics*, 6:205–221.

Kalman, R. 1960. A new approach to linear filtering and prediction. *ASME Journal of Basic Engineering*, 82D:33–45.

Loretan, M. and P. Phillips. 1994. Testing the covariance stationarity of heavy-tailed time series. *Journal of Empirical Finance*, 1:211–248.

Los, C. 1982. Discrete-time martingale convergence results and nonlinear estimation using time-series data. Technical Report 8222, Federal Reserve Bank of New York, New York, NY.

Los, C. 1998. Nonparametric testing of the high-frequency efficiency of asian foreign exchange markets. Working Paper 98-03, Centre for Research in Financial Services, Nanyang Technological University, Singapore.

Ramsey, J. and Z. Zhang. 1997. The analysis of foregn exchange data using waveform dictionaries. *Journal of Empirical Finance*, 4:341–372.

Rogers, L. 1997. Stochastic calculus and markov methods. In Dempster, M. and S. Pliska, editors, *Mathematics of Derivative Securities*, pages 15–40. Cambridge University Press, Cambridge.

Sherry, C. 1992. *The Mathematics of Technical Analysis: Applying Statistics to Trading Stocks*. Probus Publishing Co., Chicago, IL.

17 Term Structure of Interactions of Foreign Exchange Rates

John Moody and Howard Yang

We investigate the term structure of foreign exchange price movements and the interactions between currencies for a set of seven major exchange rates. The techniques used include a multi-scale decomposition (MSD) and independent component analysis (ICA). The proposed MSD facilitates a time-domain term structure analysis via a causal decomposition of the price series. The cross-sectional analysis based on ICA enables the discovery of nonlinear and nongaussian effects in the interactions between the price changes across multiple securities. A full year (1996) of half-hourly exchange rate quotes is analyzed for seven rates against the U.S. Dollar. We find that a term structure is present for currency interactions on multiple time scales ranging from 30 minutes to one week, and find evidence for nonlinearities in the joint distributions of price changes. Our MSD and ICA approach is general, and may have implications for mean-reversion based trading and risk management .

17.1   Introduction

Multi-scale analysis of price movements in the foreign exchange markets has elucidated a number of interesting phenomena for single exchange rates. These include long term memory and fractional integration effects, the existence of trends and mean reverting behaviors, nonlinear effects, and the presence of hierarchical effects in the term structure of volatility. The presence of scaling laws in foreign exchange price movements for individual exchange rates is well documented [Muller et al 1990], and demonstrates that freely-floating currencies exhibit trends, while exchange rates controlled by central banks can be mean-reverting. Nonlinear relationships between price movements at different time scales have been observed by [Bjorn 1994]. Multi-scale analyses of volatility for single securities or exchange rates include the long-term memory model of [Ding et al 1993], the FIGARCH model [Baillie et al 1993], and HARCH models [Muller et al 1995, Dacorogna et al 1998]. These models capture volatility term structure effects that can be attributed to a heterogeneous set of independent volatility components present at different time scales [Andersen and Bollerslev 1996, Dacorogna et al 1998].

In this paper, we investigate the term structure of the *interactions* of multiple foreign exchange price movements for a set of seven major exchange rates. The techniques used include a causal multi-scale decomposition (MSD) and independent component analysis (ICA). The high frequency data set analyzed is a full year (1996) of half-hourly exchange rate quotes for seven currencies against the U.S. Dollar, representing the G-7 countries, plus Australia.

17.2 Term Structure Analysis via Multi-Scale Decomposition

To investigate the interactions between different exchange rates, we first decompose each price series into price movements on a hierarchy of time scales.

A term structure of price movements on four time scales is constructed via a multi-scale decomposition (MSD) of the seven original price series. This proposed decomposition makes use of causal, overlapping band pass filters applied to the price series. These filters are constructed by taking differences of exponential moving averages (EMAs) on time scales of 30 minutes, 2 hours, 8 hours, one day, and one week. The resulting four "oscillators" are mean reverting by construction; the one week moving average contains the long term drift. This approach is motivated by a desire to characterize price movements on a spectrum of time scales using a transformation that (1) is causal, (2) can be recursively updated and (3) yields a complete representation of the original price series. In contrast, wavelet decompositions [Bjorn 1994, Ramsey and Zhang 1995, Ramsey and Zhang 1996] do not satisfy properties (1) and (2).

Define a set of integer time constants $(\tau_0, \tau_1, \cdots, \tau_K)$ measuring the number of 30 minute intervals. For example,

$$(\tau_0, \tau_1, \cdots, \tau_K) = (1, 4, 16, 48, 240). \tag{17.1}$$

These time constants correspond to the time scales of 30 minutes, 2 hours, 8 hours, one day, and one week.

Define $\eta_k = 1/\tau_k$, $k = 0, 1, \cdots, K$. Given a process x_t, we define $K+1$ EMAs of x_t, for $k = 0, 1, \cdots, K$,

$$M_{t,k} = (1 - \eta_k)M_{t-1,k} + \eta_k x_t, \tag{17.2}$$

$$M_{0,k} = x_0. \tag{17.3}$$

Define $N_{t,j} = M_{t,j-1} - M_{t,j}$, $j = 1, \cdots, K$ which is an output of the band pass filter. $N_{t,j}$ is called an oscillator in technical analysis. In this paper, we call $N_{t,j}$ the scale j oscillator. By definition, $\eta_0 = 1$ when $\tau_0 = 1$ and $M_{t,0} = x_t$. We thus obtain a multi-scale decomposition of x_t:

$$x_t = \sum_{j=1}^{K} N_{t,j} + M_{t,K}. \tag{17.4}$$

The decomposition of JPY is shown in Fig. 17.1.

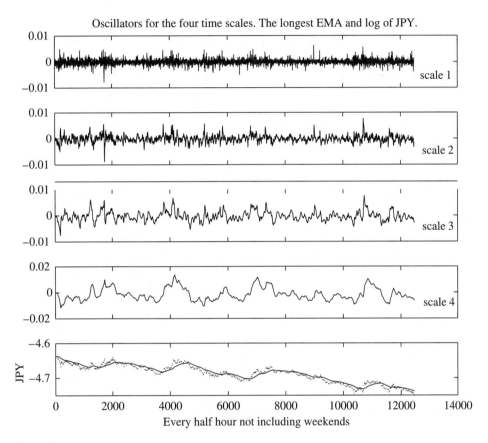

Figure 17.1
The multi-scale decomposition for JPY_USD for a full year of half-hourly data. First four panels: oscillators on the scales (30 minutes, 2hours), (2hours, 8hours), (8hours, 1day) and (1day, 1week). Last panel: the logarithm of the prices (dotted line) and its one week EMA (solid line). The magnitudes of the price movements on the four time scales increases with scale, suggesting the presence of a scaling law similar to those described in [Muller et al 1990, Moody and Wu 1996a].

17.3 Independent Component Analysis

Independent Component Analysis is a technique to transform a set of variables into a new set of variables, so that statistical dependency among the transformed variables is minimized. As pointed out by [Moody and Wu 1996b], ICA is superior to PCA (principle component analysis) for financial data, since it is able to find bases that reduce statistical dependencies, even when the data contains nongaussian innovations and nonlinearities. These bases are typically *non-orthogonal* when the joint distribution of price returns is nongaussian . ICA is sensitive to higher order moments, while PCA has an implicit assumption that the price series are jointly gaussian. The version of ICA that we use here discovers a non-orthogonal basis that minimizes mutual information between basis vectors. Other applications of ICA to financial data include [Wu and Moody 1997, Back and Weigend 1997].

ICA algorithms are nonlinear estimators . A variety of different forms have been proposed. In this paper, we use the following ICA algorithm

$$y_t = W_t x_t,$$
$$W_{t+1} = W_t + \eta(I - f(y_t)y_t)W_t, \tag{17.5}$$

where $\eta > 0$ is a learning rate, the matrix W_t which transforms the input vector x_t to the output vector y_t is updated by the above equation. There are many choices for the nonlinear function $f(\cdot)$ in the ICA algorithm. We choose $f(y) = 2tanh(y)$. The iterative learning process performs a nonlinear optimization . After the learning phase, the components of y_t become statistically independent under certain assumptions.

The above ICA algorithm was derived in [Amari et al 1996, Yang and Amari 1997] by using the natural gradient decent method to maximize entropy [Bell and Sejnowski 1995], to maximize Quasi-likelihood or to minimize mutual information. Different from some conventional ICA algorithms, the algorithm (17.5) does not need to compute the matrix inverse. It is more stable and robust due to the equivariant property [Cardoso and Laheld 1996]. At convergence, we obtain the ICA transform $W = W_\infty$.

Let w_i^T be the i-th row vector of W, v_j be the j-th column vector of W^{-1}. Then, we have two equations

$$y_i(t) = w_i^T x_t, \tag{17.6}$$
$$x_t = y_1(t)v_1 + \cdots + y_n(t)v_n. \tag{17.7}$$

The first equation shows how each ICA component is formed from the observation vector $x(t)$ and the second equation gives the decomposition of the observation vector in terms of the ICA components $y_i(t)$ and the vectors v_i.

Due to the overlap between the frequency responses of the band pass filters, the oscillators are not statistically independent. We use correlation coefficient (CC) and mutual information (MI) to measure the dependency between two random variables. The mutual information is defined by the entropies $H(X)$, $H(Y)$ and $H(X,Y)$:

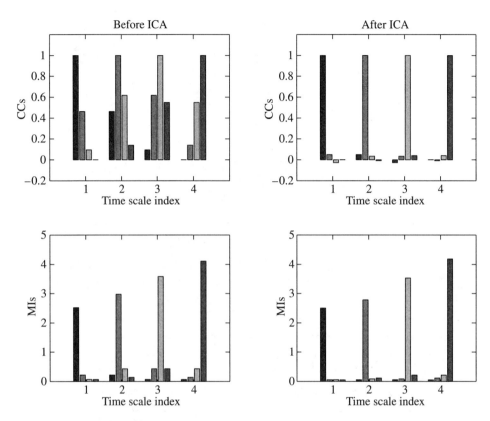

Figure 17.2
Analysis of multi-scale decomposition for USD_JPY. Correlation coefficients (CCs) and mutual information (MI) between oscillators and ICA components. Each of the four bar charts in each panel represents one row of the 4 × 4 correlation or mutual information matrix. Upper panels: on the left, CCs between oscillators; on the right, CCs between ICA components. Lower panels: on the left, MI between oscillators; on the right, MI between ICA components. From the two right panels, we see that the CCs and the MI between the ICA components are reduced.

$$I(X;Y) = H(X) + H(Y) - H(X,Y), \qquad (17.8)$$
$$I(X;X) = H(X). \qquad (17.9)$$

To reduce the dependency between oscillators, we apply the ICA algorithm to process the oscillators. The outputs of the ICA are the new representation of the oscillators.

It is shown by the two left panels in Fig. 17.2 that oscillators on adjacent scales, one and two, two and three, and three and four, are not statistically independent.

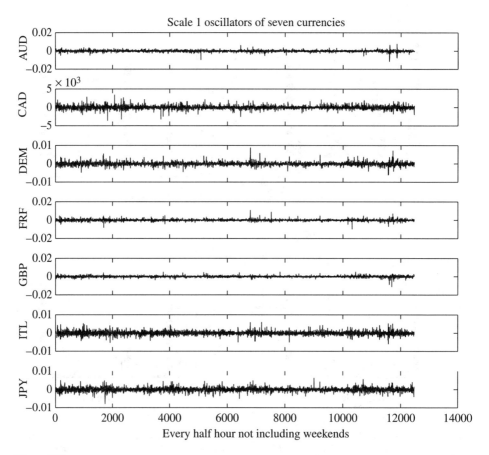

Figure 17.3
Scale1 oscillators (30minutes, 2hours) for the seven currencies during 1996. Note the visible correlation between DEM and FRF, particularly for larger price movements.

Instead, they have positive correlations. This is due to the overlap in frequency responses of the band pass filters at adjacent time scales. Oscillators on scale one and scale four, however, are statistically independent. This is true for all seven currencies, suggesting that half-hourly price movements have little relation to daily price movements.

As shown in the two right panels of Fig. 17.2, ICA can be used to construct statistically independent bases from the oscillators.

17.4   Cross-Sectional Analysis of Exchange Rate Interactions

For each currency, we decompose the logarithm of the price process. On each time scale, we obtain seven oscillators corresponding to the seven currencies. The oscillators on the scales (30minutes, 2hours) and (1day, 1week) are shown in Fig. 17.3 and Fig. 17.4 respectively. The ICA outputs of scale1 oscillators and scale2 oscillators are shown in Fig. 17.5-17.6.

A cross-sectional analysis of price movements across the seven exchange rates is performed for each time scale using independent component analysis. The motivation is to investigate the interaction between FX price movement on a spectrum of time scales. ICA is superior to PCA for financial data, since it is able to find (non-orthogonal) bases that reduce statistical dependencies, even when the data contains nongaussian innovations and nonlinearities [Amari et al 1996, Back and Weigend 1997, Moody and Wu 1996b, Wu and Moody 1997, Yang and Amari 1997].

The correlation coefficients between oscillators and their ICA components are shown in Fig. 17.7 for time scale1 and time scale4. The correlation coefficients are easy to compute, but they only measure the second order statistical dependency between variables. In contrast, the mutual informations are more difficult to compute, but they can measure the higher than second order statistical dependencies. The MI between oscillators on the time scale1 and the time scale4 and their ICA components are shown in Fig. 17.8. At all time scales, the independent components found by ICA correspond to linear combinations of exchange rates that have reduced cross-correlation and mutual information relative to the original quoted rates.

At each time scale, an ICA output is an inner product of a row vector in W and the seven oscillators. The four ICA transforming matrices are shown in Fig. 17.9. We find that a significant statistical dependency exists on all four time scales between the USD_DEM and USD_FRF exchange rates. The dependency is largest for time scales two and three, corresponding to (2 hours, 8 hours) and (8 hours, one day). The level of statistical dependency is higher than we anticipated, considering that the time period shown is for the third year prior to the 1999 European Monetary Union (EMU) and the fixing of the DEM and FRF exchange rate.

The other exchange rates exhibit less mixing after performing ICA. However, some mixing of the Italian Lira with the German Mark and French Franc occurs, with this effect growing larger from scale1 to scale4. This mixing may also be attributable to the pending inclusion of the Lira in the EMU.

The relative mixing of DEM, FRF, and ITL with Australian dollars also increases from scale1 to scale4.

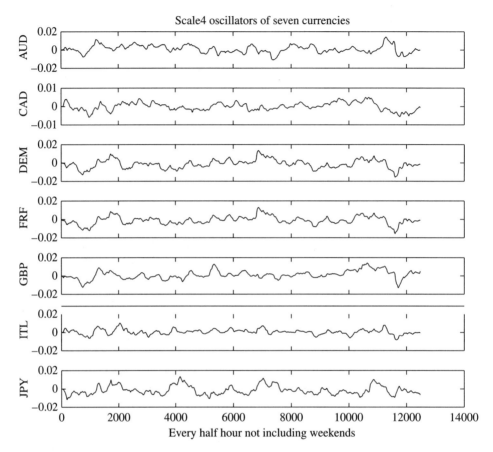

Figure 17.4
Scale4 oscillators (1day, 1week) for the seven currencies during 1996. Note that the correlation between DEM and FRF is substantially stronger at scale4 than for scale1 in Fig. 17.3. The similarity between DEM and FRF price movements at scale4 is striking, especially considering that the time period shown is for the third year prior to the 1999 European Monetary Union and the fixing of the DEM and FRF exchange rate.

The acute angles between row vectors in each ICA transforming matrix are invariant to the scaling of the row vectors. These angles are shown below to indicate the structure of each ICA matrix. The angles less than 90 degrees indicate that the row vectors in the ICA transforming matrices are not orthogonal. In contrast, standard PCA is constrained to find orthogonal bases. The ICA can find non-orthogonal, but statistically independent bases. This is important when data is

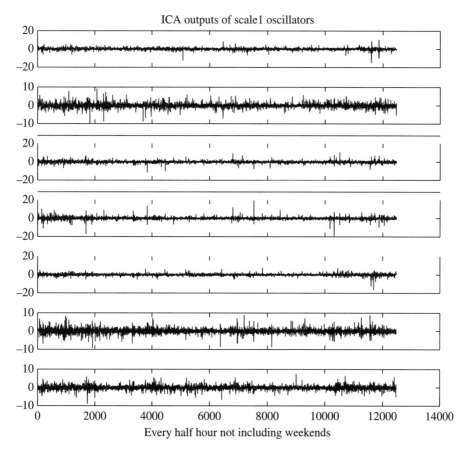

Figure 17.5
ICA outputs of the scale1 oscillators. These ICA components have less statistical dependency than
the original scale1 oscillators, as can be seen by comparing this figure to Fig. 17.3.

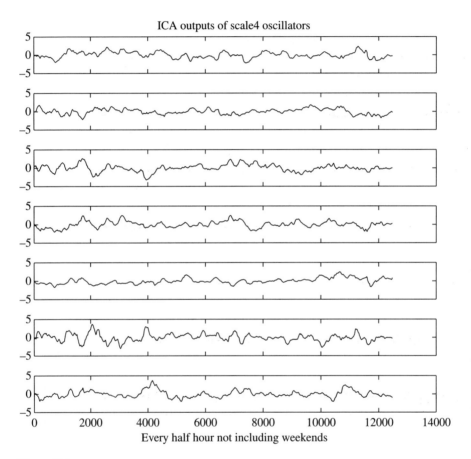

Figure 17.6
ICA outputs of the scale4 oscillators. Note the significant reduction in statistical dependencies between the ICA outputs as compared with the original scale4 oscillators in Fig. 17.4.

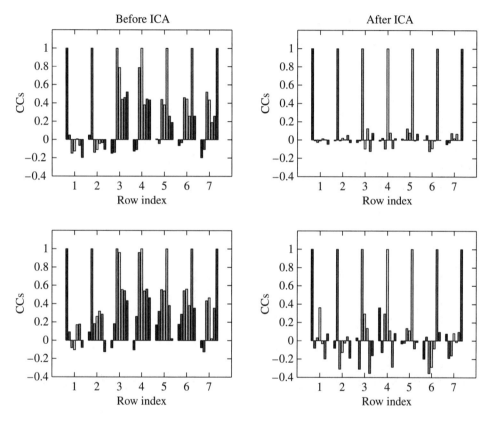

Figure 17.7
Cross-sectional interactions between currencies between time scales one (top) and four (bottom).
Correlation Coefficients (CCs) between oscillators (left) and ICA components (right). Each of the
seven bar charts in each panel represents one row of the 7×7 correlation matrix. Upper-left panel:
CCs of the scale1 oscillators; upper-right: CCs of the ICA components of the scale1 oscillators;
lower-left: CCs of the scale4 oscillators; lower-right: CCs of the ICA components of the scale4
oscillators. We see that the second order correlations between the seven ICA components are
reduced (right side panels). However, many off-diagonal elements remain non-zero, indicating the
presence of nongaussian or nonlinear effects.

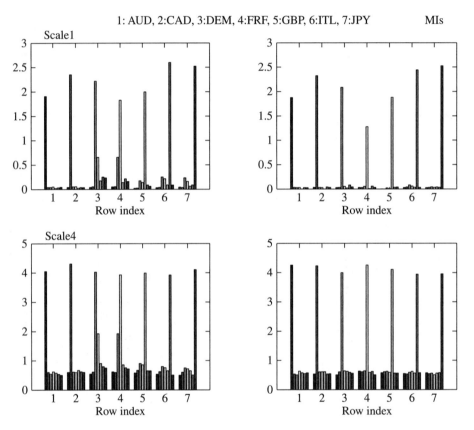

Figure 17.8
Mutual information (MI) between oscillators and ICA components. Each of the seven bar charts in each panel represents one row of the 7 × 7 mutual information matrix. Upper panels: on the left, MI of the scale1 oscillators; on the right, MI of the ICA components of the scale1 oscillators. Lower panels: on the left, MI of the scale4 oscillators; on the right, MI of the ICA components of the scale4 oscillators. We see that the MI between the ICA components are reduced to minimal values (panels on right), demonstrating that ICA discovers a (non-orthogonal) coordinate basis with minimum statistical dependencies.

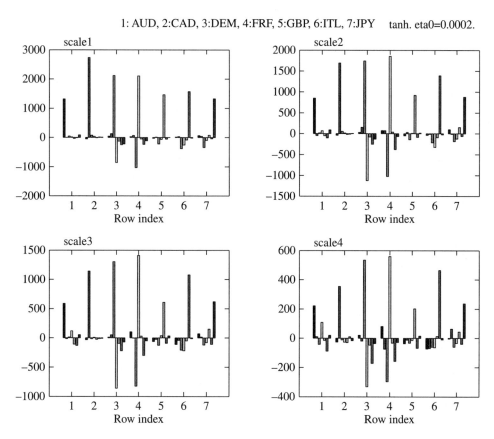

Figure 17.9
ICA transforming matrices for four different time scales. Each of the seven bar charts in each panel represents one row of the 7×7 transformation matrix. A significant statistical dependency exists on all four time scales between the USD_DEM and USD_FRF exchange rates. In order to de-mix them in the ICA outputs, the weights in the transforming matrix corresponding to USD_DEM and USD_FRF have significant amplitudes and opposite signs.

not jointly gaussian. In the following table, the rows and columns correspond to AUD, CAD, DEM, FRF, GBP, ITL, and JPY; W1, W2, W3 and W4 are the ICA transform matrices at the time scales one, two, three and four.

Row index: 1: AUD, 2:CAD, 3:DEM, 4:FRF, 5:GBP, 6:ITL, 7:JPY

Angles between rows in W1:

0	88.0252	87.8402	89.6472	87.2247	89.6040	84.1068
0	0	86.2672	89.2163	89.3675	89.8371	89.7087
0	0	0	44.8840	80.1248	75.7037	73.9604
0	0	0	0	89.4270	81.9216	89.1731
0	0	0	0	0	87.4972	85.1295
0	0	0	0	0	0	89.0944
0	0	0	0	0	0	0

Angles between rows in W2:

0	86.2256	89.5389	84.1909	84.2913	81.5562	79.0015
0	0	85.1356	89.7800	89.5669	88.3052	88.9079
0	0	0	32.5871	79.5670	83.3983	80.5622
0	0	0	0	82.8189	74.3591	88.5497
0	0	0	0	0	83.3489	79.8994
0	0	0	0	0	0	88.9234
0	0	0	0	0	0	0

Angles between rows in W3:

0	86.7148	87.0929	76.9221	77.2090	71.8013	81.6967
0	0	89.2526	88.5595	87.3066	88.5152	89.1955
0	0	0	30.8498	74.8600	79.8011	82.3614
0	0	0	0	78.9374	77.5465	89.7375
0	0	0	0	0	83.4557	73.5124
0	0	0	0	0	0	85.2162
0	0	0	0	0	0	0

Angles between rows in W4:

0	81.1641	72.1332	53.7211	81.7027	63.2201	86.0720
0	0	89.3603	81.0451	80.9511	89.9427	88.6007
0	0	0	37.8581	81.4970	76.6055	79.0215
0	0	0	0	89.0054	76.3747	87.7292
0	0	0	0	0	86.0014	73.1156
0	0	0	0	0	0	87.0230
0	0	0	0	0	0	0

The angles between DEM row vector and FRF row vector in the ICA transforming matrices are 44.9, 32.6, 30.8, and 37.9 degrees at the time scales one, two, three and four respectively. This indicates that the dependency between USD_DEM and USD_FRF is largest for time scales two and three, corresponding to (2 hours, 8 hours) and (8 hours, one day). The other exchange rates exhibit less mixing after performing ICA, however, some mixing of the Italian Lira with the German Mark

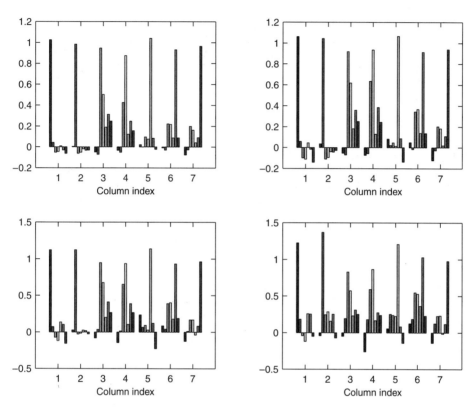

Figure 17.10
The inverse matrices of the ICA transforming matrices for four different time scales, with time scales increasing from the upper left panel to the lower right. Each of the seven bar charts in each panel represents one column of the 7 × 7 inverse transformation matrix. The column vectors of these inverse matrices form the coordinates for projecting the data. The non-orthogonality of these statistically-independent ICA components in readily apparent.

and French Franc occurs. Similarly, some mixing of DEM, FRF and ITL with AUD occurs. In both the ITL and AUD cases, the mixing increases from scale1 to scale4.

The interactions of the various exchange rates are even more striking when the angles between the columns of the inverse matrix W^{-1} is considered. These columns are the ICA vector coordinates in the original bases of observed exchange rates. Small angles between ICA vectors indicate that the statistically-independent bases are *non-orthogonal* in the original space. This is typical for distributions that have nonlinear or nongaussian mixing. One possible source of such nonlinear effects are amplitude-dependent correlations.

Angles between columns in the inverse of W1:

0	86.9156	82.9749	83.9542	88.7891	86.4941	81.2562
0	0	81.2930	82.3348	88.2803	84.8961	85.4126
0	0	0	34.1448	73.5539	55.4683	61.9269
0	0	0	0	76.6256	57.7339	66.6608
0	0	0	0	0	78.7179	86.8001
0	0	0	0	0	0	75.3294
0	0	0	0	0	0	0

Angles between columns in the inverse of W2:

0	83.8679	78.8564	77.7748	82.7605	87.3960	73.5913
0	0	78.1110	78.9783	88.8626	83.0738	84.3503
0	0	0	20.3460	79.6133	43.6727	60.7139
0	0	0	0	82.6094	42.5582	61.3599
0	0	0	0	0	78.4034	84.8164
0	0	0	0	0	0	69.9797
0	0	0	0	0	0	0

Angles between columns in the inverse of W3:

0	84.4834	81.9906	77.6446	70.5469	84.9436	73.9316
0	0	89.5992	89.3966	85.1573	87.7139	88.9647
0	0	0	18.8242	78.4756	39.8028	63.9479
0	0	0	0	83.9305	41.4816	62.9918
0	0	0	0	0	75.2004	77.4348
0	0	0	0	0	0	70.7107
0	0	0	0	0	0	0

Angles between columns in the inverse of W4:

0	81.9495	89.9500	77.9635	75.4924	75.5067	81.1799
0	0	63.5362	64.5720	68.4832	65.2220	80.4639
0	0	0	22.0129	63.8460	35.8967	57.9198
0	0	0	0	68.3177	42.3585	57.7738
0	0	0	0	0	63.2138	89.1352
0	0	0	0	0	0	65.8368
0	0	0	0	0	0	0

It is important to note that the independent components found vary with time scale. The presence of a "term structure of currency interactions" has implications for both trading and risk management. Part of this term structure may reflect geographical or time zone effects.

17.5   Conclusions

We have proposed a new approach for analyzing the term structures of security price movements and the interactions in price movements between multiple securities. The approach makes use of two key techniques: a multi-scale decomposition (MSD) and independent component analysis (ICA).

First, a multi-scale decomposition is performed, which transforms each price series into a set of filtered series corresponding to different time scales. The proposed MSD characterizes price movements on a spectrum of time scales via a transformation that (1) is causal, (2) can be recursively updated and (3) yields a complete representation of the original price series.

Secondly, interactions between price movements of different securities on each time scale are identified via independent component analysis. ICA is superior to PCA (principle component analysis) for financial data, since it is able to discover statistical dependencies not only at second order, but also at higher order moments of the returns. This is important when the joint distribution of returns is non-gaussian or when nonlinearities exist in the price dynamics, leading to amplitude-dependent interactions.

We have investigated the use of these methods for foreign exchange price movements and cross-currency interactions. The data set considered is a full year of half-hourly data for seven exchange rates, representing the G-7 countries, plus Australia. Our empirical investigations have revealed the following:

- Half-hourly price movements have little relation to daily price movements, as measured by correlation coefficient or mutual information. This statistical independence holds for all seven exchange rates examined.

- Significant statistical dependence between the USD_DEM and USD_FRF exchange rates is present during 1996 on all time scales examined. Interactions for this period between USD_ITL and both USD_DEM and USD_FRF are also identified. Statistical dependencies between USD_AUD and several European currencies are observed.

- The magnitude of these European inter-currency interactions is surprising, given that the period studied is the third year prior to the 1999 European Monetary Union and the fixing of the exchange rates between DEM, FRF and ITL.

- ICA is effective in identifying such interactions. The statistically independent components are *non-orthogonal*, indicating nongaussian or nonlinear effects. Interactions between currencies exist at higher moments and are amplitude-dependent.

- The magnitude of all of these statistical dependencies varies with the time scale considered. Hence, we observe a term structure of currency interactions.

The term structure of currency interactions revealed suggests that developing better multi-currency trading , portfolio management, and risk management strategies may require different solutions for different time scales. The nonlinear effects observed via ICA indicate that amplitude dependent interactions must be considered.

Our multi-scale decomposition and independent component analysis approach is general, and can be applied to other classes of securities and to price movement interactions on arbitrary time scales. For example, the type of analysis presented here may facilitate the development of more robust mean reverting trading strategies across security groups (e.g. equities an a particular industry). Our analyses may also enable the development of better strategies for risk management across multiple time scales. In particular, optimal hedging, portfolio management and value-at-risk estimation methods are likely to be time-scale-dependent.

Acknowledgments

We would like to thank Olsen & Associates for providing us with the data sets, and Matthew Saffell for helpful comments.

References

Amari, S., A. Cichocki, and H. H. Yang. 1996. A new learning algorithm for blind signal separation. In *Advances in Neural Information Processing Systems, 8*, eds. David S. Touretzky, Michael C. Mozer and Michael E. Hasselmo, MIT Press: Cambridge, MA., pages 757–763.

Andersen, T. G. and T. Bollerslev. 1996. Heterogeneous information arrivals and return volatility dynamics: uncovering the long-run in high frequency returns. Technical Report 216:1-42, Kellogg Graduate School of Management, Northwestern University.

Back, A. and A. Weigend. 1997. A first application of independent component analysis to extracting structure from stock returns. *Journal of Neuroscience*, 8.

Baillie, R. T., T. Bollerslev, and H.-O. Mikkelsen. 1993. Fractionally integrated generalized autoregressive conditional heteroskedasticity. Technical Report 168:1-24, Kellogg Graduate School of Management, Northwestern University.

Bell, A. J. and T. J. Sejnowski. 1995. An information-maximisation approach to blind separation and blind deconvolution. *Neural Computation*, 7:1129–1159.

Bjorn, V. 1994. Optimal multiresolution decomposition of financial time-series. In *Proceedings of the Conference on Neural Networks in the Capital Markets*, Pasadena.

Cardoso, J.-F. and B. Laheld. 1996. Equivariant adaptive source separation. *IEEE Trans. on Signal Processing*, 44(12):3017–3030.

Dacorogna, M. M., U. A. Muller, R. B. Olsen, and O. V. Pictet. 1998. Modelling short-term volatility with garch and harch models. In Dunis, C. and B. Zhou, editors, *Nonlinear Modelling of High Frequency Financial Time Series*, pages 161–176. John Wiley & Sons, Inc.

Ding, Z., C. W. J. Granger, and R. F. Engle. 1993. A long memory property of stock market returns and a new model. *Journal of Empirical Finance*, 1:83–106.

Moody, J. and L. Wu. 1996a. Improved estimates for the rescaled range and hurst exponents. In Refenes, A., Y. Abu-Mostafa, J. Moody, and A. Weigend, editors, *Neural Networks in Financial Engineering, Proceedings of the London Conference* (October 1995).

Moody, J. and L. Wu. 1996b. What is the True Price? – State Space Models for High Frequency FX Rates . In Shun-ichi Amari, Lei Xu, Laiwan Chan, Irwin King and Kwong-Sak Leung , editor, *Proceedings of the International Conference on Neural Information Processing*, pages 1069–1074. Springer Verlag, Singapore Pte. Ltd.

Muller, U. A., M. M. Dacorogna, R. D. Dave, R. B. Olsen, O. V. Pictet, and J. E. von Weizsacker. 1995. Volatilities of different time resolutions: Analyzing the dynamics of market components. Technical Report UAM.1995-01-12, Olsen & Associates Research Institute for Applied Economics.

Muller, U. A., M. M. Dacorogna, R. B. Olsen, O. V. Pictet, M. Schwatz, and C. Morgenegg. 1990. Statistical study of foreign exchange rate, empirical evidence of a price change scaling law, and intraday analysis. *Journal of Banking and Finance*, 14:1189–1208.

Ramsey, J. B. and Z. Zhang. 1995. The analysis of foreign exchange data using waveform dictionaries. In *Conference on High Frequency Dynamics*. Zurich: Olsen and Associates.

Ramsey, J. B. and Z. Zhang. 1996. The application of wave form dictionaries to stock market index data. In Kadtke, J. and Y. A. Kravtsov, editors, *Predictability of Complex Dynamical Systems*, pages 189–205. Springer-Verlag, New York.

Wu, L. and J. Moody. 1997. Multi-Effect Decompositions for Financial Data Modeling. In *Advances in Neural Information Processing Systems, 9*, eds. Michael C. Mozer, M.I. Jordan and T. Petsche. MIT Press: Cambridge, MA., pages 995–1001.

Yang, H. H. and S. Amari. 1997. Adaptive on-line learning algorithms for blind separation: Maximum entropy and minimum mutual information. *Neural Computation*, 9(7):1457–1482.

18 Exchange Rates and Fundamentals: Evidence from Out-of-Sample Forecasting Using Neural Networks

Min Qi and Yangru Wu

In this paper we employ neural networks to investigate the nonlinear predictability of exchange rates using economic fundamentals. From the four currencies studied, we find that in general the neural network model with market fundamentals cannot beat the random walk model in out-of-sample forecasting accuracy. However when fundamentals are dropped, neural networks show some ability in forecasting and market timing.

18.1 Introduction

It is widely believed among economists that exchange rates are largely unforecastable. In a seminal work, Meese and Rogoff (1983) estimate three linear structural models using monthly data for three dollar exchange rates: the British pound, the German mark and the Japanese yen. They find that in terms of out-of-sample forecasting performance, at the 1-, 6- and 12-month horizons, none of these models can outperform the naive random walk (RW) model without drift even when realized values of explanatory variables are used to form forecasts. Furthermore, they report that neither their two time-series models nor the forward exchange rate appear to improve forecasting. In Meese and Rogoff (1988), they exacerbate these negative results. The poor performance of structural models has indeed led researchers, such as Meese (1986) and Woo (1987) to suggest that speculative bubbles might have driven exchange rates.[1]

Subsequently, a number of researchers have pursued nonlinear modeling of exchange rates, yet the outcomes are also quite negative in general. Engel and Hamilton (1990) argue that exchange rates are subject to changes in regimes and they estimate a Markov switching model for 3 exchange rates. They find, however, that for the mark and the franc, their model yields higher root mean square errors (RMSEs) than the RW model. Engel (1994) extends this work to 13 exchange rates and shows that the Markov model in general does not generate superior forecasts to the RW or to the forward exchange rate.

Diebold and Nason (1990) model nonlinearities in 10 exchange rates by employing a nonparametric technique, and report that their model is unable to improve upon the simple RW model. In an independent work, Meese and Rose (1991) estimate a nonparametric flexible functional form for five structural models and find that

---

1. Theoretically, the issue of whether speculative bubbles can exist in financial markets is subject to much controversy. On the empirical front, mixed results have been produced. For example, West (1987) and Wu (1995) both report no evidence of bubbles.

all models display a general lack of ability to out-predict the RW alternative significantly. These studies constitute very strong evidence against the existence of exchange rate nonlinearities that are exploitable to improve forecasting.

With accumulating evidence documented that exchange rates are essentially unforecastable over short horizons (one year or less), recent researches have focused more on predictability over longer horizons. Mark (1995) finds that at forecast horizons of 3 and 4 years, the flexible-price monetary model produces lower RMSEs than the RW for three out of four currencies in his study. Based on both parametric and nonparametric bootstrap distributions, Mark concludes that for the German mark at the 4-year horizon, his model can beat the RW model at the 5 percent significance level. Chinn and Meese (1995) estimate three structural models using five currencies. They report that for the Japanese yen at the 3-year horizon, all three models correctly predict the direction of changes over 50 percent of the time; and one of the models produces a lower RMSE than the RW. However, results regarding the other four currencies remain largely negative.

In this paper, we re-examine the predictability of exchange rates over the short to medium forecast horizons and ask whether market fundamentals are useful at all in explaining the movements of exchange rates. We share the view with many researchers that standard linear models may be misspecified and hence unable to fully capture exchange rate dynamics. To this end, we deviate from the traditional approach, and employ artificial neural network (NN) technologies to study the forecastability of exchange rates. One main advantage of using the NN method is that NNs are universal approximators which can approximate a large class of functions with a high degree of accuracy, while most of the commonly used nonlinear models cannot. Such a flexible mapping is data based and does not need *a priori* parametric restrictions that are typically needed in traditional econometric modeling.

NN technologies have been increasingly employed to study financial data. Hutchinson, Lo and Poggio (1994), Donaldson and Kamstra (1996), Garcia and Gencay (1999), Gencay (1998), Qi and Maddala (1999) and Qi (1999) are a few of the recent contributions.[2] In the study of exchange rates, Kuan and Liu (1995) use feedforward and recurrent NNs to forecast daily exchange rates and report mixed results. They find NNs with significant market-timing ability and/or significantly lower out-of-sample RMSE relative to the RW in only two out of the five currencies they evaluate. Brooks (1997) uses NN as well as a number of other univariate

---

2. For a comprehensive survey, see Qi (1996).

time series models to forecast daily returns in three exchange rates relative to the British pound. His preferred NN model shows a modest improvement over the RW model, but has no significant market-timing ability. Gencay (1999) demonstrates that using NN, simple technical trading rules can provide significant forecast improvements for the daily returns of five exchange rates over the RW. Hu et al. (1999) document superior performance of NN using weekly exchange rate between the British pound and the dollar. Compared to the negative findings of Diebold and Nason (1990), these results suggest that NN may be more suitable than the non-parametric method for daily or weekly prediction. These studies, however, include no fundamentals as candidate explanatory variables in the forecast equation and are therefore essentially nonlinear univariate time series analysis in nature. This paper differs from the aforementioned studies in that our choices of explanatory variables are guided by economic theory. We employ a lower frequency data set (monthly) to explore a possible nonlinear relationship between exchange rates and fundamentals, in an attempt to address the issues of whether the unpredictability is caused by limitations of the linear specification and whether economic fundamentals are useful in explaining exchange rate movements. Our paper thus complements the existing studies, and in particular, offers an interesting comparison to Meese and Rose (1991) who employ a nonparametric method to predict monthly exchange rates with fundamentals.

The remainder of this paper is organized as follows. Section II provides some simple theoretical background on exchange rate determination and motivates our empirical specifications. In Section III, we introduce the NN methodology and describe various statistics to be employed to test for the forecastability of exchange rates. Section IV describes the data and reports the empirical results. Concluding remarks are offered in Section V.

18.2   Some Simple Theoretical Motivations

We employ a simple version of the monetary model of exchange rate determination, popularized by Bilson (1978), to motive our empirical work and to guide our choice of forecasting variables. Within this model, it is assumed that both the domestic and foreign countries have a transactions-type money demand function and that both countries have the same income elasticity and interest rate semi-elasticity. Combining the money-market equilibrium conditions for the two countries yields:

$$m_t - p_t = a_0 + a_1 y_t - a_2 r_t, \tag{18.1}$$

where m_t, p_t, and y_t are, respectively, natural logarithms of relative money supply, relative price level and relative real income between the domestic and foreign countries; r_t is their interest rate differential. Assuming that purchasing power parity holds[3], we obtain:

$$s_t = m_t - a_0 - a_1 y_t + a_2 r_t, \qquad (18.2)$$

where s_t is the logarithm of exchange rate (domestic currency price of one unit foreign currency).

It is well documented that Equation (2) does not hold on a period-by-period basis and that deviations from this simple relationship can be quite persistent due to, for example, nominal rigidities. However, over time there may exist a tendency for the exchange rate to gradually revert to its fundamental value in response to either nominal or real shocks, and hence market fundamentals may contain useful information in forecasting changes in future exchange rates. We follow Mark (1995) by postulating that the h-period ahead change in exchange rate is related to its current deviation from the fundamental value, namely:

$$s_{t+h} - s_t = b_h + c_h(m_t - a_0 - a_1 y_t + a_2 r_t - s_t) + \varepsilon_{t+h}, \qquad (18.3)$$

where b_h and c_h are regression parameters and ε_{t+h} is the forecast error.

Equation (3) thus provides some guidance for our forecasting experiment. It shows that the h-period ahead exchange rate should be related to the current level of the exchange rate, as well as three monetary variables, all observable at time t. In our forecasting exercises below, we choose $(s_t, m_t, y_t, r_t)'$ as our parsimonious information set. We then estimate a set of NN specifications that are highly nonlinear and of flexible functional form using these variables as explanatory variables to explain s_{t+h}. We will also estimate a simple linear regression model (LR) using these same fundamentals, and compare the forecast accuracy of our NN models with this benchmark model, as well as with the naive RW model and a neural network model without monetary fundamentals.

18.3   Empirical Methodology

NNs are a class of flexible nonlinear models inspired by the way that the human brain processes information. Given an appropriate number of hidden-layer units,

---

3. For recent empirical studies supporting purchasing power parity under the current float, see Wu (1996), among others.

NNs can approximate any nonlinear (or linear) function to an arbitrary degree of accuracy through the composition of a network of relatively simple functions (see Hornik, Stinchcombe and White, 1989, and White, 1990, among others). The flexibility and simplicity of NNs have made them a popular modeling and forecasting tool across different research areas in recent years.

There are various kinds of NNs, among which the three-layer feedforward network is most widely used and is adopted in the present study. Let f be the unknown underlying function (linear or nonlinear) through which a vector of input variables $X = (x_1, x_2, \ldots, x_k)'$ explains the output variable s, i.e.,

$$s = f(X), \tag{18.4}$$

where for simplicity superfluous time subscripts are omitted. Then f can be approximated by a three-layer NN model that can be written as a linear sum of logistic functions:

$$f(X) = \alpha_0 + \sum_{j=1}^{n} \alpha_j g(\sum_{i=1}^{k} \beta_{ij} x_i + \beta_{0j}) + \varepsilon, \tag{18.5}$$

where n is the number of units in the hidden layer, k is the number of input variables, g is a logistic transfer function defined as $g(x) = \frac{1}{1+\exp(-x)}$, $\{\alpha_j, j = 0, 1, \ldots, n\}$ represents a vector of coefficients (weights) from the hidden- to the output-layer units, $\{\beta_{ij}, i = 0, 1, \ldots, k, j = 0, 1, \ldots, n\}$ denotes a matrix of coefficients from the input- to the hidden-layer units, and ε is the error term. The error term can be made arbitrarily small if n is chosen to be large enough. However, if n is too large, the NN may overfit in which case the in-sample errors can be very small but the out-of-sample errors may be large. The choice of n is data dependent and there exists no general rule for predetermining the optimal number of hidden-layer units. Thus, we perform a sensitivity analysis with respect to n by exploring a wide range from 1 to 10.

For a given data set with T observations, the out-of-sample forecasts for a given horizon h are constructed by first estimating the NN model (5) with data up through time $t_0 < T$, so that the last observation used is (s_{t_0}, X_{t_0-h}). Let $(\hat{\alpha}_{t_0}^h, \hat{\beta}_{t_0}^h)$ be the coefficients estimated with these observations. The first h-horizon forecast is

$$\hat{s}_{t_0+h} = \hat{\alpha}_{0,t_0}^h + \sum_{j=1}^{n} \hat{\alpha}_{j,t_0}^h g(\sum_{i=1}^{k} \hat{\beta}_{ij,t_0}^h x_{i,t_0} + \hat{\beta}_{0j,t_0}^h). \tag{18.6}$$

This procedure is repeated for $t_0 + 1, t_0 + 2, \ldots, T - h$, thus yielding N forecasts, where $N = T - t_0 - h + 1$. Forecast accuracy is measured by the RMSE. To test whether the forecasts from two competing models are equally accurate, we use the Diebold and Mariano (1995, DM) test for the significance of the difference between the squared forecast errors of the two models. We also employ Wilcoxon's signed-ranks test (SR) to compare forecast accuracy. The benefit of the SR test lies in that it assigns a higher weight to an observation with a larger absolute square error differential than to an observation with a smaller differential. To compare the market-timing ability of alternative forecasts, we use the direction accuracy (DA) to measure the percentage of correct prediction in direction changes. The significance of market-timing ability of alternative models is tested by the non-parametric Pesaran and Timmermann (1992, PT) test.

18.4   Data and Empirical Results

All data are monthly and are obtained from IMF's *International Financial Statistics*. Our sample starts in March 1973, the same as in Meese and Rogoff (1983), and ends in July 1997 with 293 observations. We choose exchange rates between the U.S. dollar and the Japanese yen, the Deutsche mark, the British pound and the Canadian dollar. The Japanese yen, the Deutsche mark and the British pound along with the U.S. dollar form the core currencies in the world economy. The Canadian dollar is chosen because of Canada's close economic tie to the United States. Exchange rates are end-of-month U.S. dollar prices of the foreign currencies. Variables chosen to proxy market fundamentals are as follows. We measure money supply by M1, and real income by industrial production in each of the countries. As for interest rates, we use Treasury-bill rates for Britain, Canada and the U.S. (line 60c). Treasury-bill rate data are not available for Japan and are available for Germany only from July 1975. Therefore, for these two countries, we use call money rates (line 60b) as an alternative measure of interest rate.

To make our study comparable to Meese and Rogoff (1983, 1988) and others, the forecast horizons, h, are chosen to be 1, 6 and 12 months. All forecasting exercises are carried out using the "rolling regression" technique, where we use data from the beginning of the sample up to the month of the forecast to estimate model parameters. At each horizon, our out-of-sample forecast covers the period from January 1990 through July 1997 with 91 months.[4] For each currency, we use *ex ante* observations of the fundamentals, $X = (s_t, m_t, y_t, r_t)'$ as the explanatory

---

4. Economic theory provides little guidance on how to choose an "optimal" forecasting period in a given sample. Our "rule of thumb" here is that we use roughly the first 2/3 of the sample to estimate the first rolling regression and the remaining 1/3 for out-of-sample forecasting.

vector to estimate a set of ten NN specifications of S_{t+h}. We choose 1-10 hidden units so as to check for robustness of the results and to avoid a possible model selection bias. For comparison, we use three benchmark models: the simple RW without drift, a neural network model without monetary fundamentals (NN1), and the linear model with X as the explanatory vector (LR).

Tables 18.1 through 18.4 report the empirical results for the four currencies, respectively. Each table is organized as follows. For the three tests, namely, Pesaran-Timmermann (PT), Diebold-Mariano (DM) and signed-ranks (SR), we report only their p-values, defined as the significance levels at which the null hypothesis under investigation can be rejected. In implementing the DM test, we use two fixed lags, 0 and 24, as well as Andrews' (1991) optimal truncation lag to estimate the spectral density at frequency zero, but only report the results obtained with Andrews' lag to economize on space. Columns (1)-(4) report results for the random walk model (RW), and the NN model with monetary fundamentals at each of the ten levels of complexity. Columns (5)-(8) display results for the linear monetary model (LR), and the neural network model without market fundamentals (NN1). For each of these models, we report the RMSE (in percentage terms). For all models except the RW, a measure of market-timing ability, the direction accuracy (DA), is also reported along with the PT test for the significance of this measure. As for the RW, since it has no market-timing ability by definition and the PT test is not well defined, no PT test result is reported. Columns (9)-(10) compare the performance of our NN model with the RW, where we use, respectively, the DM and SR tests to test for the null hypothesis that the square forecast error using the RW model is larger than that using the NN. Organized in the same manner, Columns (11)-(12) exhibit the results to test the null hypothesis that the RW model yields a larger square forecast error than the NN1 model. We discuss the results currency by currency as follows.

The Japanese yen (Table 18.1). It is apparent that our NN model cannot beat the simple RW in terms of out-of-sample forecasting accuracy at any horizon, in that at all ten levels of complexity, the NN model produces higher RMSEs than those of the RW. Indeed, in most cases, the NN yields significantly higher forecast errors than the RW, as can be seen in Columns (9)-(10).[5] Second, Columns (11)-(12) show that the NN1 also does not seem to improve forecasting over the RW.

---

5. In Columns (9)-(10), a p-value no greater than 0.05 indicates that the NN yields a lower forecast error than the RW at the 5 percent significance level, while a p-value no smaller than 0.95 means that the NN produces a higher forecast error at the 5 percent level. Similar interpretation can be given for the p-values reported in Columns (11)-(12).

Table 18.1
Out-of-Sample Performance for the Japanese Yen

The table reports the performance measures of alternative forecasting models and the p-values of various test statistics. Columns (1)-(4) are results for the random walk (RW), and the neural network model with monetary fundamentals (NN). Columns (5)-(8) show results for the linear monetary model (LR) and the neural network without market fundamentals (NN1). "RMSE" is the root mean square error; "DA" is direction accuracy; and "PT" is the p-value of the Pesaran-Timmermann test. Columns (9)-(10) compare the NN and RW models with the Diebold-Mariano (DM) and the signed-rank (SR) tests. Columns (11)-(12) compare the RW and NN1 models.

(1) Model	(2) RMSE (%)	(3) DA (%)	(4) PT	(5) Model	(6) RMSE (%)	(7) DA (%)	(8) PT	(9) RW-NN DM	(10) SR	(11) RW-NN1 DM	(12) SR
Panel A 1-month horizon											
RW	3.22	–	–	LR	3.21	56.04	0.1013				
NN				NN1							
n = 1	3.47	50.55	0.4237	n = 1	3.40	47.25	0.6975	0.9292	0.9446	0.9418	0.9680
n = 2	3.65	50.55	0.3934	n = 2	3.39	46.15	0.7709	0.9925	0.9890	0.9465	0.9819
n = 3	3.67	50.55	0.4159	n = 3	3.39	45.05	0.8289	0.9965	0.9937	0.9554	0.9829
n = 4	3.72	46.15	0.7876	n = 4	3.38	45.05	0.8289	0.9998	0.9983	0.9624	0.9875
n = 5	4.03	47.25	0.7031	n = 5	3.42	45.05	0.8279	1.0000	0.9994	0.9703	0.9899
n = 6	3.86	53.85	0.1995	n = 6	3.36	45.05	0.8279	0.9999	0.9940	0.9565	0.9905
n = 7	4.26	42.86	0.9269	n = 7	3.42	45.05	0.8273	1.0000	1.0000	0.9714	0.9880
n = 8	4.36	45.05	0.8342	n = 8	3.38	48.35	0.6255	1.0000	1.0000	0.9596	0.9481
n = 9	4.13	50.55	0.4338	n = 9	3.42	46.15	0.7752	1.0000	0.9999	0.9725	0.9872
n =10	4.53	46.15	0.7703	n = 10	3.43	50.55	0.4628	1.0000	1.0000	0.9371	0.9246
Panel B 6-month horizon											
RW	8.93	–	–	LR	8.43	65.93	0.0003				
NN				NN1							
n = 1	9.89	49.45	0.4580	n = 1	9.84	37.36	0.9911	0.7698	0.9839	0.9637	1.0000
n = 2	12.53	42.86	0.9120	n = 2	11.02	34.07	0.9988	0.9999	1.0000	0.9609	1.0000
n = 3	11.25	54.95	0.0609	n = 3	11.11	39.56	0.9785	0.9670	0.9997	0.9846	1.0000
n = 4	14.67	59.34	0.0068	n = 4	11.18	40.66	0.9683	0.9892	1.0000	0.9834	1.0000
n = 5	15.33	50.55	0.3218	n = 5	11.19	41.76	0.9548	1.0000	1.0000	0.9869	1.0000
n = 6	14.59	60.44	0.0100	n = 6	11.13	41.76	0.9620	0.9999	1.0000	0.9858	1.0000
n = 7	15.31	50.55	0.3366	n = 7	11.05	48.35	0.7013	1.0000	1.0000	0.9806	0.9999
n = 8	16.83	49.45	0.4685	n = 8	11.51	42.86	0.9377	1.0000	1.0000	0.9981	1.0000
n = 9	19.82	45.05	0.7885	n = 9	11.04	43.96	0.9032	1.0000	1.0000	0.9918	0.9999
n =10	21.92	38.46	0.9849	n = 10	15.57	47.25	0.7478	1.0000	1.0000	0.9980	1.0000
Panel C 12-month horizon											
RW	11.68	–	–	LR	11.00	72.53	0.0000				
NN				NN1							
n = 1	17.43	45.05	0.2071	n = 1	13.91	23.08	1.0000	0.9235	0.9993	0.9956	1.0000
n = 2	19.15	47.25	0.1754	n = 2	17.74	28.57	1.0000	0.9953	1.0000	0.9773	1.0000
n = 3	22.39	42.86	0.3116	n = 3	16.75	30.77	1.0000	0.9981	1.0000	0.9893	1.0000
n = 4	20.27	58.24	0.0088	n = 4	17.52	35.16	0.9999	0.9108	0.9978	0.9911	1.0000
n = 5	19.22	72.53	0.0000	n = 5	17.67	36.26	0.9998	0.9630	0.9223	0.9922	1.0000
n = 6	18.96	73.63	0.0000	n = 6	17.55	36.26	0.9998	0.9822	0.9188	0.9914	1.0000
n = 7	20.77	57.14	0.0418	n = 7	23.16	35.16	0.9999	0.9999	1.0000	0.9895	1.0000
n = 8	21.77	61.54	0.0015	n = 8	17.48	35.16	0.9998	0.9999	1.0000	0.9936	1.0000
n = 9	24.22	59.34	0.0060	n = 9	17.81	38.46	0.9996	1.0000	1.0000	0.9882	1.0000
n =10	30.91	47.25	0.4020	n = 10	22.70	38.46	0.9985	0.9999	1.0000	0.9977	1.0000

Table 18.2
Out-of-Sample Performance for the Deutsche Mark

The table reports the performance measures of alternative forecasting models and the p-values of various test statistics. Columns (1)-(4) are results for the random walk (RW), and the neural network model with monetary fundamentals (NN). Columns (5)-(8) show results for the linear monetary model (LR) and the neural network without market fundamentals (NN1). "RMSE" is the root mean square error; "DA" is direction accuracy; and "PT" is the p-value of the Pesaran-Timmermann test. Columns (9)-(10) compare the NN and RW models with the Diebold-Mariano (DM) and the signed-rank (SR) tests. Columns (11)-(12) compare the RW and NN1 models.

(1) Model	(2) RMSE	(3) DA (%)	(4) PT	(5) Model	(6) RMSE (%)	(7) DA (%)	(8) PT	(9) RW-NN DM	(10) RW-NN SR	(11) RW-NN1 DM	(12) RW-NN1 SR
Panel A 1-month horizon											
RW	3.16	–	–	LR	3.20	49.45	0.5779				
NN				NN1							
n = 1	3.43	45.05	0.7961	n = 1	3.35	45.05	0.7272	0.9313	0.9975	0.8731	0.9939
n = 2	3.60	43.96	0.8152	n = 2	3.31	45.05	0.7272	0.9877	0.9977	0.8509	0.9920
n = 3	3.67	47.25	0.6875	n = 3	3.29	46.15	0.6135	0.9981	0.9986	0.8363	0.9908
n = 4	3.67	39.56	0.9701	n = 4	3.30	48.35	0.4154	0.9982	0.9993	0.9099	0.9905
n = 5	3.66	47.25	0.6100	n = 5	3.30	48.35	0.4154	0.9846	0.9936	0.9096	0.9903
n = 6	3.72	49.45	0.5000	n = 6	3.29	48.35	0.4154	0.9953	0.9941	0.9018	0.9872
n = 7	3.72	47.25	0.6875	n = 7	3.33	47.25	0.5000	0.9947	0.9892	0.9456	0.9959
n = 8	3.58	60.44	0.0235	n = 8	3.39	42.86	0.8770	0.9458	0.5939	0.9911	0.9997
n = 9	3.80	58.24	0.0626	n = 9	3.42	45.05	0.7556	0.9845	0.8653	0.9771	0.9997
n =10	3.95	49.45	0.5648	n = 10	3.46	46.15	0.6528	0.9960	0.9937	0.9903	0.9996
Panel B 6-month horizon											
RW	8.39	–	–	LR	9.30	49.45	0.6584				
NN				NN1							
n = 1	8.58	58.24	0.0379	n = 1	9.02	54.95	0.0279	0.5883	0.7787	0.7542	0.9396
n = 2	10.68	58.24	0.0379	n = 2	9.23	54.95	0.0279	0.9588	0.9945	0.8058	0.9442
n = 3	11.99	42.86	0.9332	n = 3	9.28	54.95	0.0279	0.9985	1.0000	0.8230	0.9477
n = 4	12.35	47.25	0.7156	n = 4	9.48	54.95	0.0279	0.9999	1.0000	0.8378	0.9549
n = 5	13.45	45.05	0.8246	n = 5	9.33	53.85	0.0668	1.0000	1.0000	0.8404	0.9691
n = 6	14.79	50.55	0.4812	n = 6	10.30	50.55	0.3085	0.9982	1.0000	0.9271	0.9950
n = 7	18.59	52.75	0.3168	n = 7	10.27	54.95	0.0647	0.9973	1.0000	0.9588	0.9958
n = 8	18.19	53.85	0.2370	n = 8	10.55	43.96	0.8880	0.9993	1.0000	0.9599	0.9999
n = 9	17.51	45.05	0.8504	n = 9	11.09	47.25	0.6635	0.9999	1.0000	0.9860	0.9999
n =10	20.54	43.96	0.8809	n = 10	11.11	47.25	0.6635	0.9882	1.0000	0.9837	0.9999
Panel C 12-month horizon											
RW	10.96	–	–	LR	12.70	50.55	0.4703				
NN				NN1							
n = 1	11.26	63.74	0.0001	n = 1	13.02	52.75	0.0233	0.6335	0.5939	0.9613	0.9996
n = 2	21.18	31.87	0.9999	n = 2	13.36	52.75	0.0233	0.9534	1.0000	0.9622	0.9999
n = 3	27.42	31.87	0.9999	n = 3	13.30	52.75	0.0233	0.9993	1.0000	0.9486	0.9995
n = 4	27.18	30.77	1.0000	n = 4	13.35	52.75	0.0233	1.0000	1.0000	0.9491	0.9995
n = 5	30.64	26.37	1.0000	n = 5	13.44	52.75	0.0233	1.0000	1.0000	0.9545	0.9997
n = 6	28.37	43.96	0.8727	n = 6	13.48	52.75	0.0233	0.9998	1.0000	0.9578	0.9998
n = 7	28.25	35.16	0.9977	n = 7	13.50	52.75	0.0233	1.0000	1.0000	0.9579	0.9998
n = 8	23.54	40.66	0.9620	n = 8	13.52	52.75	0.0233	1.0000	1.0000	0.9598	0.9998
n = 9	26.71	38.46	0.9861	n = 9	13.55	52.75	0.0233	0.9997	1.0000	0.9625	0.9999
n =10	27.03	32.97	0.9994	n = 10	13.56	52.75	0.0233	1.0000	1.0000	0.9644	0.9999

Third, the LR model, on the other hand, produces a lower RMSE than the RW at the 6- and 12-month horizons, consistent with the pattern documented by Mark (1995). However, this pattern does not exist for either the NN or the NN1 model. Indeed, as the forecast horizon is lengthened, both neural models perform worse and appear to be overfitted when the level of complexity increases. Four, the NN model has some market-timing ability at the 6- and 12-month horizons. In particular, at the 12-month horizon, when the number of hidden units is between 4 and 9, the DA measure is well above 50 percent, and sometimes as high as 74 percent. Statistically, this measure is better than pure chance at the 5 or 1 percent significance level. This result is in contrast with Engel (1994) who finds that using a Markov switching model, at the 12-month forecast horizon, the average DA for 13 exchange rates is only 52 percent and it is not statistically significant.

The Deutsche mark (Table 18.2). These results are quite similar to those for the Japanese yen, in that neural models in general produce higher forecasting errors than the RW at all horizons. In particular, the NN model with market fundamentals performs poorer at longer horizons and is much overfitted for larger n. At the 6- and 12-month horizons, the NN1 model has some market-timing ability, with statistically significant DA measures ranging between 53 and 55 percent.

The British pound (Table 18.3). While the NN model continues to perform poorly, interestingly, the NN1 model in general is able to produce a lower RMSE than both the RW and LR models. Indeed, except for $n = 1$ at the 1-month horizon, the RMSE from NN1 is lower than that of the RW for all other levels of complexity and at all horizons. In terms of statistical significance, however, we find that the NN1 model beats the RW only in a few cases. In particular, using the DM test, NN1 yields a lower RMSE at the 10 percent level for $n = 7$ at the 6-month horizon and for $n = 2$ at the 12-month horizon, and at the 5 percent level for $n = 1$ at the 12-month horizon. Results are somewhat stronger based on the SR test. Namely, NN1 outperforms the RW model at the 10 percentage level at the 6-month horizon for $n = 4$, 5, and 7, and at the 5 percent level at the 12-month horizon for $n = 1$ and 2.

The Canadian dollar (Table 18.4). The pattern for the Canadian dollar is quite similar to that for the British pound. Namely, the NN1 model yields a lower RMSE than that of the RW for n below 7 at the 1- and 12-month horizons, and for all n at the 6-month horizon. None of the results are, however, statistically significant. Furthermore, at the 1-month horizon, NN1 shows some significant market-timing ability.

Table 18.3
Out-of-Sample Performance for the British Pound

The table reports the performance measures of alternative forecasting models and the p-values of various test statistics. Columns (1)-(4) are results for the random walk (RW), and the neural network model with monetary fundamentals (NN). Columns (5)-(8) show results for the linear monetary model (LR) and the neural network without market fundamentals (NN1). "RMSE" is the root mean square error; "DA" is direction accuracy; and "PT" is the p-value of the Pesaran-Timmermann test. Columns (9)-(10) compare the NN and RW models with the Diebold-Mariano (DM) and the signed-rank (SR) tests. Columns (11)-(12) compare the RW and NN1 models.

(1) Model	(2) RMSE (%)	(3) DA (%)	(4) PT	(5) Model	(6) RMSE (%)	(7) DA (%)	(8) PT	(9) RW-NN DM	(10) RW-NN SR	(11) RW-NN1 DM	(12) RW-NN1 SR
Panel A 1-month horizon											
RW	3.20	–	–	LR	3.27	50.55	0.4025				
NN				NN1							
n = 1	3.34	50.55	0.4025	n = 1	3.22	43.96	0.8846	0.9354	0.9194	0.9135	0.9502
n = 2	3.29	46.15	0.7107	n = 2	3.18	53.85	0.2784	0.9967	0.9945	0.2500	0.3970
n = 3	3.43	48.35	0.6005	n = 3	3.19	52.75	0.3556	0.9603	0.9332	0.2985	0.4779
n = 4	3.53	42.86	0.9141	n = 4	3.19	51.65	0.4291	0.9857	0.9836	0.3584	0.4795
n = 5	3.41	46.15	0.8210	n = 5	3.19	51.65	0.4291	0.9800	0.9861	0.3767	0.5126
n = 6	3.46	45.05	0.8609	n = 6	3.19	52.75	0.3487	0.9693	0.9854	0.3679	0.5032
n = 7	3.46	43.96	0.9096	n = 7	3.19	50.55	0.4832	0.9832	0.9968	0.3667	0.6582
n = 8	3.58	40.66	0.9756	n = 8	3.19	51.65	0.4037	0.9457	0.9964	0.3903	0.3728
n = 9	3.68	45.05	0.8853	n = 9	3.20	51.65	0.4122	0.9866	0.9958	0.5121	0.6257
n =10	3.57	45.05	0.8768	n = 10	3.19	47.25	0.7200	0.9918	0.9966	0.3965	0.8319
Panel B 6-month horizon											
RW	8.44	–	–	LR	8.71	51.65	0.2941				
NN				NN1							
n = 1	9.02	52.75	0.2052	n = 1	8.37	53.85	0.1342	0.9311	0.9705	0.3548	0.2966
n = 2	9.06	48.35	0.1188	n = 2	7.93	56.04	0.3188	0.7089	0.9926	0.1450	0.3535
n = 3	9.90	52.75	0.0668	n = 3	7.84	61.54	0.0882	0.9709	0.9994	0.1185	0.1255
n = 4	9.39	46.15	0.2003	n = 4	7.80	62.64	0.0618	0.8145	0.9988	0.1021	0.0771
n = 5	10.84	48.35	0.3775	n = 5	7.82	62.64	0.0618	0.9689	1.0000	0.1075	0.0924
n = 6	11.81	46.15	0.5060	n = 6	7.81	60.44	0.1213	0.9723	1.0000	0.1138	0.1255
n = 7	12.47	39.56	0.8787	n = 7	7.73	62.64	0.0410	0.9592	1.0000	0.0938	0.0861
n = 8	11.42	48.35	0.6174	n = 8	7.84	52.75	0.4611	0.9281	0.9999	0.1298	0.4154
n = 9	13.04	43.96	0.8547	n = 9	7.82	56.04	0.2778	0.9988	1.0000	0.1253	0.3360
n =10	11.85	49.45	0.5077	n = 10	7.88	54.95	0.3359	0.9927	0.9999	0.1493	0.3743
Panel C 12-month horizon											
RW	10.26	–	–	LR	10.29	39.56	0.9831				
NN				NN1							
n = 1	10.76	38.46	0.9887	n = 1	9.50	62.64	0.0081	0.6912	0.9984	0.0124	0.0000
n = 2	10.45	65.93	0.0010	n = 2	9.72	58.24	0.0546	0.5460	0.5923	0.0882	0.0132
n = 3	12.62	56.04	0.1427	n = 3	9.93	49.45	0.4981	0.8603	0.9268	0.2939	0.4984
n = 4	11.88	63.74	0.0034	n = 4	9.88	54.95	0.1501	0.8719	0.8197	0.2923	0.3345
n = 5	14.63	48.35	0.5878	n = 5	9.88	54.95	0.1501	0.9677	0.9998	0.2896	0.3374
n = 6	16.33	56.04	0.1363	n = 6	9.91	53.85	0.2012	0.9379	0.9994	0.3085	0.3894
n = 7	15.37	60.44	0.0248	n = 7	9.90	54.95	0.1429	0.9468	0.9935	0.3083	0.3623
n = 8	15.16	57.14	0.0876	n = 8	9.93	56.04	0.1028	0.9706	0.9868	0.3216	0.4138
n = 9	16.44	51.65	0.4037	n = 9	9.99	53.85	0.1926	0.9811	0.9999	0.3550	0.5158
n =10	16.85	56.04	0.1284	n = 10	10.01	52.75	0.2522	0.9913	0.9960	0.3617	0.5582

Table 18.4
Out-of-Sample Performance for the Canadian Dollar

The table reports the performance measures of alternative forecasting models and the p-values of various test statistics. Columns (1)-(4) are results for the random walk (RW), and the neural network model with monetary fundamentals (NN). Columns (5)-(8) show results for the linear monetary model (LR) and the neural network without market fundamentals (NN1). "RMSE" is the root mean square error; "DA" is direction accuracy; and "PT" is the p-value of the Pesaran-Timmermann test. Columns (9)-(10) compare the NN and RW models with the Diebold-Mariano (DM) and the signed-rank (SR) tests. Columns (11)-(12) compare the RW and NN1 models.

(1) Model	(2) RMSE (%)	(3) DA (%)	(4) PT	(5) Model	(6) RMSE (%)	(7) DA (%)	(8) PT	(9) RW-NN DM	(10) SR	(11) RW-NN1 DM	(12) SR
Panel A 1-month horizon											
RW	1.22	—	—	LR	1.19	59.34	0.1004				
NN				NN1							
n = 1	1.17	59.34	0.0714	n = 1	1.20	53.85	0.2513	0.0675	0.1391	0.1096	0.3638
n = 2	1.20	52.75	0.7225	n = 2	1.20	59.34	0.0599	0.3447	0.5707	0.2101	0.2007
n = 3	1.26	49.45	0.7933	n = 3	1.20	60.44	0.0399	0.8006	0.8059	0.2094	0.2052
n = 4	1.29	49.45	0.6692	n = 4	1.20	60.44	0.0362	0.9350	0.9235	0.2579	0.2468
n = 5	1.30	47.25	0.8479	n = 5	1.20	59.34	0.0543	0.9399	0.9718	0.2213	0.2320
n = 6	1.29	49.45	0.6449	n = 6	1.20	61.54	0.0232	0.8784	0.8670	0.2119	0.2237
n = 7	1.26	52.75	0.4252	n = 7	1.22	57.14	0.1205	0.7756	0.7619	0.4891	0.4921
n = 8	1.32	56.04	0.2053	n = 8	1.26	59.34	0.0387	0.9182	0.8483	0.8285	0.5613
n = 9	1.57	51.65	0.4753	n = 9	1.30	54.95	0.1651	0.9998	0.9998	0.9457	0.8113
n = 10	1.74	56.04	0.2205	n = 10	1.29	56.04	0.0887	0.9662	0.9944	0.9137	0.6669
Panel B 6-month horizon											
RW	2.83	—	—	LR	2.75	63.74	0.0016				
NN				NN1							
n = 1	2.58	65.93	0.0025	n = 1	2.72	56.04	0.1657	0.0939	0.0013	0.1597	0.1721
n = 2	3.24	47.25	0.9820	n = 2	2.69	56.04	0.1906	0.8804	0.9956	0.1800	0.3202
n = 3	3.19	59.34	0.2181	n = 3	2.73	51.65	0.3445	0.8540	0.8703	0.2393	0.7763
n = 4	3.17	59.34	0.1109	n = 4	2.71	57.14	0.1268	0.7628	0.5300	0.2161	0.5063
n = 5	3.65	57.14	0.1474	n = 5	2.72	50.55	0.7235	0.9841	0.9808	0.2561	0.7250
n = 6	4.20	57.14	0.0759	n = 6	2.65	57.14	0.3158	0.9958	0.9948	0.1760	0.4247
n = 7	4.20	60.44	0.0327	n = 7	2.65	56.04	0.4260	0.9932	0.9295	0.1766	0.4200
n = 8	4.69	53.85	0.4052	n = 8	2.65	58.24	0.2218	0.9959	0.9982	0.1857	0.4340
n = 9	3.74	48.35	0.6920	n = 9	2.64	56.04	0.3852	0.9903	0.9880	0.1765	0.5032
n = 10	4.51	57.14	0.1945	n = 10	2.64	57.14	0.2817	0.9998	0.9995	0.1668	0.4418
Panel C 12-month horizon											
RW	4.39	—	—	LR	4.40	59.34	0.0007				
NN				NN1							
n = 1	4.28	67.03	0.0000	n = 1	4.43	52.75	0.4368	0.3884	0.0684	0.5458	0.8070
n = 2	6.51	48.35	0.5304	n = 2	4.33	53.85	0.3691	0.9826	0.9999	0.4492	0.8510
n = 3	5.04	49.45	0.7080	n = 3	4.28	48.35	0.7014	0.8569	0.9108	0.3855	0.9396
n = 4	6.72	47.25	0.7576	n = 4	4.21	50.55	0.5740	0.9965	1.0000	0.3163	0.8113
n = 5	6.81	47.25	0.7280	n = 5	4.29	42.86	0.9160	0.9998	1.0000	0.4056	0.9510
n = 6	6.91	51.65	0.3312	n = 6	4.20	42.86	0.9160	0.9972	0.9999	0.3100	0.9194
n = 7	7.98	48.35	0.6010	n = 7	4.45	45.05	0.8283	0.9982	1.0000	0.5801	0.9489
n = 8	6.90	48.35	0.6353	n = 8	4.45	45.05	0.8283	0.9922	1.0000	0.5760	0.9451
n = 9	7.69	51.65	0.3990	n = 9	4.34	45.05	0.8504	0.9907	0.9996	0.4528	0.8945
n = 10	10.85	54.95	0.2468	n = 10	4.74	42.86	0.9160	0.9128	0.9995	0.7729	0.9853

In summary, the findings on the forecastability of exchange rates using neural networks are rather negative or mixed at best. The neural model with monetary fundamentals as explanatory variables in general underperforms the RW model in out-of-sample forecasting accuracy across all four currencies. The model without market fundamentals provide limited support for the British pound and the Canadian dollar. The neural models have some market-timing ability in a number of cases, yet the evidence is not overwhelming. While Mark (1995) reports that the forecasting ability of the linear model improves as the forecast horizon lengthens, this pattern is not discovered within our framework. Furthermore, we find that our neural models do not seem to be superior to the simple linear model in terms of forecasting accuracy or market timing. This result complements those of Meese and Rose (1991) and Diebold and Nason (1990) and further demonstrates the inability of nonlinear models in forecasting exchange rate movements.

18.5   Conclusion

The goal of this paper has been to re-examine the predictability of exchange rates. We postulate that economic fundamentals are important in driving exchange rates but the underlying relationship between exchange rates and fundamentals may be inherently too complex for traditional linear models to handle adequately. Therefore, we employ the NN technique and choose, as guided by economic theory, a parsimonious set of monetary fundamentals as explanatory variables to forecast four major exchange rates. Overall, we find the general lack of ability of neural network models in forecasting future exchange rate movements. Our model with monetary fundamentals produces higher RMSE than both the random walk model and the simple linear monetary model. However, when market fundamentals are dropped from the model, the results are somewhat more supportive for the British pound and the Canadian dollar. In a number of cases, our models show some market-timing ability. Therefore, we conclude that the Meese-Rogoff results cannot be overturned even with the more complicated neural network models.

Several extensions are possible in future research. First, as our neural models show some market-timing ability in a number of occasions, it will be interesting to examine whether it is possible for some simple trading rules constructed based on our forecast to make excess profits. The outcome can be compared to those from standard buy-and-hold strategy and technical trading rules, such as in Levich and Thomas (1992). Such an exercise is useful because it can offer more insights into the economic significance of our findings. Second, it is well known that the US dollar had a cycle in the mid-eighties, and it is unclear how this cycle affects the forecasting performance of alternative models. To avoid the possible "dollar cycle" problem, one can employ a different vehicle currency, such as the German mark, and examine the forecastability of currency prices relative to the German mark. Finally, we have adopted a "rolling regression" strategy so as to make maximum use of data points in the estimation period. It will be interesting to see how a "moving regression" approach (with a fixed window size) performs as this latter strategy can better capture possible structural changes in sample and thus should do better if such structural changes do exist. These as well as others are beyond the scope of this paper and are left for future research.

18.6   Acknowledgment

We would like to thank Ramazan Gencay, Nelson Mark, John Wald and seminar participants at the Ohio State University, University of Windsor, Kent State University, the 1999 Computational Finance Conference at the Stern School of Business of New York University and INFORMS Cincinnati Spring 1999 for helpful conversations and comments. We are also grateful to Mark Holmes and Donggyu Sul for data assistance, and to Suwanna Chanyawongsak for research assistance. The usual disclaimer applies.

References

Andrews, Donald W. K., 1991, Heteroskedasticity and autocorrelation consistent covariance matrix estimation, *Econometrica* 59(3), 817-858.

Bilson, John F.O., 1978, Rational expectations and the exchange rate, in: Jacob Frenkel and Harry G. Johnson, eds., *The Economics of Exchange Rates* (Addison-Wesley Publishing Co.: Reading, Mass.).

Brooks, Chris, 1997, Linear and nonlinear (non-) forecastability of high-frequency exchange rates, *Journal of Forecasting* 16, 125-145.

Chinn, Menzie and Richard Meese, 1995, Banking on currency forecasts: How predictable is change in money? *Journal of International Economics* 38, 161-178.

Diebold, Francis and James Nason, 1990, Nonparametric exchange rate prediction, *Journal of International Economics* 28, 315-332.

Diebold, Francis and Roberto Mariano, 1995, Comparing predictive accuracy, *Journal of Business and Economic Statistics* 13(3), 253-263.

Donaldson, Glen and Mark Kamstra, 1996, A new dividend forecasting procedure that rejects bubbles in asset prices: The case of 1929's stock crash, *Review of Financial Studies* 9(2), Summer, 333-83.

Engel, Charles and James D. Hamilton, 1990, Long swings in the exchange rate: Are they in the data and do markets know it? *American Economic Review* 80, 689-713.

Engel, Charles, 1994, Can the Markov switching model forecast exchange rates? *Journal of International Economics* 36, 151-165.

Garcia, Rene and Ramazan Gencay, 1999, Pricing and hedging derivative securities with neural networks and a homogeneity hint, *Journal of Econometrics*, forthcoming.

Gencay, Ramazan, 1998, The predictability of security returns with simple technical trading rules, *Journal of Empirical Finance*, 5, 347–359.

Gencay, Ramazan, 1999, Linear, nonlinear and essential foreign exchange rate prediction with simple technical trading rules, *Journal of International Economics,* 47, 91–107.

Hornik, Kurt, Maxwell Stinchcombe and Halbert White, 1989, Multilayer feedforward networks are universal approximators, *Neural Networks* 2, 359-366.

Hu, Michael Y., Peter Zhang, Christine X. Jiang and B. Eddy Patuwo, 1999, The out-of-sample performance of neural networks in foreign exchange rate forecasting, *Decision Science*, forthcoming.

Hutchinson, James M, Andrew Lo and Tomaso Poggio, 1994, A nonparametric approach to pricing and hedging derivative securities via learning networks, *Journal of Finance* 49 (3), 851-89.

Kuan, Chung-Ming and Tung Liu, 1995, Forecasting exchange rates using feedforward and recurrent neural networks, *Journal of Applied Econometrics* 10(4), Oct.-Dec., 347-64.

Levich, Richard M. and Lee R. Thomas, 1993, The significance of technical trading-rule profits in the foreign exchange markets: A bootstrap approach, *Journal of International Money and Finance* 12, 451-474.

Mark, Nelson, 1995, Exchange rates and fundamentals: Evidence on long-horizon predictability, *American Economic Review* 85 (1), 201-218.

Meese, Richard A. and Kenneth Rogoff, 1983, Empirical exchange rate models of the seventies: Do they fit out of sample? *Journal of International Economics* 14, 3-24.

Meese, Richard A., 1986, Testing for bubbles in exchange markets: A case of sparkling rates? *Journal of Political Economy* 94, 345-373.

Meese, Richard A. and Kenneth Rogoff, 1988, Was it real? The exchange rate-interest differential relation over the modern floating-rate period, *Journal of Finance* 43 (4), 933-948.

Meese, Richard A. and Andrew Rose, 1991, An empirical assessment of non-linearities in models of exchange rate determination, *Review of Economic Studies* 58, 603-619.

Pesaran, M. Hashem and Allan Timmermann, 1992, A simple nonparametric test of predictive performance, *Journal of Business and Economic Statistics* 10, 461-465.

Qi, Min, 1996, Financial applications of artificial neural networks, in: G.S. Maddala and C.R. Rao, eds., *Handbook of Statistics, Vol. 14: Statistical Methods in Finance* (North-Holland Elsevier Science Publishers: Amsterdam), 529-552.

Qi, Min, 1999, Nonlinear predictability of stock returns using financial and economic variables, *Journal of Business and Economic Statistics* 17(4), forthcoming.

Qi, Min and G. S. Maddala, 1999, Economic factors and the stock market: A new perspective, *Journal of Forecasting,* 18(3), 151–166.

West, Kenneth, 1987, A standard monetary model and the variability of the Deutsche mark-dollar exchange rate, *Journal of International Economics* 23, 57-76.

White, Halbert, 1990, Connectionist nonparametric regression: Multilayer feedforward networks can learn arbitrary mappings, *Neural Networks* 3, 535-549.

Woo, Wing T., 1987, Some evidence of speculative bubbles in the foreign exchange markets, *Journal of Money, Credit and Banking* 19, 499-514.

Wu, Yangru, 1995, Are there rational bubbles in foreign exchange markets? *Journal of International Money and Finance* 14(1), 27-46.

Wu, Yangru, 1996, Are real exchange rates non-stationary? Evidence from a panel-data test, *Journal of Money, Credit and Banking* 28, 54-63.

IV   Dynamic Trading Strategies

19 Trading Models as Specification Tools

Ramazan Gençay, Giuseppe Ballocchi, Michel Dacorogna, and
Olivier Pictet

In this paper, a trading model based on exponential moving averages is used to evaluate the statistical properties of foreign exchange rates. The out-of-sample test period is seven years of five-minute series on three major foreign exchange rates against the US Dollar and one cross rate. The performance of the trading model is measured by the annualized return, two measures of risk corrected annualized return, deal frequency and maximum drawdown. The simulated probability distributions of these performance measures are calculated with the three traditional processes, the random walk, GARCH and AR-GARCH. The null hypothesis that the real-time performances of the foreign exchange series are generated from these traditional processes is tested under the probability distributions of the performance measures.

19.1 Performance Measures

The *total return*, R_T, is a measure[1] of the overall success of a trading model over a period T, and defined by

$$R_T \;\equiv\; \sum_{j=1}^{n} r_j \tag{19.1}$$

where n is the total number of transactions during the period T and j is the jth transaction and r_j is the return from the jth transaction. The total return expresses the amount of profit made by a trader always investing up to his initial capital or credit limit in his home currency. The annualized return, $\bar{R}_{T,A}$, is calculated by multiplying the total return with the ratio of the number of days in a year to the total number of days in the entire period.

The *maximum drawdown*, D_T, over a certain period $T = t_E - t_0$, is defined by

$$D_T \;\equiv\; \max(\; R_{t_a} - R_{t_b} \mid t_0 \le t_a \le t_b \le t_E \;) \tag{19.2}$$

where R_{t_a} and R_{t_b} are the total returns of the periods from t_0 to t_a and t_b respectively.

---

1. The performance measures of this paper are also used in Pictet et al. (1992) and Gençay et al. (1998).

The trading model performance needs to account for a high total return; a smooth, almost linear increase of the total return over time; a small clustering of losses and no bias towards low frequency trading models. A measure frequently used by practitioners to evaluate portfolio models is the Sharpe ratio. Unfortunately, the Sharpe ratio is numerically unstable for small variances of returns and cannot consider the clustering of profit and loss trades. As the basis of a risk-sensitive performance measure, a trading model return variable $\tilde{R}$ is defined to be the sum of the total return R_T and the unrealized current return r_c. The variable $\tilde{R}$ reflects the additional risk due to unrealized returns. Its change over a time interval Δt is

$$X_{\Delta t} = \tilde{R}_t - \tilde{R}_{t-\Delta t} \tag{19.3}$$

where t expresses the time of the measurement. In this paper, Δt is allowed to vary from seven days to 301 days.

A risk-sensitive measure of trading model performance can be derived from the utility function framework (Keeney and Raiffa (1976)). Let us assume that the variable $X_{\Delta t}$ follows a Gaussian random walk with mean $\overline{X}_{\Delta t}$ and the risk aversion parameter α is constant with respect to $X_{\Delta t}$. The resulting utility $u(X_{\Delta t})$ of an observation is $-\exp(-\alpha X_{\Delta t})$, with an expectation value of $\overline{u} = u(\overline{X}_{\Delta t})\exp(\alpha^2 \sigma_{\Delta t}^2/2)$, where $\sigma_{\Delta t}^2$ is the variance of $X_{\Delta t}$. The expected utility can be transformed back to the *effective return*, $X_{eff} = -\log(-\overline{u})/\alpha$ where

$$X_{eff} = \overline{X}_{\Delta t} - \frac{\alpha \sigma_{\Delta t}^2}{2}. \tag{19.4}$$

The risk term $\alpha \sigma_{\Delta t}^2/2$ can be regarded as a risk premium deducted from the original return where $\sigma_{\Delta t}^2$ is computed by

$$\sigma_{\Delta t}^2 = \frac{n}{n-1}\left(\overline{X_{\Delta t}^2} - \overline{X}_{\Delta t}^2\right). \tag{19.5}$$

Unlike the Sharpe ratio, this measure is numerically stable and can differentiate between two trading models with a straight line behaviour ($\sigma_{\Delta t}^2 = 0$) by choosing the one with the better average return[2].

The measure X_{eff} still depends on the size of the time interval Δt. It is hard to compare X_{eff} values for different intervals. The usual way to enable such a comparison is through the annualization factor, $A_{\Delta t}$, where $A_{\Delta t}$ is the ratio of the number of Δt in a year divided by the number of Δt's in the full sample.

---

2. An example for the limitation of the Sharpe ratio is its inability to distinguish between two straigth line equity curves with different slopes.

$$X_{eff,ann,\Delta t} \;=\; A_{\Delta t}\,X_{eff} \;=\; \overline{X} - \frac{\alpha}{2}\,A_{\Delta t}\,\sigma^2_{\Delta t} \tag{19.6}$$

where $\overline{X}$ is the annualized return and it is no longer dependent on Δt. The factor $A_{\Delta t}\sigma^2_{\Delta t}$ has a constant expectation, independent of Δt. This annualized measure still has a risk term associated with Δt and is insensitive to changes occurring with much longer or much shorter horizons. To achieve a measure that simultaneously considers a wide range of horizons, a weighted average of several $X_{eff,ann}$ is computed with n different time horizons Δt_i, and thus takes advantage of the fact that annualized $X_{eff,ann}$ can be directly compared

$$X_{eff} \;=\; \frac{\sum_{i=1}^{n} w_i X_{eff,ann,\Delta t_i}}{\sum_{i=1}^{n} w_i} \tag{19.7}$$

where the weights w are chosen according to the relative importance of the time horizons Δt_i and may differ for trading models with different trading frequencies. In this paper, α is set to $\alpha = 0.10$.

The risk term of X_{eff} is based on the volatility of the total return curve against time, where a steady, linear growth of the total return represents the zero volatility case. This volatility measure of the total return curve treats positive and negative deviations symmetrically, whereas foreign exchange dealers become more risk averse in the loss zone and do hardly care about the clustering of positive profits. A measure which treats the negative and positive zones asymmetrically is defined to be R_{eff} (Dacorogna et al. (1999)) where R_{eff} has a high risk aversion in the zone of negative returns and a low one in the zone of profits whereas X_{eff} assumes constant risk aversion. A high risk aversion in the zone of negative returns means that the performance measure is dominated by the large drawdowns. The R_{eff} has two risk aversion levels: a low one, α_+, for positive $\Delta\tilde{R}$ (profit intervals) and a high one, α_-, for negative $\Delta\tilde{R}$ (drawdowns)

$$\alpha \;=\; \begin{cases} \alpha_+ & for \quad \Delta\tilde{R} \geq 0 \\ \alpha_- & for \quad \Delta\tilde{R} < 0 \end{cases}$$

where $\alpha_+ < \alpha_-$. The high value of α_- reflects the high risk aversion of typical market participants in the loss zone. Trading models may have some losses but, if the loss observations strongly *vary* in size, the risk of very large losses becomes unacceptably high. On the side of the positive profit observations, a certain regularity of profits is also better than a strong variation in size. However, this distribution of positive returns is never *vital* for the future of market participant as the distribution of losses (drawdowns). Therefore, α_+ is much smaller than α_-. In this paper, we assume that $\alpha+ = \alpha_-/4$ and $\alpha_- = .20$.

Amongst annualized return, X_{eff} and R_{eff}, the last two performance measures examine the entire equity curve contrary to the annualized total return. The X_{eff} and R_{eff} are more stringent performance measures by taking into account the entire path in the equity curve. The annualized return, on the other hand, leaves a large degree of freedom to an infinite number of equity curve paths by only considering the beginning and the end points of the equity curve performance.

19.2   Simulation Methodology

The distributions of the performance measures under various null processes will be calculated by using a simulation methodology in Gençay et al. (1998). The random walk process is defined by

$$r_t = \alpha + \epsilon_t \tag{19.8}$$

where $r_t = log(p_t/p_{t-1})$ and $\epsilon_t \sim \mathrm{N}(0,\sigma^2)$. The random walk estimation involves the regression of the actual foreign exchange returns on a constant. A simulation sample for the random walk series with drift is obtained by sampling from the Gaussian random number generator with the mean and the standard deviation of the residual series. The simulated residuals are added to the conditional mean defined by $\hat{\alpha}$, to form a new series of returns. The new series of the returns has the same drift in prices, the same variance and the same unconditional distribution. From the new series of returns, the simulated price process is recovered recursively by setting the initial price to the true price at the beginning of the sample. The trading models use the bid and ask prices as inputs. Half of the average spread is subtracted (added) from the simulated price process to obtain the simulated bid and ask prices.

The GARCH(1,1) process is written as

$$r_t = \gamma_0 + \epsilon_t \tag{19.9}$$

where $\epsilon_t = h_t^{1/2} z_t$, $z_t \sim \mathrm{N}(0,1)$ and $h_t = \alpha_0 + \alpha_1 h_{t-1} + \beta_1 \epsilon_{t-1}^2$. GARCH specification (Bollerslev (1986)) allows the conditional second moments of the return process to be serially correlated. This specification implies that periods of high (low) volatility are likely to be followed by periods of high (low) volatility. GARCH specification allows the volatility to change over time and the expected returns are a function of past returns as well as volatility. The parameters and the normalized residuals are estimated from the foreign exchange returns using the maximum likelihood procedure. The simulated returns for the GARCH(1,1) process are generated from the simulated normalized residuals and the estimated parameters.

The AR(p)-GARCH(1,1) process is written as

$$r_t = \gamma + \sum_{i=1}^{p} \gamma_i r_{t-i} + \epsilon_t \tag{19.10}$$

where $\epsilon_t = h_t^{1/2} z_t$ $z_t \sim$ N(0,1) and $h_t = \alpha_0 + \alpha_1 h_{t-1} + \beta_1 \epsilon_{t-1}^2$. The estimated parameters of the AR(p)-GARCH(1,1) processes together with the simulated residuals are used to generate the simulated returns from these processes. As before, half of the average spread is subtracted (added) from the simulated price process to obtain the simulated bid (ask) prices.

19.3 Trading Models

Trading models offer a real-time analysis of foreign exchange movements and generate explicit trading recommendations. These models are based on the continuous collection and treatment of foreign exchange quotes by market makers around the clock at the tick-by-tick frequency level. There are three important reasons to utilize high frequency data in the trading models. The first one is that the model indicators acquire robustness by utilizing the intraday volatility behavior in their build-up. The second reason is that any position taken by the model may need to be reversed quickly although these position reversals may not need to be observed often. The stop-loss objectives need to satisfied and the high frequency data provides an appropriate platform for this requirement. More importantly, the customer's trading positions and strategies within a trading model can only be replicated with a high statistical degree of accuracy by utilizing high frequency data in a trading model.

The trading models imitate the trading conditions of the real foreign exchange market as closely as possible. They do not deal directly but instead instruct human foreign exchange dealers to make specific trades. In order to imitate real-world trading accurately, they take transaction costs into account in their return computation, they do not trade outside market working hours except for executing stop-loss and they avoid trading too frequently. In short, these models act realistically in a manner which a human dealer can easily follow.

The central part of a trading model is the analysis of the past price movements which are summarized within a trading model in terms of indicators. The indicators are then mapped into actual trading positions by applying various rules. For instance, a model may enter a long position if an indicator exceeds a certain threshold. Other rules determine whether a deal may be made at all. Among various factors, these rules determine the timing of the recommendation. A trading model thus consists of a set of indicator computations combined with a collection of rules. The former are functions of the price history. The latter determine the applicability of the indicator computations to generating trading recommendations. The model gives a recommendation not only for the direction but also for the amount of the exposure. The possible exposures (gearings) are $\pm\frac{1}{2}$, ± 1 or 0 (no exposure).

The trading model indicator of this paper is momentum based indicator consisting of a difference between two exponential moving averages of range $\tau = 0.5$ and $\tau = 20$ days. The gearing function for the trading model is

$$g(I_p) = sign(I_p) \ f(|I_p|)$$

where

$$I_p = EMA(\tau = 0.5) - EMA(\tau = 20)$$

and

$$f(|I_p|) \quad = \quad \begin{cases} if \ |I_p| > a & 1 \\ if \ |I_p| < a & 0 \end{cases}$$

where $a > 0$. I_p is the indicator function, EMA is the exponential moving average with a given range, $sign$ measures the sign of the indicator and f measures the size of the movements in foreign exhange. The model is subject to the open-close and holiday closing hours.

19.4 Empirical Results

The data is the five minutes ϑ-time series from January, 1, 1990 to December, 31 1996 for the three major foreign exhange rates, USD-DEM, USD-CHF (Swiss Franc), USD-FRF (French Franc), and the cross-rate DEM-JPY (Deutsche Mark - Japanese Yen). The high frequency data inherits intra-day seasonalities and requires deseasonalization. This paper uses the deseasonalization methodology advocated in Dacorogna et al. (1993) named as the ϑ-time seasonality correction method. The ϑ-time method uses the business time scale and utilizes the average volatility to represents the activity of the market. The ϑ-time method is based on three geographical markets namely the East Asia, Europe and the North America. A more detailed exposition of the business time approach is presented in Dacorogna et al. (1993.)

The optimization and the validation of the trading models are done with data prior to January 1, 1990. Therefore, our results here provide a complete *ex-ante*

Table 19.1
Trading Model Performance 1990-1996

Currency	Cumulative Return	Annualized Return
USD-DEM	20.89%	3.33%
USD-CHF	29.26%	4.40%
USD-FRF	46.81%	6.01%
DEM-JPY	55.87%	7.09%

test for the trading performance measures under the studied processes with seven years of 5 minute frequency data. The simulations for each process are done for 1000 replications.

19.4.1   Random Walk Process

The simulation results for the trading model are presented in Table 19.1. The annualized returns for the USD-DEM, USD-CHF, USD-FRF and DEM-JPY are 3.33, 4.40, 6.01 and 7.09 percent, respectively. As reported in Table 19.2, the p-values for the annualized returns are 12.6, 8.8, 6.4 and 6.6 percent for the four currencies pairs. All four p-values are greater than the 5 percent level of confidence. Therefore, it is not possible to reject the null hypothesis that the data generating process is random walk under the simulated annualized return distributions.

The examination of the p-values for the X_{eff} and R_{eff} indicate that these values are 2.8 and 2.3 percent for the USD-DEM; 0.9 and 0.4 percent for the USD-CHF; 0.6 and 0.4 percent for the USD-FRF and 1.4 and 1.0 percent for the DEM-JPY. Under these more stringent performance measures, the null hypothesis that the random walk process is the data generating process for the foreign exchange returns is rejected.

As presented in Table 19.3, the p-values for the maximum drawdown and the deal frequency indicate that the trading model's historical performance stays well below the ones generated under the random walk simulations. In other words, the random walk simulations always generate larger drawdowns relative to the historical drawdowns from the four currency pairs. In fact, the mean simulated drawdowns for the USD-DEM, USD-CHF, USD-FRF and DEM-JPY are 49.70, 60.72, 47.51 and 44.28 percent which are at least three times larger than the historical drawdowns. Similarly, the mean of the simulated deal frequencies for the random walk process stays approximately 20 percent above the historical realizations.

The overall evaluation of the trading model is that this simple technical model generate net positive returns for all currencies after taking the transaction costs into account. The simulated probability distributions of the performance measures

Table 19.2
P-value Comparisons for (%) with RW, GARCH(1,1) and AR(4)-GARCH(1,1)

Currency	Random Walk	GARCH(1,1)	AR(4)-GARCH(1,1)
Annualized Return			
USD-DEM	12.6	14.1	10.0
USD-CHF	8.8	9.6	5.9
USD-FRF	6.4	4.6	3.2
DEM-JPY	6.6	2.8	1.8
Xeffective			
USD-DEM	2.8	2.3	3.8
USD-CHF	0.9	0.7	1.7
USD-FRF	0.6	0.6	0.7
DEM-JPY	1.4	0.5	0.5
Reffective			
USD-DEM	2.3	1.8	3.7
USD-CHF	0.4	0.5	2.4
USD-FRF	0.4	0.4	0.6
DEM-JPY	1.0	0.2	0.4

Table 19.3
Random Walk Process, Maximum Drawdown Comparisons, 1990-1996

Currency	Max. Drawdown	Mean Simulated Max. Drawdown
USD-DEM	17.73%	49.70%
USD-CHF	17.10%	60.72%
USD-FRF	14.52%	47.51%
DEM-JPY	13.06%	44.28%

also indicate that the null hypothesis of whether the foreign exchange returns can be characterized by random walk process is rejected.

19.4.2   GARCH(1,1) Process

A more realistic process for the foreign exchange returns is the GARCH(1,1) process which allows for conditional heterskedasticity. The simulation performance of the trading model under the GARCH(1,1) process is presented in Table 19.2. The p-values for the annualized returns for the four currency pairs are 14.1, 9.6, 4.6 and 2.8 percent, respectively. Based on the annualized return performance, the null hypothesis that the GARCH(1,1) process is the data generating process of foreign exchange returns cannot be rejected for the USD-DEM and USD-CHF. The other currency pairs stay below the 5 percent level but relatively close to the 5 percent level providing a weak level of confidence.

The p-values of the X_{eff} and R_{eff} are 2.3, 1.8 percent for USD-DEM; 0.7, 0.5 percent for USD-CHF; 0.6, 0.4 percent for USD-FRF and 0.5, 0.2 percent for the DEM-JPY. Relative to the annualized return performance, the p-values of the X_{eff}

Table 19.4
Random Walk Process, Deal Frequency Comparisons (deal/week), 1990-1996

Currency	Deal Freq.	Mean Sim. Deal Feq.
USD-DEM	0.77	0.98
USD-CHF	0.85	1.19
USD-FRF	0.70	0.96
DEM-JPY	0.75	0.95

and R_{eff} remain statistically significant as the largest values is not greater than 2.3 percent. The annualized return is a performance measure does not utilize the entire equity curve. Rather, only first and the last points of the equity curve are used in the calculation of the annualized returns. Therefore, a straight line equity curve as well as an equity curve which is subject to extreme variations can have the same annualized returns. Based on the X_{eff} and R_{eff} p-values, it can be concluded that the GARCH(1,1) process be rejected as a data generating mechanism of foreign exchange returns. The finding of the trading model is line with the earlier literature, such as Brock et. al (1992), who also obtained similar findings.

19.4.3   AR(4)-GARCH(1,1) Process

A further direction is to investigate whether a conditional mean dynamics with GARCH(1,1) innovations would be a more successful characterization of the dynamics of the high frequency foreign exchange returns. The conditional mean of the foreign exchange returns are estimated with four lags of these returns. The additional lags did not lead to substantial increases in the likelihood value.

The performance of the trading model with the AR(4)-GARCH(1,1) process are presented in Table 19.2. The p-values are 10.0, 5.9, 3.2 and 1.8 percent for the USD-DEM, USD-CHF, USD-FRF and DEM-JPY. The p-values for the USD-DEM and USD-CHF are higher than than the 5 percent level. The results with the X_{eff} and R_{eff}, on the other hand, indicate that the p-values remain under the 5 percent levels. In fact, the p-vales for the X_{eff} and R_{eff} are 3.8, 3.7 percent for the USD-DEM; 1.7, 2.4 percent for the USD-CHF; 0.7, 0.6 percent for the USD-FRF and 0.5, 0.4 percent for the DEM-JPY. For the USD-FRF and DEM-JPY, all horizons have p-values less than 5 percent indicating the rejection of the AR(4)-GARCH(1,1) as the data generating process of the foreign exchange returns.

As presented in Table 19.5, the means of the simulations indicate that the distributions are centered at the average transaction costs. This is expected for the random walk process and can be used a reliability check of the trading model. For all currencies, the mean simulated annual return is within the proximity of the annual transaction cost for the random walk process. On the other hand, the annual returns of the trading model with actual foreign exchange series stay well above the annual transaction costs indicating net profitability.

The GARCH(1,1) and AR(4)-GARCH(1,1) models also yield simulated annualized returns which are near their annual transaction costs. Although the trading model indicate net profitability with actual foreign exchange series, the absence of any profitability with the GARCH(1,1) and AR(4)-GARCH(1,1) processes can be interpreted as the failure of these processes as potential data generating processes for the foreign exchange markets.

19.5 Conclusions

In this paper, we have used a technical trading model of foreign exchange markets as a specification test for three traditional statistical models of foreign exchange returns. The results reject the random walk, GARCH(1,1) and AR-GARCH(1,1) processes as the data generating mechanisms for the high frequency foreign exchange dynamics. One important reason for the rejection of the GARCH(1,1) process as a data generating mechanishm of foreign exchange returns is the aggregation property of the GARCH(1,1) process[3].

The GARCH(1,1) process behaves more like a homoskedastic process at lower frequencies. Since the trading model's trading frequency is less than two deals per week, the trading model does not pick up the five minute level heteroskedastic structure at the weekly frequency. Rather, the heteroskedastic structure behaves as if it is measurement noise where the model takes positions and this leads to the rejection of the GARCH(1,1) as a data generation process of the foreign exchange series.

In a GARCH process, the conditional heteroskedasticity exists in the frequency that the data has been generated. As it is moved away from this frequency to lower frequencies, the heteroskedastic structure slowly dies away leaving itself to a more homogeneous structure in time. A more elaborate processes such as the mul-

---

3. Andersen and Bollerslev (1997) analysed the intraday periodicity and volatility persistence in financial markets. They show that intraday periodicity in the return volatility in foreign exchange markets has a strong impact on the dynamic properties of high frequency returns. Múller et al. (1997) designed a multiple horizon HARCH process to address the conditionally heteroskedastic nature of the foreign exchange returns at different frequencies. Guillaume (1995) show that the use of an alternative time scale can eliminate the inefficiencies in the estimation of a GARCH model caused by intra-daily seasonal patterns. However, the temporal aggregation properties of the GARCH models do not hold at the intra-daily frequencies, revealing the presence of several time-horizon components.

Table 19.5
Mean of the Annualized Return and the Annualized Transaction Cost Based on the Mean Deal
Frequency

Currency	Annual Return	Annual Trans. Cost	Mean Annual Simulated Return
Random Walk			
USD-DEM	3.33%	-1.27%	-2.20%
USD-CHF	4.40%	-1.55%	-3.33%
USD-FRF	6.01%	-1.50%	-1.84%
DEM-JPY	7.09%	-1.24%	-0.75%
GARCH(1,1)			
USD-DEM	3.33%	-1.37%	-1.98%
USD-CHF	4.40%	-1.67%	-3.16%
USD-FRF	6.01%	-1.33%	-1.60%
DEM-JPY	7.09%	-1.21%	-1.59%
AR(4)-GARCH(1,1)			
USD-DEM	3.33%	-1.13%	-1.90%
USD-CHF	4.40%	-1.33%	-2.89%
USD-FRF	6.01%	-1.13%	-1.63%
DEM-JPY	7.09%	-1.09%	-1.58%

tiple horizon ARCH models possess conditionally heteroskedastic structure at all frequencies in general. The existence of multiple frequency heteroskedastic structure may be more in line with the heterogeneous structure of the foreign exchange markets.

Similarly, one possible explanation for the rejection of the AR(4)-GARCH(1,1) process is the relationship between the dealing frequency of the model and the frequency of the simulated data. The AR(4)-GARCH(1,1) process is generated at the 5 minutes frequency but the model's dealing frequency is one or two deals per week. Therefore, the model picks up the high frequency serial correlation as a noise and this serial correlation works against the process. This can not be treated as a failure of the trading model. Rather, this strong rejection is an evidence of the failure of the aggregation properties of the AR(4)-GARCH(1,1) process over lower frequencies.

The results also indicate that the foreign exchange series may possess a multi-frequency conditional mean and conditional heteroskedastic dynamics. The traditional heteroskedastic models fail to capture the entire dynamics by only capturing a slice of this dynamics at a given frequency. Therefore, a more realistic processes for foreign exchange returns should give consideration to the scaling behavior of returns at different frequencies and this scaling behavior should be taken into account in the construction of a representative process.

References

Andersen, T. G. and T. Bollerslev, 1997, Intraday periodicity and volatility persistence in financial markets, *Journal of Empirical Finance*, 4, 115-158.

Bollerslev, T., 1986, Generalized autoregressive conditional heteroskedasticity, *Journal of Econometrics* 31, 307-327.

Brock, W. A., J. Lakonishok and B. LeBaron, 1992, Simple technical trading rules and the stochastic properties of stock returns, *Journal of Finance* 47, 1731-1764.

Dacorogna, M. M., R. Gençay, U. A. Müller and O. V. Pictet, 1999, Effective return, risk aversion and drawdowns, Olsen Research Institute Discussion Paper.

Dacorogna, M. M., U. A. Müller, R. J. Nagler, R. B. Olsen, and O. V. Pictet, 1993, A geographical model for the daily and weekly seasonal volatility in the foreign exchange market, *Journal of International Money and Finance*, 12, 413-438.

Gençay, R., G. Ballocchi, M. Dacorogna, R. Olsen and O. Pictet, 1998, Real time trading models and the statistical properties of foreign exchange rates, Olsen Research Institute Discussion Paper.

Guillaume, D. M., O. V. Pictet and M. M. Dacorogna, 1995, On the intra-daily performance of GARCH process, Olsen Research Institute Discussion Paper, Zurich, Switzerland.

Keeney, R. L. and H. Raiffa, 1976, Decision with multiple objectives: Preferences and value tradeoffs, John Wiley & Sons, New York.

Pictet, O. V., M. M. Dacorogna, U. A. Müller, R. B. Olsen and J. R. Ward, 1992, Real-time trading models for foreign exchange rates, Neural Network World, 6, 713-744.

Müller, U. A., M. M. Dacorogna, R. D. Davé, Richard B. Olsen, O. V. Pictet and J E. von Weizsäcker, 1997, Volatilities of Different Time Resolutions - Analyzing the Dynamics of Market Components, *Journal of Empirical Finance*, 4, 213-240.

20 Statistical Arbitrage Models of the FTSE 100

A. N. Burgess

In this paper we describe a set of statistical arbitrage models which exploit relative value relationships amongst the constituents of the FTSE 100. Rather than estimating cointegration vectors of high dimensionality, a stepwise regression approach is used to identify the most appropriate subspace for the stochastic detrending of each individual equity price. A Monte Carlo simulation is used to identify the empirical distribution of the Variance Ratio profile of the regression residuals, under the null hypothesis of random walk behaviour. Both a chi-squared test on the joint distribution of the Variance Ratio profile, and additional tests based on its eigenvectors, indicate that as a whole the stochastically detrended stock prices deviate significantly from random walk behaviour and hence may contain predictable components. A combined cross-sectional and time-series model indicates that the relative "mispricing" of the equities tends to trend in the short-term and revert in the longer term. The out-of-sample performance of the models is consistently profitable using a simple trading rule, with the combined portfolio suggesting a possible annualised Sharpe Ratio of over 7 for a trader with costs of 50 basis points. Furthermore, information derived from the in-sample variance ratio profile is shown to be significantly correlated with the out-of-sample profitability of the individual models—suggesting that the performance may be improved further by modelling the time-series properties conditionally on such information.

20.1 Introduction

In many cases the volatility in asset returns is largely due to movements which are market-wide or even world-wide in nature rather than specific characteristics of the particular asset; consequently there is a risk that this "market noise" will overshadow any predictable component of asset returns. A number of authors have recently suggested approaches which attempt to reduce this effect by suitably transforming the financial time-series. Lo and MacKinley (1995) create "maximally predictable" portfolios of assets, with respect to a particular information set. Bentz et al (1996), use a modelling framework in which prices are relative to the market as a whole, and returns are also calculated on this basis; this "de-trending" removes typically 90% of the volatility of asset returns, as is consistent with the Capital Asset Pricing Model (CAPM) of finance theory. Burgess and Refenes (1996) use a cointegration framework in which FTSE returns are calculated relative to a portfolio of international equity indices, with the weightings of the portfolio given by the coefficients of the cointegrating regression. Steurer and Hann (1996) also adopt a cointegration framework, modelling exchange rates as short-term fluctuations around an "equilibrium" level dictated by monetary and financial fundamentals. This type of approach in general is characterised as "statistical arbitrage" in Burgess

(1996) where a principle components analysis is used to create a eurodollar portfolio which is insulated from shifts and tilts in the yield curve and optimally exposed to the third, "flex" component; the returns of this portfolio are found to be partly predictable using neural network methodology but not by linear techniques.

We define statistical arbitrage as a generalisation of traditional "zero-risk" arbitrage. Zero-risk arbitrage consists of constructing two combinations of assets with identical cash-flows, and exploiting any discrepancies in the price of the two equivalent assets. The portfolio Long(combination1) + Short(combination2) can be viewed as a synthetic asset, of which any price-deviation from zero represents a "mispricing" and a potential risk-free profit.[1] In statistical arbitrage we again construct synthetic assets in which any deviation of the price from zero is still seen as a "mispricing", but this time in the statistical sense of having a predictable component to the price-dynamics.

Our methodology for exploiting statistical arbitrage consists of three stages:

- constructing "synthetic assets" and testing for predictability in the price-dynamics
- modelling the error-correction mechanism between relative prices
- implementing a trading system to exploit the predictable component of asset returns

In this paper we adopt an approach to statistical arbitrage which is essentially a generalisation of the econometric concept of cointegration. We modify the standard cointegration methodology in two main ways: firstly we replace the cointegration tests for stationarity with more powerful variance ratio tests for "predictability", and secondly we construct the cointegrating regressions by a stepwise approach rather than the standard regression or principal components methodologies which are found in the literature. These two innovations are easily motivated: firstly, variance ratio tests are more powerful against a wide range of alternative hypotheses than are standard cointegration tests for stationarity, and hence are more appropriate for identifying statistical arbitrage opportunities; secondly, the high dimensionality of the problem space (approx. 100 constituents of the FTSE 100 index) necessitates the use of a methodology for reducing the models to a manageable (and tradable!) complexity, but in a systematic and principled manner—for which the "subset" approach of stepwise regression is ideally suited. The predictive model is simply a linear error-correction model using the cointegration residuals (asset

---

1. Subject to transaction costs, bid-ask spreads and price slippage.

"mispricings") and lagged relative returns to forecast future relative returns on a one-day ahead basis. The trading system described in this paper is very simple—simply taking offsetting long and short positions which are proportional to the forecasted relative return. For a discussion of more-sophisticated trading rules for statistical arbitrage, see Towers and Burgess (1998a, b).

The paper is organised as follows. Section 2 describes the stepwise cointegration methodology and the Monte Carlo experiments to determine the distribution of the variance ratio profile under the null hypothesis that the variables are all random walks. Section 3 describes the tests for predictability which are based on the variance ratio analysis, and the results of applying these tests to the statistical "mispricings" obtained from the stepwise regressions. Section 4 describes the time-series model for forecasting changes in the mispricings and section 5 analyses the out-of-sample performance of this model. Section 6 explores the relationship between the characteristics of the variance ratio for a given mispricing and the profitability of the associated statistical arbitrage model. Finally, a discussion and brief conclusions are presented in section 7.

20.2 Distribution of the Variance Ratio Profile of Stepwise Regression Residuals

Our methodology for creating statistical arbitrage models is based on the econometric concept of cointegration. Cointegration can be formally defined as follows: if a set of variables $\mathbf{y}$ are integrated of order d (i.e. must be differenced d times before becoming stationary) and the residuals of the cointegrating regression are integrated of order $d - b$ where $b > 0$ then the time-series are said to be cointegrated of order (d, b).

i.e. if each y_i is $I(d)$ and ε_t is $I(d - b) b > 0$ then $\mathbf{y} \sim CI(d, b)$

The most common and useful form of cointegration is CI(1,1) where the original series are random walks and the residuals of the regression are stationary according to a "unit root" test such as the Dickey-Fuller (DF), Augmented Dickey-Fuller (ADF), suggested by Engle and Granger (1987) or the cointegrating regression Durbin-Watson (CRDW) proposed by Sargan and Bhargava (1983). Tests based on a principal components or canonical correlation approach have been developed by Johansen (1988) and Phillips and Ouliaris (1988) amongst others.

In our case, however, the data consists of 93 constituents[2] of the FTSE 100 together with the index itself, giving a dimensionality of 94—much higher than normal for cointegration analysis, and large relative to the sample size of 400 (see section 3 for a description of the data). In order to reduce the dimensionality of the problem we decided to identify relationships between relatively small subsets of the data. There remains the problem of identifying the most appropriate subsets to form the basis of the statistical arbitrage models. In order to ensure a reasonable span of the entire space, we decided to use each asset in turn as the dependent variable of a cointegrating regression. To identify the most appropriate subspace for the cointegrating vector we use a stepwise regression methodology in place of the standard "enter all variables" approach. Before moving on to analyse these models further, we will describe the basis of the "Variance Ratio" methodology which we use to test for potential predictability.

The variance ratio test follows from the fact that the variance of the innovations in a random walk series grows linearly with the period over which the increments are measured. Thus the variance of the innovations calculated over a period τ should approximately equal τ times the variance of single period innovations. The basic $VR(\tau)$ statistic is thus:

$$VR(\tau) = \frac{\sum_t (\Delta^\tau d_t - \overline{\Delta^\tau d})^2}{\tau \sum_t (\Delta d_t - \overline{\Delta d})^2} \qquad (20.1)$$

The variance ratio is thus a function of the period τ. For a random walk the variance ratio will be close to 1 and this property has been used as the basis of statistical tests for deviations from random walk behaviour by a number of authors since Lo and McKinley (1988) and Cochrane (1988).

Rather than testing individual VR statistics, we prefer to test the variance ratio profile as a whole, firstly because there is no a priori "best" period for the comparison and secondly because it can summarise the dynamic properties of the time series: a positive gradient to the variance ratio function (VRF) indicates positive autocorrelation and hence trending behaviour; conversely a negative gradient to the VRF indicates negative autocorrelations and mean-reverting or cyclical behaviour. Figure 20.1 shows the VRFs for the Dax and Cac indices together with the VRF for the *relative* value of the two indices.

The usefulness of the variance ratio profile can be seen from the fact that it indicates the degree to which the time-series departs from random walk behaviour—

---

2. The remaining FTSE constituents were excluded from the analysis due to insufficient historical data being available (e.g. for newly quoted stocks such as the Halifax building society).

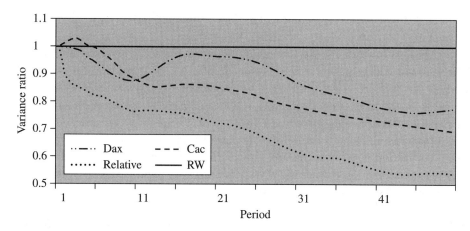

Figure 20.1
The Variance Ratio profile of the Dax and Cac indices individually and in relative terms. The x axis is the period over which asset returns are calculated (in days), the y axis is the normalised variance of the returns. In this case, the fact that the relative price deviates further from random-walk behaviour suggests that it may be easier to forecast than the individual series.

which may be taken as a measure of the potential predictability of the time-series. This is unlike standard tests for cointegration which are concerned with the related but different issue of testing for stationarity—a series may be nonstationary but still contain a significant predictable component and thus the variance ratio will identify a wider range of opportunities than the more restrictive approach of testing for stationarity. For both the Dax and the Cac the VRFs fall below 1, suggesting a certain degree of predictability—even though both series are nonstationary. Note also that the VRF for the relative price series is consistently below those of the individual series, indicating that the relative price exhibits a greater degree of potential predictability than either of the individual assets.

A problem with using the Variance Ratio test in conjunction with a cointegration methodology is that the residuals of a cointegrating regression (even when the variables are random walks) will not behave entirely as a random walk—for instance, they are forced, by construction, to be zero mean. More importantly, the regression induces a certain amount of spurious "mean-reversion" in the residuals and the impact of this on the distribution of the VR function must be taken into account. In our case, there is one further complication in that we are using stepwise regression and hence the selection bias inherent in choosing m out of $n > m$ regressors must also be accounted for. This is akin to the "data snooping" issue highlighted by Lo and McKinley (1990)

We thus performed a Monte Carlo simulation to identify the joint distribution of the variance ratio profile under the null hypothesis of regressing random walk variables on other random walks (i.e. no predictable component), accounting in particular for the impact of (a) the mean-reversion induced by the regression itself, and (b) the selection bias introduced by the use of the stepwise procedure. The distribution was calculated from 1000 simulations, in each case the parameters of the simulation match those of the subsequent statistical arbitrage modelling: namely a 400 period realisation of a random walk is regressed upon 5 similarly generated series from a set of 93 using a forward stepwise selection procedure, and the variance ratio profile calculated from the residuals of the regression.[3] The variance ratio is calculated for returns varying from one-period up to fifty periods. Note however, that by construction the value of VR(1) can only take the value 1.

From these 1000 simulations, both the average variance ratio profile and the co-variance matrix of deviations from this profile were calculated. As we are interested in the "shape" of the VR profile we also conducted a principle component analysis to characterise the structure of the deviations from the average profile. The scree plot of the normalised eigenvalues is shown in Figure 20.2.

The average profile and selected eigenvectors are shown in Figure 20.3. The average profile shows a significant negative slope which would imply a high degree of mean reversion if this were a standard variance ratio test. In our case it merely represents an artefact of the regression methodology which can be taken as a "baseline" for comparing the variance ratio profiles of actual statistical "mispricings". Note also the highly structured nature of the eigenvectors—indicating that deviations from the average profile have a tendency to be correlated across wide regions of lag-space rather than showing up as "spikes" in the VR profile. The first eigenvector represents a low frequency deviation in which the variance is consistently higher than the average profile—patterns with a positive projection on this eigenvector will tend to be trending whilst a negative projection will tend to indicate mean-reversion. The second eigenvector has a higher "frequency" and characterises profiles which mean-revert in the short term and trend in the longer term (or vice versa). Similarly the third eigenvector represents a pattern of trend-revert-trend.

---

3. Clearly it would be straightforward to repeat the procedure for other experimental parameters, sample size, number of variables etc, but the huge number of possible combinations leads towards recalibrating only for particular experiments rather than attempting to tabulate all possible conditional distributions.

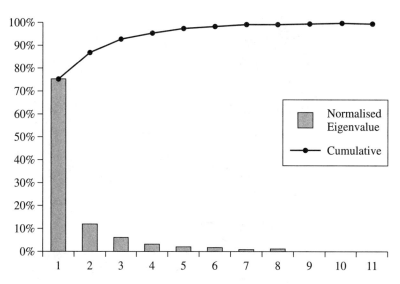

Figure 20.2
The scree plot of normalised eigenvalues for the covariance matrix of the variance ratio profile. The fact that almost the entire variability can be represented by the first few factors (out of a total of 49) shows that deviations from the average profile tend to be highly structured and can be characterised by only a small number of parameters.

The higher-order eigenvectors (not shown in the figure) tend to follow this move towards higher frequency deviations. The fact that the associated eigenvalues are large only for the first few components tells us that the residuals derived from random walk time-series tend to deviate from the average profile only in very simple ways, as represented by the low-order eigenvectors shown in the diagram.

20.3 Analysis of Variance Ratio Profiles of Statistical "Mispricings" of FTSE 100 Stocks

Given the average profile and covariance matrix of the profile under the null hypothesis of random walk behaviour, we can test the residuals of actual statistical arbitrage models for significant deviations from these profiles. The data used consist of daily closing prices of the FTSE 100 and 93 of its constituent stocks. The prices were obtained from the Reuters TS1 database and in total consist of 500 observations from 13 June 1996 to 13 May 1998. Of these, 400 observations were

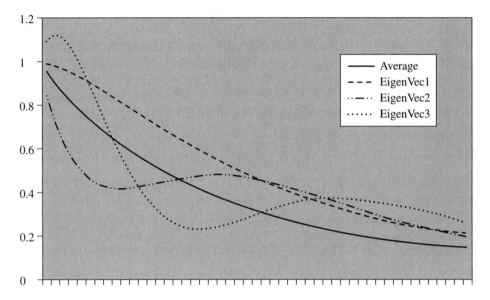

Figure 20.3
Variance Ratio profiles for: average residual of regression from simulated random-walk data; characteristic deviations from the average profile as represented by selected eigenvectors.

used to estimate the cointegrating regressions and the final 100 observations were reserved for the purposes of out-of-sample evaluation.

Each asset in turn was used as the dependent variable in a stepwise regression, with constant term and five regressors selected from the possible 93, and the VR profile of the resulting statistical mispricing tested for potential predictability in the form of deviation from random walk behaviour.

Two types of test were used, the first treating the distribution of the VR profile as multivariate normal and measuring the Mahalanobis distance of the observed profile from the average profile under the null hypothesis. This approach to joint testing of VR statistics has previously been used by Eckbo and Liu (1996) and it is easy to show that the test statistic should follow a chi-squared distribution with degrees of freedom equal to the dimensionality of the test. The second set of tests are designed to identify different types of deviation from the average profile and are based on the projection of the deviation onto the different eigenvectors—under the null hypothesis these statistics should follow a standard normal distribution. Figure 20.4 shows Variance Ratio profiles of the mispricings for selected statistical arbitrage models:

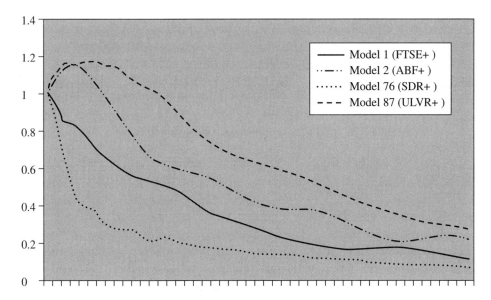

Figure 20.4
Selected variance ratio profiles for statistical mispricings obtained through stepwise regression of asset on remaining assets in FTSE 100 universe.

Table 20.1
Comparison of VR tests for random-walk simulations and actual mispricings, nominal size of test = 1%

	Chi-sq	EigCov1	EigCov2	EigCov3	EigCov4	EigCov5	EigCor1	EigCor2	EigCor3	EigCor4	EigCor5
Cal	1.8%	1.6%	1.4%	1.4%	0.9%	1.4%	1.7%	1.1%	1.7%	1.5%	1.2%
Test	4.3%	1.2%	0.9%	1.8%	1.3%	1.2%	1.3%	0.9%	1.3%	1.3%	1.6%
Model	36.2%	8.5%	1.1%	2.1%	3.2%	3.2%	8.5%	4.3%	3.2%	4.3%	8.5%

Table 20.2
Comparison of VR tests for random-walk simulations and actual mispricings, nominal size of test = 5%

	Chi-sq	EigCov1	EigCov2	EigCov3	EigCov4	EigCov5	EigCor1	EigCor2	EigCor3	EigCor4	EigCor5
Cal	6.6%	4.5%	5.1%	4.8%	5.2%	6.0%	4.7%	5.8%	4.0%	4.1%	4.8%
Test	9.9%	3.9%	5.5%	4.6%	4.8%	5.4%	4.1%	4.2%	4.3%	5.6%	6.2%
Model	53.2%	11.7%	8.5%	7.4%	12.8%	11.7%	11.7%	9.6%	8.5%	14.9%	13.8%

The test results are shown in Tables 20.1–3; in order to account for deviations from (multivariate) normality we report the nominal size but also the empirical size of the tests—calculated from the calibration data from the original simulation and also a test set from a second similar but independent simulation. Eigenvectors derived from both the correlation and the covariance matrix are used in the analysis.

Table 20.3
Comparison of VR tests for random-walk simulations and actual mispricings, nominal size of test = 10%

	Chi-sq	EigCov1	EigCov2	EigCov3	EigCov4	EigCov5	EigCor1	EigCor2	EigCor3	EigCor4	EigCor5
Cal	11.7%	8.7%	9.8%	9.5%	10.6%	10.5%	8.3%	10.0%	8.4%	9.4%	9.7%
Test	14.5%	8.2%	10.5%	9.3%	10.9%	10.7%	7.5%	10.1%	8.5%	12.1%	10.4%
Model	59.6%	20.2%	13.8%	14.9%	18.1%	18.1%	19.1%	14.9%	16.0%	19.1%	23.4%

Table 20.4
Comparison of average values of the various VR tests for random-walk simulations and actual mispricings

	Chi-sq	EigCov1	EigCov2	EigCov3	EigCov4	EigCov5	EigCor1	EigCor2	EigCor3	EigCor4	EigCor5
AveTest	50.99	-0.01	-0.01	0.00	0.01	0.00	-0.15	0.03	0.10	0.08	-0.07
VarTest	135.19	0.22	0.04	0.01	0.01	0.00	33.57	5.56	2.72	1.57	0.83
AveModel	70.79	-0.23	0.01	0.07	-0.03	-0.03	-2.34	0.32	1.02	-0.65	0.61
VarModel	676.34	0.41	0.04	0.02	0.01	0.00	62.67	7.45	3.83	1.86	1.06
z' stat	7.3	-3.2	0.5	4.0	-4.1	-5.0	-2.6	1.0	4.4	-5.0	6.3
p-value	0.00000	0.00129	0.61169	0.00006	0.00004	0.00000	0.00890	0.32816	0.00001	0.00000	0.00000

The tests indicate that the mispricings of the statistical arbitrage models deviate significantly from the behaviour of the random data—suggesting the presence of potentially predictable deviations from randomness. Table 20.4 shows 'z' tests of the average scores of the mispricings when compared to the simulated test data.

This result reinforces the findings that the actual mispricings deviate from random behaviour. In the next section we describe a forecasting model based on these mispricings.

20.4   Modelling the Dynamics of the Statistical Mispricings

In this section we describe the error-correction model which forecasts one-day-ahead changes in the statistical mispricings of the FTSE 100 stocks.

A single "pooled" model was estimated across the cross-section of 94 mispricing models and sample period of 400 observations. In order to capture any "mean reversion" effects, the one day ahead changes in the mispricings were regressed on the current level of the mispricing:

$$\text{MIS}_{s,t} = P_{s,t} - \left(\sum_{i=1}^{5} w_{s,i} P_{c(i,s),t} + c \right) \qquad (20.2)$$

where $P_{c(i,s)}$ is the price of the i'th constituent asset for the model of stock 's' and $w_{s,i}$ is the associated regression coefficient (portfolio weighting).

The remaining independent variables were selected in order to capture properties of different segments of the lag-space of mispricing dynamics and are of the form:

Table 20.5
Regression output

SUMMARY OUTPUT

Regression Statistics						
Multiple R	28.6%					
R Square	8.3%					
Adjusted R Square	8.2%					
Standard Error	0.016					
Observations	37600					

ANOVA

	df	SS	MS	F	Signigicance F	
Regression	6	0.83	0.14	559.02	0	
Residual	37593	9.31	0.0002			
Tota;	37599	10.14				
	Coefficients	Standard Error	t Stat	P-value	Lower 95%	Upper 95%
Intercept	0.000	0.0001	−2.05	0.0401	0.000	0.000
MIS	−0.188	0.0043	−43.48	0.0000	−0.197	−0.180
L1020	0.021	0.0027	7.99	0.0000	0.916	0.027
L510	0.030	0.0036	8.24	0.0000	0.023	0.037
L25	0.037	0.0043	8.76	0.0000	0.028	0.046
L12	0.018	0.0060	2.96	0.0031	0.006	0.029
L01	0.107	0.0060	17.97	0.0000	0.096	0.119

$$L(n, m)_{s,t} = \text{MIS}_{s,t-n} - \text{MIS}_{s,t-m} \tag{20.3}$$

with the resulting regression of the form:

$$\text{MIS}_{s,t+1} - \text{MIS}_{s,t} = \alpha + \beta_0 \text{MIS}_{s,t} + \beta_1 L(0, 1)_{s,t} + \beta_2 L(1, 2)_{s,t} \tag{20.4}$$

$$+ \beta_3 L(2, 5)_{s,t} + \beta_4 L(5, 10)_{s,t} + \beta_5 L(10, 20)_{s,t} + \varepsilon_{s,t+1} \tag{20.5}$$

In total, $94 * 400 = 37600$ observations were used to estimate the model, leaving $94 * 100 = 9400$ for out-of-sample evaluation. The regression output is shown in Table 20.5.

The model shows significant predictability in future changes of the statistical mispricings. This predictability derives from two sources—firstly a **short term trend** as represented by the positive coefficients for the lagged difference terms $L(n, m)$, and secondly a **long term error-correction** as represented by the negative coefficient for the mispricing MIS. Given the size of the dataset from which the model was estimated, the results are all highly significant and the adjusted R^2 suggests that the predictable component accounts for 8.2% of total variability in the mispricings. In spite of this, it is unclear how much of this effect is spuriously induced by the cointegrating regression methodology which was used to generate the mispricings—the true test of the model is on the out-of-sample performance, an evaluation of which is presented in the following section.

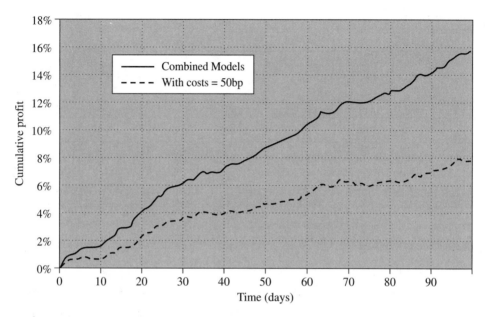

Figure 20.5
Aggregate equity curve, averaged across the performance of the 94 statistical arbitrage models.

Table 20.6
Aggregate cross-section performance of the statistical arbitrage models: the first row shows performance excluding trading costs, the second row shows performance with trading costs assumed equal to 50 basis points (0.5%) The metrics are directional ability (percentage of periods in which profits are positive), daily and annualised return and risk (measured as standard deviation of return), and Sharpe Ratio of annualised return to annualised risk.

	Profitable	Ave Ret	SD ret	Ret (Annual)	SD (Annual)	Sharpe
No costs	85%	0.16%	0.14%	31.75%	2.03%	15.7
Costs = 50bp	67%	0.08%	0.14%	15.73%	2.02%	7.8

20.5   Performance Analysis

Firstly let us consider the aggregate performance which is achieved by averaging the cross-section performance of the models—this is equivalent to trading a portfolio with an equal weight in each of the individual statistical arbitrage models.

The out-of-sample aggregate equity curve is shown in Figure 20.5.

A set of performance metrics for the aggregate performance are reported in Table 20.6.

Table 20.7
Summary of the performance metrics evaluated for individual models; the table reports the
min, max and average values of: predictive correlation (between actual and forecasted returns),
Directional forecasting ability, annualised return, risk and Sharpe Ratio, and equivalent figures
adjusted for transaction costs at a level of 50 basis points (0.5%). Note that the figures in a given
row may be derived from different models.

Model	Correlation	Direction	Return	Risk	Sharpe	Direction(Adj)	Return(adj)	Risk(adj)	Sharpe (adj)
Min	0.006	46%	-7.0%	5.8%	-0.3	26%	-38.0%	5.8%	-6.5
Max	0.386	66%	184.4%	67.6%	5.4	59%	160.3%	67.2%	4.0
Ave	0.224	56%	58.2%	21.6%	2.8	44%	25.3%	21.4%	1.0

The trading performance suggests that the model is highly successful—the diversification across models means that on this aggregate level the strategy is profitable
in 85% of the out-of-sample periods (falling to 67% when costs are included). After
costs the annualised return is just over 15% which is very satisfactory given that
the trading is market neutral and could be overlaid on an underlying long position
in the market. Alternatively the Sharpe Ratio suggests that the returns are large
when compared to the capital requirements of covering the associated risks and
that in this risk-adjusted sense the system is highly attractive. Note that the performance is highly sensitive to the assumed level of trading costs—one-way costs of
50bp reduce the return by half, with the break-even point lying close to transaction
costs of 1%. From this perspective the usefulness of such a system is conditional on
the circumstances of the user—whilst a bank may have costs as low as 10-20 basis
points, the equivalent cost for an individual is likely to be over 1%, hence negating
the information advantage provided by the model.

Table 20.7 summarises the performance metrics of the individual models:

The key feature of the results in Table 20.7 is the wide range of performance
across the individual models. Note that, after adjusting for transactions costs, the
models are only profitable in 44% of the out-of-sample periods and yet still return
positive profits—suggesting that the models are better at forecasting the larger
moves. The average Sharpe Ratio of the models is only 1.0 but notice that by
aggregating across the models the average return is unaffected whilst the average
risk is significantly reduced. From this perspective the improvement from a Sharpe
Ratio of 1.0 on an individual basis, to 7.8 on an aggregate basis (see Table 20.5)
would be expected only from models which are almost uncorrelated and hence can
significantly reduce risk by means of diversification.

20.6   Investigation of the Relationship between Variance Ratio Profile and Profitability

In the final phase of the analysis, we investigated the relationship between the insample properties of the variance ratio profiles of the different models, and the variability in their profitability during the out-of-sample period. This analysis consisted of regressing the out-of-sample Sharpe Ratios of the individual models on their VR statistics (Mahalanobis distance and eigenvector projections). A stepwise regression procedure resulted in the model shown here:

```
Multiple Regression Analysis
-----------------------------------------------------------------------------
Dependent variable: adjSharpe
-----------------------------------------------------------------------------

                                   Standard          T
Parameter               Estimate     Error       Statistic        P-Value
-----------------------------------------------------------------------------
CONSTANT                0.330649    0.166633       1.9843          0.0503
EigCor3                 0.281245    0.075705       3.71502         0.0004
EigCor5                 1.35602     0.316422       4.28548         0.0000
EigCov5                 14.3265     5.00645        2.86161         0.0052
-----------------------------------------------------------------------------

                       Analysis of Variance
-----------------------------------------------------------------------------
Source          Sum of Squares   Df   Mean Square    F-Ratio      P-Value
-----------------------------------------------------------------------------
Model              61.4094        3    20.4698        12.67        0.0000
Residual          145.455        90     1.61617
-----------------------------------------------------------------------------
Total (Corr.)     206.864        93

R-squared = 29.6858 percent
R-squared (adjusted for d.f.) = 27.342 percent
Standard Error of Est. = 1.27129
Mean absolute error = 0.915465
Durbin-Watson statistic = 1.85346
```

The regression diagnostics indicate a significant relationship between certain aspects of the variance ratio profile during the insample period, and risk-adjusted return during the out-of-sample. In particular the projections of the deviations from the average profile onto Eigenvectors 3 and 5 were found to be significantly related to profitability. In principle this information could be used in two ways: firstly to identify the models which are more likely to be profitable and weight them appropriately; secondly as additional conditioning information in an appropriate nonlinear error-correction model equivalent to (4) but allowing for interaction effects between the time-series dynamics and the information derived from the variance ratio profile. This aspect is the subject of current research.

20.7   Conclusion

The concept of cointegration provides a suitable basis for statistical arbitrage models but, being motivated by the search for theoretical understanding, is rather too restrictive if applied in the standard manner. This paper introduces two general directions in which cointegration analysis can be generalised to statistical arbitrage: the first is the method which is used to generate the "mispricing relationship"— in this case stepwise regression rather than standard regression—and the second is the nature of the tests employed—in our case tests for predictability which are based on the variance ratio profile of the mispricing time-series. In this case Monte-Carlo analysis is required in order to estimate the joint distribution of the individual variance ratio statistics and the test results indicate that the assumption of multivariate normality is almost—if not quite—accurate. In this paper, we have hardly touched upon the many options which are available for building the error-correction models, and for implementing trading systems which best exploit the information in the forecasts which they generate.

In spite of the fact that the focus of the work is placed elsewhere, the trading performance of the system appears to be impressive—returning an annualised Sharpe Ratio of 7.8 at a realistic transaction cost level of 50 basis points. From this perspective, the key feature of the system is the benefit of combining diversified models, in terms of reducing the aggregate risk—the **maximum** Sharpe Ratio of the individual models is 4.0, and the **average** only 1.0, much less impressive than the overall figure!

Finally, the underlying approach is equally applicable to a wide range of asset classes where assets share common stochastic trends and hence can be rendered more predictable by modelling in terms of relative prices rather than in raw form. Current research projects are concerned with a range of equity, fixed-income and derivatives markets, with sampling frequencies ranging between 10 minutes and daily.

References

Bentz, Y., Refenes, A. N. and De Laulanie, J-F., 1996, Modelling the performance of investment strategies, concepts, tools and examples, in Refenes et al (eds), *Neural Networks in Financial Engineering*, World Scientific, Singapore, 241–258.

Burgess, A. N., 1996, Statistical yield curve arbitrage in eurodollar futures using neural networks, in Refenes et al (eds), *Neural Networks in Financial Engineering*, World Scientific, Singapore, 98–110.

Burgess, A. N. and Refenes, A. N., 1996, Modelling non-linear cointegration in international equity index futures, in Refenes et al (eds), *Neural Networks in Financial Engineering*, World Scientific, Singapore, 50–63.

Cochrane J. H., 1988, How Big is the Random Walk in GDP?, *Journal of Political Economy* 96(5): 893–920.

Eckbo B. E., and Liu, J., 1993, Temporary Components of Stock Prices: New Univariate Results, *Journal of Financial and Quantitative Analysis* 28(2): 161–176.

Engle, R. F. and Granger, C. W. J., 1987, Cointegration and error-correction: representation, estimation and testing, *Econometrica*, 55: 251–276.

Johansen, S., 1988, Statistical analysis of cointegration vectors, *Journal of Economic Dynamics and Control* 12: 131–154.

Lo, A. W. and MacKinlay A. C., 1988, Stock Market Prices Do Not Follow Random Walks: Evidence from a Simple Specification Test, *The Review of Financial Studies* 1(1): 41–66.

Lo, A. W. and MacKinlay, A. C., 1990, Data-Snooping Biases in Tests of Financial Asset Pricing Models, *Review of Financial Studies* 3(3).

Lo, A. W., and McKinley A. C., 1995, Maximizing predictability in the stock and bond markets, NBER Working Paper #5027.

Phillips P. C. B. and Ouliaris S., 1988, Testing for cointegration using Principal Components Methods, *Journal of Economic Dynamics and Control* 12: 105–30.

Sargan, J. D. and Bhargava, A., 1983, Testing residuals from least squares regression for being generated by the Gaussian random walk, *Econometrica* 51: 153–174.

Steurer, E., and Hann, T. H., 1996, Exchange rate forecasting comparison: neural networks, machine learning and linear models, in Refenes et al (eds), *Neural Networks in Financial Engineering*, World Scientific, Singapore, 113–121.

Towers N. and Burgess, A. N., 1998, Optimisation of Trading Strategies using Parametrised Decision Rules, International Symposium on Intelligent Data Engineering and Learning (IDEAL) 1998, Hong Kong, October 14–16, 1998.

Towers N. and Burgess, A. N., 1999, Implementing Trading Strategies for Forecasting Models, in Abu-Mostafa et al. (eds.), *Computational Finance 99*, MIT Press, Cambridge, 313–326.

21 Implementing Trading Strategies for Forecasting Models

N. Towers and A. N. Burgess

In this paper we implement trading strategies for asset price forecasting models using parameterised decision rules. We develop a synthetic trading environment to investigate the relative effects, in terms of profitability, of modifying the characteristics of the forecasting model and the decision rule parameters. We show that implementation of the decision rule can be as important to trading performance as the predictive ability of the forecasting model. We apply these techniques to the dynamic trading of an intra-day "statistical mispricing" between a group of international equity indices. Results indicate that optimisation of decision rules can significantly improve trading performance, with annualised Sharpe Ratio increasing by up to a factor of two over a naive trading rule. To achieve this level of performance increase through the forecasting model alone would require a 50% improvement in prediction accuracy.

21.1   Introduction

In the last few years, a substantial amount of research has been dedicated to the development of financial forecasting models that attempt to exploit the dynamics of financial markets. A number of studies (e.g. Lo & MacKinley, 1995), have shown that predictable components exist within financial asset prices and that sophisticated forecasting models can have predictive power.

To take advantage of predictability, price forecasts need to be incorporated into a dynamic trading strategy. In the financial forecasting community, optimisation of the trading policy has often been overlooked and implementation trivialised. In this paper we show that implementation is just as important and that optimisation of parameterised trading rules can lead to a significant improvement in trading performance.

One approach to implementing decision making under uncertainty, is to decompose the problem into two stages: first the building of the forecasting model and then secondly, a decision phase that converts the forecast information into an action which, in this case, changes the trading position.

Alternative methods have been developed, (Moody et al., 1996; Choey & Weigend, 1996) that combine these two stages into one. These trading strategies use a single model to perform a joint optimisation over both the forecasting and decision stages.

In this paper we adopt the two stage decomposition approach. The advantages are potentially different information sets in the two phases, implementation of complex (non-differentiable) decision objectives, use of an existing forecasting model, trading strategies with different objectives from the same forecasting model and a more transparent trading system. We propose that a form of joint optimisation can be implemented using a high level "feedback" mechanism, which provides information from the decision module to the forecasting model.

To simulate this system we develop a synthetic trading environment that generates predictions with a controllable degree of predictability and a selection of parameterised decision rules. The inclusion of transaction costs results in trading profits that depend on sequences of interdependent decisions, and so are path dependent. Thus, to optimise the trading objective, the decision rule requires information of past actions as well as information from the forecasting model. This information is incorporated into three path dependent decision rules. We investigate the effects on the profitability of the trading system by changing the quality of the forecasting model and the decision rule parameters.

We apply our analysis to an example of a trading strategy developed from an asset price forecasting model. The predictable component is formed by combining hourly price data from a group of equity indices (FTSE, S&P, DAX, CAC, FIB, SSMI). Different decision rules are compared for two trading objectives: profit and annualised Sharpe Ratio.

21.2   Synthetic Trading System

In this section, we develop a framework for a synthetic-trading environment. The system contains a data generating process that simulates the output from a forecasting model of a single risky asset. The framework allows control of the prediction accuracy (specified as the correlation between predicted return and actual price return) and first order prediction autocorrelation.

The decision step is implemented using a parameterised trading rule that converts the forecast into a trading position. This rule is extended to path dependent trading rules by including information from recent actions.

The trading environment contains a transaction cost ratio parameter that specifies the ratio of transaction cost to the standard deviation of the asset returns. As the simulated returns are standardised, this ratio represents the relationship between the estimated volatility of the asset and cost of trading.

To formally construct the data generating process let an asset price series, y, an explanatory variable, x, and two noise variables, ε_t, and η_t be defined as

$$\Delta y_t = \beta \Delta x_t + \varepsilon_t \ where \ \varepsilon_t \sim NID(0, \sigma_\varepsilon^2) \tag{21.1}$$
$$\Delta x_t = \varphi \Delta x_{t-1} + \eta_t \ where \ \eta_t \sim NID(0, \sigma_\eta^2)$$

where the coefficient, β, represents the information between the returns of the explanatory variable and the asset price. The explanatory variable, x_t, is considered to be the deterministic component of the asset price signal and the noise variable, ε_t, the stochastic component. The coefficient, φ, represents a stability factor in the explanatory variable.

Suppose the variance of the explanatory variable returns is equal to the variance of the actual asset returns. Standardising these two returns allows the variance of the two noise terms to be defined as

$$\sigma_\varepsilon^2 = 1 - \beta^2 \tag{21.2}$$

$$\sigma_\eta^2 = 1 - \varphi^2 \ where \ \varphi < 1$$

where, φ, defines the level of autocorrelation in the returns of the explanatory variable and, β, the correlation between the asset return and the explanatory variable returns.

The predicted asset returns, $\Delta\hat{y}$, of the price series, y, are defined as

$$\Delta\hat{y} = \gamma\Delta x_t \tag{21.3}$$

where for a well specified forecasting model, $\gamma = |\beta|$. The absolute value is used so that the information content of the predictive model can be negative. If $|\gamma| \neq |\beta|$ then the model is biased. If we assume $\gamma = |\beta|$ then the correlation coefficient between predicted and actual returns equals β, and is considered to be the measure of prediction accuracy. We have now defined a data generating process for a well-specified forecasting model, with parameters β and φ controlling the degree of predictability and prediction autocorrelation.

Next, we devise some parameterised decision rules to convert predicted returns into trading positions. Parameterisation provides a convenient method of describing a family of related trading rules. Modification of the decision parameters allows selection of the trading rule that maximises the decision objective.

The basic parameterised decision rule which uses only the predicted asset return and ignores information about recent decisions is defined as

$$D_t(\Delta\hat{y}_t; k, m) = m|\Delta\hat{y}_t|^k sign(\Delta\hat{y}_t) \tag{21.4}$$

where k and m are the two decision parameters, $\Delta\hat{y}$ is the forecast return and D_t the trading position at time, t. The parameters, k and m, control the shape and magnitude of the decision function respectively.

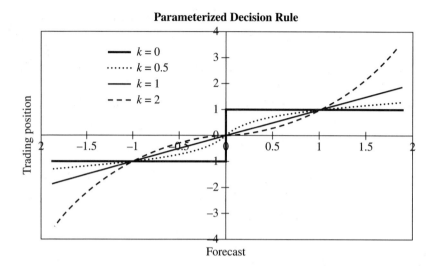

Figure 21.1
Four examples of trading rules derived from the parameterised decision rule by varying the value of k with m fixed at 1.

Examples from this parameterised decision rule are shown in Figure 21.1. The amount of the asset that must be either bought or sold is then defined as the difference between the new and previous trading position.

When $k = 1$ the trading rule is a linear function with slope m; when $k = 0$ the rule is a step function between two states $+m$ and $-m$. Other positive values of k and m give additional non-linear decision functions. To compare the average profits of different trading rules we set m to be a normalisation factor so that the average size of the trading position, D is equal to one for any value of k.

This simple parameterised decision rule, described in equation 21.4, is used to devise three path dependent decision rules to include information from the most recent decisions. These path dependent decision rules, $D(t)*$, are defined as

$$D_t * (\theta) = \theta D_t + (1 - \theta)D_{t-1}* \qquad (21.5)$$

where $D_t * (\theta)$ is an exponential moving average of D_t with decay parameter, θ.

$$D_t * (h) = \frac{1}{h} \sum_{j=0}^{h-1} D_{t-j} \qquad (21.6)$$

where $D_t * (h)$ is a moving average of D_t with the number of past observations, h.

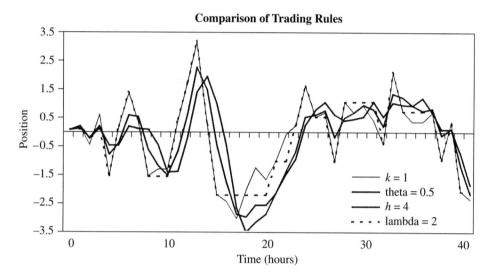

Figure 21.2
Comparison of the trading positions for an example of the four different trading rules

$$D_t * (\lambda) \;=\; D_t \qquad \text{if } |D_t - D_{t-1}*| > \lambda \qquad\qquad (21.7)$$
$$\qquad\quad\; =\; D_{t-1} * \quad \text{otherwise}$$

where $D_t*(\lambda)$ is a parameterised step rule that requires the current position, $D_{t-1}*$, to change by greater than the tolerance parameter, λ.

Figure 21.2 illustrates a simulated trading position for examples of the four decision rules over a sample of 50 predicted returns. The returns were generated for a forecasting model with a prediction accuracy of 0.25 and a prediction autocorrelation of 0.5. For all decision rules the parameter, k, was set to one with m set so that the amplitude of the average trading position was normalised to one. The other parameters of the three path dependent decision rules were set with $\theta = 0.4, h = 4$ and $\lambda = 1$ respectively.

The trading profit for each time period is defined as

$$P_t = D_t \Delta y_t - T|D_t - D_{t-1}| \qquad\qquad (21.8)$$

where T is the estimated transaction cost per unit of y, D_t is the percentage of the fund invested in asset y and P_t is the percentage trading profit.

The synthetic trading system assumes asset returns of unit variance, so to be consistent, T is scaled by the variability of the asset returns. This defines T as the ratio of transaction cost to asset variability.

21.3 Simulated Results

In this section we show results from the synthetic trading system for a number of different trading scenarios. We simulate scenarios for trading different types of assets on intra-day forecast horizons. The ratio of transaction costs to asset variability, T, was set to three values, 0.1, 0.5 and 1.0. These represent typical values of T for intra-day equity futures, long government bond futures, and interest rate futures respectively with transaction costs estimated from the typical bid/ask spread.

21.3.1 Basic decision rule

To illustrate the effect of prediction accuracy and prediction autocorrelation on average profit the decision rule parameter, k, in equation 21.4, was set to either 0 or 1. The case of $k = 0$ represents a trading rule with a fixed size trading position defined by the sign of the prediction, and $k = 1$ represents a relative size trading position proportional to the size of the predicted return. The profitability of the basic decision rule was simulated for the three scenarios of T.

Figure 21.3 shows that the average profit increases as the prediction accuracy of the forecasting model increases. Positive profits are achieved for all forecasting models with prediction accuracy above 0.1. The horizontal contours show that the effect of autocorrelation is small. Increasing prediction autocorrelation by 0.1 is approximately equal to increasing prediction accuracy by 0.01.

With the higher transaction ratio, in Figure 21.4, a prediction accuracy of at least 0.2 is required to achieve of a profit. The angled contours show that prediction autocorrelation is significant with both variables influencing profit. For both values of k, a prediction accuracy of approximately 0.6 is required to achieve a profit if the autocorrelation is zero, compared to only 0.2 if the autocorrelation is 0.9.

Figure 21.5 shows that for both these trading rules prediction accuracy of at least 0.4 is required to achieve a profit. The contours show that profitability is affected almost equally by prediction autocorrelation and prediction accuracy. For instance, the expected average profit for autocorrelation of 0.6 and predictability of 0.3 is almost equal to autocorrelation of 0.3 and predictability of 0.6.

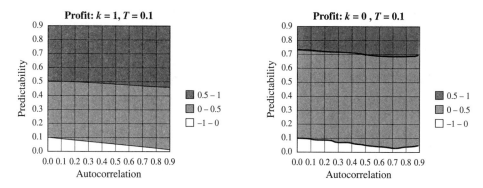

Figure 21.3
The contour profile of average profit for transaction cost, $T = 0.1$ and the two values of k.

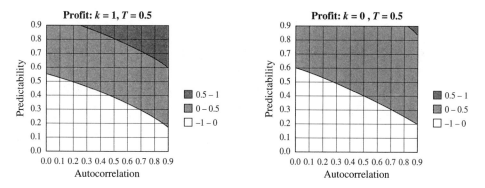

Figure 21.4
The contour profile of average profit for transaction cost, $T = 0.5$ and the two values of k

These experiments serve to illustrate the interaction between the properties of the forecasting model (predictability and autocorrelation), the decision rule parameter, k, and three different classes of assets on intra-day time scales.

21.3.2   Path dependent decision rules

In these experiments we illustrate the effect of the path dependent decision rules on the difference in profit compared to the basic decision rule with $k = 1$. The decision rule parameters θ, h, λ were not optimised but fixed at typical values.

Figure 21.6 shows the profit change for the three path dependent rules from basic decision rule with $k = 1$ for a transaction cost ratio of $T = 0.1$. The first plot shows

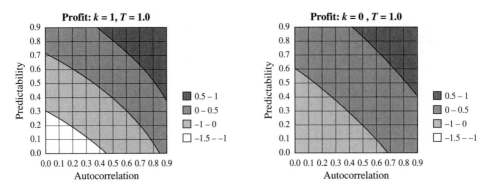

Figure 21.5
The contour profile of average profit for transaction cost, $T = 1.0$ and the two values of k

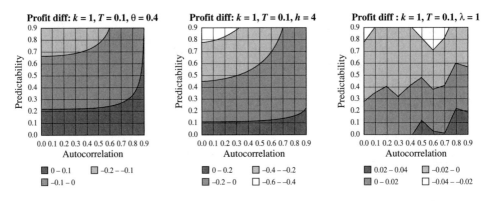

Figure 21.6
The contour profiles for changes in average profit for the three path dependent decision rules for transaction ratio $T = 0.1$.

the profit difference for the exponential moving average rule. The second plot shows the results for the moving average rule and the third plot shows the parameterised step rule. All graphs show some regions of increased profit, generally at low levels of prediction accuracy, and profit deterioration, for higher levels. In general, profits deteriorate faster with low levels of prediction autocorrelation.

Figure 21.7 shows differences in average profit for the path dependent decision rules compared to the basic decision rule with a higher transaction costs ratio of 0.5. For all levels of predictability and autocorrelation, the curved contours in the first and third plots show increased profits over the basic decision rule with

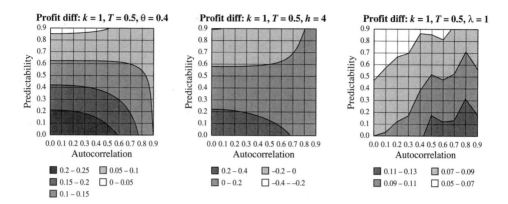

Figure 21.7
The contour profiles for changes in average profit for the three path dependent decision rules for transaction cost ratio $T = 0.5$.

higher profits at lower levels of predictability. The exponential decision rule is more effective for lower levels of autocorrelation. The second plot has contours which show decreasing profits at high levels of predictability which are further degraded by low autocorrelation. The jagged contours of the third plot show that the average profit of the parameterised step rule may be more unstable.

Further analysis shows that all three of the path dependent decision rules reduce the size of the negative profit region compared to the basic decision rule, (as shown in figure 21.4).

Figure 21.8 shows profit changes for the path dependent decision rules compared to the basic decision rule with a high transaction cost ratio of 1.0. For all characterised forecasting models, the three path dependent decision rules show increased profitability over the basic decision rule. Again the first and second plots show results for the exponential and equal weight moving average decision rules respectively. The curved contours for these two plots are similar in shape and show increasing profit differences for reductions in levels of predictability and autocorrelation. The contours in the third plot, generated using the parameterised step rule, show increasing profits for higher autocorrelation and low predictability.

The differences between the direction of contours on the three plots can be explained by examining the three path dependent decision rules. The parameterised step rule with a fixed value for λ reduces trading turnover most significantly for high levels of autocorrelation and the two moving average rules reduce turnover most

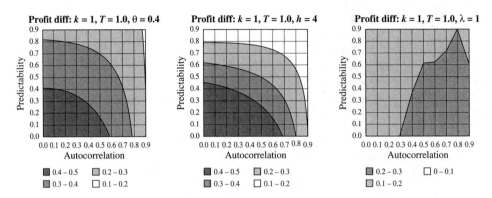

Figure 21.8
The contour profiles for changes in average profit for the path dependent decision rules with transaction cost parameter, $T = 1.0$.

with low levels of autocorrelation. This gives an opposite gradient to the slope of the contours.

The experiments above illustrate the importance of path dependent decision rules in improving the profitability of trading strategies with transaction costs. In these experiments, illustrated in Figures 21.6 to 21.8, the path dependent rules have fixed parameter values. To improve the expected average profits further the decision rule parameters can be optimised to maximise expected utility.

The path dependent decision rules are most effective with high transaction cost ratios and low levels of predictability. This can be explained by considering the variance and stability of the trading position through time. A higher variance reflects greater exploitation of the predictive ability of the forecasting model with stability in the trading position reducing relative transaction costs. The path dependent decision rules have the effect of reducing trading position variance, hence, not fully exploiting predictive ability, but they tend to increase trading position stability thereby reducing transaction costs. This effect can be described as introducing bias to the trading position while lowering variability. Under conditions of low predictability and high transaction cost, the lower trading position variability is preferable even at the expense of increasing bias.

This explanation is analogous to the well known bias/variance tradeoff in statistics where, in this case, bias refers to trading position stability and variance refers to the degree to which the predictive ability is exploited by varying the trading position. Under this analogy, the path dependent decision rule parameter is used

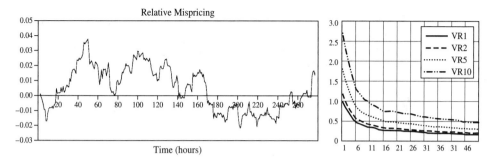

Figure 21.9
The left hand graph shows the estimated mispricing, p, between the prices of FTSE, S&P, DAX, FIB and SSMI indices. The right hand graph shows the Variance Ratio profile for the mispricing.

to find the optimal position on the bias-variance tradeoff curve and so maximise trading system performance.

21.4   Application in "Statistical Arbitrage"

We apply our techniques to a typical example of a "real" financial trading strategy. The example comes from a class of trading we describe as "statistical arbitrage". In traditional "zero risk" arbitrage trading, a mispricing between assets is detected and exploited, by trading, to achieve a profit. Similarly, in statistical arbitrage trading, a "statistical mispricing" between assets is detected and exploited. The "statistical mispricing" is not a true mispricing, but based upon statistical relationships identified from historical price data of an associated group of assets. This type of trading is no longer "risk free" and so the level of trading risk needs to be controlled with the trading strategy.

Hourly price data was collected from 15 May 1998 to 7 July 1998 for a group of equity index futures (FTSE, S&P, DAX, CAC, FIB and SSMI). A methodology using principal components was applied to the data to estimate relative weightings of the equity indices and so generate a "statistical mispricing", p, defined as

$$p = 0.58FTSE + 0.17S\&P - 0.15DAX - 0.76FIB + 0.19SSMI \qquad (21.9)$$

The left hand graph of Figure 21.9 shows the value of the "mispricing" through time and the right hand graph is the variance ratio profile for the mispricing. It shows that the combination of assets has a variance ratio function that falls below one and so signifies a degree of cyclically or mean reverting behaviour.

Table 21.1
shows the annualised return, annualised standard deviation and Sharpe Ratio for the selected
trading rules over the trading period.

Trading Rules	Annualised Profit	Annualised Std. Dev.	Annualised Sharpe Ratio
$k = 1$	0.461	0.175	2.634
$k = 0$	0.276	0.155	1.783
$k = 1, \theta = 0.67$	0.626	0.179	3.483
$k = 1, h = 5$	0.576	0.181	3.180
$k = 1, \lambda = 0.45$	0.596	0.175	3.41

Given the variance ratio profile, the forecasting model of the mispricing return
was defined as

$$\Delta \hat{p} \propto -p \tag{21.10}$$

where the predicted mispricing return is proportional to the negative of the relative
mispricing. The constant of proportionality is incorporated into the decision rule
normalisation parameter, m, and so can be ignored.

Over the sample period, this simple forecasting model is characterised by a
prediction accuracy (i.e. the correlation between the forecast and the actual change
in the mispricing) of 0.12 and prediction autocorrelation of 0.96. The transaction
cost ratio is estimated using the bid/ask spreads of the equity index futures contract
and the sample standard deviation of the mispricing return. The transaction cost for
one unit of mispricing is approximately 10 basis points and the standard deviation
of the return is 0.005. This gives a ratio of transaction cost to unit return variance
of approximately 0.2. Given these characteristics of the forecasting model and the
T ratio, the graphs from the simulations indicate that the path dependent decision
rules may give improved profitability.

The synthetic trading system was set up with a transaction cost ratio of 0.2
and the properties of the forecasting model. With decision parameter, k, set to
1, the path dependent parameters θ, h, λ were optimised to be 0.67, 5 and 0.45
respectively. These path dependent trading rules, and also two naïve rules, with k
set to 0 and 1, were then applied to the real data set and the performance metrics
calculated as shown in table 21.1 and equity curves generated as shown in Figure
21.10.

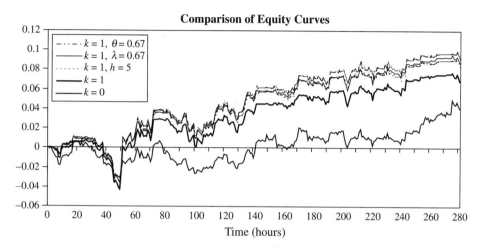

Figure 21.10
The equity curves generated for the five trading rules shown in table 1.

21.5   Conclusions

We have devised a general methodology for simulating trading systems, given an asset price forecasting model, and using the proposed parameterised decision rules. We illustrate the trading conditions that are most likely to produce positive profits and are liable to give increased profits using the path dependent decision rules. We show that, under certain trading conditions, implementation of the trading rule is as important as predictive ability.

   We apply these techniques to an example of a forecasting model that generates an intra-day "statistical mispricing" from a combination of equity indices. Analysis of the trading performance results show that profits and Sharpe Ratio are highly dependent on the choice of trading rule. Changing only the decision rule parameter, k, from 0 to 1, alters the annualised Sharpe Ratio from 1.78 to 2.63. Using any of the three path dependent decision rules produces increased profits and Sharpe Ratio. For example, using the exponential moving average trading rule ($k = 1, \theta = 0.7$) increases the annualised Sharpe Ratio from 1.78 ($k = 0$) to 3.48, a factor of 2, and from 2.63 ($k = 1$) to 3.48, over 30% improvement in performance over the naive trading rule.

   Optimisation of the trading rules relies on accurate characterisation of the forecasting model and so in the example the performance improvements from this technique can be considered an upper limit. Using a larger sample data set would allow the data to be split into two parts, one for building the forecasting model and optimising the trading parameters, and the second for out-of-sample performance.

It is proposed that decision making can be improved by "feedback" from the decision to the forecasting module. The synthetic trading system can be used to measure the sensitivity of the trading profit to changes in the characteristics of the forecasting model. This information can be used to assess the value, in terms of profitability, of improving the characteristics of the forecasting model and lead to improvements in the whole decision making methodology.

References

Burgess A. N., (1997) "Controlling nonstationary in statistical arbitrage using a portfolio of cointegration models," *Proceedings from Fifth International Conference on Computational Finance*, CF97.

Burgess A. N., N. Towers, (1998) "Statistical arbitrage models in Equity and Fixed Income markets," Technical Report, London Business School, 1998.

Choey, M., Weigend, A. S., (1996) "Nonlinear Trading Models through Sharpe Ratio Maximization," *Proceedings from Fourth International Conference on Neural Networks in the Capital Markets*, NNCM96.

Lo, A., MacKinley, C.,(1995) "Maximizing Predictiability in the stock and bond markets," *NBER*, 1995.

Moody, J., (1996) "Optimisation of Trading Systems and Portfolios," *Proceedings from the Fourth International Conference on Neural Networks in the Capital Markets*, NNCM96.

Towers, N., Burgess, A. N., (1998) "Optimisation of Trading Strategies using Parameterised Decision Rules," *International Symposium of Intelligent Data Engineering and Learning*, IDEAL98.

Towers, N, Burgess A. N., (1999) "A framework for applying Reinforcement Learning to Investment Finance," Technical Report, London Business School, 1999.

22 Using Nonlinear Neurogenetic Models with Profit Related Objective Functions to Trade the US T-bond Future

Zac Harland

Trading decision models are often designed by optimizing standard statistical measures of error to create forecasts from which trading rules are then indirectly synthesized. In the context of a bond futures trading model, we find that by directly optimizing a number of profit related objective functions, superior results are attained than when using mean square error. Moreover, by using a genetic training method we gain flexibility with regards to the choice of objective function by dispensing with the need to operate within a gradient based framework.

22.1 Introduction

Although much has been written recently on the use of neural networks and computational learning techniques in financial forecasting and the design of trading systems, the majority of this research has concentrated on minimizing standard statistical measures of predictability rather than directly optimizing a profit related objective function—for recent examples see Refenes et al.(1993). This is not altogether surprising as many of these advanced techniques have their foundation in other fields where minimizing error functions such as mean square error (MSE) is more meaningful to the task at hand. However, in financial forecasting practitioners are more interested in real trading profits and the risk associated with attaining those profits than they are in 'inferred' profitability derived from intermediate measures of predictive accuracy, whose relationship to trading returns is somewhat tenuous.

The observation that statistical error measures may be unsuitable is not new; Leitch (1991) finds that, in the context of treasury bill forecasts, predictive accuracy as measured by MSE is not strongly related to returns. A study by Caldwell (1995) shows that lower measures of MSE and Mean Absolute Error(MAE) did not correlate well with trading profits and in some cases were positively correlated (lower error resulted in lower returns and vice versa). LeBaron (1993) also finds evidence of a weak connection between MSE measures and trading profits. When minimizing traditional error measures such as MSE more emphasis is placed on reducing an error where the network predicts a positive move of +3%, compared to an actual move of +1%, than in reducing the error in a predicted move of −0.5% for the same actual move. However, from a trading perspective, the latter error is least desirable especially if the decision is to sell when the predicted move is negative. This is one reason why metrics based on direction may be more closely correlated to actual returns. Using some kind of threshold on the network output may help to alleviate the problem but it is probably more efficient to optimize the desired trading rule more directly.

In this paper we describe a trading model that utilizes neural networks trained with a genetic training algorithm to trade the 30 year US Treasury bond futures contract. To address the issue of sub-optimal objective functions we directly optimize a number of profit related functions, including the well known Sharpe Ratio (Sharpe, 1966), and compare the results with a model which minimizes MSE. The main objective was to produce a tradable model and so to this end we endeavored to keep all aspects of the model as simple as possible.

Much of the other work on training neural networks with profit related error functions has tended to concentrate on modifying the standard gradient descent learning algorithms such as backpropagation—usually designed to minimize the MSE between target and output—to minimize an objective function more directly related to the trading process. Bentz and Refenes(1994) use a technique whereby the backpropagation algorithm is modified so that, using a sigmoidal weighting function, more emphasis is placed on observations where there is directional error. Choey and Weigend(1996) present a gradient ascent method for directly optimizing the Sharpe Ratio as the cost function. Other related work in this area includes that of Bengio(1996) and Moody(1996).

Approaching the problem from a gradient based standpoint, requiring modification of the gradient descent learning algorithm, is somewhat restrictive as it requires that the function which captures the problem's optimization objective be differentiable. Moreover, this procedure can be fairly complex and limits the space of possible objective functions. What is arguably more useful is a method that is able to train a neural network on any function of interest including those that are not continuous. For example, functions such as, "if network output > 0 then long else short" are not easy to accommodate within a gradient based framework. This is where stochastic training methods such as those using genetic algorithms can be very useful. In the case of the genetic training algorithm all that is required is a comparative measure of 'fitness', without any need for gradient based information. This allows more flexibility in the choice of objective function.

22.2 Genetic Algorithms

The concept of Genetic Algorithms (GAs) was defined by John Holland (1975). Holland showed that a variety of optimization problems could be solved by a method that he called the Genetic Algorithm. GAs are especially useful when the function to be optimized is discontinuous or noisy (such as a trading related function) and does not lend itself easily to other gradient based approaches. Its effectiveness is partly based on its ability to simultaneously search large regions of the parameter space and converge to regions of high fitness (although not necessarily the global optimum).

The technique is based on the principle of Darwinian evolution and the "survival of the fittest" and follows this general pattern:

1. First a suitable representation scheme is identified for the problem of interest. In this case it is the neural network weight vectors that are encoded in such a way as to represent candidate solutions to the problem.

2. An initial randomly created population of solution candidates is created.

3. Each member of the population is assigned a fitness measure depending on the nature of the problem.

4. A new generation is then created by repeatedly iterating through the following three steps:

a. Reproduce an existing member by copying it directly into the new population.

b. Create two new offspring solutions by performing a crossover operation on two parent solutions (parents are selected randomly but biased towards high fitness).

c. Create a new solution from an existing one by random mutation—this particular operation is generally constrained to have a low probability of occurrence.

5. The process is then halted when the population has converged on an acceptable solution.

GAs can be used in a number of ways in ANN design including but not limited to, input feature selection, optimization of network architecture, training algorithms etc. In this particular application we use GAs as a training algorithm with all other network parameters being decided a priori.

22.3   Objective Functions

The decision as to which objective function to use is not so clear cut—it is unlikely that a single objective function will capture all the features relevant to the trading process. In this paper we use four different objective functions: MSE, the Sharpe Ratio (SR), Total log returns (TLR) and a variation of TLR which includes a penalty term (TLRP). Although the SR is used extensively in the financial community as measure of risk adjusted returns, it is generally criticized as it penalizes both negative and positive returns equally. TLR is somewhat similar to the SR objective but without the risk adjustment however; its drawback is that it does not take into account the total number of trades—a factor that becomes increasingly important when transaction costs are taken into account. In the end the choice of objective functions was guided by the need for simplicity.

For the MSE, SR and TLR functions the models take on either a Long or Short position $S_t \in \{1, -1\}$ in the futures contract and as such are always in the market. The MSE model simply minimizes the mean square error between the network output and the target, which in this case is one day log returns. After training the following rule is applied:

If output≥ 0.0 then long, else short.

The TLR model maximizes the following:
Define daily log returns as,

$$r_t = \log(price_{t+1}/price_t) \tag{22.1}$$

$$\text{Total log returns} = \sum_{t=1}^{N} p_t(r_t) \tag{22.2}$$

where p_t $\qquad = \qquad$ $\begin{cases} 1 & \text{if } o_t \geq 0.0 \\ -1 & \text{otherwise and} \end{cases}$

$\qquad o_t$ is the network output.

The SR model maximizes the Sharpe Ratio defined as,

$$SR = \frac{r^a - r^f}{\sigma} \tag{22.3}$$

where r^a $=$ actual returns,
$\quad r^f$ $=$ risk free returns, and
$\quad \sigma$ $=$ standard deviation of r^a.

The SR provides a measure of risk adjusted returns. Actual returns are calculated on a monthly basis, averaged and then annualized. We actually remove the risk free returns term as it cancels with the interest that is ordinary earned from margin in a trading account.

The TLRP model can be long, short or neutral $S_t \in \{1, -1, 0\}$. It has a penalty term which simply penalizes incorrect daily direction by increasing the resultant daily loss by a certain percentage in an attempt to raise overall trading accuracy.

$$\text{TLRP} = \sum_{t=1}^{N} d_t \left((r_t) + w_t(r_t) \right) \tag{22.4}$$

$$\text{where } d_t = \left\{ \begin{array}{ll} 1 & \text{if } o_t > 0.5 \\ -1 & \text{if } o_t < -0.5 \\ 0 & \text{otherwise} \end{array} \right.$$

Four values for the penalty term, g are chosen: 0.0, 0.1, 0.15 and 0.20.

22.4 Data

The data used in this study consist of the open, high, low and close of both the US Tbond and S&P500 nearest to expiry futures contracts, covering the period from 12th April 1983 to 30th June 1998–62 separate contracts in all. As explained later, S&P500 data is used for additional inputs to the models. It was necessary to create two adjusted time series from the raw prices. For total return calculations in contract points the Bond series is converted into a continuous contract series— raw contract prices adjusted to take into account the spread at rollover between the nearest contract to expiry and the next contract. This is accomplished by establishing the spread between the nearest contract and the next nearest contract at rollover and then adding the cumulative spread up to that contract to the new contract prices. Contracts are rolled over when the trading volume of the next contract is equal to, or greater than, that of the present contract. This splicing creates a new series with the contract rollover distortions removed. All exchange holidays are removed from the data.

Where first log differences are required we use the unadjusted raw prices except on the two days at rollover, where the appropriate one day overlapping prices of each contract are used to calculate the respective log difference of the data (see Eq.1).

Because futures price data are already inherently noisy, adjusting for the spread is essential. Without this adjustment a potentially large artificial drop/rise at each rollover can result. In the case of the US Bond futures price this spread is mostly negative in the period under study due to the financing rate at the time being less than the income or coupon received from the underlying bond. Over the period of

1983–1998 the total spread results in a 40 point artificial drop in the unadjusted prices. This artificial drop will tend to cause a negative bias in a model using only unadjusted prices.

22.5   The BDS Test

Before embarking on the relatively costly and time intensive task of designing a prediction model for financial time series it is prudent to ascertain whether or not the data will lend itself to such a task. With this in mind we use the test of Brock, Dechert, and Scheinkman (1987), the BDS test, as an initial diagnostic of potential predictability within the data series. The BDS test is a powerful statistic and tests the null hypothesis that a time series $\{x_t\}$ is independent and identically distributed (iid) against a non-specific alternative. Let $\{x_t, t = 1, \ldots, T\}$ be a time series, and denote $X_t^M = (x_t, x_t, \ldots, x_{t+M-1})$ a point in the M-dimensional Euclidean space. The BDS test develops a statistic based on the correlation integral, defined as:

$$C_M(\varepsilon, T) = \frac{2}{T_M(TM-1)} \sum_{t<s} I_\varepsilon(X_T^M, X_s^M) \tag{22.5}$$

where $T_M = T - M + 1$ is the number of M-histories constructed from the sample of length T, and $I_\varepsilon(X_t^M, X_s^M)$ is an indicator function defined as,

$$I_\varepsilon(X_t^M, S_s^M) = 1, \text{if } ||X_t^M - X_s^M|| < \varepsilon \tag{22.6}$$

$$= 0, \text{ otherwise} \tag{22.7}$$

and $|| \; ||$ denotes the sup norm.

The correlation integral gives us the fraction of all possible pairs of points that are within a distance ε of eachother.

The test statistic is

$$\text{BDS}_M(\varepsilon, T) = \frac{\sqrt{T_M} \left[C_M(\varepsilon, T) - C_1(\varepsilon, T)^M \right]}{\sigma_M(\varepsilon, T)} \tag{22.8}$$

and has a limiting standard normal distribution. Under the null hypothesis that $\{X_t\}$ is iid, the term, $\sqrt{T_M}[C_M(\varepsilon, T) - C_1(\varepsilon, T)^M]$, has a normal limiting distribution with mean zero and standard deviation, $\sigma_M(\varepsilon, T)$. The null hypothesis is rejected if the probability of any two M-histories being close together is greater than the Mth power of the probability of any two points being close together.

The test can also serve as a general model specification test by applying the test to the residuals of any time series model—a properly specified model should produce

Table 22.1

ε	M	Log Diff	AR(1)	AR(4)	LogDiff shuffled	AR(1) Shuffled	AR(4) Shuffled
1	2	2.16	2.32	2.33	0.35	0.166	-0.039
1	3	3.79	3.93	3.94	0.17	0.128	-0.096
1	4	4.90	5.07	5.09	0.20	0.179	-0.0165
1	5	6.15	6.33	6.35	0.24	0.207	-0.193
0.5	2	2.04	2.43	2.41			
0.5	3	3.57	3.86	3.87			
0.5	4	4.41	4.71	4.72			
0.5	5	5.36	5.64	5.64			

iid residuals. In order to test for possible nonlinear dependencies it is common practice to remove any linear dependence which may be present by filtering or prewhitening the series by fitting a linear autoregressive model and then analyzing the residuals to check for structure beyond linearity. In this case we test the log difference series, the residuals of an AR(1) and AR(4) model fitted to the series and randomly shuffled versions of all three.

Table 22.1 shows the results of the BDS statistic for embedding dimensions M ranging from 2 to 5, with $\varepsilon = 1$ and 0.5 times the standard deviation for the log first differences of the original series, the whitened AR(1) and AR(4) residuals and, for $\varepsilon = 1$, the mean of 50 shuffled (with replacement) versions of all three series.

All statistics excluding the shuffled series are significant at the 5% level ($>$ 1.96) with the majority significant at the 1% level. In the absence of a significant difference between the statistics for the raw data and the AR residuals this points to nonlinearities in the underlying data generating process of the series. The possible presence of nonlinear dependence suggests that linear methods will not be sufficient to model the data adequately. The results for the shuffled series show that the underlying structure is destroyed by this process and lends further support to the results.

22.6 Inputs

Given that many of today's financial markets are interrelated and global in nature it is possible that including inputs from related markets may help to improve performance. We decided to use both Bond and S&P500 data in the model. There is a 0.3 linear correlation between daily log differences of the Bond and S&P500 daily futures data series from 83–98—an indication that certain interrelationships may be exploitable in an effort to improve the model.

Choice of inputs is of paramount importance when building financial prediction models. Although neural networks have been proven to be powerful function approximators it is still necessary to use extensive pre-processing of the input variables—it is unlikely that simply presenting inputs derived from price data of the target series at arbitrary lags will produce usable results. Theoretical concerns aside, were this the case these 'anomalies' would quickly be priced out of the market as various participants discovered them. Almost by definition, any pre-processed variable which contains predictive accuracy must be difficult to discover or it would no longer exist. In an effort to find meaningful input features we tested a number of the popular technical indicators such as, MACD, RSI, Bollinger bands etc. We came to the conclusion that many of these more commonly known technical indicators owe their use to the promotional skills of their creators, rather than from proper analysis of their correlation to future price changes. In light of this, we ended up in using a number of digital filter design techniques from the field of signal processing in an attempt to arrive at more useful and robust input features.

Given that the models are based on daily data and will produce an output at the close of each day, we focused our attention on inputs that showed correlation with future daily prices. We reasoned that if it was possible to find inputs with stable correlation to 1 and 2 day future returns it should help to circumvent the problem of the model being biased to either trending or sideways markets—a common problem in many conventional trading models. Various statistical measures were used including parametric and non-parametric correlation, mutual information and a technique using ANOVA, similar to that proposed by Burgess and Refenes (1995). The main criteria being that any correlation exhibited by a potential input candidate had to be as constant as possible over the full length of the training set.

In all, 5 inputs were formed from 3 separate price transformations. Price transformations derived from the S&P500 futures contract consisted of a momentum type indicator at time , along with lags at $t-20$ and $t-25$. The two inputs from the bond series consisted of another momentum type indictor at time t, together with an input that measured the predictive correlation of this input with future prices (lagged appropriately). All inputs were standardized to zero mean and unit variance. In order to lessen the effect of outliers the inputs were then put through the tanh function, which has the effect of compressing outliers.

22.7   Model Design and Methodology

Neural networks can be powerful function approximators and thus lend themselves well to financial time series prediction, a form of 'weak' modeling in which the underlying equations of the system are not readily available (unlike so called 'strong' models). However, weak models gain their flexibility via the use of many parameters which can lead to the danger of overfitting the data. This concept is embodied in the so called bias/variance trade off. The modeler's objective is to produce a statistical model of the underlying data generating process which then generalizes well out of sample. If too many parameters are used there is a tendency for the model to overfit the data which leads to poor generalization (the model has a high variance in the estimated parameters and a low bias in that it has the ability to fit a wide variety of functions). Conversely, if too few parameters are used it may be too inflexible to extract the relevant features of the underlying process (it is said to have a high bias and low variance). The ultimate goal is to have a model with low variance and low bias. Given that financial time series tend to have a very low signal to noise ratio, overfitting the data is a real possibility. As such, we lean towards the low-variance/high-bias choice and constrain the network's ability to overfit the data by restricting the number of hidden neurons used.

There are different approaches when it comes to deciding how much data to use for training a network. One view is that the market is always changing and therefore one does not want to use data too far back in history as there is a danger that much of it will be redundant. The other approach is to use as much data as is available, reasoning that the only way to have confidence in the model's final results is if it has acceptable performance over as long a data history as possible. We subscribe to the latter approach and therefore use as much of the available data to train the networks whilst making sure to leave a large enough out of sample period for final analysis.

Initially, the data set was divided into training, validation and test sets as shown in table 22.2. All networks had 1 hidden layer with 5 input units and 1 output unit. Input units were linear while tanh units were used for the remaining layers. In an attempt to deal with the bias/variance trade off and to achieve *structural stabilization* within the model, networks with hidden layers of 1 to 10 units were tested. The objective was to find the network architecture which relied on the least amount of parameters (hidden units) yet delivered the most consistent performance. As we wished to use as much data to train the final networks as possible the following training regime was decided on.

Table 22.2

Set	Dates	Length
Training set	12th April 1983 to 6th January 1989	1456 days
Validation set	7th January 1989 to 7th October 1994	1456 days
Final testing set	10th October 1994 to 30th June 1998	935 days

Table 22.3

Final sets		
Training set	12th April 1983 to 7th October 1994	2912 days
Final testing set	10th October 1994 to 30th June 1998	935 days

First, all potential network architectures for each objective function were trained to convergence on the training set data with the resulting validation set performance analyzed. Then both sets were alternated and the process repeated. This allowed out of sample performance to be monitored on both training and validation data in an effort to make sure that the final architecture chosen had stable performance. It was found that networks with 2 hidden units produced the most stable results over all objective functions. Although some networks with more hidden units produced better performance, this performance varied too widely across individual trials.

Finally, networks for each objective function were trained to convergence on the joined training and validation sets (see Table 22.3) and their performance analyzed on the final 935 day testing set. Twenty training runs, each with populations of 150 networks, were used for each objective function (the total of 140 runs took approximately 170 hours on a 200Mhz PC). The outputs of the top 10 performing networks were then averaged to produce the final results for each objective.

22.8 Results

The final results for all objective functions over the training period of 2912 days are presented in Table 22.4. Also shown are the results for the benchmark buy and hold (B&H) strategy (in practice this would involve rolling over a long position at each rollover date). No slippage or transaction costs were taken into account.

Of those models that are always in the market, it is clear that the MSE objective delivers the worst performance. Apart from lower total return (approximately half that of the TLR objective) and average trade statistics, it also suffers from a comparatively large drawdown of $15450.00. Inspection of the cumulative equity

Table 22.4
In sample results for all objective functions based on data from 1983 to 1994.

	TLR	MSE	SR	TLRP 0%	TLRP 10%	TLRP 15%	TLRP 20%	B&H
Total Log Returns	88.08	44.08	79.29	66.46	52.62	45.22	50.2	28.4
Avg log trade	0.17	0.09	0.15	0.13	0.15	0.19	0.2	na
Total net profit	$177.08	$97.78	$166.22	$139.23	$113.81	$100.84	$104.80	$58.43
Gross profit	$385.14	$318.12	$381.58	$313.28	$222.29	$164.88	$162.12	na
Gross loss	−$208.06	−$220.34	−$215.36	−$174.05	−$108.48	−$64.04	−$57.32	na
Sharpe Ratio	1.46	0.98	1.30	1.23	1.23	1.26	1.43	0.54
% of time in Market	100%	100%	100%	68%	42%	30%	22%	100%
Total # of trades	511	463	538	496	349	237	252	na
Number winning trades	301	255	319	300	216	163	168	na
Number losing trades	210	208	219	196	133	74	84	na
Percent profitable	59%	55%	59%	60%	62%	69%	67%	na
Largest winning trade	$9.75	$11.63	$9.75	$9.53	$9.53	$9.53	$9.75	na
Average winning trade	$1.28	$1.25	$1.20	$1.04	$1.03	$1.01	$0.97	na
Largest losing trade	−$4.19	−$5.59	−$3.91	−$4.09	−$3.13	−$2.97	−$3.00	na
Average losing trade	−$0.99	−$1.06	−$0.98	−$0.89	−$0.82	−$0.87	−$0.68	na
Ratio avg win/avg loss	1.29	1.18	1.22	1.18	1.26	1.17	1.41	na
Avg trade(win & loss)	$0.35	$0.21	$0.31	$0.28	$0.33	$0.43	$0.42	na
Max consec. winners	9	9	10	10	12	15	13	na
Max consec. losers	9	8	6	5	7	3	8	na
Avg # days in winners	5	6	5	4	4	3	3	na
Avg # days in losers	6	6	5	4	4	4	3	na
Max intraday drawdown	−$9.67	−$15.45	−$11.65	−$9.98	−$8.47	−$5.46	−$4.98	−$20.21

Notes: All log figures are multiplied by 100. Currency figures are in thousands of US dollars. All results are based on trading one US Treasury bond futures contract.

curves for the MSE, SR and TLR objectives in Figure 22.1 also show the poor performance of the MSE objective, including a flat period in the cumulative equity curve from 1988 to 1993, followed by the large drawdown previously mentioned (the vertical line at the right of the graph shows the division between in and out of sample results). The SR and TLR objectives fair much better but are closely correlated. This is evident in the similarity of their equity curves and also in the percentage profitable figures, which are equal at 59%, with the TLR network delivering the superior performance overall. All the models outperform the B&H strategy. The fact that the SR model did not perform as well as the TLR model is a possible indication that there may not be enough information within the input features to take advantage of the inherent SR risk adjustment.

The out of sample performance of these models (see table 22.5 and figure 22.3) is fairly consistent with the in sample results. The MSE model continues to deliver relatively poor performance, including another large drawdown of $20700.00—far too high a figure for this model to be traded with real money.

Examination of the TLRP models in Tables 22.4 and 22.5, along with their respective equity curves in figure 22.2, show that as the penalty term increases from 0% to 20%, the percentage of trades that were profitable rises from 60% to 67% in sample. Average trade figures rise from $280.00 to $420.00, along with a decrease in the average days spent in each trade. Like the other models, there seems to be a fair amount of consistency between the in and out of sample results except for the 20% TLRP model, where performance drops out of sample (see figure 22.4).

Figure 22.1
Cumulative equity curves for TLR, SR and MSE objectives

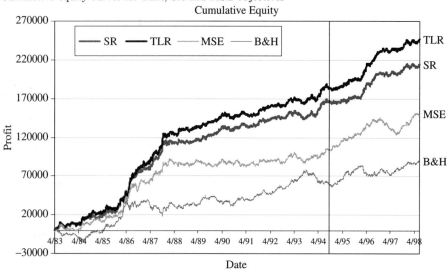

What is interesting is that it continues to have near 70% accuracy but the average
trade decreases from $420.00 to $270.00 as the avg. win/loss ratio drops from 1.41
to 1.03. Even though the TLRP models spend less time in the market than the B&H
strategy, all except the 20% objective deliver superior out of sample performance.

With an out of sample sharpe ratio of 2.0, the TLRP15% objective seems to
perform well however, on closer inspection it has an associated drawdown of $5.59,
compared with that of $6.47 for the TLR objective which gains an extra 40% in
profits by being constantly in the market. Moreover, the TLRP15% objective, with
a win/loss ratio of 1.17, relies on high trade accuracy for its profit as opposed to the
TLR model, which has a win/loss ratio of 1.30 and hence a more desirable balance
between trade accuracy and amount gained per trade. The amount of days spent
in losers and winners seems to be fairly consistent at 5 days for the TLR objective.
It may be possible to the use stops to improve this ratio.

An interesting corollary to these results can be observed by looking closely at
the cumulative equity curves for all objectives in figures 22.1 and 22.2. From 1985
to 1987 all equity curves experience a steep rise until the time of the October 1987
crash, at which point the curves flatten out, something that is especially noticeable
with the MSE objective. This flat period persists until about 1993 at which point

Figure 22.2
Cumulative equity curves for TLRP objectives

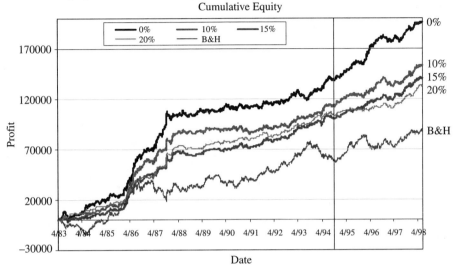

the equity curves begin to rise again at a steeper rate. This would seem to indicate that there was a structural shift in the relationship between stocks and bonds at that time. Further research is needed to gain more insight into this observation.

22.9 Implementation

It should be noted that there are some implementation problems with the final models. The day session of S&P500 futures closes 75 minutes after that of the US Tbond futures. In order to put the models into practice closing prices from both contracts are required at the time of the Tbond close, therefore a modification in the trading strategy is needed. There are a number of possible solutions to this. The simplest method is to trade the Tbond during the evening session at the close of the S&P500 day session. To give an indication of the resulting difference that could be expected we recalculated the TLR results on daily data by assuming trades were made on the following day's opening price and found a difference of less than 1% in total log returns. This difference is likely to be even less if trading took place at the time of the S&P500 close.

Figure 22.3
Out of sample cumulative equity curves for the MSE, TLR and SR objectives

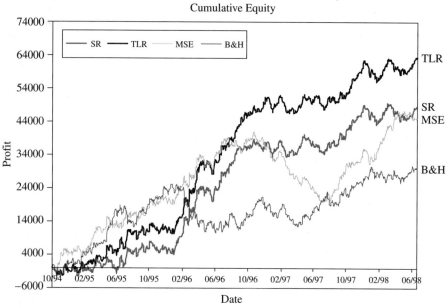

22.10   Conclusion

We have researched the feasibility of using genetically trained neural networks in conjunction with profit oriented objective functions to trade the US Tbond future. The results show some promise in this endeavor in that the networks seem to have captured an on going relationship between the two series, leading to profitable trading of the US Tbond futures contract from 1983 to 1998. Further research is required into the exact nature of this predictive relationship in order to gain additional confidence in the underlying models. Our results lend further support to previous findings that traditional statistical measures of error may be inappropriate for use as objective functions when designing trading models in this way.

Lastly, there is always a danger of 'datasnooping' when building financial forecasting models based on finite datasets. Even if all preventive measures are taken in an attempt to eliminate this possibility, one can never be absolutely certain that is has not taken place. Research and design of trading models tends to be a continual process and it is unlikely that a researcher will arrive at a successful model on the

Figure 22.4
Out of sample cumulative equity curves for the TLRP objectives

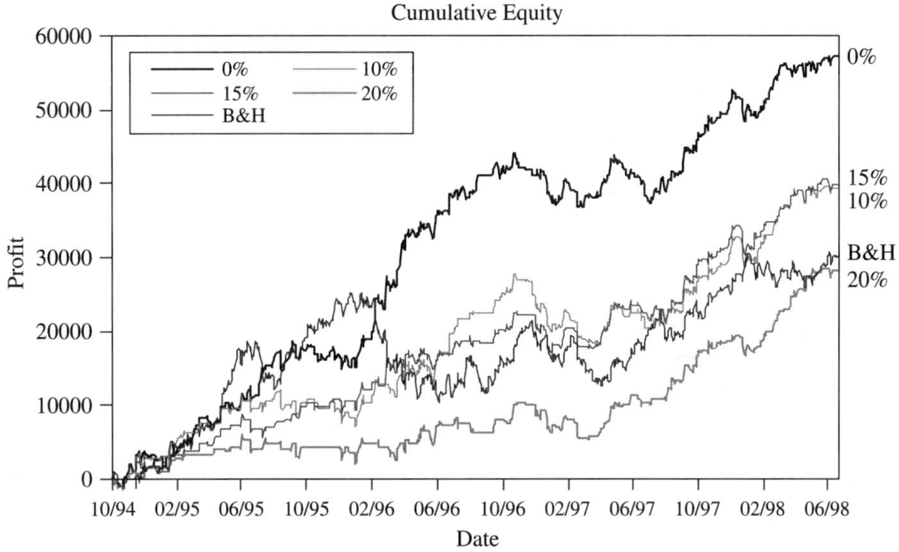

Cumulative Equity

first attempt. It is quite possible that during this ongoing process, a priori knowledge of the full dataset could lead to inadvertent 'datasnooping'. Indeed, supporters of the EMH would argue that most, if not all trading models which outperform the market on a risk adjusted basis, are the result of inadvertent 'datasnooping'.

References

Bengio, Y. 1996. Training a neural network with a financial criterion rather than a prediction criterion, *Decision Technologies for Financial Engineering* (Proceedings of the Fourth International Conference on Neural Networks in the Capital Markets 1996). World Scientific.

Bentz, Y and A.N. Refenes. 1994. Backpropagation with weighted signs and its application to financial time series, *Proceedings of Neural Networks in the Capital Markets*, 1994.

Brock, W.A., W.D. Dechert, and J. A. Scheinkman. 1987. A test for independence based on the correlation dimension, working paper, University of Wisconsin Press, Madison, WI.

Burgess, A.N. and A.N. Refenes. 1995. Modelling non-linear cointegration in international equity index futures, *Neural Networks in Financial Engineering* (Proceedings of the Third International Conference on Neural Networks in the Capital Markets 1995). World Scientific.

Caldwell, R.B. 1995. Improved prediction performance metrics for neural network-based financial forecasting systems, *Neurove$t Journal* 3(5): 13–23.

Table 22.5
Out of sample results for all objective functions based on data from 1994 to 1998.

	TLR	MSE	SR	TLRP 0%	TLRP 10%	TLRP 15%	TLRP 20%	B&H
Total Log Returns	24.22	17.26	18.35	22.4	15.42	15.02	10.83	11.94
Avg log trade	0.14	0.11	0.09	0.13	0.12	0.14	0.1	na
Total net profit	$63.04	$44.41	$48.16	$57.26	$39.48	$39.97	$28.21	$30.31
Gross profit	$120.71	$104.89	$115.14	$101.89	$77.85	$67.94	$52.63	na
Gross loss	-$57.67	-$60.48	-$66.98	-$44.63	-$38.37	-$27.97	-$24.42	na
Sharpe Ratio	1.80	1.23	1.35	1.92	1.63	2.00	1.49	0.82
% of time in Market	100%	100%	100%	72%	54%	45%	33%	100%
Total # of trades	175	154	199	166	131	113	105	na
Number winning trades	103	86	107	105	81	76	71	na
Number losing trades	72	68	92	61	50	37	34	na
Percent profitable	59%	56%	54%	63%	62%	67%	68%	na
Largest winning trade	$4.88	$4.60	$4.59	$4.59	$3.13	$3.56	$2.53	na
Average winning trade	$1.17	$1.22	$1.08	$0.97	$0.96	$0.89	$0.74	na
Largest losing trade	-$3.22	-$3.31	-$3.22	-$3.16	-$3.16	-$3.12	-$3.00	na
Average losing trade	-$0.80	-$0.89	-$0.73	-$0.73	-$0.77	-$0.76	-$0.72	na
Ratio avg win/avg loss	1.46	1.37	1.48	1.33	1.25	1.18	1.03	na
Avg trade(win & loss)	$0.36	$0.29	$0.24	$0.34	$0.30	$0.35	$0.27	na
Max consec. winners	8	14	7	7	13	10	15	na
Max consec. losers	4	5	5	4	4	5	3	na
Avg # days in winners	5	6	5	4	6	4	3	na
Avg # days in losers	5	6	4	4	4	4	3	na
Max intraday drawdown	-$6.47	-$20.70	-$5.81	-$7.75	-$9.93	-$5.59	-$5.56	-$14.78

Notes: All log figures are multiplied by 100. Currency figures are in thousands of US dollars. All results are based on trading one US Treasury bond futures contract.

Choey, M. and A.S. Weigand. 1996. Nonlinear trading models through Sharpe Ratio Maximization, *Decision Technologies for Financial Engineering* (Proceedings of the Fourth International Conference on Neural Networks in the Capital Markets 1996). World Scientific.

Holland, J.H. 1975. *Adaptation in Natural and Artificial Systems*. Ann Arbor: The University of Michigan Press.

LeBaron, B. 1993. Nonlinear diagnostics and simple trading rules for high-frequency foreign exchange rates, *Time Series Prediction: Forecasting the Future and Understanding the Past*. Santa Fe Institute Studies in the Sciences of Complexity, Proc. Vol XV. Reading, MA: Addison-Wesley.

Leitch, G. and J. Tanner. 1991. Economic forecast evaluation: Profits versus the conventional error measures. *The American Economic Review*, 580–590.

Moody, J. and W. Lizhong. 1996. Optimization of trading systems and portfolios, *Decision Technologies for Financial Engineering* (Proceedings of the Fourth International Conference on Neural Networks in the Capital Markets 1996). World Scientific.

Refenes, A.N. 1995. *Neural Networks in the Capital Markets,* ed. A. Refenes, John Wiley & Sons, Chichester.

Sharpe, W. F. Jan 1966. Mutual fund performance. *Journal of Business*, 119–138.

23 Parameter Tuning in Trading Algorithms Using ASTA

Thomas Hellström and Kenneth Holmström

This paper describes ASTA, an Artificial Stock Trading Agent, in the Matlab programming environment. The primary purpose of the project is to supply a stable and realistic test bench for the development of multi-stock trading algorithms. The behavior of the agent is controlled by a high-level language, which is easily extendable with user-defined functions. The buy and sell rules can be composed interactively and various types of data screening can be easily performed, all within the Matlab m-file language syntax.

Apart from being a Windows-based test bench for trading algorithms, the system can be also run in batch mode, where a supplied objective function maps a trading strategy to a profit measure. This can be used to tune parameters or to automate the development of trading strategies, for example with genetic methods. Examples of tuning parameters in standard technical indicators are presented using new techniques for global optimization available in the optimization environment TOMLAB. A modified Sharpe Ratio is used as a performance measure.

To improve the performance of a given algorithm, the data from the simulated trades can be output and post-processed by classification methods such as artificial neural networks or fuzzy rule bases.

The ASTA system has been applied successfully to historical stock data, and results covering 11 years of the Swedish stock market are presented.

23.1 Introduction

The idea of expressing stock prediction algorithms in the form of trading rules has gained considerable attention in academic research in the last years. The international conference NNCM-96 devoted a whole section in the proceedings to "Decision Technologies". [Bengio 1997] writes about the importance of training artificial neural networks with a financial criterion rather than a prediction criterion. [Moody and Wu 1997] use reinforcement learning to train a trading system with objective functions such as profit, economic utility and Sharpe ratio. [Atiya 1997] describes a trading system based on time-variable stop-losses and profit objectives.

This paper describes the system ASTA, which is an implementation of an Artificial Stock Trading Agent. With ASTA, trading-rule-based prediction algorithms are easily evaluated using historical data. ASTA performs a simulation of multi-stock trading, where trading rules are executed for a large number of available stocks every day in the simulation period. The situation is fundamentally different from the single-stock prediction case.

Besides being an evaluation tool, ASTA is also a development tool where trading rules can be combined and tuned. Examples of tuning parameters in the technical indicator Stochastics are presented.

The program is developed in the Matlab programming language and is used either as an ordinary objective function called from a user's program, or as an interactive tool for making benchmarks and development of trading algorithms. The ASTA system is thoroughly described in [Hellström 1998b] and in the present paper we only give a short introduction to the system.

23.1.1   The Usage of ASTA

The development of ASTA was instigated by a need for good working tools for the following research tasks:

1. *A test bench for trading algorithms.*
Many "technical indicators" for stock prediction are accepted and widely used without having ever been subject to an objective scientific analysis with historical stock data. It is true that many commercial software packages for technical analysis offer both a comprehensive programming language and a simulation mode where the performance can be computed. However, most available products do not take this task very seriously and real trading simulations with a multi-stock portfolio are seldom possible.

2. *An interactive development tool for trading rules.*
There are reasons to believe that a successful trading system consists of many disjunct parts where a buy signal may be, for example, "screened" by looking at the traded volume. A buy signal issued with a low traded volume may then be rejected. Other composite rules include looking at the general trend of the stock before accepting a signal from the system. ASTA provides the possibility to test such composite rules easily.

3. *A non-interactive development tool for trading rules.*
Furthermore, it is possible and maybe also fruitful to automate the development of trading rules. Since ASTA defines the trading strategy as symbolic Buy rules and Sell rules given as arguments to the system, it would be perfectly possible to construct buy and sell rules in a genetic framework, for example.
Even if the general look of the algorithm is fixed, there are often a lot of tunable parameters that affect the trading performance. Examples are filter coefficients, order of polynomials and levels above or below which an entity should pass to generate a trading signal. Since we believe that the actual behavior during a realistic trading situation is essential for proper selection and optimization of an algorithm, there is a need for an objective function that can be included in an optimization phase for parameter tuning.

4. *A data generating tool for post processing.*
The comprehensive and user-friendly macro language in ASTA makes it a very suitable tool for extracting data for further analysis, such as classification with neural networks or fuzzy rule bases.

23.2   Basic Approaches to Stock Predictions

Prediction algorithms for stock prices can be categorized in a number of ways. One categorization focuses on the way the points to predict are selected. Two broad classes can be identified; "The Time Series Approach" and "The Trading Simulation Approach"

23.2.1   The Time Series Approach

The traditional way to define a stock prediction problem is to view the stock returns as a time series $y(t)$. For example, one-day stock returns are defined as

$$y(t) = \frac{Close(t) - Close(t-1)}{Close(t-1)}. \tag{23.1}$$

To predict the return h days in the future, $y(t+h)$ is assumed to be a function g of the previous (lagged) values

$$y(t+h) = g(y(t), y(t-1), ..., y(t-k)). \tag{23.2}$$

The task for the learning or modeling process is to find the function g that best approximates a given set of measured data. The unknown function g can be chosen in many ways, e.g. as linear autoregressive (AR) models or feed-forward neural networks. The unknown parameters in the model are normally computed by a learning (identification) algorithm that minimizes the root mean square prediction error

$$RMSE = \sqrt{\frac{1}{N} \sum_{t=1}^{N} (g(t) - y(t+h))^2}. \tag{23.3}$$

It is most common to let the minimized RMSE measure (23.3) be the end point in the prediction task. However, to utilize the predictions, a decision-taking rule has to be created. A simple rule often used is

$$D(t) = \begin{cases} \text{Buy} & : \text{ if g(t)} > \alpha \\ \text{Sell} & : \text{ if g(t)} < -\beta \\ \text{Do nothing} & : \text{ otherwise} \end{cases}, \tag{23.4}$$

where α and β are positive valued threshold parameters for buy and sell actions depending on the predicted change in the stock price.

The time series formulation based on the minimized RMSE measure (23.3) is not always ideal for useful predictions of financial time series. Some reasons are:

1. The fixed prediction horizon h does not reflect the way in which financial predictions are being used. The ability of a model to predict should not be evaluated at one single fixed point in the future. A big increase in a stock value 14 days into the future is as good as the same increase 15 days into the future!

2. The equation (23.3) treats all predictions, small and large, as equal. This is not always appropriate. Prediction points that would never be used for actual trading (i.e. price changes too small to be interesting) may cause higher residuals at the other points of more interest, to minimize the global RMSE.

3. A small predicted change in price, followed by a large real change in the same direction, is penalized by the RMSE measure. A trader is normally happy in this case, at least if, say, the small positive prediction was large enough to give a buy signal.

4. Several papers report a poor correlation between the RMSE measure and the profit made by applying a prediction algorithm, e.g. [Leitch and Tanner 1991] and [Bengio 1997]. A strategy that separates the modeling from the decision-taking rule, such as the one in 23.4, is less optimal than modeling the decision taking directly [Moody 1992]. Arguments 2 and 3 both give some explanations to these results.

23.2.2 The Trading Simulation Approach

Instead of separating the prediction task and the decision task as was done in the "Time Series Approach", algorithms can be constructed to recognize situations where one should buy and sell stocks respectively (The approach in the ASTA system). A trading rule can be described as a time series $T(t)$ defined as

$$T(t) = \begin{cases} \text{Buy} & : \text{ if g}(\mathbf{X}(t)) > 0 \\ \text{Sell} & : \text{ if g}(\mathbf{X}(t)) < 0 \\ \text{Do nothing} & : \text{ otherwise} \end{cases}. \tag{23.5}$$

The unspecified function g determines the type of trading rule. The argument $\mathbf{X}(t)$ has the form

$$\mathbf{X}(t) = (R_1(t), ..., R_N(t)), \tag{23.6}$$

where each $R_k(t)$ is an observable feature at time t. In the case of stock predictions it may be for example the k-day returns defined as

$$R_k(t) = 100 \cdot \frac{Close(t) - Close(t - k)}{Close(t - k)} \tag{23.7}$$

or standard technical indicators such as the Stochastic Oscillator, the Relative Strength Index (RSI) or the Moving Average Convergence/Divergence (MACD) [Achelis 1995]. $R_k(t)$ can of course also simply be lagged values of the returns, i.e. $R_k(t) = y(t - k)$.

The task for the learning process in The Trading Simulation Approach is to find the function g to maximize the profit, when applying the rule on real data. Various ways to measure the profit are discussed in [Hellström 1998b]. Note the difference between this and The Time Series Approach, where the learning task is to find a function g that minimizes the $RMSE$ error (23.3) for the entire time series.

The Trading Simulation Approach avoids many of the problems previously described of the Time Series Approach but does indeed have problems of its own, primarily that of statistical significance. The trading rule $T(t)$ normally issues Buy or Sell signals only for a minor part of the points in the time series.

23.3 Design of the Artificial Trader

In this section we discuss the design and implementation of the ASTA system. The task of the Artificial Trader is to act on an artificial market with a large number of available stocks that vary in prices over time. The Trader has to execute the trading rule $T(t)$ at every time step and decide whether to buy or sell stocks.

23.3.1 Performance Evaluation

The result of the artificial trader is presented as annual profits together with the increase in index. The mean difference between these two figures constitutes the net performance for the trader. The performance is displayed in both tabular and graphical formats as shown in the table part of Figure 23.2 and in Figure 23.3. Various considerations when measuring the profit are discussed in more detail in the thesis by [Hellström 1998a]. We now turn to the general architecture of the developed system.

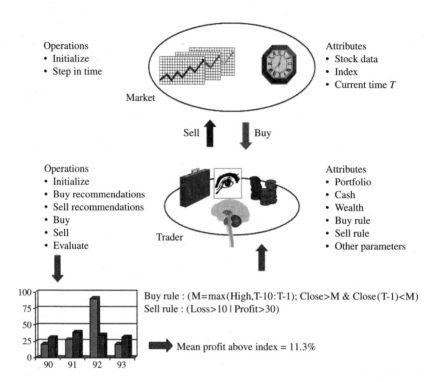

Figure 23.1
Basic Components of the ASTA System.

23.3.2   Basic Architecture

The architecture of ASTA is based on an object-oriented approach with two major objects; the Market and the Trader. The basic layout is presented in Figure 23.1.

The Market Object   The Market Object consists essentially of the total number of stocks participating in the trading simulation. A stock is defined by four time series; Close, High, Low and Volume. The basic operation on the Market Object is the simulation of changing prices as the date moves from start date to end date.

The Trader Object   The Trader Object is more complex than the Market Object, as far as both attributes and allowed operations are concerned. The Buy rule and Sell rule are the main attributes that affect the behavior of the Trader. They are expressed in a high-level language and may include calls to a large number of predefined Matlab functions that access the stock data in the Market Object. User-defined functions can also be called directly.

Other Parts of the System   The Market and Trader Objects have to be controlled by a support system that takes care of the following "meta" operations:

- Simulation.

The Step in time operation has to be applied to the Market Object in a loop for the selected time period. For each time step T, the Trader Object should also be activated. The following pseudo code describes the full ASTA system:

Trader.Initialize
Market.Initialize
loop until Market.T$\geq$EndDate
    s = Trader.Sell_Recommendations
    Trader.Sell(s) % Sell all stocks of type s
    s = Trader.Buy_Recommendations
    n = T.available_cash / length(s)
    Trader.Buy(s, n) % Buy n stocks of type s
    Market.Step in time
end loop
Trader.Evalute

- User interface.

The end user assigns values to parameters such as the Buy rule and Sell rule of the Trader and the chosen time period for simulation. After the simulation the computed performance of suggested trades is presented.

The "silent mode" makes it possible to use the system as an objective function in a parameter optimization. The Artificial Trader is then called as a standard Matlab function from the optimization program code, returning a function value for each set of input parameters.

23.3.3   Predefined ASTA Functions

ASTA has a large number of predefined functions that make it possible to express compound trading rules interactively (as Buy and Sell rules). They also provide the developer of new algorithms with basic database access functions as well as some useful high-level functions. A complete description of the predefined functions in ASTA can be found in [Hellström 1998b].

23.4   An Example

In this section one example from the Windows version of ASTA is presented. 32 major stocks with active trading from the Swedish stock market for the years 1987-1997 have been selected for analysis. The main ASTA screen is shown in Figure 23.2. The most interesting items are the lines "Buy rule" and "Sell Rule". This is where the trading algorithm is defined. The rules follow the Matlab syntax and can include the predefined functions or the users' own functions with new algorithms. The example shows a test of the Stochastics indicator, here defined as

$$Stochastics(t, K, KS, D) = mav(100 * (Close(t) - L)/(H - L), D), \tag{23.8}$$

where $L = mav(min(Low(t-K : t)), KS)$ and $H = mav(max(High(t-K : t)), KS)$. The parameter K is the length of the window, and KS and D the length of the moving average function mav. A Buy signal is issued when $Stochastics(t, K, KS, D) >$ $Buylevel$ and a Sell signal when $Stochastics(t, K, KS, D) < Sellevel$. The parameters $K, KS, D, Sellevel$ and $Buylevel$ control the performance of a trading strategy based on the indicator. Define $Stoch(K, KS, D, Buylevel, Sellevel)$ as the ASTA trading function, which will be subject to analysis in the next section.

In Figure 23.2, the "standard" values $30, 3, 3, 20, 80$ common in technical trading are used for the parameters. The results shown in Figure 23.2 and Figure 23.3 are quite stunning, with an average annual profit of 53.4% compared to the 16.3% achieved by the index. It is noteworthy that the only negative result is for the year 1997, where the strategy only made 1.7% whereas the index increased by 23.8%.

23.5   Viewing the Trader as an Objective Function

The obvious wish to maximize the profit p can be tackled in two ways:

1. Parameterizing the Buy rule and Sell rule, i.e. introducing parameters within the rules. Example:
Buy rule $= 'Close(T) > Maxx('High', N_{high}, T - 1)'$
Sell rule $= 'Loss > L \mid (Profit > P \& Close(T) < Close(T - 1))'$
The function $Maxx$ determines the maximum time series value in the interval $[T - N_{high}, T - 1]$. It is now possible to optimize the profit P with respect to the parameters N_{high}, L and P.

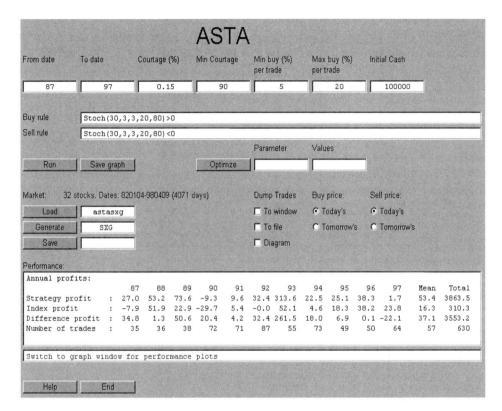

Figure 23.2
ASTA command window with buy and sell rules using the *Stoch* trading function based on the Stochastics indicator.

2. Viewing the Buy rule and Sell rule as symbolic expressions. The optimization then turns into a search problem, most naturally implemented in a genetic framework or using Inductive Logic Programming.

An optimization of one of the parameters in the Stochastics trade function serves as an example for approach 1. We set up an optimization with buy and sell rules according to:

Buy rule $=$ '$Stoch(30, 3, 3, Sellevel, 80)$'

Sell rule $=$ '$Stoch(30, 3, 3, Sellevel, 80)$'.

The excess profit P can now be optimized with respect to *Sellevel*. The graphs in Figure 23.4 are automatically generated by the "Sweep" function in the ASTA

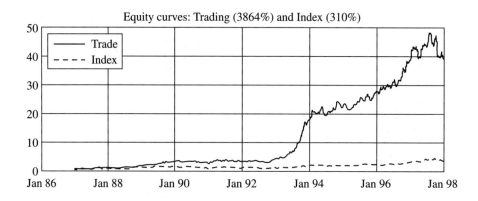

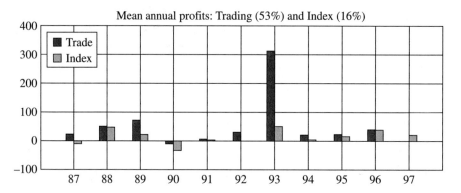

Figure 23.3
Performance of the trading function $Stoch(30, 3, 3, 20, 80)$ based on the Stochastics indicator.

system. The name of the parameter is given in the "Parameter" text box and the range in the "Values" text box.

It must be emphasized that the optimization of the performance is a multi-dimensional parameter estimation problem. The graphs presented show the profit P as a function of *one* of the involved parameters whereas the rest of the parameters are fixed. The main purpose is to illustrate the possibilities and problems involved, even in a one-dimensional optimization.

From the summary graph (top left) of the entire training period we can deduce that the highest profit is achieved for a *Sellevel* somewhere around 35. However, viewing the data at a higher resolution reveals a more complicated situation. In the bottom left diagram the same relation is plotted with one curve for each year in

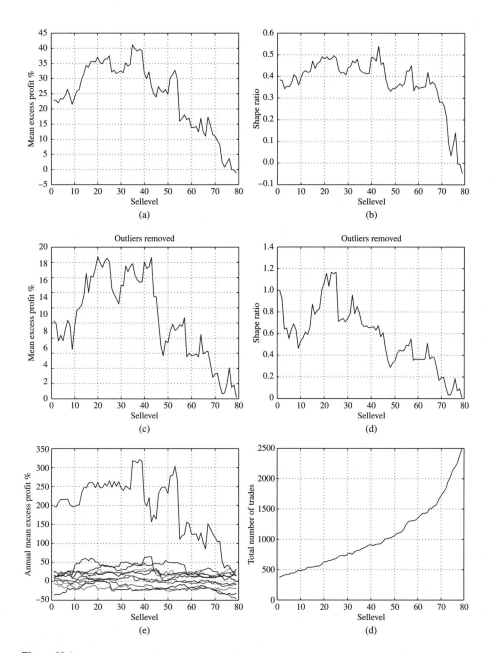

Figure 23.4
Trading results as a function of the *Sellevel* parameter. Stocks: SXG. Years: 87-97. Buy rule: $Stoch(30, 3, 3, Sellevel, 80)$. Sell rule: $Stoch(30, 3, 3, Sellevel, 80)$.

the training data set. It is clear that the mean profit is totally dominated by the results from *one* of the years (1993).

From these curves we can learn at least two important points:

1. The spread between individual years is very high.
2. The location of the maximum is not obvious.

This behavior of data is typical for most variables. The profit cannot be easily described as a function of measurable variables without introducing a dominant noise term in the function. Let us view the annual excess profit as a stochastic variable $P(\theta)$, where θ stands for one particular setting of the parameters that affect the profit. In the shown example, θ is the *Sellevel* parameter. $P(\theta)$ has been sampled once per year during the eleven years in the data set

$$\{P_1(\theta), P_2(\theta), P_3(\theta), P_4(\theta), P_5(\theta), P_6(\theta), P_7(\theta), P_8(\theta), P_9(\theta), P_{10}(\theta), P_{11}(\theta)\}. \quad (23.9)$$

Viewed this way, the task of tuning the parameter θ to find the "maximum" profit P is not well defined. P is a stochastic function and consequently has no "maximum". It has a probability distribution with an expected value E and a variance V. It's important to realize that tuning θ to maximize $E[P(\theta)]$ is just one of the available options. Maximizing $E[P(\theta)]$ provides the highest *mean* performance. Another possibility is to maximize the lower limit of a confidence interval. Since the risk factor is always a major concern in investments, and since the spread between individual years obviously can be very high, this sounds like a promising idea. A lower limit P_{low} for a confidence interval could be defined as

$$P_{low} = E[P(\theta)] - \sqrt{V[P(\theta)]}, \quad (23.10)$$

where $V[P(\theta)]$ is the variance of the stochastic variable $P(\theta)$. Yet another possibility is to use the Sharpe Ratio SR, which expresses the excess return in units of its standard deviation as

$$SR = \frac{E[P(\theta)]}{\sqrt{V[P(\theta)]}}. \quad (23.11)$$

The Sharpe Ratio is normally used to *evaluate* the performance of a trading strategy ([Sharpe 1966, Sharpe 1994]). However, [Choey and Weigend 1997] suggest to use the Sharpe Ratio as an objective function in portfolio optimization and derive a learning algorithm for artificial neural networks. The Sharpe Ratio should be as high as possible for an optimal trading algorithm.

Due to the high noise level in the data we have added a modified Sharpe Ratio where the outliers are removed. The largest and smallest $P_i(\theta)$ in the set 23.9 are removed before taking the expected value and standard deviation for each θ.

The unmodified Sharpe Ratio is shown in the top-right diagram and the one with outliers removed in the mid-right diagram. As we can see, the one with the outliers removed clearly reveals a maximum at around 20-25 followed by a clear decline. The unmodified Sharpe Ratio shows no such pattern.

23.5.1   Global Optimization

It is evident from the previous discussion that whatever performance measure we are using, the resulting objective function is very noisy. Therefore, new techniques for global optimization are needed to find the correct extreme point and optimal parameter values for a multi-variable problem.

We have made some preliminary tests using the DIRECT algorithm ([Jones et al 1993]) as implemented in the optimization environment TOMLAB ([Holmström 1999]). In Figure 23.5 we see the points sampled when trying to find the optimal buy and sell rules in the Stochastics Indicator. They cluster around $(40, 78)$, which seems to be the global optimum. In Figure 23.6 one-dimensional views of the *Net profit* (with reversed sign) versus the *Buylevel* and the *Sellevel* are shown. The optimum is more well-determined and distinct in the *Buylevel*. The global optimum is in fact very close to the standard values used in technical analysis. Further testing and analysis are needed to establish robustness properties of the parameters found.

23.6   Results and Further Development

The presented system provides a powerful tool for the development and evaluation of trading algorithms. Parameter settings can be tested and data screening can be easily performed interactively. As was mentioned in section 23.1.1, one of the reasons for the development of the ASTA system was to use it as an objective function when tuning model parameters and to find the general structure of trading rules, for example within a generic framework. The preliminary results show both possibilities and difficulties. The track can be examined considerably.

The dangers with "data snooping" got highlighted by breaking down the performance measures into shorter intervals. However, the inherent uncertainty resulting from the noisy processes involved calls for more computer-intensive simulation schemes to achieve statistically significant performance measures.

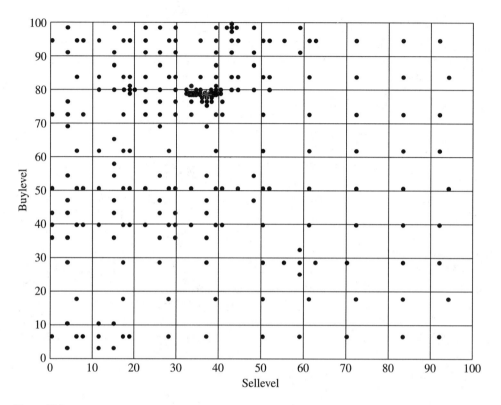

Figure 23.5
Sampled points in the parameter space by the TOMLAB global optimization solver when optimizing the buy and sell levels for the trading function $Stoch(30, 3, 3, Sellevel, Buylevel)$.

References

Achelis, S. B. 1995. *Technical Analysis from A to Z.* Irwin Professional Publishing, Chicago, 2nd edition.

Atiya, A. 1997. Design of time-variable stop losses and profit objectives using neural networks. In Weigend, A. S., Y. S. Abu-Mostafa, and A.-P. N. Refenes, editors, *Decision Technologies for Financial Engineering (Proceedings of the Fourth International Conference on Neural Networks in the Capital Markets, NNCM-96)*, pages 76–83, Singapore. World Scientific.

Bengio, Y. 1997. Training a neural network with a financial criterion rather than a prediction criterion. In Weigend, A. S., Y. S. Abu-Mostafa, and A.-P. N. Refenes, editors, *Decision Technologies for Financial Engineering (Proceedings of the Fourth International Conference on Neural Networks in the Capital Markets, NNCM-96)*, pages 36–48, Singapore. World Scientific.

Choey, M. and A. S. Weigend. 1997. Nonlinear trading models through Sharpe Ratio maximization. In Weigend, A. S., Y. S. Abu-Mostafa, and A.-P. N. Refenes, editors, *Decision Technologies*

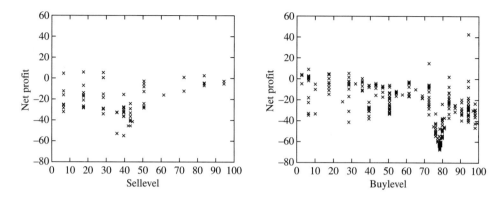

Figure 23.6
One-dimensional views of the global optimization of the parameters in the trading function
Stoch(30, 3, 3, *Sellevel*, *Buylevel*). The left graph shows the *Net profit* versus the *Buylevel* for
an equidistant grid of values of the *Sellevel*. The right graph shows the *Net profit* versus the
Sellevel for an equidistant grid of values of the *Buylevel*. Note that the sign of the *Net profit* is
reversed, making it a minimization problem.

for Financial Engineering (Proceedings of the Fourth International Conference on Neural Networks in the Capital Markets, NNCM-96), pages 3–22, Singapore. World Scientific.

Hellström, T. 1998a. Asta - a test bench and development tool for trading algorithms. Technical
Report UMINF-98.12, ISSN-0348-0542, Department of Computing Science Ume(**??**) University,
Ume(**??**) Sweden.

Hellström, T. 1998b. *A Random Walk through the Stock Market*. Licentiate Thesis, UMINF
98.16 ISSN-0348-0542, Department of Computing Science,, Ume(**??**) University, Sweden.

Holmström, K. 1999. The TOMLAB Optimization Environment in Matlab. *Advanced Modeling
and Optimization*, 1. To be published.

Jones, D. R., C. D. Perttunen, and B. E. Stuckman. 1993. Lipschitzian optimization without the
lipschitz constant. *Journal of Optimization Theory and Applications*, 79(1):157–181.

Leitch, G. and J. Tanner. 1991. Economic forecast evaluation: Profit versus the conventional error
measures. *The American Economic Review*, pages 580–590.

Moody, J. E. 1992. Shooting craps in search of an optimal strategy for training connectionist
pattern classifiers. In Moody, J. E., S. J. Hanson, and R. P. Lippmann, editors, *Advances in
Neural Information Processing Systems 4, Proceedings of the 1991 NIPS Conference*, pages 847–
854, San Mateo , CA. Morgan Kaufmann Publishers.

Moody, J. E. and L. Z. Wu. 1997. Optimization of trading systems and portfolios. In Weigend,
A. S., Y. S. Abu-Mostafa, and A.-P. N. Refenes, editors, *Decision Technologies for Financial
Engineering (Proceedings of the Fourth International Conference on Neural Networks in the
Capital Markets, NNCM-96)*, pages 23–35, Singapore. World Scientific.

Sharpe, W. F. 1966. Mutual fund performance. *Journal of Business*, pages 119–138.

Sharpe, W. F. 1994. The Sharpe Ratio. *Journal of Portfolio Management*, 21:49–58.

24 Hedge Funds Styles

David A. Hsieh

24.1 Introduction

US investors are interested in diversifying the risk of portfolios that typically have a substantial core position in US stocks and bonds. Historically, diversification involves investing in assets which have low correlation to US stocks and bonds, such as international stocks and bonds, emerging market stocks and bonds, real estate, oil and gas, venture capital, and private equities. These assets are held in the portfolio from a buy-and-hold perspective. Given that the number of assets are finite, diversification based on a buy-and-hold perspective has a natural limit.

Recently, investors have begun to examine diversification benefits from trading strategies that are not buy-and-hold. For simplicity, we use the term "dynamic trading strategies" to include all trading strategies that are different from buy-and-hold, such as short selling and market timing (frequent shifts between asset classes). Many dynamic trading strategies employ leverage and derivatives.

Different dynamic trading strategies, when applied to the same asset, can generate returns that are uncorrelated to each other and to the buy-and-hold strategy on that asset. Given that there is no limit to the number of dynamic trading strategies, the inclusion of dynamic trading strategies can potentially increase the diversification of a portfolio relative to the traditional buy-and-hold perspective, without any need to increase the number of assets in the portfolio.

In this paper, we examine managers who are generally regarded by the investment world to practice dynamic trading strategies—hedge fund managers and commodity trading advisors (CTAs). Hedge funds are private investment vehicles for wealthy individuals and institutional investors. They are typically formed as limited partnerships, in which the general partners put in a significant amount of personal wealth, and receive a substantial incentive fee. CTAs are firms or individuals who handle customer funds or provide advise on trading futures. Historically, CTA funds have been viewed as distinct from hedge funds. However, the growth of financial futures and derivatives and the deregulation of the financial markets have blurred the distinction between CTA funds and hedge funds. For the purpose of our paper, we analyze both CTA funds and hedge funds.

24.2   The Legal Environment of Hedge Funds

Hedge funds are typically exempt from the securities laws and regulations that govern the issuance and trading of publicly traded securities as enforced by the Securities Exchange Commission (SEC).

The Securities Act of 1933 requires corporations to register and to file reports with the SEC when they issue publicly traded securities. As private placements, hedge funds are exempt from these regulations.

The Securities Exchange Act of 1934 governs the behavior of securities brokerage funds that execute customer orders in public securities as well as trade from their own accounts. Under this act, the SEC requires broker dealers to file reports and maintain extensive records. Hedge funds are not securities brokerage firms, and are typically exempt from these requirements.

The Investment Company Act of 1940 sets up the foundation of the US mutual fund industry. It restricts the activities of mutual funds. By limiting their investors to wealthy individuals and institutions, hedge funds are exempt from these regulations.

The Investment Advisers Act of 1940 regulates the behavior of investment advisers to the general public. By not giving advise to the general public, a hedge fund manager may be exempt from registering as an investment adviser with the SEC.

Under the Commodity Exchange Act of 1974, individuals and firms (including hedge funds) handling customer funds and giving advise on futures trading are required to register as commodity pool operators or commodity trading advisors with the National Futures Association, a self-regulatory body approved by the Commodity Futures Trading Commission (CFTC). There are associated registration and disclosure requirements. However, some hedge fund mangers may be exempt from certain reporting and disclosure requirements to the CFTC.

24.3   A Brief History of Hedge Funds

According to Caldwell (1995), A.W. Jones created the first hedge fund in 1949, using leverage and long/short positions in equities, with a performance based fee. However, the growth of hedge funds has taken place in the 1990s as shown in Table 24.1. As of the end of 1997, there are 987 hedge funds with $65 billion of assets under management, and 291 CTA funds with $17 billion of assets under management.

Table 24.2 provides the mean and standard deviation of their returns. Hedge funds and CTA funds have comparable returns to the S&P 500 index, with some-

Table 24.1
Numbers and Assets of Hedge Funds and CTA Funds

	1985	1990	1991	1992	1993	1994	1995	1996	1997
Numbers:									
Hedge funds	37	231	310	442	644	856	1027	1076	987
CTA funds	114	404	468	557	577	558	488	363	291
Assets under management ($ billion):									
Hedge funds	na	6.5	10.1	17.9	35.8	41.3	50.4	59.4	64.6
CTA funds	5.9	34.3	36.6	41.3	49.9	41.8	22.6	12.8	17.1

Source: TASS.

Table 24.2
Annualized Mean and Standard Deviation of Returns: 1990-1997

	Mean	Std Dev	Correlation Coefficients		
			HF	CTA	S&P
Hedge funds	15.1%	5.7%	1.00	0.75	0.37
CTA funds	14.7%	9.9%		1.00	−.01
S&P 500	21.5%	11.4%			1.00
US T-Bill	4.9%	0.23%			

Source: TASS, S&P/BARRA, Ibbotson Associates.

what lower volatility. In addition, they have low correlation to the S&P 500. This raises some interesting questions. Since hedge fund and CTA fund returns have been substantially higher than the riskfree interest rate, the question is: Are these returns properly measured? If they are, how does this come about?

Table 24.3 summarizes the distribution of management fees and incentive fees. For both CTA funds and hedge funds, the typical management fee is 1-2%, and incentive fee 15-20%.

In terms of investment styles, hedge fund consultants have classified the industry based on the managers' description of their trading strategies. Table 24.4 contains the classifications of MAR/Hedge, as reported in Eichengreen et al (1998). "Event-driven" refers to funds trading on corporate events, typically restructuring and merger. "Global" funds invest in stocks and bonds around the world, including emerging market equities and debt. "Global/Macro" funds bet on macroeconomic events in interest rates, currencies, and commodities. "Market neutral" funds use pairs of long/short positions to remove major market risks but to capture spread movements. "Sector" funds specialize in segments of the economy. "Short-sellers" only take short positions on overvalued securities. 'Long-only' funds take long positions in equities, typically with leverage. Table 5 reports the MAR classification of CTA funds, based on Billingsley and Chance (1996). It shows that more than 50% of CTA funds use a "trend following" trading strategy.

Table 24.3
Distribution of Management & Incentive Fees

	MAR Hedge	Tass CTA
Management Fees:		
0%	0%	13%
0–1	63%	4%
1–2	32%	53%
2–3	4%	16%
3–4	0%	12%
4–5	0%	0%
5–6 (max)	0%	1%
Incentive Fees:		
0%	14%	1%
0–5%	2%	0%
5–10	3%	1%
10–15	13%	10%
15–20	62%	69%
20–25	5%	16%
25–30	0%	3%
30–35	1%	0%
35–40 (max)	0%	0%

Table 24.4
MAR Hedge Fund Categories: December 1997

Category	Number	Assets ($ b)	1990-1997 Mean	Std Dev
Event-Driven	120	8.6	18.9%	5.9%
Global	334	30.9	17.7%	9.4%
Global/Macro	61	29.8	28.1%	16.3%
Market Neutral	201	18.0	8.6%	2.1%
Sectors	40	1.8	29.6%	15.9%
Short-Sellers	12	0.5	7.0%	15.2%
Long-Only*	15	0.4	27.3%	15.4%

* 1994-1997.
Source: Eichengreen et al (1998).

From a quantitative perspective, hedge funds and CTA funds have returns that are quite distinct from mutual funds. Fung and Hsieh (1997a) found that hedge funds and CTA funds have very low correlation with the major asset markets. In contrast, mutual funds are strongly correlated to stocks and bonds. Furthermore, hedge funds and CTA funds contain many distinct return characteristics. To demonstrate this, Fung and Hsieh (1997a) relied on the notion that two managers with the same trading strategy should generate correlated returns. Using principal components analysis to group funds with correlated returns, they found that the five

Table 24.5
MAR CTA Trading Strategies

Strategies	% of Total
Arbitrage	1.1%
Discretionary	26.1%
Fundamental	0.5%
Mechanical	0.2%
Pattern Recognition	0.2%
Quantitative	4.9%
Statistical	0.9%
Stochastic	0.1%
Systematic	6.7%
Technical	1.1%
Trend Following	58.1%

Source: Billingsley and Chance (1996).

largest groups accounted for less than half of the cross section differences in these funds. In contrast, mutual funds have much less diversity.

Below, we examine some of the distinctive return characteristics of a few of these styles.

24.4   Trend Following CTA Funds

The term "trend following" is used by the majority of CTAs to describe their trading strategies. While these managers do not disclose details of these strategies, they typically use mechanical rules (such as moving average crosses) to generate buy and sell signals to capture "trends" in markets.

Fung and Hsieh (1997b) demonstrated that the returns of trend following CTA funds have a very interesting feature. On average, these funds perform best during extreme up and down moves in the stock market. They look like straddles on the stock market. Fung and Hsieh (1998) further showed that lookback straddles on currencies, bonds, and commodities can mimic the returns of trend following CTA funds.

This analysis shows that trend following CTA funds have directional exposure to the major asset markets. Sometimes the exposure is positive while other times it is negative. On average, the exposure is zero. This explains why their returns have very low correlation to the major asset markets.

This analysis also shows that trend following CTA funds should provide down side protection during sharp declines in the stock market. Yet they are not as costly as put protection or portfolio insurance, which have negative returns in rising stock markets.

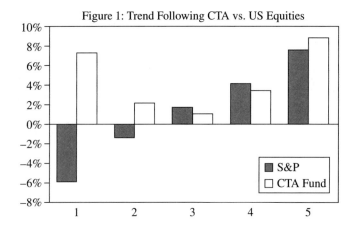

Figure 24.1

24.5 Global/Macro Funds

The largest hedge funds are typically Global/Macro funds, such as George Soros' Quantum Fund, Julian Robertson's Jaguar Fund, Leon Cooperman's Omega Overseas, Louis Bacon's Moore Global, and Mark Kingdon's Kingdon Fund.

These funds have a low degree of correlation with the major asset markets. Specifically, they tend to underperform the stock market in rallies but overperform the stock market in declines. In other words, they appear to have collar strategies on the stock market—short an out-of-the-money call and long an out-of-the-money put.

24.6 Market Neutral Funds

Market neutral funds tend to have very low return volatility, less than 20% of that of the S&P 500 index. The low volatility does not appear to depend on the stock market environment, in the sense that these funds tend to earn a positive return regardless of the market environment. This means that market neutral funds, as advertized, have very little exposure to the major asset markets.

How can market neutral funds generate persistently high return (relative to the riskfree interest rate) and low volatility? One possibility is that market neutral funds can find pure arbitrage (riskless) opportunities. Another possibility is that

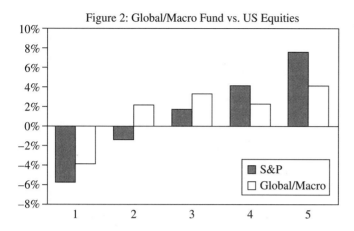

Figure 24.2

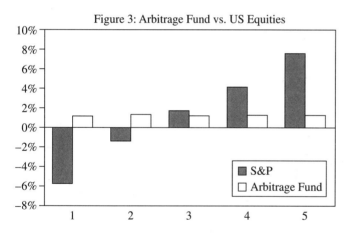

Figure 24.3

these funds sell financial catastrophe insurance. We have seen only the insurance premium but no any catastrophic payouts. The events in September and October of 1998 is consistent with this hypothesis, when the typical arbitrage fund lost more than 6% in both months.

24.7 Implications and Conclusions

Hedge funds and CTA funds have distinct return characteristics from mutual funds. In addition, there are different styles within hedge funds and CTA funds. These styles can provide useful diversification for a portfolio with a core holding of stocks and bonds.

Careful due diligence is needed to understand the style of each fund. Risk management is also more complicated, because of the lack of transparency in the typical hedge funds and CTA funds.

There are many remaining issues. For academics, the questions are: Do hedge funds earn excess return above a riskfree interest rate? If they do, then how does this come about? Why are incentive fees so different between hedge funds and mutual funds? Do incentive fees properly align a manager's interest with those of the investors?

For practitioners, the interesting issues are: Can mean-variance analysis be used in asset allocation decisions with hedge funds? How can investors manage the risk in hedge funds in face of the lack of transparency?

For regulators, the important questions are: Do hedge funds create special problems in market integrity and systemic risk?

These are questions which are open for research.

References

Billingsley, R., and D. Chance, 1996, "Benefits and Limitations of Diversification Among Commodity Trading Advisors," *Journal of Portfolio Management*, 23, 65–80.

Caldwell, Ted. 1995. "Introduction: The Model for Superior Performance" in Lederman, Jess and Robert A. Klein. (ed.), *Hedge Funds*. New York: Irwin Professional Publishing, p. 1–17.

Chicago Mercantile Exchange. "Futures and Options Trading for Hedge Funds: The Regulatory Environment." This paper can be found at the web address: (http://www.cme.com/market. institutional/strategy_papers/hedge.html)

Eichengreen, B., D. Mathieson, B. Chadha, A. Jansen, L. Kodres, and S. Sharma. 1998. Hedge Fund and Financial Market Dynamics, Washington, DC: International Monetary Fund (Occasional Paper No. 166).

Fung, William, and David A. Hsieh. 1997a. "Empirical Characteristics of Dynamic Trading Strategies: The Case of Hedge Funds." *Review of Financial Studies*, 10, 275–302.

Fung, William, and David A. Hsieh. 1997b. "Investment Style and Survivorship Bias in the Returns of CTAs: The Information Content of Track Records." *Journal of Portfolio Management*, 24, 30-41.

Fung, William, and David A. Hsieh. 1998. "A Risk Neutral Approach to Valuing Trend Following Trading Strategies." Working paper, Duke University.

Investment Company Institute, 1997, "Differences Between Mutual Funds and Hedge Funds," www.ici.org/s97_cgi.html.

Lederman, Jess and Robert A. Klein. (ed.) 1995. *Hedge Funds*. New York: Irwin Professional Publishing.

Roth, Paul. 1995. "Chapter 11: Critical Legal and Regulatory Issues," in Lederman, Jess and Robert A. Klein. (ed.), *Hedge Funds*. New York: Irwin Professional Publishing, p. 145-197.

Securities Exchange Commission. "What the SEC Is, What It Does," www.sec.gov.

Sharpe, William. 1992. "Asset Allocation: Management Style and Performance Measurement," *Journal of Portfolio Management*, 18, 7-19.

25 Optimization of Technical Trading Strategy Using Split Search Genetic Algorithms

Raymond Tsang and Paul Lajbcygier

Recently, the use of genetic algorithms for the optimization of technical trading strategies has been receiving a great deal of attention. Studies by Allen and Karjalainen (1994) and Bauer (1994) have shown genetic algorithms are capable of developing extremely profitable technical trading strategies. This paper looks at the uses of genetic algorithms in the optimization of parameter values in a technical trading strategy and proposes a novel hybrid genetic algorithm, focused on the role of mutation in the evolutionary process. The novel Split Search Genetic Algorithms (SSGAs) is assessed in performance against STanDard Genetic Algorithms (STDGAs). Results from preliminary function optimization show that this novel algorithm is more effective and efficient in locating the optimal solution. The profitability of technical trading strategies optimized with SSGAs is greater than those optimized with standard GAs.

25.1 Introduction

Genetic Algorithms are heuristic search algorithms based on concepts of Darwinian evolution, and are commonly used for the optimization of complex problems (Zhuang & Galiana 1990, Balci et al. 1992, Hiew & Nicholson 1996, Kim & Kim 1996, and McIlhagga et al. 1996). This paper, will explore the use of a "Split Search Genetic Algorithm" (SSGAs), and its performance in the optimization of a technical trading strategy.

This paper is organized into three main parts, the first part (Section 25.2–25.5) involves a brief explanation and justification for the use of genetic algorithms and the SSGA. The second part (Section 25.6–25.7) is focused on some preliminary testing performed to assess the performance of the SSGA in optimizing a test bed of complex functions. Finally, sections 25.8 to 25.10, will deal with the application of SSGA and its performance in trading a variety of currencies.

25.2 Technical Trading Strategies and Genetic Algorithms

Technical trading strategies are essentially "algorithms proposing trading recommendations for financial assets". These algorithms rely on financial data, primarily prices, as their input, and analysis is performed to form some sort of conclusion about the market trend or behavior (Murphy 1986).

Much like tuning a car engine, to maximize the performance of a technical trading model, these models need to be fine-tuned before they can operate effectively. There are a number of free parameters which must be optimized.

Each market and its commodities behave differently. It is often a very difficult task to identify the most appropriate parameter values for technical trade models analytically over several markets. It is only through trial and error that these values can be determined.

In principle, normal exhaustive search techniques can identify the global optima for optimization problems such as technical trading rule optimization, although this is often not feasible because of time and/or resource constraints. Hence, special search algorithms such as heuristic search algorithms were developed to identify local optima using a minimum amount of resource (OTC 1996).

Heuristic search algorithms such as genetic algorithms are a class of optimization that mimic the process of evolution. In their most basic form, genetic algorithms can be defined as a type of heuristic algorithm that searches the available space in a parallel fashion by simultaneously looking at a "population" of solutions (Goldberg 1989, Holland 1993).

The next section will be a brief overview of the make up of a STanDard Genetic Algorithm (STDGAs) followed by an explanation of the Split Search Genetic Algorithm (SSGA).

25.3   Standard Genetic Algorithms

In a standard GA, a population of individuals is randomly generated. An individual represents a combination of variables that shall be tested. Each individual is made up of a string of binary digits (or genes) called a chromosome. The chromosome is divided into segments of binary digits, each segment representing a variable (or allele). During optimization, this population of solutions is subjected to four important operations:

1. *Evaluation* involves assessing an individual based on an objective function which the system attempts to either maximize or minimize, depending on the user's requirement.

2. *Selection* is the choosing of parents for reproduction. In the simplest STDGAs, this is performed by randomly selecting two individuals. Other popular selection methods are schemes such as roulette wheel selection or rank based selection (Goldberg 1989, Yuret 1994).

3. *Reproduction* allows the "crossing-over" of individuals in a population. Crossover, in standard GAs involves randomly selecting a segment in the two parent's chromosomes and swapping them to create two entirely different chromosomes, or offspring.

4. *Mutation* is the act of randomly changing an individual's genes. As in nature, mutation in genetic algorithms usually occurs at very low rates.

As each generation progresses and reproduces, the chance of those with lower fitness values reproducing will decrease. Eventually, it is hoped that the population will reach "convergence", i.e. the majority of the population will have the same genetic makeup because this makeup is fittest under the test environment.

25.4 Maintaining Diversity through Mutation

Research has shown that mutation is an extremely important factor in effective genetic algorithms (Fogel 1995, Kampen 1996). Generally speaking, the mutation operation is responsible for the random re-introduction of lost genetic materials during optimization. This feature helps the algorithm to refrain from being caught in local optimum (or "premature convergence") due to a lack of genetic material.

Experiments have shown that systems with a high mutation rate (i.e. 10% or more) will in general have an adverse effect on the GA search because this will indiscriminately mutate individuals, destroying both bad and good genetic materials and thus severely interrupts convergence (Srinivas & Patnaik 1994).

On the other hand, a mutation rate set too low, will result in the system losing its diversity and, as a result, being more likely to fall victim to premature convergence due to the lack of genetic materials for the crossover operator to work on.

What is needed is a system that addresses the need for diversity using a relatively high mutation rate, while at the same time preserving individuals that has a high fitness value through the use of a low mutation rate.

25.5 The Split Search Genetic Algorithms (SSGAs)

The Split Search Genetic Algorithm (SSGAs) proposed in this work aims to minimize premature convergence. Based on what is commonly known as distributed genetic algorithms (DGAs) (Tanese 1989, Adachi 1995, and Pavel et. al. 1995), SSGAs focuses on the use of mutation as a means to maintaining diversity and the protection of strong individuals in the population.

Rather than splitting the population into many subpopulations, as in most DGAs, the population is only split into two. The first group has the aim of maintaining diversity by introducing a high level of mutation rate (the *experimental* group); and second group has the aim of protecting good genetic material using a low mutation rate (the *control* group).

During the optimization process, the two groups will perform reproduction and mutation operations independently. At the end of each generation, the two groups are allowed to communicate. The best and worst individual of the two groups will be identified and the best individual will be replicated and used to replace the other group's worst individual. The term "invasion" has been coined to describe this process as the best individual from either group invades the other group.

As the control group allows the algorithm to converge in an almost mutation free environment, the experimental group ensures the algorithm will still be exposed to new genetic material. This is particularly important during the latter stages of optimization when the population is largely made up of similar genetic material (approaching convergence).

However, by splitting the population into sub-populations, the amount of genetic material available for manipulation in each sub-population is a portion of the entire population. As a result, the gain in diversity from the high mutation rate is off-set by a reduction in the amount of genetic material represented. A balance is therefore needed to find the appropriate size allocation for the groups.

Therefore, experimentation will be carried out in two stages: Firstly, a comparison between two versions of SSGAs will be performed, these two SSGAs will have different group sizes, one with 30% of its population allocated to the control group, the other with 70%.

Secondly a comparison between the more successful version of SSGAs against the STDGA in function optimization will be completed.

25.6 Preliminary Testing

The two stages of preliminary testing is performed over a test bed of 4 functions. Functions 25.1, 25.2, and 25.3 were selected from the First International Contest on Evolutionary Optimization (Seront 1995), and chosen because they represent some extremely complex and challenging problems for the GAs to solve. Function 25.4 was chosen as a simple test of the algorithm's performance in a noisy environment (DeJong 1975).

The following is the test bed of four functions over which the algorithms will compete on:

$$f_1(\overline{x}) = \sum_{i=1}^{5} (x_1 - 1)^2 \tag{25.1}$$

$$\text{where } x_i \in [-5, 5], i = 1, \ldots, 5$$

$$f_2(\overline{x}) = \frac{1}{4000} \sum_{i=1}^{5} (x_1 - 100)^2 - \prod_{i=1}^{5} \cos\left(\frac{x_1 - 100}{\sqrt{i}}\right) + 1 \tag{25.2}$$

$$\text{where } x_i \in [-600, 600], i = 1, \ldots, 5$$

$$f_3(\overline{x}) = -\sum_{i=1}^{5} \sin(x_i) \cdot \sin^{20}\left(\frac{i \cdot x_i^2}{\pi}\right) \tag{25.3}$$

$$\text{where } x_i \in [0, \pi], i = 1, \ldots, 5$$

$$f_4(x_i) = \sum_{i=1}^{30} i \cdot x_i^4 + Gauss(0, 1) \tag{25.4}$$

$$\text{where } x_i \in [-1.28, 1.28], i = 1, \ldots, 30$$

The three GAs that were used for testing are as follows:

30-70SSGAs 30%   Control group: 70% Experimental group

70-30SSGAs 70%   Control group: 30% Experimental group[1]

STDGAs   Standard Genetic Algorithms (described in section 25.3)

To ensure that the results are comparable across the four test functions, the Relative Deviation Index (RDI), as suggested by Kim & Kim (1996), is used to grade all solutions between 0 and 1:

$$RDI = \frac{(T_w - T_a)}{(T_w - T_B)}$$

where

$$T_a = \text{the solution for a given parameter set}$$

$$T_B = \text{the parameter set which gave the best solution.}$$

$$T_W = \text{the parameter set which gave the worst solution}$$

When $T_a = T_B$, the RDI index will return 1, and 0 when $T_a = T_W$. Therefore, an RDI of 0.5 will indicate an average result.

The basis for comparison will be based on efficiency and effectiveness. To measure efficiency, the number of **fitness evaluations** will be measured; effectiveness will

---

1. The ratio 30:70 and 70:30 were arbitrarily chosen, further research into the most appropriate ratio is under way.

be measured by the **best solution** and the **RDI** performance of the algorithm in the overall tests.

The following hypotheses were first tested to identify the preferred control group size:

Effectiveness ($H_{1,0}$):   The null hypothesis is that no difference exists between the RDI fitness performance of 30-70SSGAs and 70-30SSGAs.

Efficiency ($H_{1,1}$):   The null hypothesis is that no difference exists between the number of function calls between 30-70SSGAs and 70-30SSGAs to reach at least 0.5 RDI.

Once the more optimal version of SSGAs (30-70SSGAs or 70-30SSGAs) is determined, the following hypotheses were tested:

Effectiveness ($H_{2,0}$):   The null hypothesis is that no difference exists between the RDI performance of SSGAs and STDGAs.

Efficiency ($H_{2,1}$):   The null hypothesis is that no difference exists between the number of function calls between SSGAs and STDGAs.

Finally, the parameter settings for the algorithms, i.e. the mutation rate, recombination rate, population size, etc. are derived from benchmark studies previously performed (Tsang 1997). The values used are respectively: 0.01, 0.95, and 50. For the SSGA, the two mutation rates were arbitrarily chosen as 0.008 for the control group and 0.15 for the experimental group.[2] Because of the nature of genetic algorithms, we expect variability in the solution obtained,[3] the algorithms were trailed ten times for each test function to study its behavior.

25.6.1   Preliminary Findings

Mann-Whitney U tests were used to test the performances of the two versions: 30-70SSGAs and 70-30SSGAs. The tests show that although the average RDI of the 30-70SSGAs was slightly higher, the only rejection of the null hypothesis at all three levels of statistical significance was ICEO1. The average RDI indicated a slight bias towards the 30-70SSGAs, hence it was chosen to represent SSGAs against STDGAs. (Table 25.1)

---

2. Further studies as to the optimum mutation rates for the two groups will be conducted in future.

3. The variability is mainly due to the probabilistic nature of the genetic operators as well as factors such as the initial population, etc. (Kampen 1996).

Table 25.1
($H_{1,0}$) The null hypothesis that no difference exists between the RDI performance of 30-70SSGAs and 70-30SSGAs in terms of final fitness value.

Statistical Significance		Effectiveness			Ave. RDI	Ave. RDI
		$P \leq 0.05$	$P \leq 0.01$	$p \leq 0.005$		
To Accept:	Z*	$-1.96 \leq z \leq 1.96$	$-2.58 \leq z \leq 2.58$	$-2.81 \leq z \leq 2.81$	30–70 SSGAs	30–70 SSGAs
(F_1): ICEO 1	−3.1435	Reject	Reject	Reject	0.99634	0.73443
(F_2): ICEO 2	−1.8898	Accept	Accept	Accept	0.72118	0.48841
(F_3): ICEO 4	−2.0821	Reject	Accept	Accept	0.81444	0.51354
(F_4): De Jong 4	0.98271	Accept	Accept	Accept	0.41046	0.37451
Average (RDI only)	—	—	—	—	0.73560	0.52772

Table 25.2
(H2,0) The null hypothesis that no difference exists between the RDI performance of SSGAs and STDGAs in terms of final fitness value.

Statistical Significance		Effectiveness			Ave. RDI	Ave. RDI
		$P \leq 0.05$	$P \leq 0.01$	$p \leq 0.005$		
To Accept:	Z*	$-1.96 \leq z \leq 1.96$	$-2.58 \leq z \leq 2.58$	$-2.81 \leq z \leq 2.81$	SSGAs	STDGAs
(F_1): ICEO 1	3.57624	Reject	Reject	Reject	0.99951	0.48400
(F_2): ICEO 2	3.77964	Reject	Reject	Reject	0.89959	0.31897
(F_3): ICEO 4	3.67423	Reject	Reject	Reject	0.83281	0.59813
(F_4): De Jong 4	3.02372	Reject	Reject	Reject	0.71270	0.36746
Average (RDI only)	—	—	—	—	0.86115	0.44214

Table 25.3
($H_{1,1}$) The null hypothesis that no difference exists between 30-70SSGAs and 70-30SSGAs efficiency to reach and RDIBV of 0.5 or greater.

Statistical Significance		Efficiency			Ave. RDI	Ave. RDI
		$P \leq 0.05$	$P \leq 0.01$	$p \leq 0.005$		
To Accept:	Z*	$-1.96 \leq z \leq 1.96$	$-2.58 \leq z \leq 2.58$	$-2.81 \leq z \leq 2.81$	SSGAs	SSGAs
(F_1): ICEO 1	0.68803	Accept	Accept	Accept	0.99634	0.96729
(F_2): ICEO 2	0	Accept	Accept	Accept	0.81124	0.72203
(F_3): ICEO 4	0	Accept	Accept	Accept	0.93590	0.89948
(F_4): De Jong 4	−1.8516	Accept	Accept	Accept	0.55556	0.77451
Average (RDI only)	—	—	—	—	0.82476	0.84083

The comparison between SSGAs and STDGAs, showed $H_{(2,0)}$ was rejected in all cases. The average RDI also show the SSGAs to perform significantly more effective than the STDGAs (See Table 25.2).

In terms of efficiency, $H_{(1,1)}$ was accepted in all cases (See Table 25.3). In comparing against STDGAs however, $H_{(2,1)}$ was rejected at lower confidence levels. Average of RDI shows a bias towards STDGAs, SSGAs were found to utilize more function calls than STDGAs (See Table 25.4). Hence, in terms of efficiency, STDGAs is more efficient when compared against SSGAs.

The results so far have shows that SSGAs were more effective in finding the optima than STDGAs under the test environment. The result also indicates that while STDGAs assumed it was appropriate to stop, the SSGAs had found it necessary to perform more searches to locate the optima. In other words, SSGAs have shown to have avoided premature convergence.

Table 25.4

($H_{2,1}$) The null hypothesis that no difference exists between STDGAs and 70-30SSGAs efficiency to reach and RDIBV of 0.5 or greater.

Statistical Significance		Efficiency			Ave. RDI	Ave. RDI
		$P \leq 0.05$	$P \leq 0.01$	$p \leq 0.005$		
To Accept:	Z^*	$-1.96 \leq z \leq 1.96$	$-2.58 \leq z \leq 2.58$	$-2.81 \leq z \leq 2.81$	SSGAs	STDGAs
(F_1): ICEO 1	-0.3086	Accept	Accept	Accept	0.54088	0.49476
(F_2): ICEO 2	0	Accept	Accept	Accept	0.72061	0.75991
(F_3): ICEO 4	2.43028	Reject	Accept	Accept	0.48848	0.80770
(F_4): De Jong 4	2.02837	Reject	Accept	Accept	0.47021	0.87166
Average (RDI only)	—	—	—	—	0.55505	0.73351

25.7 Application to the Foreign Exchange Market

The preliminary testing provided a general summary of the performances of SSGAs and STDGAs in function optimization. The attention now turns to their performances in the real life problem of trading strategy optimization

While an algorithm's performance in optimization is important, the solution set identified by the optimization must also perform well when used to trade. In other words, the algorithm's performance must perform well in identifying the optimal parameter values for the trading strategy for in-sample testing but the same set of parameter values must be able to do well in out-of sample environment also. To deal with this issue, data collected will be split into two samples, in-sample data set and out-of sample data set, the algorithm will then be allowed to optimize with the in-sample data but their performance will be evaluated using their out-of sample performance.

A second issue, other then performance over time, is that the solution set should also perform well across a variety of environments common to the problem, i.e. it needs to be "robust". In our case, the solution would also need to perform well in a variety of commodities. This can be achieved in two ways:

• The objective function should be based on robustness, so that the functions are optimizing with robustness and not over-fitting the data.

• The algorithm itself measures the robustness of a solution and either rewards or penalizes a solution based on its robustness.

Studies have shown that using the second option, will allow genetic algorithms to find robust parameters which "correspond to a broad regions where the fitness function is higher on average" (Pictet 1996). Whilst this article acknowledges the importance of these features it will not implement them in the current research.

To ensure that the strategy will perform well across a wide variety of market conditions, it was tested over 7 different currencies: AUD, DBM, CAD, CHF, GBP,

IDR and JPY (Figure 25.1). These currencies have been selected because of their high daily volume.

The 7 currencies' daily open, high, low, and close prices for 24th July 1996 to 24th July 1998 have been collected from Reuters and split up into 2 intervals: 24/7/1996 to 23/7/1997, and 24/7/1997 to 23/7/1998 for in-sample and out-of-sample testing respectively. As a benchmark comparison, a simple buy and hold strategy is performed across the 7 currencies and the performance of the algorithms is benchmarked using a buy and hold strategy.

25.8   Implementing GAs

There are several key issues that must be considered in the implementation of a GA for the optimization of technical trading strategies. They relate to:

- The selection of trading strategies to optimize
- The objective function

25.8.1   Trading Strategies for Optimization

In this article, a strategy is derived from concepts that are actually used by traders (Kaiser 1998). Commonly known as a "trade range break-out" strategy, and similar to the text book version of a "channel rule" (Murphy 1986, Deboeck 1994), the strategy is based on the daily high and low of a commodity and generates buy, sell or hold signals based on the current day's range. Figure 25.2 provides an explanation of how the strategy generates signals based on the trade ranges of prices. The main difference between this strategy and channel rules is that instead of focusing on support and resistance level over a period of time, the strategy emphasis is on the daily trade range (i.e. the daily high and low) the use of stop-loss and take-profit, and exit techniques.

In essence, the strategy reacts to the first sign of a market's movement out of a non-trending period. Hence the first step is to identify when the market is not trending using a time frame (dotted box in Figure 25.2), if no breaches occur for a certain period of time, the strategy will enter an alert phase. During the alert phase, the strategy is prepared to open a buy or sell position up to an amount specified by the buy percentage depending on which side of the buffer zone (gray bands in Figure 25.2) the price breaches. The strategy incorporates the use of buffers to ensure that misleading movements, which regularly occur before a major "bullish" or "bearish" move, will be filtered out (Kaiser 1998). Once a position is opened, the

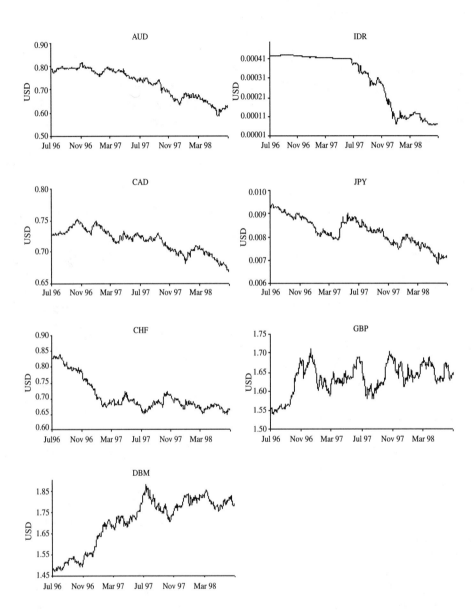

Figure 25.1
The above are the currencies that had been selected for trading. They show a variety of patterns. Note that the IDR had been included to increase the test environment's difficult as the currency was devalued severely in the out-of sample period during the Asian currency crisis in 1998.

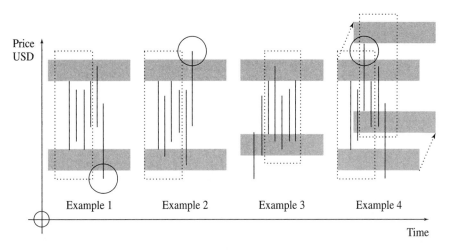

Figure 25.2
The figure shows how the trade range break rule will generate trade signals. Each verticle line represent the daily range of the price of the currency. The grey area is the buffer above and below a trade range. If the bandwidth is not breached within a certain amount of time defined by the dotted line time frame, the algorithm will be on the alert for any break out of the bandwidth. In example 1 and 2, this is highlighted by a circle. When this breach occurs above the upper (lower) bandwidth, the algorithm will return a sell (buy) signal in the anticipation of a weakening (strengthening) currency. Example 3, is an example of the algorithm returning an exit signal when price osillation occurs. As a result, the algorithm will signal to exit the market. Example 4 shows how the system will NOT return a signal if the trade range breaks out of the bandwidth before the time frame is over. As a result, the time frame will restart at the point of the breach; note the broken arrows.

Table 25.5
The strategy acts based on the signals generated by the previous price and the current price.

Previous State	Current Signal	Action taken
Hold	Buy	(Entry) Buy currency with USD
Hold	Sell	(Entry) Sell currency for USD
Buy	Buy	Do nothing
Sell	Sell	Do nothing
Buy	Hold	(Exit) Sell amount invested in currency for USD
Sell	Hold	(Exit) Buy currency with the amount invested in USD
Hold	Hold	Do Nothing

strategy will exit upon a stop-loss signal or a take-profit signal. These are activated if the stop-loss amount or the take profit amount is reached.

There are three signals that the strategy will generate: buy, hold, and sell. A complete list of transitions with the appropriate resultant signal is provided:

In summary, the variables for optimization are:

- Buy % (0.05% to 0.0001%)—This is simply the % amount of the total portfolio that will be invested on each trade.

- Time Frame (1 to 20)—This is the number of days before the algorithm goes on the alert for any breaches of the bandwidth. Any breach of the bandwidth after this period is deemed to be a signal.

- Bandwidth Size (1% to 100%)—This is the amount of bandwidth the algorithm should place above and below the daily high and low.

- Stop Losses % (1% to 50%)—This is the % of the trade that may be lost before exiting the position to minimize losses.

- Take Profits % (1% to 50%)—This is the % of the trade that is allowed to profit before exiting the trade.[4]

Transaction cost is assumed to be 0.001 USD per trade (Pereira 1998).

In total, the number of possible combinations of these five variables is:

$500 \times 20 \times 100 \times 50 \times 50 = 2,500,000,000$ combinations

It has been estimated that approximately 5 function evaluations (each function evaluation consists of testing one combination on all 7 currencies over the in-sample period) can be performed in 1 second on a Pentium100. This would mean that it would take 2,500,000,000 seconds or the equivalent of 15.85 years to exhaustively search all the possible combinations. This further establishes the need for search algorithms such as GAs.

25.8.2 The Objective Function

Perhaps one of the most important issues in the optimization of the technical trading model is determining the objective function that the algorithm aims to optimize.

As mentioned previously, to ensure the solution is robust in its performance both in and out of sample, we modified the objective function so that it aims to maximize the sum of the sharpe ratios over all seven currencies. The sharpe ratio is calculated by dividing the return by the standard deviation (Sharpe 1994). The algorithm aims to maximize the return, and minimize the variability of the return. In addition, the algorithm will also have to optimize for a high return consistently across all currencies. Solutions with high returns in one currency but poor performance in

---

4. The size of the stop-loss and take-profit had been set as between 1% to 50% for these experiments. In actual trading system the figure depends on the trader's willingness to take risk.

Table 25.6
Returns for a buy and hold strategy. Note that due to the Asian currency crisis at the end of 1997 caused the IDR to fall dramatically from 2613 to 13950 over the course of the year.

BUY AND HOLD (Out Sample) Date	USD/AUD	USD/CAD	USD/CHF	USD/DEM	USD/GBP	USD/IDR	USD/JPY	Average
24/7/97	0.7359	0.7239	0.6645	1.8334	1.6746	0.000383	0.0086	—
24/7/98	0.6215	0.6684	0.6647	1.7845	1.6510	0.000072	0.0071	—
% return p.a.	-7.773%	-3.830%	0.017%	-1.334%	-0.705%	-40.634%	-8.940%	-9.028%
Ave. Daily Return	-0.000089	-0.000043	0.000003	-0.000013	-0.000006	-0.000719	-0.000104	-0.000971
Std. Deviation	0.001095	0.000371	0.000838	0.000798	0.000704	0.007646	0.001196	0.008454
Sharpe Ratio	-0.081285	-0.117143	0.003137	-0.015906	-0.008667	-0.094054	-0.086651	-0.114907

others will not be favored (Pictet 1996). Robustness across different environment means the algorithms can be applied with more confidence.

Due to the nature of heuristic search algorithms, we would expect some variability in the solutions, as a result, each algorithm was trailed 15 times to assess its overall behavior.

25.9 Analysis of Results

Table 25.6 is the benchmark result of a buy and hold strategy which will provide an average return of –9.03% per annum (or –5.50% if excluding the IDR[5]). This will be the base line comparison for the STDGAs and SSGA.

To assess the performance of the SSGA and STDGAs require the assessment of Sharpe ratios first. The boxplots in Figure 25.3 are derived from the 15 trials of the algorithms in in-sample optimization and out-of sample trading.

As illustrated by the boxplots, the out-of sample results shows that the median of SSGAs lies around 0.3 sharpe ratio with few trials returning a negative return. STDGAs on the other hand, has a median around 0 sharpe ratio. Compared with the buy and hold strategy, the return per annum for STDGAs and SSGAs was also higher than the—9.028%, where STDGAs' median was around 0%p.a. and SSGAs' around 0.4%p.a. See Figure 25.4.

The following hypotheses were tested for out of sample results only:

Effectiveness ($H_{3,0}$): The null hypothesis is that no difference exists between the sharpe ratio of SSGAs and STDGAs.

Effectiveness ($H_{3,1}$): The null hypothesis is that no difference exists between the return of SSGAs and STDGAs.

---

5. Indonesian Rupiah was heavily involved in the Asian Currency Crisis of 1998.

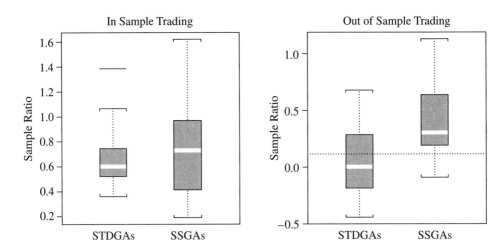

Figure 25.3
Boxplots of sharpe ratio from in-sample optimization and out of sample trading.

Table 25.7
$(H_{3,0})$, $(H_{3,1})$ & $(H_{3,2})$: No difference between the Sharpe Ratio $(H_{3,0})$ of SSGAs and STDGAs. No difference between the average return $(H_{3,1})$ of SSGAs and STDGAs. No difference between the standard deviation $(H_{3,2})$ of SSGAs and STDGAs.

		Effectiveness				
Statistical Significance		$P \leq 0.05$	$P \leq 0.01$	$P \leq 0.005$	Ave. RDI	Ave. RDI
To Accept:	Z^*	$-1.96 \leq z \leq 1.96$	$-2.58 \leq z \leq 2.58$	$-2.81 \leq z \leq 2.81$	SSGAs	STDGAs
$(H_{3,0})$ Sharpe Ratio	2.5094	Reject	Accept	Accept	0.5341	0.3279
$(H_{3,1})$ Ave. Return p.a.	2.6753	Reject	Reject	Accept	0.5099	0.3281
$(H_{3,2})$ Std. Deviation	−0.3526	Accept	Accept	Accept	0.5650	0.6343

Effectiveness ($H_{3,2}$): The null hypothesis is that no difference exists between the standard deviation of SSGAs and STDGAs.

Efficiency ($H_{3,4}$): The null hypothesis is that no difference exists between the number of function calls needed by SSGAs and STDGAs to reach at least an RDIBV of 0.5 or higher.

A test of the null hypothesis that there was no difference between the performance of SSGAs and STDGAs in the optimization of sharpe ratio ($H_{3,0}$) and average returns (H3,1) was rejected at lower confidence levels. A study of the average RDI shows that the SSGAs outperformed STDGAs at finding a profitable parameter set for the trading rule. Null hypothesis of no difference in terms of standard deviation

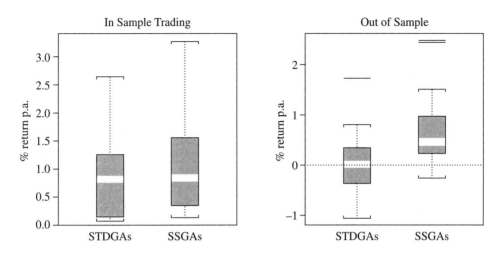

Figure 25.4
Boxplots of returns from in-sample optimization and out of sample trading.

Table 25.8
($H_{3,4}$): No difference between the number of function calls needed by SSGAs and STDGAs to reach at least an RDIBV of 0.5 or higher.

		Efficiency				
Statistical Significance		$P \leq 0.05$	$P \leq 0.01$	$P \leq 0.005$	Ave. RDI	Ave. RDI
To Accept:	Z*	$-1.96 \leq z = le1.96$	$-2.58 \leq z \leq 2.58$	$-2.81 \leq z \leq 2.81$	SSGAs	STDGAs
($H_{3,3}$) Function Calls	0.3419	Accept	Accept	Accept	0.6916	0.6222

was accepted in all cases ($H_{3,2}$), although the averages RDI indicates that STDGAs on average have a lower standard deviation (i.e. a higher RDI value) then SSGAs.

Hence, it may be concluded that SSGA is more effective at finding the optimal parameter set than a standard version of GA, with a confidence of 95%. At higher levels of confidence (p values), the results do indicate a bias towards SSGAs, as the hypothesis was only marginally accepted (Z values of 2.5094 and 2.6753 for sharpe ratio and average returns respectively). (See table 25.7.)

In terms of efficiency, the null hypothesis that there are no difference between SSGAs and STDGAs in terms of function calls to reach an above average (0.5 RDI) was tested (H3,4). The results indicates that no difference was found. (See Table 25.8.) The average RDI shows that SSGAs seem to perform slightly better then STDGAs[6].

---

6. Note that only 3 results form STDGAs was higher then 0.5 RDI, against 7 from SSGAs.

25.10   Conclusion

Heuristic search techniques are search algorithms that search the available search space and use decision rules to guide the search system to the optimum result possible. Genetic Algorithms belong to this family and are commonly used for solving general global optimization problems.

This paper has suggested a variation of the standard genetic algorithm by manipulating the mutation process. By splitting the population into two groups, a control group and an experimental group, the algorithm is able to maintain the diversity that is possible from a high mutation rate while ensuring possible local optima are not destroyed.

Results from function optimization problems prove that the SSGA was found to be statistically significantly more effective in optimization than STDGAs. In terms of efficiency, SSGAs required more function calls than STDGAs to reach an RDIBV of 0.5 or greater. Therefore, to a certain extent, SSGAs are not as efficient as STDGAs. On the other hand, this implies the SSGAs have avoided premature convergence and local optima.

In its application to finance, the results are also very promising. This article has defined a type of trade range breakout rule from concepts used by actual traders, and has found that it works well against a wide variety of currencies when benchmarked against a buy and hold strategy. The parameter values of this trade strategy were then further optimized by the use of SSGAs and STDGAs. The results once again show that the SSGA is superior in terms of being able to produce a higher return and sharpe ratio, with little difference in the standard deviation. Statistical test of the efficiency shows that there was no difference between SSGAs and STDGAs, a study of RDI shows STDGAs efficiency performs marginally better.

Further work is thus planned to study the effect of varying the mutation rate, the group sizes and various aspects of SSGAs. There is also a need for further research in SSGAs to ensure the robustness of solutions in noisy environments, such as financial markets. Further refinement to the technical trade strategy will also be made, for example, including mechanisms to minimize "drawdowns" and using other indicators to assist trading in trending periods.

25.11   Acknowledgement

We wish to thank Dr. Raymond Li, Mr. Tony Kaiser and Mr. Robert Pereira for their invaluable time and advice.

References

Adachi, N. and Y. Yoshida (1995). "Accelerating Genetic Algorithms: Protected Chromosomes and Parallel Processing". International Conference on Genetic Algorithms in Engineering Systems: Innovations and Applications, University of Sheffield, UK, The Institution of Electrical Engineers.

Allen, F. and R. Karjalainen (1994). "Using Genetic Algorithms to Find Technical Trading Rules." from Pereira R.

Balci, O., R. Sharada, et al. (1992). *Computer Science and Operations Research: New Developments in their interfaces.* New York, Pergamon Press.

Bauer(Jr), R. J. (1994). *Genetic Algorithms and Investment Strategies,* John Wiley & Sons.

Deboeck, G. J. (1994). *Trading On the Edge.* Toronto, John Wiley & Sons, Inc.

DeJong, K. A. (1975). An Analysis of the Behavior of a Class of Genetic Adaptive System. *Computer and Communication Sciences.* Michigan, University of Michigan: 256.

Deshpande, J. V., A. P. Gore, et al. (1995). *Statistical Analysis of Nonnormal Data.* New Delhi, John Wiley & Sons.

Fama, E. F. and M. E. Blume (1966). "Filter Rules and Stock-Market Trading," *Journal of Business* (Jan.): 226–241.

Fogel, D. B. (1995). *Evolutionary Computation: Toward a New Philosophy of Machine Intelligence.* New York, Institute of Electical and Electronics Engineers Press.

Goldberg, D. E. (1989). *Genetic Algorithm in Search, Optimization and Machine Learning.* Addison-Wesley Publishing Company Inc.

Hiew, C. and A. Nicholson (1996). Analysis of Simulated Annealing and Other Algorithms in Cricket Scheduling. *School of Business Systems.* Melbourne, Monash University.

Holland, J. H. (1993). *Adaptation in Natural and Artificial Systems.* London, Massachusetts Institute of Technology.

Kaiser, T. (1998). Personal Communication. Endeavour Hills, Victoria, Australia.

Kampen, A. H. C. v. and L. M. C. Buydens (1996). "The Effectiveness of Recombination". Proceedings of the 2nd Nordic Workshop on Genetic Algorihtms and their Applications (2NWGA), Vaasa (Finland), University of Vaasa.

Kim, J. and Y. Kim (1996). "Simulated Annealing and Genetic Algorithms for Scheduling Products with Multi-level Product Structure." *Computers Operations Research* **23**: 857–868.

McIlhagga, M., P. Husband, et al. (1996). "A comparison of optimization techniques on a wing-box optimization problem". Fourth Conference on Parallel problem solving from nature, Berlin, Germany, Springer.

Murphy, J. J. (1986). *Technical Analysis of the Furtures Markets: A Comprehensive Guide to Trading Methods and Applications.* New York, Prentice-Hall.

OTC (1996). (Optimization-Technology-Center) NEOS Guide Optimization Tree, http://www.mcs.anl.gov/home/oct/Guide/optWeb.

Pavel, O., S. Ivan, et al. (1995). "Multilevel Distributed Genetic Algorithms". International Conference on Genetic Algorithms in Engineering Systems: Innovations and Applications, University of Sheffield, UK, Insitution of Electical Engineers.

Pereira, R. (1998). Personal Communication. LaTrobe university, Melbourne, Victoria, Australia.

Pictet, O., M. Dacorogna, et al. (1995). "Genetic Algorithms with collective sharing for Robust Optimizsation in Financial Applications." *Neural Network World* 5(4): 573-587.

Seront, G. (1995). First International Contest on Evolutionary Optimization, http://iridia.ulb.ac.be/langerman/ICEO.html.

Sharpe, W. F. (1994). "The Sharpe Ratio." *Journal of Portfolio Management* **21**(1): 49–58.

Tanese, R. (1989). "Distributed Genetic Algorithms". Proceedings of the Third International Conference on Genetic Algorithms, Arlington, Morgan Kaufmann Publishers.

Taylor, S. J. (1994). "Trading Futures Using a Channel Rule: A study of the predictive power of technical analysis with currency examples." *The Journal of Futures Markets* **14**(2): 215–235.

Tsang, R. (1997). Genetic Algorithms and Simulate Annealing, A Baseline Comparison. *School of Business Systems*. Melbourne, Monash University: 113.

26 Trading Mutual Funds with Piece-wise Constant Models

Michael de la Maza

26.1 Introduction

In this paper, we describe the together structure system, a machine learning system that creates piece-wise constant models, and use it to create a trading strategy that switches amongst mutual funds. The daily return of the trading strategy on out-of-sample data is significantly better ($p < .05$) than the daily return of buying and holding any one of the mutual funds.

Mutual funds have become the most popular vehicle for domestic investors to invest in the stock market. With well over 6000 mutual funds in existence, the number of mutual funds rivals the number stocks listed on US exchanges. Despite this huge growth, the academic community has not studied mutual fund trading strategies with the attention that has been paid to trading stocks, bonds, or currencies. Although mutual fund returns (Rahman, Fabozzi and Lee, 1991), mutual fund managers (Lee and Rahman, 1991), and mutual fund investors (Goetzmann and Peles, 1997) have all received attention, we know of no other academic study that analyzes the performance of a mutual fund trading strategy.

Here we apply many of the same methods that have been used to study the stock market over the past few decades to the mutual fund markets and find evidence that above average returns can be achieved, thus providing some evidence that mutual fund markets are inefficient. A strategy similar to the one described in this paper has been implemented in real-time since November, 1996 in a managed account program and a hedge fund, and the real-time results support the claim that the strategy improves on buy-and-hold ($p < 0.05$).

This paper is divided into five sections. In Section 2, we describe together structures in general terms and show how they can be used to create a piece-wise constant model of mutual fund returns. In Section 3, the together structure system is applied to mutual funds in the T. Rowe Price mutual fund family. Section 4 analyzes the results and Section 5 suggests ways to extend this work. Section 6 introduces the Twiddledee/Twiddledum thought experiment which raises serious concerns about the standard method of testing trading strategies of the sort described in this paper.

26.2   Together Structures

Together structures are a representation for memory and learning that have their roots in machine learning, a sub-field of artificial intelligence. Like neural networks (Rumelhart and McClelland, 1986) and nearest-neighbor methods (Atkeson, 1990), together structures produce nonlinear models. The together structure system divides the instance space into sub-spaces and in each sub-space creates a constant model. Hence, the output of the together structure system is a piece-wise constant model that maps an arbitrary set of inputs to one output.

Together Structures Store Co-occurrence Information

Together structures store co-occurrence information about domain elements. *A domain element* is either a user-defined abstraction that specifies the level at which inference should take place (called a *primitive domain element*) or another together structure. Thus, together structures are recursive representations that can be defined with the following simple BNF grammer: T :–(P P) | (P T) where P is a primitive domain element and T is a together structure.

Each together structure stores the average value of the output variable for the instances that it *covers*. A together structure covers an instance if all of the domain elements in the together structure are true of the instance. For example, if a together structure has a single domain element that specifies that the one day change in a particular time series is between 0.0% and 0.1%, then the together structure covers all instances in which this time series has a one day change between 0.0% and 0.1%. This together structure stores the average value of the output variable for all such instances. In the mutual fund application, this output variable is the next day's return of the security that is being modeled.

A Beam Search Nests Together Structures

For the mutual fund application described in this paper, the number of domain elements is fdb where f is the number of time series, d is the number of days, and b is the number of bins. The number of days, d, is the number of days prior to the current day that the system can access and the number of bins, b, is the number of separate ranges that each time series is divided into. Because $f = 18, d = 10$, and $b = 10$ the total number of unique primitive domain elements is 1800. Hence there are $O(1800^n)$ together structures with n domain elements. Because of the exponential growth of the number of together structures, exhaustively searching all together structures with even three domain elements would be impractical. Hence, a modified beam search (Winston, 1992) is used to nest together structures.

The beam search restricts the number of together structures that are generated by eliminating branches in the search tree that are unlikely to lead to good together structures. By greatly reducing the branching factor, the beam search enables the creation of together structures with more domain elements than could be generated by an exhaustive procedure.

This feature does not come without a cost. If a together structure with $m + 1$ domain elements does not have a good precursor with m elements, then the $m + 1$ domain element together structure will never be created because none of the m domain element precursors will be extended.

Unlike a traditional beam search, the beam search used here does not fix the number of solutions that are extended. Instead, the beam search procedure uses two types of cutoffs to determine which solutions will be killed, kept, or extended. The *quality criterion* determines whether a together structure will be kept. The *extension criterion* determines whether a together structure can be nested in other together structures. No together structure that fails the quality criterion can meet the extension criterion.

The quality criterion compares the number of days which a together structure covers and the number of days which a together structure is expected to cover. If the ratio of these two numbers is above 1.5 then the together structure is kept. The number of days that a together structure is expected to cover is $n * (1/b)^\wedge m$ where n is the number of days in the sample, b is the number of bins, and m is the number of domain elements that the together structure contains.

The extension criterion is a percentage of the total number of days in the sample. If a together structure covers less than this percentage of days, then it is not extended. For the experiments described in this paper, the percentage is set to 1%.

Hence, each together structure can be killed (if it fails the quality criterion), kept (if it passes the quality criterion and fails the extension criterion), or extended (if it passes both the quality and the extension criteria). Pseudo-code for the together structure algorithm is shown in Figure 26.1.

The Most Specific Together Structure Selects the Security to Trade

Once the together structures database has been created, it is matched against the out-of-sample database and relevant performance data is recorded. For each instance (i.e., day), the most specific together structure which covers the instance is used

```
/* Initialize */
   All_P = All primitive domain elements
   Extend_T = All together structures with two primitive
              domain elements
   Kept_T = Nil
   Active_T = Nil

/* Body */
   Repeat until Extend_T = Nil
     For each T in Extend_T
       If Quality(T) = False then Kill(T,Extend_T)
          Else if Extension(T)=False then Move(T,Extend_T,Kept_T)
             Else
                 Move(T,Extend_T,Kept_T)
                 Extend(T)
       Extend_T = Active_T
       Active_T = Nil
     Output(Kept_T) /* Final list of together structures */

/* Extend Function */
Extend(T)
   For each P in all All_P
      Add(Concatenate(T,P),Active_T)
```

Figure 26.1
Pseudo-code for the together structure system.

to select the security to invest in for the following day.[1] The most specific together structure is the one with the greatest number of primitive domain elements. If there are multiple together structures with the same number of primitive domain elements, then the one that covers the most instances in the in-sample data is selected.

This selection criteria maximizes the expected daily return of the trading strategy. Many other selection criteria could have been chosen. For example, allocating the

---

1. For the mutual fund application, if the expected return of the security is less than 1, then the capital is invested in a money market fund.

```
/* Initialize */
Kept_T = All together structures in system
Instances = All instances
Best_length = 1
Best_sample = 0
Best_T = Nil

/*Body*/
For every I in Instances
   For every T in Kept_T
      If And(Cover(I,T),Length(T)>=Best_length) = False then Continue
      If Or(Length(T)>Best_length, Samples(T)>Best_sample)
         Best_sample = Samples(T)
         Best_T = T
Output(Best_T) /* The together structure chosen to estimate
                  the output*/
```

Figure 26.2
Pseudo-code for the matching procedure that selects the best together structure for each instance.

capital among several mutual funds to maximize the Sharpe ratio is a compelling alternative.

Pseudo-code for the selection method is shown in Figure 26.2.

26.3   Application to Mutual Fund Trading

In this section we show how to apply the together structure inference system to the problem of trading three mutual funds in the T. Rowe Price family of mutual funds. Table 26.1 shows standard statistical information for the three funds that the together structure strategy trades. Note the high autocorrelations. If execution at the closing price on the day a signal is generated were possible, an approach that some have adopted (LeBaron, 1998), then the strategy of buying on days when the mutual fund gains and switching into a money market fund when the mutual fund falls dominates the buy and hold strategy (results not shown). In this study, however, we assume that all trading signals are executed at the next day's closing price.

Table 26.1
Three T. Rowe Price mutual funds. Note the high autocorrelations.

Name	Science & Technology	Small Cap Value	New American
Ticker symbol	PRSCAX	PRSVX	PRWAX
Time period	1/26/89–8/8/97	1/26/89–8/8/97	1/26/89–8/8/97
Sample Size	2158 days	2158 days	2158 days
Beta vs. S&P 500	1.170	0.448	0.995
Autocorrelation	0.20	0.12	0.26
Mean daily return	1.001045	1.000622	1.000746
Skewness	−0.216010	−0.65588	−0.428730
Kurtosis	1.421136	5.007741	3.907594

Table 26.2
Six parameters. P^n is the n day moving average: $nP^n = \sum_{l=0}^{n-1} P_{t-l}$

Daily return	P_t/P_{t-1}
5 day moving average ratio	P_t/P^5
10 day moving average ratio	P_t/P^{10}
20 day moving average ratio	P_t/P^{20}
50 day moving average ratio	P_t/P^{50}
100 day moving average ratio	P_t/P^{100}

There is only one user-level decision that needs to be made when applying together structures to a domain: Defining the primitive domain elements. For this domain, each primitive element will have three components:

• A time series. For each of the three mutual funds, there are a total of six derived time series (the daily return and five moving average ratios). These time series are defined in Table 26.2.

• The number of days of historical data available. For this application, ten days of historical data will be available. So, for example, the together structure will be able to access the daily return of the Science & Technology fund seven days ago.

• The number of bins. Each of the eighteen time series will be segmented into ten ranges or bins. Bin boundaries for the daily return time series for each of the funds are shown in Table 26.3.

Hence, a primitive element might be represented internally within the together structure system as follows: (5maST 7 3). The first element, 5maST, stands for the five day moving average ratio of the Science & Technology fund; the second element, seven, is the number of days ago; and the third element, 3, is the bin number. A together structure with just this domain element will cover all instances in which seven days ago the five day moving average ratio of the Science & Technology fund fell into the third bin.

Table 26.3
Bin boundaries. This table shows the nine cutoffs for the ten daily return bins for each of the three funds. The first bin for the Small Cap Value fund is composed of all days with a return less than 0.994770, the second bin is composed of all days with a return greater than 0.994770 and less than or equal to 0.997126, and the tenth bin is composed of all days with a return greater than 1.006252. The rest of the bins are defined in an analogous manner.

Small Cap Value	Science	New American
0.994770	0.985547	0.990151
0.997126	0.991859	0.993884
0.998734	0.995889	0.997151
1.000000	0.998878	0.999335
1.000877	1.001320	1.001256
1.001866	1.003750	1.002980
1.002975	1.006721	1.004985
1.004187	1.010140	1.007636
1.006252	1.015365	1.011129

Table 26.4
The data is divided into two data sets, the in-sample data set and the out-of-sample data set. The in-sample data set is used to create the trading strategy and the out-of-sample data set is used to test the strategy.

In-sample data	1/26/89–12/31/93
Out-of-sample data	12/3/93–8/8/97

Once the primitive domain elements are defined, there are no other user-level decisions that need to be made. The together structure algorithm, shown in Figure 26.1, is run on each of the three mutual funds, and the together structures are stored so they can be applied in out-of-sample and real-time trading.

26.4   Results

The trading strategy created by the together structure system is tested using the standard in-sample / out-of-sample methodology. The data series is divided into two sets, the in-sample set and the out-of-sample set, and the trading strategy is developed on the in-sample set and tested on the out-of-sample set. The out-of-sample data is kept pristine throughout the development process, thus avoiding data snooping problems. Table 26.4 shows how the data was split it into the two sets.

Figure 26.3 shows the compound cumulative return of the trading strategy and compares it to the compound cumulative returns of the buy and hold trading strategy for each of the three mutual funds on the out-of-sample data set. Table 26.5 summarizes some of the key quantitative features of the trading strategy.

Figure 26.3
Out-of-sample performance (semi-log plot). This figure shows the cumulative return of the trading strategy (top line), the T. Rowe Price Science Technology fund (second line from top), the Small Cap Value fund (smooth line near bottom), and the New American fund (choppy line near bottom). The strategy outperforms the three funds that it trades during the out-of-sample period on an absolute return basis ($p < 0.05$).

Table 26.5
Out-of-sample statistics for the together structure trading strategy and the three mutual funds.

	Strategy	Science & Technology	Small Cap Value	New American
Number of days in market	809 (88.9%)	910 (100%)	910 (100%)	910 (100%)
Mean daily return	1.001984	1.001063	1.000693	1.000696
Standard deviation	0.009673	0.013659	0.003768	0.007525
Skewness	0.145014	−185510	−0.505046	−0.423300
Kurtosis	3.399174	1.218711	3.986721	1.660555

To test differences in the daily returns, we use the same t-test adopted by Brock, Lakonishok, and LeBaron (1992). In addition to testing the three mutual funds we also tested a blended portfolio with equal dollar amounts in each of the three funds. The p-values are given in Table 26.6.

Table 26.6
Comparison of the performance of the three mutual funds and a three fund blend with equal weightings in each of the three funds to the performance of the together structure stragegy on out-of-sample data. In all four cases, the daily return of the together structure stragegy is greater than the daily return of buy and hold by a statistically significant margin.

Small Cap	$p < 0.0001$
Science & Technology	$p < 0.05$
New American	$p < 0.001$
Three fund blend	$p < 0.005$

(NAM 0 8) (NAM 0 7) (ST 1 9)
(5maSCV 1 0) (50maST 0 6)
(NAM 3 0) (20maST 2 5)
(20maSCV 8 1) (100maNAM 9 2) (SCV 0 1)

Figure 26.4
Examples of together structures in the Small Cap Value fund strategy. The abbreviations for the first parameter are as follows: ST refers to the Science & Technology fund, SCV refers to the Small Cap Value fund, and NAM refers to the New American Fund. The prefix $n$ma refers to the n-day moving average ratio. If there is no prefix, then the daily return time series is being referenced. The second parameter is the number of days ago and the third parameter is the bin number.

What these results suggest is that the together structure strategy has been successful in uncovering significant regularities in these three T. Rowe Price funds. Results qualitatively similar to these have been found in over twenty mutual fund families (data not shown).

Since the together structure database for each of the three mutual funds contains hundreds of together structures, we cannot print the entire trading strategy here.[2] A few together structures from the Small Cap Value fund strategy are shown in Figure 26.4. Fortunately, we can arrive at a good understanding of each trading strategy by studying a generalization of each strategy that captures its most important qualitative components. These generalizations, which were created by hand by the author after examining the strategies, are shown in Figures 26.5–7.

There are several qualitative conclusions that can be drawn from these stylized together structures. First, the moving average ratios prior to the current day are unnecessary. Fewer than 1% of all together structures access these historical moving average ratios and they can be ablated without influencing the performance. In contrast, the daily return data of the last two days often appears in the together

---

2. The together structure databases, along with other relevant data, are available from the author.

```
If 20maST <= 0.9567124
ODayNAM=0.79389 + 0.423*1DayNAM - 0.243*20maST - 0.035 * 5maSCV +
0.047*50maSCV
If 20maST >= 0.9567124
ODayNAM = 0.8210 + 0.288*1DayNAM - 0.108*5maSCV
```

Figure 26.5
A generalization of the trading strategy for the New American fund. The prefix nDay refers to
the daily return of a fund n days ago. All other parameter values are as in Figure 26.4.

```
If 1DayST <= 1.006178
ODayST = 1.10004 - 0.07*2DayNAM + 0.78*5maNAM - 0.166*10maNAM -
0.004*20maNAM +   0.218*100maNAM + 0.026*1DayST -
0.004*2DayST + 0.023*20maST + 0.026*50maST - 0.026*100maSCV

If 1DayST > 1.006178
ODayST = 0.91793 + 0.002*2DayNAM + 0.026*5maNAM - 0.001*10maNAM -
0.002*20maNAM +   0.17*1DayST - 0.095*2DayST + 0.002*20maST +
0.0086*50maST - 0.023*100maSCV
```

Figure 26.6
A generalization of the trading strategy for the Science & Technology fund. Parameters are defined
as in Figure 26.5.

```
ODaySCV = 0.85195 + 0.029*2dayNAM + 0.12*1DayST
```

Figure 26.7
A generalization of the trading strategy for the Small Cap Value fund. Parameters are defined as
in Figure 26.5.

structures and is critical in achieving a high level of performance. Second, the
together structure system locates and exploits significant influences across time
series. For example, the Small Cap Value fund strategy depends primarily on time
series from the Science & Technology and the New American fund. The ability
of the together structure system to incorporate time series from multiple sources
is one of its strengths. Third, the moving average ratios play a significant role in
both the New American and Science & Technology trading strategies. Significant

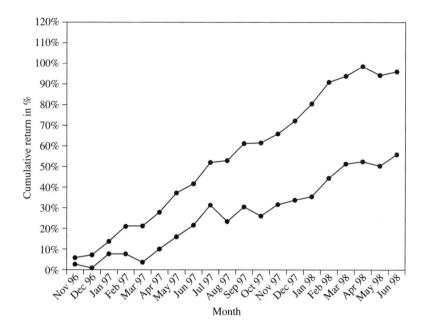

Figure 26.8
Real-time trading results. The upper line is the cumulative return of the together structure system and the lower line is the cumulative return of the S&P 500.

evidence is beginning to accumulate that moving averages can be used to create trading strategies that are economically significant (see, for example, Kuo (1998)).

Since November, 1996 we have been trading a version of this system in real time. For the first year trading took place in a set of managed accounts and in November, 1997 these accounts were rolled into a hedge fund. The compound return of the real-time trading is shown in Figure 26.8.

The monthly returns of the real-time trading are superior to the monthly returns of the S&P 500 ($p < 0.05$). There are several key differences between this real-time trading and the out-of-sample results. Most importantly, the together structure system has undergone some significant changes since it was first developed in 1996. For example, initially it stored the probability that a security's return would be in a certain bin, but, as described in this paper, it now stores the expected return of the security to be traded. Furthermore, the T. Rowe Price funds were only used during a short period. For most of the real-time trading other mutual fund families were traded. Also, because of human errors, the trading strategy was not always executed correctly. Finally, the real-time trading returns reflect a 1% management fee (charged on a monthly basis in increments of 1/12%) and a monthly 20% incentive fee.

26.5 Analysis

The results show that the together structure system has uncovered a trading system that outperforms buy and hold both in out-of-sample testing and in real-time trading. Whether mutual funds have simple regularities that are easy to locate or the together structure system is uncommonly good at finding regularities in the financial markets is difficult to determine. However, given that there is considerable evidence that simple regularities do not exist in individual stocks and that the mutual funds studied here are almost entirely invested in stocks, there is some reason to believe that the together structure system is primarily responsible for the trading performance. Nevertheless, this important question requires further study. Currently, our best hypothesis is that the together structures exploit over-reactions in stock prices of the sort described by de Bondt and Thaler (1985).

These results have straightforward implications for mutual fund investors. Such investors, which include over 30% of the adult population in the United States, should consider trading mutual funds instead of purchasing and holding them. Although there are practical limitations on this activity, such as prohibitions against excessive trading, mutual funds do exist that allow unlimited trading and exhibit significant regularities (results not shown).

Despite the positive results reported in this paper, there are at least two reasons why these findings should be treated with some caution. First, the stock market's annual return between the beginning of 1995 and the end of 1997 was approximately twice the mean annual return over the last one hundred years. This three-year period marked the first time in history that the Dow Jones Industrials gained over 20% three years running. Given that this period comprises the majority of both the out-of-sample data and the real-time trading period, there is a serious question about whether the returns achieved by the strategy will persist.

Second, the strategy is highly positively correlated with the S&P 500 index, but because the market has experienced no extended bear markets over the past decade, there is no data, either in the in-sample or out-of-sample set, which characterizes its performance in down markets. The possibility exists that while the strategy may outperform in bull markets it will significantly underperform in bear in markets and thus have a mean return that is statistically indistinguishable from buy and hold.

Both of these shortcomings are not unique to this strategy. Any US stock market strategy tested over the past decade falls prey to these two problems. Unfortunately, simply reaching back to stock data from earlier periods does not decisively solve the problem because market structure may have changed, so results that obtain in the 1970s may not obtain in the 1990s and vice versa. Hence, students of the stock market face a Catch-22 situation: Recent stock market performance may be overly bullish while previous data may be irrelevant.

The real-time trading strategy suffers from the additional problem of having to locate mutual fund families that permit very frequent trading. In the nearly two years that we have been trading this strategy in real-time, we have been asked to close our accounts multiple times due to excessive trading. Shifting capital from one fund family to another fund family reduces returns and requires the constant creation of new trading strategies.

In addition to important differences in mean returns between the buy and hold strategy and the together structure strategy, Table 5 also shows that there is a large difference in the skewness of the returns. The three mutual funds all have negative skewnesses while the trading strategy has a positive skewness. The Boos (1986) linear rank test for skewness shows that these differences are significant ($p < 0.01$). This result indicates that the trading strategy is reducing the probability of large negative returns or increasing the probability of large positive returns. This hypothesis is supported by Tables 26.7 and 26.8 which show the returns of the strategy on the five days when the blended portfolio has its worst return and the five days when the blended portfolio has its best return. On the five days when the blended portfolio has its worst return on the out-of-sample data, the together trading strategy outperforms the blended portfolio by over 0.4% per day.

We call the ability to eliminate negative skewness from a security "skew balancing." This truncation of the left side of the return distribution can also be achieved by put option strategies (Bookstaber and Clarke, 1987) but, unlike these methods, the together structure system (in this application at least) does not sacrifice return.

26.6 A Note on Out-of-Sample Results

This research, like much of the research in this area, depends critically on out-of-sample testing to validate results. This sort of testing is fraught with pitfalls, one of which is highlighted by the following thought experiment:

Professors Twiddledee and Twiddledum are in search of profitable trading strategies. Professor Twiddledee generates five trading strategies, tests them using his favorite

Table 26.7
Comparison of the average return of the three mutual funds with the return of the trading strategy on the five days of the three fund blend's worst performance in the out-of-sample period. Note that on two of these five days the trading strategy is out of the market and, on average, outperforms the average return of the three mutual funds by over 0.4% per day during these five days.

Date	Blend	Strategy
7/12/96	0.969874	0.951954
1/8/96	0.973056	0.982534
7/18/95	0.973922	0.956421
7/10/96	0.975007	1
3/27/97	0.976526	1

Table 26.8
Comparison of the average return of the three mutual funds with the return of the trading strategy on the five days of the three fund blend's best performance in the out-of-sample period. The strategy outperforms the average return of the three mutual funds by over 0.6% on these five days.

Date	Average	Strategy
4/20/94	1.020712	1
7/16/96	1.023294	1.034768
5/2/97	1.023719	1.03906
5/1/97	1.025213	1.039865
4/4/97	1.030904	1.038467
Average	1.024768	1.030432

technique,[3] and to his delight discovers a trading strategy that has above average risk-adjusted performance, thus providing evidence that the efficient market hypothesis (EMH) is false. Professor Twiddledum has a similar experience. He also generates five trading strategies, tests them using his favorite technique, and discovers a trading strategy that provides evidence that the EMH is incorrect. Professor Big observes the success of his colleagues and decides to pursue a similar line of thinking. Professor Big generates a total of ten trading strategies: the five that Professor Twiddledee produced plus the five that Professor Twiddledum produced. When he tests the significance of these ten trading strategies, he discovers that he cannot reject EMH.

In this story, Professor Twiddledee and Twiddledum were able to find better than average trading strategies because the number of trading strategies they tested was smaller than the number of trading strategies that Professor Big tested, and, hence, the threshold that the best of their trading strategies had to pass was lower than the threshold that Big's best strategy had to pass. The procedure that Twiddledee and

---

3. Critically, the statistical test does not matter. All that is required is that for a trading strategy to be considered better than average, its "goodness" must strictly increase as the number of trading strategies increases (the n in a parameterized statistical test). For example, a trading strategy that rejects EMH when $n = 1$ may not reject EMH when $n = 100$.

Twiddledum followed is qualitatively similar to the one that virtually every paper in this field (including this one) follows: When it comes time to test significance, only the trading strategies that the authors generated are considered. Instead, as this story shows, the total number of trading strategies should be considered. If Twiddledee and Twiddledum had considered the total number of trading strategies generated, then they, like Big, would have found that they could not reject EMH.

Because the number of total trading strategies that have been tested is orders and orders of magnitude greater than the number of trading strategies that any single research project considers, significance levels are over-estimated by very wide margins. This conclusion is qualitatively similar to one reached by Sullivan, Timmermann, and White (1998) for the specific case of calendar-based strategies.

To highlight the difficulty raised by the Twiddledee/Twiddledum thought experiment, we created a clairvoyant S&P 500 strategy which knows the price of the S&P 500 one hundred days in advance. If the price is higher than the current price, the strategy goes long; otherwise, it stays in a risk-free asset which produces no gain. Over the period from 1/1/90 to 12/31/98, this strategy does not have a risk-adjusted return that is sufficient to reject the efficient market hypothesis using the same t-test used previously when $n = 1,000,000,000$ (de la Maza, 1999). Since well over one billion strategies have been tested on the S&P 500 and this clairvoyant strategy is far superior to any strategy that has been published or is likely to be published, this suggests that there is no empirical test that can reject EMH.

26.7   Conclusions and Future Work

This work introduces mutual funds, which have been little studied in the academic literature, as a trading vehicle and shows how the together structure system, a type of machine learning algorithm, is able to extract statistically and economically significant regularities from mutual fund time series. On out-of-sample data the trading strategy has a higher daily return ($p < 0.05$) than any of the three mutual funds that it trades. These results are supported by twenty months of real-time trading which produced monthly returns that are superior to the returns of the S&P 500 cash index ($p < 0.05$). The significance of these results is questioned by the Twiddledee/Twiddledum thought experiment which suggests that virtually all empirical tests of trading strategies over-estimate significance levels, and by the clairvoyant strategy experiment which suggests that there is no empirical test that can disprove EMH.

Obvious extensions to this work include applying the together structure system to other markets to see if improvements in returns can be obtained. In addition, we plan to further investigate whether the together structure system can skew balance other financial time series.

References

Atkeson, C. "Memory-based approaches to approximating continuous functions," Proceedings of the Workshop on Nonlinear Modeling and Forecasting, 1990.

Bookstaber, R. and Clarke, R. (1987). "Options can alter portfolio returns," Journal of Portfolio Management, Spring, pp. 63-70.

Boos, D. D. (1986) "Comparing k populations with linear rank statistics." Journal of the American Statistical Association, 81, pp. 1018-1025.

Brock, W., Lakonishok, J. and LeBaron, B. (1992) "Simple technical trading rules and the stochastic properties of stock returns," Journal of Finance, 47, pp. 1731-64.

de la Maza, M. (unpublished) "The Twiddledee/Twiddledum thought experiment: Why no empirical test can disprove EMH."

de Bondt, W. and Thaler, R. "Does the stock market overreact?" Journal of Finance, July 1985, pp. 793-808.

Goetzmann, W. and Peles, N. (1997) "Cognitive dissonance and mutual fund investors," The Journal of Financial Research, 20, 1, pp. 145-58.

Kuo, G. (1998) "Some exact results for moving-average trading rules with applications to UK indices" in Advanced Trading Rules (eds E. Acar and S. Satchell) Oxford, England, Butterworth-Heinemann, pp. 81-102.

Lebaron, B. (1998) "Technical trading rules and regime shifts in foreign exchange" in Advanced Trading Rules (eds E. Acar and S. Satchell) Oxford, England, Butterworth-Heinemann, pp. 1-40.

Rahman, S., Fabozzi, F. and Lee, C-F. (1991) "Errors-in-variables, functional form, and mutual fund returns," Quarterly Review of Economics and Business, 31, 4, pp. 24-35.

Rahman, S. and Lee, C-F. (1991) "New evidence on timing and security selection skill of mutual fund managers," Journal of Portfolio Management, Winter, pp. 80-91.

Rumelhart, D. and McClelland, J (eds) (1986) Parallel Distributed Processing: Explorations in the Microstructure of Cognition (Volumes 1 and 2), Cambridge, MA, MIT Press.

Sullivan, R., Timmermann, A., and White, H. (1998) "Dangers of data-driven inference: The case of calendar effects in stock returns," Discussion paper 98-16, University of California, San Diego.

Winston, P. (1992). Artificial Intelligence (3rd edition). Reading, MA, Addison-Wesley Publishing Company.

27 Minimizing Downside Risk via Stochastic Dynamic Programming

John Moody and Matthew Saffell

We propose to train trading systems by minimizing measures of downside risk via stochastic dynamic programming. In [Moody and Wu 1997], we presented empirical results in controlled experiments that demonstrated the advantages of stochastic dynamic programming relative to supervised learning. Here we demonstrate the feasibility of using a stochastic dynamic programming algorithm, Recurrent Reinforcement Learning (RRL) [Moody et al 1998], to train trading systems by maximizing performance functions that incorporate downside risk. These include the Downside Deviation ratio, a downside performance function based on the Downside Deviation. The Downside Deviation (closely related to the Lower Partial Moment) can be easily used to model a variety of investing behaviors from risk-avoiding to risk-seeking, by adjusting the desirability of positive or negative skewness in the returns distribution. We discuss some of the advantages of using downside risk measures for optimizing trading systems, and show that optimizing downside risk measures fits naturally into our previously proposed recurrent stochastic dynamic programming framework. We present experimental results demonstrating the successful use of downside risk measures on artificially created data sets. We also present results for a high-frequency British Pound foreign exchange trading system that achieves a 15% unleveraged annualized return over a 6 month time period while being required to trade through the bid/ask spread.

27.1 Introduction: Stochastic Dynamic Programming for Trading

The investor's or trader's ultimate goal is to optimize some relevant measure of trading system performance such as profit, economic utility or risk-adjusted return. In this paper, we propose to use stochastic dynamic programming to directly optimize trading system performance functions that incorporate downside risk measures. Downside risk measures are interesting because they apparently model actual investor attitudes about risk more accurately than traditional symmetric risk measures such as variance [Markowitz 1959, Bawa 1975, Fishburn 1977, Nawrocki 1991, Nawrocki 1992, Sortino and van der Meer 1991, Sortino and Forsey 1996, White 1996]. For example, few investors will be heard complaining on the days when their trades post large gains, ie. large upside "risk" as measured by a symmetric risk measure such as variance. In [Moody and Wu 1997, Moody et al 1998], we demonstrate the use of symmetric risk measures in optimizing trading systems. In other recent independent work, [Kang et al 1997] demonstrate the use of the Sharpe ratio for optimizing an asset allocation system, and [Timmermann and Pesaran 1995] use wealth and the Sharpe ratio as a selection criteria for selecting between trading systems. [White 1996] has also done simulations that optimize various risk-adjusted performance measures including downside measures.

Trading system profits depend upon sequences of interdependent decisions, and are thus path-dependent. Optimal trading decisions when the effects of transactions costs, market impact and taxes are included require knowledge of the current system state, typically requiring some type of recurrent learning algorithm. [Bengio 1997] globally optimizes a system containing forecasting and trading modules using back-propagation through time. In [Moody et al 1998], we demonstrate that stochastic dynamic programming based on real-time recurrent learning provides a more elegant and effective means for training trading systems when state-dependent transaction costs are included, than do more standard supervised approaches. [Satchell and Timmermann 1995] provide a theorem that there is not necessarily any monotonic relationship between the size of mean-square forecast error and the probability of correctly forecasting the sign of a variable.

27.2 Trading Systems and Financial Performance Functions

27.2.1 The Structure of Trading Systems

We consider performance functions for systems that trade a single [1] security with price series z_t. The trader is assumed to take only long, neutral or short positions $F_t \in \{-1, 0, 1\}$ of constant magnitude. The constant magnitude assumption can be easily relaxed to enable better risk control. The position F_t is established or maintained at the end of each time interval t, and is re-assessed at the end of period $t + 1$. A trade is thus possible at the end of each time period, although nonzero trading costs will discourage excessive trading. A trading system return R_t is realized at the end of the time interval $(t - 1, t]$ and includes the profit or loss resulting from the position F_{t-1} held during that interval and any transaction cost incurred at time t due to a difference in the positions F_{t-1} and F_t.

In order to properly incorporate the effects of transactions costs, market impact and taxes in a trader's decision making, the trader must have internal state information and must therefore be recurrent. An example of a single asset trading system that takes into account transactions costs and market impact has following decision function: $F_t = F(\theta_t; F_{t-1}, I_t)$ with $I_t = \{z_t, z_{t-1}, z_{t-2}, \ldots; y_t, y_{t-1}, y_{t-2}, \ldots\}$ where θ_t denotes the (learned) system parameters at time t and I_t denotes the information set at time t, which includes present and past values of the price series z_t and an arbitrary number of other external variables denoted y_t.

---

1. See [Moody et al 1998] for a detailed discussion of multiple asset portfolios.

27.2.2 Profit and Wealth for Traders

Trading systems can be optimized by maximizing performance functions $U()$ such as profit, wealth, utility functions of wealth or performance ratios like the Sharpe ratio. The simplest and most natural performance function for a risk-insensitive trader is profit. We consider two cases: additive and multiplicative profits. The transactions cost rate is denoted δ.

Additive profits are appropriate to consider if each trade is for a fixed number of shares or contracts of security z_t. This is often the case, for example, when trading small futures accounts or when trading standard US\$ FX contracts in dollar-denominated foreign currencies. With the definitions $r_t = z_t - z_{t-1}$ and $r_t^f = z_t^f - z_{t-1}^f$ for the price returns of a risky (traded) asset and a risk-free asset (like T-Bills) respectively, the additive profit accumulated over T time periods with trading position size $\mu > 0$ is then defined as:

$$P_T = \sum_{t=1}^{T} R_t = \mu \sum_{t=1}^{T} \left\{ r_t^f + F_{t-1}(r_t - r_t^f) - \delta|F_t - F_{t-1}| \right\} \tag{27.1}$$

with $P_0 = 0$ and typically $F_T = F_0 = 0$. Equation (27.1) holds for continuous quantities also. The wealth is defined as $W_T = W_0 + P_T$.

Multiplicative profits are appropriate when a fixed fraction of accumulated wealth $\nu > 0$ is invested in each long or short trade. Here, $r_t = (z_t/z_{t-1} - 1)$ and $r_t^f = (z_t^f/z_{t-1}^f - 1)$. If no short sales are allowed and the leverage factor is set fixed at $\nu = 1$, the wealth at time T is:

$$W_T = W_0 \prod_{t=1}^{T} \{1 + R_t\} \tag{27.2}$$

$$= W_0 \prod_{t=1}^{T} \left\{ 1 + (1 - F_{t-1})r_t^f + F_{t-1}r_t \right\} \{1 - \delta|F_t - F_{t-1}|\}. \tag{27.3}$$

27.2.3 The Sharpe Ratio

For many investors, a more useful measure of trading success must take into account the risk of the trading strategy. The Sharpe ratio is a measure of risk-adjusted return [Sharpe 1966] that is often used to measure trading performance. Denoting as before the trading system returns for period t (including transactions costs) as R_t, the Sharpe ratio is defined to be

$$S_T = \frac{\text{Average}(R_t)}{\text{Standard Deviation}(R_t)} \tag{27.4}$$

where the average and standard deviation are estimated over returns for periods $t = \{1, \ldots, T\}$.

27.3   Downside Performance Functions

27.3.1   The Downside Deviation and the Downside Deviation Ratio

Symmetric measures of risk such as variance are more and more being viewed as inadequate measures due to the asymmetric attitude of most investors to price changes. Few investors consider large positive returns to be "risky", though both large positive as well as negative returns are penalized using a measure of risk such as the variance. To a large number of investors, the term "risk" refers to returns in a portfolio that decrease its profitability. [Markowitz 1959] proposed the semi-variance as a means for dealing with these downside returns. A similar risk measure that is designed to penalize such events is the Downside Deviation (DD), or the Second Lower Partial Moment (SLPM) [Nawrocki 1991, Nawrocki 1992, Sortino and van der Meer 1991, Sortino and Forsey 1996, White 1996]. The Downside Deviation is defined to be the square root of the average of the square of the negative returns:

$$DD_T = \left(\frac{1}{T} \sum_{t=1}^{T} \min\{R_t, 0\}^2 \right)^{\frac{1}{2}} . \tag{27.5}$$

Using the Downside Deviation as a measure of risk, we can now define a utility function similar to the Sharpe ratio, which we will call the *Downside Deviation ratio* (DDR):

$$DDR_T = \frac{\text{Average}(R_t)}{DD_T} \tag{27.6}$$

The Downside Deviation ratio rewards the presence of large average positive returns and penalizes risky returns, where "risky" now refers to downside returns.

In order to facilitate the use of our stochastic dynamic programming algorithm (Section 27.4), we need to compute the influence of the return at time t on the DDR. In a similar manner to the development of the differential Sharpe ratio in [Moody et al 1998], we define exponential moving averages of returns and of the squared Downside Deviation:

$$\begin{align}
A_t &= A_{t-1} + \eta(R_t - A_{t-1}) \tag{27.7} \\
DD_t^2 &= DD_{t-1}^2 + \eta(\min\{R_t, 0\}^2 - DD_{t-1}^2) ,
\end{align}$$

and define the Downside Deviation Ratio in terms of these moving averages. Then we define our performance function to be the first order term in the expansion in η of the DDR:

$$\mathrm{DDR}_t \approx \mathrm{DDR}_{t-1} + \eta \frac{d\mathrm{DDR}_t}{d\eta}\Big|_{\eta=0} + O(\eta^2) . \tag{27.8}$$

We refer to the first order term, $d\mathrm{DDR}_t/d\eta$, as the differential Downside Deviation ratio, and it has the form

$$
\begin{aligned}
D_t \equiv \frac{d\mathrm{DDR}_t}{d\eta} \quad &= \quad \frac{R_t - \frac{1}{2}A_{t-1}}{\mathrm{DD}_{t-1}} \qquad\qquad , R_t > 0 \\[2mm]
&= \quad \frac{\mathrm{DD}_{t-1}^2 \cdot (R_t - \frac{1}{2}A_{t-1}) - \frac{1}{2}A_{t-1}R_t^2}{\mathrm{DD}_{t-1}^3} \quad , R_t \leq 0 .
\end{aligned} \tag{27.9}
$$

From Equation 27.9 it is obvious that when $R_t > 0$, the utility increases as R_t increases, with no penalty for large returns such as exists when using variance as the risk measure.

27.3.2   The n–degree Downside Deviation

The analysis in the previous section can be extended in a straightforward manner to the more general n–degree Downside Deviation

$$\mathrm{DD}(n)_T = \left(\frac{1}{T} \sum_{t=1}^{T} \max\{h - R_t, 0\}^n \right)^{\frac{1}{n}} , \tag{27.10}$$

where h is a target return, and the maximum of the negative of the returns is used to ensure that DD is positive for all values of n. Previously, we set h equal to 0, though in general it will be set to some desired average return, which if not met will impact the investor negatively. Allowing the exponent n of the utility function to vary allows a wide range of investing behaviors to be modelled. That is, as n increases, investors become increasingly risk-avoiding. When $n < 1$ investors become risk seeking, ie. all other things being equal, they will prefer a negatively skewed distribution to a positively skewed distribution. It has also been shown that stochastic dominance, which does not make any distributional assumptions and assumes a very general set of utility functions, is equivalent to all degrees of the n–degree DD [Bawa 1975, Fishburn 1977].

Previous researchers have examined the use of the Downside Deviation in the construction of efficient frontier portfolios [Bawa and Lindenberg 1977, Harlow 1991, Nawrocki 1991, Sortino and van der Meer 1991, Nawrocki 1992]. In general they find that when using real market data, portfolios based on downside risk measures dominate portfolios based on symmetric risk measures. Empirical evidence also suggests that being more risk-averse, ie. $n > 2$, yields larger improvements in performance, and that the optimal degree of risk-aversion depends on the holding length of the portfolio [Nawrocki 1990]. Nawrocki also cites a study of [Laughhunn et al 1980] which finds that only 9% of a sample of corporate managers have utility functions in the general area of $n = 2$. This highlights the need for a general utility function that can model a wide range of investor preferences.

27.4   Stochastic Dynamic Programming for Trading Systems

The goal in using stochastic dynamic programming to adjust the parameters of a system is to maximize the expected payoff or reward that is generated due to the actions of the system. This is accomplished through trial and error exploration of the environment. The system receives a reinforcement signal from its environment (a *reward*) that provides information on whether its actions are good or bad. The stochastic dynamic programming algorithm we briefly summarize here is our previously proposed Recurrent Reinforcement Learning (RRL) algorithm [Moody et al 1998] based on real-time recurrent learning[Williams and Zipser 1989]. The performance functions that we consider are functions of profit or wealth $U(W_T)$ after a sequence of T time steps, or more generally of the whole time sequence of trades $U(W_1, W_2, \ldots, W_T)$ as is the case for a path-dependent performance function like the Downside Deviation ratio. In either case, the performance function at time T can be expressed as a function of the sequence of trading returns $U(R_1, R_2, \ldots, R_T)$. We denote this by U_T in the rest of this section.

27.4.1   Maximizing Immediate Utility

Given a trading system model $F_t(\theta)$, the goal is to adjust the parameters θ in order to maximize U_T. This maximization for a complete sequence of T trades can be done off-line using dynamic programming or batch versions of recurrent reinforcement learning algorithms. Here we do the optimization on-line using the RRL [Moody et al 1998] algorithm. This reinforcement learning algorithm is based on stochastic gradient ascent. The gradient of U_T with respect to the parameters θ of the system after a sequence of T trades is

$$\frac{dU_T(\theta)}{d\theta} = \sum_{t=1}^{T} \frac{dU_T}{dR_t} \left\{ \frac{dR_t}{dF_t} \frac{dF_t}{d\theta} + \frac{dR_t}{dF_{t-1}} \frac{dF_{t-1}}{d\theta} \right\} \quad . \tag{27.11}$$

The above expression as written with scalar F_i applies to the traders of a single risky asset, but can be trivially generalized to the vector case for portfolios.

The system can be optimized in batch mode by repeatedly computing the value of U_T on forward passes through the data and adjusting the trading system parameters by using gradient ascent (with learning rate ρ) $\Delta\theta = \rho dU_T(\theta)/d\theta$ or some other optimization method. A simple on-line stochastic optimization can be obtained by considering only the term in (27.11) that depends on the most recently realized return R_t during a forward pass through the data:

$$\frac{dU_t(\theta)}{d\theta} = \frac{dU_t}{dR_t}\left\{\frac{dR_t}{dF_t}\frac{dF_t}{d\theta} + \frac{dR_t}{dF_{t-1}}\frac{dF_{t-1}}{d\theta}\right\} \ . \tag{27.12}$$

The parameters are then updated on-line using $\Delta\theta_t = \rho dU_t(\theta_t)/d\theta_t$. Such an algorithm performs a stochastic optimization (since the system parameters θ_t are varied *during* each forward pass through the training data), and is an example of *immediate reward* reinforcement learning. The RRL algorithm is described in [Moody et al 1998] along with extensive simulation results.

27.5   Experimental Simulations for Maximizing the Downside Deviation Ratio

27.5.1   Artificial Price Series with Skewed Returns

We generate price series as random walks with autoregressive trend processes with *skewed* returns distributions. The two parameter model for an individual asset is thus:

$$\begin{aligned}
p(t) &= p(t-1) + \beta(t-1) + k\,\epsilon(t) \\
\beta(t) &= \alpha\,\beta(t-1) + \nu(t) \ ,
\end{aligned} \tag{27.13}$$

where α and k are constants, and $\epsilon(t)$ and $\nu(t)$ are iid random deviates drawn from a demeaned gamma distribution with shape parameter 5. We define the artificial price series as

$$z(t) = \exp\left(\frac{p(t)}{R}\right) \tag{27.14}$$

where R is a scale defined as the range of $p(t)$: $\max(p(t)) - \min(p(t))$ over a simulation with 10,000 samples. Figure 27.1 shows an example of an artificially created time series, and a histogram of the returns distribution that generated it.

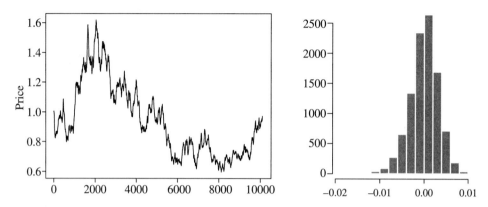

Figure 27.1
An example of the type of artificial price series used in the experiments here and the negatively skewed returns distribution that generated it. The returns are generated from a gamma distribution with shape parameter 5. The means of the distributions are removed, and here the sign of the distribution is adjusted to produce a negatively skewed distribution.

27.5.2 Long/Neutral/Short Trading System

In this section we compare trading systems that can take long, neutral and short positions in a single asset. The dataset used consists of 10 different realizations of artificially created data described in Section 27.5.1. One trading system is trained to maximize the Downside Deviation ratio, "DDR", and the other is trained to maximize the Sharpe ratio, "SR". The left panel in Figure 27.2 shows boxplots of the Sharpe ratio for 100 trading systems trained from random initial weight configurations. The right panel shows the summary results when measuring the Downside Deviation ratio. The plots show that the trading systems are successful in maximizing the performance ratios they were trained to maximize.

A very interesting property of the systems here that were trained to maximize the Downside Deviation ratio is that the maximum drawdowns incurred by these traders are consistently less than the drawdowns incurred by the Sharpe ratio traders. Figure 27.3 shows a comparison of drawdowns between the "DDR" and "SR" trading systems. The plot on the left compares the histograms of maximum drawdowns for each trading system. The figure shows that the worst drawdowns in the histogram for the "DDR" trading system are truncated at approximately half the magnitude as that of the "SR" trading system. The plots on the right show an excerpt of the behavior of the two systems on a sample test period. The top panel shows the underwater curves for the trading systems. An underwater

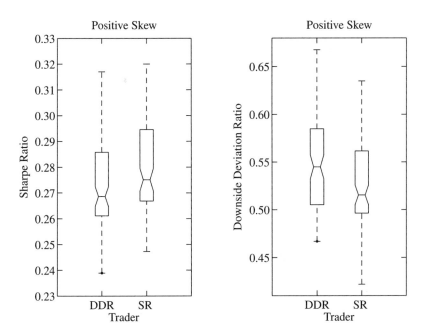

Figure 27.2
Boxplots of performance results on the artificial data series for ensembles of 100 trading systems. The set of systems labeled "DDR" were trained to maximize the Downside Deviation ratio, and the set labeled "SR" were trained to maximize the Sharpe ratio. The left panel shows summary statistics of the final Sharpe ratios and the right panel shows the summary statistics of final Downside Deviation ratios calculated for each of the 100 trials. The notches shown on the boxplots are robust confidence intervals on the medians of the distributions. The plots show that the systems trained to maximize a certain performance function do, on average, significantly outperform (according to their performance measure) trading systems trained to maximize other performance functions. The 100 trials were composed of trading system trained from 10 different random initializations for each of 10 different artificially generated price series.

curve shows the magnitude of the drawdowns, and is equal to 0 when the system is "above water", ie. when a new equity peak is achieved. The difference in behavior during drawdowns can be clearly seen here as the "DDR" trader maintains a neutral position during the worst of the "SR" trader's drawdowns. The lower panel shows a moving average calculation of the Downside and Standard Deviations calculated from the equity curves in the top panel. These are the risk penalty terms in the DDR and SR performance functions respectively. Of particular interest is the time period between 100 and 150, where even though the "SR" trading system is recovering from a severe drawdown, the penalty term (the Standard Deviation) is increasing.

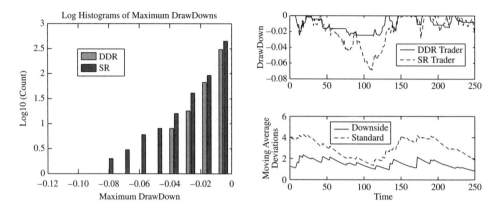

Figure 27.3
The figure on the left compares the histograms of maximum drawdown incurred by the "DDR"
and "SR" trading systems. The magnitudes of the worst drawdowns for the "DDR" system are
only half the size of those for the "SR" trading system. The figures on the right show a closeup
of the behavior of the two trading systems. The top panel shows the underwater curves for the
systems. Note that the "DDR" system avoids the large drawdowns incurred by the "SR" system.
The bottom panel shows a moving average calculation of the Downside Deviation and the Standard
Deviation. Note that the Standard Deviation, used as a penalty term in the Sharpe ratio, increases
even though the "SR" system is recovering from a severe drawdown. On the other hand, the
Downside Deviation only increases as the drawdown for the "DDR" system worsens.

Examination of the Downside Deviation shows an increase in penalty only when
the drawdown becomes worse.

27.5.3   US Dollar/British Pound Foreign Exchange Trading System

A long/short trading system is trained on half-hourly British Pound foreign exchange data[2]. The dataset used here consists of the first 8 months of quotes from
the 24 hour, 5-days a week foreign exchange market during 1996. Both bid and ask
prices are in the dataset, and the trading system is required to incur the transaction
costs of trading through the bid/ask prices. The trader is trained via the Recurrent
Reinforcement Learning (RRL) algorithm to maximize the differential Downside
Deviation ratio.

The top panel in Figure 27.4 shows the US Dollar/British Pound price series for
the 8 month period. The trading system is initially trained on the first 2000 data
points, and then produces trading signals for the next 2 week period (480 data
points). The training window is then shifted forward to include the just tested on

---

2. The foreign exchange data is part of the Olsen & Associates HFDF96 dataset.

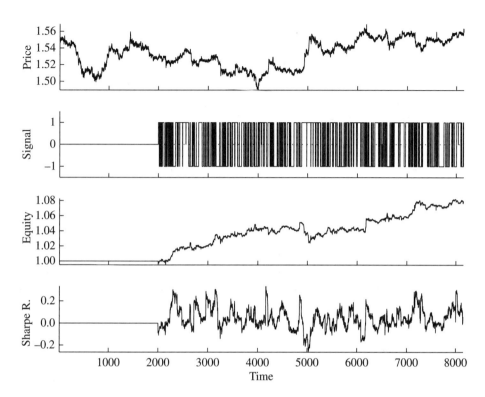

Figure 27.4
Short/long trading system of the US Dollar/British Pound that uses the bid/ask spread as transaction costs. The data consists of half-hourly quotes. The time period shown is the first 8 months of 1996. The first 2000 data points are used for training and validation.

data, is retrained and its trading signals recorded for the next 2 week out-of-sample time period. This process for generating out-of-sample trading signals continues for the rest of the data set.

The second panel in Figure 27.4 shows the out-of-sample trading signal produced by the trading system, and the third panel displays the equity curve achieved by the trader. The bottom panel shows a moving average calculation of the Sharpe ratio over the trading period with a time constant of 0.01. The trading system achieves an annualized 15% return (unleveraged) with an annualized Sharpe ratio of 2.3 over the approximately 6 month long test period. On average the system makes a trade once every 5 hours.

27.6   Conclusions

In this paper, we have demonstrated the feasibility of training trading systems via stochastic dynamic programming to maximize financial performance functions based on downside risk measures.

We have previously shown with extensive simulation results [Moody et al 1998] that trading systems trained via stochastic dynamic programming can significantly outperform systems trained using supervised methods for traders of both single securities and portfolios. Here we show that the stochastic dynamic programming algorithm can in principle accommodate the optimization of a wide range of investor utilities. In particular, we have demonstrated the use of downside risk measures such as the Downside Deviation ratio for a given level of risk aversion.

The empirical results presented include controlled experiments using artificial data with skewed returns distributions as well as a successful British Pound foreign exchange trading system. We find that the systems are able to discover successful trading strategies, and that their learned behaviors exhibit interesting risk-avoiding characteristics.

Acknowledgments

We gratefully acknowledge support for this work from Nonlinear Prediction Systems and from DARPA under contract DAAH01-96-C-R026 and AASERT grant DAAH04-95-1-0485.

References

Bawa, V. S. 1975. Optimal rules for ordering uncertain prospects. *Journal of Financial Economics*, 2:95–121.

Bawa, V. S. and E. B. Lindenberg. 1977. Capital market equilibrium in a mean-lower partial moment framework. *Journal of Financial Economics*, 4:189–200.

Bengio, Y. 1997. Training a neural network with a financial criterion rather than a prediction criterion. In Weigend, A., Y. Abu-Mostafa, and A. N. Refenes, editors, *Decision Technology for Financial Engineering*, London. World Scientific.

Fishburn, P. C. 1977. Mean-risk analysis with risk associated with below-target returns. *The American Economic Review*, 67(2):116–126.

Harlow, W. V. 1991. Asset allocation in a downside-risk framework. *Financial Analysts Journal*, pages 28–40.

Kang, J., M. Choey, and A. Weigend. 1997. Nonlinear trading models and asset allocation based on Sharpe ratio. In Weigend, A., Y. Abu-Mostafa, and A. N. Refenes, editors, *Decision Technology for Financial Engineering*, London. World Scientific.

Laughhunn, D. J., J. W. Payne, and R. Crum. 1980. Managerial risk preferences for below-target returns. *Management Science*, pages 1238–1249.

Markowitz, H. 1959. *Portfolio Selection: Efficient Diversification of Investments*. New York: Wiley.

Moody, J. and L. Wu. 1997. Optimization of trading systems and portfolios. In Weigend, A. S., Y. Abu-Mostafa, and A. N. Refenes, editors, *Neural Networks in the Capital Markets*, London. World Scientific.

Moody, J., L. Wu, Y. Liao, and M. Saffell. 1998. Performance functions and reinforcement learning for trading systems and portfolios. *Journal of Forecasting*, 17. To appear.

Nawrocki, D. 1990. Tailoring asset allocation to the individual investor. *International Review of Economics and Business*, pages 977–990.

Nawrocki, D. 1991. Optimal algorithms and lower partial moment: Ex post results. *Applied Economics*, 23:465–470.

Nawrocki, D. 1992. The characteristics of portfolios selected by n-degree lower partial moment. *International Review of Financial Analysis*, 1:195–209.

Satchell, S. and A. Timmermann. 1995. An assessment of the economic value of non-linear foreign exchange rate forecasts. *Journal of Forecasting*, 14:477–497.

Sharpe, W. F. 1966. Mutual fund performance. *Journal of Business*, pages 119–138.

Sortino, F. and H. Forsey. 1996. On the use and misuse of downside risk. *The Journal of Portfolio Management*, 22:35–42.

Sortino, F. and R. van der Meer. 1991. Downside risk – capturing what's at stake in investment situations. *The Journal of Portfolio Management*, 17:27–31.

Timmermann, A. and H. Pesaran. 1995. Predictability of stock returns: Robustness and economic significance. *Journal of Finance*, 50:1201–1228.

White, H. 1996. Personal communication. Unpublished.

Williams, R. J. and D. Zipser. 1989. A learning algorithm for continually running fully recurrent neural networks. *Neural Computation*, 1:270–280.

28 An Optimal Binary Predictor for an Investor in a Futures Market

Dirk W. Rudolph

This paper develops the economic loss function for a risk neutral investor in a futures market and his corresponding expected loss minimizing predictor which is based on his economic loss function. Unlike the quadratic statistical loss function, this economic loss function directly follows from his arbitrage rule and depends on the sign of the prediction error. The expected loss minimizing prediction rule based on the economic loss function is shown to be a binary predictor, i.e. the predictor forecasts the sign of the futures price change. Two such predictors are developed here. One is specified for very general distributional assumptions, and the second, which is termed here Truncated-Regression-Weighted-Discriminant-Analysis (TWDA), is developed for the specific assumption of truncated multivariate normality of price changes and informative signals. The TWDA predictor appears to be especially suitable for nonlinear time series with correlation structures of price changes and informative signals that differ in declining and rising markets. In using the TWDA predictor, the estimation and evaluation stages of developing price prediction models become consistent.

28.1 Introduction

The idea behind studies on the informational efficiency of futures markets is the search for a prediction model which yields average profits that are above the market return if the model is combined with the appropriate arbitrage rule. In searching for such a model, the econometric technique to be used plays a decisive role. Numerous methods have been applied in efficient market tests. Taylor (1986), Baillie (1989), and Mills (1993) surveyed the econometric methods used for such tests. Most of these methods either disregard loss considerations (maximum likelihood techniques) or minimize expected losses that arise from a statistical quadratic loss function (least-squares (LS) methods). However, the quadratic loss function that plays such a prominent role in econometrics is not derived from the arbitrage rule of an investor and, therefore, does not adequately represent the economic losses he incurs from prediction errors. As Varian (1974), Zellner (1986), Blattberg and George (1992), and Christofferson and Diebold (1997) have shown, optimal estimators and predictors for a non-quadratic loss function differ from LS techniques. Built on that insight, prediction techniques like the ones developed by Kandel and Stambaugh (1996) and Choey and Weigend (1997) are now emerging, which pay attention to the fact that the investor's economic calculus must already be taken into consideration at the stage when the prediction model is estimated and not just at the evaluation stage. To make further progress in this direction, the present paper presents two results. Firstly, the economic loss function approach, which goes back to Savage

(1954), Theil (1961) and Theil (1964) will be extended to model the economic calculus of an investor in a futures market. Secondly, based on this economic loss function an econometric prediction method, called Truncated-Regression-Weighted-Discriminant-Analysis (TWDA), will be developed which minimizes the expected losses an investor in a futures market has to incur from his price prediction errors.

The paper is organized as follows: In section 2 the economic loss function of an investor in a futures market is derived from his arbitrage rule. Then section 3 presents a binary predictor that minimizes the investor's expected economic losses. The predictor is based on the assumption that futures price changes and informative signals may be generated by two different types of market regimes, i.e. market data may come from nonlinear time series. Section 4 examines the specific case where price changes and informative signals follow two truncated multivariate normal probability distributions that may differ with respect to their mean vectors and covariance matrices in rising and declining markets. All estimators necessary for implementing TWDA are presented. TWDA combines the quadratic discriminant function and two truncated Tobit regression functions. In section 5, TWDA's potential gain in predictability is examined by means of an artificially constructed numerical example. The paper closes with a summary.

28.2   The Economic Loss Function for an Investor in a Futures Market

Econometric methods which are based on the quadratic loss function are—by design—inappropriate for solving the investor's price prediction problem. The quadratic loss function weights negative and positive prediction errors of equal absolute size equally, i.e., it is independent of the sign of the error. Thereby it disregards the most important type of variation of the variable to be predicted, namely its change of sign. The problem surfaces most clearly at the evaluation stage, when prediction errors are evaluated using the mean squared error loss criterion which disregards sign errors. Savage (1954, p. 163) defined the loss function as the difference between the consequences arising from a perfect foresight decision setting and a decision setting where the decision maker does not know the true state of the world and makes for a given but unknown state of the world some decision which is typically suboptimal. This loss function approach can be applied to derive the economic loss function of an investor from his arbitrage rule. Under perfect foresight, the investor knows the actual forthcoming futures price at the time when he buys or sells futures contracts. The perfect foresight profit function for the investor will be denoted by $\Pi(P_{t+1}, P_{t+1})$. The economic consequences for the investor, when he does not know the actual forthcoming futures price but has to base his arbitrage decision, i.e. his excess demand for futures contracts, on his point prediction $\mathcal{P}_t^{t+1}$ of tomorrow's futures price, will be denoted by by $\Pi(P_{t+1}, \mathcal{P}_t^{t+1})$. In this case the actual forthcoming futures price P_{t+1} and the predicted price $\mathcal{P}_t^{t+1}$ might differ. The economic loss function for the investor thus becomes:

$$L(P_{t+1}, \mathcal{P}_t^{t+1}) = \Pi(P_{t+1}, P_{t+1}) - \Pi(P_{t+1}, \mathcal{P}_t^{t+1}). \tag{28.1}$$

To make the arbitrage activity of the investor explicit a particularly simple trading rule will be assumed, which will be called the arbitrage rule. The investor is assumed to invest a constant fraction m of his wealth W, with $0 < m \leq 1$, in a short or long futures market position. If his prediction $\mathcal{P}_t^{t+1}$ of tomorrow's futures price exceeds today's price his excess demand for futures contracts h_t will be positive, et vice versa. His excess demand for futures contracts h_t, i.e. his trading rule, is defined to be the following function:

$$h_t \equiv \{\, mW/P_t \quad \text{if } \mathcal{P}_t^{t+1} \geq P_t - mW/P_t \quad \text{if } \mathcal{P}_t^{t+1} < P_t \,. \tag{28.2}$$

This trading rule will be called the arbitrage rule. Assuming away transaction costs such as brokerage fees and using the definition of the sign function:

$$\text{sign } (P_{t+1} - P_t) \equiv \{\, 1 \quad \text{if } P_{t+1} - P_t \geq 0 - 1 \quad \text{if } P_{t+1} - P_t < 0\,, \tag{28.3}$$

allows the derivation of the economic loss function for an investor from his profit functions for perfect foresight profits:

$$\Pi(P_{t+1}, P_{t+1}) = (P_{t+1} - P_1)(mW/P_t)[\text{sign}(P_{t+1} - P_t)], \tag{28.4}$$

and for realized profits:

$$\Pi(P_{t+1}, \mathcal{P}_t^{t+1}) = (P_{t+1} - P_t)(mW/P_t)[\text{sign } (\mathcal{P}_t^{t+1} - P_t)]. \tag{28.5}$$

Substituting eqs. (4) and (5) into eq. (1) yields the investor's economic loss function:

$$L(P_{t+1}, \mathcal{P}_t^{t+1}) = [(P_{t+1} - P_t)(mW/P_t)][\text{sign } (P_{t+1} - P_t) - \text{sign } (\mathcal{P}_t^{t+1} - P_t)]. \tag{28.6}$$

It holds that $L(P_{t+1}, \mathcal{P}_t^{t+1}) \geq 0$. Clearly, the economic loss function of an investor depends on the sign of the prediction error. In minimizing his losses he has to choose $\mathcal{P}_t^{t+1}$ in the second term in squared brackets so as to make it equal to zero. In other words, he needs to predict the sign of the futures market price change rather than its level. The investor's economic loss function does not eliminate the sign of the prediction error, as the quadratic loss function does, but instead takes a sign prediction error into account.

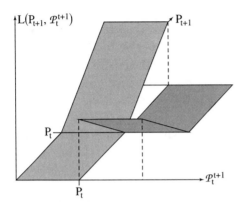

Figure 28.1

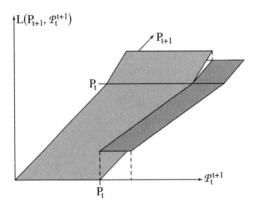

Figure 28.2

Figures 28.1 and 28.2 show economic loss functions for low and high current futures prices, respectively. The slope of the surface depends on $2(mW/P_t)$, is equal for both segments of the surface and is steeper for a smaller current futures price. Correctly predicting the sign of the price change results in zero losses. Falsely predicting the sign of a price change vis-à-vis today's futures price results in "double losses", so to speak, if measured against perfect foresight profits.

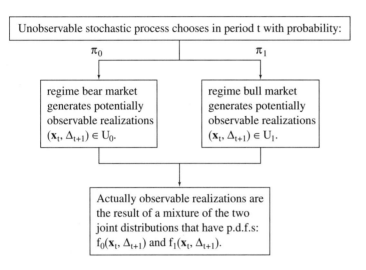

Figure 28.3

28.3   An Optimal Binary Predictor for an Investor when the Distributions Are Known

This section presents an expected loss minimizing predictor for a risk-neutral investor who knows the true joint distribution of futures price changes and informative signals, which have some value for predicting the forthcoming futures price change. An optimal binary predictor is a statistical decision function that specifies for a given vector of informative signals and price changes that sign prediction of tomorrow's futures price change which is optimal with respect to the investor's economic loss function, his predictive distribution of price changes and informative signals, and his decision criterion. Thus the problem of determining an optimal predictor for the investor has three elements. The economic loss function of the investor is stated in eq. (6). In assumption 2 it will be supposed that the predictive multivariate distribution of price changes and informative signals is known. And throughout the present paper it will be assumed that the investor minimizes the expected losses he has to incur from prediction errors, i.e. he applies Bayes' decision criterion as his decision criterion. Consequently, the predictors presented here are only optimal with respect to Bayes rule. For other decision criteria, like Roy's (1952) safety first principle or Telser's (1955) safety rule, other predictors than the ones presented here will be optimal.

28.3.1 Assumption 1

By assumption, the futures market may be in either one of two regimes. A bear market $(j = 0)$ and a bull market $(j = 1)$ is dominated by pessimistic and optimistic investors, respectively. The data generating mechanism switches stochastically between these two regimes. Each of these regimes generates realizations of price changes and informative signals. However, the true regime is unobservable. The actually observable realizations are a mixture of the two multivariate distributions that represent the probabilistic laws of the two regimes. The multivariate probability density functions (p.d.f.s) $f_0(\mathbf{x}_t, \Delta_{t+1})$ and $f_1(\mathbf{x}_t, \Delta_{t+1})$ characterize the probabilistic laws of the unobservable vectors of informative signals and price changes that rule in the bear market and bull market, respectively. Without specifying the functional type of these p.d.f.s it is only assumed that they do exist. The vector of informative signals will be denoted by $\mathbf{x_t}$ and may include variables that are lagged one or more periods, and all values of that vector are assumed to be known in period t. The size of the futures price change from t to $t+1$ is defined to be:

$$\Delta_{t+1} \equiv P_{t+1} - P_t. \tag{28.7}$$

If the stochastic process generates a vector of potentially observable realizations $\mathbf{z}'_t = (\mathbf{x}'_t, \Delta_{t+1})$, which comes from the regime bear market, i.e. $\Delta_{t+1} < 0$, then $\mathbf{z}_t \in U_0$, where U_0 denotes the sample space of that regime. Else the vector of potentially observable realizations $\mathbf{z}_t$ comes from the sample space U_1 of the bull market, i.e. $\Delta_{t+1} \geq 0$. Figure 28.3 shows the stochastic process diagrammatically which generates the observations $(\mathbf{x}'_t, \Delta_{t+1})$.

28.3.2 Assumption 2

The investor is assumed to know the joint probability densities of the two different regimes $f_0(\mathbf{x}_t, \Delta_{t+1})$ and $f_1(\mathbf{x}_t, \Delta_{t+1})$ and to know π_0 and π_1, the true probabilities of the market to be in regime bear market and bull market, respectively. The conditional expected values of the forthcoming futures price change when the market is bearish or bullish are denoted by $E_0[\Delta_{t+1}|\mathbf{x}_t]$ and $E_1[\Delta_{t+1}|\mathbf{x}_t]$, respectively, and the marginal densities $f_0(\mathbf{x}_t)$ and $f_1(\mathbf{x}_t)$ exist and can be readily computed from the multivariate densities. The investor is risk neutral and therefore uses Bayes' rule as his decision criterion.

28.3.3 Proposition 1

Provided assumptions 1 and 2 hold, then the expected loss minimizing predictor of an investor, who uses the arbitrage rule in eq. (2) is given by:

$$\hat{y}_{t+1}(\mathbf{x}_t) = \begin{cases} 1 & \text{if } \frac{f_1(\mathbf{x}_t)\pi_1}{f_0(\mathbf{x}_t)\pi_0} \geq \frac{-E_0[\Delta_{t+1}|\mathbf{x}_t]}{E_1[\Delta_{t+1}|\mathbf{x}_t]} \\ 0 & \text{if } \frac{f_1(\mathbf{x}_t)\pi_1}{f_0(\mathbf{x}_t)\pi_0} < \frac{-E_0[\Delta_{t+1}|\mathbf{x}_t]}{E_1[\Delta_{t+1}|\mathbf{x}_t]} \end{cases}. \tag{28.8}$$

Now, what is the interpretation of this optimal binary predictor? The investor must reach a decision, which is either to predict a price increase or a price decrease. His decision space $\mathcal{D}$ contains only the two elements 1 and 0, i.e. to predict a bull or a bear market, respectively. The optimal binary predictor is then a decision rule $\hat{y}_{t+1}(\mathbf{x}_t)$, which maps optimally the sample space X of informative signals into the decision space $\mathcal{D}$. Or, put differently, the investor seeks a predictor that specifies for a particular observation of $\mathcal{J}$ informative signals $(x_{1,t,...,},x_{\mathcal{J},t})$, that market regime to which the current observation $\mathbf{x}_t$ must belong. This predictor discriminates between a bull and a bear market by making use of the observation $\mathbf{x}_t$. In other words, the optimal binary predictor specifies for any vector of informative signals $\mathbf{x}_t$ whether the current trading day belongs to the regime bear market or bull market.

The left-hand side of the inequality in eq. (8) is the odds-ratio, the right-hand side gives the ratio of stakes. For example, suppose the odds that the current trading period is followed by a price increase are 2:1. And suppose further that the conditional expected value of a price decrease for the observed vector of informative signals is equal to -2, i.e. $E_0[\Delta_{t+1}|\mathbf{x}_t] = -2$, whereas $E_1[\Delta_{t+1}|\mathbf{x}_t] = 3$. Then the ratio of stakes is $2/3$, which is smaller than the odds ratio. Consequently, the optimal binary predictor predicts a price increase. Note that the optimal binary predictor of an investor in a futures market is independent of his wealth and the fraction of wealth he is willing to invest in futures contracts.

28.4 An Optimal Binary Predictor for an Investor for Estimated Multivariate Normal Probability Distributions with Unequal Covariance Matrices

In this section it will no longer be assumed that the probability distributions were known as in the previous section. Instead it will be assumed that the probability distributions which generate the observations $\mathbf{z}'_t$ are not known but have to be estimated from observed data.

28.4.1   Assumption 3

The investor is risk neutral and uses Bayes' rule as his decision criterion. In period t he has observed $T + 1$ vectors of past realizations of informative signals $\mathbf{x}'_{t-s} = (x_{1,t-s}, x_{2,t-s}, \ldots, x_{J,t-s})$, and futures prices P_{t-s} with $s = 0, 1, 2, \ldots, T-1, T$, where T is fixed and t is the index for the present time period. Past price changes of the futures contract will be denoted by:

$$\Delta_{t-s+1} \equiv P_{t-s+1} - P_{t-s}. \tag{28.9}$$

His objective is to predict the price change for $s = 0$, i.e. Δ_{t+1}.

A key practical step of estimating the parameters of the optimal binary predictor is the partitioning of the data set Ω_t into two subsets that correspond to the two observable regimes. One subset contains only those observations $\mathbf{z}_t$ that occurred on trading days that were followed by a price increase, the other subset includes observations $\mathbf{z}_t$ only that occurred on trading days which were followed by a price decrease. The criterion to partition the observations is the sign of the observed realized price change. To partition the data set means to form two subsets $\mathcal{Z}^+$ and $\mathcal{Z}^-$ which contain all observations that occurred in periods followed by a price increase and a price decrease, respectively. Out of the T trading days for which observations $\mathbf{z}_t$ are available for estimation, T_1 of these trading days were followed by a price increase and T_0 were followed by a price decrease. These two subsets and the information set of the investor will be defined as follows:

$$\Omega_t \equiv \{(\Delta_{t+1-s}, x'_{t-s}) : s = 1, 2, \ldots, T\}, \tag{28.10}$$

$$\mathcal{Z}^+ \equiv \{z'_{t-s} : z'_{t-s} \in \Omega_t, z'_{t-s}e \geq 0, s = 1, 2, \ldots, T\}, \text{ and} \tag{28.11}$$

$$\mathcal{Z}^- \equiv \{z'_{t-s} : z'_{t-s} \in \Omega_t, z'_{t-s}e < 0, s = 1, 2, \ldots, T\}, \tag{28.12}$$

where $\mathbf{e}$ is a vector of dimension $J + 1$ with $\mathbf{e}' = (1, 0, \ldots, 0)$. It holds that: $\mathcal{Z}^+ \cap \mathcal{Z}^- = \phi$ and $\mathcal{Z}^+ \cup \mathcal{Z}^- = \Omega_t$. Partitioning the data set has to be done prior to estimation. It is the investor's economic calculus which determines the criterion that is to be used in splitting up the data set. Consequently, the investor's loss considerations already affect the prediction process at the estimation stage and not just at the evaluation stage.

28.4.2   Assumption 4

The stochastic process that gives rise to the observations $\mathbf{z}_t$ can be characterized as follows. An unobservable stochastic process chooses with probability π_0 and π_1 either one of two regimes, bear or bull market, respectively. Once the process switches to bear market a potentially observable realization $\mathbf{z}_t$ of the original population of the bear market is drawn from the following multivariate normal distribution:

$$
\begin{pmatrix} \Delta \\ \mathbf{x} \end{pmatrix} \sim N_{\mathcal{J}+1}^{(0)} \left(\begin{pmatrix} \mu_\Delta^{(0)} \\ \mu_\mathbf{x}^{(0)} \end{pmatrix}, \begin{pmatrix} (\sigma_\Delta^{(0)})^2 & \sigma_{\Delta\mathbf{x}}^{(0)} \\ \sigma_{\mathbf{x}\Delta}^{(0)} & \Sigma_{\mathbf{x}\mathbf{x}}^{(0)} \end{pmatrix} \right) \tag{28.13}
$$

Similarly, a potentially observable realization $\mathbf{z}_t$ of the original population of the bull market is drawn from the multivariate normal distribution:

$$
\begin{pmatrix} \Delta \\ \mathbf{x} \end{pmatrix} \sim N_{\mathcal{J}+1}^{(1)} \left(\begin{pmatrix} \mu_\Delta^{(1)} \\ \mu_\mathbf{x}^{(1)} \end{pmatrix}, \begin{pmatrix} (\sigma_\Delta^{(1)})^2 & \sigma_{\Delta\mathbf{x}}^{(1)} \\ \sigma_{\mathbf{x}\Delta}^{(1)} & \Sigma_{\mathbf{x}\mathbf{x}}^{(1)} \end{pmatrix} \right) \tag{28.14}
$$

If $\Delta < 0$ ($\Delta \leq 0$), then the potentially observable realization $(\mathbf{x}, \Delta)$ of the original population of the bear (bull) market becomes an actually observed realization in period $t + 1$. Else the potentially observable realization is discarded and a new one is drawn from the original population of the bear market (bull market). This stochastic process continues up until a new actually observable realization is included in the selected population of the bear market (bull market). As a result of this process, the actually observable realizations $\mathbf{z}_\mathbf{t}$ contained in the two partitioned data sets $\mathcal{Z}^+$ and $\mathcal{Z}^-$ come from the selected populations of the bear and bull market, respectively. They are distributed according to two multivariate normal distributions which are truncated with respect to Δ_{t+1} from above and below at zero, respectively. These distributions may have different mean vectors and unequal covariance matrices for $j = 0, 1$. Figure 28.4 shows this data generating process diagrammatically. Consequently, $\hat{f}_0^*(\mathbf{x_t}, \Delta_{t+1}|\mathcal{Z}^-)$ and $\hat{f}_1^*(\mathbf{x_t}, \Delta_{t+1}|\mathcal{Z}^+)$ can be estimated by the truncated multivariate normal model. An asterisk (*) denotes truncation of a distribution or a density or operations on a truncated distribution. Formally,

$$
\text{if} \begin{cases} \begin{pmatrix} \Delta_{t+1} \\ \mathbf{x}_t \end{pmatrix} \in \mathcal{Z}^- & \text{then } \begin{pmatrix} \Delta_{t+1} \\ \mathbf{x}_t \end{pmatrix} \sim \mathbf{N}_{\mathcal{J}+1}^{*(0)} \left(\begin{pmatrix} \mu_\Delta^{*(0)} \\ \mu_\mathbf{x}^{*(0)} \end{pmatrix}, \begin{pmatrix} (\sigma_\Delta^{*(0)})^2 & \sigma_{\Delta\mathbf{x}}^{*(0)} \\ \sigma_{\mathbf{x}\Delta}^{*(0)} & \Sigma_{\mathbf{x}\mathbf{x}}^{*(0)} \end{pmatrix} \right) \\[2em] \begin{pmatrix} \Delta_{t+1} \\ \mathbf{x}_t \end{pmatrix} \in \mathcal{Z}^+ & \text{then } \begin{pmatrix} \Delta_{t+1} \\ \mathbf{x}_t \end{pmatrix} \sim \mathbf{N}_{\mathcal{J}+1}^{*(1)} \left(\begin{pmatrix} \mu_\Delta^{*(1)} \\ \mu_\mathbf{x}^{*(1)} \end{pmatrix}, \begin{pmatrix} (\sigma_\Delta^{*(1)})^2 & \sigma_{\Delta\mathbf{x}}^{*(1)} \\ \sigma_{\mathbf{x}\Delta}^{*(1)} & \Sigma_{\mathbf{x}\mathbf{x}}^{*(1)} \end{pmatrix} \right) \end{cases}, \tag{28.15}
$$

$$
\mu_\mathbf{x}'^{*(j)} = \left(\mu_{x_1}^{*(j)}, \dots, \mu_{x\mathcal{J}}^{*(j)} \right), \tag{28.16}
$$

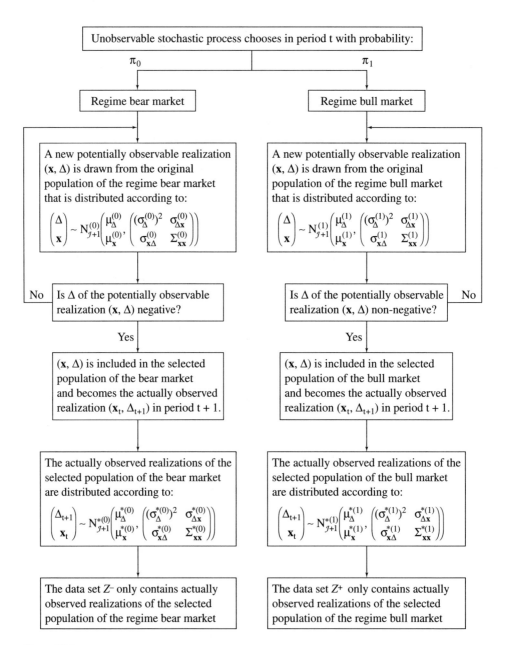

Figure 28.4

$$\sum{}_{\mathbf{zz}}^{*(j)} = \begin{pmatrix} \left(\sigma_{\Delta}^{*(j)}\right)^2 & \sigma_{\Delta,x_1}^{*(j)} & \cdots & \sigma_{\Delta,x_{\mathcal{J}}}^{*(j)} \\ \sigma_{x_1\Delta}^{*(j)} & \left(\sigma_{x_1}^{*(j)}\right)^2 & \cdots & \sigma_{x_1 x_{\mathcal{J}}}^{*(j)} \\ \vdots & \vdots & \ddots & \\ \sigma_{x_{\mathcal{J}},\Delta}^{*(j)} & \sigma_{x_{\mathcal{J}}x_1}^{*(j)} & \cdots & \left(\sigma_{x_{\mathcal{J}}}^{*(j)}\right)^2 \end{pmatrix} = \begin{pmatrix} \sigma_{\Delta\Delta}^{*(j)} & \sigma_{\Delta,x}^{*(j)} \\ \sigma_{\mathbf{x},\Delta}^{*(j)} & \sum_{\mathbf{xx}}^{*(j)} \end{pmatrix}$$

with $j = 0, 1$. $\qquad$ (28.17)

28.4.3 Proposition 2

Assumptions 3 and 4 hold. The expected loss minimizing predictor for an investor, who invests in a particular futures contract and uses the arbitrage rule stated in eq. (2), to predict price changes which are generated by a process as characterized in figure 28.4 is given by:

$$\hat{y}_{t+1}(\mathbf{x}_t) = \begin{cases} 1 & \text{if } R \geq \ln\left\{\frac{K_- \hat{\pi}_0}{K_+ \hat{\pi}_1}\right\} \\ 0 & \text{if } R < \ln\left\{\frac{K_- \hat{\pi}_0}{K_+ \hat{\pi}_1}\right\} \end{cases}, \quad \text{with} \qquad (28.18)$$

$$\begin{aligned} R = & \frac{1}{2}\ln\frac{\left|\hat{\sum}_{\mathbf{xx}}^{*(0)}\right|}{\left|\hat{\sum}_{\mathbf{xx}}^{*(1)}\right|} - \frac{1}{2}\left\{\mathbf{x}_t'\left[\left(\hat{\sum}_{\mathbf{xx}}^{*(1)}\right)^{-1} - \left(\hat{\sum}_{\mathbf{xx}}^{*(0)}\right)^{-1}\right]\mathbf{x}_t \right. \\ & \left. - 2\mathbf{x}_t'\left[\left(\hat{\sum}_{\mathbf{xx}}^{*(1)}\right)^{-1}\hat{\mu}_x^{*(1)} - \left(\hat{\sum}_{\mathbf{xx}}^{*(0)}\right)^{-1}\hat{\mu}_x^{*(0)}\right]\right\} \end{aligned} \qquad (28.19)$$

and where the weights K_- and K_+ are given in eqs. (20) and (21), respectively,

$$K_- = -\hat{E}_0^*[\Delta_{t+1}|\mathbf{x}_t; \mathcal{Z}^-] = -\hat{\mathbf{b}}_{0,\text{cols}}^{(0)} - \mathbf{x}_t'\hat{\mathbf{b}}_{\text{cols}}^{(0)} + \hat{\sigma}_{\Delta}^{(0)}\frac{Z\left(\frac{\hat{\mu}_{\Delta}^{(0)}}{\hat{\sigma}_{\Delta}^{(0)}}\right)}{1 - \phi\left(\frac{\hat{\mu}_{\Delta}^{(0)}}{\hat{\sigma}_{\Delta}^{(0)}}\right)} \quad \text{and} \qquad (28.20)$$

$$K_+ = \hat{E}_1^*[\Delta_{t+1}|\mathbf{x}_t; \mathcal{Z}^+] = \hat{\mathbf{b}}_{0,\text{cols}}^{(0)} + \mathbf{x}_t'\hat{\mathbf{b}}_{\text{cols}}^{(1)} + \hat{\sigma}_{\Delta}^{(1)}\frac{Z\left(\frac{\hat{\mu}_{\Delta}^{(1)}}{\hat{\sigma}_{\Delta}^{(1)}}\right)}{\phi\left(\frac{\hat{\mu}_{\Delta}^{(1)}}{\hat{\sigma}_{\Delta}^{(1)}}\right)}, \qquad (28.21)$$

and where the required parameter estimators are given in table 28.1.

Table 28.1

Parameter:	Regime bear market	Regime bull market
vector of sample means of informative signals in the selected population	$\hat{\mu}_{\mathbf{x}}^{*(0)} = \dfrac{\sum_{z-} \mathbf{x}_t}{T_0}$	$\hat{\mu}_{\mathbf{x}}^{*(1)} = \dfrac{\sum_{z+} \mathbf{x}_t}{T_1}$
sample mean of price changes in the selected population	$\hat{\mu}_{\Delta}^{*(0)} = \dfrac{\sum_{z-} \Delta_{t+1}}{T_0}$	$\hat{\mu}_{\Delta}^{*(1)} = \dfrac{\sum_{z+} \Delta_{t+1}}{T_1}$
sample covariance matrix of informative signals in the selected population	$\hat{\Sigma}_{\mathbf{xx}}^{*(0)} = \dfrac{\sum_{z-} (\mathbf{x}_t - \hat{\mu}_{\mathbf{x}}^{*(0)})(\mathbf{x}_t - \hat{\mu}_{\mathbf{x}}^{*(0)})'}{T_0-1}$	$\hat{\Sigma}_{\mathbf{xx}}^{*(1)} = \dfrac{\sum_{z-} (\mathbf{x}_t - \hat{\mu}_{\mathbf{x}}^{*(1)})(\mathbf{x}_t - \hat{\mu}_{\mathbf{x}}^{*(1)})'}{T_0-1}$
vector of sample covariances between price changes and informative signals in the selected population	$\hat{\sigma}_{\mathbf{x}\Delta}^{*(0)} = \dfrac{\sum_{z-} (\mathbf{x}_t - \hat{\mu}_{\mathbf{x}}^{*(0)})(\Delta_t - \hat{\mu}_{\Delta}^{*(0)})}{T_0-1}$	$\hat{\sigma}_{\mathbf{x}\Delta}^{*(1)} = \dfrac{\sum_{z+} (\mathbf{x}_t - \hat{\mu}_{\mathbf{x}}^{*(1)})(\Delta_t - \hat{\mu}_{\Delta}^{*(1)})}{T_1-1}$
sample variance of price changes in the selected population	$(\hat{\sigma}_{\Delta}^{*(0)})^2 = \dfrac{\sum_{z-} (\Delta_t - \hat{\mu}_{\Delta}^{*(0)})^2}{T_0-1}$	$(\hat{\sigma}_{\Delta}^{*(1)})^2 = \dfrac{\sum_{z+} (\Delta_t - \hat{\mu}_{\Delta}^{*(1)})^2}{T_1-1}$
relative frequency of the market to be in the respective regime	$\hat{\pi} = T_0/T$	$\hat{\pi} = T_1/T$
sample parameter vector for the slope coefficients in the selected population	$\mathbf{b}^{*(0)} = \left(\hat{\Sigma}_{\mathbf{xx}}^{*(0)}\right)^{-1} \hat{\sigma}_{\mathbf{x}\Delta}^{*(0)}$	$\mathbf{b}^{*(1)} = \left(\hat{\Sigma}_{\mathbf{xx}}^{*(1)}\right)^{-1} \hat{\sigma}_{\mathbf{x}\Delta}^{*(1)}$
sample coefficient of determination between $\mathbf{x}$ and Δ in the selected population	$\left(\hat{\rho}^{*(0)}\right)^2$ $= \hat{\sigma}_{\mathbf{x}\Delta}^{*(0)} \left(\hat{\Sigma}_{\mathbf{xx}}^{*(0)}\right)^{-1} \hat{\sigma}_{\mathbf{x}\Delta}^{*(0)} / \left(\hat{\sigma}_{\Delta}^{*(0)}\right)^2$	$\left(\hat{\rho}^{*(1)}\right)^2$ $= \hat{\sigma}_{\mathbf{x}\Delta}^{*(1)} \left(\hat{\Sigma}_{\mathbf{xx}}^{*(1)}\right)^{-1} \hat{\sigma}_{\mathbf{x}\Delta}^{*(1)} / \left(\hat{\sigma}_{\Delta}^{*(1)}\right)^2$
$\hat{\mu}_{\Delta}^{(j)}/\hat{\sigma}_{\Delta}^{*(j)}$ can be inferred from using:	$\hat{\mu}_{\Delta}^{*(0)}/\hat{\sigma}_{\Delta}^{*(0)}$ and Pearson and Lee's table	$\hat{\mu}_{\Delta}^{*(1)}/\hat{\sigma}_{\Delta}^{*(1)}$ and Pearson and Lee's table.
sample estimate of the unobserved ratio of variances of price changes in the selected and original population	$\hat{\zeta}^{(0)} = 1 + \dfrac{\hat{\mu}_{\Delta}^{(0)}}{\hat{\sigma}_{\Delta}^{(0)}} Z\left(\dfrac{\hat{\mu}_{\Delta}^{(0)}}{\hat{\sigma}_{\Delta}^{(0)}}\right) / \left[1 - \Phi\left(\dfrac{\hat{\mu}_{\Delta}^{(0)}}{\hat{\sigma}_{\Delta}^{(0)}}\right)\right]$ $- \left(Z\left(\dfrac{\hat{\mu}_{\Delta}^{(0)}}{\hat{\sigma}_{\Delta}^{(0)}}\right) / \left[1 - \Phi\left(\dfrac{\hat{\mu}_{\Delta}^{(0)}}{\hat{\sigma}_{\Delta}^{(0)}}\right)\right]\right)^2$	$\hat{\zeta}^{(1)} = 1 - \dfrac{\hat{\mu}_{\Delta}^{(1)}}{\hat{\sigma}_{\Delta}^{(1)}} Z\left(\dfrac{\hat{\mu}_{\Delta}^{(1)}}{\hat{\sigma}_{\Delta}^{(1)}}\right) / \Phi\left(\dfrac{\hat{\mu}_{\Delta}^{(1)}}{\hat{\sigma}_{\Delta}^{(1)}}\right)$ $- \left[Z\left(\dfrac{\hat{\mu}_{\Delta}^{(1)}}{\hat{\sigma}_{\Delta}^{(1)}}\right) / \Phi\left(\dfrac{\hat{\mu}_{\Delta}^{(1)}}{\hat{\sigma}_{\Delta}^{(1)}}\right)\right]^2$
sample bias correction term	$\hat{\eta}^{(0)} \equiv \hat{\zeta}^{(0)} + \left(\hat{\rho}^{*(0)}\right)^2 \left(1 - \hat{\zeta}^{(0)}\right)$	$\hat{\eta}^{(1)} \equiv \hat{\zeta}^{(1)} + \left(\hat{\rho}^{*(1)}\right)^2 \left(1 - \hat{\zeta}^{(1)}\right)$
corrected sample coefficient of determination between $\mathbf{x}$ and Δ in the original population	$\left(\hat{\rho}^{(0)}\right)^2 = \dfrac{\left(\hat{\rho}^{*(0)}\right)^2}{\hat{\eta}^{(0)}}$	$\left(\hat{\rho}^{(1)}\right)^2 = \dfrac{\left(\hat{\rho}^{*(1)}\right)^2}{\hat{\eta}^{(1)}}$
sample estimate of the variance of price changes in the original population	$\left(\hat{\sigma}_{\Delta}^{(0)}\right)^2 = \dfrac{\left(\hat{\sigma}_{\Delta}^{*(0)}\right)^2}{\hat{\zeta}^{(0)}}$	$\left(\hat{\sigma}_{\Delta}^{(1)}\right)^2 = \dfrac{\left(\hat{\sigma}_{\Delta}^{*(1)}\right)^2}{\hat{\zeta}^{(1)}}$
sample estimate of the mean of price changes in the original population	$\hat{\mu}_{\Delta}^{(0)}$ $= \hat{\mu}_{\Delta}^{*(0)} + \hat{\sigma}_{\Delta}^{*(0)} Z\left(\dfrac{\hat{\mu}_{\Delta}^{(0)}}{\hat{\sigma}_{\Delta}^{(0)}}\right) / \left(1 - \Phi\left(\dfrac{\hat{\mu}_{\Delta}^{(0)}}{\hat{\sigma}_{\Delta}^{(0)}}\right)\right)$	$\hat{\mu}_{\Delta}^{(1)} = \hat{\mu}_{\Delta}^{*(1)} - \hat{\sigma}_{\Delta}^{*(1)} Z\left(\dfrac{\hat{\mu}_{\Delta}^{(1)}}{\hat{\sigma}_{\Delta}^{(1)}}\right) / \Phi\left(\dfrac{\hat{\mu}_{\Delta}^{(1)}}{\hat{\sigma}_{\Delta}^{(1)}}\right)$
sample parameter for the intercept	$\hat{b}_0^{*(0)} = \hat{\mu}_{\Delta}^{*(0)} - \mathbf{b}^{*(0)'}\hat{\mu}_{\mathbf{x}}^{*(0)}$	$\hat{b}_0^{*(1)} = \hat{\mu}_{\Delta}^{*(1)} - \mathbf{b}^{*(1)'}\hat{\mu}_{\mathbf{x}}^{*(1)}$
corrected sample parameter for the intercept	$\hat{b}_{0,\text{cols}}^{(0)} = [\hat{b}^{(0)} + \hat{\mu}_{\Delta}^{(0)}(\hat{\eta}^{(0)}(\hat{\rho}^{*(0)})^2)$ $- \hat{\mu}_{\Delta}^{*(0)}(1 - (\hat{\rho}^{*(0)})^2]/\hat{\eta}^{(0)}$	$\hat{b}_{0,\text{cols}}^{(1)} = [\hat{b}^{(1)} + \hat{\mu}_{\Delta}^{(1)}(\hat{\eta}^{(1)} - (\hat{\rho}^{*(1)})^2)$ $- \hat{\mu}_{\Delta}^{*(1)}(1 - (\hat{\rho}^{*(1)})^2)]/\hat{\eta}^{(1)}$
vector of sample means of informative signals in the original population	$\hat{\mu}_{\mathbf{x}}^{(0)} = \hat{\mu}_{\mathbf{x}}^{*(0)} + \dfrac{\hat{\Sigma}_{\mathbf{xx}}^{*(0)} \hat{b}_{0,\text{cols}}^{(0)} \left(\hat{\mu}_{\Delta}^{(0)} - \hat{\mu}_{\Delta}^{*(0)}\right)}{\left(\sigma_{\Delta}^{(0)}\right)^2}$	$\hat{\mu}_{\mathbf{x}}^{(1)} = \hat{\mu}_{\mathbf{x}}^{*(1)} + \dfrac{\hat{\Sigma}_{\mathbf{xx}}^{*(1)} \hat{b}_{0,\text{cols}}^{(1)} \left(\hat{\mu}_{\Delta}^{(1)} - \hat{\mu}_{\Delta}^{*(1)}\right)}{\left(\sigma_{\Delta}^{(1)}\right)^2}$
sample covariance matrix of informative signals in the original population	$\hat{\Sigma}_{\mathbf{xx}}^{(0)} = \hat{\Sigma}_{\mathbf{xx}}^{*(0)} + \dfrac{\left(1 - \hat{\zeta}^{(0)}\right)\hat{\sigma}_{\Delta}^{(0)}\hat{\sigma}_{\mathbf{x}\Delta}^{*(0)}}{\left(\hat{\zeta}^{(0)}\right)^2}$	$\hat{\Sigma}_{\mathbf{xx}}^{(1)} = \hat{\Sigma}_{\mathbf{xx}}^{*(1)} + \dfrac{\left(1 - \hat{\zeta}^{(1)}\right)\hat{\sigma}_{\Delta}^{(1)}\hat{\sigma}_{\mathbf{x}\Delta}^{*(1)}}{\left(\hat{\zeta}^{(1)}\right)^2}$

Pearson and Lee's table has been reproduced in Olson (1980, pp. 1102-1103, table I). In proving the optimality of the optimal binary predictor stated in eqs. (18), (19), and (20), results can be used, which have been obtained by Anderson (1984, section 6), who developed the quadratic discriminant function for the multivariate normal distribution, and results by Goldberger (1981), Greene (1981), Greene (1983), and Olson (1980), can be applied, who solved the regression problem for a truncated multivariate normal distribution. Therefore, the optimal binary predictor stated in proposition 2 will be termed Truncated-Regression-Weighted-Discriminant-Analysis (TWDA).

28.5   What Difference Will it Make in Using the TWDA Predictor?

Now, what difference will it make in using the TWDA predictor instead of prediction methods that are based on the quadratic loss function? There is a potential gain in predictability in using TWDA instead of LS techniques if futures market data are generated by two different types of data generating mechanisms in rising and declining markets. TWDA can detect asymmetries in the correlation structure of the time series of futures price changes that cannot be detected by LS techniques. If the correlation structure of the data generating process with respect to downturns and upturns is asymmetric, then the investor will be able to discriminate between a trading day that is followed by a price decrease and a trading day that is followed by a price increase due to the differences between the estimated covariance matrices and mean vectors of informative signals and price changes. Such nonlinearities can arise, for example, from interactions among informative signals, e.g. price-volume interactions, which influence the sign of the futures market price change, that must remain undetected by LS techniques. To illustrate this point, consider the following artificially constructed data structure depicted in figure 28.5, where the head of each arrow represents a particular observation. Though the mean vectors and variances of informative signals are equal in both regimes in this example, their covariance matrices differ because of the multiplicative interaction between the two explanatory variables $x_{1,t}$ and $x_{2,t}$. The TWDA predictor can detect such asymmetries of the correlation structure in bear and bull markets. Observers of commodity futures markets, like Powers (1993, pp. 148-149), have long detected interactions between open interest and the most recent futures price change, on which they based rules of thumb that they recommend for trading. If these interactions are really present in market data then an estimated prediction model based on the TWDA predictor will reveal such patterns.

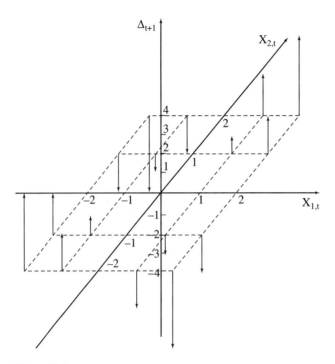

Figure 28.5

28.6 Summary

Econometric and statistical prediction methods which are based on the quadratic loss function are—by design—inappropriate for solving the investor's price prediction problem. As shown in this paper, the economic loss function for an investor in a futures market is not quadratic but depends on the sign of the prediction error. Unlike the quadratic loss function the economic loss function does not eliminate the most important type of variation of the variable to be predicted, namely its change of sign, but takes the dependence of economic losses on the sign of the prediction error into consideration.

In using Savage's (1954) loss function approach, the economic loss function of an investor in a futures market is derived in this paper from his arbitrage rule. To make the estimation and the evaluation of a prediction model consistent, the expected loss minimizing predictor to be used must be based on the economic loss function. Two such predictors are developed here. One is specified for very general distributional assumptions, and the second one, which is termed here Truncated-Regression-Weighted-Discriminant-Analysis (TWDA), is developed for the specific assumption of truncated multivariate normality of price changes and informative signals. TWDA appears to be especially suitable for nonlinear time series with correlation structures of price changes and informative signals that differ in declining and rising markets. The TWDA prediction method can exploit asymmetries of the correlation structures for predicting the sign of the forthcoming price change, whereas standard LS techniques must fail to reveal their influence. Another advantage of models using the TWDA method is the fact that their predictions directly address the investor's decision problem. They tell the investor whether to go short or long in the futures market and what are the stakes and the odds at risk of taking such a position. Furthermore, in using the economic loss function of an investor stated in eq. (6), the evaluation of an estimated prediction model can be conducted in money terms rather than in terms of the mean squared error criterion. In summarizing one may say that the economic loss function approach based on Savage's (1954) definition can be fruitfully used to develop novel prediction methods. For predictors like TWDA which are based on this approach, the criterion function that is optimized is the same function that will be used for evaluating prediction performance. Therefore, in using the economic loss function approach, estimation and evaluation become consistent.

Acknowledgments

Very helpful comments from Adusei Jumah, Thomas Kähler and Alexander Karmann are gratefully acknowledged. This article is an abbreviated version of a more elaborate paper with the same title, which can be obtained from the author upon request. In particular, the proofs of propositions 1 and 2 are contained in the appendices of the unabridged paper.

References

Anderson, T. W., 1984. *An introduction to multivariate statistical analysis*, 2nd ed., John Wiley & Sons, New York.

Baillie, R. T., 1989. Econometric Tests of Rationality and Market Efficiency, *Econometric Theory*, vol. 8, no. 2, pp. 151–186.

Blattberg, R. C. and E. I. George, 1992. Estimation Under Profit Driven Loss Functions, *Journal of Business & Economic Statistics*, Oct., vol. 10, no. 4, pp. 437–444.

Choey, M., and A. S. Weigend, 1997. Nonlinear Trading Models Through Sharpe Ratio Maximization, pp. 3-22, in: A. S. Weigend, Y. S. Abu-Mostafa, and A.-P. N. Refenes (eds.), *Technologies for financial engineering*, Proceedings of the Fourth International Conference on Neural Networks in the Capital Markets, NNCM-96, Singapore, World Scientific.

Christofferson, P. F., and F. X. Diebold, 1996. Further Results on Forecasting and Model Selection under Asymmetric Loss, *Journal of Applied Econometrics*, vol. 11, pp. 561–571.

Goldberger, A. S., 1981. Linear Regression after Selection, *Journal of Econometrics*, vol. 15, pp. 357–366.

Greene, W., 1981. On the Asymptotic Bias of the Ordinary Least Squares Estimator of the Tobit Model, *Econometrica*, vol. 49, pp. 505–513.

Greene, W., 1983. Estimation of Limited Dependent Variable Models by Ordinary Least Squares and the Method of Moments, *Journal of Econometrics*, vol. 21, pp. 195–212.

Kandel, S., and R. F. Stambaugh, 1996. On the Predictability of Stock Returns: An Asset-Allocation Perspective, *Journal of Finance*, vol. 51, no. 2, June, pp. 385–424.

Mills, T. C., 1993. *The econometric modelling of financial times series*, Cambridge University Press, Cambridge, United Kingdom.

Olson, R. J., 1980. Approximating a Truncated Normal Regression with the Method of Moments, *Econometrica*, vol. 48, pp. 1099–1105.

Powers, M. J., 1993. *Starting out in futures trading*, 5th ed., Probus Publishing Co., Chicago.

Roy, A. D., 1952. Safety First and the Holding of Assets, *Econometrica*, vol. 20, Jul., pp. 431–449.

Savage, L. J., 1954. *The foundations of statistics*, 2nd revised ed., 1972, first published 1954, Dover Publications, Inc., New York.

Taylor, S., 1986. *Modelling financial time series,* John Wiley & Sons, Chichester.

Telser, L. G., 1956. Safety First and Hedging, *Review of Economic Studies*, vol. 23, pp. 1–16.

Theil, H., 1961. *Economic forecasts and policy*, 2nd ed., North-Holland, Amsterdam.

Theil, H., 1964. *Optimal decision rules for government and industry*, North-Holland, Amsterdam.

Varian, H. R., 1974. A Bayesian Approach to Real Estate Assessment, pp. 195-208, in: S.E. Fienberg and Arnold Zellner, (eds.), *Studies in Bayesian econometrics and statistics*, North-Holland, Amsterdam.

Zellner, A., 1986. Biased Predictors, Rationality and the Evaluation of Economic Forecasts, *Economics Letters*, vol. 21, pp. 45–48.

29 An Introduction to Risk Neutral Forecasting

Spyros Skouras

Risk Neutral Forecasting refers to the use of forecasts that are optimal for a risk neutral investor. This class of forecasts is rather wide since it includes all forecasts which have the same sign as the conditional mean. We discuss the reasons for which a special estimator to be used for Risk Neutral Forecasting is required, provide such an estimator and derive some of its asymptotic properties. Finally, an algorithm that facilitates its computation is proposed. Direct applications include a formally justified method for estimating optimal investment rules such as 'technical trading' and 'market timing' rules.

29.1 The forecasting problem of a risk neutral investor

Consider a *risk neutral investor* forecasting uncertain returns r obtained from holding a single financial asset (or portfolio) for one period. Returns may be described as a random variable satisfying:

$$r = g(x) + u \tag{29.1}$$
$$E(u|x) = 0$$

where $x \in X \subseteq \mathrm{R}^K$ is a vector random variable containing the agent's available information, $g : X \to \mathrm{R}$ is a possibly nonlinear function, u is a disturbance term and $E(*|x)$ is the mathematical expectation conditional on x.

Suppose the risk neutral investor uses some forecast for returns to solve a standard *single period cash-asset allocation decision*:

$$\max_{\mu \in [-s, l]} E\{W'|x\} \tag{29.2}$$
$$s.t. \ W' = \mu W(1 + r) + (1 - \mu)W$$

where W' is next period's wealth, W is current wealth, μ determines the proportion of wealth invested in the asset and $\{s, l\}$ are scalars describing the agent's borrowing and short selling constraints.

When this agent's forecast for returns is θ and the actual realization is r, he incurs a pecuniary loss (in that his wealth is less than what it would have been had his forecast been correct) described by a *Loss Function* $L : \mathrm{R} \times \mathrm{R} \to \mathrm{R}_+$. This function has the form:

$$L(r, \theta) = W\left((l + s) \cdot \mathbf{1}\left[\mathbf{r} > \mathbf{0}\right] - \mathbf{s}\right)r - \tag{29.3}$$
$$W\left((l + s) \cdot \mathbf{1}\left[\theta > \mathbf{0}\right] - \mathbf{s}\right)r$$

The risk neutral investor's decision problem described in (29.2) can be recast as a prediction problem in which the objective is to find a mapping from each realization ξ of x to a prediction that minimizes expected loss conditional on this ξ. Such mappings $p : X \to \mathrm{R}$ are usually called *best predictors*[1]. It is easy to show that for the risk neutral investor's loss function, the best predictor is a mapping $p : X \to \mathrm{R}$ satisfying:

$$p(x) \in \arg \min_{\theta \in \mathrm{R}^1} - \int r \cdot \mathbf{1} \left[\theta > \mathbf{0} \right] \mathbf{dP} | \mathbf{x} \tag{29.4}$$

where $1 \left[E \right]$ is one if E is a true statement and zero otherwise, and $P|x$ denotes the c.d.f. of r conditional on x.

We will call any $p(x)$ satisfying (29.4) a *Risk Neutral Best Predictor*; *Risk Neutral Forecasting* refers to the associated use of Risk Neutral Best Predictors to forecast the value of an asset's return. To make Risk Neutral Forecasting feasible in practice, a technique for using data to estimate an unknown Risk Neutral Best Predictor is required. Such a technique could be used by a risk neutral investor to *learn* how to forecast optimally.

It is straightforward to show[2] that the conditional mean $g(x)$ is only one of the many mappings that are Risk Neutral Best Predictors (all mappings which have the same sign as $g(x)$ for all x are Risk Neutral Best Predictors). The objective of this paper is to propose statistical and computational techniques for estimating a Risk Neutral Best Predictor when we do not require that the Risk Neutral Best Predictor coincides with the conditional mean.

29.2   The importance of the risk neutral investor's forecasting problem

The risk neutral investor's decision problem has a natural dual interpretation as a problem of optimal *point* forecasting. By contrast, most risk averse agents solving standard investment problems cannot make optimal decisions based on point forecasts because their decisions require information about the conditional distribution of returns which cannot be captured by such a forecast. The risk neutral setting therefore provides a natural starting point for analyzing optimal forecasting problems in the context of financial decisions (as also been noted by [Granger and

---

1. Prediction under broad classes of loss functions has recently attracted renewed interest. See for example, [Christofferson and Diebold 1996] and [Weiss 1996] inter alia.

2. Proofs of all results mentioned can be found in a more complete version of this paper [Skouras 1998].

Pesaran 1996]) so as to see how optimal predictors in this setting will differ to the 'generic' predictors we are more familiar (such as predictors which minimize expected squared errors). Like many other instances in financial economics, this is a case in which risk neutrality serves as a convenient benchmark.

The development of estimation techniques for Risk Neutral Forecasting can also serve as a normative model of how a restricted class of agents *should* estimate forecasts for returns. Indeed, there is some evidence that certain institutional investors and some individuals who invest a very small proportion of their wealth behave in a fashion well approximated by risk neutrality (at least in making their decisions at the margin). Additionally, in the spirit of the learning literature, such models also have a dual interpretation as positive models of how agents *do* learn to forecast[3]. However, since funds invested according to an approximately risk neutral objective function constitute a fairly small proportion of total invested funds, a positive model of this form is probably of limited interest.

Risk Neutral Forecasting may also be of interest because Risk Neutral Best Predictors can be used to construct binary 'investment rules' (i.e. rules which restrict an investor's choice set (position size) to two positions - usually of opposite sign) which are optimal for a wide class of agents. Investment rules with this structure, including technical trading rules [Sullivan et al 1998] and market timing rules [Henriksson and Merton 1981] have received extensive attention in the literature, perhaps because they represent a boundedly rational mode of investment which not only results in a considerable simplification of investment decisions but is also *empirically observed*. These rules simplify decisions by allowing a broad class of agents to reduce their decision problem to a problem of Risk Neutral Forecasting. This occurs because of a remarkable property of binary investment rules which implies that the rule that maximizes expected profits also minimizes the variance of profits[Skouras 1997]. Hence, the same rule is optimal for all mean-variance agents and they will take positions identical to those of a risk neutral investor. That binary investment rules can provide useful information for risk averse agents is a robust fact that has been shown to hold in general settings [Merton 1981].

A number of economists have stressed the importance of evaluating the performance of econometric models according to metrics which capture their 'economic value'. Typically, the 'economic value' of a model is measured by using the forecasts it generates to measure its out of sample 'profitability'. Profitability of a model is typically measured by a procedure which is equivalent to measuring the average

---

3. See [Sargent 1993] for an excellent discussion of the role of learning models in Economics.

losses of an investor using this model's forecasts to solve (29.2) (see for example [Pesaran and Timmerman 1995], [Satchell and Timmerman 1995] and [Breen et al 1989]).

Finally, it has also been noted ([Granger 1993]) that, in general, estimating a model according to the metric by which it will be evaluated out of sample should improve its performance according to this metric. If this also applies to the performance metric derived from the risk neutral investor's loss function, it follows that econometric models should also be *estimated* to maximize their 'economic value'. The techniques developed here provide the requisite estimation methods.

29.3   Semiparametric estimation of Risk Neutral Best Predictors

The estimator we propose is based on the 'analogy principle'[4] and in particular the idea that there must be some general conditions under which, as the size of a sample increases, the model maximizing mean sample profits should also maximize expected profits in the population. The intuitiveness of this estimation procedure is probably responsible for its use in the estimation of a variety of investment rules (e.g. [Moody et al 1998], [LeBaron 1998], [Pictet et al 1992]) even before its statistical properties were formally studied by [Skouras 1998]. This section describes the estimator in detail, discusses some of its properties and proposes an algorithm for its computation.

29.3.1   Semiparametric estimation

Suppose the risk neutral investor's uncertainty about $g(x)$ can be summarized in a finite dimensional parameter c, i.e. he knows of a mapping $s : X \times B \to \mathrm{R}^1$ such that there exists an (unknown) parameter c' in the parameter space $B \subseteq \mathrm{R}^{K+1}$ for which $s(x, c') = g(x)$. Suppose also that the distribution of $u|x$ is completely unknown beyond the normalization $E(u|x) = 0$ (allowing for unknown and arbitrary heteroskedasticity). This structural model for $g(x)$ involves the unknown function $E(u|x)$ and the unknown finite dimensional parameter c; this makes the associated problem of estimating $g(x)$ *semiparametric*.

A population property of Risk Neutral Best Predictors and its sample analog   It can be shown [Skouras 1998] that if the mapping $s(x, c)$ is a Risk Neutral Best Predictor for some c' (a much weaker condition than the assumption

---

4. A lucid exposition of this principle is provided by [Manski 1988] and [Manski 1994].

that for some c', $s(x, c') = g(x)$), a necessary and sufficient condition for $s(*, b)$, $b \in B$ to be a Risk Neutral Best Predictor *almost everywhere* on X is:

$$b \in \arg\min_{c \in B} - \int r \cdot \mathbf{1}\left[\mathbf{s}(\mathbf{x}, \mathbf{c}) > \mathbf{0}\right] d\mathbf{P} \tag{29.5}$$

where P is the joint c.d.f. of (r, x). This condition says that the Risk Neutral Best Predictor must maximise expected profits unconditional on x; this follows from the application of the law of iterated expectations to the fact that (by definition) it maximises expected profits conditional on each x.

This population property of the parameter b is a moment extremum condition. Its *sample analog* is:

$$B^N \in \arg\min_{c \in B} - \int r \cdot \mathbf{1}\left[\mathbf{s}(\mathbf{x}, \mathbf{c}) > \mathbf{0}\right] d\mathbf{P^N} \tag{29.6}$$

where P^N is the empirical probability measure given by a sequence of observations $\{r_i, x_i\}_{i=1}^N$. The rest of this section discusses the properties of B^N as an estimator for b.

Asymptotic consistency: analytic results   Under assumptions discussed elsewhere [Skouras 1998] requiring that the strong law of large numbers holds for (r, x), B is compact as well as regularity conditions that guarantee identification of b and continuity of $\int r \cdot \mathbf{1}\left[\mathbf{s}(\mathbf{x}, \mathbf{c}) > \mathbf{0}\right] d\mathbf{P}$, it can be shown - based on results in [Manski 1988] - that $B^N \longrightarrow b$ almost surely.

The regularity conditions are *un*necessary for this result to go through when B is a set with finite cardinality as in studies such as [Skouras 1997] which optimize technical trading rules according to a metric equivalent to (29.5). However, if $s(x, c)$ is a highly nonlinear function (as it has been in studies mentioned in the introduction to this section) and B is a continuous parameter set, the requirements on P for the derived estimators to be consistent may be unrealistic. It is therefore not necessarily a good idea to postulate a very general model for $p(x)$ and maximize its profitability because the derived estimators may be *inconsistent*[5].

Asymptotic distribution: simulation evidence   The estimator defined in (29.6) is the minimum of a discontinuous function of c. Unfortunately, there exists no general theory describing the properties of estimators of this type. The few estimators with this structure that have been analyzed have been studied on a

---

5. This may be either due to identification problems or because $\int r \cdot \mathbf{1}(\mathbf{s}(\mathbf{x}, \mathbf{c}) > \mathbf{0}) d\mathbf{P}$ is discontinuous in a way that prohibits $\int r \cdot \mathbf{1}(\mathbf{s}(\mathbf{x}, \mathbf{c}) > \mathbf{0}) d\mathbf{P^N}$ from converging uniformly in x.

case-by-case basis. Structurally, the closest estimator to the one herein proposed is the maximum score estimator of [Manski 1975]. [Kim and Pollard 1990] show that the asymptotic distribution of this estimator is given by the maximum of a Gaussian process to which it converges at a cube-root rate. Based on the loose similarity of the maximum score estimator to the one presented here, it seems reasonable to conjecture that our estimator might behave in a similar way; we check this using a simple simulation.

Consider the following DGP:

$$r_{t+1} = 0.00015 + 0.0330 \cdot r_t + u$$
$$u \sim N(0, 0.0108) \text{ iid}$$

where the parameters of this DGP were determined using OLS to estimate an AR(1) model on a series drawn from the empirical distribution of 2049 observations on IBM daily closing prices[6] from 1st January 1990 through to 6th November 1997.

Suppose the parametric model to be estimated is $s(x, c) = c_0 + c_1 x$. Our estimator can only identify the parameters of this model to scale. We therefore use the model:

$$s(x, c) = c + x$$

which leads to an estimator:

$$B^N \in \min_c - \int r_{t+1} \cdot \mathbf{1} \left[\mathbf{c} + \mathbf{r_t} > \mathbf{0} \right] d\mathbf{P^N}$$

Asymptotic consistency ensures that B^N converges to $\frac{0.00015}{0.0330} = 4.5455 \times 10^{-3}$ as N becomes large. We have generated 10^4 series of size N from this DGP and estimated the parameter B^N on each of these series. We have repeated this experiment setting $\{N_k\}_{k=1}^7 = \{100 \cdot 2^{k-1}\}_{k=1}^7$ and observed how the distribution of B^N varied across these different values of N. Figure 29.1 indicates that convergence is achieved at cube-root rate.

While it is difficult to show that the asymptotic distribution of B^N is the same as that of the maximum score estimator, the QQ-plot in Figure 29.2 (based on the distribution of B^N for $N = 6400$) provides a strong indication that the estimator's asymptotic distribution is non-normal.

Alternative estimation techniques   We would like to know how this somewhat irregular estimator compares to others. One prominent alternative estimator can be based on the fact that the conditional mean $g(x)$ is a Risk Neutral Best Predictor;

---

6. Obtained from DATASTREAM on the last day in the dataset.

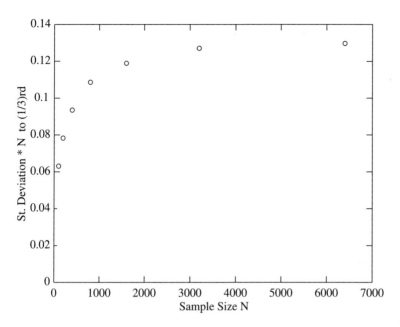

Figure 29.1
This figure provides supportive evidence for the conjecture that convergence occurs at cube-root rate since it indicates that $\lim_{N\to\infty} N^{\frac{1}{3}} \cdot \sigma_{B_N} = \sigma \simeq 0.13$

it therefore seems plausible that any 'good' estimator $\widehat{g}(x)$ for $g(x)$ should also be a 'good' estimator for a Risk Neutral Best Predictor $p(x)$. Unfortunately, this is not usually the case.

The primary cause of this is the nature of financial data which is such that most estimation techniques deliver estimates $\widehat{g}(x)$ that are only crude approximations to $g(x)$ and which differ greatly with the technique used. It is therefore relevant to choose an approximation that is 'good' in terms of a metric relevant for the application in which the estimate will be used (at least when - as is the case here - this is known).

The expected loss of a risk neutral agent using an estimate $\widehat{g}(x)$ is determined by how closely the subspace $\widehat{\overline{X}} = \{x : \widehat{g}(x) > 0\}$ matches $\overline{X} = \{x : g(x) > 0\}$. If, for example, $\widehat{g}(x)$ and $g(x)$ are strictly monotonic (and are both increasing or decreasing), this closeness will be determined by the closeness of $\{x : g(x) = 0\}$ to $\{x : \widehat{g}(x) = 0\}$. In this case, an estimation technique that performs well in terms of the profit metric must also be good at estimating the zeros of $g(x)$. However, this

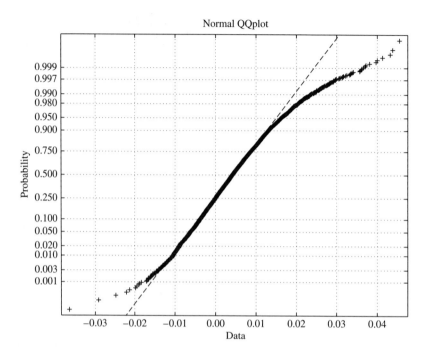

Figure 29.2
Normality requires that the observations drawn from the 10^4 draws from the distribution of B^N roughly lie on the straight line.

is a property which standard estimation techniques[7] such as OLS do not achieve successfully (as has been observed by contributors to the literature on calibration estimators, e.g. [Kruthckoff 1967], [Williams 1969], [Shukla 1972]). This suggests that standard estimation techniques may not perform well in terms of profitability because they are not accurate in the required sense. Indeed [Skouras 1998] confirms this by simulation.

The reasons for which standard estimators are not good at determining the set $\overline{X}$ are two. First, the accuracy with which this set is determined does not directly influence the value of the estimated quantity. Secondly, they do not exploit the fact that there are many mappings other than $g(x)$ which are Risk Neutral Best Predictors.

---

7. This example also indicates that special estimation techniques for determining the zeros of a regression function such as those proposed by [Hardle and Nixdorf 1987] and [Tsybakov 1988] may be good at delivering models appropriate for use by a risk neutral investor.

By contrast, the semiparametric estimation technique presented here chooses the model which is best at determining $\overline{X}$ according to the desired metric. Also, it is more *robust* than estimation methods based on structural models for $g(x)$ because consistency is obtained even in circumstances where this model is mis-specified for $g(x)$. Finally, even when the model is imperfectly specified for $p(x)$, it will have the desirable property of (asymptotically) minimizing the expected loss of a risk neutral investor subject to the constraints imposed by the restriction of predictors to the class $s(x, c)$, $c \in B$.

29.3.2   Computation

Apart from making standard results on estimators' properties inapplicable, the discontinuity of the integrand in (29.6) makes the computation of B^N non-trivial. A direct implication of this discontinuity is that the objective function must necessarily have finite cardinality. This is reassuring in as much as it implies that required estimate always exists; but it is also what makes its computation difficult because it means that the objective function to be optimised will be set-valued and discontinuous. Considering that the randomness inherent in the sampling process is also carried over to the objective function, it becomes evident that $\int r \cdot \mathbf{1}\left[\mathbf{s}(*, \mathbf{c}) > \mathbf{0}\right] d\mathbf{P^N}$ will be a highly rugged object with many local extrema even when $\int r \cdot \mathbf{1}\left[\mathbf{s}(*, \mathbf{c}) > \mathbf{0}\right] d\mathbf{P}$ is itself continuous.

To get a feel for the properties of the objective functions we typically deal with, consider Figure 29.3 which is a plot of $\int r_{t+1} \cdot \mathbf{1}\left[\mathbf{c_0} + \mathbf{0.1 r_t} + \mathbf{c_2 r_{t-1}} > \mathbf{0}\right] d\mathbf{P^N}$ where P^N is the empirical distribution of IBM returns previously described.

We have tried a variety of optimization techniques (such as simplex search, gradient descent and a genetic algorithm) on this type of problem but they have drastically failed to converge to a value for B^N which does not heavily depend on initial conditions. This problem has also been noted by [LeBaron 1998] and [Pictet et al 1996] for similar objective functions and, along with the lack of a theory for the statistical properties of B^N, has probably been the most important obstacle to the empirical application of the intuitive estimation procedure we propose.

An algorithm for computing the estimator B^N The computational procedure we propose is based on deriving B^N without actually minimizing $-\int r \cdot \mathbf{1}\left[\mathbf{s}(\mathbf{x}, \mathbf{c}) > \mathbf{0}\right] d\mathbf{P^N}$. It is sometimes possible to achieve this by finding an objective function which *(a)* has a minimum close to B^N and *(b)* does not have the undesirable features that make B^N difficult to compute[8]. Our algorithm does better than

---

8. This drives the minimisation procedure independently developed by [LeBaron 1998].

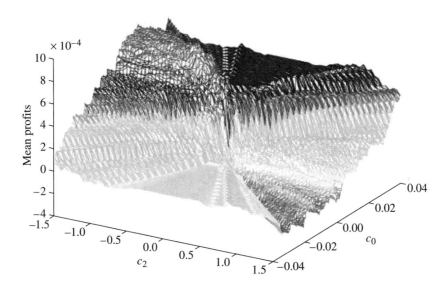

Figure 29.3
This objective function has a large number of local extrema and its discontinuities preclude the
use of most sophisticated optimization procedures to find its global maximum.

this by side stepping the trade-off between *(a)* and *(b)* typically characterizing such
a procedure.

To achieve this, suppose there exists a sequence of functions $\{f_j\}_{j=1}^J$ s.t. *(i)* f_1
is easy to minimize globally, *(ii)* the minima of f_j and f_{j+1} are 'close' for all j
and *(iii)* $f_J = -\int r_{t+1} \cdot \mathbf{1}\left[\mathbf{s}(\xi, \mathbf{c}) > \mathbf{0}\right] d\mathbf{P^N}$. If we can find such a sequence, we can
minimize f_j globally using only a local search and the global minimum of f_{j-1} as
a starting point. Hence, a global search is required only for f_1 and by construction
this is 'easy'. The difficult optimization problem is thus replaced with a sequence
of easy optimization problems.

A sequence conjectured to have these properties is defined by

$$f_j\left(c\right) = -\int r \cdot \left(1 + \exp\left(-\frac{s(x, c)}{m_j}\right)\right)^{-1} dP^N$$

where $\{m^j\}_{j=1}^J$ is a strictly decreasing sequence of positive constants with m^J
sufficiently small to ensure $f_J\left(c\right) = \int r \cdot \mathbf{1}\left[\mathbf{s}(*, \mathbf{c}) > \mathbf{0}\right] d\mathbf{P^N}$ and m_0 derived as
described in [Skouras 1998] to ensure that a large proportion of the values of $\frac{s(x,c)}{m_0}$

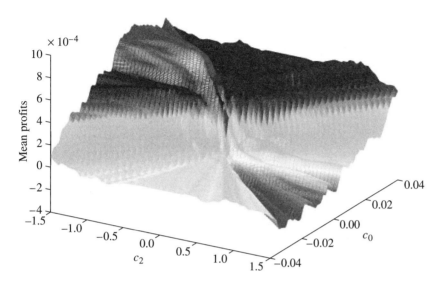

Figure 29.4
Although this objective function has more than one maximum it is sufficiently smooth for standard optimization procedures to be able to locate its global maximum.

lie in a region of the domain of $(1 + \exp(-y))^{-1}$ in which this function has a degree of curvature facilitating computation of $f_0(c)$. We illustrate the impact of smoothening our objective function in this way in Figure 29.4 which is a plot of $-f_0(c)$ with $s(*, *)$ and P^N as in Figure 29.3.

To compute the minimum of $f_0(c)$ we propose the use of a genetic algorithm to find an initial minimum (see [Dorsey and Mayer 1995] for evidence on the suitability of such an algorithm) to be used as a starting point for a simplex search. The minimum obtained from the simplex search is then used as a numerical estimate for the minimum of $f_0(c)$; having obtained this, we enter a loop in which the minimum of f_i is used as a starting point in a local search for a local minimum of f_{i+1}. The loop ends when we have obtained a minimum for f_J, and thus a numerical value for the estimator B^N.

An empirical investigation of the properties this algorithm [Skouras 1998] confirms its performance is good in that it shifts the speed-accuracy trade-off significantly outwards relative to standard techniques.

29.4 Conclusions

This paper has described the relationship between risk neutral investment decisions and optimal financial forecasting. This should be interpreted as a benchmark for studying the relationship between financial decision making and financial forecasting. However, the techniques proposed can also be applied for other purposes, notably the estimation of optimal binary investment rules including 'technical trading rules' and 'market timing' rules.

Standard estimators for the conditional mean of returns may not perform particularly well as estimates of a risk neutral investor's optimal forecasts and we therefore propose an estimator specially designed for this purpose. Its properties are discussed and an algorithm for its computation is proposed.

The results developed permit estimation of a Risk Neutral Forecasting model combining the structure of popular econometric models for returns with the structure of the most profitable investment rules. Estimation of such a hybrid model should lead to parametrizations which uncover more of the structure present in financial series, particularly of the type which has 'economic value'. In so doing, it should also improve our understanding of the features of returns processes which constitute the most important determinants of investment behaviour.

References

Breen, W., L. R. Glosten, and R. Jagannathan. 1989. Economic significance of predictable variations in stock index returns. *Journal of Finance*, Vol XLIV(No. 5):1177–1189.

Christofferson, P. F. and F. X. Diebold. 1996. Further results on forecasting and model selection under asymmetric loss. *Journal of Applied Econometrics*, 11:561–571.

Dorsey, R. E. and W. J. Mayer. 1995. Genetic algorithms for estimation problems with multiple optima, nondifferentiability and other irregular features. *Journal of Business and Economic Statistics*, 13(1).

Granger, C. W. 1993. On the limitations of comparing mean squared forecast errors: Comment. *Journal of Forecasting*, 12:651–652.

Granger, C. W. and H. Pesaran. 1996. A decision theoretic approach to forecast evaluation. Working paper, University of California San Diego.

Hardle, W. and R. Nixdorf. 1987. Nonparametric sequential estimation of zeros and extrema of regression functions. *IEEE Transactions on information systems*, IT-33(3):367–372.

Henriksson and R. Merton. 1981. On market timing and investment performace II: Statistical procedures for evaluating forecasting skills. *Journal of Business*, 54:513–533.

Kim, J. and D. Pollard. 1990. Cube root asymptotics. *Annals of Statistics*, 18:191–219.

Kruthckoff, R. 1967. Classical and inverse regression methods of calibration. *Technometrics*, pages 425–439.

LeBaron, B. 1998. An evolutionary bootstrap method for selecting dynamic trading strategies. Working paper, University of Wisconsin.

Manski, C. 1975. Maximum score estimation of the stochastic utility model of choice. *Journal of Econometrics*, (3):205–228.

Manski, C. 1988. *Analog Methods in Econometrics*, volume 39 of *Monographs on Statistics and Applied Probability*. Chapman and Hall.

Manski, C. 1994. *Analog Estimation of Econometric Models*, volume 4, chapter 43, pages 2559–2582. Elsevier.

Merton, R. 1981. On market timing and investment performance, i: An equilibrium theory of market forecasts. *Journal of Business*, 54:363–406.

Moody, J., M. Saffell, Y. Liao, and L. Wu. 1998. Reinforcement learning for trading systems and portfolios: Immediate vs. future rewards. mimeo, Oregon Graduate Institute of Science and Technology.

Pesaran, H. M. and A. Timmerman. 1995. Predictability of stock returns: Robustness and economic significance. *Journal of Finance*, L(4):1201–1228.

Pictet, O., M. Dacorogna, R. Dave, B. Chopard, R. Schirru, and M. Tomassini. 1996. Genetic algorithms with collective sharing for robust optimization in financial applications. mimeo, Olsen Associates.

Pictet, O., M. Dacorogna, U. Muller, R. Olsen, and W. J.R. 1992. Real time trading models for foreign exchange rates. *Neural Network World*, 2(6):713–744.

Sargent, T. J. 1993. *Bounded Rationality in Macroeconics*. Oxford University Press.

Satchell, S. and A. Timmerman. 1995. An assesment of the economic value of non-linear foreign exchange rate forecasts. *Journal of Forecasting*, 14:477–497.

Shukla, G. 1972. On the problem of calibration. *Technometrics*, 14:547–553.

Skouras, S. 1997. Analysing technical analysis. working paper 97-36, European University Institute. Revised 1998 as 'Financial returns and market efficiency as seen by an artificial technical analyst'.

Skouras, S. 1998. Risk neutral forecasting. Working paper 98-40, European University Institute. Revised 1999.

Sullivan, R., A. Timmerman, and H. White. 1998. Dangers of data driven inference. Working paper 98-16, University of California at San Diego.

Tsybakov, A. 1988. Passive stochastic approximation. Working paper A-207, University of Bonn.

Weiss, A. A. 1996. Estimating time series models using the relevant cost function. *Journal of Applied Econometrics*, 11:539–560.

Williams, E. 1969. A note on regression methods in calibration. *Technometrics*, 11:189–192.

30 Temporal–Difference Learning and Applications in Finance

Benjamin Van Roy

In principal, problems of sequential decision making under uncertainty can be formulated in terms of stochastic control and solved by dynamic programming algorithms. However, due to the curse of dimensionality, stochastic control problems that arise in practice are often intractable. This paper overviews temporal–difference learning, which offers an approach to approximating solutions of intractable stochastic control problems. Two application areas important to the finance industry – options pricing and portfolio optimization – are presented together with variants of temporal–difference learning designed to address intractable problems in these areas.

Problems of sequential decision making under uncertainty (stochastic control) arise in many areas of finance. Examples include dynamic portfolio optimization, price–impact optimization, and the pricing and exercising of American options. In principle, such problems can be solved by dynamic programming algorithms. These algorithms compute a *value function*, which evaluates expected future reward as a function of current state. Used as a tool for ranking alternative actions, the value function enables optimal decision–making.

For a problem with a state space S, dynamic programming algorithms represent the value function $J^* : S \mapsto \Re$ in terms of a lookup table with one numerical value $J^*(x)$ per state $x \in S$. For this reason, practical applications are limited to problems with manageably small state spaces. Unfortunately, due to the curse of dimensionality, the size of a state space grows exponentially in the number of state variables, and consequently, dynamic programming algorithms are impractical for many realistic problems.

One sensible way of dealing with the curse of dimensionality is to generate an approximation $\tilde{J} : S \times \Re^K \mapsto \Re$ parameterized by a vector $r \in \Re^K$. In particular, instead of representing and computing the value function exactly, one might attempt to compute a vector r such that $\tilde{J}(\cdot, r)$ approximates J^*. The intention would be to alleviate the need to compute as many values as there are states.

There are two important preconditions to the development of an effective approximation. First, we need to choose an approximator $\tilde{J}$ that can closely approximate the desired value function. In this respect, the choice of a suitable approximator requires some practical experience or theoretical analysis that provides rough information on the shape of the function to be approximated. Second, we need effective algorithms for tuning the parameters r.

In this paper, we will focus on approximations $\tilde{J}$ that are comprised of weighted combinations of preselected basis functions. The idea is to customize a selection of basis functions to a problem at hand and then compute weights so that the weighted combination is close to the value function.

It is important to note that methods of selecting suitable parameters for statistical regression are inadequate for value function approximation. In statistical regression, we are given training data pairs $\{(x_1, y_1), \ldots, (x_m, y_m)\}$ and must construct a function $y = f(x)$ that "explains" these data pairs. In dynamic programming, we are interested in approximating a value function $y = J^*(x)$ mapping states to optimal expected future rewards. An ideal set of training data would consist of pairs $\{(x_1, J^*(x_1)), \ldots, (x_m, J^*(x_m))\}$. However, we have no way of obtaining such data pairs. To approximate a value function, we need more sophisticated algorithms. Such algorithms constitute the central topic of research in neuro-dynamic programming and reinforcement learning.

This paper is meant to provide a tutorial on neuro-dynamic programming and reinforcement learning with an emphasis on application areas in finance. However, rather than discussing the conglomeration of algorithms and ideas under development in these fields, we will focus on temporal–difference learning, which is probably the most popular of the algorithms.

We will begin by reviewing stochastic control and the use of dynamic programming value functions. We then discuss approximations comprised of weighted combinations of basis functions. We describe in Section 30.3 temporal–difference learning as applied to tuning basis function weights. We also discuss the current state of the art with regards to both theory and practice. Finally, in Sections 30.4 and 30.5, we present variants of temporal–difference learning designed to address problems in derivatives pricing and portfolio optimization.

The exposition in this paper is neither comprehensive not rigorous. Emphasis is placed on conveying basic ideas at an intuitive level. We refer the reader to the texts of Bertsekas and Tsitsiklis [Bertsekas and Tsitsiklis 1996] and Sutton and Barto [Sutton and Barto 1998] for more extensive introductions pertaining to broader classes of algorithms.

30.1 Stochastic Control

We consider a discrete–time dynamic system that, at each time t, takes on a state x_t and evolves according to

$$x_{t+1} = f(x_t, u_t, w_t),$$

where w_t is a disturbance and u_t is a control decision. Each disturbance w_t is independently sampled from a fixed distribution. Though finance problems with more general (infinite/continuous) state spaces will be considered in Sections 30.4 and 30.5, to keep the exposition simple we restrict attention for the time being to finite state, disturbance, and control spaces, denoted by S, W, and U, respectively.

A function $g : S \times U \mapsto \Re$ associates a reward $g(x_t, u_t)$ with a decision u_t made at state x_t. A *policy* is a mapping $\mu : S \mapsto U$ that generates state–contingent decisions. For each policy μ, we define a value function $J^\mu : S \mapsto \Re$ by

$$J^\mu(x) = \mathrm{E}\left[\sum_{t=0}^{\infty} \alpha^t g(x_t, \mu(x_t)) \Big| x_0 = x\right],$$

where $\alpha \in [0, 1)$ is a discount factor and the state sequence is generated according to $x_0 = x$ and $x_{t+1} = f(x_t, \mu(x_t), w_t)$. Each $J^\mu(x)$ can be interpreted as an assessment of long term rewards given that we start in state x and control the system using a policy μ. The optimal value function J^* is defined by $J^*(x) = \max_\mu J^\mu(x)$. A standard result in dynamic programming states that any policy μ^* given by

$$\mu^*(x) = \underset{u \in U}{\mathrm{argmax}}\, \underset{w}{\mathrm{E}}\left[g(x, u) + \alpha J^*(f(x, u, w))\right],$$

where $\underset{w}{\mathrm{E}}[\cdot]$ denotes expectation with respect to the distribution of disturbances, is optimal in the sense that $J^*(x) = J^{\mu^*}(x)$, for every state x (see, e.g., [Bertsekas 1995]).

Classical dynamic programming algorithms compute the optimal value function J^*. The result is stored in a "look–up" table with one entry $J^*(x)$ per state $x \in S$. When the need arises, the value function is used to generate optimal decisions. In particular, given a current state $x_t \in S$, a decision u_t is selected according to

$$u_t = \underset{u \in U}{\mathrm{argmax}}\, \underset{w}{\mathrm{E}}\left[g(x_t, u) + \alpha J^*(f(x_t, u, w))\right].$$

Unfortunately, in many practical situations, state spaces are intractable. and it is essentially impossible to compute (or even store) one value $J^*(x)$ per state.

30.2   Approximations

The intractability of state spaces calls for value function approximation. In this paper, we will restrict attention to linearly parameterized approximations, which take form

$$\tilde{J}(x,r) = \sum_{k=1}^{K} r(k)\phi_k(x),$$

where $\phi_1,\ldots,\phi_K$ are "basis functions" mapping S to $\Re$, and $r = (r(1),\ldots,r(K))'$ is a vector of scalar weights. In a spirit similar to that of statistical regression, the basis functions $\phi_1,\ldots,\phi_K$ are selected by a human user based on intuition or analysis specific to the problem at hand. One interpretation that is useful for the construction of basis functions involves viewing each function ϕ_k as a "feature" – that is, a numerical value capturing a salient characteristic of the state that may be pertinent to effective decision making.

30.3 Temporal–Difference Learning

After selecting basis functions for a given stochastic control problem, we are left with the task of computing weights. In this section, we introduce temporal–difference learning as an algorithm for computing such weights. Though temporal–difference learning, sometimes called TD(λ), provides a continuum of algorithms parameterized by a scalar $\lambda \in [0,1]$, we will restrict attention to the case of $\lambda = 0$, which is referred to as TD(0).

30.3.1 The Basic Algorithm

Let us begin by presenting the algorithm as one for approximating the value function J^μ corresponding to a fixed policy μ. Let $\phi_1,\ldots,\phi_K$ be the collection of basis functions we choose to employ. Suppose that we observe a sequence of states $x_0, x_1, x_2,\ldots$ evolving according to $x_{t+1} = f(x_t,\mu(x_t),w_t)$ and that, at time t, the weight vector has been set to some value r_t. We define the *temporal difference* d_t corresponding to the transition from x_t to x_{t+1} by

$$d_t = g(x_t) + \alpha\tilde{J}(x_{t+1},r_t) - \tilde{J}(x_t,r_t). \tag{30.1}$$

Then, given an arbitrary initial weight vector r_0, TD(0) generates subsequent weight vectors according to

$$r_{t+1} = r_t + \gamma_t d_t \phi(x_t), \tag{30.2}$$

where γ_t is a scalar step size and $\phi(x) = (\phi_1(x),\ldots,\phi_K(x))'$. A formal analysis of temporal–difference learning (with a fixed policy) is presented in (Tsitsiklis and

Van Roy, 1997a). Under suitable technical conditions, the iterates r_t converge to a limit r^*, and the resulting function $\tilde{J}(\cdot, r^*)$ approximates J^μ.

Any function $J : S \mapsto \Re$ can be used to generate a policy

$$\bar{\mu}(x) = \operatorname*{argmax}_{u \in U} \operatorname*{E}_{w} \Big[g(x, u) + \alpha J(f(x, u, w)) \Big].$$

In this respect, one can view J as a guide for decision–making. A well–known result in dynamic programming states that, given a policy μ, the corresponding value function J^μ generates an improved policy $\bar{\mu}$. It therefore seems plausible that an approximation $\tilde{J}(\cdot, r)$ to J^μ similarly generates a policy that improves on μ. Now recall that, when TD(0) is executed on a system controlled by a fixed policy μ, the iterates $\tilde{J}(\cdot, r_t)$ converge to an approximation of J^μ. One might therefore expect that policies generated by $\tilde{J}(\cdot, r_t)$ tend to bear improvements on the policy μ. This intuitive idea motivates an algorithm for approximating J^*: rather than controlling the system with a fixed policy μ, at any time t, make decisions based on $\tilde{J}(\cdot, r_t)$.

Let us now provide a more precise description of TD(0) as applied to approximating J^*. As before, we simulate a state trajectory $x_0, x_1, x_2, \ldots$ and generates weight vectors $r_0, r_1, r_2, \ldots$. The initial state x_0 and weight vector r_0 can be arbitrary. Given a state x_t and a weight vector r_t, a decision u_t is generated according to

$$u_t = \operatorname*{argmax}_{u \in U} \operatorname*{E}_{w} \Big[g(x_t, u) + \alpha \tilde{J}(f(x_t, u, w), r_t) \Big].$$

The next state x_{t+1} is then given by $x_{t+1} = f(x_t, u_t, w_t)$, and the weight vector is updated according to (30.1) and (30.2).

30.3.2 Active Exploration

In practice, temporal–differnece learning often suffers from getting "stuck" in "dead-lock" situations. In particular, there is a possibility that only a small subset of the state space will ever be visited and that the value of states outside that region will never be "learned" – the unexplored is never explored because values learned from the explored do not promote further exploration. A modification that has been found to be useful in alleviating this shortcoming involves adding "exploration noise" to the controls. In particular, during execution of temporal–difference learning, one might generate decisions according to

$$u_t = \operatorname*{argmax}_{u \in U} \operatorname*{E}_{w} \Big[g(x_t, u) + \alpha \tilde{J}(f(x_t, u, w), r_t) \Big] + \eta_t,$$

where η_t is a random perturbation that induces exploration of the state space.

Approximating the Q–Function   Given the optimal value function J^*, the generation of optimal control decisions

$$u_t = \operatorname*{argmax}_{u \in U} \operatorname*{E}_{w} \Big[g(x_t, u) + \alpha J^*(f(x_t, u, w)) \Big],$$

requires computing one expectation per element of the decision space U, which requires in turn repeated evaluation of the system function f. One approach to avoiding this computation involves obtaining a "Q–function," which maps $S \times U$ to $\Re$ and is defined by

$$Q^*(x, u) = \operatorname*{E}_{w} \Big[g(x, u) + \alpha J^*(f(x, u, w)) \Big].$$

Given this function, optimal decisions can be computed according to

$$u_t = \operatorname*{argmax}_{u \in U} Q^*(x_t, u),$$

which no longer involves taking expectations or evaluating the system function. The Q–learning algorithm capitalize on conveniences associated with the use of a Q–function. It is a variant of temporal–difference learning that approximates Q–functions, rather than value functions.

30.3.3   State of the Art

There is a long history behind the algorithms discussed in the preceding sections. We will attempt to provide a brief account of items that are particularly relevant to understanding the current state of the art, and we refer the reader to the books of Sutton and Barto [Sutton and Barto 1998] and Bertsekas and Tsitsiklis [Bertsekas and Tsitsiklis 1996] for further discussions of the historical development.

A major development in reinforcement learning was the temporal–difference learning algorithm, which was proposed by Sutton [Sutton 1988], but draws on earlier work by Barto and Sutton [Sutton and Barto 1981, Barto and Sutton 1982] on models for classical conditioning phenomena observed in animal behavior and by Barto, Sutton, and Anderson on "actor–critic methods." Another major development came with the thesis of Watkins [Watkins 1989], in which "Q–learning" was proposed, and the study of temporal–difference learning was integrated with classical ideas from dynamic programming and stochastic approximation theory. The work of Werbos [Werbos 1987, Werbos 1992a, Werbos 1992b] and Barto, Bradtke, and Singh [Barto et al 1995] also contributed to this integration.

In addition to advancing the understanding of temporal–difference learning, the marriage with classical engineering ideas furthered the view of the algorithm as one for addressing complex engineering problems and lead to a number of applications. The practical potential was first demonstrated by Tesauro [Tesauro 1992, Tesauro 1994, Tesauro 1995], who used a variant of temporal–difference learning to produce a world–class Backgammon playing program. Several subsequent case studies (e.g., [Singh and Bertsekas 1997, Crites 1996, Crites and Barto 1995, Van Roy et al 1997, Zhang and Dietterich 1995]) have also shown signs of promise.

Despite a growing literature, the exist theory does not provide adequate support for applications, as we will now explain. In temporal–difference learning, approximation accuracy is limited by the choice of a parameterization. The hope, however, is that the iterative computation of parameters should lead to a good approximation relative to other possibilities allowed by this choice. Unfortunately, there is a shortage of theory that ensures desirable behavior of this kind. Most results involving temporal–difference learning apply either to cases where the optimal value function is represented exhaustively (i.e., by as many parameters as there are states) or the system is autonomous. Exceptions include work involving very restrictive types of parameterizations [Singh et al 1994, Tsitsiklis and Van Roy 1996, Gordon 1995] or overly restrictive assumptions.

Due to the absence of adequate theory, there is a lack of streamlined and widely accepted algorithms. Instead, there is a conglomeration of variants to temporal–difference learning, and each one is parameterized by values that must be selected by a user. It is unclear which algorithms and parameter settings will work on a particular problem, and when a method does work, it is still unclear which ingredients are actually necessary for success. As a result, applications often require trial and error in a long process of parameter tweaking and experimentation.

One exception to this general state of affairs involves an algorithm for solving complex optimal stopping problems such as those arising in the pricing of exotic price dependent options [Tsitsiklis and Van Roy 1997]. Here, there is a variant of temporal–difference learning accompanied by an analysis that ensures certain desirable behavior. This algorithm and its application constitute the topic of the next section.

30.4 Pricing Exotic American Options

The pricing of American options poses one stochastic control problem of significant commercial interest to the financial industry. Such tasks give rise to problems of optimal stopping, which constitute a special case of the more general stochastic control problem we have discussed. Vanilla options such as American puts and calls involve one–dimensional optimal stopping problems and can therefore be addressed by finite difference methods. However, many exotic American options such as those involving multiple assets or path dependencies lead to high–dimensional optimal stopping problems that require approximation methods.

In this section, we introduce a variant of TD(0) that addresses optimal stopping problems and discuss theoretical results that support its application. We also present a simple case study illustrating its use. The work discussed in this section is due to [Tsitsiklis and Van Roy 1997]. To maintain a simple exposition we restrict attention to a particular class of optimal stopping problems that only accommodate the pricing of certain perpetual options. However, the ideas easily generalize to address standard (non–perpetual) exotic American options. Such extensions are discussed in [Van Roy 1998].

30.4.1   Optimal Stopping

Let us begin by describing the simple class of optimal stopping problems under consideration. Let $\{x_t | t = 0, 1, 2, \ldots\}$ be an ergodic Markov process taking on values in a state space $\Re^d$. Let $G : \Re^d \mapsto \Re$ be a reward function, representing the reward received upon termination of the process (the reward is contingent on state at the time of termination) and let $\alpha \in [0, 1)$ be a discount factor. In this context, a policy is a mapping from states in $\Re^d$ to decisions in $\{\text{stop}, \text{continue}\}$. Given a policy, we can define a random variable τ, called a stopping time, which represents the first time at which the decision is to stop. The expected reward under the decision policy is then $\mathrm{E}\left[\alpha^\tau G(x_\tau)\right]$, where $G(x_\tau)$ is taken to be 0 if $\tau = \infty$. Similarly with general stochastic control problems, an optimal strategy can be generated from the optimal value function $J^* : \Re^n \mapsto \Re$, which provides the optimal expected reward contingent on the initial state.

30.4.2   An Approximation Algorithm

Let us now present a variant of temporal–difference learning designed for the formulated problem. Instead of the value function J^*, the algorithm approximates the Q–function. Recall that the Q–function has as its domain the product of the state and decision spaces. In optimal stopping, there are two possible decisions: "stop" or "continue." The Q–function for an optimal stopping problem would map a state x and the stopping decision to the reward contingent on stopping, which is $G(x)$. On the other hand, a state x and the continuation decision would map to the optimal reward starting at x contingent on continuing for one time step. Since $G(x)$ is readily available, we need only concern ourselves with approximating the Q–function over the portion of the domain corresponding to continuation decisions. Accordingly, we define Q^* as a mapping from $\Re^d$ to $\Re$ (the domain excludes the decision component, since we need only store values corresponding to the continuation decision).

The algorithm is initialized with a weight vector $r_0 \in \Re^K$. During the simulation of a trajectory $\{x_t | t = 0, 1, 2, \ldots\}$ of the (unstopped) Markov chain, the algorithm generates a sequence $\{r_t | t = 1, 2, \ldots\}$ according to

$$r_{t+1} = r_t + \gamma_t \phi(x_t)\Big(\alpha \max\{(\Phi r_t)(x_{t+1}), G(x_{t+1})\} - (\Phi r_t)(x_t)\Big), \tag{30.3}$$

where each γ_t is a positive scalar step size.

One desirable aspect of the algorithm we have described is that there exists a theory that ensures certain soundness properties under appropriate technical conditions [Tsitsiklis and Van Roy 1997]:

1. There exists a vector r^* such that r_t converges to r^* for any initial r_0 (almost surely).

2. The resulting approximation differs from Q^* by at most a constant factor times the minimal possible error given the selection of basis functions.

3. The resulting policy generates expected rewards that differ from the optimal by at most a constant factor times the minimal possible error given the selection of basis functions.

The presence of such results greatly facilitates implementation and application of the algorithm.

30.4.3 A Case Study

A case study that illustrates the use of the approximation algorithm for pricing high–dimensional American options is provided in [Tsitsiklis and Van Roy 1997]. The study involved a path–dependent option that gave rise to a one–hundred–dimensional state space. Sixteen basis functions were selected to capture what were believed to be salient features of the path, and weights were generated by the approximation algorithm presented in the previous section. The quality of the resulting policy significantly outperformed a heuristic strategy, which was used as a benchmark. Due to space limitations, we will not discuss the details of the case study. Instead, we refer the reader to [Tsitsiklis and Van Roy 1997].

30.5   Portfolio Optimization

The problem of portfolio optimization can be viewed as one of finding a desirable combination of risks and returns. Whenever possible, portfolio strategies should seek to reduce risks without significantly decreasing expected returns. Diversification among assets is probably the best known approach to risk reduction. The problem of selecting an appropriately diversified portfolio is addressed by single period portfolio optimization models such as Markowitz's. Such models lead to portfolio strategies that are *myopic*. In particular, a portfolio to be held over the impending time period is selected without regard to investment opportunities that may subsequently materialize.

A complementary approach to risk reduction involves the use of intertemporal strategies that, in addition to diversification, take advantage of correlations between immediate returns and events that influence future investment opportunities. Such strategies are produced when one considers multiperiod portfolio optimization models, and potential benefits have been identified and studied by Brennan, Schwartz, and Lagnado [Brennan et al 1997]. In their work, the problem of synthesizing an intertemporal strategy is formulated in terms of stochastic control and solved by dynamic programming algorithms. Due to the curse of dimensionality, this approach becomes intractable in the context of problems of practical scale.

In this section, we present a variant of temporal–difference learning designed to approximate solutions of multiperiod portfolio optimization problems. The hope is that this will offer a practical method enabling investors to realize benefits of intertemporal strategies.

30.5.1   Problem Formulation

We consider a situation in which an investor is initially endowed with a level of wealth w_0 and, at each nonnegative integer time t, chooses a consumption rate c_t and portfolio weights θ_t that determine how his remaining wealth is invested among n assets in the market. His wealth evolves according to

$$w_{t+1} = (\theta_t' r_t)(1 - c_t)w_t.$$

Here, θ_t is a vector in the n–dimensional unit simplex Δ^n with each component representing the fraction of wealth to be invested in a particular asset, r_t is an n–dimensional vector representing returns realized by the various assets during the interval $[t, t+1]$, and $c_t \in [0, 1]$ is a fraction of wealth that the investor consumes.

We assume that the initial wealth w_0 and each rate of return $r_t(i)$ are in $\Re^+$, the set of nonnegative reals.

The asset returns are stochastic, and we now discuss our assumptions concerning the nature of this process. A simple model of asset returns might assume that the vectors $r_0, r_1, r_2, \ldots$ are independent and identically distributed (see, e.g., Samuelson, 1969). However, we will work with a more realistic setting where the returns can be influenced by an underlying Markov process $\{x_t\}$ taking on values in a state space S. With regards to the dependency of returns on the process, we will assume that each random vector r_t is given by a deterministic function R of x_t and x_{t+1}. In particular,

$$r_t = R(x_t, x_{t+1}).$$

At each time t, the investor selects his rate of consumption c_t and portfolio θ_t based on knowledge of his wealth w_t and the current state x_t. His goal is to optimize an infinite discounted sum of utility derived from consumption:

$$\mathrm{E}\left[\sum_{t=0}^{\infty} \alpha^t U(c_t w_t)\right].$$

Here, $\alpha \in (0, 1)$ is a discount factor that defines the investor's time–relative preferences. We will restrict attention to the class of policies (i.e., consumption–investment strategies) that take the form of a function μ that maps $\Re^+ \times S$ to $[0, 1] \times \Delta^n$. In particular, an investor employing a policy μ chooses consumption rates and portfolio weights according to

$$(c_t, \theta_t) = \mu(w_t, x_t).$$

We will only consider isoelastic utility functions, which take the form

$$U(w) = \frac{w^\beta}{\beta},$$

for $\beta \in (-\infty, 1]$. It is well known that this utility function gives rise to constant relative risk aversion. In particular, the Arrow–Pratt measure of risk aversion, defined for general utility functions by

$$-\frac{d^2 U(w)/dw^2}{dU(w)/dw},$$

is equal $(1 - \beta)/w$, which is inversely proportional to the level of wealth.

30.5.2   Value Function Decomposition

As is generally the case in stochastic control, an optimal policy can be generated based on a value function J^*. In our current context, the value function is defined by

$$J^*(w, x) = \sup \mathrm{E}\left[\sum_{t=0}^{\infty} \alpha^t \frac{(c_t w_t)^\beta}{\beta} \Big| x_0 = x\right],$$

where the supremum is taken over all permissable investment/consumption strategies. Note that the state incorporates a combination of the investor's wealth and the state of the operating environment, since both can influence the investor's future utility. Due to special structure of the problem at hand, the value function can be decomposed. In particular,

$$J^*(w, x) = \frac{w^\beta}{\beta} V^*(x),$$

for some function V^*. This decomposition makes our task of computing the value function more convenient – we need only compute the function V^*. The variant of temporal–difference learning that we will present approximates this function V^*.

30.5.3   The Approximation Algorithm

We will once again generate approximations of the form

$$V^*(x) \approx \sum_{k=1}^{K} z(k)\phi_k,$$

where each ϕ_k is a basis function and $z \in \Re^K$ is the vector of weights. (We use z instead of r to denote the weight vector because, in this section, r represents the vector of returns.)

The algorithm is initialized with a weight vector $z_0 \in \Re^K$. During the simulation of a trajectory $\{x_t | t = 0, 1, 2, \ldots\}$ of the Markov chain, the algorithm generates a sequence $\{z_t | t = 1, 2, \ldots\}$ according to

$$z_{t+1} = z_t + \gamma_t \phi(x_t)\left(c_t^\beta + (1 - c_t)^\beta (\theta_t' r_t)^\beta \phi'(x_{t+1})z_t - \phi'(x_t)z_t\right),$$

where each γ_t is a positive scalar step size. At each iteration the consumption and investment decisions are based on the current approximate value function (the structure of the dependence is not straightforward and we will omit its description).

Similarly with the algorithm for optimal stopping, this algorithm bears a strong resemblance to TD(0). Though this is a newly proposed algorithm and its behavior is not yet well understood, experiments with small (two–dimensional) problems have delivered promising results [Rusmevichientong and Van Roy 1999].

30.6   Closing Remarks

Many problems in financial decision–making are naturally formulated in terms of stochastic control. In principle, such problems can be solved using the methods of dynamic programming. However, the "curse of dimensionality" presents an obstacle prohibiting effective use of dynamic programming. It is interesting to note that an analogous impediment arises in statistical regression. In particular, given an ability to collect data pairs of the form $(x, J(x))$, the problem of producing an accurate approximation $\tilde{J}$ to the underlying function J becomes computationally intractable as the dimension of the domain increases. Similarly with the context of stochastic control, difficulties arise due to the curse of dimensionality. In the setting of statistical regression, a common approach to dealing with this limitation involves selecting a set of basis functions $\phi_1, \ldots, \phi_K$, collecting a set of input–output pairs $\{(x_1, J(x_1)), \ldots, (x_m, J(x_m))\}$, and using the least–squares algorithm to compute weights $r(1), \ldots, r(K)$ that minimize

$$\sum_{i=1}^{m} \left(J(x_i) - \sum_{k=1}^{K} r(k)\phi_k(x_i) \right)^2.$$

The result is an approximation of the form

$$\tilde{J}(x) = \sum_{k=1}^{K} r(k)\phi_k(x).$$

Though there is no systematic and generally applicable method for choosing basis functions, a combination of intuition, analysis, guesswork, and experimentation often leads to a useful selection. In fact, the combination of basis function selection and least–squares is a valuable tool that has met prevalent application.

   The utility of least–squares statistical regression provides inspiration for the flavor of methods studied in neuro–dynamic programming and reinforcement learning. For example, temporal–difference learning can be viewed as an analog to the least–squares algorithm that is applicable to stochastic control rather than statistical regression – given a stochastic control problem and a selection of basis functions

$\phi_1, \ldots, \phi_K$, the intent is to compute weights $r(1), \ldots, r(K)$ such that the function

$$\tilde{J}(x) = \sum_{k=1}^{K} r(k)\phi_k(x)$$

approximates the value function. In special cases such as pricing exotic American options, there are analyses that ensure desirable qualities for resulting approximations. In these settings, the streamlined character of the algorithms and results makes them accessible and useful.

Though such results provide a starting point, the development of streamlined methods and analyses for general classes of stochastic control problems remains largely open. Our hope, however, is that the range of problems we can address in such a manner will broaden with future research. A goal might be to eventually produce an algorithm that is as useful and widely accessible in the context of stochastic control as is least–squares in the context of statistical regression.

References

Barto, A. G., S. J. Bradtke, and S. P. Singh. 1995. Real–Time Learning and Control Using Asynchronous Dynamic Programming. *Artificial Intelligence*, 72:81–138.

Barto, A. G. and R. S. Sutton. 1982. Simulation of Anticipatory Responses in Classical Conditioning by a Neuron–Like Adaptive Element. *Behavioural Brain Research*, 4:221–235.

Bertsekas, D. P. 1995. *Dynamic Programming and Optimal Control*. Athena Scientific, Bellmont, MA.

Bertsekas, D. P. and J. N. Tsitsiklis. 1996. *Neuro-Dynamic Programming*. Athena Scientific, Bellmont, MA.

Brennan, M. J., E. S. Shwartz, and R. Lagnado. 1997. Strategic Asset Allocation. *Journal of Economic Dynamics and Control*, 21:1377–1403.

Crites, R. H. 1996. *Large–Scale Dynamic Optimization Using Teams of Reinforcement Learning Agents*. PhD thesis, University of Massachusetts, Amherst, MA.

Crites, R. H. and A. G. Barto. 1995. Improving Elevator Performance Using Reinforcement Learning. In *Advances in Neural Information Processing Systems 8*, Cambridge, MA. MIT Press.

Gordon, G. J. 1995. Stable Function Approximation in Dynamic Programming. Technical Report CMU-CS-95-103, Carnegie Mellon University.

Rusmevichientong, P. and B. Van Roy. 1999. unpublished work.

Singh, S. P. and D. P. Bertsekas. 1997. Reinforcement Learning for Dynamic Channel Allocation in Cellular Telephone Systems. In *Advances in Neural Information Processing Systems 10*, Cambridge, MA. MIT Press.

Singh, S. P., T. Jaakkola, and M. I. Jordan. 1994. Reinforcement Learning with Soft State Aggregation. In *Advances in Neural Information Processing Systems 7*, Cambridge, MA. MIT Press.

Sutton, R. S. 1988. Learning to Predict by the Methods of Temporal Differences. *Machine Learning*, 3:9–44.

Sutton, R. S. and A. G. Barto. 1981. Toward a Modern Theory of Adaptive Networks: Expectation and Prediction. *Psychological Review*, 88:135–170.

Sutton, R. S. and A. G. Barto. 1998. *Reinforcement Learning: An Introduction*. MIT Press, Cambridge, MA.

Tesauro, G. J. 1992. Practical Issues in Temporal Difference Learning. *Machine Learning*, 8:257–277.

Tesauro, G. J. 1994. TD–Gammon, a Self–Teaching Backgammon Program, Achieves Master–Level Play. *Neural Computation*, 6(2):215–219.

Tesauro, G. J. 1995. Temporal Difference Learning and TD–Gammon. *Communications of the ACM*, 38:58–68.

Tsitsiklis, J. N. and B. Van Roy. 1996. Feature–Based Methods for Large Scale Dynamic Programming. *Machine Learning*, 22:59–94.

Tsitsiklis, J. N. and B. Van Roy. 1997. Optimal Stopping of Markov Processes: Hilbert Space Theory, Approximation Algorithms, and an Application to Pricing High-Dimensional Financial Derivatives. Technical Report LIDS-P-2389, MIT Laboratory for Information and Decision Systems. To Appear in the IEEE Transactions on Automatic Control.

Van Roy, B. 1998. *Learning and Value Function Approximation in Complex Decision Processes*. PhD thesis, Massachusetts Institute of Technology, Cambridge, Massachusetts.

Van Roy, B., D. P. Bertsekas, Y. Lee, and J. N. Tsitsiklis. 1997. A Neuro–Dynamic Programming Approach to Retailer Inventory Management. preprint.

Watkins, C. J. C. H. 1989. *Learning From Delayed Rewards*. PhD thesis, Cambridge University, Cambridge, UK.

Werbos, P. J. 1987. Building and Understanding Adaptive Systems: a Statistical/Numerical Approach to Factory Automation and Brain Research. *IEEE Transactions on Systems, Man, and Cybernetics*, 17:7–20.

Werbos, P. J. 1992a. Approximate Dynamic Programming for Real–Time Control and Neural Modeling. In White, D. A. and D. A. Sofge, editors, *Handbook of Intelligent Control*.

Werbos, P. J. 1992b. Neurocontrol and Supervised Learning: An Overview and Evaluation. In White, D. A. and D. A. Sofge, editors, *Handbook of Intelligent Control*.

Zhang, W. and T. G. Dietterich. 1995. A Reinforcement Learning Approach to Job Shop Scheduling. In *Proceeding of the IJCAI*.

V Heterogeneous Agents

31 Technical Trading Creates a Prisoner's Dilemma: Results from an Agent-Based Model

Shareen Joshi, Jeffrey Parker, and Mark A. Bedau

The widespread use and proven profitability of technical trading rules in financial markets has long been a puzzle in academic finance. In this paper we show, using the Santa Fe artificial stock market market, that widespread technical trading can arise due to a multi-person prisoners' dilemma in which the inclusion of technical trading rules to a single agent's repertoire of rules is a dominant strategy. The use of this dominant strategy by all agents in the market creates a symmetric Nash equilibrium in which wealth earned is lower and the volatility of prices is higher than in the hypothetical case in which all agents rely only on fundamental rules. Our explanation of this lower wealth and higher volatility is that the use of technical trading rules worsens the accuracy of the predictions of all agents' market forecasts by contributing to the reinforcement of price trends, augmenting volatility, and increasing the amount of noise in the market.

31.1 Introduction

Technical and fundamental forecasting rules are widely used by traders in financial markets. While fundamental rules are based on the assumption that prices should stay close to their true worth (the discounted worth of future returns), technical rules are based on the assumption that prices move in predictable historical patterns [Acar and Satchell 1997, Schwager 1995].

The usefulness of fundamental trading rules is adequately explained by the standard theory of efficient markets [Samuelson 1965, Cootner 1967, Fama 1970 Malkiel 1992, or Campbell 1997]. In informationally efficient markets consisting of homogeneous agents with rational expectations, the theory predicts that prices should closely track fundamental values, and so it should be possible for an agent to make higher-than-normal profits only in the case that she successfully forecasts changes in stock fundamentals. Thus fundamental rules might provide accurate forecasts of stock values. Technical trading rules on the other hand, can not be useful forecasters in such markets. Since historical patterns yield no useful information about future stock prices beyond their implications for the stream of dividends, attempting to forecast future prices based on historical patterns should not be profitable. Thus, traditional theoretical models have a difficult time explaining the proven profitability of technical trading rules in financial markets [Brock , Lakonishok and LeBaron 1992, Keim and Madhaven 1995 , Shiller 1989, Werner , deBondt and Thaler 1995].

A wide variety of theoretical and empirical models have been developed to explain this [Delong, Shleifer, Summers and Waldman 1990a, Delong, Shleifer, Summers and Waldman 1991, Kirman 1991, Kurtz 1994, Marengo and Tordjman 1995, Farmer 1998, Rieck 1994, Soros 1994]. We use an agent-based model of a stock market to explore an explanation of this phenomenon. The key characteristic of this model is that agents' expectations do not follow a fixed rule such as a rational expectations rule. Instead agents choose among an evolving set of expectation rules depending on which ones have proved to be the most successful predictors of recent stock-price changes.

Using this framework, we show first that in a market in which all other traders follow strictly fundamental rules of the kind that would characterize an efficient-market equilibrium, an individual agent might gain from adding technical trading rules to her repertoire of forecasting techniques. Second, using a game theoretic analysis, we show that while the use of technical trading rules (in addition to fundamental rules) is the optimal strategy of a single agent, the use of this strategies by all agents in the market drives the market to a symmetric Nash equilibrium at which wealth is lower for all agents than in a hypothetical equilibrium where all agents use only fundamental rules.

Our explanation of this phenomenon is that the adoption of technical-trading rules by all agents in the market adds to the noise in the market and thus make it more difficult for everyone to predict future stock-price movements than in a regime where only fundamental rules are used. Because their predictions are less accurate, the presence of technical trading makes agents in the market worse off. Thus, our results suggest that technical trading leads to a prisoners' dilemma in which individual decisions lead to an inefficient social outcome.

Section 2 below describes the Santa Fe Artificial Stock Market model that we use in our argument, section 3 explains our experimental framework, sections 4 and 5 present and explain the results of our experiment, and section 6 concludes by explaining the relevance of these results to the real world.

31.2   The Santa Fe Artificial Stock Market

The Santa Fe Artificial Stock Market described in this paper was developed by Brian Arthur, John Holland, Blake LeBaron, Richard Palmer, and Paul Taylor [Palmer, Arthur, Holland, LeBaron and Tayler 1994, Arthur, Holland, LeBaron, Palmer and Tayler 1997, LeBaron, Arthur and Palmer 1998]. It is an agent-based artificial model in which agents continually explore and develop forecasting models, buy and sell assets based on the predictions of those models that perform best, and confirm or discard these models based on their performance over time. At each time period in the market, each agent acts independently, following her currently best models, but the returns to each agent depend on the decisions made simultaneously by all the other agents in the market.

The following sections provide a brief introduction to the Santa Fe Artificial Stock Market model. More detailed descriptions are available elsewhere [Palmer et al. 1994, Arthur et al. 1997, Lebaron et al. 1998, Joshi and Bedau 1998b, Joshi, Parker and Bedau 1999]. When mentioning model parameters below, we indicate the specific parameter values we used in the work reported here with typewriter font inside brackets [like this].

31.2.1 The Market

The market contains a fixed number N [25] of agents each of whom is endowed with an initial sum of money (in arbitrary units) [10000]. Time is discrete. At a given time period each agent decides how to invest between a risky stock and a risk-free asset. The risk-free asset is perfectly elastic in supply and pays a constant interest rate r [10%]. The risky stock, of which there are a total of N shares, pays a stochastic dividend d_t that varies over time according to a stationary first-order autoregressive process with a fixed coefficient [0.95]. The past and current-period realization of the dividend is known to the agents at the time they make their investment decisions.

Agents make their investment decision by forecasting the future price of a stock (described in the next section), and performing a risk aversion calculation. Each agent possesses a constant absolute risk-aversion (CARA) utility function of the form

$$U(W_{i,t+1}) = -\exp(-\lambda W_{i,t+1})$$

where $W_{i,t+1}$ is the wealth of agent i at time $t+1$, and $0 < \lambda[0.5] \leq 1000$. This utility function is maximized subject to the following constraint:

$$W_{i,t+1} = x_{i,t}(p_{t+1} + d_{t+1}) + (1 + r_f)(W_{i,t} - p_t x_{i,t})$$

where $x_{i,t}$ is agent i's the demand for the stock at time period t. Under the assumption that agent i's predictions at time t of the next period's price and dividend are normally distributed with (conditional) mean and variance, $E[p_{t+1} + d_{t+1}]$, and $\sigma^2_{i,t,p+d}$, and the distribution of forecasts is normal, agent i's demand for the stock at time t, should be [Arthur et al. 1997]:

$$x_{i,t} = \frac{E_{i,t}(p_{t+1} + d_{t+1}) - p(1 + r)}{\lambda \sigma^2_{i,t,p+d}}$$

The bids and offers submitted by agents need not be integers; the stock is perfectly divisible. The aggregate demand for the stock must equal number of shares in the market.

Agents submit their decisions to the market *specialist*—an extra agent in the market who functions as a market maker (see [Arthur et al. 1997] for details of the market clearing process).

31.2.2   Market Forecasting Rules

Forecasts made by agents, are based on one of a set of [100] forecasting rules, each of which has the following form:

IF (the market meets state D_i) THEN ($a = a_j, b = b_l$)

where D_i is a description of the state of the market, a_j and b_l are constants, and a and b are forecasting parameters. The values of the variables a and b are used to make a linear forecast of next period's price and dividend using the equation:

$$E(p_{t+1} + d_{t+1}) = a(p_t + d_t) + b.$$

The forecasting parameters a and b are initially selected randomly from a uniform distribution of values centered on the values that would create a homogeneous rational-expectations equilibrium in the market [Arthur et al. 1997].

Market descriptors $\{D_i\}$ match certain states of the market by an analysis of the price and dividend history. The descriptors are boolean functions that are represented as an array of bits in which 1 signals that the state has been matched, 0 indicates that the state is not matched, and # indicates that that state is irrelevant for the application of the rule.[1]

The breadth and generality of the market states to which a specific rule applies depends positively on the number of # symbols in its market descriptor; rules with descriptors with many 0s and 1s recognize more narrow and specific market states. An appropriate reflection of the complexity of the population of forecasting rulesis the number of specific market states that their rules can distinguish. This

---

1. Since there are 14 boolean market descriptors, it is possible to distinguish 2^{14} different market states.

is measured by calculating the number of bits that are set to 0 or 1 in the rules' market descriptors.

There are two main categories of market conditions to which descriptors are attached. One pertains to the recent history of the stock price; the descriptors associated with these conditions are called *technical* trading bits. The other main kind of conditions pertains to the relationship between the stock's price and its fundamental value; the descriptors of these conditions are called *fundamental* trading bits. (Two aditional condition bits were set at "always on" and "always off" to reflect the extent to which agents act on useless information.) While trading rules based solely on fundamental conditions and descriptors detect immediate over- or under-valuation of a stock, technical trading rules detect recent patterns of increase or decrease in stock prices and might predict a continuation or reversal of the trend (depending on the associated values of a and b).

The market conditions corresponding to the descriptors in the technical forecasting rules (i.e., rules with some fundamental trading bits set) take one of these two forms:

"Is the price greater than an n period moving-average of past prices?" where $n \in \{5, 20, 100, 500\}$.
"Is the price higher than it was n periods ago?" where $n \in \{5, 20\}$.

The conditions in the fundamental rules (i.e., rules with only fundamental bits set) all take this form:

"Is the price greater than n times its fundamental value?" where $n \in \{\frac{1}{4}, \frac{1}{2}, \frac{3}{4}, \frac{7}{8}, 1, \frac{9}{8}\}$.

In an equilibrium corresponding to the predictions of the efficient markets theory, agents would use only an optimal fundamental rule (based on the actual parameters of the time-series process driving dividends) which would outperform all rules based on technical conditions. Our model differs from this in that agents do not know the parameters of the dividend process, and thus they must experiment with alternative forecasting rules based on fundamental (and perhaps technical) conditions in seeking to improve their forecasts.

Each rule is assigned a meausure of *accuracy*, where the accuracy is defined as the moving-average of the variance of the error (the difference between the forecasted price and the true price). An 'accuracy updating parameter' controls the length of time over which the moving-average is calculated.

If the market state in a given period matches the descriptor of a forecasting rule, the rule is said to be *activated*. A number of an agent's forecasting rules may be activated at a given time, thus giving the agent many possible forecasts to choose from. An agent decides which of the active forecasts to use by choosing at random among the active forecasts with a probability proportional to accuracy. Once the agent has chosen a specific rule to use, the rule's a and b values determine the agent's investment decision.

31.2.3   Evolution of Market Forcasting Rules

A genetic algorithm (GA) provides for the evolution of the population of forecasting rules over time. Whenever the GA is invoked, it substitutes new forecasting rules for a fraction [12%] of the least fit forecasting rules in each agent's pool of rules. A rule's success, or "fitness" is determined by its accuracy and by how complex it is (the GA has a bias against complex rules). New rules are created by first applying the genetic operators of mutation and crossover to the bit strings of the more successful rules in the agent's rule pool. The forecasting parameters a and b of the offspring are a linear combination of the forecasting parameters of the parent rules. New rules are assigned an initial accuracy rating by averaging the accuracy of their parent rules.

The GA may be compared to a real-world consultant. It replaces current poorly performing rules with rules that are likely to perform better much the same way as a consultant urges her client to replace poorly performing trading strategies with those that are likely to be more profitable.

It is important to note that agents in this model learn in two ways: First, as each rule's accuracy varies from time period to time period, each agent preferentially uses the more accurate of the rules available to her; and, second, on an evolutionary time scale, the pool of rules as a whole improves through the action of the genetic algorithm.

31.3   Experimental Methods

In this paper we study one particular aspect of an agent's general strategy for trading in the market: whether technical rules should be included in her collection of forecasting rules. So, in this framework an agent's *strategy* is either to include technical trading rules in her repertoire of trading rules, or to exclude them entirely and instead use only fundamental rules. We restrict our attention to just these two strategies to make our argument simple but realistic. In particular, we exclude the strategy of using *only* technical rules as unrealistic; no matter how much faith people have in technical trading rules, they generally seem to take economic fundamentals into consideration as well.

To investigate whether or not including technical trading rules is advantageous for traders, we contemplate a single agent confronted with a choice between our two strategies. The agent assumes that other traders in the market all follow one or the other of these two strategies—either all include technical trading rules or all exclude them—but the agent does not know which of these two possibilities occurs. Thus, the agent confronts a classic 2×2 decision problem.

To make a rational decision, the agent needs to know the relative value or payoff of each choice in each situation. Our criterion for social and individual welfare is terminal or final wealth.[2] So, to determine the payoffs in the decision matrix, we observed the final wealth of the agent in four different conditions:

A   The agent *includes* technical rules and all other traders *include* them.

B   The agent *includes* technical rules and all other traders *exclude* them.

C   The agent *excludes* technical rules and all other traders *include* them.

D   The agent *excludes* technical rules and all other traders *exclude* them.

By comparing the agent's payoffs in these four possible situations, we can determine whether there is a dominant strategy for this decision.[3]

Note that, since all agents in the market act independently and simultaneously, each time period in the market can be considered to be a multi-person simultaneous-move game. Furthermore, each agent's decision can be construed in exactly the form of the single agent considered above. So, if the single-agent decision considered above has a dominant strategy, it will be rational for all agents to use it and the simultaneous-move game will reach a symmetric Nash equilibrium [Bierman et al. 1993]. Thus, situations **A** and **B** above are the only potential symmetric Nash equilibria in our context.

Expected payoffs in situations **A**–**D** were determined by simulating the artificial market 45 times in the four corresponding circumstances. In each simulation, there were 26 agents in the market: one agent following a given strategy and 25 other agents all following another given strategy (possibly the same strategy as the single agent). Each simulation was run for 300,000 time periods to allow the asymptotic properties of the market to emerge and to reduce the dependence of the results

---

2. The final wealth of an agent in the market includes wealth from all sources: interest payments from the risk free asset, returns from stocks, and cash holdings (money not invested).

3. A dominant strategy is defined as one that outperforms all other strategies *regardless* of the strategies being used by other agents [Bierman and Fernandez 1993].

Table 31.1
The decision table for an agent contemplating whether to include technical trading rules to make her market forecasts, when she is uncertain whether or not the other traders in the market are doing so. The agent's payoff in each of the four situations **A–D** is her expected final wealth (divided by 10^4, to make more readable), derived by averaging the results of 45 simulations of each situation. Errors bounds are calculated using standard deviations of the 45 simulations.

| | | ALL OTHER TRADERS | |
		Technical rules included	Technical rules excluded
THE AGENT	include technical rules	**A**: 113 ± 6.99	**B**: 154 ± 6.68
	exclude technical rules	**C**: 97 ± 6.68	**D**: 137 ± 5.10

on initial conditions. The same 45 random sequences for dividends and initial distributions of rule descriptors among agents were used for all four experiments.

Previous work has shown that the evolutionary learning rate is a crucial parameter controlling the behavior of this model. All our simulations here were carried out at a learning rate of 100, i.e., with the genetic algorithm invoked for each agent once every 100 time periods. We chose this learning rate for two related reasons. First, we wanted to insure that agents had a realistic possibility of *using* technical trading rules. Since previous work [Palmer et al. 1994, Arthur et al. 1997, LeBaron et al. 1998, Joshi et al. 1998a, Joshi et al. 1999] has firmly established that high (statistically significant) technical trading actually occurs in the market only at learning rates in this neighborhood, our experimental design requires us to use such a rate. Furthermore, recent work [Joshi et al. 1999] has shown that agents will *choose* this learning rate if given the choice, for this learning rate maximizes their wealth. Thus, market behavior at radically different learning rates has dubious relevance to our investigation.

31.4   Results

Table 1 shows the expected payoffs to the agent in the four situations **A–D**. These payoffs were calculated by averaging the agent's final wealth in repeated simulations of each of the four situations. This decision matrix supports three conclusions.

First, note that since the payoff in **A** exceeds that in **C** and the payoff in **B** exceeds that in **D**, the agent's dominant strategy is to *include* technical trading rules. No matter what strategy the other agents in the market might be using, it is always advantageous for the agent to include technical trading rules.

Second, since *each* agent in the market faces decision problem described in Table 31.1, a multi-person simultaneous-move game is created. Since including technical trading rules is each agent's dominant strategy, the situation in which all agents include technical trading rules is the one and only symmetric Nash equilibrium of the simultaneous-move game.

Third, note that the expected payoff in situation **A** is less than the expected payoff in situation **D**. Thus, the expected aggregate wealth is less if everyone includes technical trading rules than if everyone excludes them. In other words, everyone is better off if no one includes technical trading rules to their set of forecasting rules. In other words, engaging in technical trading leads the market to a sub-optimal equilibrium.

Thus, technical trading creates a prisoner's dilemma problem in the market. Although it is to the social advantage if everyone foregoes technical trading, each individual has an incentive to cheat. In the aggregate, then, if everyone does what is rational for her, all will engage in technical trading and thus make themselves all worse off.[4]

Figure 31.1 shows time series data from typical simulations of each of the four situations in the decision matrix of our agents and compare how the accumulated wealth of the individual agent compares with that of the rest of the traders. We see the significant advantage in accumulated wealth that technical trading creates in situations **B** and **C**, and we see illustrations of the different final wealth reported in Table 31.1.[5]

31.5 Discussion

These results raise two important questions: (i) Why are agents led to an equilibrium in which everyone uses technical trading rules? (ii) Why is everyone worse off when everyone engages in technical trading rules?

---

4. In [Joshi et al. 1998b], we explore the possibility of a mixed strategies, and show that no mixed strategy is likely to lead the market to the optimal equilibrium.

5. Elsewhere [Joshi et al.1998b] we confirm that in the situations where technical trading is an option (in addition to fundamental trading), technical trading rules are used overwhelmingly. Thus, it is precisely the levels of technical trading that explain the differences in wealth in the four situations.

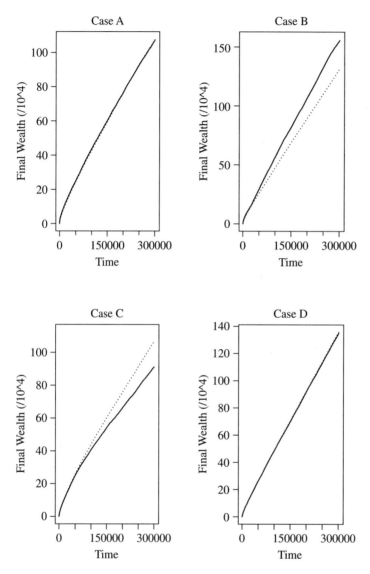

Figure 31.1
Time series data of accumulated wealth from a typical simulation of situation **A-D**, in which all agents *include* technical rules. Solid line shows the wealth of a single agent, and the dotted lines shows the average wealth of all other agents. Note that all agents accumulate equivalent wealth in situations **A** and **D**, the single agent earns significantly lower levels of wealth in situation **C**, and significantly higher wealth than other agents in situation **C**.

We are attracted to the following answer to question (i). Assume that the price stream contains some definite trends. (In the present case, the price trends are due in part at least to the autoregressive form of the dividend stream; recall section 2.1 above. But the same argument applies no matter what causes the price trends.) Assume, further, that some technical trading rules can detect these trends. Then if only a single agent discovers the technical trading rules, she can exploit these trends without dissipating them and thus "beat the market," earning huge profits. But now, as more agents begin to adopt technical rules, the incentives for technical trading can reinforce themselves in a new way. Detailed descriptions of the mechanisms for this are provided elsewhere [Arthur 1988, Arthur 1989, Delong et al. 1990a, Delong et al. 1991, Kirman 1991, Rieck 1994, Youssefmir et al. 1998]. In effect, if enough traders in the market buy into similar enough technical trading rules, positive feedback can make the rules self-fulfilling prophecies. This self-reinforcement process can make technical trading rules more successful in forecasting prices than fundamental rules, which generally predict that prices will return to value. (Evidence of positive-feedback in the Santa Fe stock market has been provided elsewhere [Arthur et al. 1997].)

The mechanism behind this process in the Santa Fe Artificial Stock Market would be the genetic algorithm by which agents' trading rules evolve. If technical trading rules become more successful, even if merely because they happen to be self-fulfilling prophecies, they will be likely to survive the culling process of the GA, and new rules introduced by the GA, their "offspring", will also be technical trading rules.

This answer to question (i) implies an answer to question (ii). The self-fulfilling prophecies created by technical trading dramatically increase the volatility of prices in the market, causing bubbles and crashes [Palmer et al. 1994, Arthur et al. 1997, Joshi et al. 1998a, Joshi et al. 1999]. Though the accuracy of some rules *increases* (those that cause the positive re-enforcement), increased noise over extended periods of time, *decreases* the average accuracy of the forecasting rules being used by agents in the market. The decreased accuracy of forecasting rules, in turn, drives down agents' wealth; less accurate rules are less profitable. The gains from self-reinforcing technical trends are thus short lived; in the long run, correction toward fundamental value bursts the bubbles.

The use of a technical trading rule in the market thus poses a negative externality. It worsens everyone else's strategies by driving prices away from the fundamental value and increasing noise. When all agents choose to perform high technical trading, they worsen each others strategies, there is a loss of efficiency and the average returns in the market are lowered.

These explanations fit well with the results of our experiments. In situation **A** (Figure 31.1a), high technical trading by all agents lowers everyone's wealth, presumably because everyone's predictors are less accurate. In situation **B** (Figure 31.1b), in which only one agent engages in technical trading, she accumulates significantly more wealth than the other agents, but since only one agent is cashing in on price patterns, everyone else's forecasting rules are not rendered inaccurate, so the price patterns do not dissipate in noise. This lack of noise makes the single agent's trend detectors stronger, which is reflected in her high final wealth.

If one agent uses only fundamental rules but everyone else uses technical rules (situation **C**, Figure 31.1c), the fundamental trader is worse off than the other agents. The market is so noisy that fundamental strategies have little value; technical traders are driving short-term price patterns so prices do not obey her fundamental predictions and she ends up worse off.

Situation **D** (Figure 31.1d) is the best global state. All agents in this case rely solely on fundamental rules. The absence of technical trading rules reduces the noise in the market, strengthening the accuracy of agent's predictors, thus leading them to accumulate higher levels of wealth over time.

Statistics of the price stream in the Santa Fe Artificial Stock Market provide further support for these explanations. When all agents use fundamental trading rules alone, agents show behavior that is consistent with the theory of rational expectations. When the price is over-valued, agents predict that the price will fall and thus drive the price down. Consequently, the volatility of prices is low and prices stay close to fundamental values. Trading still occurs because the market is constantly changing. But when agents include technical rules in their pool of forecasting rules, the market becomes unstable. Bubbles and crashes occur frequently. The volatility of prices roughly doubles and prices deviate from fundamental values for extended periods of time, having about a third the correlation compared to when only fundamental trading rules are used.

An alternate explanation of our results reported above is that, when only one agent exploits these patterns in the market, this agent beats the market (as we described above), but if all agents use technical trading rules, they dissipate the patterns, thereby making the market more efficient and allowing the agents to accumulate less wealth. However, we find it difficult to reconcile this explanation with the bubbles, crashes and positive-feedback observed in the market [Palmer et al. 1994, Arthur et al. 1997, Joshi et al. 1998a, Joshi et al. 1999].

We should reiterate that the observed advantage enjoyed by a singular technical trader is no surprise. The autoregressive dividend stream creates structure in the price stream that fundamental traders cannot detect, so a single technical trader can exploit this structure without destroying it. What *is* notable is that the wholesale adoption of technical trading worsens everyone's earnings so much that a prisoner's dilemma is created. Furthermore, the explanation for this result in no way depends what causes price patterns that technical trading exploits. Both real and artificial markets can have many kinds of patterns in prices. No matter how these patterns arise, our results suggest that, while a single trader who discovers these patterns can profit significantly, if all traders discover the patterns they dissipate them by exploiting them, thus lowering profits for all.

31.6   Summary and Conclusion

Our simulations using the Santa Fe Artificial Stock Market suggest that financial markets can end up in a prisoner's dilemma, creating a sub-optimal strategic equilibrium in which extensive technical trading creates market volatility and thus reduces earnings. We show that each agent will choose to include technical trading rules in her repertoire of forecasting rules, even if other traders use only rules based on stock-price fundamentals. Including technical rules is the dominant strategy of the game because it makes each agent better off regardless of what strategy other traders in the market follow.

Because this singular agent's decision is mirrored by a decision for every other trader in the market, we have a multi-person game in which each agent has a dominant strategy. The use of this dominant strategy by all agents in the population, however, drives the market to a symmetric Nash equilibrium at which the average final wealth of agents in the market is lower than in the hypothetical equilibrium in which everyone uses only fundamental trading rules. Our explanation of this reduced wealth is that the wide-spread use of technical trading rules worsens the accuracy of the predictions of all agents by reinforcing price trends, augmenting volatility, and making the market more noisy.

Though the model considered in this paper is an extreme simplification of real-world stock markets, we believe that it captures some essential elements of such markets. Moving away from assumption of rational expectations, with its implication that agents *know* the underlying structure of the stochastic processes driving the model, allows us to mimic the kind of asymmetric model uncertainty and learning that we observe in actual markets. Our market models the process of searching for the ideal forecasting rule explicitly through a mechanical, yet quite sophisticated, learning process. Our analysis leads to an equilibrium outcome of this process—a volatile market in which the use of technical trading rules is pervasive—that mirrors some key aspects of real markets that are contrary to the predictions of some of the most widely accepted models of stock markets.

Much research remains to be done in establishing the robustness of these results to variations both in the model's parameters and in the structural design of the model itself. However, the results obtained in our early explorations point to a conclusion of great potential importance: that technical trading might be inevitable, yet traders would end up better off if it were possible to prevent it.

Acknowledgments

Thanks to the authors of the Santa Fe Artificial Stock Market, especially Richard Palmer and Blake LeBaron, for making their source code available to us and helping us to use it productively. For helpful discussion, thanks to Doyne Farmer, Blake LeBaron, John Moody, Norman Packard, Richard Palmer, and Robert Seymour.

References

Acar, E. and S. Satchell. 1997. *Advanced Trading Rules* (Butterworth-Heinemann, Woburn).

Arthur, W.B. 1988. Self-reinforcing mechanisms in economics, in: P.W. Anderson, K. J. Arrow and D. Pines, eds., *The Economy as an Evolving, Complex System I: Proceedings of the Evolutionary Paths of the Global Economy Workshop* (Addison-Wesley, Redwood City) 15-44.

Arthur, W.B. 1989. Positive feedbacks in the economy, *Scientific American* (February), 92–99.

Arthur, W.B., J.H. Holland, B. LeBaron, R. Palmer, and P. Tayler. 1997. Asset pricing under endogenous expectations in an artificial stock market, in: W. B. Arthur, D. Lane, and S.N. Durlauf, eds., *The Economy as an Evolving, Complex System II*, (Menlo Park, Addison-Wesley).

Bierman, S.H, and L. Fernandez. 1993. *Game Theory with Economic Applications* (Redwood City: Addison-Wesley).

Brock, W., J. Lakonishok, and B. LeBaron. 1992. Simple technical trading rules and the stochastic properties of stock returns, *Journal of Finance* 47,1731–1764.

Campbell, J. Y. and A. Lo. 1997. *The Econometrics of Financial Markets* (Princeton, Princeton University Press).

Cootner, P. 1967. *The Random Character of Stock Market Prices* (Cambridge, MIT Press).

Delong, J.B., A. Shleifer, L.H. Summers, and J. Waldmann. 1990a. Positive feedback and destabilizing rational speculation, *Journal of Finance* 45, 379–395.

Delong, J.B., and A. Shleifer, L.H. Summers and J. Waldmann. 1990b. Noise trader risk in financial markets, *Journal of Political Economy* 98, 703–738.

Delong, J.B., A. Shleifer, L.H. Summers, and J. Waldmann. 1991. The survival of noise traders in financial markets, *Journal of Business* 64, 1–18.

Fama, E.F. 1970. Efficient capital markets: A review of theory and empirical work. *Journal of Finance* 25, 383–420.

Farmer, J.D. 1998. Market force, ecology and evolution, Working Paper 98-12-116E, Santa Fe Institute, Santa Fe NM.

Frankel, J.A., and K.A. Froot. 1990. Chartists, fundamentalists, and trading in the foreign exchange market. *AEA Papers and Proceedings* 80, 181–185.

Joshi, S., and M.A. Bedau. 1998a. An explanation of generic behavior in an evolving financial market, in: R. Standish, B. Henry, S. Watt, R. Marks, R. Stocker, D. Green, S. Keen, and T. Bossomaier, eds., *Complex Systems '98, Complexity Between the Ecos: From Ecology to Economics* (Complexity Online, Sydney) 326–332.

Joshi, S., J. Parker, and M.A. Bedau. 1998b. Technical trading creates a prisoner's dilemma: Results from an agent-based model, Working Paper No. 98-12-115E, Santa Fe Institute, Santa Fe NM, to appear in the proceedings of the *Conference on Computational Finance 1999*.

Joshi, S., J. Parker, and M.A. Bedau. 1999. Financial markets can be at sub-optimal equilibria. Working Paper No. 99-03-023E, Santa Fe Institute, Santa Fe NM.

Keim, D.B. and A. Madhaven. 1995. Anatomy of the trading process: Empirical evidence of the behaviour of institutional traders. *Journal of Financial Economics* 37, 371-398.

Kirman, A. 1991. Epidemics of opinion and speculative bubbles in financial markets. in: M. Taylor, ed., *Money and Financial Markets* (London: Macmillan).

Kurtz, M. 1994. On the structure and diversity of rational beliefs. *Economic Theory* 4, 877–900.

LeBaron, B. 1997. Technical trading rules and regime shifts in foreign exchange markets, in: E. Acar and S. Satchell, eds., *Advanced Trading Rules* (Woburn, Butterworth-Heinemann).

LeBaron, B., W.B. Arthur, and R. Palmer. 1998. Time series properties of an artificial stock market, *Journal of Economic Dynamics and Control*, forthcoming.

Malkiel, B., 1992. Efficient market hypothesis. in: P. Newman, M. Milgate, and J. Eatwell, eds., *New Palgrave Dictionary of Money and Finance* (London: Macmillan Press Limited).

Marengo, L., and H. Tordjman. 1995. Speculation, heterogeneity, and learning: A model of exchange rate dynamics, Working Paper, WP-95-17, IIASA.

Palmer, R.G., W.B. Arthur, J.H. Holland, B. LeBaron, and P. Tayler. 1994. Artificial economic life: a simple model of a stock market, *Physica D* 75, 264–274.

Rieck, C. 1994. Evolutionary simulation of asset trading strategies, in: E. Hillenbrand and J. Stender, eds., *Many Agent Simulation and Artificial Life* (Washington DC: IOS Press).

Samuelson, P. 1965. Proof that properly anticipated prices fluctuate randomly, *Industrial Management Review* 6, 41-49.

Shleifer A. and L.H. Summers. 1990. The noise trader approach to finance. *Journal of Economic Perspectives* 4, 19–33.

Schwager, J.D. 1995. *Technical Analysis* (New York, John Wiley and Sons).

Shiller, R. 1989. *Market Volatility* (Cambridge, MIT Press).

Soros, G., 1994, *The Theory of Reflexivity* (New York: Soros Fund Management).

Werner, F.M., deBondt, and R. H. Thaler. 1995. Financial decision making in markers and firms: A behavioral perspective, in: R. Jarrow et al., eds., *Handbooks in OR & MS*, Vol. 9 Elsevier Science.

Youssefmir M., B. Huberman, and T. Hogg. 1998. Bubbles and market crashes. *Computational Economics* 12, 97-114.

32 Cycles of Market Stability and Instability Due to Endogenous Use of Technical Trading Rules

David Goldbaum

A model is examined in which traders endogenously select from available information sources in order to maximize expected profits. The information options include fundamentals and a technical trading rule. The trading rule earns profits for the users as long as the demand of the fundamental traders sets the market price. Under certain model parameters, success by the trading rule increases its popularity. Excessive popularity of the trading rule destabilizes the market, causing a price bubble to develop. The bubble's collapse reduces the trading rule's popularity and returns the market to stability as the fundamental traders again set the price.

Academics in economics and finance typically discount evidence of the usefulness of technical trading rules. The Efficient Markets Hypothesis provides the theoretical foundation with which technical trading rules are rejected. Market efficiency suggests that market prices reflect the most recently available information. Thus, in an environment of efficient markets, past price patterns cannot be used to forecast future returns. Technical trading rules, which provide the user with a signal of when to buy or sell an asset based on such price patterns, should not be useful for generating excess returns.

Despite academic admonitions, as Taylor and Allen (1992) document, use of technical trading rules is widespread. The users of technical trading rules (e.g. technical traders and chartists) tend to put little faith in strict efficient markets. In particular, users of trend following rules describe how the market can be slow to reach a new equilibrium after the arrival of new information. Evidence of slow asset price adjustment can be found in Rendleman, Jones, and Latané (1982). Users claim that technical trading rules provide an indication of when those with the superior information have begun to trade and what position they are taking in the market. With a quick enough response, the technical trader is able to imitate the actions of those with the superior information, before the market price completes its adjustment, without necessarily learning what changed in the fundamental value of the asset. The opportunity to make a profit is lost if the trader waits to receive the fundamental information, since he will not likely receive it until long after the price adjustment is complete, if at all.

For this paper, a model is developed and examined in which individual boundedly rational optimizing behavior leads to inefficiencies in an asset market which can be exploited through use of a technical trading rule. The objectives for this paper are to examine the profitability of the technical trading rules in the market and to examine the impact of the technical trading rule on the market. In the model, each trader chooses from a menu of information sources, selecting the one he or she believe to be the most beneficial for the next period of trading. In selecting an information source, traders consider which information source appears to be best for the period dependent on the current state of the market. The examination of the model is accomplished through a computer simulation.

32.1   The Model

The model is developed with the aim of creating an environment in which market participants reasonably choose to rely on a technical trading rule, at least under certain conditions. A thorough mathematical derivation of the model and the governing equations that are used in the computer simulation are provided in Goldbaum (1999). The text that follows summarizes this model.

32.1.1   The Market

A large but finite number of agents, indexed by $i = 1, \ldots, N$, trade a risky asset and a risk free asset. In time period t, after receiving a private information signal, the trader purchases $a_{i,t}$ units of the risky asset at price p_t and $b_{i,t}$ units of the risk free bond. The risk free bond, with a price of one, pays R. In period $t+1$, the risky asset pays a stochastic dividend d_{t+1} and traders sell the asset for the market determined price, p_{t+1}. The dividend follows a random walk:

$$
\begin{aligned}
d_{t+1} &= d_t + \varepsilon_{t+1}, & (32.1) \\
\varepsilon_{t+1} &\sim IIDN(0, \sigma_d^2).
\end{aligned}
$$

The available sources of information include two signals based on fundamental information about the risky asset. One of these is free and the other is costly but superior. A third option is to use a technical trading rule (TTR) which provides the investor with a buy or sell signal based on past and present price patterns.

32.1.2   The Fundamental Trader

Traders who choose to receive a signal based on fundamental information are modeled as selecting a portfolio to maximize a negative exponential utility function, conditional on the given information set $H_{i,t}$,

$$
\begin{aligned}
&\max\{E[-\exp(-\gamma w_{i,t+1})|H_{i,t}]\} \\
&\text{s.t., } p_t a_{i,t} + b_{i,t} = w_{i,t} & (32.2) \\
&\qquad w_{i,t+1} = (p_{t+1} + d_{t+1})a_{i,t} + R b_{i,t}.
\end{aligned}
$$

Let z_{t+1} be the excess payoff of risky asset over what would have been earned purchasing bonds, $z_{t+1} = p_{t+1} + d_{t+1} - Rp_t$. Under the assumption that returns are normally distributed, the demand for the risky asset is the expectation of z_{t+1} divided by γ time the variance of z_{t+1}. Demand is thus

$$a_{i,t} = \frac{E[z_{t+1}|H_{i,t}]}{\gamma \text{var}(p_{t+1} + d_{t+1}|H_{i,t})}. \tag{32.3}$$

A subset of $H_{i,t}$ is the shared common information set $I_t = \{d_t, p_{t-1}, vol_{t-1}\}$ where *vol* stands for the volume of trading. The private component of $H_{i,t}$ is the signal, $y_{i,t}$. The private signal provides the recipient with an indication of next period's dividend payment. Each trader's signal has an idiosyncratic component. In addition, all signals received by the traders are subject to a shared random "macro" bias. Further, the inferior information source is subject to a market "fad," or rumor bias. Those who spend the resources can avoid the rumor by obtaining the superior signal:

Superior Signal 1: $y1_{i,t} = d_{t+1} + \omega_t + e1_{i,t}$, with $e1_{i,t} \sim IIDN(0, \sigma_1^2)$, $\tag{32.4}$

Inferior Signal 2: $y2_{j,t} = d_{t+1} + \omega_1 + \psi_t + e2_{j,t}$, with $e2_{j,t} \sim IIDN(0, \sigma_2^2)$.

The macro bias, ω_t, is distributed $IIDN(o, \sigma_\omega^2)$ and the rumor bias evolves based on the process

$$\psi_t = \phi_t \psi_{t-1} + \eta_t, \tag{32.5}$$

$\eta_t \sim IIDN(0, \sigma_\eta^2), \phi_t = (n_t^2)^{1/2}\varphi$, and $0 \le \varphi \le 1$.

The rumor in period t is built upon the rumor of period $t - 1$. The strength of this interaction is based on n_t^2, the proportion of the population using the inferior Signal 2 at time period t.

Recognizing that both private signals are noisy signals of the future dividend, the trader's optimal forecast of d_{t+1} relies on a weighted combination of the received signal and the unconditional expectation. The combination minimizes the expected squared error of the forecast.

$$E[d_{t+1}|H_{i,t}^k] = (1 - \beta_k)d_t + \beta_k yk_{i,t}, k = \{1, 2\} \tag{32.6}$$

with

$$\beta_1 \equiv \text{cov}(d_{t+1}, y1_{i,t})/\text{var}(y1_{i,t}) = \frac{\sigma_d^2}{\sigma_d^2 + \sigma_\omega^2 + \sigma_1^2} \tag{32.7}$$

$$\beta_2 \; \equiv \; \mathrm{cov}(d_{t+1}, y2_{i,t})/\mathrm{var}(y2_{i,t}) = \frac{\sigma_d^2}{\sigma_d^2 + \sigma_\omega^2 + \sigma_\psi^2 + \sigma_2^2}.$$

32.1.3   The Technical Trader

One easily implemented and commonly computed technical trading rule is a Simple Moving Average rule. The rule provides a "buy" or "sell" signal based on whether the current price is above or below a moving average of the price computed over a given length of time. The time-series created, ttr_t, has a value of 1 in the event that p_t is greater than the moving average (buy) or -1 in the event that p_t is less than the moving average (sell). A number of variations of the moving average trading rule were examined, including different length moving averages and using bands around the moving average (the "Envelope" trading rule). There are some interesting differences in the profitability of the trading rules explored in Goldbaum (1999), but with regards to the present limited investigation, they all have essentially the same impact on the market. The trading rule discussed in the results section has a moving average length of 12 periods.

The individual trader using the TTR needs a demand function based on the signal. For simplicity of implementation, I set the volume of demand of each technical trader (vol^3) to a fixed value. The trader using the trading rule has demand

$$a_t^{TTR} = vol^3 \cdot ttr_r. \tag{32.8}$$

32.1.4   Determining the Market Price

Let $\bar{a}_t^1$, $\bar{a}_t^2$, and $\bar{a}_t^3$ represent the period t average demand by Group 1 traders using Signal 1, by Group 2 traders using Signal 2, and by Group 3 traders using the TTR respectively. The proportion of the population in each group is represented by n_t^1, n_t^2, and n_t^3. With supply set exogenously to zero, equilibrium market clearing conditions require

$$0 = n_t^1 \bar{a}_t^1 + n_t^2 \bar{a}_t^2 + n_t^3 \bar{a}_t^3 \tag{32.9}$$

in each period t. In forming expectations of the next period's price as part of determining demand, traders conjecture that the price is determined by a linear function of the distinguishable group level informations underlying the private signals:

$$p_t = b_0 + b_1 d_t + b_2(d_{t+1} + \omega_t) + b_3 \psi_t. \tag{32.10}$$

In the posterior, this conjecture is correct. The last three terms of the price equations capture the influence of the fundamental traders. The intercept, b_0, reflects the impact of the demand by the group of technical traders.

32.1.5 Selecting an Information Source

Prior to receiving one's private signal, the trader must select a source. Based on the shared information in I_t, traders form an expectation of the profitability of relying on each of the information sources for the next period of trading, $E(\pi_t^k), k = 1, 2, 3$. A comparison of these forecasts determines which information signal the trader receives. In considering between the two fundamental signals, the trader's concern is in the quality of Signal 2, i.e. how far the rumor is from reality. In order to ascertain the quality of Signal 2, the trader recognizes that trading volume increases with the discrepancy in the beliefs of the traders. Since period t's rumor is based on the rumor circulating during $t - 1$, the traders can make an estimate at the magnitude of the rumor based on observed trading volume. With the estimate of the magnitude of the bias, the trader can compute expected profits of receiving each signal. Expected profits for Signal 1 are increasing in the magnitude of the bias, and expected profits for Signal 2 are decreasing,

$$E[\pi_t^1] = f_1 \left(\frac{n_{t-1}^1}{n_{t-1}^1 + n_{t-1}^2}, \beta_1 - \beta_2, \hat{\psi}_t^2, c \right) \tag{32.11}$$

$$\qquad\qquad\quad - \qquad\quad + \quad + \ -$$

$$\text{and } E[\pi_t^2] = f_2 \left(\frac{n_{t-1}^1}{n_{t-1}^1 + n_{t-1}^2}, \beta_1 - \beta_2, \hat{\psi}_t^2 \right).$$

$$\qquad\qquad\qquad\quad + \qquad\quad - \quad -$$

Of course, in estimating profits, the trader must account for the cost, c, of obtaining a rumor free signal.

The expected profit from using each of the fundamental information sources is compared to the performance evaluation of the technical trading rule. Traders use a weighted average of the past performance of the trading rule to form an estimate of its success in the present period.

$$E_t[\pi_t^3] = v\pi_{t-2}^3 + (1 - v)E_{t-1}[\pi_{t-1}^3], \tag{32.12}$$

where v indicates the weight placed on the most recent observations of profits.[1]

The individual trader's final choice is modeled as a randomized discrete choice in the nature of Manski and McFadden (1981) and Anderson, de Palma, and Thisse (1992). Applying the LLN to the individual probabilities, the proportion of the population choosing each signal is equal to the probability that individual traders choose that signal. Thus,

$$n_t^1 = \frac{\exp(\rho \cdot E_{t-1}[\pi_t^1])}{Z_t}, n_t^2 = \frac{\exp(\rho \cdot E_{t-1}[\pi_t^2])}{Z_t}, n_t^3 = \frac{\exp(\rho \cdot E_{t-1}[\pi_t^3])}{Z_t} \quad (32.13)$$

$$Z_t = \exp(\rho E_{t-1}[\pi_t^1]) + \exp(\rho E_{t-1}[\pi_t^2]) + \exp(\rho E_{t-1}[\pi_t^3]).$$

The greater the expected benefit of one signal over the others, the higher the proportion of traders who choose to use that signal. How sensitive the population is to differences in the expected profits is set according the "intensity of choice" parameter, ρ.[2] The greater the value of ρ, the greater the sensitivity of traders to differences in expected profits of each signal. With $\rho \to \infty$, small differences in the expected profits are very important to the traders so that the model choice approaches full rationality with all traders choosing the signal with the highest expected profit for that period. With ρ set to zero, differences in the expected profits are ignored. The population of traders split evenly between the information options, regardless of which has the highest expected profit.

Once traders select their information source for the period, individual signals are received. Equation 32.3 indicates how the fundamental traders use their expectations of excess returns to determine a demand function. Equation 32.8 indicates the shared demand of the technical traders. All traders submit their demand function to the market. The market price for the risky asset, p_t, is determined to clear the demand of all three trading groups. The period ends with traders carrying out their transactions, selling their holdings from the previous period and purchasing their portfolio to hold into the next period.

32.2 Simulation Results

The main result discussed in this section is how the "intensity of choice" parameter influences the market. A number of the parameters are kept unchanged for the

1. The $t-2$ profit is the most recently observed. The $t-1$ profit has yet to be determined since the time t price is, as yet, undetermined.

2. Setting ρ identifies the standard deviation of the randomized component of the individual agent's expectations of profit.

different executions. These are:

$$\sigma_d^2 = 1, \varphi = 0.9, \sigma_\eta^2 = 0.057, \sigma_\omega^2 = 0.7, \sigma_2^2 = 1, \sigma_1^2 = \sigma_2^2 \sigma_\psi^2 + 0.08 = 1.38,$$
$$R = 1.02, \gamma = 1, v = 0.3, vol^3 = 0.0002, \beta_1 = 0.3247, \beta_2 = 1/3, T = 20,000.$$

For consistency, each simulation is executed using the same set of underlying stochastic shocks.

Figures 32.1 and 32.3 plot the time trends of a number of variables during a 50 period window of the simulation. The differences between Figures 32.1 and 32.3 demonstrate how ρ impacts the functioning of the market. Each figure displays the same 50 periods, from $t = 8150$ to 8200. The top frame in each figure plots the market price (solid line), and the Rational Expectations Equilibrium (REE) price. The middle frame shows the average profits for the traders using each trading strategy: π_t^1, π_t^2, and π_t^3. The bottom frame plots the proportion of the population using each of the strategies: n_t^1, n_t^2, and n_t^3. In the second and third frame, the solid line represents traders using Signal 1, the long dashed line represents traders using Signal 2, and the short dashed line represents traders using the TTR.

In adjusting ρ, the simulation results fall into two categories. A low ρ causes the population proportions to remain near one third for each information source since traders have little concern over the differences in expected profits between the information sources. As a result, the popularity of the technical trading rule remains small. Traders using the TTR have only a small influence on the market price with the price primarily set by the demand of the fundamental traders. The primary source of disagreement on the value of the stock is from the two groups of fundamental traders so that they always take opposite positions in the market. The technical traders simply follow whichever fundamental group is trading consistent with the TTR signal.

These market characteristics are captured in Figure 32.1 where ρ is set to 80. In the bottom frame, it can be seen that each information source is used by roughly one third of the population. The top frame shows that the market price stays relatively close to the REE. The middle frame shows that the two groups of fundamental traders typically make opposite signed profits. This reveals that they are taking opposing positions in the market.

In the simulation that generates Figure 32.1, selective use of the TTR can generate superior average profits over reliance on the fundamental information sources. In an environment where the price is near the REE, price movements are primarily the result of changes in the underlying fundamental value of the asset. The TTR exploits this to earn a profit. Figure 32.2 shows average profits based

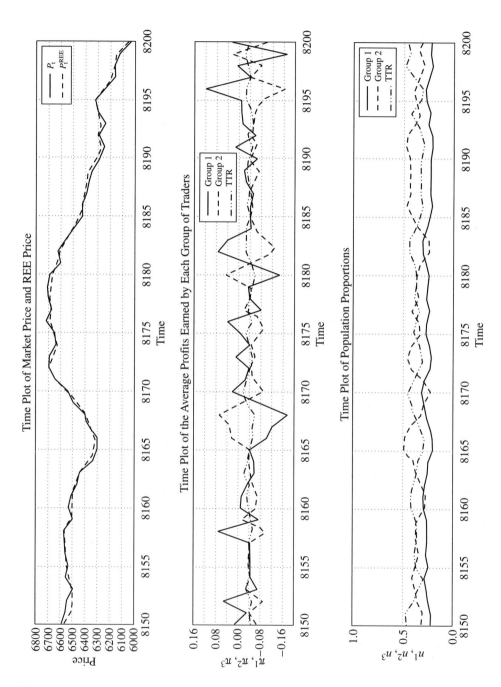

Figure 32.1
Selected time-series: $\rho = 80$

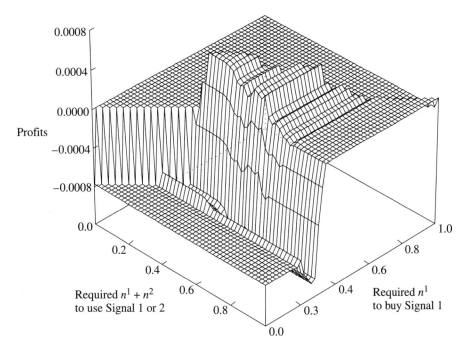

Figure 32.2
Average profits earned through selective use of each information source

on the propensity of a trader to use each of the three information sources. Along the front left edge of the surface is the return based on sole reliance on Signal 1. Along the front right edge is sole reliance on the TTR. Across the middle along the diagonal are the average returns from relying on Signal 2. Within these boundaries are the average profits received through selective use of each information source. The raised triangular region in the middle of the surface indicates that mixed use of the TTR and the fundamental information earns competitively high profits.

When ρ is set to a higher level, the popularity of each of the information sources is more sensitive to its expected performance. As can be seen in Figure 32.3, with ρ set to 250, there is more substantial movement in the population switching between the information sources. At times the TTR is the dominant choice. Most of the movement is between the TTR and the fundamental information sources, with Signal 2 being preferred to Signal 1. The large influence the technical traders have on price and expected profit dwarfs the differences in the beliefs of the fundamental traders caused by the rumor bias. This results in little movement between the two fundamental information sources.

A trend in the dividend process, either increasing or decreasing, creates the potential for a price bubble to develop. This, in turn, increases the popularity of the trading rule. Consider an example of increasing dividends. During the dividend's growth, the TTR correctly issues a series of buy signals. The popularity of the TTR grows with the repeated correct signals to the extent that a large population of technical traders develops, all buying as a result of the signal. The impact on the market is to push the price to rise more quickly than does the underlying value so that a price bubble forms. The growth of the price bubble and the popularity of the TTR are interdependent. The bubble increases the profits of the TTR and thus contributes to its popularity and the popularity of the TTR increases the magnitude of the bubble. The bubble collapses if the trend in the dividend reverses, or it may simply dissipate if dividend growth slows or stops without reversing. The negative returns during a collapse again reduce the attractiveness of the trading rule and the market returns to a more stable condition.

An example of a (negative) price bubble induced by the popularity of the TTR occurs between the times $t = 8163$ to 8166 during which the market price undervalues the risky asset as its true value falls. The bubble's collapse takes place during 8167 and 8168 when the trend in dividends reverses. Based on their holdings set in 8166, the few remaining fundamental traders earn extraordinary profits when the bubble begins to collapse in 8167. An example of a price bubble which deflates rather than bursting runs from 8189 through 8193.

When ρ is set high enough for price bubbles to develop, those traders who stay exclusively with the fundamental information earn, on average, positive profits while those who employ the trading rule earn, on average, negative profits.

32.3   Concluding Remarks

The technical trading rule can perform well in a market which is dominated by fundamentals. Employing a noisy fundamental signal generates a degree of precautionary skepticism about the private signal. This prevents a trader, or any group of traders, from employing unlimited resources to instantaneously move the market to the new REE. Technical traders then have the opportunity to engage in trading that replicates that of the better informed traders by observing price movement to indicate the direction of trade.

David Goldbaum

491

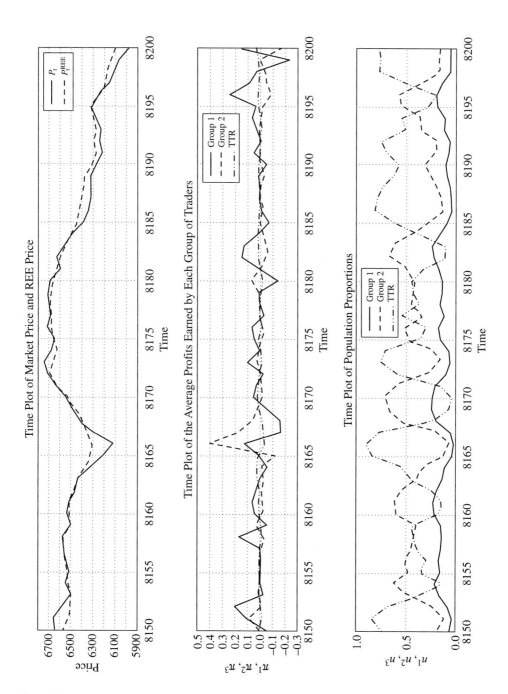

Figure 32.3
Selected time-series: $\rho = 250$

The TTR is profitable and the market remains stable as long as the popularity of the TTR does not grow to dominate the market price. When the traders' information selection decisions are highly influenced by recent successes of the TTR, a cycle can develop. A series of successful TTR signals can increase the popularity of the TTR to a level where it exerts a distortionary force on the market, moving the price away from its fundamental value. Thus, the TTR can cause price bubbles to develop. The TTR performs particularly poorly when these bubbles collapse. The poor performance leads to a decrease in the popularity, returning the market to a condition where the price is dominated by fundamentals.

Acknowledgments

I wish to thank Blake LeBaron, William Brock, Mark Ready, and Ka-fu Wong for their useful comments during the early stages of this project. This work was partially conducted while visiting at George Washington University and I am grateful for its hospitality.

References

Anderson, Simon P., André de Palma, and Jacques-François Thisse, 1992. *Discrete Choice Theory of Product Differentiation* (MIT Publishers, Cambridge, MA.).

Arthur, W. Brian, John H. Holland, Blake LeBaron, Richard Palmer, and Paul Tayler, 1997. "Asset Pricing Under Endogenous Expectations in an Artificial Stock Market," in W.B. Arthur, D. Lane, and S.N. Durlauf, eds., *The Economy as an Evolving, Complex System II* (Addison-Wesley, Menlo Park, CA) pp. 15–44.

Blume, Lawrence, David Easley, and Maureen O'Hara, 1994. "Market Statistics and Technical Analysis: The Role of Volume," *The Journal of Finance*, 49(1), pp. 153–181.

Brock, William A, and Cars H. Hommes, 1995. "Rational Routes to Randomness" *Econometrica*, 65(5), pp. 1059–1095.

Brock, William, Josef Lakonishok, and Blake D. LeBaron, 1992. "Simple Technical Trading Rules and the Stochastic Properties of Stock Returns" *The Journal of Finance*, 47(5), pp. 1731–1764.

Brock, William A., and Blake D. LeBaron, 1996. "A Dynamic Structural Model for Stock Return Volatility and Trading Volume," *The Review of Economics and Statistics*, 78(1), pp. 94–110.

Brown, David P., and Robert H. Jennings, 1989. "On Technical Analysis" *The Review of Financial Studies*, 2(4), pp. 527–551.

Goldbaum, David H., 1999, "Profitability and Market Stability: Fundamentals and Technical Trading Rules," Rutgers University at Newark Working paper.

Grundy, Bruce D., and Maureen McNichols, 1989. "Trade and the Revelation of Information through Prices and Direct Disclosure," *The Review of Financial Studies*, 2(4), pp. 495–526.

Manski, C.F., and McFadden, D., 1981. *Structural Analysis of Discrete Data with Econometric Applications* (MIT Press, Cambridge, MA.).

Rendleman, R., C. Jones, and H. Latané, 1982. "Empirical Anomalies Based on Unexpected Earnings and the Importance of Risk Adjustments" *Journal of Financial Economics*, 10(3), pp. 269–287.

Sargent, Thomas, 1993. *Bounded Rationality*, (Oxford Press, New York, NY.).

Taylor, Mark P., and Helen Allen, 1992. "The Use of Technical Analysis in the Foreign Exchange Market." *Journal of International Money and Finance*, 11, 304–314.

Treynor, Jack L., and Robert Ferguson, 1985. "In Defense of Technical Analysis" *Journal of Finance*, 40, 757–772.

33 Relative Performance of Incentive Mechanisms in Delegated Investments: A Computational Study

T. S. Raghu, H. R. Rao, and P. K. Sen

This paper addresses the issue of motivating investment managers in a delegated investment setting where moral hazard is present due to effort and risk aversion of agents. Specifically, we evaluate the relative performance of two incentive mechanisms, both of which are linear in outcome but differ in agent's liability in case of a loss. The multi-period nature of the problem makes it analytically intractable and therefore, we use a computational modeling approach under controlled experimental conditions to simulate comparative solutions for the contracts under different parametric settings. We consider multiple homogeneous agents who decide their investment strategy over several consecutive periods. Agents learn about estimation uncertainty through repeated realizations of investment returns. Results of the computational experiments are presented. Our results indicate a significant improvement in the investment performance results from offering a limited liability contract to the agents.

33.1 Introduction

We examine the problem of delegated portfolio investment when a number of homogeneous agents compete for capital in a multi-period setting. Agents are subject to moral hazard due to their effort and risk aversion and they learn about the estimation environment through past realization of investment returns. The very nature of this problem makes it analytically intractable and we use computational modeling to simulate comparative solutions for the specific contracts. Specifically, we evaluate the implications of limited liability in the agent's contract by comparing investment performance under two contracts, which are linear in outcome but differ in the way they impose liability to the investment managers in the event of a loss. By studying the investment performance of the agents over a period of time we make statistical inferences on how these two contracts, that differ only in the liability placed on the agents, influence investor welfare. In addition, we examine how the risk sharing and incentive effects under different levels of market uncertainty affect the investment managers' investment strategy. We find that under different conditions of risk aversion and market uncertainty, the agency problems induce the agents to substitute between unsystematic and systematic risk, thereby resulting in an inefficient resource allocation in their portfolio.

Though, the problem of delegated investments has been studied under a number of different settings, we focus our attention on the use of linear contracts. Cohen and Starks (1988) investigate the impact of a linear contracting scheme on the principal-agent relation. They use a variant of the Capital Asset Pricing Model (CAPM) where the investment manager chooses the distribution parameters of the portfolio.

The investment manager's effort reduces the risk associated with the estimation of the beta of the portfolio. The model uses a mean-variance utility function with a linear contract. For a linear contract, the model predicts that the principal would choose an agent who is less risk averse than the principal. An important result of the paper is that the agent would choose higher risk and higher effort than what the principal prefers when the manager is globally less risk averse than the principal.

The model used in this paper closely follows that of Cohen and Starks (1988), yet is different in two important ways. First, in spite of the popularity of linear contracts in analytical papers [Cohen and Starks (1988), Stoughton (1993)], these contracts are somewhat removed from reality since they assign unlimited liability to the agents. Therefore, in our paper we specifically introduce limited liability such that although the incentive contract is linear in portfolio returns on the positive side, it does not result in any loss to managers in case of portfolio losses. Second, we consider multiple homogeneous agents who learn about the estimation uncertainty through their investments over multiple periods.

The rest of the paper is organized as follows: in Section 2, we describe the economic scenario and the model formulation. Section 3 presents the computational implementation of the economic model presented in Section 2. Section 4 describes the experimental setup. Section 5 presents and discusses the results of the computational experiment. Finally, we make some concluding remarks and note some future research issues in Section 6.

33.2   Model Formulation

33.2.1   The Economic Scenario

The economic model used here closely follows that of Cohen and Starks (1988), with an important exception. As explained earlier, we also consider a linear contract with limited liability. The delegated investment process is organized in the form of a two level organizational hierarchy, with an investor (principal) at one level and several investment analysts (homogeneous agents) at the other, who together as a team constitute the set of decision-makers. The principal's decision-problem is to allocate resources (capital) among the investment analysts and select incentive contracts so as to maximize the returns from the investment analysts' actions. The interaction between the principal and the agents takes place over multiple periods.

The sequence of activities between the agents and the principal in each period is depicted in Figure 33.1.

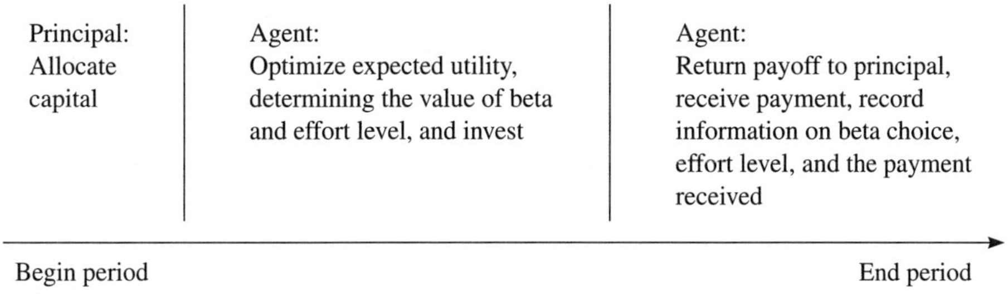

Principal:	Agent:	Agent:
Allocate capital	Optimize expected utility, determining the value of beta and effort level, and invest	Return payoff to principal, receive payment, record information on beta choice, effort level, and the payment received

Begin period   End period

Figure 33.1
Sequence of activities performed by the principal and the agents

33.2.2 Model Formulation

Consider a firm with an owner (principal) and N investment analysts (agents). Let **A** denote the actions of the individuals and $\mathbf{A}_o$ denote the action of the principal. The principal's action is to allocate some resource Q to the N agents (the resource is the capital in the delegated investments scenario) [Radner (1987)]. Thus,

$$\mathbf{A}_o = (Q_0, Q_1, Q_2, Q_3 \ldots Q_N), \tag{33.1}$$

Where Q_i is the resource allocated to the ith agent (index $i = 0$, implies the reference is made to the principal). Q_0 is the amount the principal retains to invest in a risk free asset.

$$Q \;=\; Q_0 + Q_1 + Q_2 + Q_3 \ldots + Q_N \text{ and} \tag{33.2}$$
$$Q_i \;\geq\; 0 \qquad \forall i = 0, 1, 2, \ldots N.$$

The returns on the capital allocated is assumed to be normally distributed and are modeled according to the Capital Asset Pricing Model (CAPM) as shown below:

$$E(R_i) = R_f + (E(R_m) - R_f)\text{Beta}_i, \text{ where} \tag{33.3}$$

$$
\begin{aligned}
R_i &= \text{Rate of return for portfolio } i, \\
R_f &= \text{Risk free rate of return,} \\
R_m &= \text{Market rate of return, and} \\
\text{Beta}_i &= \text{Portfolio } i\text{'s beta value.}
\end{aligned}
$$

We assume investors hold a well-diversified portfolio and therefore, the correlation coefficient between the market rate of returns and the portfolio returns is assumed to be 1 [Cohen and Starks (1988)]. The portfolio's beta value, Beta_i, from Cohen and

Starks (1988) is considered to be random variable with mean β_1 and variance β_i^2. Further, it is assumed that the agent's effort reduces the estimation risk associated with the Beta$_i$ value, and the resulting variance of the Beta$_i$ value is given by β_i^2/A_i. Where, A_i is the effort exerted by the agent i.

The equation 33.3 can therefore be rewritten as [Cohen and Starks (1988)],

$$R_i = R_f + (R_m - R_f + \sigma_m z_m)(\beta_i + z_i\beta_i/\sqrt{A_i}) \tag{33.4}$$

where, z_m, and z_i are i.i.d. standard normal random variables. The term σ_m, denotes the market uncertainty which the agent does not control and which is assumed to be unknown to both the principal and the agents at the time of specifying the incentive contract.

An investment analyst's effort is assumed to include all activities involved in the analysis of investment opportunities, trading the investment products in the markets to minimize transaction costs as well as to maximize returns from the portfolios. It is assumed that an investment analyst's effort reduces the risk (variance) involved in the estimation of the beta of the portfolio and thus has an effect on the magnitude of returns generated as well. The principal's problem is to maximize the returns generated by the team of investment analysts by motivating them to make prudent investment decisions and provide an appropriate level of effort.

From equations 33.2 and 33.4, the outcome generated by agent i, is given by

$$M_i = R_i * Q_i, and \tag{33.5}$$

the total return of the principal

$$M = M_0 + M_1 + M_2 + M_3 \ldots + M_N \tag{33.6}$$

The principal pays the agents some compensation C_i, based on the outcome that is generated by the agents.

Therefore, agent i's compensation C_i is given by

$$C_i = W_i(M_i, R_i), \text{ where } W \text{ is an incentive function.} \tag{33.7}$$

Note that $W_0(M_0) + W_1(M_1) + W_2(M_2) + \ldots + W_N(M_N) = M$, i.e., the principal only shares a portion of the wealth generated with the agents. This budget breaking property is a desirable feature for team incentives as argued by Holmstrom (1982).

The agent's decision-problem is to choose an appropriate level of portfolio β_i and a level of effort A_i. The agent is assumed to be risk averse and effort averse and maximizes a utility function that is additively separable in payoff and effort for a given incentive contract. We assume a negative exponential utility function in wealth and a quadratic function of effort aversion as follows.

$$U_i(C_i, A_i) = U(\text{Wealth}) - U(\text{Effort}) \tag{33.8}$$
$$U_i(C_i, A_i) = -e^{-\gamma C_i} - K A_i^2$$

Here, γ is the constant absolute risk aversion (CAR) parameter and K is scaling parameter for effort aversion. The agents maximize the above utility function by choosing an appropriate value of β_i (See equations 33.4 and 33.7) and A_i. Therefore, the agent's action set is defined as

$$\mathbf{A}_i = (\beta_i, A_i) \tag{33.9}$$

The principal's utility is assumed to be linear in returns minus the payments made to the agents. We assume repeated interaction between the principal and the agents over a number of periods. Further, when several choices for agent action, $\mathbf{A}_i$, exist, it is assumed that the agent will choose the action that maximizes the principal's utility.

It is clear from the above formulation that the agent's choice set $\mathbf{A}_i$, is influenced by the type of incentives set in place by the principal. The two specific incentive contracts tested in this paper are described in the section below.

33.2.3   Incentive Contracts

We test two different linear incentive contracts in this paper, namely, the pure linear contract of [Cohen and Starks (1988)] (Unlimited liability) and that of linear contract with limited liability as used in papers such as [Feltham and Xie (1994)]. The contracts are explained in detail below.

1. **Limited-liability:** Under this incentive scheme the agent receives a commission based on the portfolio return. No commission is paid if the portfolio return results in a loss. Thus, the payment received by the agent is linear in returns if returns are positive. The contract is expressed as follows.

$$C_i = 0 \qquad \text{for } R_i \leq 0 \tag{33.10}$$
$$C_i = \alpha R_i \qquad \text{elsewhere.}$$

2. **Unlimited-liability:** Under this incentive scheme the agent's payment is linear in portfolio returns. Thus, any portfolio loss results in the agent making payments to the principal based on the slope of the linear rate. The contract is expressed as follows.

$$C_i = \alpha R_i \qquad \forall R_i \tag{33.11}$$

33.2.4   Agent's Expected Utility Optimization

Under our scenario, each agent uses the information from investments and payoffs
realized in the previous periods and regresses his choice of beta level and effort
level against derived utility to make an expected utility maximizing choice. Agents
record information related to returns generated, payments received, their effort and
portfolio beta choices privately, i.e., each agent has his own information repository.
Therefore, while agents are ex-ante homogeneous in their utility functions, their
particular choice of effort and portfolio beta levels in subsequent periods may be
dependent on the outcome of the payoff function and beta realization in equation
33.4. Since the agents are assumed to have an approximate knowledge of this payoff
function, the payoff is estimated by a regression function, that regresses the choice
of portfolio beta levels and effort levels against the realized returns. Using the
expected returns and the incentive contract terms, the agent estimates his expected
utility as in equation 33.8. The agent maximizes his expected utility by choosing an
appropriate value of β_i and A_i. Conceptually, each agent i believes that the security
returns are generated by a regression function of the following form:

$$E(R_i) = C_1 + C_2\beta_i + C_3\beta_i^2 + C_4\beta_i^2/A_i + e \text{ where,} \tag{33.12}$$

C_1, C_2, C_3, and C_4 are regression coefficients, which are estimated during each
period, e is the regression residual term.

The following algorithm is followed by each agent.

1. Estimate regression coefficients C_1, C_2, C_3, and C_4 with the data gathered
   from period 0 to the current period.
2. Set Optimal_utility $= -\infty$
3. For β_i = Min. Beta to Max. Beta Do {
        For A_i = Min. Effort to Max. Effort Do {
/* The step sizes are chosen to be sufficiently small enough to exhaustively
search the solution space of allowed values for β_i and A_i */
            Compute the value of equation 33.12
            Compute the value of equation (33.8 into Current_utility
            If (Current_utility > Optimal_utility) {
/* In case of a tie, agent's choice maximizes expected returns to the principal */
                Set Optimal_utility = current_utility
                Set Beta_choice = β_i
                Set Effort_choice = A_i
        }

}
}

4. Receive Capital

5. Use Beta_choice and Effort_choice for β_i and A_i values in equation 33.4 and sample z_m and z_i to determine the returns from the investment.

6. Return the realized investment value to the principal.

33.2.5   Research Hypotheses

We test the following hypotheses when experimenting with the two incentive contracts.

Both Limited-liability and Unlimited-liability are purely commission based contracts. However, Limited-liability contract limits the liability of the investment analysts, hence shields the agents from investment risk compared to the Unlimited-liability contract. Considering that the agents are risk averse, the Limited-liability contract provides some insurance to agents that would generate at least, the risk sharing benefits to the principal. The protection of downside risk should also induce the agents to take more risk. Thus, the Limited-liability contract should perform better than a Unlimited-liability contract. In fact, we predict that the Unlimited-liability contract exposes the agent to "too much" risk for which they need to be compensated and for that reason, it would consistently under-perform. This leads to our first hypothesis.

Hypothesis 1: The Limited-liability contract will perform consistently better than the Unlimited-liability contract.

The intention of commission based contracts is to provide better incentives for risk taking behavior. Therefore, higher rates of commission should lead to better risk taking behavior among the agents, which may result in higher returns. Therefore, we state our second hypothesis as follows.

Hypothesis 2: The incentive effect of both the contracts should increase with higher rates of commission thus improving performance at higher commission rates.

It is well known that the effect of moral hazard increases with risk aversion. Thus, a less risk-averse agent would choose a higher level of beta than a more risk averse agent when subjected to the same environmental condition. Hence, the average returns generated from such investment behavior should yield higher realized returns. This leads to our third hypothesis.

Hypothesis 3: For the same incentive contract, a less risk-averse agent would perform better than a more risk averse agent.

33.3   The Computational Model

Our computational model consists of a single principal and a number of agents. It is assumed that the agents are homogeneous in that they maximize identical utility functions and are all offered the same incentive contract. Pilot simulation experiments with different number of agents indicates the necessity of multiple agents (> 3) in order to sustain a steady stream of returns to the principal, perhaps generating a diversification effect to the principal. We further assume that the principal and the agents are not aware of the *precise nature* of relation between portfolio choice (beta level) and effort choice on the returns generated. The agents are allowed to *learn* about the estimation environment by repeating the investment process over a number of periods. Thus, each agent is assumed to utilize the information from investments and payoffs realized in the previous periods to regress his choice of beta level and effort level against expected utility.

The combination of repeated interaction and the presence of multiple agents necessitate the choice of an appropriate capital allocation mechanism. The initial allocation of capital is based on Einhorn's (1977) unit weighted composite model (i.e. the one member-one vote principle used in the literature of consensus formation), where each agent is allocated an equal amount of capital. It is important to note that this is only one of many plausible methods of initial allotment of resources. Many other methods exist in resource allocation literature [Radner (1972), Bellman (1991)]. Our rule is a credible allocation rule, especially if we assume that the principal has no prior knowledge, or biases about the effectiveness of any of the agents. It may be argued that factors such as the environment, the economy, political and cultural situations need to be considered when making capital allocation decision, but to limit the number of factors in the computational experiments we assume that the principal makes capital allocation decisions based *only* on the returns in the immediately preceding period [Rao, Chaudhury, Chakka (1995)] .

The market uncertainty is captured by the z_m term in equation (2.4) of the model, which generates the return on individual investment. Estimation risk is captured by the term z_i in equation 33.4. It is to be noted that the Gaussian noise in market uncertainty characterizes noise that cannot be controlled by the agent. The level of uncertainty is assumed to be a constant over any single experimental run. The estimation risk, however, can be reduced by the agent's effort. In addition, estimation risk increases with increase in portfolio beta level. By adding two risk factors in the payoff function, we are able to model several different effects (i) intentional inclusion of randomness in decision procedure, (ii) heterogeneity in payoffs among the population of agents, and (iii) imperfections or uncertainties in the information [Kephart, Hogg and Huberman (1990)].

33.4   Experiment Details

The computational model of the previous section is run under different parametric settings to investigate the performance of the incentive contracts as measured by the average returns generated in a given period.

Sample Size   Typically the total sample size in simulation studies runs into thousands and for the same sample size it is preferable to have a smaller number of replications and a larger run length [Law and Kelton (1984)]. Each experiment is replicated 4 times and each replication consists of 1250 periods. The sample size for each experiment is 5000. In order to prevent bias and provide sufficient data points for regression, the first 500 periods of each replication are ignored for performance comparisons, and data from period 501 to 1750 is collected for evaluation purposes. In the first 500 periods, agents make random selection of beta and effort levels and record the payoffs for regression purposes. The principal during the first 500 periods allocates capital equally among the agents.

Parameter Settings   Different parameter values are used in the simulation experiment. These include two different levels of risk aversion, 6 different levels of market uncertainty (defined by the standard deviation of z_m), 3 levels of wealth sharing ratios (the portion of the returns that the principal shares with the agents). With 2 different incentive contracts the total number of simulation experiments amounts to $2 \times 6 \times 3 \times 2 = 72$. The different parameter values tested are listed in Table 33.1.

In all the experiments, the mean value of market rate of return (R_m) is fixed at 15% [Jacob and Pettit (1988)]. The risk free rate of interest is set at 6%. This is a justifiable assumption, because the market risk premium, ($R_m - R_f$) has averaged 8.4 percent a year over the last 63 years [Brealey and Myers (1991)]. We test for market uncertainty at 6 different levels. For convenience purposes, we combine the results of the simulation runs at low uncertainty with standard deviation of the market return set at (0%, 10%), medium uncertainty (20%, 30%), high uncertainty

Table 33.1
Different parameter values in the simulation experiments

Factors	Values
Incentive Contracts	Limited-liability, Unlimited-liability
Market Uncertainty (Standard Deviation)	0.0, 0.1, 0.2, 0.3, 0.4, 0.5
Risk Aversion (value of γ in equation 33.8)	3.0, 5.0
Sharing Ratio (Value of α and (adjusted value) of ρ in Equations 33.10–33.14)	0.02, 0.05, 0.10

(40%, 50%). Historical U.S. stock market data indicate market uncertainty to be as high as 35% though it may vary over a period of time [Brealey and Myers (1991)].

The mean of the portfolio beta value is allowed to range from 0.5 to 2.0. We choose these representative betas because "most betas are in the range of 0.50 to 1.50" [Brigham and Gapenski (1988)]. The variance of beta is the square of the mean of the beta value. The effort level values are set such that the lowest level of effort leaves the standard deviation of estimation risk unaffected. While, the highest level of effort reduces the standard deviation of estimation risk by 10 times. Thus, we let the effort level to range from 1 to 10. The value of constant absolute risk aversion for the agents is tested for at two different levels, namely, 3.0 and 5.0 [Tew, Reid, and Witt (1991)]. The percentage of returns that is shared with the agent is arrived at such that the incentive payments made to the agents near peak levels of returns is as similar as possible. Since incentive contracts are not arrived after maximizing principal and agent utilities, the sharing ratios are carefully chosen to test for performance variations when incentive payments are positioned at certain points on the utility function of wealth. Since, negative exponential utility functions are utilized here, the utility value asymptotically converges to 0, and the sharing ratio of 0.1 is chosen such that the utility of wealth is near this asymptotically maximum value. The effort aversion constant, K, in equation 33.8 is chosen such that the values of utility in wealth and disutility of effort are well balanced. Pilot runs indicate that minor variations in the chosen value of K had no significant effect on the relative performances in the experiments. However, order of magnitude changes in K can cause the effort level values chosen by the agents to lie in the extremes.

33.5   Results and Discussion

The results of the computational experiments are presented in Tables 33.2 to 33.7. Table 33.2 presents the mean and standard deviations of the average return per period in the different experiments. Table 33.3 tabulates the average portfolio beta in each period for all the experiments. Table 33.4 presents the average effort level in each period in the experiments. Further, paired comparisons for the incentive contracts are carried out for each experiment and the significance levels of the differences in the performances of incentives are presented in Tables 33.5, 33.6, and 33.7 for sharing ratios of 0.02, 0.05, 0.1 respectively.

The salient features of the results are as follows.

1. We find very significant support for Hypothesis 1. The Limited-liability contract consistently outperforms Unlimited-liability contract under all levels of sharing ratio, market uncertainty and risk aversion (except at low market uncertainty and higher sharing ratios).

2. Hypothesis 2 is not supported from our computation experiments. Irrespective of the incentive mechanism, it is clearly seen that as the sharing ratio increases, the portfolio beta (Table 33.3) and effort levels (Table 33.4) actually decline! Thus, the computational experiments do not provide for higher performance levels from agents due to higher commissions.

3. We find partial support for Hypothesis 3. The experimental results suggest that risk aversion level is a significant factor in the selection of the portfolio beta and effort levels. However, the effect of this choice on the returns generated is mixed. For instance, we see that CAR effect on the returns generated is significant under lower levels of market uncertainty. However, as market uncertainty increases, the CAR effect on returns is seen to wear off slightly. It is to be noted that there is a significant effect of risk aversion on the choice of portfolio beta and effort levels. However, this effect does not translate to a significant difference in average returns.

4. The average returns generated per period decreases as market uncertainty increases for both the incentive mechanisms. This is accompanied by changes in beta and effort level changes as well.

5. As the market uncertainty level increases, the beta levels of both the contracts decrease with corresponding decrease in effort. The extent of this decrease, however, is dependent on the sharing ratio employed by the principal.

The individual effects are detailed below:

33.5.1   Effect of Sharing Ratio

As mentioned in Section 3, sharing ratio is the rate at which the principal shares the returns generated with the agent. The three different sharing ratio values are chosen at certain regions on the utility curve in wealth. For instance a sharing ratio of 0.02

Table 33.2
Mean and standard deviation values for Returns

		Sharing Ratio = 0.02					
		Market Uncertainty					
		LOW		MED		HIGH	
	Incentive	Mean	Std. Dev	Mean	Std. Dev	Mean	Std. Dev
CAR=5	Limited-Liability	19.37	4.34	16.25	13.47	16.34	25.5
	Unlimited-Liability	16.36	4.28	12.76	9.33	12.7	17.09
CAR=3	Limited-Liability	20.23	4.58	18.15	15.11	17.5	27.47
	Unlimited-Liability	17.81	4.44	12.48	8.9	12.83	17.15

		Sharing Ratio = 0.05					
		Market Uncertainty					
		LOW		MED		HIGH	
	Incentive	Mean	Std. Dev	Mean	Std. Dev	Mean	Std. Dev
CAR=5	Limited-Liability	15	3.86	13.6	11.41	13.27	20.09
	Unlimited-Liability	15.24	3,8	11.54	8.22	9.93	10.99
CAR=3	Limited-Liability	17.18	4.05	15	12.68	15.06	24.86
	Unlimited-Liability	15.52	3.85	12.35	9.25	11.28	14.15

		Sharing Ratio = 0.01					
		Market Uncertainty					
		LOW		MED		HIGH	
	Incentive	Mean	Std. Dev	Mean	Std. Dev	Mean	Std. Dev
CAR=5	Limited-Liability	12.94	3.28	12.7	11.33	12.52	21.71
	Unlimited-Liability	13.77	3.53	9.57	6.3	9.36	10.9
CAR=3	Limited-Liability	13.78	3.68	12.56	11.29	12.48	21.72
	Unlimited-Liability	14.43	3.7	10.55	7.5	9.37	10.91

lies at the lower regions of the utility curve. This is to simulate the different levels of commission rates that may be paid to the agents. The performance of the incentive contracts seen to depend on the value of the sharing ratio. Sharing a larger pie with the agents results in lesser returns to the principal. The issue is whether sharing a larger portion of the pie with the agent leads to better performance. The evidence from the computational experiments is overwhelmingly against such a conjecture. As can be seen in Table 33.2, The highest returns to the principal results in the case where the sharing ratio is the lowest. As the sharing ratio increases, the returns to the principal decrease. Irrespective of the incentive mechanism, it is clearly seen that as the sharing ratio increases, the portfolio beta (Table 33.3) and effort levels (Table 33.4) actually decline. Thus, the computational experiments do not provide for higher performance levels from agents due to higher commissions.

33.5.2 Effect of Market Uncertainty

We have tested for six different levels of market uncertainty. However, to keep the tables more readable we have combined two adjacent levels of market uncertainty

Table 33.3
Mean and standard deviation values for Portfolio beta

		Sharing Ratio = 0.02					
		Market Uncertainty					
		LOW		MED		HIGH	
	Incentive	Mean	Std. Dev	Mean	Std. Dev	Mean	Std. Dev
CAR=5	Limited-Liability	1.35	0.11	1.08	0.12	1.09	0.12
	Unlimited-Liability	1.06	0.3	0.73	0.12	0.72	.016
CAR=3	Limited-Liability	1.43	0.08	1.25	0.06	1.2	0.09
	Unlimited-Liability	1.2	0.26	0.7	0.11	0.73	0.16

		Sharing Ratio = 0.05					
		Market Uncertainty					
		LOW		MED		HIGH	
	Incentive	Mean	Std. Dev	Mean	Std. Dev	Mean	Std. Dev
CAR=5	Limited-Liability	0.98	0.25	0.87	0.15	0.88	0.17
	Unlimited-Liability	1	0.24	0.65	0.1	0.5	0.03
CAR=3	Limited-Liability	1.19	0.16	1	0.14	1.05	0.13
	Unlimited-Liability	1.03	0.25	0.73	0.13	0.62	0.13

		Sharing Ratio = 0.01					
		Market Uncertainty					
		LOW		MED		HIGH	
	Incentive	Mean	Std. Dev	Mean	Std. Dev	Mean	Std. Dev
CAR=5	Limited-Liability	0.85	0.21	0.87	0.13	0.92	0.19
	Unlimited-Liability	0.94	0.21	0.52	0.05	0.5	0
CAR=3	Limited-Liability	0.94	0.26	0.86	0.18	0.91	0.18
	Unlimited-Liability	1	0.23	0.61	0.12	0.5	0

into one. We observe from the results that market uncertainty results in higher variance in the returns per period. The Unlimited-liability contract has lower standard deviations compared to the Limited-liability contract at higher levels of market uncertainty. This is reflected in the significantly lower values of beta and effort levels for the Unlimited-liability incentive mechanism.

Market uncertainty is seen to affect the contracts in such a way that the returns decline steadily with increasing uncertainty. This is associated with decrease in agent choices of beta and effort levels. The variations in beta and effort levels with market uncertainty appears to be more at a low sharing ratio (0.02, see Tables 33.4 and 33.5) than at higher sharing ratios. We conjecture that when agent's utility in wealth is more sensitive to agent's decision choices (which is so at lower sharing ratios), the agents response to market uncertainty is also more pronounced. The general decline in beta and effort levels is also attributable to the loss of control the agent perceives with his ability to control the average returns as the market uncertainty increases.

Table 33.4
Mean and standard deviation values for effort level

		Sharing Ratio = 0.02					
		Market Uncertainty					
		LOW		MED		HIGH	
	Incentive	Mean	Std. Dev	Mean	Std. Dev	Mean	Std. Dev
CAR=5	Limited-Liability	5.83	1.03	4.03	0.75	4.1	0.93
	Unlimited-Liability	6.54	1.4	4.46	1.43	3.09	1.66
CAR=3	Limited-Liability	6.06	1.01	4.66	0.93	4.44	1.01
	Unlimited-Liability	6.3	1.33	5.13	1.44	4.2	1.63

		Sharing Ratio = 0.05					
		Market Uncertainty					
		LOW		MED		HIGH	
	Incentive	Mean	Std. Dev	Mean	Std. Dev	Mean	Std. Dev
CAR=5	Limited-Liability	3.9	1.03	3.42	0.79	3.41	0.84
	Unlimited-Liability	6.04	1.39	2.78	1.43	1.03	0.24
CAR=3	Limited-Liability	5	1.1	3.88	0.74	4.1	0.86
	Unlimited-Liability	6.57	1.22	3.83	1.26	2.44	1.42

		Sharing Ratio = 0.01					
		Market Uncertainty					
		LOW		MED		HIGH	
	Incentive	Mean	Std. Dev	Mean	Std. Dev	Mean	Std. Dev
CAR=5	Limited-Liability	3.34	0.8	3.28	0.69	3.55	0.85
	Unlimited-Liability	5.4	1.69	1.3	0.69	1	0
CAR=3	Limited-Liability	3.65	0.88	3.33	0.91	3.53	0.95
	Unlimited-Liability	5.73	1.6	2.44	1.27	1	0

The Unlimited-liability contract is seen to perform comparably well at lower uncertainty levels. However, at higher market uncertainty levels, the risk aversion effect causes this contract to degenerate into corner solutions. It is no surprise that contracts of this nature are not observed in business organizations.

33.5.3   Effect of Risk Aversion

We have tested for two different levels of agent risk aversion, namely 5 and 3. The higher value indicates a greater level of risk aversion on the part of the agent. The results in Tables 33.5, 33.6, and 33.7 show that risk-aversion affects agents' performance to some degree.

In general, the choice of portfolio beta and effort levels is affected by risk aversion parameter at all levels of market uncertainty. However, this variation in choice is not uniformly reflected in the average returns generated. The variation caused by risk aversion is more pronounced at lower levels of market uncertainty as opposed to higher levels of market uncertainty. We believe that at higher levels of uncertainty, the variation caused by risk aversion is masked by market variance.

Table 33.5
T-Test Significance Results: Sharing Ratio = 0.02

A. Relative Performance of Incentive Mechanisms

	Incentive		Market Uncertainty		
			LOW	MED	HIGH
CAR=5	Limited-Liability v/s	Returns	***+ve	***+ve	***+ve
	Unlimited-Liability	Beta	***+ve	***+ve	***+ve
		Effort	***−ve	***−ve	***−ve
CAR=3	Limited-Liability v/s	Returns	***+ve	***+ve	***+ve
	Unlimteded-Liability	Beta	***+ve	***+ve	***+ve
		Effort	***−ve	***−ve	***+ve

B. Effect of CAR on the Same Incentive Mechanisms

		CAR = 5v/s CAR = 3		
		LOW	MED	HIGH
Limited-Liability	Returns	***−ve	***−ve	***−ve
	Beta	***−ve	***−ve	***−ve
	Effort	***−ve	***−ve	***−ve
Unlimited-Liability	Returns	***−ve	***+ve	NoSigEff
	Beta	***−ve	***+ve	***−ve
	Effort	***+ve	***−ve	***−ve

Table 33.6
T-Test Significance Results: Sharing Ratio = 0.05

A. Relative Performance of Incentive Mechanisms

	Incentive		Market Uncertainty		
			LOW	MED	HIGH
CAR=5	Limited-Liability v/s	Returns	***−ve	***+ve	***+ve
	Unlimited-Liability	Beta	***−ve	***+ve	***+ve
		Effort	***−ve	***+ve	***+ve
CAR=3	Limited-Liability v/s	Returns	***+ve	***+ve	***+ve
	Unlimteded-Liability	Beta	***+ve	***+ve	***+ve
		Effort	***−ve	***+ve	***+ve

B. Effect of CAR on the Same Salary Policy

		CAR = 5v/s CAR = 3		
		LOW	MED	HIGH
Limited-Liability	Returns	***−ve	***−ve	***−ve
	Beta	***−ve	***−ve	***−ve
	Effort	***−ve	***−ve	***−ve
Unlimited-Liability	Returns	***−ve	***−ve	***−ve
	Beta	***−ve	***−ve	***−ve
	Effort	***−ve	***−ve	***−ve

For the Limited-liability contract, at the lower sharing ratio, higher risk aversion causes low beta and high effort. At higher sharing ratios, both beta and effort are lower at low and medium uncertainty levels and both are higher at high uncertainty level for increased risk aversion. The Limited-liability contract shows reduced beta

Table 33.7
T-Test Significance Results: Sharing Ratio = 0.1

A. Relative Performance of Incentive Mechanisms

	Incentive		\multicolumn{3}{c}{Market Uncertainty}
			LOW	MED	HIGH
CAR=5	Limited-Liability v/s	Returns	***−ve	***+ve	***+ve
	Unlimited-Liability	Beta	***−ve	***+ve	***+ve
		Effort	***−ve	***+ve	***+ve
CAR=3	Limited-Liability v/s	Returns	***−ve	***+ve	***+ve
	Unlimteded-Liability	Beta	***−ve	***+ve	***+ve
		Effort	***−ve	***+ve	***+ve

B. Effect of CAR on the Same Salary Policy

		\multicolumn{3}{c}{CAR = 5v/s CAR = 3}	
		LOW	MED	HIGH	
Limited-Liability	Returns	***−ve	NoSigEff	NoSigEff	
	Beta	***−ve	***+ve	***+ve	
	Effort	***−ve	***−ve	***−ve	
Unlimited-Liability	Returns	***−ve	***−ve	NoSigEff	
	Beta	***−ve	***−ve	***−ve	
	Effort	***−ve	***−ve	NoSigEff	

and effort levels for higher risk aversion in general for all sharing ratios and all levels of uncertainty.

33.6 Conclusion

The paper has described the computational results of the test on how Limited-liability feature of incentive mechanisms affect agent performance in delegated investment settings. While the usual caveat of generalizability applies to the results obtained in the paper, we believe that the results from our computational experiments provide us several useful insights about the effect of incentive mechanism features on the performance and behavior of investment managers. We find that the Limited-liability contract consistently outperforms Unlimited-liability contract under all levels of sharing ratio, market uncertainty and risk aversion. We also find that there is a significant effect of risk aversion on the choice of portfolio beta and effort levels. However, this effect does not translate to a significant difference in average realized returns. As demonstrated from our experiments, the specification of limited liability seems to be a sufficient risk shielding mechanism for risk averse investment managers. The results focus our attention to the level of payments made to the agents. In general, paying higher commissions do not result in comparable improvements in performance.

Several useful future research directions emerge from the problem studied here. For instance, would similar performance characteristics be observed when agent's decision choices affect the mean and variance of the outcome in a different manner? How do other incentive mechanisms such as target-based contracts, communication-based contracts and group incentive schemes compare with the contracts tested in this paper? We are currently investigating these issues.

Acknowledgments

This research has been supported by NSF under grant 9505790 and the research of the second author has been supported in part by NSF under grant 9907325.

References

Bellman, R. E., (1991) *Adaptive Control Processes*: A Guided Tour, Princeton University Press, Princeton, N. J.

Brealey R. A. and S. C. Myers, (1991) *Principles of Corporate Finance*, McGraw Hill, New York.

Brigham E. F. and L. C. Gapenski, (1988) *Financial Management: Theory and Practice*, The Dryden Press, Chicago.

Cohen, S. I., and Starks, L. T., (1988) "Estimation Risk and Incentive Contracts For Portfolio Managers," *Management Science*, 34(9), 1067–1079.

Einhorn, H. J., Hogarth, R. M., and Klempner, E., (1977) "Quality of Group Judgment", *Psychological Bulletin*, Vol 84.

Feltham, G. A., and Xie, J., (1994) "Performance Measure Congruity and Diversity in Multi-task Principal/Agent Relations," *The Accounting Review*, Vol. 69(3), 429–453.

Holmstrom, B., (1982) "Moral Hazard in Teams," *Bell Journal of Economics*. (Autumn).

Law, A. M., and Kelton, W. D., (1984) "Confidence Intervals for Steady State Simulation: I. A Survey of fixed sample size procedures." Operations Research, 32, 1221–1239.

Radner, R., (1972) "Allocation of a Scarce Resource under Uncertainty: An Example of a Team," C. M. McGuire and R. Radner (eds) *Decision and Organization*.

Radner, R., (1987) *Decentralization and Incentives*, University of Minnesota Press, Minneapolis, MN.

Rao, H. R., Chaudhury, A., with Chakka M., (1995) "Modeling Team Processes: Issues and a Specific Example.", *Information Systems Research*, 6(3).

Stoughton, N. M., (1993) "Moral Hazard and the Portfolio Management Problem," *Journal of Finance*, 48(5), 2009–2028.

Tew, B. V., Reid, D. W., and Witt, C. A., (1991) "The Opportunity Cost of a Mean-Variance Efficient Choice," *The Financial Review*, 26(1), 31–43.

VI   Credit Risk

34 Rules Extractions from Banks' Bankrupt Data Using Connectionist and Symbolic Learning Algorithms

Edmar Martinelli, André de Carvalho, Solange Rezende, and Alberto Matias

This article investigates the use of connectionist and symbolic learning algorithms in the problem of Bankruptcy Prediction. This problem is regarded in this paper as a classification problem. Its main goal is the classification of banks in two classes, bankrupt and non-bankrupt, based on indicators of their financial situation. This paper is also concerned with the knowledge that can be extracted from the data sets used. For such, the performance of a connectionist model is compared to those achieved by symbolic learning techniques both in terms of correct classification rates and the quality of the knowledge extracted. Since Neural Networks are seen as black box, due to the difficulty of understanding the underlying process behind their decisions, a technique to extract knowledge from trained networks, the TREPAN algorithm is used in this paper. The main difficulty in this work was the different number of examples belonging to the classes of bankrupt and non-bankrupt banks.

34.1 Introduction

The recent process of the Brazilian economy stabilisation demanded a rigorous adaptation from the bank institutions to the new situation. The accentuated fall of the inflation and increase of the credit rates provoked the failure declaration of 34 banks from 1994 to 1996. Associated to the movement towards economic blocks and the growing globalisation, a strong demand has been created for robust and reliable systems for banks bankruptcy forecasting. This demand comes from different sources, such as managers, investors and government organisations.

Several techniques have been investigated for bankruptcy forecasting [2,7]. Among the recent methods proposed, Artificial Intelligence techniques, based on connectionist and symbolic learning, have provided efficient alternatives for financial modelling. For bankruptcy prediction, the domain investigated in this paper, several applications using intelligent techniques have been successfully accomplished, as the bankruptcy forecasting of Texas banks [19] and of Brazilian banks [1].

This paper is organised as follows. Section 2 presents the methods investigated in this paper, the symbolic learning algorithms CN2 [5] and C4.5 [17] and the MLP neural network model [10], respectively. A technique to extract knowledge from Artificial Neural Networks [8] is described in Section 3. The experiments carried out the results achieved are discussed in Sections 4 and 5. Finally, Section 6 presents the conclusion.

34.2   Artificial Intelligence Methods

Bankruptcy risk has been carried out by using regression and discriminant analysis techniques [12]. Recently, Artificial Neural Networks have been successfully applied [1]. This article investigates the use of Symbolic Learning Algorithms—SLAs—and Artificial Neural Networks—ANNs—for Brazilian banks bankruptcy forecasting. This problem was regarded as a pattern recognition problem: given a group of input attributes representing the financial situation of a bank, the ANNs and SLAs must identify which class (bankrupt or non-bankrupt) this bank belongs to. The Symbolic Learning Algorithms used in this paper are the CN2 [5] and C4.5 [17]. The connectionist model used was the Multi Layer Perceptron—MLP—network [10].

34.2.1   Symbolic Algorithms

The symbolic learning algorithms are very efficient in the extraction of meaningful knowledge from a data set. Two such symbolic algorithms are investigated in this paper: The CN2 [5] and C4.5 [17] learning algorithms. Next, these algorithms are described.

The CN2 Algorithm   The CN2 algorithm induces a list of ordered and unordered classification rules from real-world examples. There are two versions of the CN2 algorithm. The CN2 algorithm with ordered classification rules, which was developed by Clark and Niblett [5], uses the entropy measure as a heuristic search method. It generates rules ordered by their generality. Clark and Boswell proposed a modification in the original algorithm in order to generate unordered rules. This modified algorithm uses the Laplacian method [6].

The original CN2 algorithm employs the *beam-search* method. Initially, it removes the dependencies among the examples during the search. Next, it increases its search space in order to include rules that do not accurately represent the training data. CN2 works iteratively. At each iteration, it looks for a condition that covers the largest number of examples from a particular class C and a few examples from the other classes. When the condition is considered good by an evaluation function, the examples it covers are removed from the training set and a *if condition then class C* rule is added to the end of the rules list. Thus, the conditions are selected to cover the training examples of a certain class through general-to-specific search. The last rule in the list is the default rule that classifies new examples in the most frequent class. This process is repeated until no more satisfactory conditions are found.

The C4.5 Algorithm   The main feature of the C4.5 algorithm [17] is the construction of decision trees. In a classification problem, the leave nodes of a tree correspond to classes. The other nodes are attributes of the examples used for classification. The branches are labeled with either the discrete attributes values or continuous attributes intervals. A decision tree can be later pruned. The knowledge extracted can also be described by production rules. The generation of decision trees is based on the Hunt algorithm [11] which, given a test set T containing examples from the classes $C_1, C_2, \ldots, C_k$:, takes one among three possible decisions:

- T contains one or more examples, all of them belonging to the class C_j. The generated decision tree for T is a leaf that identifies the class C_j.

- T does not contain examples. The decision tree is also a leaf, but the class associated to this leaf must be defined through information defined by other sources than T. As an example, the node can be associated to the class with the largest number of occurrences.

- T contains examples belonging to more than one class. In this case, T is divided in subsets, where each subset should have examples from the smallest number of classes possible. A criterion to divide T is chosen and its application generates the subsets $T_1, T_2, \ldots, T_n$. The decision tree for the set T is then composed by a decision node and a set of child nodes. For each of these child nodes, one of these three decisions is recursively applied.

34.2.2   Artificial Neural Networks

Artificial Neural Networks—ANNs—are distributed computational models based on the nervous system. They have achieved a good performance when applied to patterns classification tasks. Their generalisation capacity, adjustment through a learning process and ability to perform non-linear mappings can be regarded as contribute to their successful application to a large variety of tasks.

This paper uses MLP networks trained by the Resilient Backpropagation learning algorithm [18]. Resilient Backpropagation, or Rprop, is a local adaptive learning scheme. Its basic principle is to eliminate the negative influence of the size of the partial derivative on the weight update step. Thus, only the sign of the partial derivative is considered to indicate the direction of the weight update.

34.3   Rules Extraction from Artificial Neural Networks

A strong limitation of Artificial Neural Networks is their inability to express their stored knowledge in a meaningful way. The main difficulty of understanding the knowledge acquired by ANNs is due to their representation of the stored knowledge as a set of numerical values (weights and bias), which are manipulated through mathematical equations. In contrast to ANNs, the knowledge represented by symbolic algorithms is generally friendlier and easier to understand.

There are several algorithms for rules extraction from ANNs, such as: KT [9], EN [14], MofN [20], RULEX [3] and TREPAN [8]. This paper describes and uses the TREPAN algorithm to extract knowledge from trained ANNs. This algorithm represents the knowledge stored in an ANN as a decision tree. In order to produce a decision tree, TREPAN uses a trained ANN and its training data set. By not taking into account network architecture, TREPAN is generic enough to be applied to several ANN models. TREPAN builds a decision tree by asking the class of each example to an oracle, which is composed by the trained network.

It must be pointed out that the class indicated by the oracle for a particular example may be, in some cases, different from the class associated to this sample in the training set. This happens because even after trained, the network classification of the training input data might not agree with the related training desired output data for all the patterns. On the other hand, since the TREPAN algorithm aims only to extract the knowledge acquired by the ANN, it is not concerned with the correct sample classification, but only with the network classification. TREPAN try to build the decision tree that best represents the ANN stored knowledge.

TREPAN first steps are similar to those used by conventional algorithms of induction decision trees, like CART (Classification and Regression Tree) [4] and C4.5 [17], which construct a decision tree by partitioning the examples recursively.

One advantage of TREPAN when compared to C4.5 is that TREPAN can randomly create new examples when building the decision tree. New examples are created using the current decision tree and the trained network. This guarantees that the choice of the division test to be applied to the tree deepest nodes will be based on a large number of examples. The division test carried out by TREPAN can follow three different approaches:

• Original or *m-of-n*—extracts trees whose internal nodes present tests of the *m-of-n* type.

• Disjunctive or *1-of-n*—variation of the original method, uses disjunctive (OR) tests to generate the trees.

- *True-False*—the decision tests have only one attribute, which is evaluated as true or false.

34.4 Experiments

This article compares the use of symbolic and connectionist learning algorithms for Brazilian banks failure forecasting. This comparison will take into consideration the error rates obtained by each method and the knowledge extracted by them.

The data set used in this paper consists of data from 246 Brazilian banks. There are micro (44%), small (22%), medium (23%) and large (11%) Brazilian banks. The origin of the capital of these institutions is national private, foreigner, official federal, official state and foreigner association. From these 246 examples, there are 212 non-bankrupt Institutions (86,2%) and 34 bankrupt Institutions (13,8%). As can be noticed, there is a very small amount of examples from the bankruptcy institutions. To overcome this problem, the number of samples in this class was increased by adding noise.

All the information about non-bankrupt banks were collected in June 1995. The information about the bankrupt banks were obtained in the closest date previous to their bankruptcy, from December 1993 to July 1995. In the data set employed, a bank is considered as bankrupt if either it is under intervention, or it was sold or liquidated. This data set was supplied by the Business Department, School of Economy and Administration of the University of Sao Paulo (FEA—USP Ribeirao Preto).

Two groups of attributes from the original data set were considered for the classification. The first group consisted of all the 26 attributes. The second group consisted of only 10 attributes, selected among the original ones through the t-student test [13]. These attributes describe the current financial situation of the banks.

34.4.1 Data Set Organisation

As suggested by the report PROBEN1 [15], the split sample technique was used, with the data set was divided in three subsets: training, validation and test subsets. The proportion of samples proposed for these subsets are: 50% for training, 25% for validation and 25% for test. For the symbolic methods, the validation subset was added to the training subset. To make the results more reliable, this report also suggests the use of three different divisions. In these divisions, the same proportion of examples present in each classes for the training, validation (for the experiments with ANNs) and test subsets should be preserved. For the experiments carried out for each phase, the average and standard deviation values are presented.

However, as pointed out previously, the amount of data belonging to each class in the banks bankruptcy data set was very unbalanced. The number of samples of non-bankrupt institutions is six times larger than the number of samples of bankrupt institutions. The use of different numbers of examples in each class can reduce the ANNs and SLAs classification performance for those examples belonging to the smaller class. Two techniques can be applied in an attempt to deal with this problem:

• Elimination of class samples: examples from the larger class can be randomly eliminated in order to create a more balanced training subset.

• Noise addition: addition of noise into the examples of the smallest class to generate new patterns.

In this paper, noisy samples were added to the class with the smaller number of examples.

34.4.2 Experimental Results

In order to evaluate the performance achieved by these techniques, this work compares the knowledge extracted from ANN and the knowledge obtained by using symbolic techniques. There are three different ways to evaluate the quality of a knowledge extraction technique:

• Classification accuracy;

• Comprehensibility;

• New interesting knowledge.

This work will evaluate the performance of three knowledge extraction techniques in terms of their correct classification rates and comprehensibility of the knowledge extracted. It verifies if the knowledge acquired presents any new information previously unknown. Next, the correct classification performances achieved by CN2, C4.5, ANN and TREPAN for different noise levels are shown.

ANN Results   The performance achieved by the ANN using different noise levels are presented on Table 34.1. This table shows the correct recognition rates for the learning, validation and test stages when 26 attributes were used. For each situation, it shows the average and standard deviation values. According to these results, the addition of noise improved the correct classification rates achieved in

Table 34.1
ANN performance for 26 attributes

	Correct classification rates (%)		
Noise level (%)	Training	Validation	Test
0	59.2 ± 41.7	45.8 ± 39.7	49.8 ± 43.7
10	66.1 ± 8.9	65.0 ± 5.8	50.8 ± 4.6
20	64.3 ± 7.9	61.4 ± 2.0	52.8 ± 4.9
30	57.0 ± 19.9	51.8 ± 23.5	44.6 ± 7.5

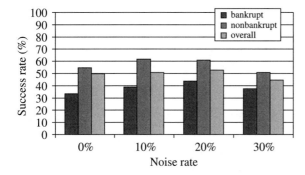

Figure 34.1
ANN success rates

the learning, validation and test phases. It can be seen that, although the best correct validation rate was achieved with 10% of noise, the best test performance was achieved with a 20% noise level.

Figure 34.1 shows the bankrupt, non-bankrupt and overall average correct classification rates for the experiments using the 26 attributes without noise and with 10%, 20% and 30% noise rates respectively.

The performance achieved in a pattern classification task can be improved by selecting the best features from the set of original features. Thus, 10 attributes were selected from the original set of 26 attributes. Table 34.2 illustrates the correct classification rates obtained when these 10 attributes were used. As can be seen, this selection improved the classification performance for all noise levels. The best correct classification rates were obtained with 30% of noise.

A common practice used to improve the network performance is to run a few additional epochs using both the validation subset and the training subset to update the network weights. Table 34.3 illustrates the results obtained with the same ANNs from Table 34.2, now retrained with additional 350 cycles using both training and

Table 34.2
ANN Performance for 10 attributes.

Noise level (%)	Correct classification rates (%)		
	Training	Validation	Test
0	66.7 ± 24.0	68.8 ± 6.3	55.0 ± 4.6
10	64.8 ± 18.5	60.7 ± 10.9	54.4 ± 15.5
20	59.7 ± 18.2	60.4 ± 10.4	48.2 ± 13.2
30	71.5 ± 19.9	68.3 ± 16.3	64.7 ± 11.4

Table 34.3
ANN performance using 10 attributes and final training with the training and validation subsets.

Noise level (%)	Correct classification rates (%)	
	Training	Test
0	90.4 ± 5.1	62.0 ± 1.6
10	76.6 ±?7.3	67.7 ± 1.16
20	75.7 ± 4.8	69.3 ± 5.5
30	79.7 ± 6.6	73.2 ± 2.6

validation subsets. The results show a large improvement in the correct classification rates and more uniformity. The reason for these improvements seems to be the larger number of bankrupt banks used in that last cycles to train the neural networks. The validation samples were used only in the last 350 training cycles, thus avoiding the overfitting.

Figure 34.2 shows the bankrupt, non-bankrupt and overall average success rate for the experiments using 10 attributes without noise and with 10%, 20% and 30% noise rates, respectively. It also shows the results achieved in the test stage by the network trained by both the validation subset and the training subset. The smaller number of examples from the non-bankrupt class undermined the correct classification for this class. The increment of noise levels caused an improvement in the classification rates of non-bankrupt banks. According to Figure 34.2, the higher correct rates were obtained by using a noise level of 30% and adding the validation subset to the training set.

Once the best performance was achieved by using the 10 selected attributes, this set of attributes will be used in the next experiments.

CN2 Results   The average performance achieved by CN2 using the Laplacian method is illustrated by Table 34.4. It shows that the best and second best correct classification rates were achieved by the data with 30% and 20% of noise level, respectively.

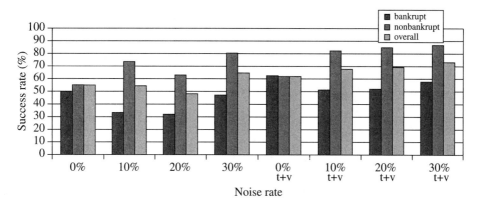

Figure 34.2
Network performance in the test subset using 10 attributes

Table 34.4
CN2 performance for the subsets using 10 attributes.

	Correct classification rates (%)	
Noise level (%)	Training	Test
0	97.5 ± 1.1	68.7 ± 7.4
10	91.2 ± 2.4	66.3 ± 9.6
20	90.4 ± 1.6	73.6 ± 10.9
30	90.5 ± 3.7	74.9 ± 12.4

Figure 34.3 shows the average performance reached by each class. It can be noticed that the best performance was achieved by adding 30% of noise. It should also be noticed that the two classes achieved very similar performances when 10% of noise was added to the data set.

Figure 34.4 presents the rules set extracted from the data set with 30% of noise level. This set has 19 rules, including the default rule. These rules are non-ordered, which allows an independent analysis of each one of them, thus easier to understand than the set ordered rules.

34.4.3 C4.5 Results

Table 34.5 shows the performance reached by the trees generated by the C4.5 algorithm. It can be seen that the best performance was achieved by adding 20% of noise. For the data set without noise, the test subsets had only 8 examples of insolvent banks and 186 examples of solvent banks, which bias the results towards the class of solvent banks.

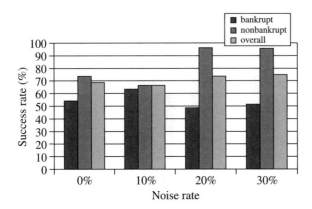

Figure 34.3
C4.5 performance for the test subset with 10 attributes.

Table 34.5
C4.5 trees performance for the data with 10 attributes.

Noise level (%)	Correct classification rates (%)	
	Training	Test
0	78.2 ± 4.0	91.6 ± 1.6
10	97.0 ± 3.2	67.0 ± 8.7
20	98.1 ± 1.1	77.2 ± 7.5
30	92.2 ± 5.9	75.2 ± 9.1

Table 34.6
C4.5 rules performance for the data with 10 attributes.

Noise level (%)	Correct classification rates (%)	
	Training	Test
0	80.1±± 4.4	91.6 ± 1.6
10	95.1±? 5.8	67.0 ± 8.7
20	97.9±? 1.0	78.1 ± 8.0
30	91.6±? 4.6	77.9 ± 4.7

Table 34.6 shows the performance achieved by the rules generated by C4.5. The performance achieved was very similar to that obtained by the decision tree produced by C4.5 for the same data set.

As can be seen in Figure 34.5, the performance achieved by the C4.5 algorithm for the test sets using different noise levels and 10 attributes. It can be seen that the best training performance was reached with 20% of noise. The large majority

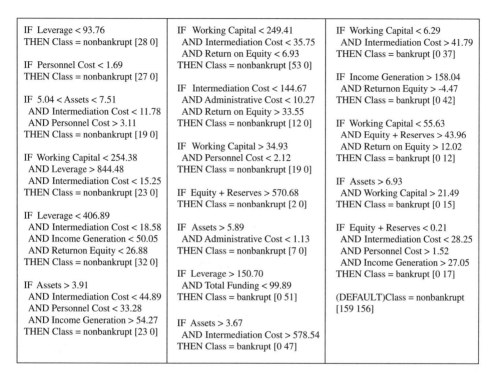

IF Leverage < 93.76
THEN Class = nonbankrupt [28 0]
 	
IF Personnel Cost < 1.69
THEN Class = nonbankrupt [27 0]
 	
IF 5.04 < Assets < 7.51
  AND Intermediation Cost < 11.78
  AND Personnel Cost > 3.11
THEN Class = nonbankrupt [19 0]
 	
IF Working Capital < 254.38
  AND Leverage > 844.48
  AND Intermediation Cost < 15.25
THEN Class = nonbankrupt [23 0]
 	
IF Leverage < 406.89
  AND Intermediation Cost < 18.58
  AND Income Generation < 50.05
  AND Returnon Equity < 26.88
THEN Class = nonbankrupt [32 0]
 	
IF Assets > 3.91
  AND Intermediation Cost < 44.89
  AND Personnel Cost < 33.28
  AND Income Generation > 54.27
THEN Class = nonbankrupt [23 0]
	IF Working Capital < 249.41
	  AND Intermediation Cost < 35.75
	  AND Return on Equity < 6.93
	THEN Class = nonbankrupt [53 0]
	
	IF Intermediation Cost < 144.67
	  AND Administrative Cost < 10.27
	  AND Return on Equity > 33.55
	THEN Class = nonbankrupt [12 0]
	
	IF Working Capital > 34.93
	  AND Personnel Cost < 2.12
	THEN Class = nonbankrupt [19 0]
	
	IF Equity + Reserves > 570.68
	THEN Class = nonbankrupt [2 0]
	
	IF Assets > 5.89
	  AND Administrative Cost < 1.13
	THEN Class = nonbankrupt [7 0]
	
	IF Leverage > 150.70
	  AND Total Funding < 99.89
	THEN Class = bankrupt [0 51]
	
	IF Assets > 3.67
	  AND Intermediation Cost > 578.54
	THEN Class = bankrupt [0 47]
		IF Working Capital < 6.29
		  AND Intermediation Cost > 41.79
		THEN Class = bankrupt [0 37]
		
		IF Income Generation > 158.04
		  AND Returnon Equity > -4.47
		THEN Class = bankrupt [0 42]
		
		IF Working Capital < 55.63
		  AND Equity + Reserves > 43.96
		  AND Return on Equity > 12.02
		THEN Class = bankrupt [0 12]
		
		IF Assets > 6.93
		  AND Working Capital > 21.49
		THEN Class = bankrupt [0 15]
		
		IF Equity + Reserves < 0.21
		  AND Intermediation Cost < 28.25
		  AND Personnel Cost > 1.52
		  AND Income Generation > 27.05
		THEN Class = bankrupt [0 17]
		
		(DEFAULT)Class = nonbankrupt
		[159 156]

Figure 34.4
Set of rules produced by the CN2 algorithm.

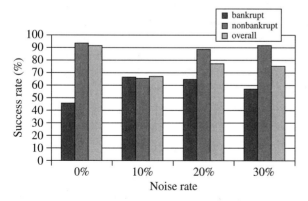

Figure 34.5
C4.5 performance for the test subset with 10 attributes.

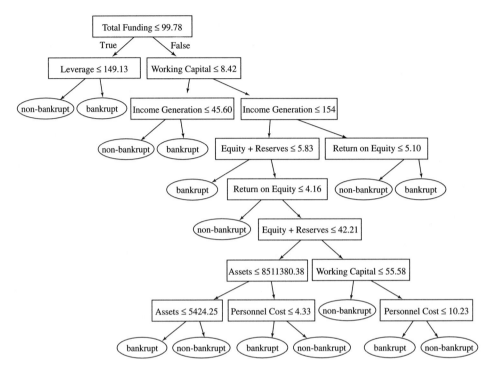

Figure 34.6
Decision tree generated by C4.5.

of the correct classifications obtained for the data without noise were obtained for the solvent class, so the performance is very biased towards this class.

The decision tree extracted by C4.5 for the data with 30% of noise is illustrated by Figure 34.6. Since tree data set partitions were used, three different trees were produced. The tree presented is the one whose performance is nearer to the average of the three performances achieved.

Figure 34.7 shows the set of non-ordered rules produced by the C4.5 algorithm. These rules were extracted from the data set with 30% of noise. A total of 14 rules were found, including the default rule.

34.4.4   TREPAN Results

The performance achieved by the TREPAN algorithm by the m-of-n, 1-of-n e True-False and using different noise levels is illustrated by Table 34.7. The networks used were those trained with training and validation set, whose performance was shown

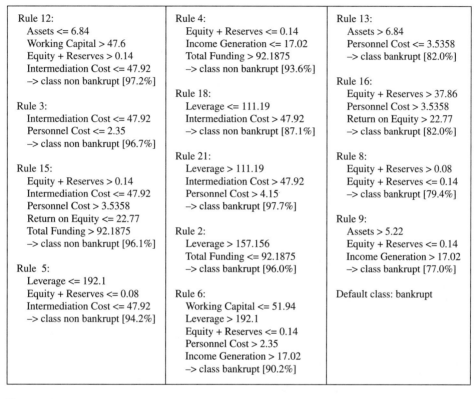

Figure 34.7
Non-ordered rules generated by C4.5.

by Table 34.3. All the three methods achieved a good performance. Among the trees generated by the three methods, the tree extracted by true-false method was the easiest to understand. In this method, the division criterion used by each node involves a test of only one attribute.

According to Figure 34.8, the performances achieved by the TREPAN methods for each class were very similar when using the test subsets. The experiments using a noise level of 30% achieved a superior performance.

Figures 34.9, 34.10, and 34.11 show the decision trees produced by the methods *m-of-n*, *1-of-n* and *True-False*. These trees were generated using the partition with the average performance and 30% noise level. The tree illustrated by Figure 34.9 was produced by the *True-False* method. The tree produced by this method was simple to understand because it is small and has a simple division test. The tree

Table 34.7

Performance achieved by TREPAN using 10 attributes and training final with the training and validation subsets.

		Correct classification rates (%)	
Method	Noise level (%)	Training	Test
True-False	0	71.8 ± 4.0	82.0 ± 23.2
	10	71.9 ± 2.7	74.6 ± 5.0
	20	73.0 ± 1.6	70.9 ± 3.7
	30	71.5 ± 2.9	74.6 ± 3.7
1-of-n	0	72.4 ± 6.7	77.8 ± 29.9
	10	73.4 ± 5.8	66.6 ± 6.8
	20	75.3 ± 2.5	74.6 ± 2.5
	30	66.9 ± 4.9	73.2 ± 3.4
m-of-n	0	73.1 ± 1.9	88.7 ± 11.6
	10	71.6 ± 3.9	71.6 ± 3.8
	20	76.6 ± 2.1	76.2 ± 10.0
	30	73.7 ± 3.6	73.9 ± 4.9

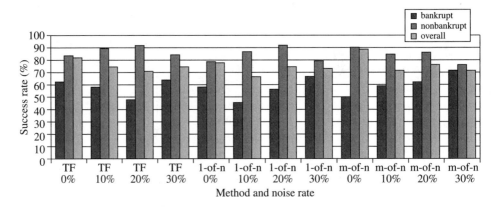

Figure 34.8

TREPAN performance in the test subset using 10 attributes

produced by the *1-of-n* is illustrated by Figure 34.10. The tree nodes have *OR* tests, what makes the understanding of the knowledge extracted more difficult.

34.4.5 Comparing the Results

Figure 34.11 shows the tree extracted by the *m-of-n* method. In spite of the good classification rates accomplished, it is even more difficulty to understand the knowledge represented by the extracted tree. This difficulty is due to the size of the tree and *m-of-n* tests.

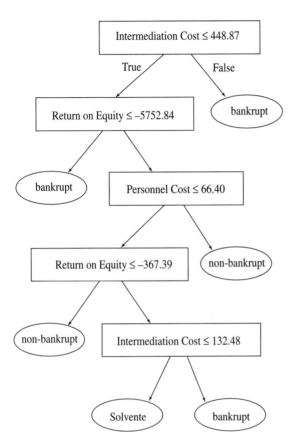

Figure 34.9
Decision tree produced by the True-False method

Table 34.8 resumes the best results achieved by C4.5, CN2, ANN and TREPAN for the test subsets. It can be seen the best performance was achieved by the C4.5 algorithm, followed by CN2, TREPAN and ANN. The results achieved by TREPAN suggest their efficiency in the knowledge extraction from the ANNs.

Figure 34.12 illustrates the performance for each class, by each algorithm, for the test subsets. According to this figure, the C4.5 algorithm achieved the best overall performance. The TREPAN m-of-n method achieved a more uniform performance for the two classes and good correct classification rates for the insolvent class. Thus, the best performances were achieved by C4.5 and TREPAN m-of-n method.

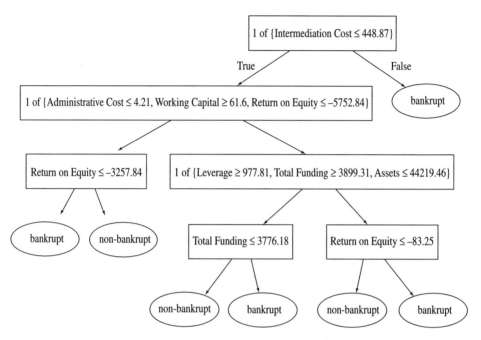

Figure 34.10
Decision tree produced by the 1-of-n method.

Table 34.8
Correct classification rates achieved by the C4.5, CN2, ANN and TREPAN in the test file.

Algorithm	Average
C4.5	78.1 ± 8.0
CN2	74.9 ± 12.4
ANN	73.2 ± 2.6
TREPAN (True-False)	74.6 ± 3.7
TREPAN (1-of-n)	73,9 ± 4.9
TREPAN (m-of-n)	74.6 ± 2.5

34.5   Conclusion

This paper compared the performance achieved by artificial neural networks and symbolic learning techniques in the classification of non-bankrupt and bankrupt Brazilian banks based on indicators of their current financial situation.

The comparison considered both the correct classification rates achieved by each technique and the "quality" of the knowledge extracted by them. In the experiments

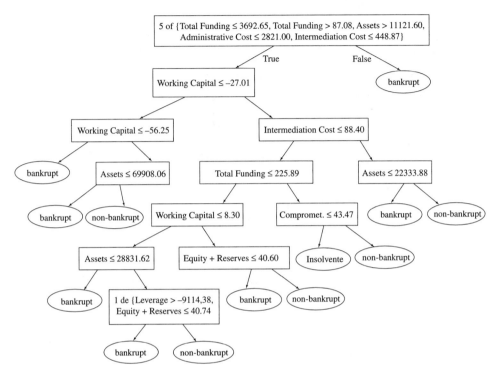

Figure 34.11
Decision tree produced by the *m-of-n* method.

carried out, the small number of samples in the non-bankrupt class was the main difficulty faced by the authors. As the results presented suggest, the addition of noise can be an interesting alternative to liven up the problems provoked by this difference.

Acknowledgments

The authors would like to thank the support received from CAPES, CNPq, FAPESP and FINEP, and the contribution received from Mr. Hélio Diniz.

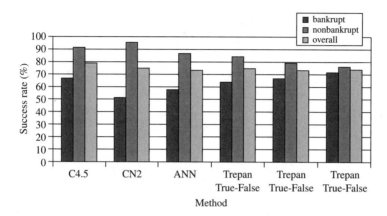

Figure 34.12
Best average results achieved by each method for the test subsets.

1. Almeida, F.; Matias, A. "Bankruptcy Prediction of Brazilian Banks Using Neural Networks", School of Business Administration, University of Sao Paulo, Brazil, 1997.

2. Altman, E.; Haldeman, R. and Narayanan, P. "Zeta Analysis", *Journal of Banking and Finance*, pp. 29-54, June, 1977.

3. Andrews, R.; Geva, S. "RULEX & CEBP Networks As the Basis for a Rule Refinement System". In *Hybrid Problems Hybrid Solutions*, Hallam J.(Ed), IOS Press, pp. 1–12, 1995.

4. Breiman, L.; Olshen, R.; Stone, C. *Classification and Regression Trees*. Wadsworth and Brooks, Monterey, CA, 1984.

5. Clark, P. and Niblet, T. "The CN2 Induction Algorithm", *Machine Learning Journal* 3, n. 4, Netherlands, pp. 261–283, 1989.

6. Clark, P. and Boswell, R. "Rule Induction with CN2: Some Recent Improvements", *Proceedings of Fifth European Conference Machine Learning*, Springer-Verlag, Berlin, Germany, pp. 151–163, 1991.

7. Cohen, I.; Gilmore, T. and Singer, F. "Bank procedures for analysing business loan applications", *Analytical Methods in Banking*, Cohen, K. and Hammer, F. Eds., Homewood, Ill., R.D. Irwin, 1966.

8. Craven, M. W. "Extracting Comprehensible Models from Trained Neural Networks", PhD thesis, University of Wisconsin, Madison, 1996.

9. Fu, L. "Rule Generation from Neural Networks", *IEEE Transactions on Systems, Man, and Cybernetics*, 24, n. 8, pp. 1114-1123, August, 1994.

10. Haykin, S. *Neural Networks—A Comprehensive Foundation*, Second edition. Prentice Hall. 1999.

11. Hunt, E. B.; Marin, J. and Stone, P. J. *Experiments in Induction*, New York: Academic Press, 1966.

12. Lachenbruch, P. A. "An Almost Unbiased Method of Obtaining Confidence Intervals for the Probability of Misclassification in Discriminant Analysis", *Biometrics*, December, 1967.

13. Miller, I.; Freund, J. and Johnson, R. *Probability and Statistics for Engineers*, Prentice-Hall Editions, 1990.

14. Pau, L. F. and Götzche, T. "Explanation Facility for Neural Networks", *Journal of Intelligent and Robotic Systems*, 5, pp. 193-206, 1992.

15. Prechelt, L. "PROBEN1, A Set of Neural Network Benchmark Problems and Benchmarking Rules", University of Karlsruhe, Technical Report 21, Germany, 1994.

16. Quinlan, J. R. *C4.5 Programs for Machine Learning*, Morgan Kaufmann Publishers, San Mateo, California, 1993.

17. Riedmiller, M. and Braun, H. "A direct adaptive method for faster backpropagation learning: the RPROP algorithm", *Proceedings of the IEEE International Conference on Neural Networks*, pp. 586–591, 1993.

18. Tam, K. and Kiang, M. "Predicting Bank Failures: A Neural Network Approach", *Management Science* 38, n. 7, pp. 926–947, 1992.

19. Towell, G. G. and Shavlik, J. W. "Extracting Refined Rules from Knowledge-Based Neural Networks". *Machine Learning*, 13, pp. 71–101, 1993.

35 Evaluating Bank Lending Policy and Consumer Credit Risk

Tor Jacobson and Kasper F. Roszbach

In this chapter a bivariate probit model is used to evaluate bank lending policy. The first equation models the bank's decision to grant a loan, the second the probability of default. The results confirm that banks provide loans in a way that is not consistent with default risk minimization. The lending policy is thus either inefficient or the product of some other type of optimizing behavior than expected profit maximization. Value at Risk, provides a more adequate measure of the credit risk on a portfolio of loans than default risk. Therefore we derive a Value at Risk measure for the sample portfolio of loans. We show how analyzing Value at Risk can enable financial institutions to compare alternative lending policies with respect to their credit risk and implied loss rate, and allow them to adjust lending rates to the incurred risk.

35.1   Introduction

Consumer credit has come to play an increasingly important role as an instrument in the financial planning of households. The quantitative importance of consumer credit may be illustrated by the fact that total lending, excluding residential loans, by banks and financial companies to Swedish households amounted to SEK 207 bn., or SEK 22.698 per capita, by the end of 1996. That is the equivalent of 12 percent of Swedish GDP or 22.7 percent of total private consumption. Viewed from the perspective of financial institutions, consumer credit also constitutes a significant part of their activities, making up 25 percent of total lending to the public. If one includes residential loans in total lending, this figure drops to 11 percent. When looking at the risk involved in these loans instead of their volume, their importance is even greater, however. Rules by the Basle Committee on Banking Supervision, that works under the umbrella of the Bank for International Settlements, stipulate an 8 percent capital requirement on consumer credit compared to, for example, 4 percent on residential loans. The above numbers make it clear that lending institutions' decision to grant a loan or not and their choice for a specific loan size can thus greatly affect a great many households' ability to smooth consumption over time, and thereby their welfare.

At a more aggregate level, consumer credit makes up a significant part of financial institutions' assets and the effects of any loan losses on lending capacity will be passed through to other sectors of the economy that rely on borrowing from the financial sector. Consequently, investigating the properties of banks' lending policies is not merely of interest because it enables us to examine how households' ability to smooth consumption is affected; these policies also have indirect implications for welfare, through financial markets. We will restricts ourselves to the first channel, however.

When a lender cannot observe borrowers' probabilities of default, credit scoring models - by enabling a lending institution to rank potential customers according to their default risk - can improve the allocation of resources, from a second best towards the first best equilibrium. Boyes, Hoffman and Low [Boyes et al 1989] investigate if the provision of credit takes place in an efficient way. For this purpose they estimate a bivariate probit model with two sequential events as the dependent variables: the lender's decision to grant the loan or not, and - conditional on the loan having been provided - the borrower's ability to pay it off or not. The parameters on variables like duration of job tenure, education and credit card ownership are, however, found to carry equal signs in both equations. Variables that increase (decrease) the probability of positive granting decision thus reduce (raise) the likelihood of a default. In addition, *unexplained* tendencies to extend credit, as measured by the regression error, were found to be positively correlated with default frequencies. Both these observations are inconsistent with a policy of default risk minimization.

In this chapter, we construct an alternative risk measure for loans and present two problems to which it can be applied. Instead of an unweighted sum, a value weighted sum of all individual default risks is a more suitable measure of the risk on a portfolio of loans for a financial institution to consider when it needs to balance risk and return.

First, we re-estimate the model of Boyes et al. on a bigger data set that contains both more reliable and more extensive financial and personal information on the loan applicants. This allows us to investigate the robustness of the finding that banks' lending policies are not consistent with default risk minimization. Next, we take Value at Risk as the relevant risk measure and study how marginal changes in a default risk based acceptance rule would shift the size of the bank's loan portfolio, its VaR exposure and average credit losses. Finally, we compare the risk on the sample portfolio with that on an efficiently provided portfolio of equal size.

The rest of the chapter is organized as follows. The data set and its sources are described in section 35.2. In section 35.3, we present the parameter estimates of the econometric workhorse model. In section 35.4, these estimates are used in the Value at Risk experiments we described earlier.

35.2 Data

The data set consists of 13,338 applications for a loan at a major Swedish lending institution between September 1994 and August 1995. All loans were granted in stores where potential customers applied for instant credit to finance the purchase of a consumer good. The evaluation of each application took place in the following way. First, the store phoned to the lending institution to get an approval or a rejection. The lending institution then analysed the applicant with the help of a database with personal characteristics and credit variables to which it has on-line access. The database is maintained by Upplysningscentralen AB, the leading Swedish credit bureau which is jointly owned by all Swedish banks and lending institutions. If approval was granted, the store's salesman filled out a loan contract and submitted it to the lending institution. The loan is revolving and administered by the lending institution as any other credit facility. It is provided in the form of a credit card that can only be used in a specific store. Some fixed amount minimum payment by the borrower is required during each month. However, since the loan is revolving, there is no predetermined maturity of the loan. Earnings on the loan come from three sources: a one-time fee paid by the customer; a payment by the store that is related to total amount of loans granted through it; and interest on the balance outstanding on the card.

For this study, the lending instutution provided us with a data file with the personal number of each applicant, the date on which the application was submitted, the size of the loan that was granted, the status of each loan (good or bad) on October 9, 1996, and the date on which bad loans gained this status.

Although one can think of several different definitions of a 'bad' loan, we classify a loan as bad once it is forwarded to a debt-collecting agency. We do not study what factors determine the differences in loss rates, if any, among bad loans.

Upplysningscentralen provided the information that was available on each applicant at the time of application and which the financial institution accessed for *its* evaluation. By exploiting the unique personal number that each resident of Sweden has, the credit bureau was able to merge these two data sets. Before handing over the combined data for analysis, the personal numbers were removed. The database included publicly available, governmentally supplied information, such as sex, citizenship, marital status, postal code, taxable income, taxable wealth, house ownership, and variables reported by Swedish banks like the total number of inquiries made about an individual, the number of unsecured loans and the total amount of unsecured loans. In total we disposed of some 60 different variables.

Table 35.1
Definition of variables

Variable	Definition
AGE	age of applicant
MALE	dummy, equals 1 if applicant is male
MARRIED	dummy, equals 1 if applicant is married
DIVORCE	dummy, equals 1 if applicant is divorced
HOUSE	dummy, equals 1 if applicant owns a house
BIGCITY	dummy, 1 if applicant lives in one of the three greater metropolitan areas around Göteborg, Malmö and Stockholm.
NRQUEST	no. of requests for information on applicant that the credit agency received during past 36 months
ENTREPR	dummy, equals 1 if applicant has taxable income from a registered business
INCOME	annual wage income as reported to Swedish tax authorities (in 10k SEK)
DIFINC	change in *INCOME*, relative to preceding year, as reported to Swedish tax authorities (in 10k SEK)
CAPINC	dummy, equals 1 if applicant has taxable income from capital
BALANCE	total collateral free credit facilities actually utilized
BALINC	$DUMMY_{\{income > 0\}} * BALANCE / INCOME$ (as a fraction)
ZEROLIM	dummy, equals 1 if applicant has no collateral-free loans outstanding
LIMIT	total amount of collateral free credit facilities already outstanding (in th. SEK)
NRLOANS	number of collateral free loans already outstanding
LIMUTIL	percentage of *LIMIT* that is actually being utilized
LOANSIZE	amount of credit granted (in th. SEK)
COAPPLIC	dummy, equals 1 if applicant has a guarantor

Tables 35.1 - 35.3 contain definitions and descriptive statistics for the variables that have been selected for the estmation of the final model in Section 35.3. Note that *BALINC* in Tables 35.2 - 35.3 only refers to the 5197 rejected and 5086 approved applications with *BALINC* >0. Of all applicants, 6,899, or 51.7 percent, were refused credit. The remaining 6,439 obtained a loan ranging from 3,000 to 30,000 Swedish kronor (approximately US$ 375 - 3750). The lending institution's policy was that no loans exceeding 30,000 kronor were supplied. Although there is an indicated amortization scheme, the loans have no fixed maturity - they are revolving.

On 9 October 1996, the people in the sample were monitored by the lending institutution. On that day 388 (6.0 %) of those who obtained a loan had defaulted and been forwarded to a debt collection agency. All other borrowers still fulfilled their minimum repayment obligations at that time.

Table 35.2
Descriptive statistics for all loan applicants ($N = 13338$)

Variable	Rejections ($N = 6899$)				Granted loans ($N = 6439$)			
	mean	stdev	min	max	mean	stdev	min	max
AGE	38.65	12.76	18	84	41.02	12.08	20	83
MALE	.62	.48	0	1	.65	.48	0	1
DIVORCE	.13	.34	0	1	.14	.35	0	1
HOUSE	.34	.47	0	1	.47	.50	0	1
BIGCITY	.41	.49	0	1	.37	.48	0	1
NRQUEST	4.69	2.60	1	10	4.81	2.68	1	19
ENTREPR	.04	.21	0	1	.02	.16	0	1
INCOME	12.99	7.04	0	73.8	18.95	7.57	0	109.3
DIFINC	.54	3.41	-43.9	25.3	.90	3.46	-62.3	50.1
CAPINC	.12	.32	0	1	.07	.25	0	1
BALINC	1.14	10.00	<.01	415.3	.36	4.32	<.01	223.9
ZEROLIM	.15	.36	0	1	<.01	.05	0	1
LIMIT	79.89	93.69	0	1703.0	50.47	51.07	.0	949.2
NRLOANS	2.99	2.42	0	18	3.65	2.04	0	16
LIMUTIL	64.34	38.88	0	278.0	53.22	33.94	0	124.0
COAPPLIC	.16	.36	0	1	.14	.35	0	1

35.3 Econometric model

In this section we present the econometric model, that will be used as a workhorse in the experiments of Section 35.4. The model consists of two simultaneous equations, one for the binary decision to provide a loan or not, y_{1i}, and another for the binary outcome, 'default' or 'proper repayment', of each loan, y_{2i}. We let the superscript $*$ indicate an unobserved variable and assume that y_{1i}^* and y_{2i}^* follow:

$$y_{1i}^* = \mathbf{x_{1i}}.\alpha_1 + \varepsilon_{1i}, \tag{35.1}$$
$$y_{2i}^* = \mathbf{x_{2i}}.\alpha_2 + \varepsilon_{2i} \tag{35.2}$$

for i=1,2,.....,N, where the $\mathbf{x_{ji}}$, $j = 1, 2$, are $1 \times k_j$ vectors of explanatory variables. The disturbances are assumed to be bivariate normal distributed with $\sigma_j = var(\varepsilon_j) = 1$ and $\sigma_{12} = cov(\varepsilon_1, \varepsilon_2)$. The binary choice variable y_{1i} is observed according to:

$$y_{1i} = \begin{cases} 0 & \text{if loan not granted} \quad (y_{1i}^* < 0) \\ 1 & \text{if loan granted} \quad (y_{1i}^* \geq 0) \end{cases} \tag{35.3}$$

The binary variable, y_{2i}, takes the value 0 if the loan defaults and 1 if not:

Table 35.3
Descriptive statistics for granted loans.

Variable	Defaulted loans ($N = 388$)				Good loans ($N = 6051$)			
	mean	stdev	min	max	mean	stdev	min	max
AGE	36.11	11.03	21	75	41.33	12.07	20	83
MALE	.67	.47	0	1	.65	.48	0	1
DIVORCE	.20	.40	0	1	.14	.35	0	1
HOUSE	.28	.45	0	1	.48	.50	0	1
BIGCITY	.41	.49	0	1	.36	.48	0	1
NRQUEST	6.15	2.85	1	14	4.72	2.64	1	19
ENTREPR	.02	.13	0	1	.03	.16	0	1
INCOME	16.54	8.24	0	109.3	19.10	7.50	0	103.2
DIFINC	.35	3.90	-13.5	44.0	.94	3.43	-62.3	50.1
CAPINC	.04	.20	0	1	.07	.26	0	1
BALINC	.46	3.38	<.01	60.4	.38	4.38	<.01	223.9
ZEROLIM	.04	.20	0	1	<.01	.02	0	1
LIMIT	41.44	57.98	0	511.5	51.05	50.54	0	949.2
NRLOANS	2.34	1.64	0	11	3.74	2.04	0	16
LIMUTIL	75.69	33.37	0	124.0	51.78	33.47	0	112.0
LOANSIZE	7.08	3.95	3.0	24.5	7.12	3.83	3.0	30.0
COAPPLIC	.07	.26	0	1	.14	.35	0	1

Table 35.4
Observation rule for y_{1i} and y_{2i}. Entries in the table show pairs (y_{1i}, y_{2i}) that are observed for all ranges of y_{1i}^* and y_{2i}^*

	$y_{2i}^* < 0$	$y_{2i}^* \geq 0$	
$y_{1i}^* < 0$	$(0,.)$	$(0,.)$	
$y_{1i}^* \geq 0$	$(1,0)$	$(1,1)$	

$$y_{2i} = \begin{cases} 0 & \text{if} \quad \text{loan defaults} \quad\quad (y_{2i}^* < 0) \\ 1 & \text{if} \quad \text{loan does not default} \quad (y_{2i}^* \geq 0) \end{cases} \tag{35.4}$$

Because one can only observe whether a loan is good or bad if it was granted, there is not only a censoring rule for (y_{1i}, y_{2i}) but even an *observation* rule, as shown in Table 35.4.

Because we have three types of observations: no loans, bad loans and good loans, the likelihood function will take the following form:

$$\ln L = \prod_{no\ loans} \Pr(no\ loan) \cdot \prod_{bad\ loans} \Pr(bad\ loan) \cdot \\ \prod_{good\ loans} \Pr(good\ loan) \tag{35.5}$$

Table 35.5
Bivariate probit MLE of $\widehat{\alpha}_1$ **and** $\widehat{\alpha}_2$

Variable	P(obtain a loan)			P(loan does not default)		
	$\widehat{\alpha}_1$	std. error	t-stat.	$\widehat{\alpha}_2$	std. error	t-stat.
CONSTANT	-.237	.0665	-3.57	2.290	.146	15.65
AGE	-.00430	.00117	-3.69	.00689	.00262	2.63
MALE	-.200	.0282	-7.10	-.0246	.0581	-.43
DIVORCE	-.0259	.0370	-.70	-.238	.0713	-3.34
HOUSE	.0639	.0276	2.32	-.0202	.0583	.35
BIGCITY	-.238	.0266	-8.96	-.0372	.0540	-.69
NRQUEST	-.00812	.00515	-1.58	-.100	.0102	-9.84
ENTREPR	.522	.0629	8.30	.207	.161	1.28
INCOME	.000893	.0000182	49.17	-.000239	.0000497	-4.81
DIFINC	-.000234	.0000345	-6.78	.000223	.0000735	3.04
CAPINC	-.278	.0507	-5.48	.119	.123	.97
BALINC	.00655	.00181	3.48	-.00914	.00592	-1.54
ZEROLIM	-2.244	.105	-21.40	-.659	.289	-2.23
LIMIT	-.00838	.000153	-54.94	.00506	.000493	10.28
NRLOANS	.0842	.00688	12.23	.270	.0187	14.41
LIMUTIL	-.00775	.000437	-17.72	-.0129	.000927	-12.91
COAPPLIC	.130	.0340	3.83	.437	.0972	4.50
LOANSIZE	-	-	-	-.00664	.00679	-.98
ρ	-	-	-	-.923	.0533	-17.34

In combination with the observation rule, (35.5) implies the following loglikelihood:

$$\ln L = \sum_{i=1}^{N}(1-y_{1i})\cdot \ln[1-\Phi(\mathbf{x_{1i}}\alpha_1)]+ \\ \sum_{i=1}^{N}y_{1i}\cdot(1-y_{2i})\{\Phi(\mathbf{x_{1i}}\alpha_1)-\Phi_2(\mathbf{x_{1i}}\alpha_1,\ \mathbf{x_{2i}}\alpha_2;\ \rho)\} \\ \sum_{i=1}^{N}y_{1i}\cdot y_{2i}\ \ln\Phi_2(\mathbf{x_{1i}}\alpha_1,\ \mathbf{x_{2i}}\alpha_2;\ \rho) \quad (35.6)$$

where $\Phi(\cdot)$ and $\Phi_2(\cdot,\cdot,\rho)$ represent the univariate and bivariate standard normal c.d.f., the latter with correlation coefficient ρ. The estimated parameters, their standard errors and t-statistics are presented in Table 35.5. Notice that *LOANSIZE* cannot be used as an explanatory variable in the first equation because no data on this variable is available for rejected applicants. The effect of many variables on the probability of obtaining a loan seems in accordance with the behavior banks commonly display. *INCOME, HOUSE, ENTREPR, NRLOANS* and having a *COAPPLIC*ant confirm their role as important factors that contribute positively while *ZEROLIM, LIMIT*, and *LIMUTIL* weigh negatively in the bank's decision.

Striking is the fact that only four variables have the equal signs in both equations that one would expect when banks are minimizing default risk. Exploiting the credit facilities one disposes of to a greater extent (a higher *LIMUTIL*) or lacking experience with servicing debt (*ZEROLIM*) reduces an applicant's odds of obtaining a loan from the bank and increases the likelihood of a default. Having more experience in borrowing money and servicing a debt, as reflected by a higher *NRLOANS,* or applying together with a *COAPPLIC*ant makes it more likely that somebody will receive a loan and also add to the chances that the loan will be paid back.

Four variables have opposite coefficients in the loan granting and default equations. *INCOME*, notwithstanding a large positive weight in the decision to grant a loan by the bank, actually increases a loan's probability of default. Table 35.3 clearly shows that people who default on their loans have a lower average income than those who do not. This may well lead us to infer - if we disregard the rejected applicants, who have lower incomes than those who were granted a loan - that higher income reduces default risk. Suppose, however, that it is actually the case that other factors than *INCOME* determine a loan's survival. Then the selection of applicants may be taking place on the basis of a negative bivariate correlation between *INCOME* and defaults rather than on grounds of a negative partial correlation, which controls for both the sample selection effect and the correlation with other variables. It may, for example, be the case that people with higher income have other characteristics that are associated with greater default risk. The positive coefficient on *DIFINC* in combination with the negative coefficient on *INCOME* illustrate how popularly assumed relations can lack factual support.

Furthermore, it is wortwhile to take notice of the large number of variables that are significant in only one equation and thus witness of inefficient use of information in the evaluation of applicants. *NRQUEST* is a proxy for people's eagerness to obtain additional credit and as such adds to the probability of a default. In the decision to grant a loan it has no role of importance, however. Being *DIVORCE*d, which can bring about a mismatch between financial obligations and income, has an effect similar to that of *NRQUEST*. Five variables, *MALE, HOUSE, BIGCITY, CAPINC* and *BALINC* carry either positive or negative weight in the bank's decision but do not affect a loan's risk of default. Finally, we point out that *LOANSIZE* has no influence whatsoever on default risk. On the margin, an extra credit with a maximum of SEK 30,000 apparently does not affect default probability. Because the average *LIMIT* is between six and seven times the the average *LOANSIZE*, the relevant variable to study in this context is *LIMIT*, the total amount of credit facilities.

The only parameter we have not yet reviewed is the correlation coefficient. The value of $-.923$ implies that non-systematic tendencies to grant loans are almost perfectly correlated with non-systematic increases in default risk.[1] In other words: the subjective elements - that conflict with the systematic policy described by (35.1) - in the bank's lending policy that increase individuals' odds of being granted a loan, are positively related to increases in default risk that cannot be unexplained by a systematic relation with the covariates x_{2i}.

If we compare the above results with those in [Boyes et al 1989] we can make three observations. Firstly, our results confirm the conclusion in [Boyes et al 1989] that banks do not appear to be minimizing default risk. Many of the variables that make the bank approve loan applications are not among those that reduce the probability of default. Secondly, non-systematic tendencies to grant loans are indeed associated with greater default risk. Thirdly, we find that the *size* of a loan does *not* affect default risk. This contradicts the interpretation of Boyes et al. that banks pick out loans with higher default risk because they have higher returns. They suggest that banks actually prefer *bigger*, not riskier, loans for the one reason that they offer higher expected earnings. Because they think of bigger loans as generally also being riskier, maximizing earnings would imply deviating from risk minimization. Here we *control* for *LOANSIZE* by including it in the set of explanatory variables and find that it has no significant impact on default risk. Bigger loans are thus not riskier.

As a consequence, the fact that bank behavior is not consistent with risk minimization cannot be ascribed to a disregarded relation between loan size and return. Because all loans in this sample pay the same rate of interest, there remain only two sources of differences in the expected rate of return between loans: survival time - and the amortizations and interest payments that result from it - and the loss rate on bad loans. To get a good forecast of profitability, banks may be evaluating survival and the loss rate simultaneously. In a study of the survival of bank loans, [Roszbach 1998] finds, however, that loans are not provided in a way that is consistent with survival time maximization. As an alternative, banks have been maximizing some other objective than the rate of return on their loan portfolio; for example, the number of customers or lending volume subject to a minimum return constraint, or total profits from a range of financial products.

---

1. Although the value of $-.92324$ for ρ is quite close to -1, and more than twice as large as what [Boyes et al 1989] found it to be, this is no symptom of problems with convergence for the algorithm. The correlation coefficient varied between $-.51$ and $-.97$ depending on the number and the type of variables that we let x_{ji} consist of.

35.4   Lending policies and Value at Risk

Estimating individual default risks is of limited help, because their linkage with credit losses is unclear. We will shift our attention in the remainder of the chapter from the estimation of default risk to the construction of a Value at Risk (VaR) measure. First, we derive a VaR measure using a Monte-Carlo simulation of the bivariate probit model of Section 35.3. After that, we show how it can be applied in a typical problem that a lending institution may be confronted with when supplying loans.

We define Value at Risk as "the loss that is expected to be exceeded with a probability of only x percent during the total holding period of the loan portfolio", where the relevant risk measure x needs to be chosen in advance. If one sets x equal to 5 percent, for example, a Value at Risk of SEK 10 mn. means that total credit losses on the loan portfolio will be greater SEK 10 mn. with a probability of 5 percent. Observe that our VaR concept differs from more conventional types in that the computed losses concern credit risk rather than market risk.

One of the purposes of this section is to illustrate how using Value at Risk instead of default risk can be auxiliary in optimizing bank lending policy. We will therefore carry out two experiments, in which the bivariate probit model from Section 35.3 will serve as a workhorse. First, we analyse how the Value at Risk is affected by marginal changes in the bank's acceptance rule. Second, we construct a hypothetical portfolio of loans that would be granted if the bank had a default risk based decision rule instead of its current policy. Comparing the distribution of credit losses on this hypothetical portfolio with those on the actual portfolio may supply us with a crude estimate of the efficiency losses that the bank's lending gives rise to.

In the first experiment we study how the bank can affect its Value at Risk exposure by making its acceptance criterion more or less restrictive. Here, we abandon the bank's current lending policy, as described by (35.1) and (35.3). In section 35.3 we showed that this policy is not consistent with risk minimization. Instead, we construct a default risk based acceptance rule of the form:

$$
\left. \begin{array}{l} \text{loan not granted} \\ \text{loan granted} \end{array} \right\} \ \text{if} \ \left\{ \begin{array}{l} pr\,(y_{2i} = 0) \geq \delta' \\ pr\,(y_{2i} = 0) < \delta' \end{array} \right. \tag{35.7}
$$

By means of a Monte-Carlo simulation similar to the one described above, we can derive the probability distribution of bank credit losses associated with the acceptance/rejection rule (35.7) for any value of the threshold parameter δ'. The Monte-Carlo simulation consists of the following 5 steps:

1. Pick a value for δ'.

2. Draw one observation $\mathbf{x_{2i}}\widetilde{\alpha_2}$ from $N\left(\mathbf{x_{2i}}\widehat{\alpha_2}, \sigma_{\mathbf{x_{2i}}\widehat{\alpha_2}}\right)$ for $i = 1, 2, .., 13338$, where $\sigma^2_{\mathbf{x_{2i}}.\widetilde{\alpha_{2i}}} = \mathbf{x_{2i}} \cdot \Sigma_{\widehat{\alpha_2}} \cdot \mathbf{x'_{2i}}$. Number them $i = 1, 2, .., 13338$;

3. To determine which applicants will be granted a loan, calculate the expected default probabilities $E\left[pr\left(y_{2i} = 0\right)\right]$ as

$$E\left[\widetilde{p_i}\right] = 1 - \Phi\left(\mathbf{x_{2i}}.\widetilde{\alpha_{2i}} \middle/ \left(1 + \sigma^2_{\mathbf{x_{2i}}.\widetilde{\alpha_{2i}}}\right)^{1/2}\right)$$

and then apply (35.7). Number the approved applications $i = 1, 2, ..., N_A$;

4. For the N_A approved applications, compute the total credit losses λ on this portfolio as

$$\lambda = \sum_{i=1}^{N_A} E\left[\widetilde{p_i}\right] \cdot q_i$$

where q_i is the size of the loan individual i applied for. Because q_i is not available for the rejected applicants, we impute $\overline{q} = \frac{1}{N_{A, \, true}} \sum_{i=1}^{N_{A, \, true}} q_i$ in steps 1-4. Here, $N_{A, \, true}$ is the number of accepted applicants in the original sample.

5. Repeat steps 1-4 M times and compute the approximate probability distribution over losses from the M values one obtains for λ. M should be chosen such that the distribution is invariable for $M' \geq M$.

For our purpose we have picked a series of values δ' in the interval $[.01, \ .20]$. The results from these simulations are displayed in Table 35.6. The second column shows how expected loan losses increase as the bank relaxes its lending policy. The most restrictive policy, $\delta' = .01$, results in lending between 36.6 mn. and 37.2 mn. kronor, whereas the most generous policy, $\delta' = .20$, leads to approximately two and a half times as much lending. As the lending volume grows, losses increase at an accelerating rate. For the most risk averse decision rule loan losses range from .3 to .6 mn. kronor, compared to SEK 3 mn. - up to 9 times as much - on the riskiest loan portfolio.

Applying a Value at Risk analysis before selecting a lending policy thus allows the lending institution to decide explicitly on either its aggregate credit risk exposure or its loss rate. Alternatively, it could choose to pick a desirable loss rate conditional on the Value at Risk not exceeding some maximum allowable amount of money. Doing so has several advantages. First, compared to current practice, the risk involved in lending becomes more transparent. Instead of registering loans that have already become non-performing, the financial institution will be able to create provisions for expected losses. This offers gains from both a private and a social perspective. From

Table 35.6
95 percent confidence intervals for total loan losses, total lending (both in th. SEK) and the loss rate (total credit losses/total lending), all for a given rejection threshold δ'

δ'	loan losses	total lending	loss rate
.01	$131 - 137$	$36,583 - 37,226$	$.36 - .37$
.02	$339 - 551$	$51,124 - 51,763$	$.66 - .68$
.03	$548 - 564$	$59,705 - 60,318$	$.92 - .94$
.04	$751 - 773$	$65,641 - 66,248$	$1.14 - 1.17$
.05	$948 - 947$	$70,083 - 70,683$	$1.35 - 1.38$
.06	$1,143 - 1,174$	$73,678 - 74,276$	$1.55 - 1.58$
.07	$1,334 - 1,370$	$76,672 - 77,225$	$1.74 - 1.77$
.08	$1,516 - 1,555$	$79,138 - 79,703$	$1.91 - 1.95$
.09	$1,687 - 1,730$	$81,181 - 81,730$	$2.08 - 2.12$
.10	$1,849 - 1,895$	$82,916 - 83,449$	$2.23 - 2.27$
.11	$2,003 - 2,053$	$84,411 - 84,923$	$2.37 - 2.42$
.12	$2,149 - 2,201$	$85,699 - 86,190$	$2.51 - 2.55$
.13	$2,285 - 2,339$	$86,812 - 87,279$	$2.63 - 2.68$
.14	$2,414 - 2,470$	$87,785 - 88,230$	$2.75 - 2.80$
.15	$2,285 - 2,339$	$88,641 - 89,066$	$2.85 - 2.91$
.16	$2,648 - 2,709$	$89,389 - 89,793$	$2.96 - 3.02$
.17	$2,752 - 2,814$	$90,034 - 90,416$	$3.06 - 3.11$
.18	$2,847 - 2,909$	$90,586 - 90,945$	$3.14 - 3.20$
.19	$2,932 - 2,995$	$91,057 - 91,398$	$3.22 - 3.28$
.20	$3,009 - 3,073$	$91,467 - 91,789$	$3.29 - 3.35$

a private perspective because provisions for loan losses on banks' balance sheets will be forward-looking and only lag *un* expected events. This should facilitate a correct valuation of the firm. At an aggregate level, there would be less risk for bankruptcy of financial institutions and therefore less risk for financial disturbances to the economy. See for example [Bernanke and Gertler 1995]. Secondly, unless the bank sets interest rates individually, this methodology also enables a bank to pick a risk-premium on top of the risk free rate of interest that is consistent with average credit risk over the maturity in question.

In the second experiment our aim is to produce an estimate of the monetary losses that the inefficiency in the current lending policy gives rise to. Table 35.6 has given us an impression of how lending volume, loan losses and the loss rate covary, and can help a bank choose one specific efficient lending policy from a larger set. However, before switching to a new policy, a financial institution will first want to quantify the potential gains from doing so. For this purpose, we construct the 'efficient' portfolio of loans that would be granted if the bank used a default risk based decision rule, instead of its current policy, but preferred a lending volume (approximately) equal to that of the actual portfolio. Executing steps 1-3 in the above Monte-Carlo

Table 35.7
Value at Risk at different risk levels computed for the sample portfolio and an efficiently provided portfolio of equal size (amounts × th. SEK)

Portfolio	Risk level		
	1%	5%	10%
Sample	1,513	1,506	1,503
Efficient	263	262	261

experiment and picking δ' such that the simulated lending volume equals actual lending gives us the desired portfolio.

By inspecting Table 35.6 one can already infer that the implied value of δ' will lie between .01 and .02. We find that δ' equals .012. We then repeat steps 2-5 of the Monte-Carlo experiment for both the actual and the 'efficient' portfolio - but do not apply (35.7) in step 3 since we already know which individuals make up our sample. From the credit loss distributions that we obtain along these lines, we extract three different Value at Risk measures for each portfolio. These are displayed in Table 35.7. Credit losses on the two portfolios clearly differ greatly. At the 10 percent risk level, the value at risk amounts to SEK 1,503 thousand for the actual portfolio compared to 261 thousand for the efficient portfolio. At the 1 percent risk level these amounts are 1,513 and 263 respectively. By shifting to a default risk based decision rule and abandoning its current lending policy, the bank can can reduce its expected credit losses significantly. Continuing providing loans in the same way as has been done leads to a VaR exposure that is six times higher than with a policy consistent with default risk minimization. Switching to one of the 'efficient' lending policies displayed in Table 35.7 thus involves large potential benefits for the financial institution.

35.5   Discussion

In this chapter we have applied the bivariate probit model from [Boyes et al 1989] to investigate the implications of bank lending policy. With a larger and more extensive data set we confirm earlier evidence that banks provide loans in a way that is not consistent with default risk minimization. It had been suggested that banks prefer *bigger* loans because they offer higher expected earnings. Since bigger loans are generally thought to be riskier, maximizing expected earnings would then imply deviating from risk minimization. However, with the data on the size of all loans that we have at our disposal, size has been shown not to affect the default risk associated with a loan. Banks, even if they are risk averse, are thus not faced with a trade-off between risk and return. The inconsistency in banking behavior can thus not be ascribed to some relation between loan size and return, that earlier models had not accounted for. The banking behavior must be either a symptom of an inefficient lending policy or the result of some other type of optimizing behavior. Banks may, for example, be forecasting survival time, loss rates or both. Another alternative is that they are maximizing another objective than the rate of return on their loan portfolio. Current banking technology does not yet allow for the pursuit of a composite objective such as the return on a range of products, however. In addition, the above suggestions are not in agreement with the practices reported to us by the lending institution that provided our data. Rather, the results bear the evidence of a lending institution that has attempted to minimize risk or maximize a simple return function without success.

By means of Monte-Carlo simulation with the bivariate probit model, we have obtained a Value at Risk measure for the sample portfolio of loans. Studying VaR offers several gains. It enables financial institutions to evaluate alternative lending policies on the basis of their implied credit risks, so that they can choose a risk-premium that is *consistent with* the average credit risk and can make provisions for loan losses more forward-looking. This should reduce the risk of bankruptcy for financial institutions and the likelihood of financial disturbances to the economy.

Acknowledgments

We thank Georgina Bermann, Kenneth Carling and Anders Vredin for their helpful comments and Björn Karlsson and Yngve Karlsson at Upplysningscentralen AB for providing and discussing the data. Roszbach gratefully acknowledges financial support from the Jan Wallanders and Tom Hedelius Foundation for Research in the Social Sciences.

References

Bernanke, B. and M. Gertler. 1995. Inside the black box: The credit channel of monetary policy transmission. *Journal of Economic Perspectives*, 9(4):27–48.

Boyes, W., D. Hoffman, and S. Low. 1989. An econometric analysis of the bank credit scoring problem. *Journal of Econometrics*, 40:3–14.

Roszbach, K. 1998. Bank lending policy, credit scoring and the survival of loans. Working Paper Series in Economics and Finance no.261, Stockholm School of Economics, Stockholm, Sweden.

36 Loan Duration and Bank Lending Policy

Kasper F. Roszbach

To evaluate loan applicants, banks use a large variety of credit scoring models. Traditional models typically minimize default rates. They fail to take into account that loans are multiperiod contracts. From a utility maximizing perspective it is not only important to know *if* but also *when* a loan will default. A Tobit model with a variable censoring threshold and sample selection effects is estimated for (1) the decision to provide a loan or not, and (2) the survival of granted loans. The model is an affective tool to separate applicants with short survival times from those with long survivals. The bank's loan provision process is shown to be inefficient: loans are granted in a way that conflicts with both default risk minimization and survival time maximization; there is no trade-off between risk and return in the policy of banks.

36.1   Introduction

Consumer credit has come to play an increasingly important role as an instrument in the financial planning of households. Its quantitative importance may be illustrated by the fact that total lending, excluding residential loans, by banks and finance companies to Swedish households amounted to SEK 207 bn., or SEK 22.698 per capita, by the end of 1996. That is equivalent to 12% of Swedish GDP or 22.7% of total private consumption. Viewed from the perspective of financial institutions, consumer credit also constitutes a significant part of their activities, making up 25% of total lending to the public. If one includes residential loans in total lending, this figure drops to 11%. When looking at the risk involved in these loans instead of their volume, their importance is even greater, however. BIS rules stipulate an 8 percent capital requirement on consumer credit compared to, for example, 4 percent on residential loans.

From these numbers, it may be clear that a lending institution's decision to grant a loan or not and its choice for a specific loan size can greatly affect households' ability to smooth consumption over time, and thereby even households' welfare. At an aggregate level the effects of any loan losses on lending capacity will be passed through to other sectors of the economy that rely on borrowing from the financial sector.

The process by which lending institutions evaluate loan applications varies greatly in its degree of sophistication, ranging from a non-formalized analysis of applicants' personal characteristics to statistical 'credit scoring' models that separate loan applicants that are expected to pay back their debts from those who are likely to fall into arrears or go bankrupt. The most commonly used methods [1] tend to suffer from problems with either the calibration, estimation or interpretation of their parameters and from a sample selection bias. Moreover, they fail to account for the multiperiod character of a debt contract and the implications this should have for the credit-granting decision.

In financial markets with perfect information, a one-period debt contract is optimal [Townsend 1982]. If single-period agreements were optimal and only the probability of default were unobservable to the lender, traditional credit scoring models - by enabling a lending institution to rank potential customers according to their default risk - could improve the allocation of resources, from a second best towards the first best equilibrium. In a more general context, with asymmetric information, a lender cannot solve his profit maximization problem this way, because an optimal debt contract will stretch out over several time periods [Townsend 1982]. A loan then generates a flow of funds until it either is paid off or defaults, in which case a part of the principal may still be recovered. The net present value of a loan is thus determined by the duration of the repayments, the amortization scheme, collection costs and any possible collateral value. Even if one is certain that it will default, it may well be profitable to grant a loan, Credit scoring models thus leave much room for subjective judgement in the loan approval process. In a sense, banks use statistical models to forecast bankruptcy, but - conditional on this forecast - resort to ad-hoc methods to predict profitability.

[Boyes et al 1989] address this deficiency and investigate if the provision of credit currently takes place in an efficient way. For this purpose they estimate a bivariate probit model with two sequential events as the dependent variables: the lender's decision to grant the loan or not, and the borrower's ability to pay it off or not. If the lending institution is minimizing credit risk, one ought to find opposite signs for the parameter of one particular explanatory variable in the two different equations. This would imply that variables that increase the probability of positive granting decision also decrease the likelihood of a default, or vice versa. [Boyes et al 1989] find, however, that variables like duration of job tenure, education and credit card ownership carry equal signs, indicative of a policy that conflicts with default risk. As we noted earlier, lenders may nevertheless prefer such a policy of supplying loans with a higher default risk because they have a higher expected rate of return (either the interest rate is higher or the default is expected to occur after a long

---

1. A good review of the literature on discriminant analysis is provided in [Altman et al 1981]. More recent studies have employed k-nearest-neighborhood [Henley and Hand 1996] and count data models [Dionne et al 1996], classification trees [Arminger et al 1997] and neural networks.

period with regular installments and interest payments). [Boyes et al 1989] also show that unexplained tendencies to extend credit are positively correlated with default frequencies - another fact consistent with a policy that trades off default risk against profitability.

This paper deals with two issues. First, in order to improve upon the currently available methods for evaluating loan applications, I construct and estimate a Tobit model with sample selection and variable censoring thresholds. This model can be used to predict the expected survival time on a loan for any potential applicant. This allows for a more realistic evaluation of the return on a loan than a simple default risk estimate froma traditional credit scoring model does. Secondly, I take up the question about the efficiency of banks' loan provision process raised by [Boyes et al 1989].

The rest of this paper is organized as follows. Section 36.2 describes the data set and its sources. In Section 36.3, I derive the econometric model. Section 36.4 contains the empirical results and Section 36.5 concludes the paper with a discussion of the results and possibilities for future research.

36.2 Descriptive statistics and the lending process

The data set consists of 13,337 applications for a loan that were processed by a major Swedish lending institution between September 1994 and August 1995. All applications were submitted in stores where potential customers applied for instant credit to finance the purchase of a consumer good. The evaluation of each application took place in the following way. First, the store phoned to the lending institution to get an approval or a rejection. The lending institution then analysed the applicant with the help of a database with personal characteristics and credit variables to which it has on-line access. The database is maintained by Upplysningscentralen AB,

the leading Swedish credit bureau which is jointly owned by all Swedish banks and lending institutions. If approval was given, the store's salesman filled out a loan contract and submitted it to the lending institution. The loan is revolving and administered by the lending institution as any other credit facility. It is provided in the form of a credit card that can only be used in a specific store. Some minimum payment by the borrower is required during each month. However, since the loan is revolving, there is no predetermined maturity of the loan. Earnings on the loan come from three sources: a one-time fee paid by the customer; a payment by the store that is related to total amount of loans granted through it; and interest on the

Table 36.1
Definition of variables

Variable	Definition
SURVIVAL	days between granting of a loan and its default
MALE	dummy, equals 1 if applicant is male
MARRIED	dummy, equals 1 if applicant is married
DIVORCE	dummy, equals 1 if applicant is divorced
HOUSE	dummy, equals 1 if applicant owns a house
BIGCITY	dummy, 1 if applicant lives in one of the three greater metropolitan areas around Göteborg, Malmö and Stockholm.
NRQUEST	no. of requests for information on applicant that the credit agency received during past 36 months
ENTREPR	dummy, equals 1 if applicant has taxable income from a registered business
INCOME	annual wage income as reported to Swedish tax authorities (in 10k SEK)
DIFINC	change in INCOME, relative to preceding year, as reported to Swedish tax authorities (in 10k SEK)
CAPINC	dummy, equals 1 if applicant has taxable income from capital
ZEROLIM	dummy, equals 1 if applicant has no collateral-free loans outstanding
LIMIT	total amount of collateral free credit facilities already outstanding (in th. SEK)
NRLOANS	number of collateral free loans already outstanding
LIMUTIL	percentage of LIMIT that is actually being utilized
LOANSIZE	amount of credit granted (in th. SEK)
COAPPLIC	dummy, equals 1 if applicant has a guarantor

balance outstanding on the card. For this study, the lending institution provided a data file with the personal number of each applicant, the date on which the application was submitted, the size of the loan that was granted, the status of each loan (good or bad) on October 9, 1996, and the date on which bad loans gained this status.

Upplysningscentralen provided the information that was available on each applicant at the time of application and which the financial institution accessed for *its* evaluation. By exploiting the unique personal number that each resident of Sweden has, the credit bureau was able to merge these two data sets. Before handing over the combined data for analysis, the personal numbers were removed. Overall, the database includes a total 60-70 variables. The major part consists of publicly available, governmentally supplied information such as sex, citizenship, marital status, postal code, taxable income, taxable wealth, house ownership. The remaining variables, like the total number of inquiries made about an individual, the number of unsecured loans and the total amount of unsecured loans, are reported to

Table 36.2
Descriptive statistics for all loan applicants ($N = 13337$)

Variable	Rejections ($N = 6899$)				Granted loans ($N = 6438$)			
	mean	stdev	min	max	mean	stdev	min	max
MALE	.62	.48	0	1	.65	.48	0	1
MARRIED	.47	.50	0	1	.47	.50	0	1
DIVORCE	.13	.34	0	1	.14	.35	0	1
HOUSE	.34	.47	0	1	.47	.50	0	1
BIGCITY	.41	.49	0	1	.37	.48	0	1
NRQUEST	4.69	2.60	1	10	4.81	2.68	1	19
ENTREPR	.04	.21	0	1	.02	.16	0	1
INCOME	12.99	7.04	0	73.8	18.95	7.57	0	109.3
DIFINC	.54	3.41	-43.9	25.3	.90	3.46	-62.3	50.1
CAPINC	.12	.32	0	1	.07	.25	0	1
ZEROLIM	.15	.36	0	1	<.01	.05	0	1
LIMIT	79.89	93.69	0	1703.0	50.33	49.83	.0	627.0
NRLOANS	2.99	2.42	0	18	3.65	2.04	0	16
LIMUTIL	64.34	38.88	0	278.0	53.22	33.94	0	124.0
COAPPLIC	.16	.36	0	1	.14	.35	0	1

Upplysningscentralen by the Swedish banks. Table 36.1 contains definitions of all variables that are used in the analysis in Section 36.4. Some descriptive statistics on the explanatory variables are provided in Tables 36.2 and 36.3.

Of the applicants, 6,899 (51.7%) were refused credit. The remaining 6,438 obtained a loan ranging from 3,000 to 30,000 Swedish kronor (approximately US$ 375 - 3750) . The lending institution's policy was that no loans exceeding 30,000 kronor were supplied. Although there is an indicated amortization scheme, the loans have no fixed maturity - they are revolving. On 9 October 1996, all people in the sample were monitored by the lending institutution. At that moment 388 (6.0%) of those who had obtained a loan had defaulted (forwarded to a debt-collecting agency). All other borrowers still fulfilled their minimum repayment obligations at that time. Descriptive statistics for survival time are provided in Table 36.4. The table may create the impression that the distribution of logarithmized survival time for bad loans is more skewed than untransformed survival. A QQ normality graph (not shown here), that compares a variable's sample distribution with a normal distribution with equal mean and variance, shows, however, that the transformation reduces the skewedness of survival time and improves the match with the normal distribution slightly.

Table 36.3
Descriptive statistics for granted loans.

Variable	Defaulted loans ($N = 388$)				Good loans ($N = 6051$)			
	mean	stdev	min	max	mean	stdev	min	max
MALE	.67	.47	0	1	.65	.48	0	1
MARRIED	.23	.43	0	1	.48	.50	0	1
DIVORCE	.20	.40	0	1	.14	.35	0	1
HOUSE	.28	.45	0	1	.48	.50	0	1
BIGCITY	.41	.49	0	1	.36	.48	0	1
NRQUEST	6.15	2.85	1	14	4.72	2.64	1	19
ENTREPR	.02	.13	0	1	.03	.16	0	1
INCOME	16.54	8.24	0	109.3	19.10	7.50	0	103.2
DIFINC	.35	3.90	-13.5	44.0	.94	3.43	-62.3	50.1
CAPINC	.04	.20	0	1	.07	.26	0	1
ZEROLIM	.04	.20	0	1	<.01	.02	0	1
LIMIT	41.44	57.98	0	511.5	50.90	49.21	0	627.0
NRLOANS	2.34	1.64	0	11	3.74	2.04	0	16
LIMUTIL	75.69	33.37	0	124.0	51.78	33.47	0	112.0
LOANSIZE	7.08	3.95	3.0	24.5	7.12	3.83	3.0	30.0
COAPPLIC	.07	.26	0	1	.14	.35	0	1

Table 36.4
Descriptive statistics for survival time. Percentiles for survival time and the natural logarithm of survival time. The sample has been split up into defaulted and non-defaulted loans.

Sample	min	Percentiles							max
		5	10	25	50	75	90	95	
t, bad loans	130	156	192	278	403	514	606	648	789
t, good loans	34	470	497	564	652	704	746	767	795
$\ln(t)$, bad loans	4.87	5.05	5.26	5.63	6.00	6.24	6.41	6.47	6.67
$\ln(t)$, good lns	3.53	6.15	6.21	6.34	6.48	6.56	6.61	6.64	6.68

36.3   Econometric model

Under ideal conditions evaluating loan applicants or studying efficiency in the provision of bank loans would entail modelling the revenue on each loan as a function of a set of personal characteristics and macro-economic indicators. However, since few banks store complete time series of interest payments and amortizations on loans, the information presently available and useful for such a study is limited to the current balance and status (good or bad) of each loan. Therefore, I will instead model the survival time of each loan. With some simplifying assumptions imposed on the amortization scheme and cost structure, one can then in principle calculate an estimate of the return on each loan as a function of survival time.

The econometric model consists of two simultaneous equations, the first one a probit for the decision to provide a loan or not, y_i, and the second one a Tobit for the natural logarithm of survival time of a loan (in days), for reasons of notational simplicity denoted by t_i. Because the bank from which we obtained our data merely considered whether it would accept an application or not, all people who were granted a loan received the amount of credit they applied for at the going rate of interest. The first equation therefore models a binary decision. I do not model how individuals determine the amount of credit they apply for. I use the superscript $*$ to indicate an unobserved variable and let y_i^* and t_i^* follow

$$y_i^* = \mathbf{x_{1i}}.\beta_1 + \varepsilon_{1i}, \tag{36.1}$$
$$t_i^* = \mathbf{x_{2i}}.\beta_2 + \varepsilon_{2i} \tag{36.2}$$

where the disturbances are assumed to be bivariate normal distributed with $\sigma_j = var\left(\varepsilon_j\right)$, $\sigma_{12} = cov\left(\varepsilon_1, \varepsilon_2\right)$, and $\sigma_1 = 1$. The binary choice variable y_i has the following censoring rule:

$$y_i = \begin{cases} 0 & if \quad y_i^* < 0 \\ 1 & if \quad y_i^* \geq 0 \end{cases} \qquad \text{for i=1,2,3,...,N} \tag{36.3}$$

The exact survival time can only be observed for loans that turn bad. For loans that are still performing on the day of monitoring, survival is censored because we do not know if and when they will turn bad. Because all loans are monitored on October 9, 1996, but are granted anywhere between September 1994 and August 1995, good loans' survival times will be censored at varying thresholds. If one denotes the censoring threshold by $\overline{t_i}$, then the censoring rule for the observed survival time t_i is:

$$t_i = \begin{cases} t_i^* & if \quad t_i^* < \overline{t_i} \\ \overline{t_i} & if \quad t_i^* \geq \overline{t_i} \end{cases} \qquad \text{for i=1,2,3,...,N} \tag{36.4}$$

Due to the fact that one only observes survivals for loans that are actually granted, there is not only a censoring rule for t_i but even an *observation* rule. This is shown in Table 36.5.

Because there are three types of observations (no loans, defaulted loans with survival t_i^*, and good loans with survival $\overline{t_i}$), the likelihood function will take the following form:

Table 36.5

Observation rule for y_i and t_i. Entries in the table show pairs $(y_i,\ t_i)$ that are observed for all ranges of y_i^* and y_i^*

	$t_i^* \le \overline{t_i}$	$t_i^* > \overline{t_i}$	
$y_i^* < 0$	$(0,.)$	$(0,.)$	
$y_i^* \ge 0$	$(1, t_i^*)$	$(1, t_i)$	

$$
\ln L \;=\; \prod\nolimits_{no\ loans} \Pr\left(no\ loan\right) \cdot \prod\nolimits_{bad\ loans} \Pr\left(bad\ loan\right) \cdot \\
\prod\nolimits_{good\ loans} \Pr(good\ loan) \tag{36.5}
$$

In combination with the observation rule in Table 36.5 and equations (36.1) - (36.2), (36.5) implies the following loglikelihood:

$$
\begin{aligned}
\ln L \;=\; & \sum_{i=1}^{N} (1 - y_i) \cdot \ln\left[1 - \Phi\left(\mathbf{x_{1i}}\beta_1\right)\right] + \\
& \sum_{i=1}^{N} y_i \cdot (1 - d_i) \; \left\{ \ln \Phi\left(\frac{\mathbf{x_{1i}}\beta_1 - \frac{\sigma_{12}}{\sigma_2^2}\left(t_i - \mathbf{x_{2i}}\beta_2\right)}{\sqrt{(1-\rho^2)}} \right) + \right. \\
& \left. -\tfrac{1}{2}\ln 2\pi + \ln\left(\tfrac{1}{\sigma_2}\right) - \tfrac{1}{2}\left(\frac{t_i - \mathbf{x_{2i}}\beta_2}{\sigma_2} \right)^2 \right\} + \\
& \sum_{i=1}^{N} y_i \cdot d_i \; \ln \Phi_2\left(\mathbf{x_{1i}}\beta_1,\ \frac{\mathbf{x_{2i}}\beta_2 - \overline{t_i}}{\sigma_2};\ \rho \right)
\end{aligned} \tag{36.6}
$$

Here $\Phi\left(\cdot\right)$ and $\Phi_2\left(\cdot, \cdot, \rho\right)$ represent the univariate and bivariate standard normal c.d.f., the latter with correlation coefficient ρ. The dummy d_i splits up the granted loans into good ones (1) and bad ones (0). The first term, for rejected applications, is a standard probit likelihood. The other terms resemble bivariate probit likelihoods, that are modified for the fact that t_i is a continuous, albeit censored, variable.

36.4 Empirical results

Table 36.6 contains the FIML estimates and t-statistics of the model parameters. Column one shows that the effect of most variables on the probability of obtaining a loan is as one might have expected. *INCOME* and *HOUSE* confirm their role as important factors that contribute positively, while *LIMIT*, *LIMUTIL* and *DIVORCE* have the traditional negative effects. More surprising are the coefficients on *MAR-RIED*, *DIFINC* and *CAPINC*. The parameter on *MARRIED* may be capturing the positive correlation between age and marriage. In preliminary regressions where age was one of the explanatory variables, it consistently had a negative effect on the probability of being granted a loan. Its parameter estimate failed to gain significance, though. *LOANSIZE* could not be used as an explanatory variable because no data on this variable were available for rejected applications.

Columns two and three compare two different estimators of β_2 and σ_2. The estimates in the second column are from a Tobit model with a variable censoring threshold that ignores the sample selection effect one generates by disregarding the rejected loan applications. This is equivalent to estimating β_2 and σ_2 in (36.2) under the hypothesis that $\rho = 0$. One is, in other words, assuming that the likelihood of a survival of a certain length is not affected in any systematic way by the inferences one can make from observing y_i and x_{1i}. If the hypothesis is true, then the parameters in equations (36.1) - (36.2) can be estimated separately from each other. However, if the disturbances ε_1 and ε_2 *are* correlated, then the estimators of β_2 and σ_2 will be biased. The third column contains the consistent parameters estimates of β_2 and σ_2 obtained by estimating the complete model $(36.1) - (36.4)$.

The purpose of this comparison is to investigate to what extent any misunderstandings about the relation between people's characteristics and financial discipline may have originated in an incorrect way of sampling data for profitability analyses by financial institutions, and vice versa. It will also help us to determine whether inconsistencies in bank lending policy find their origin in a sample selection bias and to what extent this is a quantitatively importannt phenomenon.

All explanatory variables enter the model linearly. I have checked for the presence of non-linear effects by adding quadratic terms of all continuous variables. Their coefficients were never significant, however. Out of 16 explanatory variables, four lose or reduce their significance and three turn significant or increase their level of significance when the sample selection effect is disregarded. So although accounting for the sample selection effect never reverses the sign of any of the coefficients, it does clearly affect their magnitude. The influence of the variable *ZEROLIM*, for example, will be badly overestimated if one does not account for the sample selection effect. Tables 36.2 and 36.3 may help us to understand this phenomenon. Although having no loans outstanding is rather uncommon among the granted loans, it is stronger associated with defaulting than with proper repayment behavior. However, this overlooks the fact that 15% of all rejected applicants did not have any loan yet. If rejected applications are not so much different from approved ones, then the actual impact of having a zero limit may well be much smaller than one would expect by merely looking at granted loans.[2] Similarly, *INCOME* is not significant in the column with biased estimators, whereas the consistent parameter estimate has a

---

2. Rejected applications will differ very little from approved ones if the lending institution grants loans to applicants on the basis of characteristics that have little impact on survival.

Table 36.6
Bivariate Tobit MLE of β_1, univariate and bivariate Tobit MLE of β_2 and bivariate probit MLE of α_2. Univariate MLE are computed under the hypothesis $\rho = 0$.

Variable	β_1	univ. β_2	biv. β_2	α_2
CONSTANT	-0.328	8.246	9.065	2.454
	(-6.40)	(53.05)	(47.08)	(21.69)
MALE	-0.196	-0.106	0.0240	-0.0234
	(-7.00)	(-1.74)	(0.41)	(-0.40)
MARRIED	-0.233	0.187	0.345	0.253
	(-7.89)	(2.74)	(5.22)	(3.85)
DIVORCE	-0.179	-0.124	-0.00873	-0.0702
	(-4.54)	(-1.58)	(-0.13)	(-0.95)
HOUSE	0.103	0.0607	-0.0233	-0.0100
	(-3.63)	(0.99)	(-0.38)	(-0.17)
BIGCITY	-0.222	-0.128	0.0233	-0.0407
	(-8.37)	(-2.21)	(0.44)	(-0.74)
NRQUEST	-0.00429	-1.155	-0.967	-0.104
	(-0.85)	(-9.48)	(-8.87)	(-10.10)
ENTREPR	0.570	0.136	0.162	0.135
	(8.88)	(0.75)	(1.02)	(0.86)
INCOME	0.00086	0.00379	-0.0286	0.000227
	(48.63)	(0.90)	(-5.71)	(-4.52)
DIFINC	-0.000237	0.0147	0.0185	0.000205
	(-6.80)	(1.96)	(2.35)	(2.80)
CAPINC	-0.272	-0.0571	0.195	0.148
	(-5.44)	(-0.46)	(1.95)	(1.17)
ZEROLIM	-2.218	-2.244	-0.328	-0.680
	(-19.54)	(-5.60)	(-2.34)	(-2.28)
LIMIT	-0.00848	0.00582	0.561	0.00482
	(-40.71)	(0.10)	(11.27)	(8.47)
NRLOANS	0.0864	3.288	2.587	0.270
	(12.41)	(12.85)	(11.50)	(13.89)
LIMUTIL	-0.759	-12.950	-12.230	-1.208
	(-16.89)	(-10.76)	(-10.58)	(-13.00)
COAPPLIC	0.146	0.509	0.374	0.419
	(4.26)	(4.68)	(3.60)	(4.28)
LOANSIZE		-0.0686	-0.0670	-0.00658
		(-0.94)	(-1.00)	(-0.96)
σ_2		0.919	1.096	$\equiv 1$
		(20.50)	(15.68)	(-)
ρ		$\equiv 0$	-0.986	-0.911
			(-46.11)	(-16.20)

significantly negative coefficient. Although one should be careful not to rationalize each counter-intuitive finding, we can look for a tentative explanation. Tables 36.2 and 36.6 clearly show that people with higher incomes are more likely to be granted a loan. This may well lead us to infer - if we disregard the rejected applicants, who have low incomes, and consider only approved ones - that income does not influence a loan's default risk. Suppose, however, that actually other factors than *INCOME* determine a loan's survival. Then the selection of applicants may be taking place on the basis of a negative bivariate relation between *INCOME* and defaults (see Table 36.3) that disappears when one controls for the sample selection effect and the correlation with other variables. It is not unusual to find people with higher incomes taking greater risks.

It is also worthwhile to take notice of the sign of some other parameter estimates in the fourth column of Table 36.6. *NRQUEST* is considered to be quite good an indicator of a person's efforts to obtain additional credit and as such expected to contribute negatively to survival. Not having any loan at all, as indicated by *ZEROLIM*, is a sign of inexperience with servicing debt and has a negative effect on survival. The reverse holds for *NRLOANS* and *LIMIT*. The positive effect on survival of two granted loan evens out the negative effect of five questions. Although one might expect *LIMIT* to have a negative influence, one should keep in mind that it is merely the ceiling of a person's credit facility. *LIMUTIL* captures the extent to which he or she actually uses it, while *LIMIT* proxies for experience with servicing debt in the same way as *NRLOANS* does. A rise in income between years increases expected survival while a higher utilization degree of the available credit facility by an applicant reduces survival. Finally, it is worth commenting the value of the correlation coefficient. Its value of -.98 may create the impression that the algorithm had problems converging. In extensive tests of the model with different sets of explanatory variables and varying sample sizes, ρ took values between -.55 and -.98. [Boyes et al 1989] report -.35. As is common with limited dependent variable models [Bermann 1993], the computations for the tobit and probit models did not converge for some configurations of explanatory variables. When the computations broke down, divergence always took place after relatively few iterations, however, with ρ breaking its constraint before any of the other parameters had stabilized around a final value. In the estimation of the model reported in Table 36.6, all parameters settled down around their final values rather quickly.

Overall, the conclusion one can draw from these results is that ignoring rejected applicants in an analysis of the duration of loans leads to large biases in the parameter estimates. Although the signs of parameters are never reversed, some of the variables that are generally thought to be among the most important determinants of creditworthiness, like income, outstanding loans, and income from assets, appear to have no relationship whatsoever with survival time when disregarding the sample selection effect. Such misunderstandings may well be the origin of inefficient lending policies at financial institutions.

Finally, in column four of Table 36.6, I present parameters of the bivariate probit model of [Boyes et al 1989], re-estimated with the data used for model (36.1) - (36.2). When comparing the probit parameters that determine the probability of a loan *not* defaulting (α_2) with those that determine logged survival time (β_2) one notes that each variable has coefficients with identical signs in both models.[3] [4] Variables that increase (decrease) the probability of a default thus also decrease (increase) the expected survival time of a loan and thus - since survival time proxies for return - reduce (raise) its expected return. Moreover, variables like *MALE, DIVORCE, HOUSE, BIGCITY* and *ENTREPR* that are given significant weights in the loan granting decision actually do not affect default risk and survival. *NRQUEST* on the other hand does have a significant effect on survival but is not given any weight in the decision process. For variables like *MARRIED, INCOME, DIFINC, CAPINC* and *LIMIT*, the parameter estimates for the loan granting decision and the probability of a loan not defaulting have opposite signs. These variables are thus used in such a way by the bank in the loan granting process that they increase (decrease) the likelihood of a loan being granted although they in fact increase (decrease) the risk of default. Because the parameters in the survival equation have the same sign as the bivariate probit parameters, these variables also reduce (raise) expected survival and return on the loan. In other words: if the bank is not minimizing default risk in its loan granting policy, it is not doing so because loans with higher default risk have higher expected returns. Moreover, the negative value of ρ indicates that any non-systematic propensity to grant loans is associated with shorter survival times and higher default risk. This is consistent with the behavior of a bank that does not trade off risk against return: the loan granting policy appears to be inefficient and contain non-systematic components that are strongly negatively correlated with survival. In the estimation of α_2 and β_2, we controlled for the size of the loan. Table 36.6 shows that neither default risk nor survival is affected by *LOANSIZE*. This has two implications. First, bigger loans do not carry greater default risk nor do they imply either shorter or longer survivals. Secondly, greater default risk is associated with shorter survival, not with *longer* survival as [Boyes et al 1989] suggest. Riskier loans thus have *lower* expected returns. The

---

3. As a matter of fact, all variables with significant parameters in the survival equation of the Tobit model with sample selection also have significant coeffficients in the 'probability that loan doesn't default' equation of the bivariate probit model. The reverse, however, does not hold! Variables that would have been sigificant in a bivariate probit model but are not in the Tobit model like (36.1) - (36.2) have therefore been omitted.

4. The bivariate probit model implicitly assumes that loans which are still good, will not turn bad later on.

lending institution that we study, however, always extended loans with size equal to the amount applied for - independent of the risk associated with the applicant - and was thus indifferent between alternative loan sizes. Such behavior is not consistent with the hypothesis that the financial institution is trading off higher default risk against higher expected earnings (that supposedly come with bigger loans). The lending institution's behavior is neither compatible with return maximization due to a (previously assumed) positive relation between loan size and rate of return nor is it in agreement with the maximization of survival time in general. If the lending institution is minimizing default risk, it would be strictly better off granting either nothing at all or the maximum amount possible for the type of loan in question. After all, granting a bigger loan does not increase risk but it does raise revenues. For the same reason, the lending institution would also be better off with this corner solution policy if it is maximizing survival time. It raises revenues without changing the riskiness.

Model $(36.1) - (36.4)$ can now be used to examine the lending policy of the bank. Loans with the longest expected survival time also have the greatest gross returns. The estimated model shown from Table 36.6 will therefore be used to calculate the expected survival time for all loan applicants. Table 36.7 shows the outcome from an experiment where all loan applications are ranked and approved according to their predicted survival time $E\left[t_i^* \mid \mathbf{x_{2i}}\right]$. The first column in the table shows that only 3,156 out of the 6,438 granted loans (49%) would have been approved if selection had taken place according to expected survival time. This strongly suggests that the current lending policy is not efficient, because it selects loans with short survivals. These results could, however, also be indicative of the model's inability to separate good from bad loans. Another means to evaluate the reliability of the results in Table 36.7 is to check how many of the bad loans would have been granted with a survival time selection criterion. This way, lending to 349 of the 388 defaulted applicants in the sample could have been avoided. This seems to confirm that the model is an effective tool to evaluate loan applicants.

36.5   Discussion

To take into account the multiperiod nature of loan contracts, a Tobit model with sample selection and variable censoring thresholds has been constructed and estimated. This model is shown to be a useful tool for predicting for expected survival time on loans. A comparison with a nested model that disregards rejected applications - as has been common in studies of creditworthiness - shows that

Table 36.7
Selecting applications by predicted survival times. Entries in the first 2 columns and rows show how many applicants who were granted a loan would even be so if applicants were ranked according to predicted survival time $E\left[t_i^* \mid \mathbf{x_{2i}}\right]$ and the number of granted loans were equal to that in the data set.

p		actual			# failed loans
r		granted	rejected	sum	among predicted
e	granted	3, 156	3, 282	6, 438	39
d	rejected	3, 282	3, 617	6, 899	349
i	sum	6, 438	6, 899	13, 337	388
c					
t					

ignoring the sample selection effect leads to a large bias in the parameters estimates. The empirical results not only confirm the finding of [Boyes et al 1989] that financial institutions' lending policies are not consistent with default risk minimization, but even show that they are not trading off higher default risk against higher returns. The lending policy does not favor people that survive longer and thus have a higher rate of return: there is no evidence that the bank maximizes profit. Unless the bank is maximizing some other objective function, like provision income from the turnover on credit cards, the number of customers or lending volume subject to a minimum return constraint, the displayed lending behavior must be a symptom of an inefficient lending policy. None of these suggestions agree, however, with the practices reported to us by the lending institution who provided our data. Rather, the results bear strong evidence of a lending institution that has attempted to minimize risk or maximize a simple return function without success.

Acknowledgments

I would like to thank Marcus Asplund, Kenneth Carling, Luigi Ermini, Lennart Flood, Dennis Hoffman, Tor Jacobson, Sune Karlsson, Jesper Lindé, Rickard Sandin, Patrik Säfvenblad, Paul Söderlind, Anders Vredin and seminar participants at the Stockholm School of Economics, the Bank of Sweden, De Nederlandsche Bank and the EARIE 1998 meeting for their helpful comments and Yngve Karlsson and Björn Karlsson at Upplysningscentralen AB for providing and discussing the data. Financial support from the Jan Wallander and Tom Hedelius Foundation is gratefully acknowledged.

References

Altman, E., R. Avery, R. Eisenbeis, and J. Sinkey. 1981. *Application of classification techniques in business, banking and finance*. JAI Press, Greenwich, CT.

Arminger, G., D. Enache, and T. Bonne. 1997. Analyzing credit risk data: a comparison of logistic discrimination,classification tree analysis and feedforward networks. *Computational Statistics*, 12:293–310.

Bermann, G. 1993. *Estimation and inference in bivariate and multivariate ordinal probit models*. PhD thesis, Uppsala University, Uppsala, Sweden. Department of statistics,.

Boyes, W., D. Hoffman, and S. Low. 1989. An econometric analysis of the bank credit scoring problem. *Journal of Econometrics*, 40:3–14.

Dionne, G., M. Artis, and M. Guillen. 1996. Count data models for a credit scoring system. *Journal of Empirical Finance*, 6:303–325.

Henley, W. and D. Hand. 1996. A k-nearest neighbor classifier for assessing consumer credit risk. *The Statistican*, 45:77–95.

Townsend, R. 1982. Optimal multiperiod contracts and the gain from enduring relationships under private information. *Journal of Political Economy*, 90(6):1166–1186.

VII Option Pricing

37 Estimation of Stochastic Volatility Models for the Purpose of Option Pricing

Mikhail Chernov and Eric Ghysels

In this paper we review the recent advances on the estimation of stochastic volatility (henceforth SV) models for the purpose of option pricing. For SV models, it is impossible to estimate the risk-neutral parameters using only the data from the underlying asset pricing process. We focus on the recent attempts which try to exploit optimally the information in the panel data of options and the information in the underlying fundamental. The fulfillment of this goal, which we have not yet fully accomplished, yields risk neutral parameters as well as the temporal dynamics under both measures.

Introduction

The literature on the subject of stochastic volatility models and on option pricing is huge. There are several recent surveys, notably by Bates (1996b) and Ghysels *et al.* (1996), which cover many of the early and more recent developments. This paper complements the recent literature and focuses on one very specific, and very important topic, namely the estimation of SV models for the purpose of option pricing. It raises several issues, some old and some new ones, which have been addressed with new methods of estimation. In order to implement option pricing formula one has to know the estimates of the parameters under the risk-neutral measure. In the world of Black and Scholes (1973) the no arbitrage portfolio argument determines an exact mapping between the so called physical measure and the risk neutral one. Both the risk neutral and physical parameters can be recovered from observing the dynamics of the underlying fundamental process. For SV models, however, the preference structure of agents is required to make a transition to the risk-neutral world because volatility is not a traded asset. It is therefore impossible to estimate the risk-neutral parameters using only the data from the asset pricing process underlying the option contracts.

The estimation of SV models typically involves the underlying fundamental asset prices. Estimation methods such as Generalized, Simulated and Efficient Methods of Moments (respectively GMM, SMM and EMM), Bayesian MCMC, as well as other simulated likelihood procedures were applied to a multitude of models belonging to the SV class. The differences in model specification, like the time structure (discrete versus. continuous) and the specification of the volatility process, make it very hard to compare the empirical results.

From the time series properties of the fundamental we can price an option only if we are willing to assume that the volatility risk is idiosyncratic as in Hull and White (1987). However, multiple studies find evidence of a nonzero volatility risk premium (see Bates (1996b) for references). This implies in turn that one needs some extra input to make the transition from the physical to the risk neutral measure. Observing only the underlying fundamental and estimating SV models with this information will not deliver derivative security pricing. One solution is to use the options data instead of the underlying fundamental for SV model estimation. It yields directly an estimate of the required risk-neutral parameters. Options data are essentially panel data, i.e. frequent (e.g. daily) observations through time of quotes or transaction prices are recorded. The moneyness and time to maturity of contracts create the cross-sectional heterogeneity. The use of option cross-sections yields estimates of the parameters, but it does not accommodate well the temporal dynamics of the model. Relying exclusively on the cross-section essentially makes the SV model a sophisticated version of the ad-hoc implementation of the Black-Scholes model. This paper focuses on the recent attempts to reconcile these shortcomings by incorporating the time series of the options data into the estimation strategy. Ultimately the goal is to exploit optimally the information in the panel data of options and the information in the underlying fundamental, realizing that some of the information is redundant. The fulfillment of this goal yields risk neutral parameters as well as the temporal dynamics under both measures.

Most of the recent attempts to address these issues use the variants of the Heston (1993) SV model which yields analytical option pricing formula. His approach was extended by many authors and generalized by Bakshi and Madan (1998) and Duffie *et al.* (1998). It applies to jump-diffusions of the affine class.[1] This imposes a certain uniformity on the empirical studies in option pricing because the models are easier to compare as they are nested in the general model specification described in Duffie *et al.* (1998). The parallel development of estimation techniques, including the Simulated Method of Moments (SMM) of Duffie and Singleton (1993) and its recent extension in Gallant and Tauchen (1996) known as the Efficient Method of Moments (EMM), allows one to deal with the issue of filtering the non-observable spot volatility and to achieve the efficiency of maximum likelihood without the knowledge of the likelihood function. Finally, typical econometric diagnostics are not enough. The size of option pricing errors is the ultimate test and object of interest. The out-of-sample performance of any model therefore becomes very important.

Table 37.1 provides a summary of the papers on the subject of estimating SV models for the purpose of option pricing. In the table we provide information about the estimation method, the type of data used, the volatility filter and the type of

---

1. The Bakshi and Madan (1998) approach extends beyond the affine class. They, however, do not specify the mapping between the objective and risk-neutral measures.

Table 37.1

Estimation Methodology: The recent empirical work on the SV model estimation for the purpose of option pricing is summarized. The class of an adopted model, type of data used for estimation, estimation method, spot volatility filter and an approach to the estimated volatility dynamics assessment are reported for each paper. Notations: iv - BS implied volatility, giv - volatility implied from an SV model, sv - spot volatility, o - objective measure parameters, n - risk-neutral measure parameters.

Paper	Model	Type of data	Estimation	SV filtering	SV dynamics
Pastorello *et al* (1994)	Hull-White	daily iv time series	indirect inference	—	—
Bates (1996, 1998)	affine	weekly options panel (transactions)	NL-GLS, options group specific + individual errors	weekly giv together with n	estimation constrained by the sv pdf, but applied to the giv
Nandi (1996)	affine	intradaily options panel	NL-GLS, AR(1) errors	daily giv together with n	—
Bakshi *et al* (1997)	affine	intradaily calls cross-section	NL-OLS	daily giv together with n	—
Bakshi *et al* (1998)	affine	daily puts panel	SMM	daily giv given n	—
Jiang and van der Sluis (1998)	discrete time	daily returns + daily calls cross-section	EMM for o, NL-OLS for n given o	daily sv reprojected from returns	fully model consistent
Chernov and Ghysels (1998)	affine	daily returns jointly with iv time series	EMM	daily sv reprojected from returns and iv	fully model consistent
Benzoni (1998)	affine and Scott	daily returns + daily calls panel	EMM for o, NL-OLS/ SMM for n given o	daily giv with n given o/ Kalman filter	—/ linearized model consistent
Pan (1998)	affine	daily returns jointly with calls time series	GMM with giv used for sv (L-GMM)	daily giv together with $o+n$	giv vs. the realized volatility
Poteshman (1998)	non-para-metric	daily options panel+returns	EM-type algorithm+ kernel reg.	daily giv together with $o+n$	—

model estimated. The content of the table will be a guidance for the discussion through the remainder of the paper. Section 37.1 provides a summary review of SV models which have been considered. The next section discusses estimation techniques. Section 37.3 surveys approaches to volatility filtering and section 37.4 reviews the empirical findings. The last section concludes.

37.1   Characterizations of the Risk Premium

The continuous time affine class of SV models is the most popular because it features analytical solutions for pricing option contracts. Therefore, the majority of empirical studies adopt a specification which is affine.[2] This motivates us to provide some details about this class of models. Comparisons with non-affine models will be addressed in the next section when we discuss particular implementations.

We adopt a simplified version of the Duffie *et al.* (1998) description of an affine jump-diffusion. We assume that the logarithm of an asset price is the first factor in the following system:

$$dX_t = \mu(X_t, t)dt + \sigma(X_t, t)dW_t + dZ_t \tag{37.1}$$

All the models we consider here can be described by a three-dimensional vector X_t with up to four independent Brownian innovation shocks W_t. In particular,

$$\mu(x, t) = \begin{pmatrix} \mu_0 \\ \theta_2 \\ \theta_3 \end{pmatrix} + \begin{pmatrix} 0 & \mu_1 - \frac{1}{2} & c\left(\mu_2 - \frac{1}{2}\right) \\ 0 & -\kappa_2 & 0 \\ 0 & 0 & -\kappa_3 \end{pmatrix} x \tag{37.2}$$

$$\sigma(x, t)\sigma(x, t)^\top = \underbrace{\begin{pmatrix} 1 & \rho_2\sigma_2 & 0 \\ \rho_2\sigma_2 & \sigma_2^2 & 0 \\ 0 & 0 & 0 \end{pmatrix}}_{\Sigma_2} x_2 + \underbrace{\begin{pmatrix} c & 0 & \rho_3\sigma_3 \\ 0 & 0 & 0 \\ \rho_3\sigma_3 & 0 & d\sigma_3^2 \end{pmatrix}}_{\Sigma_3} x_3 \tag{37.3}$$

where x_i is the ith component of the vector x. The univariate jump part is described in the following way:

$$dZ_t = -\lambda(X_t, t)\mu_J dt + \log(1 + J_t)dq_t \tag{37.4}$$

$$\log(1 + J_t) \sim N\left(\log(1 + \mu_J) - \frac{1}{2}\sigma_J^2, \sigma_J^2\right) \tag{37.5}$$

$$dq_t \sim Poi(\lambda(X_t, t)dt) \tag{37.6}$$

$$\lambda(x, t) = \lambda_0 + \lambda_2 x_2 + \lambda_3 x_3 \tag{37.7}$$

Finally, the risk-free interest rate is determined by:

$$r(x, t) = r_0 + r_2 x_2 + r_3 x_3 \tag{37.8}$$

---

2. It is worth noting that there are compelling empirical reasons to focus on the affine class of models. For instance, Benzoni (1998) finds only marginal differences between the performance of the Heston (1993) model, which is in this class, and the Scott (1987) model, which is not affine.

The most general constant interest rate model is the one with $r_2 = r_3 = 0$, $c = d = 1$ and four innovation shocks was considered by Bates (1998). The most frequently used models are nested within the above model specification and can be obtained by setting some of the parameters equal to zero. For example, $c = \mu_1 = \theta_3 = \kappa_3 = \sigma_3 = \rho_3 = \lambda_3 = \lambda_2 = 0$ yields the model introduced in Bates (1996a). In addition, setting $\lambda_0 = 0$ yields the original Heston (1993) model. Scott (1997) considers the stochastic interest rate model with $c = \rho_3 = r_0 = \lambda_2 = \lambda_3 = 0$ and $d = r_2 = r_3 = 1$. Finally, Bakshi *et al.* (1997, 1998) investigate a slightly less general model with $r_2 = 0$.[3] All of these models have as many innovation shocks as factors.

In order to price options we need to characterize the transformation from the objective measure P to the risk-neutral measure P^*. If $\exp(X_{1t})$ is the underlying asset price, then we know from financial theory that the drift of the asset price process under P^* should be equal to $r(X_t, t)$. One can not identify restrictions on the drifts of other factors because they are not traded. Consequently, one must rely on some (parametric) specification of the transformation between P and P^*. One commonly used mapping is:

$$\mu^*(x,t) \;=\; \mu(x,t) - \Sigma \eta x \qquad\qquad (37.9)$$

$$\theta(\psi) \;=\; (1 + \mu_J) \exp\left\{ \frac{\sigma_J^2}{2} \psi(\psi - 1) \right\} \qquad\qquad (37.10)$$

$$\lambda^*(x,t) \;=\; \lambda(x,t)\theta(\zeta) \qquad\qquad (37.11)$$

$$\theta^*(\psi) \;=\; \theta(\psi + \zeta)/\theta(\zeta) \qquad\qquad (37.12)$$

where Σ is a tensor comprised of Σ_i's, the vector η represents the assumed market prices of the factors risks, the scalar ζ represents the market price of the jump risk and $\theta(\psi)$ is the moment generating function of the jump size, J_t, distribution (see for instance Duffie *et al.* (1998), Ho *et al.* (1996) for details). The models specified in (1.1) through (1.12) are all special cases of the general option pricing theory developed in Bakshi and Madan (1998) and Duffie *et al.* (1998). They provide pricing formula for European-type as well as several other types of option contracts.

The above theoretical setup defines the task an econometrician faces. In particular, one has to estimate the objective measure parameters of the diffusion (37.1) and the market prices of risk $(\eta^\top, \zeta)^\top$. To execute this task one faces two important problems. The presence of unobservable (latent) variables and absence of the

---

3. Note that most of the three factor models have the stochastic interest rate as a third factor. The exception is Bates (1998) who considers another latent process as a third factor.

closed-form solution of the system of stochastic differential equations in (37.1) do not allow one to use the maximum likelihood estimation. This problem is well known and discussed in detail in the econometrics literature on the estimation of SV models (see Ghysels *et al.* (1996) for further details). Since Maximum Likelihood is not available, parameter estimates will not be most efficient. Hence, we need to find an estimation procedure with minimal efficiency losses. The second problem one faces is that in order to estimate the prices of factor risk one has to use the options data to estimate these risks.[4] We noted already that it is unclear at this point how one can utilize the available data optimally. For instance, the options cross-section will provide an excellent fit to the current date, but does not contain any information about the dynamics of the system. For instance, Bakshi *et al.* (1997) specify their model under P^* right away and re-fit it every day, foregoing any possibility to predict more than one step ahead. We know that the dynamics can be uncovered from the underlying returns time series. It is not obvious nor straightforward, however, how to combine options and returns data and which options data from the cross-section to select for this combination. Moreover, the data selection is also inherently related to the estimation methodology which is used.

37.2   Estimation Methodology

The first factor of the X_t vector process appearing in (37.1) is the logarithm of the stock price process. As is the case for any stochastic volatility process, there is no analytical expression for the likelihood function for X_{1t}. Hence, estimation has to proceed along different principles, such as method of moments or simulated likelihood methods. The Efficient Method of Moments of Gallant and Tauchen (1996) is at the intersection of full-blown maximum likelihood and moment-based estimation. More specifically, the EMM estimation procedure relies on moments, which are selected from a score of an auxiliary model which converges (in terms of the Sobolev norm) asymptotically to the true probability density of the data. Benzoni (1998) and Jiang and van der Sluis (1998) apply EMM using returns data. Chernov and Ghysels (1998) estimate the Heston (1993) model using the joint process of daily returns and at-the-money options implied volatility time

---

4. The alternative approach is to determine the measure transformation via the general equilibrium consumption-based model argument as for instance in Bates(1996a, 1998). However, unless one is willing to estimate the relevant parameters from, say monthly consumption data, one can estimate the risk-neutralized parameters only from the options data. See also Scott (1997) for the case when the S&P 500 index is the fundamental process.

series data. The estimation strategy proposed by Chernov and Ghysels (1998), in principle, applies to more complex models as well, involving panels of options data featuring different moneyness and maturity.[5] In such a setting one combines the information in the options cross-section with that in time series dynamics of options and the underlying fundamental (see Chernov *et al.* (1999) for further details). The major drawback of the EMM estimation procedure is that its implementation is computationally demanding and is currently infeasible for auxiliary densities of more than four series. Hence, for large systems (panels) one has to rely on less efficient moment-based procedures.

Several GMM (Hansen (1982)) strategies involving multiple assets were recently proposed and applied in the context of affine diffusion models. Liu (1998) estimates a stochastic interest rate extension of the Heston (1993) model using monthly yields and returns data. The GMM procedure requires analytical expressions for the unconditional moments of the model, which he derives under the assumption that the process is stationary. The stationarity assumption is warranted provided the initial value is drawn from a stationary marginal distribution. It is not feasible, however, to derive this distribution analytically.[6] Therefore, Liu assumes that the starting value is a constant. However, this may lead to the non-stationarity of the stock price process distribution, which in turn violates the regularity conditions required for implementing the GMM estimator and guarantee its standard root-T asymptotics. In one particular case one can derive the marginal distribution, though it involves the unappealing assumption that there is no leverage effect. Ho *et al.* (1996) derive analytical unconditional moments using this restriction. Another application of GMM involving the Heston model is discussed in Pan (1998). Her approach involves daily returns and options data, as in Chernov and Ghysels (1998). Pan derives analytical conditional moments for the model which depend on the spot latent volatility process. The presence of unobservable variables precludes the direct implementation of GMM (both in discrete time or in continuous time as suggested by Hansen and Scheinkman (1995)). Pan proposes an elegant modified GMM procedure, coined as L-GMM, which uses the Heston option pricing formula to imply the spot volatility from observed option prices. She invokes the implicit function theorem to obtain the asymptotic covariance estimator of the moment conditions which involve implied volatilities. The fact that latent spot volatilities

---

5. Pastorello *et al.* (1994) is an early paper which used exclusively options data and the indirect inference method of Gouriéroux *et al.* (1993), an estimation method very similar to EMM.

6. See the discussion in Hansen and Scheinkman (1995) along the same line with regard to the stationarity of multivariate diffusions.

are replaced by implied ones, still introduces a bias however, as discussed recently by Ledoit and Santa-Clara (1998). Earlier papers have often relied on GMM-type procedures, such as nonlinear ordinary and generalized least squares. Examples include Bates (1996a, 1998), Nandi (1996) and Bakshi et al. (1997). In general the estimation procedures in these papers are consistent but do not fully exploit the optimal implementation of GMM.

The aforementioned difficulties encountered with the applications of GMM can be resolved with the Simulated Method of Moments estimation procedure. Duffie and Singleton (1993) derive the asymptotic properties of SMM estimators in the context of time-homogeneous Markov processes. While there are many similarities with GMM, the fact that simulations are used to compute moment conditions has several advantages. In addition to resolving the problems of starting values and the presence of latent processes it also allows for moment conditions which are analytically intractable.[7] This last feature is particular relevant here, since moment conditions based on options prices cannot be computed analytically. While there are clear advantages to the use of SMM, there is a cost associated with the simulation uncertainty which entails a loss of efficiency. One can easily control such losses, however, by augmenting the number of simulations (see e.g. Duffie and Singleton (1993) for further details). For example, even a small number of simulated paths, say ten, increases confidence intervals by no more than 5% relative to GMM with the same moment conditions. The recent applications of SMM to options valuation include Bakshi et al. (1998), who use options panel data to estimate a Heston-type model with stochastic interest rates and jumps, and Benzoni (1998), who uses the SMM procedure as a second stage estimator of the market price of volatility risk in the context of the Heston (1993) and Scott (1987) models.

An interesting deviation from the Method of Moments approach is suggested by Poteshman (1998). His approach does not involve a parametric specification for μ and σ in a bivariate version of (37.1). The procedure involves iterations between implying volatilities from the options cross-section and non-parametric estimation of the model based on the time-series of these volatilities via an EM-type algorithm. Poteshman (1998) assumes constant risk-free interest rate, to avoid non-parametric estimation of the interest rate process, and imposes a constant correlation coefficient as well. His method has similarities with Pastorello et al. (1994) who also iterate between simulated instantaneous volatilities and the ML estimation of the model parameters.

---

7. Please note that EMM and SMM are closely related procedures. The EMM procedure is a particular SMM estimator where the choice of moment conditions is guided by an auxiliary model.

37.3 Volatility Filtering

The distinguishing feature of SV models is the latent volatility process. While it is possible to estimate SV models, using for instance the underlying fundamental, without filtering the volatility process, it is impossible to price options based only on the estimated parameters. Therefore, filtering volatility is intimately related to the pricing of options. Early studies of SV models considered filters based on returns data (see Ghysels *et al.* (1996) for a discussion). Several filters involving exclusively the return process have been proposed in the literature. Harvey *et al.* (1994) suggested to make use of the Kalman filter based on a discrete time SV model. Nelson and Foster (1994) showed how diffusion limit arguments applied to the class of EGARCH models provided a justification of EGARCH models as filters of the instantaneous volatility. French *et al.* (1987) suggest volatility filters based on squared returns. Along the same lines Nelson and Foster (1996) provide the theoretical foundations for using rolling regressions. Some attempts were made to extend these filters to a multivariate context, see in particular Harvey *et al.* (1994), Jacquier *et al.* (1995) and Nelson (1996). These multivariate extensions all involve exclusively return series and cannot accommodate derivative security market information.

The Kalman filter is known to be suboptimal because the volatility filtering problem is inherently non-Gaussian and nonlinear. The exact filter was derived by Jacquier *et al.* (1994) using Bayesian Markov Chain Monte Carlo methods. One advantage of the Bayesian MCMC methods is that filtering spot volatility is a natural by-product of estimation. The EMM estimation procedure has similar features. Gallant and Tauchen (1998) proposed an extension of EMM which yields asymptotically unbiased filters as well, based on a reprojection procedure (which will be described shortly). Bayesian MCMC methods are not easy to extend to options data, either involving simultaneously returns data and options or a panel of options. The EMM procedure in its generic form can be multivariate, (i) only involving a vector of returns, (ii) only involving a vector of options, and (iii) a mixture of the previous two.

Most studies involving options data proposed filters, which are generalized implied volatilities based on inverting the SV option pricing formula (see Table 37.1). There are at least two disadvantages to the use of implied volatilities as filters. First, implied volatilities obtained from European options are biased estimates of spot volatility as they are related to the expected volatility over the remaining life of the option contract. Second, the time series dynamics of estimated volatility are muted since implied volatilities are extracted from options cross-sections. Bates

(1996a, 1998) tries to remedy this by augmenting the NL-GLS estimation procedure with restrictions pertaining to the dynamics of the spot volatility process. Since his method still involves implied volatilities, however, it does not resolve the bias due to replacing spot volatility by implieds. For the same reasons, this bias also affects the methods proposed by Pan (1998) and Poteshman (1998).

To proceed further we need to briefly describe the reprojection method of Gallant and Tauchen (1998). Denote the vector of contemporaneous and lagged observed variables by x_t and the vector of contemporaneous unobserved variables by y_t, Θ is the parameters vector. The filtering problem is equivalent to computing the following conditional expectation:

$$\tilde{y}_t = E(y_t|x_t) = \int y_t p(y_t|x_t, \Theta) dy_t \qquad (37.13)$$

This expectation involves the conditional probability density of y_t. If we knew the density implied by the system dynamics, we could estimate it by $\hat{p}(y_t|x_t) = p(y_t|x_t, \hat{\Theta})$. Unfortunately, for SV models there is no analytical expression for the conditional density available. Therefore, we need to estimate this density as $\hat{p}(y_t|x_t) = f_K(\hat{y}_t|\hat{x}_t)$, where $\hat{y}_t, \hat{x}_t$ are simulated from the SV model with parameters set equal to $\hat{\Theta}$ and where f_K is the SNP density of Gallant and Tauchen (1989). Gallant and Long (1997) show that:

$$\lim_{K \to \infty} f_K(\hat{y}_t|\hat{x}_t) = p(y_t|x_t, \hat{\Theta}) \qquad (37.14)$$

where the index K is related to the dimension of the SNP density parameter vector and grows at the appropriate rate with the sample size. Hence, as noted earlier, reprojection provides an unbiased estimate of the spot volatility.

The reprojection method for the purpose of option pricing is applied by Chernov and Ghysels (1998) and Jiang and van der Sluis (1998). The latter consider univariate filters involving returns data. Chernov and Ghysels (1998) use the reprojection method in a univariate context, involving at-the-money options, and a bivariate setup involving returns data in addition to options.[8] Their results show that the univariate approach only involving options by and large dominates. A by-product of this finding is that they uncover a remarkably simple volatility extraction filter based on a polynomial lag structure of Black-Scholes implied volatilities. The

---

8. Gallant *et al.* (1998) adopt a strategy similar to the bivariate approach in Chernov and Ghysels (1998) though not involving options. Namely, they consider the bivariate process of the fundamental and the daily high/low spread, which provides extra information about the course of volatility.

simplicity of this scheme is rather surprising if one thinks of the complexity of the task. Indeed, alternative filters based on returns involve highly nonlinear functions of returns. Hence, the virtue of using volatility data to predict future spot volatility is that one can limit the filter to a linear structure. It should be noted, however, that the construction of the filter is unfortunately not as simple as running a linear regression model. Since spot volatility is a latent process one can only recover the filter weights via the reprojection procedure.

37.4   Evaluation and Empirical Findings

It is standard econometric practice to evaluate models on the basis of the in-sample fit. Diagnostics like overidentifying restrictions tests are among the most commonly used. Obviously, one also looks at the parameter estimates and their economic interpretation. The empirical studies reported in Table 37.1 use quite a variety of model specifications and data. The results are therefore difficult to compare directly. However, there are some findings which are robust. For instance, there is no doubt that volatility risk is priced and that volatility is negatively correlated with the asset returns (leverage effect). In this regard there are some unsettled issues. For instance, using Heston's model Chernov and Ghysels (1998) find only a small, albeit statistically significant, leverage effect regardless whether it is estimated with S&P 500 returns data or SPX options or both together. In contrast, Bakshi *et al* (1998), Benzoni (1998), Nandi (1996) and Pan (1998), using different sample periods, find much larger (though with wide range) point estimates of the leverage effect parameter for the same model. On the other hand, the parameter estimate of the price of volatility risk in Benzoni (1998) and Pan (1998) implies that the volatility process is non-stationary under risk neutral distribution while it is stationary under the objective measure. Such a discrepancy is not found in Bakshi *et al* (1998), Chernov and Ghysels (1998) and Nandi (1996). At this point, there is no clear understanding yet of these widely different results. Both theoretical and empirical developments are necessary here.

At the theoretical level, the appropriate affine model specification analysis in Dai *et al* (1998) becomes important. In particular, they show that the models considered in empirical studies impose unnecessary zero restrictions on the parameters. Removing such restrictions will help uncovering the dynamics present in the data. On the empirical side, the next logical step is to use a genuine panel of options and the fundamental returns jointly to estimate a sufficiently rich model. This line is pursued in Chernov *et al.* (1999).

Statistical criteria for model selection are one thing, financial criteria such as pricing and hedging performance out-of-sample are obviously the ultimate scope of model selection. A model rejected by the data may provide more accurate option pricing compared to one with a good in-sample fit. Hence estimated models should also be evaluated out-of-sample. Typically one uses the relative or absolute mean-squared pricing error, which corresponds to the quadratic utility-based loss function.[9] An alternative way to compare models is to appraise the performance of their volatility filters. Chernov and Ghysels (1998) suggest to substitute different volatility filters into the Black-Scholes formula. This comparison allows one to separate the role of volatility filtering from that of the pricing kernel in the valuation of derivative contracts. This comparison also allows one to see whether pricing formula more advanced than BS add any improvement in pricing performance.

There is a vast literature which studies whether the BS implied volatility is a good forecast of the realized volatility (see Bates (1996b) for a review). The premise of these studies is based on the insight of the Hull-White model that implied volatility is the expected value of the average integrated spot volatility. Most of these studies find that implied volatility is biased upwards as compared to the realized volatility. We can explain these findings by the fact that Hull and White (1987) do not model the leverage effect and volatility risk premium, which are found to be present in the data.

Overall, we still find that standard SV models are rejected, on the basis of their statistical fit, by the data whatever the source of observations is, i.e. returns or options. There is improvement in the out-of-sample option pricing performance according to some criteria, like volatility filtering and compared to naive applications of the Black-Scholes model. These improvements are not always spectacular and may not justify the additional complications that SV models bring along. Moreover, all studies involving a bivariate model find that one latent factor is not enough to explain the variability in the fundamental process and options prices. A second latent variable or a jump component are necessary to improve pricing performance. Bates (1998) made a first contribution in this direction by considering a three-factor model with jumps. Chernov *et al* (1999) and Duffie *et al* (1998) pursue the extensions of this line of research.

---

9. It would be interesting to use the representative investor utility as a loss-function. For instance, the constant interest rate affine models can be supported by the economy with logarithmic preferences (see Bates(1996a)). Brandt (1998) uses the exponential utility to evaluate hedging errors.

Conclusion

We reviewed the recent advances on the estimation of multi-factor latent volatility models for the purpose of option pricing. Important theoretical developments and improvements in econometric methods were the main reason of the recent surge of research interest in this area.

The multitude of theoretical models, of data sets used and of performance evaluation still does not allow us to make general conclusions about model specification and fitting stylized facts like the volatility smile. We tried to assess where progress was made in recent years. While advances were made in the formulation and estimation of affine SV models we still need to go a long way on their practical implementation. We expect that much of the literature will ultimately converge to a consensus SV model which passes the rigorous tests of statistical fit and outperforms conventional ad hoc pricing schemes.

References

Bakshi, G., C. Cao, and Z. Chen. 1997. Empirical performance of alternative option pricing models. *Journal of Finance*, 52:2003–2049.

Bakshi, G., C. Cao, and Z. Chen. 1998. Pricing and hedging long-term options. *Journal of Econometrics*. Forthcoming.

Bakshi, G. and D. Madan. 1998. Spanning and derivative-security valuation. *Journal of Financial Economics*. Forthcoming.

Bates, D. 1996a. Jumps and stochastic volatility: Exchange rate processes implicit in deutsche mark options. *Review of Financial Studies*, 9:69–107.

Bates, D. 1996b. Testing option pricing models. In Maddala, G. and C. Rao, editors, *Handbook of Statistics, Vol. 14*. Elsevier Science B.V.

Bates, D. 1998. Post-'87 crash fears in the S&P 500 futures option market. *Journal of Econometrics*. Forthcoming.

Benzoni, L. 1998. Pricing options under stochastic volatility: An econometric analysis. Working paper, Northwestern University.

Black, F. and M. Scholes. 1973. The pricing of options and corporate liabilities. *Journal of Political Economy*, 81:637–659.

Brandt, M. 1998. Multiperiod hedging of contingent claims. Working paper, University of Pennsylvania.

Chernov, M., A. R. Gallant, E. Ghysels, and G. Tauchen. 1999. Estimating Jump Diffusions with a Panel of Options and Returns. Working Paper, Pennsylvania State University.

Chernov, M. and E. Ghysels. 1998. A study towards a unified approach to the joint estimation of objective and risk neutral measures for the purpose of options valuation. Working paper, Pennsylvania State University.

Dai, Q., J. Liu, and K. Singleton. 1998. Admissibility and identification problems of affine asset pricing models. Working paper, Stanford University.

Duffie, D., J. Pan, and K. Singleton. 1998. Transform analysis and option pricing for affine jump-diffusions. Working Paper, Stanford University.

Duffie, D. and K. Singleton. 1993. Simulated moments estimation of Markov models of asset prices. *Econometrica*, 61:929–952.

French, K., G. W. Schwert, and R. Stambaugh. 1987. Expected stock returns and volatility. *Journal of Financial Economics*, 19:3–29.

Gallant, A. R., C.-T. Hsu, and G. Tauchen. 1998. Calibrating volatility diffusions and extracting integrated volatility. Working Paper, Duke University.

Gallant, A. R. and J. Long. 1997. Estimating stochastic differential equations efficiently by minimum chi-square. *Biometrika*, 84:125–141.

Gallant, A. R. and G. Tauchen. 1989. Seminonparametric estimation of conditionally constrained heterogeneous processes: Asset pricing applications. *Econometrica*, 57:1091–1120.

Gallant, A. R. and G. Tauchen. 1996. Which moments to match? *Econometric Theory*, 12:657–681.

Gallant, A. R. and G. Tauchen. 1998. Reprojecting partially observed systems with application to interest rate diffusions. *Journal of American Statistical Association*, 93:10–24.

Ghysels, E., A. Harvey, and E. Renault. 1996. Stochastic volatility. In Maddala, G. and C. Rao, editors, *Handbook of Statistics, Vol. 14*. Elsevier Science B.V.

Gouriéroux, C., A. Monfort, and E. Renault. 1993. Indirect inference. *Journal of Applied Econometrics*, 85:85–118.

Hansen, L. P. 1982. Large sample properties of generalized method of moments estimators. *Econometrica*, 50:1029–1054.

Hansen, L. P. and J. Scheinkman. 1995. Back to the future: Generating moment implications for continuous-time Markov processes. *Econometrica*, 63:767–804.

Harvey, A., E. Ruiz, and N. Shephard. 1994. Multivariate stochastic variance models. *Review of Economic Studies*, 61:247–264.

Heston, S. 1993. A closed-form solution for options with stochastic volatility with applications to bond and currency options. *Review of Financial Studies*, 6:327–343.

Ho, M., W. Perraudin, and B. Sørensen. 1996. A continuous-time arbitrage-pricing model with stochastic volatility and jumps. *Journal of Business and Economic Statistics*, 14:31–43.

Hull, J. and A. White. 1987. The pricing of options on assets with stochastic volatilities. *Journal of Finance*, 42:281–300.

Jacquier, E., N. Polson, and P. Rossi. 1994. Bayesian analysis of stochastic volatility models (with discussion). *Journal of Business and Economic Statistics*, 12:371–417.

Jacquier, E., N. Polson, and P. Rossi. 1995. Stochastic volatility: Univariate and multivariate extensions. Working Paper, Boston College.

Jiang, G. and P. van der Sluis. 1998. Pricing stock options under stochastic volatility and interest rates with Efficient Method of Moments estimation. Working Paper, University of Groningen.

Ledoit, O. and P. Santa-Clara. 1998. Relative pricing of options with stochastic volatility. Working Paper, UCLA.

Liu, J. 1998. Portfolio selection in stochastic environments. Working Paper, Stanford University.

Nandi, S. 1996. Pricing and hedging index options under stochastic volatility. Working Paper, Federal Reserve Bank of Atlanta.

Nelson, D. 1996. Asymptotic filtering theory for multivariate arch models. *Journal of Econometrics*, 71:1–47.

Nelson, D. and D. Foster. 1994. Asymptotic filtering theory for univariate arch models. *Econometrica*, 62:1–41.

Nelson, D. and D. Foster. 1996. Continuous record asymptotics for rolling sample variance estimators. *Econometrica*, 64:139–174.

Pan, J. 1998. "Integrated" time-series analysis of spot and option prices. Working Paper, Stanford University.

Pastorello, S., E. Renault, and N. Touzi. 1994. Statistical inference for random variance option pricing. *Journal of Business and Economic Statistics*. Forthcoming.

Poteshman, A. 1998. Estimating a general stochastic variance model from option prices. Working Paper, University of Chicago.

Scott, L. 1987. Option pricing when the variance changes randomly: Theory, estimation and an application. *Journal of Financial and Quantitative Analysis*, 22:419–438.

Scott, L. 1997. Pricing stock options in a jump-diffusion model with stochastic volatility and interets rates: Applications of Fourier inversion methods. *Mathematical Finance*, 7:413–426.

38 Option Pricing via Genetic Programming

N. K. Chidambaran, Chi-Wen Jevons Lee, and Joaquin R. Trigueros

We propose a methodology of Genetic Programming to approximate the relationship between the option price, its contract terms and the properties of the underlying stock price. An important advantage of the Genetic Programming approach is that we can incorporate currently known formulas, such as the Black-Scholes model, in the search for the best approximation to the true pricing formula. Using Monte Carlo simulations, we show that the Genetic Programming model approximates the true solution better than the Black-Scholes model when stock prices follow a jump-diffusion process. We also show that the Genetic Programming model outperforms various other models when pricing options in the real world. Other advantages of the Genetic Programming approach include its low demand for data, and its computational speed.

The Black-Scholes model is a landmark in contingent claim pricing theory and has found wide acceptance in financial markets. The search for a better option pricing model continues, however, as the Black-Scholes model was derived under strict assumptions that do not hold in the real world and model prices exhibit systematic biases from observed option prices. We propose the Genetic Programming methodology for better approximating the elusive relationship between option prices, option contract terms, and properties of the underlying stock price.

Many researchers have attempted to explain the systematic biases of the Black-Scholes model as an artifact of its assumptions [Hull 1997]. The most often challenged assumption is the normality of stock returns[1]. Merton (1976) and Ball and Torous (1985) propose a Poisson jump-diffusion returns processes. French, Schwert and Stambaugh (1987) and Ballie & DeGennaro (1990) advocate GARCH [Bollerslev 1986] processes. It is not possible to derive closed-form analytical solutions in all cases, in which cases numerical solutions are used.

The difficulty in finding an analytical closed-form parametric solution has also led to non-parametric approaches. Rubinstein (1997) suggests that we examine option data for the implied binomial tree to be used for pricing options. Chidambaran and Figlewski (1995) use a quasi-analytic approximation based on Monte Carlo simulation. Hutchinson, Lo and Poggio (1994) build a numerical pricing model using neural networks. We apply Koza's (1992) Genetic Programming to develop an adaptive evolutionary model of option pricing. This method is well suited to the

---

1. Normality of stock returns has been repeatedly rejected. Indeed, Kim and Kon (1994) have ranked candidates for return distributions and found normality to be the least likely. Their rankings are: 1) Intertemporal dependence models (ARCH, GARCH), 2) Student t, 3) Generalized mixture of normal distributions, 4) Poisson jump, and 5) Stationary normal.

task and can operate on small data sets, circumventing the large data requirement of the neural network approach noted by Hutchinson, Lo, and Poggio (1994).

The philosophy underlying Genetic Programming is to replicate the stochastic process by which genetic traits evolve in offspring through a random combination of the genes of the parents, in the biological world. A random selection of functions of the option contract terms and basic statistical properties of the underlying stock price will have among them some elements that will ultimately make up the true option pricing formula. By selectively "breeding" the functions, these elements will be passed onto future generations of functions that price options more accurately.

Since it is impossible to ex-ante determine which element is the best, we instead focus on parent-selection, that is, the method of selecting equations to serve as parents for the next generation. Equations are chosen probabilisitically based on the pricing errors of the functions. We examine six alternative parent-selection methods: Best, Fitness, Fitness-overselection, Random, Tournament with 4 individuals and Tournament with 7 individuals. We find that the Fitness-overselection method seems to offer the best results for option pricing. We also explore the effect of varying other model parameters, such as the properties of the data set required to train the genetic programs, on model efficiency.

An important advantage of the Genetic Programming approach over other numerical techniques is its ability to incorporate known approximate solution into the initial "gene pool" to be used in evolving future generations, for example, we can include the Black-Scholes model. We illustrate how this approach quickly adapts the Black-Scholes model to a jump-diffusion process, where the Black-Scholes assumption of returns normality does not hold and for pricing options in the real world. We find that the Genetic Programming formulae beats the Black-Scholes equation in 9 out of 10 runs when the underlying stock prices are generated by a jump-diffusion process and in 10 out of 10 runs when we apply the analysis to the S&P Index options. The method also outperforms the Black-Scholes model for four out of five equity stock options in our sample.

38.1 Genetic Programming—A Brief Overview

Genetic Programming is a technique that applies the Darwinian theory of evolution to develop efficient computer programs[2]. We use a variant of Genetic Programming

---

2. Genetic Programming is an offshoot of Genetic Algorithms. Genetic Algorithms have been used to successfully develop technical trading rules by Allen and Karlajainen (1993) for the S&P 500 index and by Neely, Weller, and Dittmar (1997) for foreign exchange markets. In a paper similar

called Genetic Regression, where the desired program is a function that relates a set of inputs such as stock price, option exercise price, etc., to one output, the option price.

38.1.1 Basic Approach

The set of data on which the program operates to determine the relationship between input parameters and the options price is called the training set. The set of data on which the resulting formula is tested is called the test set. The procedure of the basic approach is as follows.

• Given a training set of matched inputs and outputs, a set of possible formulas is randomly generated. The formulas are represented as trees and we allow a maximum tree depth of 17^3. Each formula is an individual and the set of individuals is called the population. The size of the population is held constant and is a control variable for optimizing the genetic program.

• Every individual in the population is evaluated to test whether it can accurately price options in the training data set. Based on individual fitness, a subset of the population is selected to act as the parents for the next generation of formulas.

• A pair of the parents generates a pair of offspring. Components of the parent formulas are crossed to generate offspring formula. A random point is selected in each parent tree. The sub-trees below that random point are switched between the two parent formulas. This operation creates a new pair of individuals, the offspring. It is possible that no crossover is performed and the parents themselves are placed in the new population (a clone). The process of selection and crossover is repeated until the new generation is completely populated.

• The steps above are repeated for a pre-specified number of times, or generations. Evolutionary pressure in the form of fitness-related selection combined with the crossover operator eventually produce populations of highly fit individuals. The best-fit individual is the solution to the option pricing problem.

---

in spirit to our study, Keber (1998) uses Genetic Programming to value American put options. Genetic Programming has also been used in multi-agent financial markets by Lettau (1997) and in multi-agent games by Ho (1996).

3. A 17 deep tree is a popular number used to limit the size of tree sizes Koza(1992). Practically, we chose the maximum depth size possible without running into excessive computer run times. Note that the Black-Scholes formula is represented by a tree of depth size 12. A depth size of 17, therefore, is large enough to accommodate complicated option pricing formulas and works well in practice.

38.1.2   Parent Selection Criteria

The method of selecting parents for the next generation can affect the efficiency of genetic programs. We analyze six different selection methods: Best, Fitness, Fitness-overselection, Random, Tournament with 4 individuals and Tournament with 7 individuals. These methods represent various attempts to preserve a degree of "randomnes" in the evolutionary process. In the Best method, individuals are ranked in terms of their fitness, ascending in order of the magnitude of their errors. The individuals with the smallest errors are thus picked to serve as parents of the next generation. In the Fitness method, individuals are selected randomly with a probability that is proportional to their fitness. In the Fitness-overselection method, 400 individuals are classified into two groups. Group 1 has 320 best-fit individuals and Group 2 has the remainder. Individuals are selected randomly with an 80% probability from Group 1 and a 20% probability from Group 2. In the Random method, the fitness of the individuals is completely ignored and parents are chosen at random from the existing population. Finally, in the Tournament method, n individuals are selected at random from the population and the best-fit individual is chosen to be a parent. We examine Tournament method with n=4 and n=7.

38.2   Performance Analysis in a Jump-Diffusion World

We first examine how well the Genetic Programming model can adapt and out-perform the Black-Scholes model under controlled conditions. We choose a jump-diffusion world described by Merton (1976), since the closed form solution for the option prices in a jump-diffusion world is known and is a convenient benchmark. We can therefore measure the pricing errors of the Genetic Programming model and the Black-Scholes model.

The jump-diffusion process is a combination of a Geometric Brownian diffusion process and a Poisson jump process and can be written as:

$$\frac{dS(t)}{S(t)} = (\mu - \lambda k)dt + \sigma dW(t) + dq \tag{38.1}$$

where dq is the Poisson-lognormal jump process. The Poisson process determines when a jump occurs, with the jump size being lognormally distributed.

We simulate the price path of daily stock prices over a 24 month period with the initial price set at $S_0 = 50$. Each month is assumed to have 21 trading days. The diffusion parameters m (mean) and σ(standard deviation) were set at 10% and 20% respectively, and jump parameters k(jump size), λ (jump rate), and δ (standard

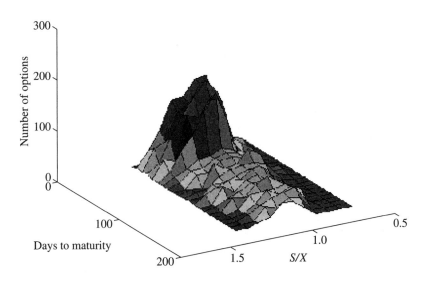

Figure 38.1
Distribution of options simulated in the jump-diffusion world

deviation of the log-jumps), were set at $0.02, 25$, and 0.05 respectively. These values are well within the range estimated by stock price data. Thus 504 stock prices, $S(t)$, are simulated using random daily returns $z_t \sim N[(m - \sigma^2/2 - k)/252, \sigma/252]$ and $n(t) \sim Poisson[\lambda t]$ jumps, each of magnitude Y_j (where $lnY_j \sim N[ln(1+k) - 0.5\delta^2, \delta]$) for each $t \in 1 \ldots 504$:

$$S(t) = S_0 e^{\sum_{i=1}^{t} z_t} Y(n(t)), \quad t = 1, \ldots, 4 \tag{38.2}$$

where, $Y(0) = 1$ and $Y(n(t)) = \prod_{i=1}^{n(t)} Y_i$, $n(t) > 0$

We use CBOE rules to create call options from the simulated stock price path. Figure 38.1 shows the distribution of option prices in a jump-diffusion world.

Options are priced using Merton's (1976) jump-diffusion formula, truncated at the point when the marginal contribution of additional terms is negligible.

$$F(S, X, r, \sigma, \tau, \lambda, k, \delta) = \sum_{n=0}^{\infty} \frac{e^{-\lambda' \tau}(\lambda' \tau)^n}{n!} C_{B-S}(S, X, r_n, v_n, \tau) \tag{38.3}$$

where, $\lambda' = \lambda(1 + k)$, $r_n = r - \lambda k + \frac{n ln(1+k)}{\tau}$, $v_n = \sigma^2 + \frac{n\delta^2}{\tau}$, and τ is the option's time to maturity. C_{B-S} is the Black-Scholes option value given by,

$$C_{B-S}(S, X, r, \sigma, \tau) = SN(d_1) - Xe^{-rT}N(d_2) \tag{38.4}$$

Table 38.1
Genetic Programming Model Specification in a Jump-Diffusion World - Training Variables.

Name	Source	Definition
S	Option Contract	Stock price
X	Option Contract	Exercise price
S/X	Option Contract	Option moneyness
τ	Option Contract	Time to maturity (years)
Max(S-X)	Boundary Condition	Intrinsic value Max (S-X,0)
Black-Scholes	Analytical Model	Black Scholes value
$+$	Standard arithmetic	Addition
$-$	Standard arithmetic	Subtraction
$*$	Standard arithmetic	Multiplication
$\%$	Standard arithmetic	x%y = 1 , if y = 0
		= x/y , otherwise
Exp	Black-Scholes	Exponent: $exp(x) = e^x$
$plog$	Black-Scholes	$plog(x) = ln(\|x\|)$
$psqrt$	Black-Scholes	$psqrt(x) = sqrt(\|x\|)$
$Ncdf$	Black-Scholes	Normal CDF

where $d_1 = (ln[S/X] + (r + \sigma^2/2)T)/(\sigma\sqrt{T})$, $d_2 = d_1 - (\sigma\sqrt{T})$. $N[d_1]$ and $N[d_2]$ are the cumulative standard normal distribution values at d_1 and d_2.

Table 38.1 presents the set of operations and variables used to develop the Genetic Programs. Note that we include the Black-Scholes option value as a possible component of the tree. This serves as a good starting point and information from known analytical models can thus be used to find a better solution. We do correct for the volatility estimate an investor would have used based on a history of prices generated by a combination of the diffusion and jump processes. This reflects the approach of a naive investor who is unaware of the true nature of the returns' underlying process when using the Black-Scholes model to price the option. The estimated call option value with the modified Black-Scholes model is therefore (Merton 1976):

$$C_{AdjB-S} = C_{B-S}(S, X, r, \sigma_{adj} = \sqrt{\sigma^2 + \lambda\delta^2}, \tau) \tag{38.5}$$

Table 38.2 and Table 38.3 present the size of the training sets used and the algorithm training criteria. We implement an additional step in setting the size of the population and the number of generations. Using an independent set of 25% of the options as a training set, we determine that a minimum population size of 5000 functions and 10 generations is needed to get a formula that outperforms the Black-Scholes model. We use these parameters on ten new 25% subsets of the

Table 38.2
Genetic Programming Model Specification in a Jump-Diffusion World - Size of Training Sets. For each training set (option pricing formula), the price path of a stock with beginning value $S_0 = 50$ was simulated through 24 21-day months. Options were created according to CBOE rules and valued using the Black Scholes formula. Each training set consisted of the daily values of these options.

Training Set	1	2	3	4	5	6	7	8	9	10
Data Points	311	350	364	308	288	420	318	387	409	319

Table 38.3
Genetic Programming Model Specification in a Jump-Diffusion World - Training Parameters. Genetic Programming algorithm training parameters used in the non-Black-Scholes world where stock prices are generated by a jump-diffusion process.

Fitness Criterion	Sum of absolute dollar and percentage errors
Population Size	5,000
Number of Generations	10

options created to develop the genetic program for option pricing in a jump-diffusion world.

The formulas generated by the genetic program are adaptations of the Black-Scholes model, for example, one of the formulas generated is:

$$C(S, X, \tau) = \sqrt{C_{B-S} * \left[0.11734 + \sqrt{0.95461 * C_{B-S} * (C_{B-S} + \tau)}\right]} \qquad (38.6)$$

where, C_{AdjB-S} is the adjusted Black-Scholes model given in Equation 38.5 and τ is the option's time to maturity.

We examine the performance of our genetic program on ten out-of-sample test sets of option data. The Fitness-overselection method gives the lowest pricing errors and beats the modified Black-Scholes model in each of the ten out-of-sample tests. The next best performance is the Tournament method with n=7. The Genetic Programming model based on Fitness-overselection clearly outperforms the Black-Scholes model in out-of-sample tests[4]. The Genetic Programming formula performs better than the Black-Scholes model for each of the 10 out-of-sample test sets.

An important criticism usually leveled at complex numerical methodologies is, Can the method perform any better than a simple linear regression model? We

---

4. The only measure in which the original Black-Scholes model ever beats the Genetic Programming formula is in the training-set sum of percentage errors, and this occurs for only 1 out of the 10 Genetic Programming formulas. However, the error is large enough to blow up the average percentage error. We attribute this fluke to our decision to ignore during training all percentage errors for options worth less than $0.01.

Table 38.4
Average Absolute Pricing Errors of the Genetic Programming models (GP), the Black-Scholes model (BS), and Linear Models in a Jump-Diffusion World. Pricing errors are presented for six Genetic Programming formulas using alternate methods for generating new populations from the previous generation and for four linear models that are a function of the initial stock price, exercise price, and time to maturity. Each cell in the table presents the average pricing errors over ten sets of stock and option prices and for the entire sample of options generated in each set. Parameter values used to generate stock price and options data and the Genetic Programming parameters are given in Table 38.1.

	GP	B-S	1-stage, with B-S	1-stage, no B-S	2-stage, with B-S	2-stage, no B-S
Best	0.0655	0.0888	0.0350	0.9357	0.0158	0.4049
Fitness	0.0517	0.0888	0.0350	0.9357	0.0158	0.4049
Fitness-Overselection	0.0393	0.0888	0.0350	0.9357	0.0158	0.4049
Random	0.0704	0.0888	0.0350	0.9357	0.0158	0.4049
Tournament, Size = 4	0.0534	0.0888	0.0350	0.9357	0.0158	0.4049
Tournament, Size = 7	0.0464	0.0888	0.0350	0.9357	0.0158	0.4049

therefore run single-stage and two-stage linear regression with and without Black-Scholes model as an independent variable. The two-stage model represents separate equations for in-the-money and out-of-the-money options.

Table 38.4 presents the pricing errors for the Genetic Programming formulas, the Black-Scholes equation, and for the linear models. The absolute and average errors for the Genetic Programming formulas are the average pricing error for all options which is again averaged across the ten Genetic Program runs. Results are presented for all six parent-selection methods considered. The modified Black-Scholes equation has the largest errors compared to all other models. The linear models give very good results when we include the naive Black-Scholes model as an independent variable with the two-stage linear model giving the lowest errors. Among the Genetic Programming formulas, the Fitness-overselection parent selection method provides the smallest absolute pricing error and one of the smaller percentage pricing errors. The magnitudes are comparable to the two-stage linear model with Black-Scholes as an independent variable[5].

5. The linear models that have the Black-Scholes model as an independent variable however have one major draw back – the partial derivatives of the pricing equation are equal to the Black-Scholes partial derivatives with a constant adjustment term. In a related paper (see Chidambaran, Lee, and Trigueros (1998)), we test the hedging effectiveness of the Genetic Program model and the Black-Scholes model by constructing a hedge portfolio of the Option, Stock, and Bonds. The

Table 38.5

Mean Absolute Pricing Errors of Genetic Programming models (GP), the Black-Scholes model (BS), and Neural Networks (NN) in a Jump-Diffusion world. The numbers in each cell are the average pricing errors from the models across 10 test sets. For each test set, the error value for each cell is calculated by taking the average pricing errors over five options. Rows in the table represent days-to-maturity and columns represent the degree-of-moneyness, S/X.

Maturity		0.9	0.95	1	1.05	1.1	1.15
				Moneyness S/X			
	BS=	0.05	0.08	0.03	0.03	0.01	0.00
5 days	GP=	0.03	0.02	0.12	0.06	0.01	0.01
	NN=	0.23	0.18	0.12	0.21	0.23	0.26
	BS=	0.08	0.09	0.00	0.04	0.01	0.00
10 days	GP=	0.03	0.02	0.08	0.07	0.03	0.02
	NN=	0.17	0.08	0.12	0.22	0.22	0.26
	BS=	0.13	0.12	0.07	0.02	0.00	0.01
30 days	GP=	0.03	0.03	0.02	0.03	0.05	0.04
	NN=	0.09	0.17	0.17	0.19	0.21	0.26
	BS=	0.15	0.14	0.10	0.06	0.03	0.01
45 days	GP=	0.04	0.04	0.03	0.02	0.03	0.04
	NN=	0.17	0.18	0.16	0.18	0.22	0.26
	BS=	0.16	0.15	0.12	0.09	0.05	0.03
60 days	GP=	0.04	0.05	0.03	0.03	0.03	0.04
	NN=	0.19	0.16	0.15	0.19	0.21	0.26
	BS=	0.19	0.18	0.16	0.13	0.10	0.07
90 days	GP=	0.06	0.06	0.05	0.05	0.05	0.06
	NN=	0.14	0.14	0.18	0.20	0.21	0.28

We further evaluate the performance of the Genetic Programming formula by comparing its pricing errors with that of the Black-Scholes model and Neural Networks for options of various maturities and moneyness. The details of the Neural Networks we use are reported in Chidambaran, Lee, and Trigueros (1998). Results are reported for the network that gives the best results among the various normalization and initialization schemes considered.

Table 38.5 shows the absolute pricing errors and the percentage pricing errors for the Genetic Programming formula developed with Fitness-overselection, for the Black-Scholes model, and for the best Neural Network, on an out-of-sample two-dimensional grid. Each cell in the table represents the average across ten out-of-sample test data sets and the value in each cell is the average over 5 options.

---

hedging performance is calculated to be the deviation from zero in the portfolio value. Overall, the Genetic Program beats the Black-Scholes model in over 50% of the cases.

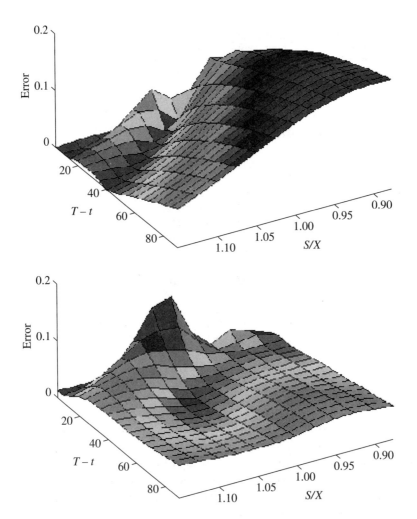

Figure 38.2
Mean absolute pricing error for the Black-Scholes (top figure) and Genetic Programming (bottom figure) models.

Figure 38.2 plots the absolute pricing errors for the Black-Scholes equation and the Genetic Programming formulas.

The Genetic Programming formula tends to do better with in-the-money and short-maturity options whereas the Black-Scholes model seems to perform relatively better with out-of-the money and long-term options. This result is consistent with the notion that the jump term influences prices of short-maturity in-the-money options more, relative to long-term and out-of-the-money options. Genetic Programming beats Neural Networks overall, however in 9 out of the 72 cases considered Neural Networks do show marginally lower errors.

To take advantage of Genetic Programming's ability to learn with small training sets [Koza 1992] and reduce computational time, we tested its performance using random samples of 5% of the options generated in the simulation, without updating the algorithm parameters. We found that the training formulas with the smaller data sets resulted in only a minimal reduction in out-of-sample performance (see Chidambaran, Lee, and Trigueros (1998)). Our tests support the notion that Genetic Programming needs only small training sets in order to arrive at a good solution.

38.3   Application in the Real World

We next apply Genetic Programming to price real-world options data. Call options data for the S&P 500 Index and 5 different stocks were obtained from the Berkeley Options Data Base (BODB). BODB's data is time stamped to the nearest second and ensures a good match between the values of an option and its underlying asset[6]. Option prices are set to be the average of the bid and ask prices. The option's time to maturity is set to be the number of trading days between the trade date and the expiration date of the option. Interest rates from the term structure of zero-coupon treasuries (Bliss 1997) were used to calculate the risk-free rate between two calendar dates.

We use a two step process to develop the Genetic Program. We first determine the optimal set of algorithm parameters using a training and validation step. That is, we vary algorithm parameters when training the program and test the performance on a validation data set of options prices from a later date. The parameters that give the best results in the validation step are the optimal algorithm parameters. These parameters are then used in the next stage when the genetic programs are

---

6. Raw BODB records are screened as follows. We do not include records from the first 2,500 seconds after 8:30 am or in the last 2,500 seconds before 3:00pm and required at least 300 seconds within a 1% deviation for the underlying index/equity price. We also reject data when the option bid-ask spread is greater than $0.25 or is greater than 5% of option value. The first restriction eliminates artificial pricing that may occur due to the structure of the market at the beginning and the ending of the day. The second restriction is to allow the options market to adjust to changes in underlying asset value. The third gives us a tighter handle on the option's equilibrium price.

developed. A separate training data set and out-of-sample data set of options prices are used for the subsequent training/test step.

Ten Genetic Programming formulas were developed using ten sets of training/validations sets and ten sets of training/test data sets. The training/validation data sets were created by randomly sampling April 3-4, 1995 screened S&P 500 Index Option data. The training/test data sets are separately created from April 6-10, 1995 screened S&P 500 Index Options data. All out-of-sample validation and test data occurred later in time than the training data. Training sets contained a mere 50 points each and training time do not exceed 3 minutes per formula.

The sets of operations, functions and variables allowed in our formulas are those used in the jump-diffusion world (given in Table 38.1), augmented by the risk-free rate and historical volatility. As in Hutchinson, Lo, and Poggio (1994), we estimate the S&P 500 Index volatility by computing the standard deviation of the 60 most recent continuously compounded daily S&P 500 returns using 3.00pm (CST) prices. We adjusted for dividends by subtracting the present value of actual dividends between the record date t_0 and the option maturity date T.

The formulas generated by the genetic program for the index options were adaptations of the Black-Scholes model. For example, one formula is,

$$C(S, X, \tau) = C_{B-S} + 3\tau \qquad\qquad (38.7)$$

where, C_{B-S} is the Black-Scholes formula and τ is the option's time to maturity.

Table 38.6 presents the average absolute pricing error and the average percentage pricing error for the 10 Genetic Programming formulas and for the Black-Scholes model when pricing the S&P Index options. The out-of-sample performance of these Genetic Programming adaptations of Black-Scholes model is remarkable: 9 out of the 10 Genetic Programming formulae beat the Black-Scholes model in both average absolute and percentage pricing errors.

For testing the performance of Genetic Programming in pricing equity options, we choose five stocks that had options volume of at least 1500 contracts and which never paid cash dividends. The stocks are: Best Buy Company Inc., Broderbund Software Inc., CompUsa Inc., Digital Equipment Corporation, and Novellus Systems Inc. For each stock, we develop ten Genetic Programming formulas. The training/validation data sets are constructed using BODB records for April 3-4, 1995. The training/test data sets are constructed from options traded during the period April 6-13, 1995.

The formulas generated by the genetic program for the equity options were also adaptations of the Black-Scholes model. In most cases, the formulas are of the form,

$$C(S, X, \tau) = C_{B-s} + Constant * \tau \qquad\qquad (38.8)$$

Table 38.6
This table shows the mean absolute pricing errors for ten Genetic Programming Formulas, the Black-Scholes model, and Neural Networks, on ten out-of-sample data sets of the S&P 500 Index (SPX) option and five equity options. Each formula came from a separate training set and was evaluated on a separate test set, each set having a sample of 50 options. The parameter search was performed using April 3-4 data to find algorithm parameters that give formulas with good out-of-sample performance. All training and test sets for SPX came from April 6-10 BODB data and those for five equity options came from April 6-13.

Run #	GP	B-S	NN	GP	B-S	NN
		S&P 500			Best Buy	
1	1.9555	3.2301	1.2371	0.0927	0.1181	0.0583
2	3.0323	4.6736	1.1773	0.0605	0.0859	0.0633
3	2.3617	3.3248	1.2008	0.1150	0.0794	0.0771
4	1.5177	3.2884	1.0456	0.0996	0.1019	0.0583
5	2.4803	3.5442	2.0528	0.1262	0.0868	0.0743
6	2.0220	3.0111	0.7804	0.1046	0.0895	0.0621
7	2.3358	3.1802	1.6938	0.1012	0.1145	0.0527
8	2.1766	3.3159	1.2111	0.1189	0.0786	0.0701
9	1.6305	3.2846	1.0720	0.0855	0.1011	0.0601
10	3.0803	4.1809	0.9376	0.1181	0.0780	0.0766
Average	2.2590	3.5030	1.2409	0.1022	0.0933	0.0653
		Broderbund			Comp USA	
1	0.1346	0.1346	0.7407	0.1475	0.1892	0.1640
2	0.1255	0.1255	0.6099	0.1919	0.1856	0.1396
3	0.1074	0.1074	0.5695	0.2145	0.1487	0.2774
4	0.1418	0.1415	0.5975	0.1622	0.1870	0.1395
5	0.1448	0.1448	0.6821	0.1592	0.1656	0.1620
6	0.1279	0.1279	0.6916	0.2133	0.1843	0.2652
7	0.1253	0.1253	0.6114	0.1665	0.1856	0.1211
8	0.1211	0.1211	0.5610	0.1502	0.1886	0.1583
9	0.1475	0.1475	0.7252	0.1796	0.1922	0.1453
10	0.1074	0.1158	0.6349	0.1519	0.1870	0.1724
Average	0.1283	0.1291	0.6424	0.1737	0.1814	0.1745
		DEC			Novellus	
1	0.1595	0.1595	0.4301	0.1423	0.2531	0.4756
2	0.1462	0.1462	0.4140	0.1976	0.2840	0.5227
3	0.1435	0.1435	0.4544	0.2249	0.2850	0.4574
4	0.1148	0.1148	0.4056	0.1817	0.2692	0.5035
5	0.0880	0.1223	0.4336	0.1882	0.2772	0.4485
6	0.1254	0.1254	0.4076	0.2049	0.2344	0.4389
7	0.1236	0.1236	0.4302	0.1668	0.3217	0.4507
8	0.1286	0.1286	0.3329	0.2006	0.1979	0.5819
9	0.1454	0.1454	0.4343	0.1953	0.3096	0.5859
10	0.1063	0.1063	0.4105	0.1617	0.2973	0.4420
Average	0.1281	0.1316	0.4153	0.1864	0.2729	0.4907

where, C_{B-S} is the Black-Scholes formula and τ is the option's time to maturity. The constant takes values from 1 to 4 depending on the stock underlying the option that is being priced.

Table 38.6 also presents the average absolute pricing errors and average percentage pricing errors for the ten Genetic Programming formulas, the Black Scholes formula, and for Neural Networks, when pricing equity options. When there is no difference between the errors for the Genetic Programming formula and the Black-Scholes model, it indicates that the Genetic Program converged on the Black-Scholes model. Except for Best Buy, the Genetic Programming method produced formulas that outperform the Black-Scholes model on average, though the results are not as strong as the case of S&P Index options. We attribute the results for Best Buy to the fact that the data set used for the parameter search is much smaller than the data sets used for the other four stocks. The resulting training and validation sets were thus not independent enough to yield an insight on satisfactory parameters.

Neural Network pricing errors, though higher, are comparable to those of Genetic Programming formulas for the S&P 500 index option. On the other hand, Neural Network pricing errors are a magnitude higher than that of Genetic Programming formulas when pricing equity options. Equity options are more thinly traded and there is less data available to train Neural Networks and Genetic Programs in comparison to the S&P 500 index option.

Note that for Broderbund and DEC, a majority of the Genetic Programs converge on the Black-Scholes model as the best possible pricing formula. This highlights the advantage of the Genetic Programming approach – it can easily converge on existing known models, if they are indeed the best solutions. By including known analytical solutions in the parameter set, we thus increase the efficiency of Genetic Programming by using it to improve on existing solutions.

38.4   Conclusion

In this paper we have developed a procedure to apply the principles of Genetic Programming to option pricing. Our results, from controlled simulations and real world data, are strongly encouraging and suggest that Genetic Programming work well in practice.

Genetic Programming is a non-parametric data driven approach and, using options data, extracts the implied pricing equation. Genetic Programming thus overcomes the need to make specific assumptions about the stock price process. Researchers have attributed the systematic biases in Black-Scholes prices to the assumption that stock prices follow a diffusion process. We show that Genetic Programming formulas beat the Black-Scholes model in 10 out of 10 cases in a simulation study where the underlying stock prices were generated using a jump-diffusion process. They work almost as well in pricing S&P Index options with genetic programs beating the Black-Scholes model in 9 out of 10 cases. For equity options, genetic programs beat or match the Black-Scholes model for 4 of the 5 stocks considered.

The Genetic Programming method requires less data than other numerical techniques such as Neural Networks (Hutchinson, Lo, and Poggio (1994)). We show this by simulation studies that use smaller subsets of the data and by using both genetic programs and neural networks to price relatively thinly traded equity options. The time required to train and develop the genetic programming formulas is also relatively short.

Genetic Programming can incorporate known analytical approximations in the solution method. For example, we use the Black-Scholes model as a parameter in the genetic program to build a better option pricing model. The flexibility in adding terms to the parameter set used to develop the functional approximation can also be used to examine whether factors beyond those used in this study, for example, trading volume, skewness and kurtosis of returns, and inflation, are relevant to option pricing. Finally, since the Genetic Programming method is self-learning and self-improving, it is an ideal too for practitioners.

References

Allen, F. and Karjalainen, R., 1999, "Using Genetic Algorithms to find technical trading rules," *Journal of Financial Economics,* Vol. 51(2), (February).

Ball, C.A. and Torous, W.N., 1985, "On jumps in common stock prices and their impact on call option pricing," *Journal of Finance,* Vol. 40 (March).

Ballie R. and DeGennaro, R., 1990, "Stock returns and volatility," *Journal of Financial and Quantitative Analysis,* Vol. 25 (June).

Black, F. and Scholes, M., 1972, "The valuation of option contracts and a test of market efficiency," *Journal of Finance,* Vol. 27 (May).

Black, F. and Scholes, M., 1973, "The pricing of options and corporate liabilities," *Journal of Political Economy,* Vol. 81.

Bliss, R., 1997, "Testing term structure estimation methods", *Advances in Futures and Options Research,* Vol 9(1).

Bollerslev T., 1986, "Generalized Autoregressive conditional Heteroskedasticity," *Journal of Econometrics,* Vol. 31 (April).

Chidambaran, N. K., Lee, C. W. J., and Trigueros, J., 1998, "An Adaptive Evolutionary Approach to Option Pricing via Genetic Programming," Working paper, New York University.

Chidambaran, N. K. and Figlewski S., 1995, "Streamlining Monte Carlo Simulation with the Quasi-Analytic Method: Analysis of a Path-Dependent Option Strategy," *Journal of Derivatives,* Winter.

French, K. R., Schwert, G.W., and Stambaugh, R.F., 1987, "Expected stock returns and volatility," *Journal of Financial Economics,* Vol. 19 (September).

Ho, T. H., 1996, "Finite automata play repeated prisoner's dilemma with information processing costs," *Journal of Economic Dynamics and Control,* Vol. 20 (January-March)

Hull, J., 1997, *Options, Futures, and Other Derivative Securities,* 3rd Ed., (Prentice-Hall, Englewood Cliffs, New Jersey).

Hutchinson, J., Lo A., and Poggio, T., 1994, "A Nonparametric approach to the Pricing and Hedging of Derivative Securities Via Learning Networks," *Journal of Finance,* Vol. 49 (June).

Keber, C., 1998, "Option valuation with the genetic programming approach," Working paper, University of Vienna.

Kim, D. and Kon, S. J., 1994, "Alternative models for the conditional heteroscedasticity of stock returns," *The Journal of Business,* Vol. 67 (October).

Koza, J. R., 1992, *Genetic Programming,* (MIT Press, Cambridge, Massachusetts).

Lettau, M., 1997, "Explaining the facts with adaptive agents," *Journal of Economic Dynamics and Control,* Vol. 21.

Merton, R. C., 1973, "Theory of rational option pricing," *Bell Journal of Economics and Management Science,* Spring.

Merton, R. C., 1976, "Option pricing when underlying stock returns are discontinuous," *Journal of Financial Economics,* Vol. 3 (January-March).

Neely, C., Weller P., and Dittmar R., 1997, "Is Technical Analysis in the Foreign Exchange Market Profitable? A Genetic Programming Approach," *Journal of Financial and Quantitative Analysis,* Vol. 32(4), pp.405-426.

Rubinstein, M., 1997, "Implied Binomial Trees", *Journal of Finance,* Vol. 49.

Trigueros, J. 1997, "A Nonparametric Approach to Pricing and Hedging Derivative Securities Via Genetic Regression," Proceedings of the Conference on Computational Intelligence for Financial Engineering, March.

39 Nonparametric Testing of ARCH for Option Pricing

Peter Christoffersen and Jinyong Hahn

This chapter nonparametrically examines the relevance of ARCH models in the specific context of option pricing. We argue that a stochastic interpretation of various option pricing formulae for econometric models of changing volatility implies the mean-sufficiency property of current volatility: No variable in the information set should have additional explanatory power given the volatility and other relevant variables. Based on this intuition, we apply the nonparametric specification tests of [Aït-Sahalia et al 1994], and [Fan and Li 1996] to European call option data where the volatility is estimated using various ARCH models. We find that ARCH models pass the nonparametric test of sufficiency. We then examine whether ARCH volatility has additional explanatory power given other relevant variables. Although the tests were somewhat sensitive to the bandwidth choice, we cautiously conclude that it may fail this test of necessity.

39.1   Introduction

Derivative securities are widely traded financial instruments which inherit their properties from the underlying assets. The well-known Black and Scholes formula [Black and Scholes 1973] is one of the few cases where the price of a derivative asset (a European call option) can be analytically expressed. Unfortunately, the set of assumptions underlying the Black-Scholes economy are rarely met in practice. Among many possible extensions of the Black-Scholes assumptions, modification of the constant volatility assumption has perhaps received the most attention in the econometric community. The ARCH model developed for discretely sampled data by [Engle 1982] and its many variants have received a lot of attention, perhaps because they were expected to capture the spirit of continuous time models as in [Hull and White 1987]. This intuition was apparently confirmed by [Nelson 1996] and [Nelson and Foster 1994], who established that the continuous-record asymptotics for some discrete-time ARCH processes converge to the continuous-time processes of [Hull and White 1987].[1]

The purpose of this chapter is to nonparametrically examine the relevance of ARCH models in option pricing. We ignore the predictive aspects of ARCH models and examine them solely based on their performance in option pricing. It is interesting to note that much of the ARCH literature verbally emphasizes the potential

---

1. Important competitors to the ARCH models include the discrete-time stochastic-volatility models discussed by [Melino and Turnbull 1990], [Wiggins 1987], [Harvey et al 1994], [Jacquier et al 1994], and [Shephard et al 1998]. Due to the ease of implementing ARCH models, and their corresponding dominance among practitioners we focus attentions on ARCH in this study.

of ARCH volatility in option pricing, but not many studies statistically test the relation between the ARCH models and option pricing. Lacking statistical testing, a few authors do investigate the link between ARCH models and option pricing, these include [Duan 1995], [Engle and Mustafa 1992], [Engle et al 1996], [Bollerslev and Mikkelsen 1995], and [Amin and Ng 1993]. All the results seem to imply at least two assumptions. The first assumption, which we will call the sufficiency assumption, is that the volatility is a mean-sufficient statistic for the option price of interest given other relevant variables. The second assumption, which we will call the necessity assumption, is that the ARCH volatility has additional explanatory power given other relevant variables. This amounts to the assumption that the changing volatility model described by ARCH better explains the option price than the constant volatility model.[2] Recent developments in the nonparametric specification literature allow us to test both assumptions. In this chapter, we test the necessity and sufficiency of ARCH models for European option pricing. We apply the tests of [Aït-Sahalia et al 1994] and [Fan and Li 1996] to examine the relevance of ARCH models in pricing European options. We try to examine the usefulness and relevance of ARCH models in option pricing taking a purely *reduced form* statistical approach. Such a reduced form strategy complements the theoretical developments of [Engle and Mustafa 1992], [Amin and Ng 1993], and [Duan 1995].

Nonparametric specification tests have an interesting practical implication. Recently, [Broadie et al 1996b] and [Broadie et al 1996a] have suggested nonparametric *estimation* of American option prices. They suggest estimating the pricing functional given a parametrically estimated volatility and other relevant variables. Given their popularity in volatility extraction and prediction, ARCH models are a natural choice in such procedure. We thus believe that our nonparametric testing results form nice complements to results on nonparametric estimation by [Broadie et al 1996b].

39.2 Sufficiency and Necessity

In this section, we elaborate on the sufficiency and necessity arguments introduced in the previous section. We first make a very brief review of European option pricing under changing volatility. In the simple Black-Scholes economy with constant

---

2. By constant volatility based option pricing, we do not restrict ourselves to the standard Black-Scholes formula. We interpret constant volatility based option pricing to mean any nonparametric specification of the option price which does not include time-varying volatility as one of the explanatory variables.

volatility, the European call option price C, on an asset without dividend payments, can be written as

$$C = P(K, S, r, T - t, \sigma). \qquad (39.1)$$

Here, $K, S, r, T - t$, and σ denote the strike price, the underlying asset price, the (constant) risk-free interest rate, the time-to-maturity, and the (constant) volatility. When the volatility is characterized by a continuous-time stochastic-volatility model and when the volatility is uncorrelated with aggregate consumption, then following [Hull and White 1987], we may write,

$$C = E\left[P(K, S, r, T - t, \sigma_T) \middle| \mathcal{F}_t \right], \qquad (39.2)$$

where the conditional expectation, given all the information available at time t, $\mathcal{F}_t$, is taken over σ_T, the random volatility at maturity. On the other hand, when volatility follows a GARCH process, and when the equivalent martingale measure Q is such that the log of the underlying asset price follows a particular random walk, [Duan 1995] establishes that the European call can be priced by

$$C_t = \exp\left(-r(T - t)\right) E^Q \left[\max(S_T - K, 0) \middle| \mathcal{F}_t \right]. \qquad (39.3)$$

Observe that all (39.1), (39.2), and (39.3) are all *deterministic* relations. We do not believe that any of them will survive a common sense test against a real data set if we strictly impose this deterministic interpretation. We thus freely depart from this deterministic interpretation, and interpret each of them in the stochastic way: we are going to read (39.1), (39.2), and (39.3) as "The conditional expectation of the left hand side of the equation given all the available information is equal to the right hand side."[3]

The stochastic interpretation of (39.1), (39.2), and (39.3) has an interesting implication. Observe that all of them imply that, given all the available information $\mathcal{F}_t$, only five variables $K, S, r, T - t, \sigma$ are relevant for option pricing. We may compactly write it as

$$E\left[C \middle| \mathcal{F}_t\right] = E\left[C \middle| K, S, r, T - t, \sigma\right]. \qquad (39.4)$$

Among the five variables of interest, the first four variables $K, S, r, T - t$ are observed. Only σ is unobserved in the option pricing relationship. This implies that

---

3. Although we do not have any finance-economic justification for this stochastic interpretation, we adopt this convention due to the seeming lack of results in the econometrics of option pricing errors. We refer to Renault (1996) for a recent attempt to resolve the difficulties, although we note that the deterministic relation implies the conditional expectation relation in any case.

σ is some real-valued mapping whose argument is an infinite-dimensional collection of all the available information. To be more specific, (39.4) implies that there exists a one-dimensional statistic which we write (with some abuse of notation) as $\sigma\left(\mathcal{F}_t\right)$ such that

$$E\left[C|\,\mathcal{F}_t\right] = \Pi\left(K, S, r, T - t, \sigma\left(\mathcal{F}_t\right)\right) \tag{39.5}$$

for *some* function Π. We are now ready to obtain the mean sufficiency and necessity of the *statistic* $\sigma\left(\mathcal{F}_t\right)$ given $(K, S, r, T - t)$.

As for sufficiency, observe that (39.5) implies that the conditional expectation given $(K, S, r, T - t)$ and $\sigma\left(\mathcal{F}_t\right)$ is equal to the conditional expectation given the filtration $\mathcal{F}_t$: No component of the filtration $\mathcal{F}_t$ has any additional explanatory power for the option price of interest. In the application, we will choose some sensible variable, say V, in the filtration $\mathcal{F}_t$, and try to examine whether

$$E\left[C|\, K, S, r, T - t, \sigma\left(\mathcal{F}_t\right)\right] \neq E\left[C|\, K, S, r, T - t, \sigma\left(\mathcal{F}_t\right), V\right].$$

As for necessity, we observe that the statistic $\sigma\left(\mathcal{F}_t\right)$ is useless in nonparametric option pricing if we further have

$$E\left[C|\,\mathcal{F}_t\right] = E\left[C|\, K, S, r, T - t\right],$$

i.e., if the exclusion of $\sigma\left(\mathcal{F}_t\right)$ does not entail any loss of information. No statistical procedure is available to test such a general implication. We thus restrict our attention to the following implication of the necessity condition:

$$E\left[C|\, K, S, r, T - t\right] \neq E\left[C|\, K, S, r, T - t, \sigma\left(\mathcal{F}_t\right)\right].$$

The necessity simply asserts that $\sigma_t\left(\theta\right)$ has additional explanatory power, thus no subjectivity is involved in practice given a parametric volatility model.

With the interpretation of $\sigma\left(\mathcal{F}_t\right)$ as just *some* statistic, consider the stochastic interpretation of (39.1), (39.2), and (39.3) again. Equation (39.1) implies that $\sigma\left(\mathcal{F}_t\right)$ is a constant valued function under the constant volatility model. Equations (39.2) and (39.3) imply that $\sigma\left(\mathcal{F}_t\right)$ may be expressed using a parametric expression in the cases of continuous-time stochastic-volatility model and discrete-time GARCH model, respectively. In every case, the "statistic" takes the form of the "volatility" of the corresponding econometric model parameterized by θ, say. With some abuse of notation again, we may thus write that $\sigma\left(\theta_0; \mathcal{F}_t\right)$ is the necessary and sufficient statistic for the option price of interest given $(K, S, r, T - t)$, where θ_0 denotes the true value of the parameter.

It should be noted that a failure of necessity does not necessarily invalidate a parametric econometric model associated with $\sigma(\theta_0; \mathcal{F}_t)$. For example, we may find that $\sigma(\theta_0; \mathcal{F}_t)$ is nonparametrically unnecessary, but it could be the case that $\sigma(\theta_0; \mathcal{F}_t)$ is constant: Under the Black-Scholes formula, the (constant) volatility is nonparametrically unnecessary. The failure may also be due to a high correlation of $\sigma(\theta_0; \mathcal{F}_t)$ with the other explanatory variables. This may happen if the alternative continuous record asymptotics by [Corradi 1997] is more relevant than that of [Nelson 1996] and [Nelson and Foster 1994]: $\sigma(\theta_0; \mathcal{F}_t)$ would be a deterministic function of t, and hence, $T - t$. Therefore, results from the necessity test should be more cautiously interpreted than those from the sufficiency test: a parametric, changing volatility model could be a reasonable model of the volatility process itself, but may turn out to be unnecessary for nonparametric option pricing.

39.3   Nonparametric Specification Tests

In this section, we briefly review the intuition of the nonparametric specification tests developed by [Aït-Sahalia et al 1994] (the ABS test) and [Fan and Li 1996], and then discuss the implementation of the tests. Consider the conditional expectation of Y given X, where Y is a one-dimensional random variable and X is a random vector consisting of a p-dimensional random vector W and a q-dimensional random vector V. The null hypothesis that V is does not have any explanatory power given W can be written as $E[Y|W,V] = E[Y|W]$. Letting $M(w) = E[Y|W = w]$ and $m(w,v) = E[Y|(W,V) = (w,v)]$, we can rewrite the hypothesis as

$$\Pr[M(W) = m(W,V)] = 1.$$

The intuition of the test by [Aït-Sahalia et al 1994] is based on the following implication of the null hypothesis:

$$E\left[(M(W) - m(W,V))^2\right] = 0.$$

Now, if we are given a relatively large data set consisting of (Y_i, X_i) $i = 1, \ldots, n$, we may be able to estimate $M(w)$ and $m(w,v)$ by any nonparametric method, say, a kernel regression. Denote the regression estimates by $\hat{M}^\omega(w)$ and $\hat{m}^\omega(w,v)$, respectively, i.e.,

$$\hat{M}^\omega(w) = \frac{\sum_{i=1}^n Y_i K\left(\frac{w - W_i}{\omega}\right)}{\sum_{i=1}^n K\left(\frac{w - W_i}{\omega}\right)}, \qquad \hat{m}^\omega(w,v) = \frac{\sum_{i=1}^n Y_i K\left(\frac{w - W_i}{\omega}, \frac{v - V_i}{\omega}\right)}{\sum_{i=1}^n K\left(\frac{w - W_i}{\omega}, \frac{v - V_i}{\omega}\right)},$$

where ω is a suitably chosen bandwidth. As the sample size gets large, we would expect

$$\Gamma_n = \frac{1}{n} \sum_{i=1}^{n} \left(\hat{M}^\omega \left(W_i \right) - \hat{m}^\omega \left(W_i, V_i \right) \right)^2 \to 0 \tag{39.6}$$

under the null. If Γ_n is substantially bigger than zero, it can be interpreted as evidence against the hypothesis.[4] Note that the test statistic is based on kernel regressions which use the *same* bandwidth, ω, under the null and the alternative. [Fan and Li 1996] develop an alternative test using similar intuition.

To see how these tests can be implemented in the volatility specification test, suppose that a theory suggests that the volatility process is governed by a parametric model $\sigma \left(\theta; \mathcal{F}_t \right)$ with the true value of the parameter equal to θ_0. For simplicity of notation, write $\sigma_t \left(\theta \right) = \sigma \left(\theta; \mathcal{F}_t \right)$. If this theory is correct, then we should observe option prices such that

$$E \left[C | \mathcal{F}_t \right] = \Pi \left(K, S, r, T - t, \sigma_t \left(\theta_0 \right) \right),$$

for *some* function Π. Suppose temporarily that we know the true value θ_0. Then the discussion of necessity and sufficiency in the previous section immediately implies the tests to be conducted. For necessity, we can test whether

$$E \left[C | K, S, r, T - t, \sigma_t \left(\theta_0 \right) \right] = E \left[C | K, S, r, T - t \right],$$

and for sufficiency, we can test whether

$$E \left[C | K, S, r, T - t, \sigma_t \left(\theta_0 \right) \right] = E \left[C | K, S, r, T - t, \sigma_t \left(\theta_0 \right), V \right]$$

for any relevant $V \in \mathcal{F}_t$.

Without knowledge of the exact value of θ_0, it is natural to rely on an estimated value, for example, MLE. Under the null of correct parametric specification of the volatility process, we can usually obtain a $\sqrt{n}$-consistent estimator, call it $\hat{\theta}$. An interesting and useful aspect of the specification test by [Aït-Sahalia et al 1994] is that the asymptotic distribution of the test statistic under the null is not changed even when we replace θ_0 by a $\sqrt{n}$-consistent estimator.[5] Although [Fan and Li 1996] does not explicitly consider such a case, it is reasonable to expect this

4. The test statistic by [Aït-Sahalia et al 1994] differs from the intuitive equation (39.6) in order to accommodate a technicality related to kernel regression: Their test static involves trimming based on the estimated density, as is customary in econometric applications of kernel estimation.

5. See Lemma 4.2 in [Aït-Sahalia et al 1994].

behavior in their test as well.[6] This observation suggests the following strategy for
the nonparametric test of relevance of ARCH models for option pricing:

1. Estimate an ARCH model.

2. For sufficiency, choose V in the information set which is expected to have
additional explanatory power, and apply the nonparametric specification test where
the regressor under the null is $\left(K, S, r, T - t, \sigma_t(\hat{\theta})\right)$ and the regressor under the
alternative additionally includes V.

3. For necessity, apply the nonparametric specification test where the regressor
under the null is $(K, S, r, T - t)$ and the regressor under the alternative additionally
includes $\sigma_t(\hat{\theta})$.

It is to be noted that the test by [Aït-Sahalia et al 1994] is originally developed
for *i.i.d.* observations, but it applies to dependent data without modification.[7] It is
reasonable to expect the same property from the test by [Fan and Li 1996].[8]

39.4   European Options on the S&P 500 Index

In this section we apply the testing methodology laid out above to European option
contracts written on the S&P 500 index.

39.4.1   The Data

We apply the data set from [Aït-Sahalia and Lo 1998], graciously provided to us
by the authors. The original data set contains 16,923 pairs of call- and put-option
prices (bid-ask averages) on the S&P 500 index recorded between January 1, and
December 31, 1993. From this, we eliminate contracts with less than one day-to-
maturity, implied volatility greater than 70%, or a price less than \$1/8. This filtering
leaves 14,431 observations.

Due to problems of infrequent trading of in-the-money options, the need for simultaneous observations of the underlying index, and unobserved dividend streams
from the index, we use the implied futures price of the index as opposed to the ac-

---

6. The intuition is the same as in [Aït-Sahalia et al 1994]. The rate of convergence of parametric
estimation is much faster than in the nonparametric case, and the asymptotic distribution of the
test statistic by [Fan and Li 1996] is based on the asymptotic distribution of the kernel estimator
whose rate of convergence is much slower than $\sqrt{n}$.

7. See Section 4.3.2 in [Aït-Sahalia et al 1994].

8. This is because, as in the test by [Aït-Sahalia et al 1994], the covariations induced by a *reasonable*
amount of dependence in the data are expected to be of small order.

Table 39.1
Descriptive Statistics of [Aït-Sahalia and Lo 1998] Data Set

Variable	Mean	Std. Dev.	Min.	Med.	Max.
Call Price	24.23	25.41	0.13	16.68	121.93
Put Price	9.75	12.57	0.13	4.73	102.08
Implied Volatility	11.36	3.29	5.07	10.71	36.43
Implied ATM Volatility	9.37	0.86	6.10	9.36	16.47
Time to Maturity	86.64	72.32	1.00	66.00	350.00
Strike Price	440.80	33.02	350.00	440.00	550.00
Futures Prices	455.42	10.26	428.70	457.82	474.44
Risk Free Rate	3.07	0.08	2.85	3.08	3.21

tual spot price. Our procedure follows [Aït-Sahalia and Lo 1998]. The spot-futures parity links the two by,

$$F_{t,T} = S_t \exp((r_{t,T} - \delta_{t,T})(T - t)),$$

where $T - t$ is the number of days-to-maturity, $r_{t,T}$ is the risk-free rate, and $\delta_{t,T}$ is the (constant) dividend rate between time t and T. The implied futures price given from the call-put parity at-the-money is,

$$
\begin{aligned}
F_{t,T} = {}& K^* + \exp(r_{t,T}(T - \tau)) \\
& \times (H(S_t, K^*, T - t, r_{t,T}, \delta_{t,T}) - G(S_t, K^*, T - t, r_{t,T}, \delta_{t,T})),
\end{aligned}
$$

where $H(\cdot)$ and $G(\cdot)$ are the call and put prices respectively. In order to get reliable futures prices, call and put contracts are used where the strike price, $K = K^* \approx S_t$, is close to at-the-money. Now, given the implied at-the-money futures price, $F_{t,T}$, the prices from the illiquid in-the-money call contracts can be calculated as,

$$
\begin{aligned}
H(S_t, K, T - t, r_{t,T}, \delta_{t,T}) = {}& G(S_t, K, T - t, r_{t,T}, \delta_{t,T}) \\
& + (F_{t,T} - K) \exp(-r_{t,T}(T - t)),
\end{aligned}
$$

since a strike price, K, corresponding to an illiquid (liquid) in-the-money call contract, automatically corresponds to a liquid (illiquid) out-of-the-money put contract.

Descriptive statistics of the data set are provided in Table 39.1.

39.4.2   Implementation of the Tests

The nonparametric regression under consideration involves many regressors even under the null: We have at least 5 regressors $(K, S_t, r_{t,T}, T - t, \delta_{t,T})$. Even though the nonparametric specification tests work asymptotically, the asymptotic approximation may be poor in finite samples when the number of regressors is large. We thus make a series of assumptions to reduce the number of regressors. In the end, the specification we test is

$$E\left[\frac{C_{t,T,K}}{F_{t,T}}\,\middle|\,\mathcal{F}_t\right] = H\left(\frac{K}{F_{t,T}}, T - t, \sigma_t\left(\theta_0\right)\right)$$

for some nonparametric function H, where $F_{t,T}$ is the implied futures price computed via the put-call parity. The specification can be derived under the assumption that

- The current underlying asset price S_t, and the dividend rate $\delta_{t,T}$ enter into Π only through the implied futures price;

- The function Π is homogeneous of degree one in $(F_{t,T}, K)$; and

- The interest rate, $r_{t,T}$, is constant.

Observe that the first two assumptions are satisfied under the standard Black-Scholes formula. As for the second assumption of homogeneity, [Broadie et al 1996b] derived similar results for American option pricing. The second assumption is important not only because of the dimension reduction implication but also because of the presumed stationarity implication. The test by [Aït-Sahalia et al 1994] applies without modification for a general class of *stationary* processes.[9] But the test does not easily accommodate the nonstationarity that is expected to be present in the underlying asset price level, S_t. Faced with this challenge, it seems reasonable to follow the standard practice of assuming stationarity of $\frac{C_{t,T,K}}{F_{t,T}}$ and $\frac{K}{F_{t,T}}$. Supporting this assumption, we do not find any significant trends in the two ratios in our data set.

We take our benchmark variance specification to be the EGARCH(1,1) model from [Nelson 1991]. Thus we estimate

$$\ln(\sigma_t^2) = \omega + \alpha\left|\frac{\varepsilon_t}{\sigma_{t-1}}\right| + \gamma\frac{\varepsilon_t}{\sigma_{t-1}} + \beta\ln(\sigma_{t-1}^2).$$

---

9. See their Assumption 4 and related discussion.

Table 39.2
EGARCH(1,1) Estimation

Parameter	Estimate	Standard error	Robust S.E.
Mean	.0268	.0195	.0202
ω	-.0398	.0074	.0131
α	.0481	.0096	.0166
γ	-.0171	.0072	.0205
β	.9923	.0022	.0042

Table 39.3
GARCH(1,1) Estimation

Parameter	Estimate	Standard error	Robust S.E.
Mean	.0388	.0198	.0201
ω	.0031	.0011	.0018
α	.0179	.0032	.0058
β	.9760	.0038	.0067

Estimating EGARCH models on the S&P 500 index returns (ex dividends) yields strongly persistent—close to integrated—specifications.[10] In Table 39.2 we show the estimation results from our benchmark specification.

We will also be employing a symmetric GARCH(1,1) model below. In this case, the estimation results are as in Table 39.3:

Finally, let us turn to the actual hypotheses tested. We carry out the following experiments: Cases 1 through 3 test the sufficiency part of our hypothesis:

• In Case 1 we take the EGARCH(1,1) specification to be the null, and include $|\Delta S_{t-1}|$ as an explanatory variable under the alternative hypothesis, testing for a more elaborate lag structure in volatility.

• A variable describing the number of days since the last trading day is sometimes included in the conditional variance specification. [French and Roll 1986] suggest the specification, $\omega_t = \omega + \ln(1 + \delta N_t)$, where N_t is the number of calendar days since the last trading day. In Case 2, we include N_t under the alternative calling it the "Monday Effect," and retain the standard EGARCH(1,1) specification under the null.

---

10. The underlying stock index data are drawn from the CRISP tapes (series SPINDX). We estimate on daily data from April 1988 through December 1993 which gives 1,500 observations. We note that the stock index prices are recorded at a slightly different time of day than are the options. But, any *deterministic* intraday volatility pattern should be captured well in the subsequent nonparametric regression. Since we use the stock prices only to obtain a parametric estimate of the conditional variance, this is not of major concern.

- In Case 3 we test for asymmetry under the alternative using a symmetric GARCH(1,1) specification under the null. It is interesting to note that the standard inference in Table 39.2 implies significant asymmetry in the EGARCH(1,1) specification, whereas the Bollerslev-Wooldridge robust inference rejects asymmetry.

Cases 4a and b test the sufficiency part of our hypothesis[11]:

- In Case 4a, we test the necessity of ARCH using a simple homoskedastic, nonparametric regression including just time-to-maturity and strike price over the futures price under the null. The alternative includes an EGARCH(1,1) volatility measure. Although we call the null 'Homoskedasticity', it is somewhat of a misnomer: As noted above, the null includes the case where the volatility is changing, but in a deterministic fashion.
- Case 4b is similar to 4a only it applies a symmetric GARCH(1,1) model under the alternative.
- In Cases 5a and b, we restrict Case 4 further, and take the regressor under the null to be the standard parametric Black-Scholes price with homoskedastic innovations. The alternative here includes the benchmark EGARCH(1,1) and GARCH(1,1) conditional volatility respectively. Case 5 is included to check the parametric Black-Scholes specification, but also to check the power of ABS tests in the actual sample at hand.

39.4.3 Test Results

Both test statistics are asymptotically standard normal: the null is rejected in favor of the alternative under 5% significance level if the test statistic exceeds 1.64. To compute the test statistics, we use a Gaussian kernel, where the bandwidth is chosen via cross-validation on a grid of possible values under the alternative, using standardized regressors. The results of the various experiments using the ABS test are summarized in Table 39.4.

Observe that the ARCH model of our choice passes the test of mean sufficiency: In Cases 1, 2, and 3, the nulls which only include the ARCH volatilities cannot be rejected under 5 % significance level. Furthermore, the asymmetry does not seem to matter for options pricing. On the other hand, the ARCH model does not pass the test of necessity. In Cases 4a and b, we see that the nonparametric model which does not include any ARCH volatility is accepted. As expected, we get a resounding

11. In case 1 through 4, the regression under the null includes the time-to-maturity as well as the strike price normalized by the futures price.

Table 39.4
Test Results

Case	Null	Alternative	$p+q$	ω	ABS test
1	EGARCH(1,1)	$\|\Delta S_{t-1}\|$	3+1	.128	-25.4
2	EGARCH(1,1)	Monday Effect	3+1	.094	-26.2
3	GARCH(1,1)	ΔS_t	3+1	.125	-25.7
4a	Homoskedasticity	EGARCH(1,1)	2+1	.061	-12.1
4b	Homoskedasticity	GARCH(1,1)	2+1	.054	-5.5
5a	Black-Scholes	EGARCH(1,1)	1+1	.052	77.0
5b	Black-Scholes	GARCH(1,1)	1+1	.041	90.8

rejection of the parametric Black-Scholes pricing formula in cases 5a and 5b. We take this result as evidence that the ABS test is quite powerful in the sample at hand.

The reduced-form nature of our approach refrains us from speculation as to the financial economic reason why the ARCH models do not pass the test of necessity. We conjecture that the volatility process has a high correlation with the other regressors included in the null, so that it does not have any additional explanatory power over and above the homoskedastic, nonparametric regression. Another possible explanation, namely sensitivity of our results with respect to bandwidth choice is explored in the next section. Finally, we remark that the application of the test by [Fan and Li 1996] yielded similar results.[12]

39.4.4 Robustness of Test Results to the Choice of Bandwidth

In order to avoid arbitrariness in the choice of bandwidth, every experiment above builds on a cross-validated bandwidth parameter. To complement this data-based bandwidth choice, we conducted some sensitivity analysis of the test results in Table 39.4 to the choice of bandwidth. First, consider the sufficiency test of GARCH, i.e. cases 1-3. In neither of the three experiments conducted, did we reject the null hypothesis of sufficiency for any reasonable bandwidth choice. Thus the sufficiency results seem robust.

Second, consider the necessity tests of GARCH in case 4a and b. The rejection of the neccesity of GARCH is somewhat sensitive to the choice of bandwidth. For a

---

12. We again used the Gaussian kernel in this application. [Fan and Li 1996] test requires that the bandwidth a under the null be different the bandwidth h under the alternative: We need $a/h \to \infty$ asymptotically. Because we would have $a/h \to 0$ if we chose both a and h by crossvalidation, we chose h by cross validation and experimented with $a = h$, $5h$, and $10h$. Although it is possible that our bandwidth choice was misleading, we find that the power of [Fan and Li 1996] rather low: We accepted the nulls for every case we considered, including the null of parametric Black-Scholes price.

bandwidth markedly different from the cross-validated one, namely larger than 0.1, the test rejects the null that the nonparametric Black-Scholes model is sufficient, and thus concludes that GARCH or EGARCH is necessary for options pricing.

Finally, the rejection of Black-Scholes in case 5a and b in Table 39.4 is robust to any reasonable choice of bandwith.

39.5   Summary and Concluding Remarks

We have considered the relevance of ARCH models in nonparametric option pricing. Relevance was decomposed into two components: sufficiency and necessity. Using the tests by [Aït-Sahalia et al 1994] and [Fan and Li 1996], we conclude that ARCH models do pass the test of sufficiency. As for the test of necessity, we find the test result to be somewhat sensitive to the bandwidth choice, although ARCH volatility fails to pass the necessity test in a fairly large region around the cross-validated bandwidth. We thus tentatively conclude that ARCH models might be irrelevant for European option pricing in a nonparametric statistical sense.

An ever open question in statistical hypothesis testing is the power of the applied tests in the particular situation under investigation. While we have a reasonably large sample at hand, the power of the nonparametric tests applied might not be as high as would be desired. Some rigorous Monte Carlo experiments or higher order expansions are necessary to validate or invalidate this concern. This, however, is beyond the scope of the present chapter.

Despite our conclusions, market participants and academics might still be interested in ARCH models since the nonparametric option pricing relationship in population cannot be hurt by the inclusion of additional variables. ARCH models may be interesting in practice solely in an economic sense. This tentative conclusion is supported by the fact that ARCH models pass the test of sufficiency, and that they do offer significant improvement over parametric Black-Scholes prices.

References

Aït-Sahalia, Y., P. Bickel, and T. Stoker. 1994. Goodness-of-fit tests for regression using kernel methods. Unpublished manuscript.

Aït-Sahalia, Y. and A. Lo 1998. Nonparametric estimation of state-price-densities implicit in financial asset prices. *Journal of Finance*, pages 499–547.

Amin, K. and K. Ng. 1993. Option valuation with systematic stochastic volatility. *Journal of Finance*, 48:881–910.

Black, F. and M. Scholes. 1973. The pricing of options and corporate liabilities. *Journal of Political Economy*, 81:637–659.

Bollerslev, T. and H. Mikkelsen. 1995. Long-term equity anticipation securities and stock market volatility dynamics. Unpublished Manuscript.

Broadie, M., J. Detemple, E. Ghysels, and O. Torrés. 1996a. American options with stochastic dividends and volatility: A nonparametric investigation. Unpublished Manuscript.

Broadie, M., J. Detemple, E. Ghysels, and O. Torrés. 1996b. Nonparametric estimation of american options exercise boundaries and call prices. Unpublished Manuscript.

Corradi, V. 1997. Degenerate continuous time limits for GARCH and GARCH-type processes. Unpublished Manuscript.

Duan, J. 1995. The GARCH option pricing model. *Mathematical Finance*, 5:13–32.

Engle, R. 1982. Autoregressive conditional heteroscedasticity with estimates of the variance of UK inflation. *Econometrica*, 50:987–1008.

Engle, R., A. Kane, and J. Noh. 1996. Index-option pricing with stochastic volatility and the value of accurate variance forecasts. *Review of Derivative Research*, 1:139–157.

Engle, R. and C. Mustafa. 1992. Implied ARCH models from option prices. *Journal of Econometrics*, 52:289–311.

Fan, Y. and Q. Li. 1996. Consistent model specification tests: Omitted variables and semiparametric functional forms. *Econometrica*, 64:865–890.

French, K. and R. Roll. 1986. Stock return variances: The arrival of information and the reaction of traders. *Journal of Financial Economics*, 17:5–26.

Harvey, A., E. Ruiz, and N. Shephard. 1994. Multivariate stochastic variance models. *Review of Economic Studies*, 61:247–264.

Hull, J. and A. White. 1987. The pricing of options on assets with stochastic volatilities. *Journal of Finance*, 42:281–300.

Jacquier, E., N. Polson, and P. Rossi. 1994. Bayesian analysis of stochastic volatility models. *Journal of Business and Economic Statistics*, 12:371–389.

Melino, A. and S. Turnbull. 1990. Pricing foreign currency options with stochastic volatility. *Journal of Econometrics*, 45:239–265.

Nelson, D. 1991. Conditional heteroskedasticity in asset returns: A new approach. *Econometrica*, 59:347–370.

Nelson, D. 1996. Asymptotically optimal smoothing with ARCH models. *Econometrica*, 64:561–573.

Nelson, D. and D. Foster. 1994. Asymptotic filtering theory for univariate ARCH models. *Econometrica*, 62:1–41.

Shephard, N., S. Kim, and S. Chib. 1998. Stochastic volatility: Likelihood inference and comparison with ARCH models. *Review of Economic Studies*, 65:361–393.

Wiggins, J. 1987. Option values under stochastic volatility: Theory and empirical estimates. *Journal of Financial Economics*, 19:351–372.

40 A Computational Framework for Contingent Claim Pricing and Hedging under Time Dependent Asset Processes

Les Clewlow and Russell Grimwood

This work proposes a general computational framework for pricing exotic options in the presence of volatility smiles. The work extends and unifies Dupire's work on implied trinomial trees with fully explicit, fully implicit and Crank Nicolson finite difference methods. We investigate the computational efficiency of this framework with the example of pricing an American barrier option.

40.1 Introduction: Trees Consistent with Observed Market Volatilities

The objective of this work is to outline a new robust algorithm which is capable of pricing exotic options in a finite difference framework consistent with market volatilities. A current popular approach to pricing exotic options consistent with market volatilities is to use a recombining implied tree. Barle and Cakici [Barle and Cakici 1995] review three methods in the recent literature which take different approaches to this problem: Rubinstein [Rubinstein 1994], Derman-Kani [Derman and Kani 1994] and Dupire [Dupire 1994]. Rubinstein's approach uses only the terminal set of option maturities observed in the market and so does not incorporate all available information. Derman-Kani build a binomial tree[1] which has the disadvantage of not being able to keep a fixed asset level due to the limited number of degrees of freedom[2]. Dupire uses a trinomial tree; this permits him to specify different local volatilities and drifts at each node. Unlike Rubinstein's method the procedure suggested by Dupire uses all the observed European[3] option prices and not just the terminal values, thus it incorporates more market information. Because of its advantages we use a trinomial tree based on the method sketched out by Dupire as our starting point. Once an implied tree for a given set of input options is built, it can be used repeatedly for pricing options other than those from the input set. The tree has to be rebuilt only when the volatility smile evolves, however as the smile shape changes daily the frequency of rebuilding the tree must be controlled carefully by the practitioner.

---

1. They were later to use trinomial trees themselves, Derman-Kani-Chriss[Derman et al 1996]

2. Their algorithm reproduces the volatility smile accurately but fails if interest rates are high.

3. We can use American style options if we use a model which explicitly takes account of the early exercise premium. Skiadopoulos, Hodges and Clewlow[Skiadopoulos et al 1998] use Barone-Adesi and Whaley's [Barone-Adesi and Whaley 1987] quadratic approximation model. Neil Chriss [Chriss 1996] uses another iterative procedure each step of which demands the valuation of an American option on a binomial tree.

The work is organised as follows: In Section 40.2, we review the work of Dupire on implied trinomial trees. We propose an improvement to Dupire's sequential method for calculating the state prices and transition probabilities, utilising matrix algebra, which is more robust and less susceptible to build up of numerical errors. Section 40.3 shows how the implied trinomial tree model can be extended to the θ-method to solve the underlying partial differential equation (PDE). The θ-method has nested within it the fully explicit, fully implicit and Crank-Nicolson finite difference methods. The computational efficiency and accuracy of these methods are compared in Section 40.4 for the example of pricing American barrier options. Finally we present our conclusions in Section 40.5.

40.1.1   The Scope of the Pricing Framework

Our framework is an extension to that proposed by Hull and White [Hull and White 1993]. They have a procedure to price a general path dependent option in a Cox, Ross and Rubinstein [Cox et al 1979] binomial tree. Our extension uses finite difference methods and takes into account information about the market's expectation of future volatility. The framework can handle American and European style path dependent derivatives as long as certain conditions are satisfied[4]. For an illustration of how to apply Hull and White's procedure to Asian and look-back options in trinomial trees see Clewlow and Strickland [Clewlow and Strickland 1998]. The framework can be viewed as an engine which can be used for the pricing, hedging and risk management of a portfolio of exotic options based on a common underlying asset like the S&P 500 or FTSE 100 indices.

40.2   Constructing Implied Trinomial Trees

40.2.1   The Tree Framework

The trinomial tree[5] was constructed in the natural logarithm of the underlying asset price x and time t. Where the underlying asset price was represented by S and therefore $x = ln(S)$, with time steps Δt_i and underlying price steps $\Delta x_{i,j}$. The node (i,j) in the tree corresponds to the time $t_i = \sum_{i=0}^{i} \Delta t_i$ from today and to

---

4. Two conditions must be satisfied: firstly that the payoff from the derivative depends on only a single function, F, of the path followed by the underlying stochastic variable, and secondly that the value of F at time $t + \Delta t$ can be calculated from the value of F at time t and the value of the underlying asset at time $t + \Delta t$.

5. The procedure for building the implied tree outlined in the following subsections is based on Chapter 5 of Clewlow and Strickland [Clewlow and Strickland 1998].

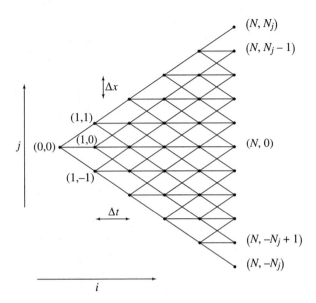

Figure 40.1
The implied trinomial tree structure.

the asset price $S_{i,j} = S_{0,0} \exp\left(\sum_{k=0}^{j} \Delta x_{i,k}\right)$ where $\Delta x_{i,1}$ was the distance between the central asset price at $(i, 0)$ and at $(i, 1)$ and where $S_{0,0}$ was the initial value of the underlying asset, i.e. the value at the root $(0, 0)$ of the tree. The underlying asset price was calculated for the whole of the trinomial tree in one forward sweep. Figure 40.1 shows the construction of an implied trinomial tree with N time steps and $2Nj + 1$ asset price steps at maturity.

For clarity we simplify this general framework by fixing the values of $\Delta x_{i,j}$ and Δt_i to be constant, i.e. Δx and Δt. The asset price at node (i, j) is then given by $S_{0,0}e^{j\Delta x}$. We then use the relationship between the time steps and the asset price steps recommended by Hull and White [Hull and White 1990][6],

$$\Delta x = \sigma_{max}\sqrt{3\Delta t}, \tag{40.1}$$

---

6. Hull and White point out that there are some theoretical advantages to choosing the above relationship: it ensures both stability and convergence. A stable procedure is one where the results are relatively insensitive to roundoff and other small computational errors. Convergence ensures that as $\Delta t, \Delta S \to 0$ the estimated value of the derivative security converges on its true continuous time value.

where the value of σ_{max} is the highest implied volatility of any of the European options in the tree[7]. If the market smiles are not too large it should be possible to use the relationship without generating negative transition probabilities[8].

40.2.2 The Diffusion Process

The implied tree is a discrete approximation of the following stochastic differential equation,

$$\frac{dS}{S} = (r(t) - \delta(S,t))\,dt + \sigma(S,t)dz, \tag{40.2}$$

$r(t)$ is the expected risk neutral rate of return, $\delta(S,t)$ is the dividend yield rate, dz is an increment in a Wiener process with a mean of zero and a variance equal to dt and $\sigma(S,t)$ is the local volatility function which is dependent on both the underlying price and time. The functional form of $\sigma(S,t)$ is inferred by requiring that option prices calculated from the tree fit the smile[9]. For ease of exposition through out this work we will assume that the interest rate is constant and the dividend yield is zero.

40.2.3 Interpolation of Option Prices

Out-of-the-money (OTM) European call prices were used to construct the upper half of the trinomial tree and OTM European put prices to construct the lower half[10]; the central row of nodes were arbitrarily chosen to be call options. Each node of the tree was labelled with an option price $C(i\Delta t, K)$, the value of which corresponded to today's value (i.e. with an underlying asset price at $S_{0,0}$) of a European option, with maturity of $i\Delta t$ and a strike price of K.

As in the papers by Dupire, Derman-Kani and Rubinstein it has been assumed that market option prices exist for all the maturities and strike prices corresponding

---

7. This is the value of σ_{max} which Dupire uses to control the openness of the tree; by using the maximum implied volatility we ensure that the asset price steps are large enough to allow for the local variance of the underlying process. This prevents negative transition probabilities.

8. Avoiding negative transition probabilities is one of the most difficult aspects of successfully implementing an implied trinomial tree for contingent claim pricing.

9. However, the form of $\sigma(S,t)$ is not unique as an infinite number of processes can produce the same probability density.

10. Aparicio and Hodges [Aparicio and Hodges 1996] recommended using OTM and at-the-money (ATM) calls and puts because this avoids the measurement problems which arise with in-the-money (ITM) options. ITM calls and puts have a high delta relative to their option prices therefore their implied volatilities are sensitive (have large confidence intervals) to synchronisation differences between the underlying asset and option markets.

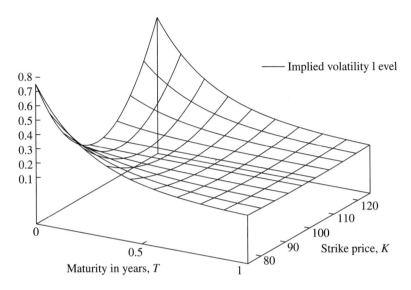

Figure 40.2
Functional form representation of a volatility smile.

to every node in the tree; in reality this is not the case. What we require is a smooth function of option prices against strike prices and maturity, so that for any strike price and maturity an option price can be recovered. To get smooth functions one must interpolate the available option prices. Shimko [Shimko 1993] states that the prices recovered from interpolation are very sensitive to the choice of interpolation method and that smoother functions can be recovered by interpolating the implied volatility figures rather than option prices themselves. The Black-Scholes formula is used to translate back and forth between interpolated implied volatilities and option prices. The option prices for the whole tree need only be computed once.

For simplicity and as we are primarily interested in the properties of the algorithm we have used a mathematical function to approximate the implied volatility surface. Figure 40.2 shows a function which is quadratic across strike prices with the function curvature decreasing with increasing time to maturity[11].

11. See Taylor and Xu [Taylor and Xu 1993] for a theoretical and empirical discussion of the magnitude of implied volatility smiles.

40.2.4   Calculating the Implied State Prices

With each node of the trinomial tree we associate a state price $Q_{i,j}$ this is the price today of an instrument which pays 1 unit of cash if the state (i, j) is reached, and zero otherwise. To calculate the state price at each node in the tree we use a method which involves varying the strike price K. The state prices at the ith time step are related to the price of a European call and its payoff by the following equation,

$$C(i\Delta t, K) = \sum_{j=-i}^{i} Q_{i,j} \max(S_{i,j} - K, 0). \tag{40.3}$$

The same equation applies for the puts, except we make the relevant change to the option payoff, $\max(K - S_{i,j}, 0)$. For a set of strike prices $K_l = S_{i,l}$, where $l = -i+1, \ldots, i-1$, Equation 40.3 gives a set of linear equations which we solve to determine the state prices[12]. Writing Equation 40.3 in more compact matrix and vector form,

$$\bar{c}_i = \bar{S}_i \times \bar{q}_i, \tag{40.4}$$

where $\bar{c}_i$ is a vector of call and put prices for each node in the column at the ith time step, $j = 0, \ldots, i$ are calls and $j = -1, \ldots, -i$ are puts, $\bar{S}_i$ is the matrix of option payoffs. The payoffs are calculated by starting at the top (bottom) of a column of nodes and setting the strike price in the call (put) payoff function to match that of the underlying asset value at the node below (above) $S_{i,j-1}$ ($S_{i,j+1}$), this collapses onto a single node in the continuous time framework. Finally we have a vector of state prices $\bar{q}_i$ which we wish to determine. Rewriting Equation 40.4 we obtain an expression for the state prices vector,

$$\bar{q}_i = \bar{S}_i^{-1} \times \bar{c}_i, \tag{40.5}$$

which is equal to the inverse of the payoff matrix multiplied by the option prices vector. The corresponding matrix calculation is repeated at each time step to retrieve all the state prices in the tree. The solution to Equation 40.5 was determined using LU decomposition - see Press, Teukolsky, Vetterling and Flannery [Press et al 1995].

Dupire uses a sequential method to solve for the state prices in Equation 40.3. Starting at the nodes on the edge of the tree he moves towards the centre solving for the state prices. This whole process is then repeated at every time step.

---

12. State prices can be also be recovered directly from butterfly spreads.

40.2.5 Calculating the Transition Probabilities

Except at maturity, each node (i,j) has three branches: up, middle and down which have associated transition probabilities $p_{u,i,j}$, $p_{m,i,j}$ and $p_{d,i,j}$. The three unknown probabilities are determined by making use of three local no-arbitrage relationships[13]. Two of these are standard backward relationships, which link the value of a claim at a node to its value at the immediate successors. The first is the price of a Δt maturity pure discount bond (i.e. a bond which pays 1 unit of cash at Δt),

$$1 = p_{u,i,j} + p_{m,i,j} + p_{d,i,j}. \tag{40.6}$$

The second relationship is the price of the underlying asset $S_{i,j}$,

$$S_{i,j} = S_{i+1,j+1}p_{u,i,j} + S_{i+1,j}p_{m,i,j} + S_{i+1,j-1}p_{d,i,j}. \tag{40.7}$$

The third relationship makes use of a technique used by Jamshidian [Jamshidian 1991], called forward induction. Here the state price of a node is related to the state prices of its immediate predecessors,

$$Q_{i+1,j} = Q_{i,j-1}p_{u,i,j-1} + Q_{i,j}p_{m,i,j} + Q_{i,j+1}p_{d,i,j+1}. \tag{40.8}$$

To determine the transition probabilities we can again use matrix algebra. However for transition probabilities this is more complicated than for the state prices as we have to solve three sets of equations rather than one. Figure 40.3 shows the matrix form of a set of linear equations equivalent to the sequential Equations 40.6, 40.7 and 40.8. This can be rewritten more compactly with matrix and vector notation,

$$\bar{v}_i = \bar{M}_i \times \bar{p}_i, \tag{40.9}$$

where the first vector is $\bar{v}_i$, the sparse matrix is $\bar{M}_i$ and the transition probability vector is $\bar{p}_i$. Rearranging this we get an expression in terms of the transition probability vector such that,

$$\bar{p}_i = \bar{M}_i^{-1} \times \bar{v}_i. \tag{40.10}$$

We use LU decomposition once more to solve Equation 40.10 which has a band diagonal structure. For band diagonal matrices it is more efficient to use LU decomposition than to invert the matrix and then to store the inverted matrix in

---

13. For clarity we will use the bank account as numeraire to avoid cluttering our equations with discount factors.

memory[14]. This calculation is repeated for each column of nodes to determine the transition probabilities for the whole tree.

Dupire uses an sequential method to calculate the implied transition probabilities working from edge of the tree down a column of nodes. The transition probabilities calculated using the sequential method depend on the values of the previous set of transition probabilities. A problem can therefore arise with the build up of roundoff errors. Dupire suggests it is better to work from the two edges of the tree towards the middle (rather than from the top all the way to the bottom or vice versa) because this helps limit the error size. Despite this the sequential method produces errors which grow in size towards the centre of the tree. In contrast the LU decomposition method from Press *et al* which we choose to use to solve the system of linear equations uses partial pivoting[15] of the matrix rows which prevents the build up of roundoff errors caused by the finite precision of computer calculations. It is partial pivoting which gives this method superior stability in the presence of roundoff error compared to a naive sequential method without partial pivoting. Figure 40.4 shows the relative error in the solution of a set of linear equations. The flat line is a comparison between LU decomposition and Gauss-Jordan elimination both with pivoting. It demonstrates that both methods produce numerically similar results as the relative errors are not visible at the scale shown. However, if we compare the Gauss-Jordan method with and without pivoting the instability of solving a set of linear equations without pivoting becomes clear. Large relative errors become visible which would produce errors in the transition coefficients. In Dupire's method this could cause negative transition probabilities.

Once the transition probabilities have been calculated we can price a target exotic option in a framework consistent with the market implied volatilities. The target options payoff at maturity is determined for each level of the underlying asset $S_{N,j}$ at the final set of nodes (N, j). We then discount these option prices back to the next time step using the transition probabilities. This process is repeated for each time step until we have recovered the option's price today at $t = 0$. Computing standard dynamic hedge sensitivities proceeds along the usual lines for lattices.

---

14. An inverted band diagonal or tridiagonal matrix will not be a sparse matrix and it will therefore require more memory space. Sparse matrices like the ones we will encounter throughout this work can be held efficiently in memory by just storing the non-zero elements and their co-ordinates - see again Press *et al.*

15. Partial pivoting involves the interchange of matrix rows so that the highest magnitude element is in the diagonal position.

$$
\begin{pmatrix}
Q_{i,i} \\
S_{i-1,i-1} \\
1 \\
Q_{i,i-1} \\
S_{i-1,i-2} \\
1 \\
Q_{i,i-2} \\
\vdots \\
Q_{i,-i+1} \\
1 \\
S_{i-1,-i+1} \\
Q_{i,-i}
\end{pmatrix}
$$

$$
=
\begin{pmatrix}
Q_{i-1,i-1} & 0 & 0 & 0 & 0 & 0 & 0 & \cdots & 0 & 0 & 0 & 0 \\
S_{i,i} & S_{i,i-1} & S_{i,i-2} & 0 & 0 & 0 & 0 & \cdots & 0 & 0 & 0 & 0 \\
1 & 1 & 1 & 0 & 0 & 0 & 0 & \cdots & 0 & 0 & 0 & 0 \\
0 & Q_{i-1,i-1} & 0 & Q_{i-1,i-2} & 0 & 0 & 0 & \cdots & 0 & 0 & 0 & 0 \\
0 & 0 & 0 & S_{i,i-1} & S_{i,i-2} & S_{i,i-3} & 0 & \cdots & 0 & 0 & 0 & 0 \\
0 & 0 & 0 & 1 & 1 & 1 & 0 & \cdots & 0 & 0 & 0 & 0 \\
0 & 0 & Q_{i-1,i-1} & 0 & Q_{i-1,i-2} & 0 & Q_{i-1,i-3} & \cdots & 0 & 0 & 0 & 0 \\
\vdots & \vdots & \vdots & \vdots & \vdots & \vdots & \vdots & \ddots & \vdots & \vdots & \vdots & \vdots \\
0 & 0 & 0 & 0 & 0 & 0 & 0 & \cdots & Q_{i-1,-i+2} & 0 & Q_{i-1,-i+1} & 0 \\
0 & 0 & 0 & 0 & 0 & 0 & 0 & \cdots & 0 & 1 & 1 & 1 \\
0 & 0 & 0 & 0 & 0 & 0 & 0 & \cdots & 0 & S_{i,-i+1} & S_{i,-i+1} & S_{i,-i} \\
0 & 0 & 0 & 0 & 0 & 0 & 0 & \cdots & 0 & 0 & 0 & Q_{i-1,-i+1}
\end{pmatrix}
$$

$$
\times
\begin{pmatrix}
P_{u,i-1,i-1} \\
P_{m,i-1,i-1} \\
P_{d,i-1,i-1} \\
P_{u,i-1,i-2} \\
P_{m,i-1,i-2} \\
P_{d,i-1,i-2} \\
P_{u,i-1,i-3} \\
\vdots \\
P_{d,i-1,-i+2} \\
P_{u,i-1,-i+1} \\
P_{m,i-1,-i+1} \\
P_{d,i-1,-i+1}
\end{pmatrix}
$$

Figure 40.3
Representation of the system of linear equations used to recover the transition probabilities in an implied trinomial tree; the band diagonal structure of the matrix is clear.

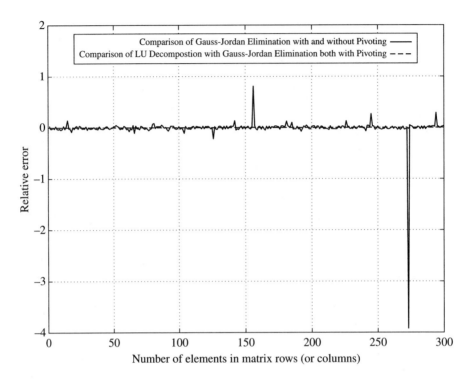

Figure 40.4
Roundoff errors in the solutions to a set of linear equations caused by using a method which does
not use pivoting.

40.3 The θ-Method: Recovering Implied Transition Coefficients Using Finite Difference

Starting with the Black-Scholes PDE,

$$\frac{\partial C(S,t)}{\partial t} + \frac{1}{2}\sigma^2 S^2 \frac{\partial^2 C(S,t)}{\partial S^2} + rS\frac{\partial C(S,t)}{\partial S} = rC(S,t), \tag{40.11}$$

we use the natural logarithm of the underlying asset price i.e., $S = ln(x)$ and
$W(x,t) = C(S,t)$ to transform the PDE so that we have constant coefficients for
the partial derivatives,

$$\frac{1}{2}\sigma^2 \frac{\partial^2 W(x,t)}{\partial x^2} + \left(r - \frac{1}{2}\sigma^2\right)\frac{\partial W(x,t)}{\partial x} + \frac{\partial W(x,t)}{\partial t} = r\,W(x,t). \tag{40.12}$$

In finite difference methods we replace the partial derivatives with difference equations[16]. Depending on whether the difference equations are centred around time step $i + 1$, i or $i + \frac{1}{2}$ determines whether the finite difference method is fully explicit, fully implicit[17] or Crank-Nicolson[18] respectively, see Figure 40.5. These three finite difference methods are nested within the θ-method. The Black-Scholes difference equation for the θ-method is,

$$
1/2 \, \frac{\sigma^2 \, (W_{i+1,j+1} - 2 \, W_{i+1,j} + W_{i+1,j-1})}{(\Delta x)^2} (1 - \theta)
$$
$$
+ 1/2 \, \frac{(r - 1/2 \, \sigma^2) \, (W_{i+1,j+1} - W_{i+1,j-1})}{\Delta x} (1 - \theta)
$$
$$
+ \frac{W_{i+1,j} - W_{i,j}}{\Delta t} - r W_{i+1,j} (1 - \theta)
$$
$$
= 1/2 \, \frac{\sigma^2 \, (W_{i,j+1} - 2 \, W_{i,j} + W_{i,j-1})}{(\Delta x)^2} \theta
$$
$$
+ 1/2 \, \frac{(r - 1/2 \, \sigma^2) \, (W_{i,j+1} - W_{i,j-1})}{\Delta x} \theta + r W_{i,j} \theta, \tag{40.16}
$$

where $0 \leq \theta \leq 1$. Wilmott, Dewynne and Howison [Wilmott et al 1993] point out that this can be thought of as a θ weighted average of the explicit and fully implicit

---

16. For the partial derivative with respect to time we use a forward difference equation,

$$
\frac{\partial W(x,t)}{\partial t} \approx \frac{W_{i+1} - W_i}{\Delta t} + O(\Delta t), \tag{40.13}
$$

for the first order partial derivative with respect to asset price we use a central difference equation,

$$
\frac{\partial W(x,t)}{\partial x} \approx \frac{W_{j+1} - W_{j-1}}{2\Delta x} + O((\Delta x)^2), \tag{40.14}
$$

and for the second order partial derivative with respect to asset price we use a symmetric central difference equation,

$$
\frac{\partial W(x,t)}{\partial x^2} \approx \frac{W_{j+1} - 2W_j + W_{j-1}}{(\Delta x)^2} + O((\Delta x)^2). \tag{40.15}
$$

The $O(\cdot)$ terms in the above difference equations represent the rest of the Taylor series expansion. Henceforth we will truncate the expansions by not including these terms. The smaller the Δt and Δx terms become (i.e., the finer the discretization) the more accurate our approximations become, that is to say the truncation errors become smaller.

17. The explicit and implicit finite difference frameworks were first used in option pricing by Brennan and Schwartz [Brennan and Schwartz 1978]

18. The Crank Nicolson method was first introduced into the contingent claim pricing literature by Courtadon [Courtadon 1982]

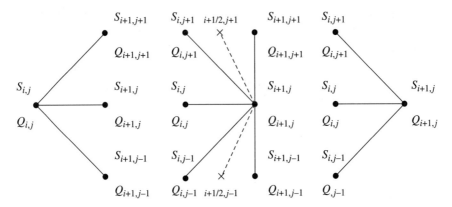

Figure 40.5
Fully explicit element centred around $i+1, j$, Crank-Nicolson element centred around $i+\frac{1}{2}, j$ and a fully implicit element centred around i, j.

finite difference methods. When $\theta = 0$, it gives the explicit method, when $\theta = \frac{1}{2}$ it gives the Crank-Nicolson method and when $\theta = 1$ it gives the implicit method. The fully explicit finite difference method has the disadvantage that it is only stable and convergent with the imposition of the restriction $\Delta x \geq \sigma \sqrt{3 \Delta t}$. The restriction implies that in order to have the large number of asset price steps necessary for accurate prices ridiculously small time steps are required. The accuracy of the fully explicit and fully implicit methods is $O((\Delta x)^2 + \Delta t)$ whereas the Crank-Nicolson method has a superior accuracy of $O\left((\Delta x)^2 + \left(\frac{\Delta t}{2}\right)^2\right)$. As it has superior convergence and is unconditionally stable our exposition will continue using the Crank-Nicolson method as our example.

Setting $\theta = \frac{1}{2}$ in equation 40.16 gives,

$$1/4 \frac{\sigma^2 \left(W_{i+1,j+1} - 2 W_{i+1,j} + W_{i+1,j-1} + W_{i,j+1} - 2 W_{i,j} + W_{i,j-1}\right)}{(\Delta x)^2}$$

$$+ 1/4 \frac{\left(r - 1/2\, \sigma^2\right) \left(W_{i+1,j+1} - W_{i+1,j-1} + W_{i,j+1} - W_{i,j-1}\right)}{\Delta x}$$

$$+ \frac{W_{i+1,j} - W_{i,j}}{\Delta t} - r \left(1/2\, W_{i+1,j} + 1/2\, W_{i,j}\right) = 0, \tag{40.17}$$

which can be rewritten as,

$$\left(1/4 \frac{\Delta t r}{\Delta x} - 1/8 \frac{\Delta t \sigma^2}{\Delta x} + 1/4 \frac{\Delta t \sigma^2}{(\Delta x)^2}\right) W_{i+1,j+1}$$

$$+ \left(1 - 1/2\,\frac{\Delta t\sigma^2}{(\Delta x)^2} - 1/2\,\Delta tr\right)W_{i+1,j}$$

$$+ \left(1/4\,\frac{\Delta t\sigma^2}{(\Delta x)^2} + 1/8\,\frac{\Delta t\sigma^2}{\Delta x} - 1/4\,\frac{\Delta tr}{\Delta x}\right)W_{i+1,j-1}$$

$$+ \left(1/4\,\frac{\Delta tr}{\Delta x} - 1/8\,\frac{\Delta t\sigma^2}{\Delta x} + 1/4\,\frac{\Delta t\sigma^2}{(\Delta x)^2}\right)W_{i,j+1}$$

$$+ \left(-1/2\,\Delta tr - 1/2\,\frac{\Delta t\sigma^2}{(\Delta x)^2} - 1\right)W_{i,j}$$

$$+ \left(1/4\,\frac{\Delta t\sigma^2}{(\Delta x)^2} + 1/8\,\frac{\Delta t\sigma^2}{\Delta x} - 1/4\,\frac{\Delta tr}{\Delta x}\right)W_{i,j-1} = 0. \tag{40.18}$$

If we separate the terms at time step i and $i+1$ onto either side of the equality, write the coefficients of W as $P_{u,i+1,j}$, $P_{m,i+1,j}$ and $P_{d,i+1,j}$ and use the bank account as numeraire we get,

$$P_{u,i+1,j}W_{i,j+1} + P_{m,i+1,j}W_{i,j} + P_{d,i+1,j}W_{i,j-1}$$
$$= -P_{u,i+1,j}W_{i+1,j+1} - (P_{m,i+1,j} - 2)W_{i+1,j} - P_{d,i+1,j}W_{i+1,j-1}. \tag{40.19}$$

The RHS of the above Equation 40.19 is made up of known option prices (we know the option's payoff at maturity $i = N$) and (once we have calculated them) known transition coefficients $P_{u,i+1,j}$, $P_{m,i+1,j}$ and $P_{d,i+1,j}$; the RHS can therefore be considered as a known constant, $Z_{i+1,j}$,

$$P_{u,i+1,j}W_{i,j+1} + P_{m,i+1,j}W_{i,j} + P_{d,i+1,j}W_{i,j-1} = Z_{i+1,j}. \tag{40.20}$$

To calculate the transition coefficients, consistent with the market implied volatilities, for the Crank-Nicolson method we must reformulate Equations 40.6, 40.7 and 40.8. The one period bond price for Δt maturity pure discount bond gives us,

$$1 = P_{u,i+1,j} + P_{m,i+1,j} + P_{d,i+1,j}. \tag{40.21}$$

For the fully explicit finite difference method the transition coefficients can be interpreted as probabilities whereas with the implicit methods there is no such interpretation. From Equation 40.21 they must sum to unity but they are not constrained to $\in [0,1]$. The price of the underlying asset $S_{i+1,j}$ is related to its immediate predecessors by,

$$S_{i+1,j} = \frac{S_{i,j+1} + S_{i+1,j+1}}{2}P_{u,i+1,j} + \frac{S_{i,j} + S_{i+1,j}}{2}P_{m,i+1,j}$$

$$+ \frac{S_{i,j-1} + S_{i+1,j-1}}{2} P_{d,i+1,j}. \tag{40.22}$$

Finally the state price[19] of a node $(i + 1/2, j)$ is given by,

$$\frac{Q_{i,j} + Q_{i+1,j}}{2} = Q_{i+1,j+1}P_{d,i+1,j+1} + Q_{i+1,j}P_{m,i+1,j} + Q_{i+1,j-1}P_{u,i+1,j-1}. \tag{40.23}$$

The values of the state prices are computed in the same manner as for the trinomial tree. The above set of linear equations cannot be solved sequentially and we must instead determine the whole vector of transition coefficients at each time step by matrix algebra. The system represented in Figure 40.6 can rewritten using more compact notation,

$$\bar{v}_i = \bar{M}_i \times \bar{p}_i, \tag{40.24}$$

where the first vector is $\bar{v}_i$, the band diagonal matrix is $\bar{M}_i$ and the transition coefficient vector is $\bar{p}_i$. Rearranging this we get an expression in terms of the transition coefficient vector such that,

$$\bar{p}_i = \bar{M}_i^{-1} \times \bar{v}_i. \tag{40.25}$$

LU decomposition is used to solve Equation 40.25. This calculation is repeated for each time step to determine the transition coefficients for the whole grid. Once the transition coefficients have been recovered they can be used with the option's boundary conditions to determine the option price by backward induction.

40.4   Results

40.4.1   Introduction

We examine the convergence properties of prices derived from the fully explicit, fully implicit and Crank Nicolson finite difference methods. Specifically we look at a European put, an American put, an up-and-out European put and an up-and-out American put both with constant volatility and in the presence of a volatility smile. For the European put we compare the prices with the Black-Scholes price and for the up-and-out European put we compare the prices with the price from an analytical formula due to Hull [Hull 1993].

---

19. Jamshidian states that the Green's function satisfies two fundamental differential equations, the Kolmogorov backward equation and the Fokker-Plank forward equation. In discrete time finance the Green's function has the interpretation of state prices. We can therefore relate state prices to each other in both forward and backward equations.

$$\begin{pmatrix} 1 \\ S_{i,Nj} \\ \frac{Q_{i-1,Nj} + Q_{i,Nj}}{2} \\ 1 \\ S_{i,Nj-1} \\ \frac{Q_{i-1,Nj-1} + Q_{i-1,Nj-1}}{2} \\ \\ \frac{Q_{i-1,-Nj} + Q_{i,-Nj}}{2} \\ S_{i,-Nj} \\ 1 \end{pmatrix}$$

$$= \begin{pmatrix}
1 & 1 & 0 & 0 & 0 & 0 & \cdots & 0 & 0 & 0 \\
\frac{S_{i-1,Nj} + S_{i,Nj}}{2} & \frac{S_{i-1,Nj-1} + S_{i,Nj-1}}{2} & 0 & 0 & 0 & 0 & \cdots & 0 & 0 & 0 \\
Q_{i,Nj} & 0 & Q_{i,Nj-1} & 0 & 0 & 0 & \cdots & 0 & 0 & 0 \\
0 & 0 & 1 & 1 & 1 & 0 & \cdots & 0 & 0 & 0 \\
0 & 0 & \frac{S_{i,Nj} + S_{i,Nj}}{2} & \frac{S_{i-1,Nj-1} + S_{i,Nj-1}}{2} & \frac{S_{i-1,Nj-2} + S_{i,Nj-2}}{2} & 0 & \cdots & 0 & 0 & 0 \\
0 & Q_{i,Nj} & 0 & Q_{i,Nj-1} & 0 & Q_{i,Nj-2} & \cdots & 0 & 0 & 0 \\
\vdots & \vdots & \vdots & \vdots & \vdots & \vdots & \ddots & \vdots & \vdots & \vdots \\
0 & 0 & 0 & 0 & 0 & 0 & \cdots & Q_{i,-Nj+1} & 0 & Q_{i,-Nj} \\
0 & 0 & 0 & 0 & 0 & 0 & \cdots & 0 & \frac{S_{i-1,-Nj+1} + S_{i,-Nj+1}}{2} & \frac{S_{i-1,-Nj} + S_{i,-Nj1}}{2} \\
0 & 0 & 0 & 0 & 0 & 0 & \cdots & 0 & 1 & 1
\end{pmatrix} \times \begin{pmatrix} P_{m,i,Nj} \\ P_{d,i,Nj} \\ P_{u,i,Nj-1} \\ P_{m,i,Nj-1} \\ P_{m,i,Nj-1} \\ P_{d,i,Nj-2} \\ \vdots \\ P_{d,i,-Nj+1} \\ P_{u,i,-Nj} \\ P_{m,i,-Nj} \end{pmatrix}$$

Figure 40.6
Representation of the system of linear equations used to recover the transition coefficients in a Crank Nicolson finite difference framework; the band diagonal structure of the matrix is clear.

In all the price convergence plots the Crank Nicolson method has oscillatory behaviour for small N, i.e. large Δt. Although the fully implicit and Crank Nicolson methods are unconditionally stable there are other conditions related to the size of Δx and Δt which need to be satisfied to prevent spurious oscillation; see Zvan, Vetzal and Forsyth [Zvan et al 1998] for a fuller discussion of this point. Suffice it to say, that it is because Δt is large for small N that we find oscillations in the Crank Nicolson method.

40.4.2 Option Prices with Constant Volatility Across Strike Prices and Maturities

The first figure in Table 40.1 shows that all three finite difference methods converge towards the Black-Scholes solution as we would expect. The second figure shows again that all three methods converge towards a common price which dominates the European price reflecting the early exercise premium associated with American options.

Table 40.1

The table of figures show the convergence properties for the finite difference methods for the following contracts: a European put, an American put, an up-and-out European put and an up-and-out American put. The contracts have the following specifications: $S = 100$, $K = 100$, $T = 0.5$, $r = 0.05$, where there is a barrier it is at a level $H = 105$ and the volatility is constant at $\sigma = 0.2$.

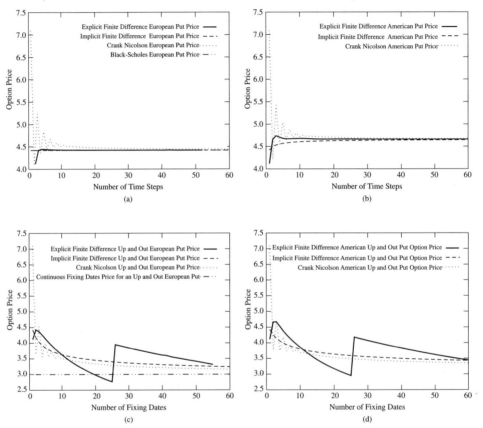

For the European and American barrier option plots the x-axis represents the number of fixing dates (i.e., the monitoring times). For this analysis we have used the same number of time steps as fixing dates to highlight the different convergence properties of the three methods. However, to achieve penny accuracy one would need to have more time steps than fixing dates. Both the third and forth figures demonstrate the well known feature that for down-and-out options the price of the option decreases as the number of fixing dates is increased, as there is a higher likelihood that if the barrier is crossed (even temporarily) it will be on a fixing date and therefore the option will be knocked out. The plots also demonstrate the fact that barrier options are always worth less than their vanilla counterparts as there is always a chance that they will be knocked out or fail to be knocked in.

The explicit finite difference line shows the characteristic saw tooth shape convergence which we associate with pricing barrier options in trinomial trees. Boyle and Lau [Boyle and Lau 1994], Derman-Kani-Ergener and Bardhan [Derman et al 995b] and Heynen-Kat [Heynen and Kat 1997] have all suggested methods for avoiding or correcting this saw tooth convergence[20].

The fully implicit and Crank Nicolson methods converge smoothly and asymptotically towards the price with a continuous number of fixing dates, this price is shown for the up-and-out European put where an analytical formula exists. The accuracy of the Crank Nicolson method is superior in these plots to the implicit method because of its faster convergence $O((\Delta t)^2)$ rather then $O(\Delta t)$.

40.4.3 Option Prices with Non-Constant Volatilities Across Strike Prices and Maturities

The four figures in Table 40.2 show the same option contracts as above except in the presence of a volatility smile. For this size of volatility smile the explicit finite difference method fails. This is because the size of the asset price step Δx is controlled (to insure stability) by Equation 40.1 which relates the size of Δx to the maximum implied volatility σ_{max}. If Δx is large for stability reasons then a conflict can arise with our accuracy requirements[21]. The resulting prices for the explicit finite difference method were very noisy and unusable.

All the contracts priced in the presence of a volatility smile have prices which dominate the contracts with constant volatility. This is expected as the minimum level of volatility in the smile was 20% which was the level for the constant volatility contracts. The higher overall level of volatility of the contracts with the volatility smile gives them a higher price.

---

20. The uneven convergence is the product of the barrier level and the position of the nearest node. For the fully explicit finite difference method the size of the asset price step Δx and therefore the position of the nodes in asset-space are related to the size of the time step Δt via Equation 40.1. In our plot Δt decreases in size as N increases and therefore the position of the nearest node changes relative to the fixed barrier level, H. As the node approaches the barrier the price of the option becomes more accurate reaching its most accurate when the node level is equal to the barrier level, conversely as the node moves away from the barrier level the accuracy deteriorates, finally the next node becomes the closest to the barrier at which point the price jumps.

21. Remember for the explicit finite difference method the accuracy is $O((\Delta x)^2)$.

Table 40.2
The table of figures show the convergence properties for the finite difference methods for the following contracts: a European put, an American put, an up-and-out European put and an up-and-out American put. The contracts have the following specifications: $S = 100$, $K = 100$, $T = 0.5$, $r = 0.05$ and where there is a barrier it is at a level $H = 105$. The contracts are priced in the presence of a volatility smile with a minimum value of $\sigma = 0.2$.

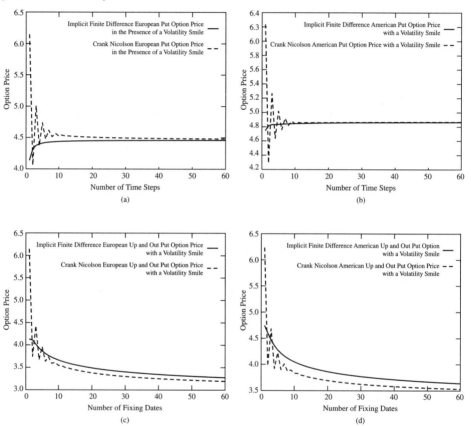

40.4.4   Computational Efficiency and Accuracy

If we have a portfolio of exotic options on a common underlying asset, for example the S&P 500 then we can think of the pricing framework as having two stages. The first stage building a grid of transition coefficients (calibrating the model to the volatility smile); this is the pricing engine and has a one off run time cost[22]. The second stage is using the transition coefficients together with the target option's boundary conditions to calculate the price, this stage must be repeated for each different option. The time for building the grid of coefficients is $\approx 100s$ for $N = 60$ and $Nj = 50$ on a Sun UltraSPARC workstation. The time for pricing an American barrier option once the coefficients have been calculated is $\approx 3.70s$ for Crank Nicolson method and $\approx 3.67s$ for fully implicit finite difference method.

The accuracy of the implied grid has already be demonstrated by checking its convergence towards Black-Scholes prices; the example given was for a European put with constant volatility.

Once the model has been calibrated the explicit finite difference method requires the least number of executions as it does not use a routine for solving band diagonal matrices[23] to determine option prices at the preceding time step. However, because it is not unconditionally stable it requires more time steps (larger N) to achieve the resolution in Δx which is needed for penny accuracy. The Crank Nicolson method requires additional arithmetic operations per time step over the fully implicit method because of the need to calculate the vector of $Z_{i+1,j}$ values from option prices and transition coefficients.

40.5   Conclusions

In this work we have outlined three finite difference methods for pricing and hedging contingent claims in the presence of volatility smiles. Our findings suggest that it is difficult to use the explicit finite difference method when volatility smiles are very pronounced. Hence, although the fully implicit and Crank Nicolson methods require

---

22. The coefficients only have to be recomputed when the implied volatility smile changes shape beyond some defined tolerance level or time period.

23. When fully implicit and Crank Nicolson finite difference methods are conventionally implemented with fixed value coefficients, a routine which takes advantage of the tridiagonal nature of the linear set of equations can be employed. We tried solving the linear set of equations for the option prices using a tridiagonal routine rather than a general routine for solving band diagonal matrices as the tridiagonal routine requires less memory and fewer arithmetic operations. However, the tridiagonal routine does not use pivoting and therefore it can sometimes fail when the matrix is non-singular (i.e., it can encounter a zero pivot); we found this to occur for $N > \approx 20$. For the tridiagonal algorithm, to avoid a zero pivot we need $|P_{m,j}| > |P_{u,j}| + |P_{d,j}|$ where $j = 1, \ldots, 2Nj + 1$; this is *diagonal dominance*. Although this condition is satisfied near the centre of the tridiagonal matrix (and for conventional implementation of the implicit and Crank Nicolson methods) it is not satisfied near the top and bottom of the tridiagonal matrix where a down or an up movement may dominate a middle movement. The band diagonal routine uses pivoting unlike the tridiagonal routine and so should only fail if the matrix is singular.

more computer operations they offer more promising results for pricing contingent claims in the presence of realistic volatility smiles. The fully implicit method requires slightly fewer computer operations than the Crank Nicolson method however the Crank Nicolson method has faster convergence. The choice between the Crank Nicolson method or the fully implicit finite difference method is problem dependent.

The work has also highlighted the importance of using pivoting when solving linear equations in order to prevent instability due to the build up of roundoff errors.

The example of pricing an American barrier option using fully implicit and Crank Nicolson finite difference methods demonstrates their superiority over unadjusted trinomial tree and fully explicit finite difference methods which have very poor convergence properties for barrier options.

References

Aparicio, S. and S. Hodges. 1996. Estimating implied distributions and issues in static hedging. Proceedings of the 9th Annual Financial Options Research Centre Conference at the University of Warwick.

Barle, S. and N. Cakici. 1995. Growing a smiling tree. *Risk*, 8:76–81.

Barone-Adesi, G. and R. Whaley. 1987. Efficient analytic approximations of American option values. *The Journal of Finance*, 42:301–320.

Boyle, P. and S. Lau. 1994. Bumping up against the barrier with the binomial method. *The Journal of Derivatives*, 1:6–14.

Brennan, M. and E. Schwartz. 1978. Finite difference methods and jump processes arising in the pricing of contingent claims: A synthesis. *Journal of Financial and Quantitative Analysis*, 13:462–474.

Chriss, N. 1996. Transatlantic trees. *Risk*, 9.

Clewlow, L. and C. Strickland. 1998. *Implementing Derivative Models*. John Wiley and Sons Ltd.

Courtadon, G. 1982. A more accurate finite difference approximation for the valuation of options. *Journal of Financial and Quantitative Analysis*, XVII(5).

Cox, J., S. Ross, and M. Rubinstein. 1979. Option pricing: A simplified approach. *Journal of Financial Economics*, 7:229–264.

Derman, E. and I. Kani. 1994. The volatility smile and its implied tree. Technical report, Goldman Sachs, Quantitative Strategies Research Notes.

Derman, E., I. Kani, and N. Chriss. 1996. Implied trinomial trees of the volatility smile. Technical report, Goldman Sachs, Quantitative Strategies Research Notes.

Derman, E., I. Kani, D. Ergener, and I. Bardhan. 1995b. Enhanced numerical methods for options with barriers. Quantitative Strategies Research Notes, Goldman Sachs.

Dupire, B. 1994. Pricing with a smile. *Risk*, 7:18–20.

Heynen, R. and H. Kat. 1997. *Exotic Options the State of the Art*, chapter 6: Barrier Options. International Thomson Business Press.

Hull, J. 1993. *Options, Futures, and Other Derivative Securities*, chapter 16, pages 418–420. Prentice-Hall, second edition.

Hull, J. and A. White. 1990. Valuing derivative securities using the explicit finite difference method. *Journal of Financial and Quantitative Analysis*, 25(1):87–100.

Hull, J. and A. White. 1993. Efficient procedures for valuing European and American path dependent options. *The Journal of Derivatives*, pages 21–31.

Jamshidian, F. 1991. Forward induction and construction of yield curve diffusion models. *Journal of Fixed Income*.

Press, W., S. Teukolsky, W. Vetterling, and B. Flannery. 1995. *Numerical Recipes in C: The Art of Scientific Computing*. Cambridge University Press, second edition.

Rubinstein, M. 1994. Implied binomial trees. *The Journal of Finance*, 69(3):770–818.

Shimko, D. 1993. Bounds of probability. *Risk*, 6:33–37.

Skiadopoulos, G., S. Hodges, and L. Clewlow. 1998. The dynamics of smiles. FORC Preprint, Financial Options Research Centre, University of Warwick.

Taylor, S. and X. Xu. 1993. The magnitude of implied volatility smiles: Theory and empirical evidence for exchange rates. FORC Preprint, Financial Options Research Centre, University of Warwick.

Wilmott, P., J. Dewynne, and S. Howison. 1993. *Option Pricing: Mathematical Models and Computation*. Oxford Financial Press.

Zvan, R., K. Vetzal, and P. Forsyth. 1998. Swing low swing high. *Risk*, 11:71–75.

41 A Framework for Comparative Analysis of Statistical and Machine Learning Methods: An Application to the Black–Scholes Option Pricing Equation

J. Galindo–Flores

The objective of the study is twofold. On the one hand, it attempts to define an specific framework to make comparative studies of different statistical and machine learning methods in the context of regression analysis. On the other, it takes a specific known economics problem and apply this framework using different algorithms—OLS, neural network, decision tree, and k–nearest neighbor. This methodology is based on the study of the error curves—the behavior of the root mean square error (RMSE) when varying the sample size and the capacity (degrees of freedom) of each analytical method. Using state–of–the–art techniques we build more than 13,920 models to test the methodology by recovering a restricted version of the Black–Scholes call option pricing formula with noise—where the instantaneous standard deviation of the noise is 0.78. The results show that—given the level of noise—neural networks provide the best estimation with an average RMSE of 0.7825 for a training sample of 6,000 records. OLS is the second best with an average RMSE of 0.7861 and its first best for sample sizes smaller than 1,125. The k–Nearest Neighbor achieved an average RMSE of 0.8380 which is comparable to the worst performer CART which attained an average RMSE of 0.8721.[1]

41.1 Introduction

Over the recent past, a number of different data–driven techniques have been developed for modeling and finding non–linear statistical relations by means of non–parametric methods. Examples of these techniques are decision trees, neural networks, vector machines, k–nearest neighbor classifiers, genetic algorithms, multivariate adaptive regression splines, projection pursuit, etc. Originally, statisticians, computer or physical scientists used many of these algorithms and methods. But their use has now spread successfully to many applications [Adriaans and Zantinge 1996, Bigus 1996, Bourgoin 1994, Bourgoin and Smith 1995, Trippi and Lee 1996][2].

Important ingredients to efficiently use non–parametric non–linear methods are: i) to understand the characteristics of the algorithms, ii) a rational methodology to find the optimal degrees of freedom (capacity) for each method, and iii) a specific rational framework to compare the different methods. In this study, we focus on the last two ingredients in the context of regression analysis. We test

1. I would like to acknowledge my indebtedness to CONACYT (Mexico) for grants #84537, which gave financial support to this project and to Thinking Machines Corporation for providing computer time and access to the Darwin tool set.

2. An interdisciplinary *Knowledge Discovery* approach to find the patterns and regularities in data has taken form over the last five years. See for example [Piatetsky-Shapiro and Frawley 1991, Fayyad et al 1996, Simoudis et al 1996].

the methodology proposed in Section 41.2 on data generated accordingly to the Black–Scholes call option pricing formula. Using state–of–the–art techniques we build more than 13,920 models as part of the study.

The studies within economics are rather few in number and limited in scope. [Hutchinson and Poggio 1994] (HLP) simulate Black and Scholes (B–S) option prices and use it to train and recover the formula by means of parametric and nonparametric methods—neural network, radial basis function, projection pursuit, and OLS. The question arises: why do we revisited nonparametric estimation of the B–S call option pricing formula?.

1. HLP fundamental question is: can learning networks "learn" the Black–Scholes pricing formula?; The study finds that "yes": learning networks indeed are able to recover the formula with "remarkable accuracy". The study does not attempt to find the best technique and therefore does not need to have a framework for comparison. In our study we are concern in making a comparative analysis of the different methods, therefore the objective of our study is twofold. On the one hand, it attempts to define an specific framework to make comparative studies of different statistical and machine learning methods in the context of regression analysis. On the other, it takes a specific inference problem—to recover the Black–Scholes equation—and apply this framework using different algorithms—OLS, neural network, decision tree, and k–nearest neighbor.

2. HLP does not make explicit how the capacity of each model is chosen—*e.g.*, the number of non–linear units, the number of iterations, the number of nodes, the number of parameters; The study argues that the choice for model complexity is motivated by minimizing error and maximizing fit for out–of–sample data but fails to describe how this criterion is implemented. Here, we make explicit the rationale used to choose the capacity for each model.

3. HLP do not explore the relationship between sample size and approximation error. The methodology we use explores the relationship between error rate, sample size, and model's capacity; it provides insight of the problem and allow us to answer important questions such as: what is the appropriate model capacity for each method given a specific data set? what is the trade–off between sample size and approximation error? how noisy is the data set? and, what is the best technique for this problem?.

4. HLP uses noise–less data and thus, the analysis is not exposed to the overfitting problem, here we include additive noise that makes us face the trade–off between under– and over–fitting.

5. HLP restricts the Black–Scholes pricing equation by keeping fixed the interest rate and the instantaneous standard deviation of the stock price. In this study we choose to work in a similar restricted set up to test the methodology and focus in the points (1) – (4) above. Work in progress show that when all the variability is allowed in the equation the results might be quite different.[3]

There is a trade off between using nonparametric versus parametric methods. Nonparametric techniques are data driven methods that make minimal assumptions on the underlying distributions of the explanatory variables and the structural relationship between these variables and the dependent variable. Data driven algorithms may capture structural changes in the data that may be induced by changes in the markets (*e.g.*, changes in liquidity); but in some cases data is scarce and may not be sufficient to adequately train the nonparametric method. Nonparametric methods are prone to overfitting the data (memorizing accidents of the data set rather than general regularities). Overfitting is a problem related to choosing the optimal degrees of freedom for each method (*e.g.*, the structure for the neural network, the size of the decision tree, the k number of neighbors, etc.). This suggest that parametric models may be more suitable in cases where the distribution of the explanatory variables is well understood and there is an adequate statistical distribution to model it. Neither approach strictly dominates the other, rather they complement each other. One should be aware of the limitations and strengths of each.

Section 41.2 sets up the strategy and methodology that will follow in the rest of the paper. Section 41.3 describes how the data is generated and applies the methodology described in Section 41.2 to the problem of recovering the Black–Scholes pricing equation under the restricted set up. This section includes the results for each algorithm and the final comparison between the methods. Section 41.4 contains the conclusions.

41.2 Strategy and Methodology

In this section we briefly review some of the algorithms, inductive principles, and empirical problems associated with model construction[4]. We also review a particular

---

3. For the interested reader these preliminary results can be found at:
http://www.geocities.com/WallStreet/Market/9587/Papers.html

4. Details of the review can be found in [Galindo and Tamayo 1999].

methodology for model building, selection and evaluation that we will follow in the rest of the paper.

41.2.1   A Multi–Strategy Statistical Inference Approach to Modeling

The general problem one encounters is that of finding effective methodologies and algorithms to produce mathematical or statistical descriptions (models) to represent the patterns, regularities or trends in financial or business data. This is not a new subject and basically extends the methods used for decades by statisticians. For complex real–world data, where noise, non–linearity and idiosyncrasies are the rule, a good strategy is to take an interdisciplinary approach that combines statistics and machine learning algorithms. This interdisciplinary, data–driven, computational approach, sometimes referred as *Knowledge Discovery in Databases* [Fayyad et al 1996, Simoudis et al 1996, Bigus 1996, Adriaans and Zantinge 1996], is specially relevant today due to the convergence of three factors: I) *Large size databases* that has opened the possibility for modeling at an unprecedented scale [Landy 1996, Small and Edelstein 1997]. II) *Progress in the theoretical front* as we can witness from the results of the last years the existence of more mature statistical and machine learning technologies and algorithms [Michie and Taylor 1994, Vapnik 1995, Mitchell 1997]. III) *Affordable computing resources* including high performance multi–processor servers, powerful desktops, and large storage and networking capabilities. The standardization of operating systems and environments has facilitated the integration and interconnection of data sources, repositories and applications.

There are many algorithms available for model construction, so one of the main problems in practice is that of algorithm selection or combination. Unfortunately it is hard to choose an algorithm a priori because one might not know the nature and characteristics of the data set, *e.g.* its intrinsic noise, complexity, or the type of relationships it contains. Each algorithm employs a different method to fit the data and approximate the regularities or correlations according to a particular structure or representation. Algorithms vary enormously in their basic structure, parameters and optimization landscapes, we do not review them here but if the reader is interested some good references in the literature are: [Michie and Taylor 1994, Weiss and Kulikowski 1991, Mitchell 1997]. In this study we choose four different algorithms that represent four important classes of estimation methods: CART decision–trees, feedforward neural networks, k–nearest–neighbors, and ordinary least squares (OLS).

Algorithms have been introduced in the context of different disciplines where the problem of data fitting or model building is approached from a particular perspective. These approaches can be classified as traditional and modern statistics [Eaton 1983, Fisher 1950, Hand 1981, Lachenbruch and Mickey 1968], Bayesian Inference and the Maximum Entropy Principle [Jeffreys 1931, Jaynes 1983, Berger 1985, Carlin and Louis 1996], Pattern Recognition and Artificial Intelligence [McLachan 1992, Fukunaga 1990, Weiss and Kulikowski 1991], Connectionist and Neural Network Models [McClelland and Rumelhart 1986, Hassoun 1995, White 1992], Computational Learning Theory and Probably Approximately Correct (PAC) Model [Valiant 1983, Kearns 1994, Mitchell 1997] , Statistical Learning Theory [Vapnik 1995], Information Theory [Cover and J. 1991, Li and Vitanyi 1997], Algorithmic and Kolmogorov Complexity [Rissanen 1989, Li and Vitanyi 1997], and Statistical Mechanics [Seung et al 1993, Opper and Haussler 1995]. We do not review them here, but make the reader aware of their existence. Historically many were developed independently but recent studies help to understand their relationships and equivalences in some cases [Li and Vitanyi 1997, Rissanen 1989, Vapnik 1995, Keuzenkamp and McAleer 1995, Wolpert 1995].

Within each perspective, the process of choosing and fitting (or training) a model is usually done according to formal or empirical versions of *inductive principles*. These principles have been developed in different contexts, but all share the same conceptual goal of finding the "best," the "optimal," or the most parsimonious model or description that captures the structural or functional relationship in the data (potentially subject to additional constraints such as those imposed by the model structure itself). Examples of these principles are Fisher's Maximum Likelihood principle [Hand 1981, Lachenbruch and Mickey 1968], Bayesian inference [Jeffreys 1931, Jaynes 1983, Berger 1985, Carlin and Louis 1996], structural risk minimization [Vapnik 1995], and Occam's razor (*choose the most parsimonious model that fits the data*) represented by the Minimum Description Length (MDL) principle, [Rissanen 1989], or Kolmogorov complexity [Li and Vitanyi 1997].

The analysis used in this study allows us to view the problem from the perspective of structural risk minimization [Vapnik 1995] and bias/variance decomposition [Breiman 1996, Friedman 1997].

Bias plus variance decomposition for regression analysis— A well known decomposition shows the bias/variance tradeoff that arises when estimating a parameter. Say we want to estimate a parameter θ, then, the mean–squared error of the estimator ($\hat{\theta}$) is

$$MSE[\hat{\theta}] = E\left[(\hat{\theta} - \theta)^2\right] = Var[\hat{\theta}] + \left(Bias[\hat{\theta}]\right)^2$$

MSE is an important criterion although is rarely operational, since computing the explicit formula is not always possible and when it exists, MSE might depend upon unknown parameters[5]. In practice we usually rely on a less demanding criterion such as the minimum variance unbiased estimators.

A similar decomposition exists for function estimation (*e.g.* regression analysis) [Breiman 1996, Friedman 1997]. When doing function estimation we usually assume the following relation $y = f(\mathbf{x}) + \varepsilon$, where y is the output variable, $f(\mathbf{x})$ is a function, usually unknown, that depends upon the vector of n explanatory variables $(\mathbf{x} = (x_1, x_2, \ldots, x_n))$, and ε is a random variable with zero mean and standard deviation σ_ε. Then, it can be shown that averaging over different samples of size N generates the MSE of the prediction,

$$\begin{aligned}
MSE[\hat{f}] &= E_T\left[(y - \hat{f}(\mathbf{x}|T))^2\right] \\
&= \left[f(\mathbf{x}) - E_T\hat{f}(\mathbf{x}|T)\right]^2 + E_T\left[\hat{f}(\mathbf{x}|T) - E_T\hat{f}(\mathbf{x}|T)\right]^2 + E_\varepsilon[\varepsilon|\mathbf{x}]^2
\end{aligned}$$

This decomposition has three components: i) *Square bias* $\left[f(\mathbf{x}) - E_T\hat{f}(\mathbf{x}|T)\right]^2$— This component measures how closely, on average over training samples of size N, the estimation method gets to the target function, $f(\mathbf{x})$. In general the bias decreases when we increase the capacity of the estimating method; ii) *Variance* $E_T\left[\hat{f}(\mathbf{x}|T) - E_T\hat{f}(\mathbf{x}|T)\right]^2$— This term shows how our estimating function, $\hat{f}(\mathbf{x}|T)$, deviates from its mean, $E_T\hat{f}(\mathbf{x}|T)$, over different samples of size N. In general the variance increases as model capacity increases and decreases as sample size increases; and iii) *Noise* $E_\varepsilon[\varepsilon|\mathbf{x}]^2$— The noise term is the irreducible component of the error and a lower bound for the $MSE[\hat{f}]$.

As is the case in parameter estimation, the regression bias/variance decomposition in function approximation is rarely operational. The problem is that the explicit form of the MSE usually depends upon unknown functions and parameters. Nonetheless, is an important criterion that provides guidelines for model estimation: i) measure and analyze the prediction MSE, ii) be aware of the bias/variance tradeoff as we increase the capacity of the estimation method, the bias usually decreases but the variance increases, iii) as we increase the sample size the error must decrease due to its effect on the variance term.

---

5. See [Greene 1993] p. 95.

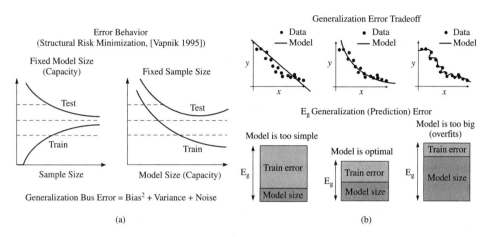

Figure 41.1

Figure a shows the error behavior and error curves. The graph on the left shows the behavior for fixed capacity: as the sample size increases the training error starts to increase since the model has more difficulties "memorizing" the training sample when the numbers of records increases; The generalization (test) error decreases because the model finds more support to characterize regularities and therefore generalizes better. For a fixed model size as the training data set increases the train and generalization (test) errors converge to an asymptotic value that represents the limit imposed by the bias of the model and the intrinsic noise in the data. The graph on the right shows the behavior for fixed sample size: if the model size is increased the generalization error decreases because a larger model has less bias and fits the data better; However, at some point the model becomes too large, producing overfitting which results in the curve moving upwards. Figure b shows the generalization error trade–off in terms of model size (capacity).

Statistical learning theory [Vapnik 1995]— This is a formalism that generalizes the problem of statistical inference from estimating some finite number of parameters to estimate the functional relationship in the data. Imagine we want to estimate an unknown functional dependency on the basis of some given i.i.d. observations $(\mathbf{x} = (x_1, x_2, \ldots, x_n))$. Under the Classical paradigm the researcher must known a lot of *a priori* information before doing the estimation. Namely, he or she must assume the form of the functional dependency (f) and then estimate the value of a finite number of parameters (θ). For example, in Classical Regression we assume f to be the multivariate normal distribution and then estimate the set of parameters $[\theta = (\mu, \Sigma)]$ from the available data. Under the Statistical and Machine Learning[6] approach the problem becomes finding the function f from a predetermined set functions and at the same time estimate the parameters that describe the function.

---

6. For machine learning see [Valiant 1983, Kearns 1994].

Figure 41.1.a describes the basic phenomenology of error curves. For fixed model size, as the training data set increases, the train and test errors converge to an asymptotic value determined by the bias of the model and the intrinsic noise in the data. The test error decreases because the model finds more support (data instances) to characterize regularities and therefore generalizes better. The train error increases because with more data, the model with its pre–determined fixed size finds greater difficulty fitting and memorizing. For very small sample sizes the train error could be zero —the model performs a "lossless" compression of the training data. For a given training sample size, there is an optimal model size for which the model neither under– nor overfits the data.

Another way to view these trade–offs is shown Figure 41.1.b. If the model is too small, it will not fit the data very well and its generalization power will be limited by missing important trends. If the model is too large, it will overfit the data and lose generalization power by incorporating too many accidents in the training data not shared by other data sets. This behavior is also shown in Figure 41.1.a. As the model size is increased the generalization error decreases because a larger model has less bias and fits the data better. However, at some point the model becomes too large, producing overfitting which results in the curve moving upwards. This fundamental behavior is shared generally by finite–sample inductive models [Kearns 1994, Vapnik 1995] and agrees well with the empirical behavior we observe in all of our models.

Conceptually, statistical and machine learning models are not all that different [Michie and Taylor 1994, Weiss and Kulikowski 1991]. Many of the new computational and machine learning methods generalize the idea of parameter estimation in statistics. Machine learning algorithms tend to be more computational–based and data–driven, and, by relying less on assumptions about the data (normality, linearity, etc.), are more robust and distribution–free. These algorithms not only *fit the parameters* of a particular model but often change the *structure* of the model itself, and in many instances they are better at generalizing complex non–linear data relationships. On the other hand machine learning algorithms provide models that can be relatively large, idiosyncratic, and difficult to interpret. The moral is that no single method or algorithm is perfect or guaranteed to work, so one should be aware of the limitations and strengths of each. For an interesting discussion about statistical themes and lessons for machine learning methods we refer the reader to [Glymor and Smyth 1997]. The new algorithms also have more explicit means for accounting for the actual complexity, size, or capacity of a model than do the traditional approaches.

41.2.2   Methodology for Model Building and Analysis of Errors Curves

In this Section we describe the basic elements of the model building methodology and the analysis that we employ in the four algorithms considered here. The main elements of the analysis are: i) Basic model parameter exploration; and ii) Analysis of error curves and estimates of noise and rate of convergence parameters.

Basic model parameter exploration. This is done at the very beginning by building a few preliminary models to get a sense for the appropriate range of parameter values.

Analysis of error curves and rate of convergence. This exploratory approach computes average values of train (in–sample) and test (out–of–sample) errors for given values of training sample and model size. By fitting simple algebraic scaling models to these curves, one can model the behavior of the learning process and obtain rough estimates of the rate of convergence and of noise in the data set. The results help to understand the intrinsic complexity of the problem, the quality of data, and provide insight into the relationship between error rates, model capacity, and optimal training set sizes. This information is also useful in planing larger modeling efforts relevant to production rather than exploratory data sets.

The methodology we use for the analysis of error curves is as follows: for each data set size, and fixed model size, we build 30 models with different random samples from the original data set. We then average the in– (train) and out–of–sample (test) error rates. These averaged errors are then fitted to an inverse power law: $E_{\text{test}} = \alpha + \beta/m^{\delta}$, where α estimates the noise/bias, β and δ estimate the complexity, and m is the sample size. Based on our experience and other work in the literature —*e.g.* [Cortes et al 1994a, Cortes et al 1994b], this model works well in describing the empirical learning curve behavior for fixed model size. A typical empirical learning curve curves —for the Black–Scholes estimated models— as a function of the sample size is shown in Figure 41.5.b and Figure 41.7, empirical error curves as a function of the capacity can be seen in Figure 41.5.a and Figure 41.9. This analysis is not entirely phenomenological because the functional forms are motivated by theoretical models [Vapnik 1995, Amari 1993, Seung et al 1993, Opper and Haussler 1995]. The inverse power law functional form of our approach is similar to the one used by Cortes and co–workers [Cortes et al 1994a, Cortes et al 1994b], but we fit directly to averaged test error curves alone rather than combining them with training curves. The computation of exact functional forms is a very difficult combinatorial problem for most non–trivial models, but functional dependencies (*e.g.* inverse power laws) and worse–case upper

Table 41.1
Format for the results of learning curve analysis fitting the model: $E_{\text{test}} = \alpha + \beta/m$

Model	Test Error at maximum training sample (standard dev. in parenthesis)	Noise/Bias α	Complexity β	Optimum training sample size [recs]

bounds have been calculated [Kearns 1994, Vapnik 1995]. These theoretical models suggest that the value for the exponent δ will be no worse than $1/2$ [Vapnik 1995]. Other formulations, in the context of computational learning theory and statistical mechanics using average rather than worst case, suggest a value of $\delta \approx 1$ [Opper and Haussler 1995, Amari 1993]. There is also empirical support for this value from earlier work [Cortes et al 1994a, Cortes et al 1994b, Galindo and Tamayo 1999]. For our data set, we find that $\delta = 1$ provides a reasonable fit for the error curves, and therefore we assume $\delta = 1$ when fitting the data[7]. Table 41.1 shows the basic format we use to report the curve analysis results.

The error curve analysis methodology describe here is still under investigation, so we recommend it with caution. It has been used by the authors to study several data sets with good results[8]. Similar methodologies have been reported in the literature [Cortes et al 1994a, Cortes et al 1994b] but their widespread use has been limited by high computational cost. The scaling analysis can be improved in many ways, particularly by extending it to account for model size to describe the entire learning manifold. This is a subject for future work.

41.3   Application of the Analysis to the Black–Scholes Option Pricing Formula with Constant Interest Rate and Constant Instantaneous Standard Deviation

Here we apply the methodology from Section 41.2 to recover of the Black–Scholes pricing equation of a call option.

---

7. However as expected the inverse power law model does not describe well the learning curve behavior for small samples so we excluded small training samples from the fit (this is done consistently for all the algorithms).

8. See [Galindo and Tamayo 1999]. Some aspects of the model building and methodology have been developed at Thinking Machines Corporation by J. Berlin, N. Dayanand, G. Drescher, D. R. Mani, C. Wang, and P. Tamayo.

41.3.1   Data Preparation

The Black–Scholes (1973) formula allow us —under certain assumptions— to calculate the price for an *european call option* which gives the owner the right to buy the underlying security at some pre–specified date at a certain pre–specified price (*i.e.* the strike price.) Under these assumptions the dynamics of the price of the underlying security is,

$$dS = \mu S dt + \sigma S dz$$

where S is the price of the asset, μ is the instantaneous expected return of the proportional change in the asset per unit of time, and σ^2 is the instantaneous variance of the proportional change in the asset price. The Black–Scholes pricing equation for an *european call option* with strike price X, and time to maturity T$-t$, is given by

$$C = SN(d_1) - Xe^{-r(\mathrm{T}-t)}N(d_2) \tag{41.1}$$

where

$$d_1 = \frac{\ln(S/\mathrm{X}) + (r + \sigma^2/2)(\mathrm{T}-t)}{\sigma\sqrt{\mathrm{T}-t}}, d_2 = \frac{\ln(S/\mathrm{X}) + (r - \sigma^2/2)(\mathrm{T}-t)}{\sigma\sqrt{\mathrm{T}-t}}$$

and $N(y)$ is the cumulative density function for a standard normal variable y.

We generated 24,096 instances of equation (41.1) which are used to train (in–sample) and test (out–of–sample) the different methods. First, we performed a Monte Carlo simulation to get a time series of stock price $S(t)$. To start the simulation we chose the following values for the variables: $S(0) = 60$, $\mu = 0.08$, $\sigma = 0.20$, and $r = 0.10$.

We got a two–year time series —assuming 254 trading days per year— for the stock path $S(t)$ by generating 507 pseudorandom instances Z_i from a Normal distribution with mean $\mu/254$ and variance $\sigma^2/254$ which correspond to the continuously compounded daily returns. These returns are transformed to the stock price $S(t)$ by using the formula $S(t) = S(0)e^{(\Sigma_{i=1}^t Z_i)}, 1 \leq t \leq 507$.

To generate the instances of equation 41.1 we need to know (on every particular day) the specifications of the options that are alive. Following the specifications in [Hull 1993], and using three stock price paths and strike prices (X) equal to 30, 35, 40, and 45, we generated the 24,096 instances of equation 41.1 by simulating the trading period starting in January, 1997 through December, 1998.

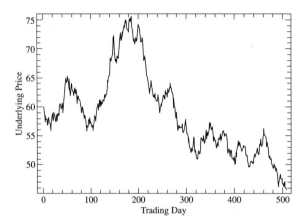

Figure 41.2
An example of a simulated training path for a stock.

We introduce additive noise $[C = f(S, \mathrm{X}, r, \mathrm{T} - t, \sigma) + \varepsilon\,]$ where ε is distributed Normal with mean zero and variance equal to 0.10 times the variance of the target function $[i.e.\ \varepsilon \sim N(0, 010 \times Var[C])$ which it turned out to have a standard deviation equal to 0.78. The motivation for the inclusion of noise is that in a noiseless environment there is no overfitting problem since the more fit you make to the training sample the closer you get to the target function. Since the Black–Scholes equation is an abstraction of the real option pricing, the noise could also be interpreted as the unexplained variation from the model when confronted to empirical data (spreads, omitted variables, or bad model specification). Although this noise has high frequency and would not be easy to capture ("memorize") by methods with few parameters, it worked under our analysis (for nonparametric models to fit the noise the number of parameters should be in the order of the number of data points).

41.3.2   OLS

A traditional tool for regression analysis is the linear regression being the simplest form the ordinary least squares (OLS). The assumptions of the linear regression model impose well known restrictions on the estimated model[9], however we use it as a benchmark for comparing the other three algorithms. The model we use is a regression of the option price (C) on the stock price (S), the strike price (X), and

---

9. See [Greene 1993] pp. 170-172.

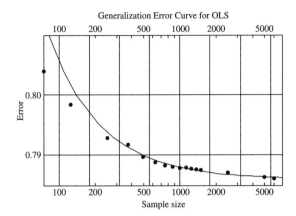

Figure 41.3
The (out–of–sample) generalization error curve as a function of the sample size for OLS. The inverse power law model describes relatively good the behavior of the RMSE.

the time to maturity $(\mathrm{T}-t)$,

$$C_i = b_0 + b_1 S_i + b_2 X_i + b_3 (\mathrm{T} - t)_i + \varepsilon_i, i = 1, \ldots, N.$$

For each modeling technique, the generalization error curve is computed. Each point is the average root mean squared error (RMSE) from 30 bootstrap samples for a given training set size. As can be seen from Figure 41.4 the inverse power model describes generally well the behavior of the curve for samples sizes of 250 records and higher.

The average RMSE for the OLS model begins about 0.83 and gradually declines to 0.786 practically converging to its asymptotic value. This is confirmed by the results of fitting the inverse power law model given in Table ($E_{\mathrm{test}} = \alpha + \beta/m$). The estimated noise/bias parameter α —the constant in the model— gives the estimated minimum asymptotic value of the error rate. This means that the asymptotic intrinsic noise in the data plus the model bias is about 0.786, and this could be achieved (within 0.1 %) with 1,950 records. The average RMSE for sample size 1,500 is 0.787 and 0.7861 when the sample size is 6,000. The number of records is calculated from the functional form of the error curve fit by solving for the sample size (m) and allowing for an error equal to the convergence value plus the arbitrary value 0.001 (in other words, we assume convergence at 0.1% of the asymptotic value).

Table 41.2

Error curve results for OLS model— The results are obtained from fitting the inverse power law model to the average RMSE values of different sample sizes. The second column shows the generalization error rate at 6,000 sample size (standard deviation inside the parenthesis). The third and fourth columns show the estimated parameters α and β. Finally the last column shows the number of records needed to obtain an error rate of $\alpha + 0.001$

OLS	Test Error at m=6,000	Noise/Bias α	Rate of convergence β	Optimum training sample size [recs]
	0.7861 (0.0018)	0.7860	1.95	1,950

The OLS model requires a few records relatively to the other algorithms to attain the asymptotic value. This is confirmed by the relatively small value of the rate of convergence ($\beta = 1.95$).

41.3.3   Decision–Tree CART Model

Classification And Regression Trees (CART) are powerful non–parametric models that produce accurate predictions and easily–interpretable rules that characterize them [Breiman 1996]. They are good representatives of the decision–tree, rule–based class of algorithms. Other members of this family are C5.0, CHAID, NewID, Cal5 etc. [Michie and Taylor 1994]. Most people are familiar with *decision trees* since they are used in other areas (*e.g.,* decision theory, game theory). Decision trees algorithms create branches or splits along restricted domains of explanatory variables trying to homogenize the value of the output variable (in regression analysis minimizes the variance within the group.) The capacity of CART increases with the number of nodes or with the degree of *purity* (homogeneity in variance) in the group. A nice feature of this type of model is *transparency*; they can be represented as a set of rules in almost plain English.

In this analysis we use 8 different tree model sizes. Each size is specified by the maximum number of nodes allowed for the CART tree: 40, 80, 120, 250, 400, 1200, 1600, and 2400. For each size, 16 different training set sample sizes are used: 75, 125, 250, 375, 500, 625, 750, 875, 1000, 1125, 1250, 1375, 1500, 2500, 5000, and 6000 records. For each sample size, 30 bootstrap averages are made. In total 3,840 tree models are used for the analysis.

In Figure 41.4.a we show the generalization error curves for trees of different sizes. The lines correspond to the fit of the inverse power law model described in Section 41.2 ($E_{\text{test}} = \alpha + \beta/m$). As expected the out–of–sample RMSE decrease as the training sample is increased, and the asymptotic value for each of the curves decreases with increasing model size. This is the implied behavior by [Vapnik 1995] and bias/variance decomposition [Breiman 1996, Friedman 1997] (see Figure

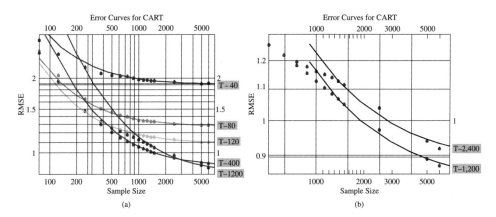

Figure 41.4
Figure a shows the generalization (test) error curves for CART trees under and up to optimal
capacity (size). The error curves decrease as the size of the trees increases from 40 to 1,200 nodes.
Figure b shows the generalization (test) error curves for CART trees on an over optimal capacity
(size). The error curves increase as the size of the trees increases from 400 to 2,400 nodes.

41.1.a). In Figure 41.4.b, the graph shows the out–of–sample RMSE curves for tree
of maximum size set to 1,200 and 2,400. As before the RMSE decreases as the
sample size increases but here the asymptotic value for each of the curves increases
with increasing model size. This suggest a procedure to find the optimal capacity
(size) of a CART model, one that neither under– nor over–fits the problem. As can
be seen from the curves for large model sizes (1,200 and 2,400 nodes), the fitted
curve does not fit the small sample sizes, so we left out sample sizes 75 to1,000
from all the curve fittings. For consistency the same criterion is applied to all the
techniques. We can see the over all behavior illustrated by Figure 41.1.a. Trees with
400 nodes or less are short on capacity and trees with 1,600 nodes or more have
excess capacity. A summary of the RMSE curve behavior for all the tree models
is shown in Table 41.3. The minimum noise/bias is achieved by the 1,200–node
tree (0.8721). Note that this modeling technique requires a large amount of data
(334,900 records) to achieve the optimal training sample size (see Section 41.2).

Figure 41.5.a shows the out–of–sample error curve as a function of the tree size
(capacity) while keeping the sample size fixed at 6,000 records. This is the empirical
form of the curve shown in the second graph of Figure 41.1.a. As we increase the
capacity of the CART model the RMSE curve first decreases, achieves a minimum
and then increases. It is important to note that there is an asymmetric behavior of
the RMSE, it decreases faster in the under–fitting area than what it increases in

Table 41.3

Error curve results for different model sizes— The results are obtained from fitting the inverse power law model to the average RMSE values of different sample sizes. The second column shows the generalization error rate at 6,000 sample size (standard deviation inside the parenthesis). The third and fourth columns show the estimated parameters α and β. Finally the last column shows the number of records needed to obtain an error rate of $\alpha + 0.001$

Size # of nodes	Test Error at m=6,000 α	Noise/Bias α	Rate of convergence β	Optimum training sample size [recs]
40	1.9041 (0.0273)	1.883	104.78	104,780
80	1.2926 (0.0162)	1.278	84.46	84,460
120	1.1079 (0.0159)	1.090	91.25	91,250
250	0.9472 (0.0055)	0.925	128.51	128,510
400	0.9074 (0.0064)	0.878	181.96	181,960
1200	0.8721 (0.0055)	0.828	334.90	334,900
1600	0.8883 (0.0060)	0.841	348.60	348,600
2400	0.9183 (0.0067)	0.875	348.69	348,690

the over–fitting region. Based on these graphs and Table 41.3, we conclude that the optimal size (capacity) for the tree model is 1,200 nodes with an asymptotic value of 0.828 and that the convergence of test and train errors takes place at 334,900 records. This high optimal number of nodes is expected from the CART decision tree algorithm since it is very difficult to describe a nonlinear continuous function with hyperplanes perpendicular to the axes.

Finally in Figure 41.5.b, we show both the generalization (out–of–sample) and the training (in–sample) error curves for the best CART tree model (1,200 nodes). We see that for small samples (75 to 500 records) the tree memorizes the training data perfectly with an error training rate equal to zero. This is the expected full memorization ("lossless" compression) effect. As the sample size increases, the training error starts to increase; the model has more and more difficulties "memorizing" the training sample. This results also help to explain why the inverse power model does not fit well for small sample sizes since the training (and therefore the testing) models are practically the same for large size models (*e.g.* 1,200, 1,600, and 2,400 nodes).

41.3.4 Neural Networks

This method is an example of a *learning network*. We choose to use the standard feedforward neural network architecture—see for example [Hassoun 1995, White 1992]—; and applied to several training algorithms: *backpropagation, steepest descent, conjugate gradient, and modified Newton.* Second–order methods, such as conjugate gradient, allow for faster training than standard back–propagation. In addition to manual training we used the *train and test* mode (it implements a

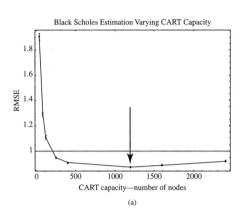

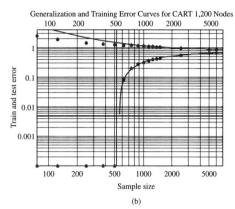

(a)   (b)

Figure 41.5

Figure a shows the generalization error curve for different capacities (sizes) when sample size is fixed at 6,000 records. At the beginning, when the model size is increased the generalization error decreases because a larger model has less bias and fits the data better; However, at some point the model becomes too large, producing overfitting which results in the curve moving upwards. Note how the error decreases faster for increases in capacity (size) under optimal capacity (underfitting area) than what the error increases beyond optimal capacity (overfitting area). The best tree size of 1,200 nodes is marked by the arrow in the graph. Error bars indicate one standard deviation from our estimates. Figure b shows the generalization (test) and training error curves for the best CART tree model (1,200 nodes). As the sample size increases the training error starts to increase; The model has more difficulties "memorizing" the training sample when the numbers of records increases. The generalization (test) error decreases because the model finds more support to characterize regularities and therefore generalizes better. For a fixed model size as the training data set increases the train and generalization (test) errors converge to an asymptotic value that represents the limit imposed by the bias of the model and the intrinsic noise in the data.

Table 41.4

Preliminary exploration for neural networks

Number of nodes	Activation function	Training algorithm	Average number of iterations	Standard deviation	Test error	Standard deviation
18	Linear	Back Propagation	500	0	1.19	0.0461
18	Linear	Steepest descent	346	136.6	0.84	0.0028
18	Linear	Conjugate gradient	63	33.7	0.81	0.0199
18	Linear	Modified Newton	49	7.8	0.78	0.0012

smoothing method for automatic termination of training when the test error starts to increase). The results are summarized in Table 41.4.

From the result of this preliminary network analysis, we concentrate on the best performing training algorithm for the rest of the analysis: this is the modified Newton. As the other methods we generate the average RMSE for 16 sample sizes and for two different network architectures with seven different number of iterations.

Table 41.5
Neural nets with 6 nodes in hidden layer (3–6–1)— The results are obtained from fitting the inverse power law model to each of the different number of iterations (model sizes). The first column shows the number of iterations, the second column presents the generalization error rate at 6,000 sample size (standard deviation inside the parenthesis). The third and fourth columns show the estimated parameters α and β. Finally the last column shows the number of records needed to obtain an error rate of $\alpha + 0.001$.

Iterations	Test Error at m = 6,000	Noise/Bias α	Rate of Convergence β	Optimum training sample size[recs.]
20	0.7942 (0.0025)	0.793673	2.01	2,010
35	0.7835 (0.0025)	0.782763	3.75	3,750
50	0.7831 (0.0025)	0.782276	4.3	4,300
100	0.7827 (0.0025)	0.781714	5.24	5,240
150	0.7827 (0.0025)	0.781561	5.85	5,585
300	0.7827 (0.0025)	0.781569	6.31	6,310
450	0.7828 (0.0025)	0.781512	6.79	6,790

A total of 6,720 models are used for this part of the analysis. The results are shown in Table 41.5, Table 41.6, Figure 41.6.a, Figure 41.6.b, and Figure 41.7.

First we explore the architecture with 3 input nodes that correspond to the explanatory variables (the stock price, the strike price, and the maturity), 6 nodes in the hidden layer, and one node as the dependent variable (the call price), we call this a neural network with a 3–6–1 architecture. We explore changing the number of iterations from 20 to 450. Table 41.5 shows a summary of the results. The RMSE decreases up to 100 iterations, then levels off (the curves with 100, 150, and 300 iterations have the same RMSE of 0.7827 at 6,000 records), and finally increases slightly. The curve with 450 iterations achieves the second lowest average RMSE (0.7828) but the lowest estimate for the noise/bias parameter.

All things considered, the RMSE changes little (in the order of 0.001 and 0.0001) and the standard deviations are small but far from making significant statistical differences beyond the 20.

The second approach explores the effect of changing the number of iterations while keeping the architecture constant at 3–18–1 —this change in architecture effectively changes the capacity of the network. Table 41.6 and Figure 41.6.a show the results.

The curve with 20 iterations has the highest average RMSE (0.7913) at 6,000 records, and it also achieves the highest asymptotic error value (0.7906). The error decreases as we increase the number of iterations and so does the asymptotic noise/bias estimate. The curve with 450 iterations achieve the lowest average RMSE at 6,000 records (0.7825) and the lowest asymptotic error value (0.7810). Although the differences are relative small and noting that for 35 iterations or more the error

Table 41.6
Neural nets with 18 nodes in hidden layer (3–18–1).- The results are obtained from fitting the
inverse power law model to each of the different number of iterations (model sizes). The first
column shows the number of iterations, the second column presents the generalization error rate
at 6,000 sample size (standard deviation inside the parenthesis). The third and fourth columns
show the estimated parameters α and β. Finally the last column shows the number of records
needed to obtain an error rate of $\alpha + 0.001$.

Iterations	Test Error at m = 6,000	Noise/Bias α	Rate of Convergence β	Optimum training sample size[recs.]
20	0.7913 (0.0025)	0.790636	3.27	3,270
35	0.7842 (0.0025)	0.783379	3.65	3,650
50	0.7831 (0.0025)	0.782264	4.8	4,800
100	0.7827 (0.0025)	0.781499	6.25	6,250
150	0.7827 (0.0025)	0.781447	6.45	6,450
300	0.7826 (0.0026)	0.781348	7.02	7,020
450	0.7825 (0.0025)	0.781023	8.16	8,160

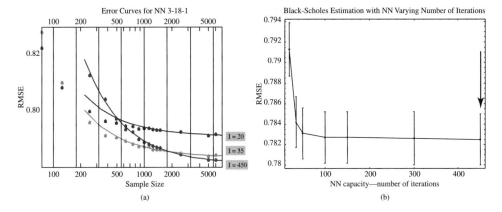

Figure 41.6
Figure a shows the generalization error curves for the 3–18–1 neural network for different number
of iterations as a function of the sample size. The figure shows that as we increase the number
of iterations the asymptotic value of the curve decreases and the rate of convergence increases.
Figure b shows the generalization error curve as a function of capacity (number of iterations)
for the neural network 3–18–1 while keeping fixed the number of records at 6,000 records. Error
bars show one standard deviation from our estimate. Our "best" neural network (3–18–1 with 450
iterations) is marked by the arrow.

bars overlap, we choose the 3–18–1 neural network with 450 iterations as our "best"
net.

Finally in Figure 41.7, we show both out–of–sample (generalization) and in–
sample error curves for the "best" neural network. As expected, as the sample size
increases the in–sample error increases and the out–of–sample error decreases. The

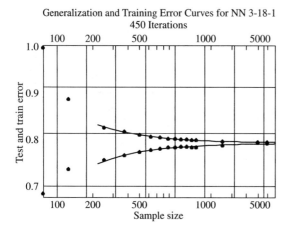

Figure 41.7
Generalization (test) and training error curves for the best neural network model (3–18–1 with 450 iterations). As the sample size increases the training error starts to increase; The model has more difficulties "memorizing" the training sample when the numbers of records increases. The generalization (test) error decreases because the model finds more support to characterize regularities and therefore generalizes better. For a fixed model size as the training data set increases the train and generalization (test) errors converge to an asymptotic value that represents the limit imposed by the bias of the model and the intrinsic noise in the data.

final results of this analysis suggest that the convergence value is 0.7810 and that it takes place at 8,160 records.

41.3.5 k–Nearest Neighbors

k–nearest neighbors (k–NN) is an algorithm that differs from the others in that the data themselves provide the "model." To predict a new record, it finds the neighbors nearest in Euclidean distance and then performs a weighted average or majority vote to obtain the final prediction. It works well for cases with relatively low dimensionality and complicated decision boundaries. The toolset we use[10] also supports the capability to "train" global attribute weights so they are optimal in maximizing the prediction accuracy of the algorithm. For this purpose, one uses a small training set of a few hundred additional records (350). This modification improves the results relative to the standard k–NN, but the algorithm retains its main characteristics. In practice, k–NN works better than expected, which may be due to the benign effect of its high–bias as has been suggested by [Friedman 1997].

---

10. We use *Darwin* for implementing CART, NN, and K– NN, see http://www.think.com/

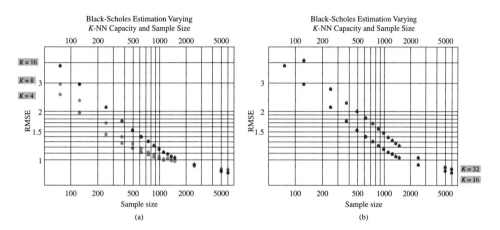

Figure 41.8
Figure a shows the generalization (test) error curves for K–nearest neighbors under and up to optimal capacity (size). The error curves decrease as K goes from 4 to 16. Figure b shows the error behavior for k–NN models. Generalization (test) error curves for CART trees on an over optimal capacity (size). The error curves increase as the value of K increases from 16 to 32.

We perform a error curve analysis similar to those described above. The results are shown in Figure 41.8.a, Figure 41.8.b, and Table 41.7. In this case, the train error is not reported; it is always zero since the "model" is the data. Since the model increases with the size of the data set, it is impossible to fit fixed–capacity error–curve models as was done for the other cases (the inverse power law fit). It is, however, possible to account for the change in model size in the fitting, but we did not attempt to do so here.

Figure 41.8.a shows the RMSE plot for different values of k (4, 8, and 16). As before the generalization errors decrease as the training sample is increased, and the asymptotic value for each curve decreases with increasing values of k (see Table 41.7). The error rates for this model are comparable to those of CART but less than the neural net or OLS.

In Figure 41.8.b, the graph shows the out–of–sample RMSE curves for values of k equal to 16 and 32. For large values of k the curve and its asymptotic value start to increase. This is the symptom of the overfitting problem. A summary of the error curve behavior for the different values of K is shown in Table 41.7.

Figure 41.9 shows the testing (out–of–sample) error plot as a function of the different values of k while keeping fixed the sample size at 6,000 records. Based on these graphs and Table 41.7 we can conclude that the optimal value of k is 16, for

Table 41.7
Error Rates for k–NN

k	Test error for 6,000 records
2	2.1205 (0.2773)
4	1.9614 (0.3231)
8	0.8384 (0.0142)
16	0.0838 (0.0127)
24	0.8558 (0.0110)
32	0.8766 (0.0110)

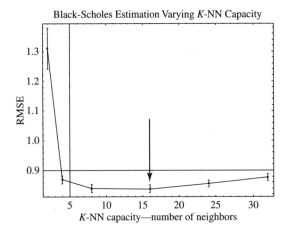

Figure 41.9
Generalization error curve for different K (number of neighbors) values when sample size is fixed at 6,000 records. At the beginning, when K is increased the generalization error decreases, however, at some point the model produces overfitting which results in the curve moving upwards. The best K value is equal to 16 and is marked by the arrow. Standard deviations are represented by the error bars.

values less than 16 we see an improvement on the predictive power and for higher values we see a worsening behavior of the RMSE.

41.3.6   Summary and Comparison of Results

Before we discuss the results it is important to keep in mind that the data we use was generated from a restricted version of the Black–Scholes call option pricing formula (with fixed interest rate and standard deviation for the stock price), these restrictions remove some non–linearity from the Black–Scholes formula. The results are not likely to hold in a richer environment.

Table 41.8 summarizes the performances of the best models (error rates, rate of convergence, and optimal sample sizes). The best overall model is the neural net-

Table 41.8
Summary of best models' performance, rate of convergence and optimal sample sizes.

Model	Test Error at m = 6,000	Noise/Bias α	Rate of Convergence β	Optimum training sample size[recs.]
CART (1200 nodes)	0.8721 (0.0055)	0.824117	334.89	334,890
k–NN (16)	0.8380 (0.0127)	—	—	—
OLS	0.7861 (0.0018)	0.786	1.953	1,953
Neural Net (18–450I)	0.7825 (0.0025)	0.781	8.16	8,160

work with architecture 3–18–1 and 450 iterations, which attains an average RMSE of 0.7825 when the sample size is 6,000 records. The asymptotic test error for this model is 0.7810. The second position is for OLS which attains an average test error of 0.7861 when sample size is 6,000 records. The asymptotic test error for this model is 0.7860 which gives the limit of predictability obtainable with this type of model. The reason for the difference with the convergence value for the best network results from the bias in the OLS model, and the ability of the NN to exploit the remaining non–linearity in the equation. The best k–NN, using 16 neighbors, holds the third position; it attains an average RMSE of 0.8380 at 6,000 records. This is considerably higher that OLS and NN models, we speculate that the reason for this higher error is likely due to the low density in the explanatory variable (input) space. Finally the CART model attains an mean RMSE of 0.8721, a result that is comparable with the k–NN but considerably higher than the NN and OLS models. The relatively poor performance of CART may be due the limitations of approximating a continuous function with hyperplanes partitions, this may also explain why the CART algorithm needs a high number of parameters (1,200 nodes) for optimal prediction; CART models seem to work better for classification problems[11].

Figure 41.10.a and Figure 41.10.b show graphically the comparison of results for the four algorithms use in the study. The comparison between the NN and the OLS is only appreciated by looking at Figure 41.10.b, we see that OLS is generally competitive and best for small sample sizes (under 1,125). For large sample sizes the NN is able to exploit the remaining non–linear regularity that exists in this restrictive regime towards increasing its predictive power [12].

---

11. CART performed best in a comparative analysis estimating the probability of default, see [Galindo and Tamayo 1999].

12. We explore the results when applying the methodology to a data set that incorporates variability for the interest rate and the standard deviation in the Black–Scholes equation and find that this ranking —as expected— breaks down in this richer set up. The interest reader may find these preliminary results at
http://www.geocities.com/WallStreet/Market/9587/Papers.html

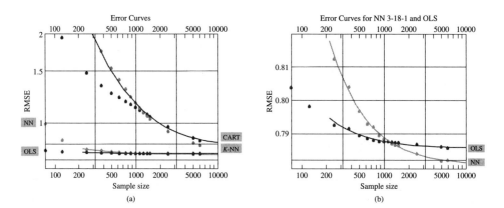

Figure 41.10
Figure a shows the comparison of results for the four algorithms (Neural Network, OLS, $K-$ NN, and CART). We see that CART model is the worst performer followed by $K-$ NN. Figure b shows the comparison of results for Neural Network and OLS.

41.4   Conclusions

A new approach to the problem of statistical inference has been introduced by Machine and Statistical Learning methods. Many of these methods generalize the idea of parameter estimation in statistics. There are many algorithms for model construction, so one of the main problems in practice is that of algorithm selection or combination. Unfortunately, it is hard to choose an algorithm a priori because on might not know the nature and characteristics of the data set, *e.g.* its intrinsic noise, complexity, or the type of relationships it contains. In this study we focus in a rational methodology to find the optimal capacity of the algorithms —*e.g.*, number of iterations, number of nodes, or number of neighbors— and a specific rational framework to compare the different methods. The methodology is based on the analysis of the RMSE as a function of the sample size and the capacity of each method. The analysis used in this study allow us to view the problem from the perspective of structural risk minimization [Vapnik 1995] and bias/variance decomposition [Breiman 1996, Friedman 1997]. The methodology is tested by recovering a restricted version of the Black–Scholes call option pricing formula in a similar set up as [Hutchinson and Poggio 1994]. We find that:

• The empirical forms of the error curves are similar to the ones implied by the statistical learning theory (see Figure 41.3, Figure 41.5.a, Figure 41.5.b, and Figure 41.7).

• This behavior allows to chose the optimal capacity for each method which in turn, forms the base for the comparative analysis between the different algorithms (see Figure 41.10.a and Figure 41.10.b).

• Under the restricted regime the results show that neural networks provide the best estimation with an average RMSE of 0.7825 for a training sample of 6,000 records. OLS is the second best with an average RMSE of 0.7861 and its first best for sample sizes smaller than 1,125. The k–Nearest Neighbor achieved an average RMSE of 0.8380 which is comparable to the worst performer, CART which attained an average RMSE of 0.8721 (see Table 41.8, Figure 41.10.a, and Figure 41.10.b).

References

Adriaans, P. and D. Zantinge. 1996. *Knowledge Discovery and Data Mining.*

Amari, S. 1993. A universal theorem on learning curves. *Neural Networks*, 6:161–166.

Berger, J. O. 1985. *Statistical Decision Theory and Bayesian Analysis.* Springer series in Statistics.

Bigus, J. P. 1996. *Data Mining with Neural Networks: Solving Business Problems from Application Development to Decision Support.*

Bourgoin, M. 1994. Applying machine-learning techniques to a real-world problem on a connection machine CM-5. Technical report.

Bourgoin, M. and S. Smith. 1995. *Leveraging Your Hidden Data to Improve ROI: A Case Study in the Credit Card Business.* Probus Publishing.

Breiman, L. 1996. Bias, variance, and arcing classifiers. Technical Report 460, Statistics Dept. U. of California Berkeley.

Carlin, B. P. and T. A. Louis. 1996. *Bayes and Empirical Bayes Methods for Data Analysis.* Chapman and Hall.

Cortes, C., L. D. Jackel, and Chiang. 1994a. *W-P Limits on Learning Machine Accuracy Imposed by Data Quality*, volume 7, page 239. MIT Press.

Cortes, C., L. D. Jackel, S. A. Solla, and V. Vapnik. 1994b. *Learning Curves: Asymptotic Values and Rate of Convergence*, volume 6, page 327. MIT Press.

Cover, T. and T. J. 1991. *Elements of Information Theory.* Wiley & Sons, New York.

Eaton, M. L. 1983. *Multivariate Statistics.* Wiley, New York.

Fayyad, U. M., G. Piatetsky-Shapiro, S. P., and U. R., editors 1996. *Advances in Knowledge Discovery and Data Mining.* AAAI Press / The MIT Press.

Fisher, R. A. 1950. *Statistical Methods for Research Workers.* 11 edition.

Friedman, J. H. 1997. *On Bias, Variance, 0/1 - Loss, and the Curse of Dimensionality*, pages 55–77.

Fukunaga, K. 1990. *Introduction to Statistical Pattern Recognition.*

Galindo, J. and P. Tamayo. 1999. Credit risk assessment using statistical and machine learning basic methodology and risk modeling applications.
also in http://www.geocities.com/WallStreet/Market/9587/Papers.html.

Glymor, C., M. D. P. D. and P. Smyth. 1997. *Statistical Themes and Lessons for Data Mining*, pages 11–28.

Greene, W. H. 1993. *Econometric Analysis*. Macmillan, 2nd edition.

Hand, D. J. 1981. *Discrimination and Classification*. John Wiley.

Hassoun, M. H. 1995. *Fundamentals of Artificial Neural Networks*. MIT Press.

Hull, J. C. 1993. *Options, Futures, and Other Derivative Securities*. Prentice Hall, 2nd edition.

Hutchinson, J. M., L. A. W. and T. Poggio. 1994. A non-parametric approach to pricing and hedging derivative securities via learning networks. *The Journal of Finance*, XLIX(3).

Jaynes, E. 1983. *Papers on Probability, Statistics and Statistical Physics*. D. Reidel Pub. Co.

Jeffreys, H. 1931. *Scientific Inference*. Cambridge Univ. Press.

Kearns, M.J., V. U. V. 1994. *An Introduction to Computational Learning Theory*. MIT Press.

Keuzenkamp, H. A. and M. McAleer. 1995. Simplicity, scientific inference and econometric modeling. *The Economic Journal*, (105):1–21.

Lachenbruch, P. A. and M. R. Mickey. 1968. *Discriminant Analysis*. Hafner press, New York.

Landy, A. 1996. An scalable approach to data mining. *Informix Tech Notes*, 6:51. Issue 3.

Li, M. and P. Vitanyi. 1997. *An Introduction to Kolmogorov Complexity and Its Applications*. Springer-Verlag, New York, 2nd edition.

McClelland, J. L. and D. E. Rumelhart. 1986. *Parallel Distributed Processing*. MIT Press.

McLachan, G. L. 1992. *Discriminant Analysis and Statistical Pattern Recognition*. John Wiley, New York.

Michie, D., S. D. J. and C. C. Taylor. 1994. *Machine Learning, Neural and Statistical Classification*. Ellis Horwood series in Artificial Intelligence.

Mitchell, T. 1997. *Machine Learning*. McGraw Hill.
Also in http://www.cs.cmu.edu/ tom/mlbook.html.

Opper, M. and D. Haussler. 1995. Bounds for predictive errors in the statistical mechanics of supervised learning. *Phys. Rev. Lett*, 75:3772.

Piatetsky-Shapiro, G. and Frawley. 1991. *Knowledge Discovery in Databases*. MIT Press.

Rissanen, J. J. 1989. *Stochastic Complexity and Statistical Inquiry*. World Scientific.

Seung, H. S., H. Sompolinsky, and T. N. 1993. Statistical mechanics of learning from examples. *Physical Review*, 45:6056.

Simoudis, E., J. Han, and F. U. 1996. *Proceedings of the Second International Conference on Knowledge Discovery and Data Mining KDD'96*. AAAI Press.
See also KDD Nuggets: http://info.gte.com/ kdd/.

Small, R. D. and H. Edelstein. 1997. *Scalable Data Mining in Building, Using and Managing the Data Warehouse*. Prentice Hall.

Trippi, R. R. and Lee. 1996. *Artificial Intelligence in Finance and Investing*.

Valiant, L. G. 1983. A theory of the learnable. *Comm. of the ACM*, 27:1134.

Vapnik, V. 1995. Springer-Verlag.

Weiss, S. M. and C. A. Kulikowski. 1991. *Computer Systems That Learn: Classification and Prediction Methods from Statistics, Neural Networks, Machine Learning and Expert Systems*. Morgan Kaufmann, San Mateo CA.

White, H. 1992. *Artificial Neural Networks*. Blackwell, Cambridge, MA.

Wolpert, D. H. 1995. *The Relationship Between PAC, the Statistical Physics Framework, the Bayesian Framework, and VC Framework*. Santa Fe Institute, Studies in the Sciences of Complexity.

42 Option Pricing with the Efficient Method of Moments

George J. Jiang and Pieter J. van der Sluis

While the stochastic volatility (SV) generalization has been shown to improve the explanatory power over the Black-Scholes model, empirical implications of SV models on option pricing have not yet been adequately tested. The purpose of this paper is to investigate the respective effect of stochastic interest rates, systematic volatility and idiosyncratic volatility on option prices. We compute option prices using reprojected underlying historical volatilities and implied stochastic volatility risk to gauge each model's performance through direct comparison with observed market option prices.

42.1 Introduction

Numerous recent studies on option pricing have acknowledged the fact that volatility changes over time in time series of asset returns as well as in the empirical variances implied from option prices through the Black-Scholes model [Black and Scholes 1973]. Many of these studies focused on modeling the asset-return dynamics through *stochastic volatility* (SV) models[1]. Due to analytically intractable likelihood functions and hence the lack of available efficient estimation procedures, SV models were until recently viewed as an unattractive class of stochastic processes compared to other time-varying volatility processes, such as ARCH/GARCH models. Moreover, to calculate option prices based on SV models we need, besides parameter estimates, a representation of the unobserved historical volatility, which is again far from straightforward. Therefore, while the SV generalization of option pricing has, thanks to advances in econometric estimation techniques, recently been shown to improve over the Black-Scholes model in terms of the explanatory power for asset-return dynamics, its empirical implications on option pricing itself have not yet been adequately tested due to the aforementioned lack of a representation of the unobserved volatility. Can the SV generalization of the option pricing model help resolve well-known systematic empirical biases associated with the Black-Scholes model, such as the volatility "smile" (e.g. [Rubinstein 1985]) and asymmetry of such "smile" or "smirk" (e.g. [Stein 1989])? How substantial is the gain, if any, from such generalization compared to relatively simpler models? The purpose of this paper is to answer the above questions by studying the empirical performance of SV models in pricing stock options, and investigating the respective effect of

---

1. Review articles on SV models are e.g. [Ghysels et al 1996] and [Shephard 1996].

stochastic interest rates, stochastic volatility and asymmetric volatility on option prices in a multivariate SV model framework.

The structure of this paper is as follows. Section 42.2 outlines our methodology; Section 42.3 reports our estimation results for our general model and various sub-models; Section 42.4 compares among different models the performance in pricing options and analyzes the effect of each individual factor; Section 42.5 concludes.

42.2 Methodology

42.2.1 The Model

We specify and implement a dynamic equilibrium model for asset returns extended in the line of [Amin and Ng 1993]. Our model incorporates both the effects of idiosyncratic volatility and systematic volatility of the underlying stock returns into option valuation and at the same time allows interest rates to be stochastic. In addition, we model the short-term interest rate dynamics and stock return dynamics simultaneously and allow for asymmetry of conditional volatility in both stock return and interest rate dynamics.

Let S_t denote the stock price at time t and r_t the interest rate at time t, we model the dynamics of daily stock returns and daily interest-rate changes simultaneously as a multivariate SV process. Assuming a constant conditional mean of asset returns, the de-meaned or the unexplained stock return y_{st} is defined as

$$y_{st} = 100 \times (\Delta \ln S_t - \mu_S - \phi_S r_{t-1}) \tag{42.1}$$

and the de-meaned or the unexplained interest-rate change y_{rt} is defined as

$$y_{rt} = 100 \times (\Delta \ln r_t - \mu_r - \phi_r \ln r_{t-1}) \tag{42.2}$$

and, y_{st} and y_{rt} are modeled as SV processes

$$y_{st} = \sigma_{st}\epsilon_{st}, \qquad \ln \sigma_{st+1}^2 = \alpha \ln r_t + \omega_s + \gamma_s \ln \sigma_{st}^2 + \sigma_s \eta_{st}, \qquad |\gamma_s| < 1 \tag{42.3}$$

$$y_{rt} = \sigma_{rt}\epsilon_{rt}, \qquad \ln \sigma_{rt+1}^2 = \omega_r + \gamma_r \ln \sigma_{rt}^2 + \sigma_r \eta_{rt}, \qquad |\gamma_r| < 1 \tag{42.4}$$

where

$$\begin{bmatrix} \epsilon_{st} \\ \epsilon_{rt} \end{bmatrix} \sim IIN(\begin{bmatrix} 0 \\ 0 \end{bmatrix}, \begin{bmatrix} 1 & \lambda_1 \\ \lambda_1 & 1 \end{bmatrix}) \tag{42.5}$$

so that $\text{Cor}(\epsilon_{st}, \epsilon_{rt}) = \lambda_1$. Here IIN denotes identically and independently normally distributed. The asymmetry, i.e. the correlation between η_{st} and ϵ_{st} and between η_{rt} and ϵ_{rt}, is modeled through λ_2 and λ_3 as follows

$$\eta_{st} = \lambda_2 \epsilon_{st} + \sqrt{1 - \lambda_2^2} u_t, \qquad \eta_{rt} = \lambda_3 \epsilon_{rt} + \sqrt{1 - \lambda_3^2} v_t \qquad (42.6)$$

where u_t and v_t are assumed to be $IIN(0, 1)$. Since ϵ_{st} and η_{st} are random shocks to the return and volatility of the index and, moreover, both are subject to the same information set, it is reasonable to assume that u_t is purely idiosyncratic, or, in other words, u_t is independent of other random noises including v_t. This implies

$$\text{Cor}(\eta_{st}, \epsilon_{st}) = \lambda_2, \qquad \text{Cor}(\eta_{rt}, \epsilon_{rt}) = \lambda_3 \qquad (42.7)$$

and imposes the restriction $\text{Cor}(\eta_{st}, \eta_{rt}) = \lambda_1 \lambda_2 \lambda_3$.

The SV model specified above offers a flexible distributional structure in which the correlation between volatility and stock returns or interest-rate movements serves to control the level of asymmetry and the volatility variation coefficients serve to control the level of kurtosis. The above model setup is specified in discrete time and includes continuous-time models as special cases in the limit. Furthermore, the above model is specified to catch the possible systematic effects through parameters ϕ_S in the trend and α in the conditional volatility. It is only the systematic state variable that affects the individual stock returns' volatility, not the other way around. The interest rate model admits possible mean-reversion in the drift and allows for stochastic conditional volatility. Finally, the above model specification allows the movements of de-meaned return processes to be correlated through random noises ϵ_{st} and ϵ_{rt} via their correlation λ_1. When ϵ_{st} and η_{st} are allowed to be correlated with each other, the model can pick up the kind of asymmetric behavior which is often observed in asset price changes and to a lesser degree in index returns and interest rate movements. In particular, a negative correlation between η_{st} and ϵ_{st} ($\lambda_2 < 0$) induces the *leverage effect* (see [Black 1976]). It is noted that the above model specification will be tested against alternative nested specifications. Statistical properties of SV models are summarized in [Ghysels et al 1996], and [Shephard 1996].

Advantages of the proposed model include: First, the model explicitly incorporates the effects of a systematic factor on option prices. Empirical evidence shows that the volatility of stock returns is not only stochastic, but also highly correlated with the volatility of the market as a whole, see e.g. [Conrad et al 1991], [Jarrow and Rosenfeld 1984], and [Ng et al 1992]. The empirical evidence also shows that the biases inherent in the Black-Scholes option prices are different for options on high and low risk stocks, see, e.g. [Black and Scholes 1972], [Gultekin and Rogalski 1982], and [Whaley 1982]. Inclusion of systematic volatility in the option prices valuation model thus has the potential contribution to reduce the empirical biases associated with the Black-Scholes formula; Second, since the variance of consumption growth is negatively related to the interest rate in equilibrium, the dynamics of the consumption process relevant to option valuation are embodied in the interest rate process. The model thus naturally leads to stochastic interest rates and we only need to directly model the dynamics of interest rates. Existing work of extending the Black-Scholes model has moved away from considering either stochastic volatility or stochastic interest rates but to considering both, examples include [Baily and Stulz 1989], [Amin and Ng 1993], and [Scott 1997]. Third, the above proposed model allows the study of the simultaneous effects of stochastic interest rates and stochastic stock return volatility on the valuation of options. It is documented in the literature that when the interest rate is stochastic the Black-Scholes option pricing formula tends to underprice the European call options, see [Merton 1973], while in the case that the stock return's volatility is stochastic, the Black-Scholes option pricing formula tends to overprice at-the-money European call options, see [Hull and White 1987]. The combined effect of both factors depends on the relative variability of the two processes, see [Amin and Ng 1993]. Based on simulation Amin and Ng show that stochastic interest rates cause option values to decrease if each of these effects acts by themselves. However, this combined effect should depend on the relative importance (variability) of each of these two processes; Finally, when the conditional volatility is symmetric, i.e. there is no correlation between stock returns and conditional volatility or $\lambda_2 = 0$, the closed form solution of option prices is available and preference free under quite general conditions, i.e., the stochastic mean of the stock return process, the stochastic mean and variance of the consumption process, as well as the covariance between the changes of stock returns and consumption are predictable. Let C_0 represent the value of a European call option at $t = 0$ with exercise price K and expiration date T, in [Amin and Ng 1993] the following option pricing formula is derived

$$C_0 = \mathsf{E}_0[S_0 \cdot \Phi(d_1) - K \exp(-\sum_{t=0}^{T-1} r_t)\Phi(d_2)] \qquad (42.8)$$

where

$$d_1 = \frac{\ln(S_0/(K\exp(-\sum_{t=0}^{T} r_t)) + \frac{1}{2}\sum_{t=1}^{T} \sigma_{st}}{(\sum_{t=1}^{T} \sigma_{st})^{1/2}}, \qquad d_2 = d_1 - \sum_{t=1}^{T} \sigma_{st}$$

and $\Phi(\cdot)$ is the CDF of the standard normal distribution, the expectation is taken with respect to the risk-neutral measure and can be calculated from simulations.

As is pointed out in [Amin and Ng 1993], several option-pricing formulas in the available literature are special cases of the above option formula. These include the Black-Scholes formula with both constant conditional volatility and interest rate, the [Hull and White 1987] stochastic volatility option valuation formula with constant interest rate, the [Baily and Stulz 1989] stochastic volatility index option pricing formula, and the [Merton 1973], [Amin and Jarrow 1992], and [Turnbull and Milne 1991] stochastic interest rate option valuation formula with constant conditional volatility.

42.2.2 Testing Option Pricing Models

Instead of implying parameter values from market option prices through option pricing formulas, we directly estimate the model specified under the objective measure from the observations of underlying state variables. By doing so, the underlying model specification can be tested in the first hand for how well it represents the true data generating process (DGP), and various risk factors, such as systematic volatility risk, interest rate risk, are identified from historical movements of underlying state variables. We employ the EMM estimation technique of [Gallant and Tauchen 1996] to estimate some candidate multivariate SV models for daily stock returns and daily short-term interest rates. The EMM technique shares the advantage of being valid for a whole class of models with other moment-based estimation techniques, and at the same time it achieves the first-order asymptotic efficiency of likelihood-based methods. In addition, the method provides information for the diagnostics of the underlying model specification. Next, we examine the effects of different elements considered in the model on stock option prices through direct comparison with observed market option prices. We compute option prices using reprojected underlying historical volatilities and implied stochastic volatility risk to gauge each model's performance through direct comparison with observed market option prices. Inclusion of both a systematic component and an idiosyncratic component in the model provides information for whether extra predictability or uncertainty is more helpful for pricing options. In gauging the empirical performance of alternative option pricing models, we use both the relative difference and the implied Black-Scholes volatility to measure option pricing errors as the latter is less sensitive to the maturity and moneyness of options.

Note that every option pricing model has to make at least two fundamental assumptions: the stochastic processes of underlying asset prices and efficiency of the markets. While the former assumption identifies the risk factors associated with the underlying asset returns, the latter ensures the existence of market price of risk for each factor that leads to a "risk-neutral" specification. The joint hypothesis we aim to test in this paper is: *The underlying model specification is correct and option markets are efficient.* If the joint hypothesis holds, the option pricing formula derived from the underlying model under equilibrium should be able to correctly predict option prices. Obviously such a joint hypothesis is testable by comparing the model predicted option prices with market observed option prices. The advantage of our framework is that we estimate the underlying model specified in its objective measure, and more importantly, EMM lends us the ability to test whether the model specification is acceptable or not. Test of such a hypothesis, combined with the test of the above joint hypothesis, can lead us to infer whether the option markets are efficient or not.

The framework in this paper is different in spirit from the implied methodology often used in the finance literature. As Bates points out [Bates 1996], the major problem of the implied estimation method is the lack of associated statistical theory, thus the implied methodology based on solely the information contained in option prices is purely objective driven, it is rather a test of stability of certain relationship (the option pricing formula) between different input factors (the implied parameter values) and the output (the option prices). As a result, the implied methodology can at best offer a test of the joint hypotheses, it fails going any further to test the model specification or the efficiency of the market. Our methodology is also different from other research based on observations of underlying state variables. First, different from the method of moments or GMM used in [Wiggins 1987], [Scott 1987], [Chesney and Scott 1989], [Jorion 1995], [Melino and Turnbull 1990], the efficient method of moments (EMM) used in this paper yields efficient estimates of SV models as we shall see below, and the parameter estimates are not sensitive to the choice of particular moments; Second, our model allows for a richer structure for the state variable dynamics, for instance the simultaneous modeling of stock returns and interest rate dynamics, the systematic effect considered in this paper, and asymmetry of conditional volatility for both stock return and interest rate dynamics.

42.2.3   Estimation

In this paper we employ EMM of [Gallant and Tauchen 1996]. This is a recent simulation-based estimation technique for models for which standard direct maximum likelihood techniques are infeasible or analytically intractable, but from which one can simulate data on a computer. Examples are general-equilibrium models, auction models and Stochastic Volatility (SV) models. As is apparent from its name EMM is a moment-based estimation technique. The adjective *efficient* is motivated by the fact that for a specific choice of the moments the EMM estimator is first-order asymptotically efficient: so EMM is a GMM-type[2] estimation technique that does as well as maximum likelihood. The common practice in the GMM literature is to select a few low-order moments on an ad hoc basis. Recognizing the need for higher statistical efficiency, Gallant and Tauchen propose EMM in an article entitled — "Which Moments to Match?" —. The answer to this question is given in the paper: the score vector of an auxiliary probability model that fits the data well. In case this auxiliary model is chosen well in [Gallant and Long 1997] it is shown that maximum-likelihood efficiency can be obtained. In the EMM jargon the auxiliary model is also called *score generator*. For efficiency EMM requires that the auxiliary model *embeds* the original (or *structural*) model, so that first-order asymptotic efficiency is achieved. While the embedding is hard to verify in practice, we have the additional result from [Gallant and Long 1997] that in case the score generator has a specific data-dependent expansion, it closely approximates the actual distribution of the data and therefore provides under very general conditions nearly fully efficient estimators. Monte Carlo studies for SV models in [Andersen et al 1997] and [van der Sluis 1999] confirm the efficiency claim for finite samples, provided a proper *leading term* is chosen in the expansion. We refer to [Jiang and van der Sluis 1998] for details on the leading term and the expansion chosen in this application. The leading term in the SNP expansion is a multivariate generalization of the EGARCH model of [Nelson 1991]. Further terms in the expansion are Hermite polynomials which pick up time homogeneous non-Gaussianity beyond the leading term[3]. Estimation in this paper was done using EmmPack of [van der Sluis 1997], and procedures used in [van der Sluis 1999].

Under the null hypothesis that the structural model is true, one may deduce an omnibus test from the EMM criterion function similar to the J test for overidentifying restrictions in the GMM literature. The direction of the mis-specification is indicated by individual components of this test corresponding to the elements of the expansion. In particular if elements corresponding to the Hermite polynomial

---

2. Generalized Method of Moments

3. With a proper leading term the coefficients in the Hermite polynomial corresponding to the time-heterogeneity non-Gaussianity are insignificantly different from zero. This indicates that the leading term picks up all the time-heterogenetic non-Gaussianity in the data, relieving the Hermite polynomial of some of its task and thus improving the small-sample properties of EMM.

cause rejection of the model, we know this is due to unexplained time-homogeneous non-Gaussianity.

In principle one should simultaneously estimate all structural parameters, including the mean parameters μ_S, μ_r, ϕ_S and ϕ_r in (42.1) and (42.2) and the volatility parameters of $y_{s,t}$ and $y_{r,t}$. This is optimal but too cumbersome and not necessary given the low order of autocorrelation in stock returns. Therefore estimation is carried out in the following way: Estimate μ_S and ϕ_S, retrieve $y_{s,t}$, Estimate μ_r and ϕ_r retrieve $y_{r,t}$. Both using standard regression techniques; Next we simultaneously estimate parameters of the SV model, including λ_1 via EMM.

42.2.4 Volatility Reprojection

One of the criticisms on EMM and on moment-based estimation methods in general has been that the method does not provide a representation of the observables in terms of their past, which can be obtained from the prediction-error-decomposition in likelihood-based techniques. In the context of SV models this means that we lack a representation of the unobserved volatilities $\{\sigma_{st}\}_{t=1}^{T}$ and $\{\sigma_{rt}\}_{t=1}^{T}$ as we need these series in our option pricing formula (42.8). The *reprojection* technique of [Gallant and Tauchen 1998] overcomes this problem. The main idea is to get a representation of the observed process in terms of past (and present) observables.

Reprojection is projecting a long simulated series from the estimated structural model p on the auxiliary model f. In short reprojection is as follows. We define the estimator $\widetilde{\beta}$, different from $\widehat{\beta}$, as follows

$$\widetilde{\beta} = \arg\max_{\beta} \mathsf{E}_{\widehat{\theta}_n} f(y_t | y_{t-1}, ..., y_{t-L}, \beta) \tag{42.9}$$

note $\mathsf{E}_{\widehat{\theta}_n} f(y_t | y_{t-1}, ..., y_{t-L}, \beta)$ is calculated using one set of simulations $y(\widehat{\theta}_n)$ from the structural model. Results in [Gallant and Long 1997] show that

$$\lim_{K \to \infty} f(y_t | y_{t-1}, ..., y_{t-L}, \widetilde{\beta}_K) = p(y_t | y_{t-1}, ..., y_{t-L}, \widehat{\theta}) \tag{42.10}$$

where K is the overall order of the leading term and the Hermite polynomials should grow with the sample size T, either adaptively as a random variable or deterministic, similarly to the estimation stage of EMM. Due to (42.10) the (conditional) moments under the structural model in $\widehat{\theta}$ can be calculated using the auxiliary model in $\widetilde{\beta}$.

A more common notion of filtration is to use the information on the observable y up to time t, instead of $t-1$, since we want a representation for unobservables in terms of the past *and present* observables. Indeed for option pricing it is more natural to include the present observables y_t, as we have current stock price and interest rate in the information set. Following [Gallant and Tauchen 1998] we can repeat the

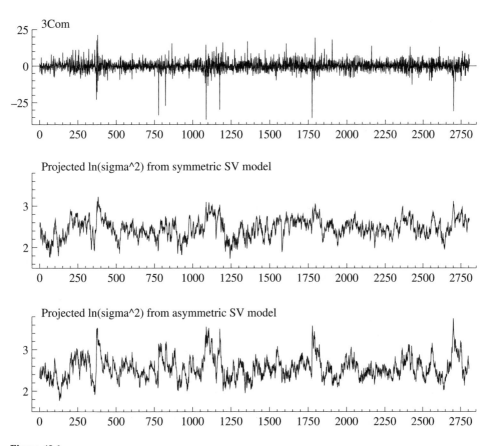

Figure 42.1
Daily returns on 3Com and filtered volatility of 3Com returns from symmetric and asymmetric
SV models using reprojection

above derivation with y_t replaced by σ_t, and y_t included in the information set at time t. In this case we need a different auxiliary model $f^*(\sigma_t | y_t, y_{t-1}, ..., y_{t-L^*}, \beta)$ from the one used in the estimation stage, $f(y_t | y_{t-1}, ..., y_{t-L}, \beta)$, see [Jiang and van der Sluis 1998] for details on the specific implementation.

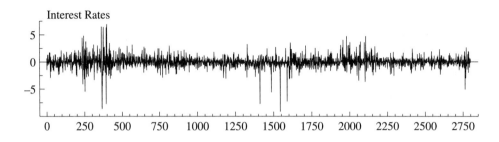

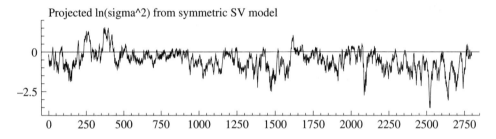

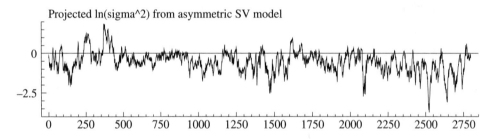

Figure 42.2
Daily interest rate movements and filtered interest returns volatility from the symmetric and asymmetric SV models using reprojection

42.3   Empirical Results

42.3.1   Description of the Data

The interest rates used in this paper as a proxy of the riskless rates are daily U.S. 3-month Treasury bill rates and the underlying stock considered in this paper is 3Com Corporation which is listed in NASDAQ. Both the stock and its options are actively traded. The stock claims no dividend and thus theoretically all options on the stock can be valued as European type options. The data covers the period from

March 12, 1986 to August 18, 1997 providing 2,860 observations. The data as well as the reprojected underlying historical volatility is displayed in Figures 42.1 and 42.2. Details on this data set can be found in [Jiang and van der Sluis 1998]. We find for the estimates of the trend parameters in the general model that for stock returns, interest rate has significant explanatory power, suggesting the presence of systematic effect or certain predictability of stock returns. For logarithmic interest rates, there is an insignificant linear mean-reversion, which is consistent with many findings in the literature. Since the score generator should give a good description of the data, we further look at the data through specification of the score generator or auxiliary model. We use the score generator as a guide for the structural model, as there is a clear relationship between the parameters of the auxiliary model and the structural model. If some auxiliary parameters in the score generator are not significantly different form zero, we set the corresponding structural parameters in the SV model *a priori* equal to zero. Various model selection criteria and *t*-statistics of individual parameters of several auxiliary models indicate that (i) The counterpart in the score generator of the correlation parameter λ_1 is clearly rejected on basis of the model selection criteria and the *t*–values. We therefore set the corresponding SV parameter λ_1 a priori equal to zero. This implies $\mathsf{Cor}(\eta_{st}, \eta_{rt}) = 0$; (ii) The counter part in the score generator of the parameter α was marginally significant at a 5 level. On basis of the BIC[4], however, inclusion of this parameter in the score generator is not justified. This rejects that the short-term interest rate is correlated with conditional volatility of the stock returns. A direct explanation of this finding is that either the volatility of the stock returns truly does not have a systematic component or the short-term interest rate serves as a poor proxy of the systematic factor. We believe the latter conjecture to be true as we re-ran the model with other stock returns and invariably found this factor to be insignificantly different from zero. We therefore set the corresponding SV parameter α a priori equal to zero; (iii) As far as the choice of a suitable order for the Hermite polynomial in the SNP expansion, we observe that for all models the terms corresponding to the time-heterogeneous non-Gaussianity are insignificantly different from zero but according to the most conservative model selection criterion, i.e. the BIC we should take up a considerable high order of the Hermite polynomial corresponding to the time-homogeneous non-Gaussianity. This is undesirable because Monte Carlo results in [van der Sluis 1999] indicate that for sample sizes encountered here the order of the Hermite polynomial should be low, say 4 or 5 and that under the

---

4. Bayesian Information Criterion

null of a *Gaussian* SV model, setting the order to zero will yield virtually efficient estimates. Still we can learn something from the Hermite polynomial in the J test. Inspection of the individual components of the J test provide information of the source of misspecification of the model.

42.3.2 Structural Models and Estimation Results

The general model: the model specified in Section 42.2.1 assumes stochastic volatility for both the stock returns and interest rate dynamics as well as systematic effect on stock returns. This model nests the [Amin and Ng 1993] model as a special case when $\lambda_2 = 0$. Following are four alternative model specifications:

- Submodel 1: No systematic effect, i.e. $\phi_S = 0$ and $\alpha = 0$, i.e. a bi-variate stochastic volatility model;

- Submodel 2: No stochastic interest rates, i.e. interest rate is constant, $r_t = r$, which is the Hull-White model and the Bailey-Stulz model[5];

- Submodel 3: Constant stock return volatility but stochastic interest rate, $\sigma_{st} = \sigma$, which is the model considered in [Merton 1973], [Turnbull and Milne 1991] and [Amin and Jarrow 1992];

- Submodel 4: Constant stock return volatility and constant interest rate, $\sigma_{st} = \sigma, r_t = r$, which is the Black-Scholes model.

Estimates of the parameters for all models can be found in [Jiang and van der Sluis 1998]. The models have also been estimated using the leading term and using the leading term with low order Hermite polynomial but no substantial differences were found in the estimation results. However the values of the individual components of the J test corresponding to the parameters of the Hermite polynomial cause rejection of the SV model. This is because the time homogeneous non-Gaussianity in the data cannot be explained by the Gaussian SV model. The conclusion of the specification test is that a *Gaussian* SV model may not be adequate and one should consider a fatter-tailed SV model or a *jump* process. Unfortunately such a non-Gaussian SV model will make option pricing much more complicated, and we leave it for future research.

From the $t-$values in the different SV models corresponding to the asymmetry parameter we can deduce that the null hypothesis of symmetry is rejected in favor of the alternative asymmetric model for both the stock returns and the interest rate movements. For submodel 1 we obtain similar results.

---

5. [Baily and Stulz 1989]

42.4   Pricing of Stock Options

The effects of SV on option prices have been examined by simulation studies[6] as well as empirical studies[7]. In this paper we will investigate the implications of model specification on option prices through direct comparison with observed market option prices, with the Black-Scholes model as a benchmark. It is documented in the literature that the Black-Scholes model generates systematic biases in pricing options, with respect to the call option's exercise prices, its time to expiration, and the underlying common stock's volatility.

42.4.1   Description of the Option Data

The sample of market option quotes covers the period of June 19, 1997 through August 18, 1997, which overlaps with the last part of the sample of stock returns. Since we do not rely solely on option prices to obtain the parameter estimates through fitting the option pricing formula, such a sample size is adequate for our comparison purpose. Note that to ease computational burden, for each business day in the sample only one reported bid-ask quote during the last half hour of the trading session of each option contract is used in the empirical test. We avoid the issue of non-synchronous prices and the data only include options with at least 5 days to expiration to reduce biases induced by liquidity-related issues. Details of our processing of the data set can be found in [Jiang and van der Sluis 1998]. We divide the option data into several categories according to either moneyness or time to expiration. Following [Ghysels et al 1996] we define,

$$x_t = \ln(S_t/Ke^{-\int_t^T r_\tau d\tau}) \tag{42.11}$$

In our partition, a call option is said to be *at-the-money* (ATM) if $-0.03 < x \le 0.05$; *out-of-the-money* (OTM) if $x \le -0.03$; and *in-the-money* (ITM) if $x > 0.05$. A finer partition resulted in six moneyness categories as in Table 42.1. According to the time to expiration, an option contract can be classified as: i) short-term ($T - t \le 30$ days); ii) medium-term ($30 < T - t < 180$ days); and iii) long-term ($T - t \ge 180$ days). The partition according to moneyness and maturity results in 18 categories as in Table 42.1.

---

6. [Hull and White 1987], [Johnson and Shanno 1987], [Baily and Stulz 1989], [Stein and Stein 1991] and [Heston 1993]

7. See e.g. [Scott 1987], [Wiggins 1987], [Chesney and Scott 1989], [Melino and Turnbull 1990], and [Bakshi et al 1997]

Table 42.1
Sample Properties of Stock Call Option Prices

	Moneyness $x = \ln(S/KB(t,T))$ [$-0.68,\ 1.11$]	Days-to-Expiration T-t [5, 215]			
		≤ 30	$30 - -180$	≥ 180	Subtotal
OTM	$x \leq -0.20$	0.223 (0.112) 0.066 (0.035) {33}	1.760 (0.819) 0.137 (0.033) {85}	1.892 (0.911) 0.274 (0.038) {146}	264
	$-0.20 < x \leq -0.03$	0.817 (0.577) 0.090 (0.040) {76}	3.140 (1.364) 0.149 (0.047) {164}	5.231 (0.989) 0.173 (0.065) {59}	299
ATM	$-0.03 < x \leq 0.00$	1.783 (1.023) 0.114 (0.054) {47}	4.911 (1.440) 0.183 (0.061) {48}	7.042 (0.584) 0.250 (0.000) {46}	151
	$0.00 < x \leq 0.05$	2.997 (0.876) 0.143 (0.050) {32}	5.843 (1.318) 0.195 (0.058) {65}	7.976 (0.559) 0.190 (0.060) {21}	118
ITM	$0.05 < x \leq 0.30$	9.114 (3.030) 0.264 (0.091) {182}	10.61 (2.736) 0.294 (0.089) {283}	11.90 (2.178) 0.306 (0.109) {101}	566
	$x > 0.30$	21.23 (5.403) 0.361 (0.053) {176}	23.99 (6.004) 0.369 (0.049) {394}	25.93 (6.135) 0.375 (0.066) {152}	722
Subtotal		556	1039	525	2120(total)

Note: In each cell from top to bottm are: the average bid-ask midpoint call option prices with standard error in parentheses; the average effective bid-ask spread (ask price minus the bid-ask midpoint) with standard error in parentheses; and the number of option price observations (in curly brackets) for each moneyness-maturity category.

It is noted that for this data set the Black-Scholes implied volatility exhibits obvious U-shaped patterns (*smiles*) as the call option goes from deep OTM to ATM and then to deep ITM, with the deepest ITM call option implied volatilities taking the highest values. The volatility smiles are more pronounced and more sensitive to the term to expiration for short-term options than for the medium-term and long-term options. Furthermore, the volatility smiles are obviously skewed to the left, indicating a downside risk anticipated by option traders. These observations indicate that the short-term options are the mostly severely mispriced ones by the Black-Scholes model and present perhaps the greatest challenge to any alternative option pricing model. The asymmetry, however, indicates a possible skewness due to such as the leverage effect or a negative random jump is expected by the option traders on the dynamics of stock returns. These findings of clear moneyness- and maturity-related biases associated with the Black-Scholes model are consistent with the findings for many other securities in the literature[8].

---

8. See e.g. [Rubinstein 1985], [Clewlow and Xu 1993] and [Taylor and Xu 1994]

42.4.2   Empirical Performance of Alternative Option Pricing Models

In judging the empirical performance of alternative models in pricing options, we perform two tests. First we assume, as in [Hull and White 1987] among others, that stochastic volatility risk is diversifiable and therefore has zero risk premium. The underlying volatilities are directly estimated for submodels 3 and 4 as constants, and are obtained through reprojection methods for the general model and submodels 1 and 2. Based on the historical volatility, we calculate option prices with given maturities and moneyness. The model-generated option prices are compared to the observed market option prices in terms of relative percentage differences and implied Black-Scholes volatility. Second, we assume a non-zero risk premium for stochastic volatility, which is estimated from observed option prices in the previous day. The estimates are used in the following day's volatility process to calculate option prices, which again are compared to the observed market option prices. Throughout the comparison, all the models only rely on information available at given time, thus the study can be viewed as out-of-sample comparison. In particular, in the first comparison, all models rely only on information contained in the underlying state variables, while in the second comparison, the models use both information contained in the underlying state variables (i.e. the *primitive* information) and in the observed (previous day's) market option prices (i.e. the *derivative* information). Our study is clearly different from those which use option prices to imply all parameter values of the "risk-neutral" model, e.g. [Bakshi et al 1997]. In their analysis, all the parameters and underlying volatility are estimated through fitting the option pricing model into observed option prices. Then these implied parameters and underlying volatility are used to predict the same set of option prices. Obviously models with more factors (or more parameters) are given extra advantage. In our comparison, the risk factors are identified from underlying asset return process and the preference parameters for option traders are inferred from observed market option prices.

Under the "risk-neutral" distribution of the general framework, a European call option on a non-dividend paying stock that pays off $\max(S_T - X, 0)$ at maturity T for exercise price X is priced as

$$C_0(S_0, r_0, \sigma_{r0}, \sigma_{S0}; T, X) = \mathsf{E}_0^*[e^{-\int_0^T r_t dt} \max(S_T - X, 0)|S_0, r_0, \sigma_{r0}, \sigma_{S0}] \quad (42.12)$$

where E_0^* is the expectation with respect to the "risk-neutral" specification for the state variables conditional on all information at $t = 0$. In particular, when $\lambda_2 = 0$ in the general model setup, i.e. Assumption 2 of [Amin and Ng 1993] is satisfied, the option pricing formula can be derived as in (42.8). The call option price is the expected Black-Scholes price with the expectation taken with respect to the stochastic variance over the life of the option, i.e. the European call option prices depend on the average expected volatility over the length of the option contract. Furthermore, if stock volatility is also constant, we obtain the Black-Scholes formula. Since the underlying stock we consider in this paper claims no dividend, all options on the stock can be valued as European type options. Option prices given in the formula can be computed based on direct simulations.

42.4.3 Comparison Based on Diversifiable Stochastic Volatility Risk

In this section, we assume that the risk premium in both interest rate and stock return processes as well as the conditional volatility processes are all zero. The SV option prices are calculated based on Monte Carlo simulation using (42.12) for asymmetric models and both (42.8) and (42.12) for symmetric models. The only approximation error involved is the Monte Carlo error which can be reduced to any desirable level by increasing the number of simulations. The estimation error involved in our study is also minimal as we rely on large number of observations over long sampling period to estimate model parameters. In our simulation, 100,000 sampling paths are simulated to reduce the Monte Carlo error and to reflect accurately the fat-tail behavior of the asset return distributions, and the antithetic variable technique is used to reduce the variation of option prices, see [Boyle et al 1997]. The results show that option prices generated using different methods are almost the same, with the largest differences less than a penny for even long term deep ITM options. The accuracy is further reflected in the small standard derivations of the simulated option prices.

Option pricing biases are compared to the observed market prices based on the mean relative percentage option pricing error (MRE) and the mean absolute relative option pricing error (MARE), given by

$$MRE = \frac{1}{n}\sum_{i=1}^{n}\frac{C_i^M - C_i}{C_i} \quad \text{and} \quad MARE = \frac{1}{n}\sum_{i=1}^{n}\frac{|C_i^M - C_i|}{C_i}$$

where n is the number of options used in the comparison, C_i and C_i^M represents respectively the observed market option price and the theoretical model option price. The MRE statistic measures the average relative biases of the model option prices, while the MARE statistic measures the dispersion of relative biases of the model prices. The difference between MARE and MRE suggests the direction of the bias of the model prices, namely when MARE and MRE are of the same absolute values, it suggests that the model systematically misprices the options to the same direction as the sign of MRE, while when MARE is much larger than MRE in absolute magnitude, it suggests that the model is inaccurate in pricing options but the mispricing is less systematic. Since the percentage errors are very sensitive to the magnitude of option prices which are determined by both moneyness and length of maturity, we also calculate MRE and MARE for each of the 18 moneyness-maturity categories in Table 42.1.

Table 42.2 reports the relative pricing errors (%) based on underlying volatility for alternative models. In each cell, from top to bottom are the MRE (mean relative error) and MARE (mean absolute relative error) statistics for: 1. the asymmetric general SV model with $\lambda_2 \neq 0, \lambda_3 \neq 0$; 2. the symmetric general SV model with $\lambda_2 = \lambda_3 = 0$; 3. the asymmetric submodel I with $\lambda_2 \neq 0, \lambda_3 \neq 0$; 4. the symmetric submodel I with $\lambda_2 = \lambda_3 = 0$; 5. the asymmetric submodel II with $\lambda_3 \neq 0$; 6. the symmetric submodel II $\lambda_3 = 0$; 7. submodel III; and 8. submodel IV. The conclusions we draw from the above comparison are summarized as follows. First, all models appear to perform very poorly in pricing options, especially the long-term options. The models in general over-price medium- and long-term options, and under-price short-term deep ITM and deep OTM options. For short-term options, our results are consistent with simulation results in e.g. [Hull and White 1987] and others, i.e. the symmetric SV models tend to predict lower prices than the Black-Scholes model for ATM options and higher prices than the Black-Scholes model for deep ITM options. Second, the effect of stochastic interest rates on option prices is minimal in both cases of stochastic stock return volatility and constant stock return volatility, i.e. the differences between submodels I and II and those between submodels III and IV. Third, the systematic effect on the "mean" of stock returns, namely the additional predictability of stock returns, has a noticeable effect on option prices as evidenced in the simulation results between the general model and submodel I. This is due to the fact that the reprojected underlying volatilities are different in magnitude under alternative specifications of the "mean" functions. As discussed in [Lo and Wang 1995], predictability of asset returns can have significant impact on option prices, even though the exact effect is far from being clear. Fourth, SV models overall underperform the Black-Scholes model, even though all the models share similar patterns of mispricing as the Black-Scholes model. While the asymmetric SV models do outperform all other models for pricing short-term options, overall they underperform both the Black-Scholes model and the symmetric SV models, i.e. they tend to have higher relative option pricing errors. Finally, a further look at the implied Black-Scholes volatility of the asymmetric model prices, however, reveals that the implied volatility curve of the asymmetric models against maturity, reported in Figure 42.3, has a curvature closer to the implied volatility

Table 42.2
Relative Pricing Errors (%) of Alternative Models with Diversifiable Stochastic Volatility Risk

Moneyness $x = ln(S/KB(t,T))$ $[-0.68, 1.11]$	Days-to-Expiration T-t [5, 215]			
	≤30	30 − −180	≥ 180	Overall
OTM $x \leq -0.20$	-2.21 40.25	66.49 68.80	91.53 91.53	67.77 79.19
	-2.83 39.16	72.92 74.73	99.80 99.80	78.92 84.37
	-3.04 34.15	65.56 68.46	91.20 91.20	67.26 77.55
	-3.06 39.19	71.86 73.72	99.75 99.75	77.73 83.34
	-3.01 34.18	65.49 68.39	91.01 91.01	67.12 77.43
	-3.05 39.19	71.89 73.75	99.78 99.78	77.76 83.37
	-19.32 38.66	47.79 49.70	64.31 64.31	48.61 56.07
	-19.63 38.73	47.51 49.43	63.96 63.96	48.29 55.80
$-0.20 < x \leq -0.03$	9.40 29.40	35.85 37.73	44.81 44.81	32.10 36.07
	17.94 29.83	34.10 34.56	40.70 40.70	31.41 34.61
	9.83 25.16	35.90 36.52	44.37 44.37	31.16 35.22
	17.41 29.82	33.63 34.10	40.27 40.27	30.93 34.20
	9.76 25.12	35.85 36.47	44.31 44.31	31.10 35.17
	17.42 29.83	33.64 34.11	40.29 40.29	30.94 34.22
	18.18 27.16	24.13 24.51	27.73 27.73	23.36 25.57
	17.93 26.98	23.98 24.36	27.59 27.59	23.18 25.59
ATM $-0.03 < x \leq 0.00$	12.87 14.36	23.71 24.77	32.45 32.45	21.82 23.29
	12.00 14.60	19.90 20.69	27.53 27.53	18.71 19.91
	13.44 15.95	23.68 24.29	32.40 32.40	21.96 23.04
	11.84 14.46	19.65 20.45	27.24 27.24	18.48 19.69
	13.40 15.91	23.65 24.26	32.39 32.39	21.94 23.01
	11.84 14.46	19.66 20.46	27.24 27.24	18.48 19.70
	13.58 15.75	13.49 14.08	18.71 18.71	14.28 15.24
	13.47 15.66	13.40 14.00	18.62 18.62	14.18 15.16
$0.00 < x \leq 0.05$	12.97 14.89	19.84 19.84	28.58 28.58	20.24 21.46
	10.23 12.70	14.95 15.16	23.50 23.50	15.33 16.05
	12.62 14.68	19.81 19.93	27.70 27.70	19.47 20.04
	10.12 12.62	14.64 14.85	23.16 23.16	15.06 15.79
	12.60 14.67	19.79 19.91	27.67 27.67	19.45 20.02
	10.12 12.62	14.65 14.85	23.17 23.17	15.07 15.80
	11.06 13.01	10.37 10.53	15.67 15.67	11.49 12.05
	10.99 12.95	10.36 10.52	15.64 15.64	11.46 12.03
ITM $0.05 < x \leq 0.30$	1.46 3.20	11.42 11.44	17.47 17.47	9.83 10.16
	0.24 2.09	6.94 7.08	13.56 13.56	6.17 6.78
	1.32 2.51	10.65 10.71	17.27 17.27	9.12 9.50
	0.22 2.08	6.83 6.98	13.45 13.45	6.09 6.71
	1.32 2.50	10.64 10.70	17.25 17.25	9.11 9.49
	0.22 2.08	6.84 6.99	13.46 13.46	6.09 6.71
	0.04 1.83	4.28 4.47	8.81 8.81	3.85 4.47
	0.04 1.83	4.23 4.43	8.73 8.73	3.81 4.44
$x > 0.30$	-0.45 0.55	1.67 1.86	3.88 3.90	1.86 2.12
	-0.56 0.64	0.51 1.04	2.00 2.34	0.62 1.24
	-0.49 0.58	1.66 1.86	3.58 3.65	1.66 2.00
	-0.56 0.65	0.49 1.02	1.95 2.30	0.60 1.22
	-0.49 0.58	1.66 1.86	3.58 3.64	1.66 1.99
	-0.56 0.65	0.49 1.02	1.95 2.30	0.60 1.22
	-0.57 0.65	-0.06 0.74	0.77 1.35	0.02 0.85
	-0.56 0.65	-0.06 0.74	0.76 1.34	0.02 0.85
Overall	1.12 13.00	19.24 19.75	41.03 41.14	19.91 22.93
	3.86 10.16	15.78 16.30	40.49 40.60	19.02 20.72
	0.70 10.00	17.27 17.76	39.45 39.47	18.88 21.21
	3.65 10.11	15.55 16.07	39.99 40.10	18.73 20.47
	0.67 10.00	17.25 17.74	39.38 39.40	18.85 21.18
	3.65 10.11	15.56 16.08	40.01 40.11	18.74 20.48
	2.65 9.60	10.46 11.08	25.92 26.10	12.41 14.33
	2.57 9.57	10.39 11.01	25.78 25.96	12.32 14.25

Note: In each cell, from top to bottom are the MRE (left-hand side) and MARE (right-hand side) statistics for: 1. The asymmetric general SV model with $\lambda_2 \neq 0, \lambda_3 \neq 0$; 2. The symmetric general SV model with $\lambda_2 = \lambda_3 = 0$; 3. The asymmetric submodel I with $\lambda_2 \neq 0, \lambda_3 \neq 0$; 4. The symmetric submodel I with $\lambda_2 = \lambda_3 = 0$; 5. The asymmetric submodel II with $\lambda_3 \neq 0$; 6. The symmetric submodel II with $\lambda_3 = 0$; 7. Submodel III; and 8. Submodel IV.

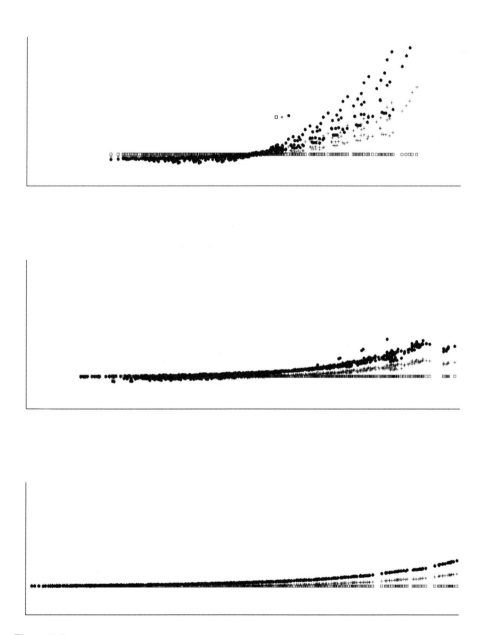

Figure 42.3
Implied Black-Scholes Volatility from Model Predicted Option Prices based on Diversifiable Stochastic Volatility

from observed market options prices in its shape, suggesting such pricing biases may be easier to correct.

42.4.4   Comparison Based on Implied Stochastic Volatility Risk

Since the short-term interest rate fails to be a good proxy of the systematic volatility of the market, the empirically insignificant correlation between interest rates and stock return volatility can not lead to conclude that there is no systematic component in the stock return volatility. The assumption that the stock return volatility is diversifiable in the previous section is very likely to be invalid. In this section, we assume that there is a non-zero risk for stochastic stock return volatility, and we use market option prices observed in the previous day $(t-1)$ to imply such risk which is then used in the following day's (t) volatility processes. Since the estimation only uses option prices at a single point of time, we can assume a general functional form for the price of stochastic volatility risk, namely $\lambda_t(\sigma_s)$ and $\lambda_{t+\tau}(\sigma_s) = \lambda_t(\sigma_s), \forall \tau \geq 0$. For simplicity and for the reason that stochastic interest rates only have limited effect on option prices on the asset considered in this paper, we assume that both the stochastic interest rate volatility and stochastic interest rate have zero risk premium. Thus, for each pricing model, a parameter $\theta_t = \lambda_t(\sigma_s)$, i.e. the implied volatility risk for stochastic volatility models or $\theta_t = \sigma_{st}$, i.e. the implied volatility for constant volatility models can be obtained by minimizing the sum of squared error (SSE), i.e.

$$\tilde{\theta}_{t-1} = \text{Argmin}_{\theta_{t-1}} \sum_i (C^M_{t-1}(S_{t-1}, r_{t-1}, \theta_{t-1}; T_i, X_i) - C_{t-1}(T_i, X_i))^2 \qquad (42.13)$$

where $C_{t-1}(T_i, X_i)$ is the option price observed at $t-1$ with maturity date T_i and strike price X_i. The implied volatility risk or volatility at $t-1$ are then used to price the options at t

$$C^M_t(S_t, r_t, \sigma_{rt}, \sigma_{St}; T, X) = \mathsf{E}^*_t[e^{-\int_0^T r_t dt} \max(S_T - X, 0)|S_t, r_t, \tilde{\theta}_{t-1}] \qquad (42.14)$$

For the SV models, the implied volatility risk can be interpreted as the option traders' revealed preference from observed market option prices, while the implied volatility in the constant conditional volatility model is purely *ad hoc* and inconsistent with the underlying model setup even though it is a common practice in the literature. To estimate θ_{t-1} through (42.13) is straightforward for constant conditional volatility models with closed form option pricing formula, but involves two problems for stochastic conditional volatility models. First, when the closed form solution of option prices is not available, the optimization involves enormous amount of simulation; Second, when the theoretical model price is replaced by the average simulated option prices, the estimate of θ_{t-1} is biased for finite number of simulations. The bias can be reduced by increasing the number of simulations, which induces extra computational burden. Note that the adjustment of stochastic volatility risk alters only the drift term of the SV process in the objective measure to the following risk-neutral specification:

$$\ln \tilde{\sigma}_{st+1}^2 = \omega_s + \lambda_t(\sigma_s) + \gamma_s \ln \tilde{\sigma}_{st}^2 + \sigma_s \eta_{st}, \qquad |\gamma_s| < 1 \qquad (42.15)$$

From the discussion on the statistical properties of SV models in e.g. [Ghysels et al 1996], we notice that, given the value of $\lambda_{t+\tau}(\sigma_s) = \lambda_t(\sigma_s) = \lambda_s, \forall \tau \geq 0$ (i.e. once it is implied from option prices at a particular point of time, the volatility risk is treated as a constant thereafter), $\mathsf{Var}[\tilde{y}_{st}] = \exp\{\mathsf{E}[\ln \tilde{\sigma}_{st}^2] + \mathsf{Var}[\ln \tilde{\sigma}_{st}^2]/2\}$ where $\mathsf{E}[\ln \tilde{\sigma}_{st}^2] = (\omega_s + \lambda_s)/(1 - \gamma_s)$, $\mathsf{Var}[\ln \tilde{\sigma}_{st}^2] = \sigma_s^2/(1 - \gamma_s^2)$. It suggests that the parameter $\lambda_t(\sigma_s)$ can be inferred from the unconditional variance of the SV process. Based on our simulations, the unconditional volatility of the symmetric SV model is approximately the same as the average implied Black-Scholes volatility of long-term options $(T - t \geq 180)$, and that of the asymmetric SV model with negative correlation is slightly higher than the average implied Black-Scholes volatility of long-term options $(T - t \geq 180)$. Thus, we can simply match the unconditional volatility of the SV model to the average implied Black-Scholes volatility from observed long-term options at each day to infer the implied stochastic volatility risk. The downward bias for the asymmetric model is adjusted based on simulations. Our results suggest that, similar to the findings in [Melino and Turnbull 1990], there exists a non-zero risk premium for stochastic volatility of stock returns. The price of volatility risk $\lambda_t(\sigma_s)$ appears to be consistently negative and rather stable over time. This finding is also consistent with the conjecture in [Lamoureux and Lastrapes 1993] and explains why the implied volatility is an inefficient forecast of the underlying volatility.

Table 42.3 reports the relative pricing errors (%) based on implied volatility or volatility risk for alternative models. In each cell, from top to bottom are the MRE (mean relative error) and MARE (mean absolute relative error) statistics for various models as listed in Table 42.2. The basic conclusions we draw from the comparison are summarized as following. First, all models have substantially reduced the pricing errors due to the use of implied volatility or volatility risk. The Black-Scholes model exhibits similar pattern of mispricing, namely underpricing of short-maturity options and over-pricing of long-maturity options, and overpricing of deep OTM options and underpricing deep ITM options. The pricing errors of long-term deep ITM options are dramatically decreased due to the larger weights

42. Option Pricing with the Efficient Method of Moments

Table 42.3
Relative Pricing Errors (%) of Alternative Models with Implied Volatility or Volatility Risk

	Moneyness $x = ln(S/KB(t,T))$ [-0.68, 1.11]	Days-to-Expiration T-t [5, 215]			
		≤30	30 − −180	≥ 180	Overall
OTM	$x \leq -0.20$	-20.18 41.40	6.41 15.76	2.69 13.63	-3.33 19.98
		-27.99 46.16	25.80 29.20	23.35 23.89	18.22 28.40
		-25.34 45.83	3.90 13.18	-3.15 13.74	-8.97 19.64
		-28.64 46.44	25.16 28.64	22.67 23.28	17.56 27.91
		-25.33 45.82	3.90 13.18	-3.26 13.76	-9.04 19.64
		-28.64 46.44	25.19 28.68	22.69 23.30	17.58 27.93
		-42.12 46.45	17.76 21.48	50.34 50.72	27.85 39.75
		-42.12 46.46	17.79 21.51	50.35 50.72	27.87 39.76
	$-0.20 < x \leq -0.03$	-14.21 21.12	3.17 8.64	7.38 7.97	-.26 11.54
		-12.42 21.65	10.73 12.68	11.53 11.62	7.87 14.66
		-16.74 22.61	1.48 8.18	6.14 7.01	-2.07 11.46
		-12.16 21.61	10.49 12.50	11.26 11.38	7.61 14.50
		-16.70 22.61	1.47 8.18	6.08 6.97	-2.08 11.45
		-12.16 21.61	10.50 12.51	11.27 11.39	7.62 14.50
		-10.07 20.42	11.60 12.78	23.64 23.64	11.27 16.63
		-10.07 20.42	11.60 12.78	23.65 23.65	11.28 16.64
ATM	$-0.03 < x \leq 0.00$	1.08 10.45	1.12 5.91	2.93 2.93	1.37 6.80
		4.61 10.16	4.19 7.05	4.04 4.04	4.29 7.52
		1.06 10.47	0.89 5.73	2.63 2.66	1.19 6.67
		4.57 10.14	4.07 7.01	3.86 3.86	4.18 7.46
		1.09 10.51	0.87 5.72	2.60 2.63	1.18 6.66
		4.57 10.14	4.08 7.01	3.87 3.87	4.19 7.47
		7.58 13.49	10.03 11.58	9.86 9.86	9.29 11.89
		7.58 13.49	10.03 11.59	9.86 9.86	9.29 11.89
	$0.00 < x \leq 0.05$	4.18 9.10	2.48 4.66	4.33 4.92	3.23 5.79
		5.41 9.50	3.37 5.20	5.21 5.79	4.20 6.36
		4.36 9.20	2.38 4.57	4.11 4.70	3.17 5.73
		5.37 9.49	3.21 5.10	5.08 5.67	4.07 6.27
		4.38 9.22	2.38 4.85	4.07 4.66	3.17 5.73
		5.37 9.49	3.21 5.10	5.09 5.68	4.08 6.28
		6.59 9.22	4.92 6.03	13.19 13.40	6.81 8.13
		6.59 9.22	4.95 6.06	14.14 14.36	6.99 8.31
ITM	$0.05 < x \leq 0.30$	-0.42 1.76	1.52 2.59	3.01 3.17	1.22 2.45
		-0.72 1.87	1.00 2.47	2.71 3.07	0.80 2.40
		-0.31 1.79	1.73 2.66	3.11 3.22	1.39 2.51
		-0.74 1.87	0.94 2.45	2.64 3.03	0.75 2.38
		-0.31 1.79	1.73 2.66	3.08 3.20	1.38 2.50
		-0.73 1.87	0.95 2.45	2.65 3.03	0.76 2.38
		-0.80 1.91	2.09 3.12	7.63 7.70	2.23 3.58
		-0.81 1.92	2.10 3.13	7.40 7.46	2.20 3.54
	$x > 0.30$	-0.46 0.59	-0.06 0.68	0.10 0.77	-0.10 0.68
		-0.58 0.67	-0.46 0.75	-0.48 0.90	-0.49 0.77
		-0.46 0.59	0.04 0.70	0.23 0.80	-0.01 0.70
		-0.50 0.67	-0.47 0.75	-0.50 0.91	-0.50 0.77
		-0.46 0.59	0.04 0.70	0.23 0.81	-0.01 0.70
		-0.59 0.67	-0.47 0.75	-0.49 0.91	-0.49 0.77
		-0.58 0.67	-0.40 0.73	0.52 1.47	-0.24 0.88
		-0.58 0.67	-0.40 0.73	0.52 1.47	-0.24 0.88
Overall		-1.36 8.18	1.69 4.27	2.59 6.26	0.03 5.96
		-1.57 8.83	4.53 6.21	9.19 9.89	4.29 7.67
		-1.51 8.37	0.99 3.98	0.70 6.18	-0.96 5.91
		-1.67 8.85	4.40 6.12	8.91 9.66	4.13 7.56
		-1.50 8.37	0.99 3.98	0.65 6.17	-0.97 5.91
		-1.67 8.85	4.41 6.12	8.92 9.66	4.14 7.57
		-2.69 8.75	4.50 5.86	20.61 21.05	6.75 10.11
		-2.69 8.75	4.51 5.87	20.62 21.05	6.75 10.12

Note: See Table 42.2.

put on these options in the minimization of the sum of squared option pricing errors; Second, the interest rate still only has minimal impact on option prices for both the cases of stochastic stock return volatility and constant stock return volatility; Third, all SV models outperform non-SV models due to the introduction of non-zero risk premium for conditional volatility. Compared to the Black-Scholes model, the symmetric SV models have overall lower pricing errors; Fourth, the asymmetric SV models further outperform the symmetric SV models significantly, especially for deep OTM and deep ITM and long-term options. Again, measured by the implied volatility the asymmetric SV models exhibit implied volatility very close to those implied from observed option prices, its plot has the same curvature as that in Figure 42.3 but with different level; Finally, the asymmetric models, however, still exhibit systematic pricing errors, namely underpricing of short-term deep OTM options, overpricing of long-term deep OTM options, and underpricing of deep ITM options. This is consistent with our diagnostics of the SV model specification, i.e. the SV models fails to capture the short-term kurtosis of asset returns. The big downside risk anticipated by option traders may be related to the historical large negative returns. These large negative returns induce a very long but thin left tail, which the SV models fail to capture. More importantly, such consistent findings in the diagnostics of the underlying model specification and the performance of option pricing model only suggest that the option pricing errors of the SV models do not provide sufficient evidence to reject the hypothesis of market efficiency. It should be noted that while statistically these pricing errors appear to be large, as high as 20% for short-term OTM options, its economic implications may not be so significant. For instance, for short-term deep OTM options, a 20% relative pricing errors correspond to absolute error of $0.05 on the average, which is smaller than the average effective bid-ask spread. Furthermore, the MARE statistics, a measure of the dispersion of the relative pricing errors, are not reduced as much as the MRE statistics.

42.5 Conclusion

In this paper, we specify a SV process in a multivariate framework to simultaneously model the dynamics of stock returns and interest rates. The model assumes a systematic component in the stock return volatility and "leverage effect" for both stock return and interest rate processes. The proposed model is first estimated using the EMM technique based on observations of underlying state variables. The estimated model is then utilized to investigate the respective effect of systematic volatility, idiosyncratic volatility, and stochastic interest rates on option prices. The empirical results are summarized as follows.

While theory predicts that the short-term interest rates are strongly related to the systematic volatility of the consumption process, our empirical results suggest that the short-term interest rate fails to be a good proxy of the systematic factor. However, the short-term interest rate is significantly correlated with the "mean" of the stock returns, suggesting stock return is predictable to certain extent. Such predictability is shown to have a noticeable impact on option prices as the reprojected underlying volatilities are different in magnitude in alternative model specifications. While allowing for stochastic volatility can reduce the pricing errors and allowing for asymmetric volatility or "leverage effect" does help to explain the skewness of the volatility "smile", allowing for stochastic interest rates has minimal impact on option prices in our case. Similar to [Melino and Turnbull 1990], our empirical findings strongly suggest the existence of a non-zero risk premium for stochastic volatility of stock returns. Based on implied volatility risk, the SV models can largely reduce the option pricing errors, suggesting the importance of incorporating the information in the options market in pricing options. Both the model diagnostics and option pricing errors in our study suggest that the Gaussian SV model is not sufficient in modeling short-term kurtosis of asset returns, an SV model with fatter-tailed noise or jump component may have better explanatory power. An important implication of the consistent findings in the diagnostics of the underlying model specification and the performance of option pricing model is that the option pricing errors of the SV models do not provide sufficient edidence to reject the hypothesis of market efficiency.

Finally, the failure of short-term interest rate as a valid proxy of systematic volatility component suggests that in the future study, an alternative state variable, say a market index, should be used to study the impact of systematic volatility on option prices. Our empirical results also suggest that normality of the stochastic volatility model may not be adequate for this data set and other data sets as well. We leave it in our future research to explore a richer structural model, for example the jump-diffusion and/or the SV model with Student-t disturbances, to describe the dynamics of asset returns.

Acknowledgments

This paper is a shortened version of [Jiang and van der Sluis 1998] that has been presented at the Econometric Institute Rotterdam, Nuffield College Oxford, CORE

Louvain-la-Neuve, Tilburg University and at CF99 at the Stern School of Business, New York University. We thank seminar participants for useful comments. We also thank Bent J. Christensen and Gary W. Geng for helpful suggestions. Pieter J. van der Sluis acknowledges financial support from NWO grant NCF/98.5538 "Option Pricing under Stochastic Volatility".

References

Amin, K. I. and R. A. Jarrow. 1992. Pricing options on risky assets in a stochastic interest rate economy. *Mathematical Finance*, 2:217–237.

Amin, K. I. and V. Ng. 1993. Option valuation with systematic stochastic volatility. *Journal of Finance*.

Andersen, T. G., H. J. Chung, and B. E. Sørensen. 1997. Efficient method of moments estimation of a stochastic volatility model: A Monte Carlo study. Working paper No. 229, Northwestern University.

Baily, W. and E. Stulz. 1989. The pricing of stock index options in a general equilibrium model. *Journal of Financial and Quantitative Analysis*, 24:1–12.

Bakshi, G., C. Cao, and Z. Chen. 1997. Empirical performance of alternative option pricing models. *Journal of Finance*, 52:2003–2049.

Bates, D. S.. 1996. Testing option pricing models. In [Maddala and Rao 1996], pages 567–611.

Black, F.. 1976. Studies of stock price volatility changes. *Proceedings from the American Statistical Association, Business and Economic Statistics Section*, pages 177–181.

Black, F. and M. Scholes. 1972. The valuation of option contracts and a test of market efficiency. *Journal of Finance*, 27:399–418.

Black, F. and M. Scholes. 1973. The pricing of options and corporate liabilities. *Journal of Political Economy*, 81:637–654.

Boyle, P., M. Broadie, and P. Glasserman. 1997. Monte Carlo methods for security pricing. *Journal of Economic Dynamics and Control*, 21:1267–1321.

Chesney, M. and L. O. Scott. 1989. Pricing European currency options: A comparison of the modified Black-Scholes model and a random variance model. *Journal of Financial and Quantitative Analysis*, 24:267–284.

Clewlow, L. and X. Xu. 1993. The dynamics of stochastic volatility. Discussion paper, University of Warwick.

Conrad, J., G. Kaul, and M. Gultekin. 1991. Asymmetric predictability of conditional variances. *Review of Financial Studies*, 4:597–622.

Gallant, A. R. and J. R. Long. 1997. Estimating stochastic differential equations efficiently by minimum chi-square. *Biometrika*, 84:125–141.

Gallant, A. R. and G. E. Tauchen. 1996. Which moments to match? *Econometric Theory*, 12:657–681.

Gallant, A. R. and G. E. Tauchen. 1998. Reprojecting partially observed systems with application to interest rate diffusions. *Journal of the American Statistical Association*, 93:10–24.

Ghysels, E., A. Harvey, and E. Renault. 1996. Stochastic volatility. In [Maddala and Rao 1996].

Gultekin, N. B. and S. M. Rogalski, R. J.and Tinic. 1982. Option pricing model estimates: Some empirical results. *Financial Management*, 11:58–69.

Heston, S. I.. 1993. A closed form solution for options with stochastic volatility with applications to bond and currency options. *Review of Financial Studies*.

Hull, J. and A. White. 1987. The pricing of options on assets with stochastic volatilities. *Journal of Finance*, 42:281–300.

Jarrow, R. and E. Rosenfeld. 1984. Jump risks and the intertemporal capital asset pricing model. *Journal of Business*, 57:337–351.

Jiang, G. J. and P. J. van der Sluis. 1998. Pricing of stock options under stochastic volatility and interest rates with efficient method of moments estimation. Revision of Tinbergen Institute Discussion Paper TI98-067/4.

Johnson, H. and D. Shanno. 1987. Option pricing when the variance is changing. *Journal of Financial and Quantitative Analysis*, 22:143–152.

Jorion, P.. 1995. Predicting volatility in the foreign exchange market. *Journal of Finance*, 50:507–528.

Lamoureux, C. G. and W. D. Lastrapes. 1993. Forecasting stock-return variance: Toward an understanding of stochastic implied volatilities. *Review of Financial Studies*, 6:293–326.

Lo, A. and J. Wang. 1995. Implementing option pricing models when asset returns are predictable. *Journal of Finance*, 50:87–129.

Maddala, G. S. and C. R. Rao, editors 1996. *Handbook of Statistics: Statistical Methods in Finance*, volume 14. Elsevier, Amsterdam.

Melino, A. and S. M. Turnbull. 1990. Pricing foreign currency options with stochastic volatility. *Journal of Econometrics*, 45:239–265.

Merton, R. C.. 1973. Theory of rational option pricing. *Bell Journal of Economics and Management Science*, 4:141–183.

Nelson, D. B.. 1991. Conditional heteroskedasticity in asset returns: A new approach. *Econometrica*, 59:347–370.

Ng, V., R. F. Engle, and M. Rothschild. 1992. A multi-dynamic-factor model for stock returns. *Journal of Econometrics*, 52:245–266.

Rubinstein, M.. 1985. Nonparametric tests of alternative option pricing models using all reported trades and quotes on the 30 most active CBOE options classes from August 23, 1976 through August 31, 1978. *Journal of Finance*, 40:455–480.

Scott, L. O.. 1987. Option pricing when the variance changes randomly: Theory, estimators, and applications. *Journal of Financial and Quantitative Analysis*, 22:419–438.

Scott, L. O.. 1997. Pricing stock options in a jump-diffusion model with stochastic volatility and interest rates: Application of Fourier inversion methods. *Mathematical Finance*, 7:413–426.

Shephard, N. G.. 1996. Statistical aspects of ARCH and stochastic volatility. In Cox, D. R., D. V. Hinkley, and O. E. Barndorff-Nielsen, editors, *Time Series Models: In econometrics, finance and other fields*, pages 1–67. Chapman and Hall, London.

Stein, E. and J. Stein. 1991. Stock price distributions with stochastic volatility: An analytic approach. *Review of Financial Studies*, 4:727–752.

Stein, J.. 1989. Overreactions in the options market. *Journal of Finance*, 44:1011–1023.

Taylor, S. J. and X. Xu. 1994. The magnitude of implied volatility smiles: Theory and empirical evidence for exchange rates. *Review of Futures Markets*, 13:215–235.

Turnbull, S. and F. Milne. 1991. A simple approach to interest-rate option pricing. *Review of Financial Studies*, 4:87–121.

van der Sluis, P. J.. 1997. Emmpack 1.01: C/C++ code for use with Ox for estimation of univariate stochastic volatility models with the efficient method of moments. *Studies in Nonlinear Dynamics and Econometrics*, 2:77–94. Version 1.04.

van der Sluis, P. J.. 1999. *Analysis with the Efficient Method of Moments: With Applications to Stochastic Volatility Models and Option Pricing.* PhD thesis, University of Amsterdam, Thela Thesis, Amsterdam. Forthcoming.

Whaley, R. E.. 1982. Valuation of American call options on dividend paying stocks. *Journal of Financial Economics*, 10:29–58.

Wiggins, J. B.. 1987. Option values under stochastic volatility: Theory and empirical estimates. *Journal of Financial Economics*, 19:351–72.

43 Option Valuation with the Genetic Programming Approach

Christian Keber

In this contribution we derive analytical approximations for the valuation of American put options on non-dividend paying stocks using the genetic programming approach. Using experimental data sets we can show that the genetically determined formulas outperform other formulas presented in the literature. Furthermore, we derive a pure analytical approximation for determining the killing price used in several classical option valuation models. We can show that the results obtained by our formula are very close to the numerically calculated killing prices.

43.1 Introduction

In their seminal papers Black and Scholes (1973) and Merton (1973) derived an analytical solution for the valuation of European call options on stocks paying no dividends during the time to expiration. Merton additionally showed that premature exercising of American call options on this type of stocks is never optimal and that the valuation can also be made using the Black/Scholes/Merton method. If in the case of an American call option, dividends are paid, and these are known with certainty, its value can be obtained using the analytically exact valuation model of Roll (1977) (see also [Geske 1977] and [Whaley 1981]).

In comparison to American call options, premature exercise of American put options on non-dividend paying stocks may produce benefits, if the stock price falls below a certain, permanently variable critical value (*killing price*). As a result of this difference between the premature exercising of American call options and of American put options, ascertaining the optimal time for premature exercising, or the killing price, is a part of the problem to be solved, for which there was previously no exact model. Thus, the valuation of American put options is based on numerical procedures or analytical approximations. The best-known numerical procedures are the *lattice approach* of Cox, Ross, and Rubinstein (1979) and the *finite difference method* of Brennan and Schwartz (1977). However, getting accurate results by using numerical procedures normally requires long calculation time. A simple analytical approximation for the valuation of American put options on non-dividend paying stocks was presented by Johnson (1983) and consists of a linear combination of the values of two European put options (see, e.g., [Margrabe 1978]) with differing exercise prices, but otherwise identical parameters. This simple analytical approximation has the disadvantage that the approximation is not very accurate, so that many more ambitious analytical approximations have been developed. The best-known of these come from MacMillan (1986) and Geske and Johnson (1984).

MacMillan's analytical approximation for the valuation of American put options consists of raising the value of a suitable European put option by the value of the approximately calculated premature exercising of the option. This method forms the basis for analytical approximations used to evaluate a range of other American options, such as index options, currency options, and options on futures (see, e.g., [Barone-Adesi and Whaley 1987] and [Stoll and Whaley 1986]). Geske and Johnson's analytical approximation works on the assumption that premature exercise is possible only at particular, discrete points in time. Accordingly, for each of these moments an option value is calculated, and, based on this, the value of the American put option is ascertained using the polynomial extrapolation method. This method treats American put options both with and without dividends. The MacMillan method, however, deals only with put options on stocks paying no dividend during the maturity of the options, although it was extended by Barone-Adesi and Whaley (1988) and Fischer (1993) to include the dividend paying case.

It is characteristic of most approximations for the valuation of American put options found in the literature that they approximate either the stochastic stock price process, or the partial differential equation (with the appropriate boundaries) which implicitly describes the option price. In contrast to these approximation methods, Geske and Johnson (1984) as well as Kim (1990) formulate a valuation equation which represents an exact solution of the partial differential equation, and then solve it either by analytical approximation (Geske and Johnson) or by numerical techniques (Kim). Hutchinson, Lo, and Poggio (1994) abandon such traditional techniques and present a non-parametric method for the valuation of European options and employ an *artificial neural network* as the method of solution (see also, e.g., [Hanke 1997] and [Hanke 1999]).

In this contribution we derive analytical approximations exclusively for the valuation of American put options on non-dividend paying stocks using the *genetic programming* approach. An extension for the dividend paying case is straightforward. Genetic programming is an approach designed to generate computer programs as well as formulas using a random oriented search technique based on principles of evolution and heredity. Hence, in our context an option pricing formula should itself evolve during the evolution process. Using experimental data sets we can show that the genetically derived analytical approximations, used for the valuation of American put options on non-dividend paying stocks, outperform alternative formulas found in the literature, and lead to significant improvements in option valuation.

In the second section we focus on the concept of genetic programming. The third section presents the genetically derived put option pricing formulas as well as a pure analytical approximation for calculating the killing price which is normally calculated using numerical procedures. In the fourth section we show the experimental results. The contribution concludes with a summary and a few closing remarks.

43.2   Genetic Programming

The genetic programming (GP) methodology comes from Koza (1992) and is based on genetic algorithms, which were originally presented by Holland (1975) and subsequently used to solve a great variety of differing problems (an overview is given in [Alander 1994]). Genetic programming is an approach designed to generate computer programs as well as formulas using a random oriented search technique based on principles of natural evolution and heredity. The fundamental philosophy of genetic algorithms lies in the imitation of the strategy that determines the evolution process: The fittest survive and pass their genetic material, and thus their strengths, to the next generation. By imitating this process we get individuals which are ever more suited to their environment. In our GP-application we start with a defined programming language $\mathcal{L}$ (see, e.g., [Aho and Ullman 1972]). $\mathcal{L}$ is to be seen simply as the set of all analytical expressions which can be produced from a start symbol $\mathcal{S}$ under application of *substitution rules* $\mathcal{P}$ and a finite set or vocabulary of *terminal symbols* $\mathcal{T}$. Thus,

$$\mathcal{L} = \{c \mid \mathcal{S} \Longrightarrow c \ \wedge \ c \in \mathcal{T}^*\} \tag{43.1}$$

where $\mathcal{T}^*$ represents the set of all analytical expressions which can be produced from the symbols of the vocabulary $\mathcal{T}$. In the sense of genetic programming, $\mathcal{L}$ is the *search space* of all potential analytical expressions to be generated, $c \in \mathcal{L}$ is a *chromosome* or *individual*, and $P_\tau \subset \mathcal{L}$ is the *population* of the τ-th generation ($\tau = 0, \ldots, \tau_{\max}$). Furthermore, the terminal symbols contained in c represent the *genes* of the chromosome c.

The genetic structure of an individual is evaluated by using the *fitness concept*. Fitness is here used as a measure of suitability of the individual to its environment. Each chromosome (analytical expression, computer program) $c \in \mathcal{L}$ can be seen as a function $c : \mathcal{E}_i \rightarrow \mathcal{A}_i$ because c transforms input data $\mathcal{E}_i$ into the solution or output data $\mathcal{A}_i$. Related to this, a fitness function $f : \mathcal{A} \rightarrow \mathbb{R}$ has to be defined in a way that it awards a higher fitness value to those individuals which represent a good solution to the task in hand, and a lower fitness value to less suitable individuals. The fitness is usually measured using a representative set of test records $\mathcal{E}_i$, for $i = 1, \ldots, n$. If these input data are processed using the program $c \in P_\tau$, the result will be the output data $\mathcal{A}_i$, which can then be compared to the target output data

$\mathcal{A}_i^S$. Using a deviation function $\Delta(\mathcal{A}_i, \mathcal{A}_i^S)$ in a way that it delivers higher values the more the output data differ from the target output data, the aggregated deviation is the so-called *raw fitness* f_r of the program c:

$$f_r(c) = \sum_{i=1}^{n} \Delta(\mathcal{A}_i, \mathcal{A}_i^S) \quad \text{with} \quad \mathcal{A}_i = c(\mathcal{E}_i). \tag{43.2}$$

The raw fitness function delivers smaller fitness values the better the individual c accomplishes its tasks. As in most applications, the raw fitness is modified in a way that the fitness values lie between zero and one, and larger fitness values represent better individuals (*adjusted fitness*).

A high fitness value expresses the ability of an individual to produce offspring more frequently (*fitness-proportional selection*), whereby the genetic material is passed on to the following generation (*reproduction/recombination*). The direct result of this is that genes which are advantageous to the individual in its environment are inherited more frequently than those from less well-suited individuals, so that in the course of evolution, populations arise which are ever more suited to their environment. Accordingly, a new population $P_{\tau+1}$ is formed by selecting $|P_\tau|$ individuals proportionally to their fitness and altering some survivors using *crossover* and *mutation*. By applying crossover—based on a given crossover rate p_c—we select pairs of formulas (individuals), swap randomly selected sub-expressions and get a new pair of offspring. By using mutation—based usually on a low mutation rate p_m—we alter formulas (chromosomes) by exchanging operators or operands (genes) randomly. Crossover as well as mutation can be interpreted as search operators. The crossover operator crosses between two individuals and enables the exchange of genetic material; the task of the mutation operator consists primarily of opposing a premature convergence on local optima. As formulated in Holland's (1975) *schema theorem* (a proof is given in [Goldberg 1989]), the performance of genetic programming can be measured as the ability of individuals to make themselves better suited to the environment (by fitness-proportional selection, reproduction, and recombination) with over-proportional speed relative to the number of generations.

43.3   The genetic determination of the analytical approximations

43.3.1   Implementation and parameter specification

By applying the genetic programming approach to option pricing we have to specify some parameters. In the fitness concept we used a (randomly generated) training sample of 1,000 American put options on non-dividend paying stocks described by the tuple $\langle P_0, S_0, X, r, T, \sigma \rangle$. P_0 refers to the "exact" value of an American put option on a non-dividend paying stock at $t = 0$, S_0 denotes the stock price at $t = 0$, X is the exercise price, r represents the annual continuous risk-free interest rate (in %), T is the time to expiration (in years), and σ is the annual volatility of the stock price (in %). Each option price P_0 was calculated by using the finite difference method[1] and served as the exact value of the American puts. The corresponding parameters were drawn randomly based on uniform distributions. In accordance with the literature as well as realistic circumstances we defined the following domains: $10 \leq S_0 \leq 100$, $3 \leq r \leq 7$, $0 < T \leq 1$, $5 \leq \sigma \leq 50$, and $0.9 \leq \alpha \leq 1.1$, where $\alpha = S_0/X$ describes the moneyness[2] of the option. In accordance with the genetic programming approach we transformed each tuple $\langle P_0, S_0, X, r, T, \sigma \rangle$ into an input data record $\mathcal{E}_i$ $(\hat{=} \langle S_0, X, r, T, \sigma \rangle)$ and a corresponding target output data record $\mathcal{A}_i^S$ $(\hat{=} \langle P_0 \rangle)$, for $i = 1, \ldots, 1000$.

For the fitness function we used the sum of the squared errors $\sum_{i=1}^{1000} (\mathcal{A}_i - \mathcal{A}_i^S)^2$. In the terminal symbol set we included the variables S_0, X, r, T, σ, α as well as the numerical constants π and e as the possible operands, the commonly used mathematical operators $+$, $-$, $*$, $\div$, $\sqrt{x}$, $\ln(x)$, x^2, x^y, the cumulative distribution function of the univariate standard normal distribution $\Phi(x)$, the logical operators $<, \leq, =, >, \geq$, and the case-differentiating symbols IF, THEN, ELSE. Furthermore, we defined a population size of 50 individuals, a crossover rate $p_c = 0.9$, a mutation rate $p_m = 0.01$, and stopped the evolution process after 20,000 generations. With this combination of values, a balanced relationship between convergence speed, calculation effort and effectiveness of the genetic algorithm was obtained.

43.3.2   The genetically determined analytical approximations

Applying the genetic programming approach as described a raw fitness of 5.1339×10^{-5} is obtained for the best individual after $\tau_{\max} = 20,000$ generations. The analytical expression of this individual represents an approximation $P_0^{(1)}$ for the valuation of American put options on non-dividend paying stocks (for the parameters contained in (43.3) see the appendix):

---

1. With $\Delta t = (1/365)/5 = 0.00054795$, $\Delta S = 0.01$, and $S_{\max} = 2 \cdot S_0$.

2. The α-domain is based on the consideration that option trading always starts near-the-money. Additionally, Barone-Adesi and Whaley's (1986) study shows that the moneyness lies between 0.9 and 1.1 in approx. 67 % of cases in a sample of 697,733 stock option transactions. Furthermore, Stephan and Whaley (1990) look at a sample of 950,346 stock option transactions and report that the moneyness is between 0.9 and 1.1 in approx. 78 % of cases.

$$P_0 \approx P_0^{(1)} = \begin{cases} p_0 - X \frac{A}{B(\beta)} \left(\frac{\alpha}{\beta}\right)^c & \text{if } \alpha > \beta \\ X - S_0 & \text{otherwise.} \end{cases} \qquad (43.3)$$

In the analytical approximation $P_0^{(1)}$ a structural similarity to the approximations by Barone-Adesi and Whaley (1988) and MacMillan (1986) (BAWMM-approximation) can be found: in all three approximations there is a case differentiation, whereby the calculation $P_0 \approx X - S_0$ is identical for all three. From (43.3) it can be seen for the genetically determined approximation, too, that the value of the American put option on non-dividend paying stocks results from a correction of the value of the corresponding European put option on non-dividend paying stocks (p_0). The formulas differ from each other just in the "correction value" and in the case-differentiation-related logical condition, and it seems appropriate to make a closer investigation.

Numerical studies have revealed the relationship

$$S^* \approx S^*_{proxy} = \beta X. \qquad (43.4)$$

This was a surprising by-product because S^*_{proxy} is a pure analytical approximation for calculating the so called *killing price* S^* used in several classical option valuation models and which is normally calculated using numerical procedures.

Using the approximation $\beta \approx S^*/X$ and the relationship $\alpha = S_0/X$ in (43.3) yields an option pricing formula (for the parameters contained in (43.5) see the appendix)

$$P_0 \approx P_0^{(2)} = \begin{cases} p_0 - \frac{A'}{B(S^*/X)} \left(\frac{S_0}{S^*}\right)^c & \text{if } S_0 > S^* \\ X - S_0 & \text{otherwise} \end{cases} \qquad (43.5)$$

and it is noticeable that the approximation $P_0^{(2)}$ except for the parameters $B(\cdot)$ and c is in accordance with the BAWMM-approach.

The analytical approximation (43.5) arises not directly from the application of genetic programming, but rather from the subsequent use of traditional elements of approximate option valuation. $P_0^{(2)}$ can thus be seen as a genetically determined, *ex post* hybridised analytical approximation for the valuation of American put options on non-dividend paying stocks. The corresponding (ex post calculated) raw fitness is 3.2419×10^{-5}. This is an improvement when compared to $P_0^{(1)}$.

Because of this improvement we applied the genetic programming algorithm as described using the numerical exact killing price S^* as an additional operand in the terminal symbol set. S^* was calculated numerically according to the procedure used in the BAWMM-approach. Using S^* (*ceteris paribus*), $\mathcal{E}_i$ is henceforth represented by the tuple $\langle S_0, S^*, X, r, T, \sigma \rangle$. This *ex ante* hybridisation of the genetic programming approach resulted in a genetically derived option pricing formula $P_0^{(3)}$ (for the parameters contained in (43.6) see the appendix):

$$P_0 \approx P_0^{(3)} = \begin{cases} p_0 - \frac{A'}{B'} \left(\frac{S_0}{S^*}\right)^{c_1} & \text{if } S_0 > S^* \\ X - S_0 & \text{otherwise.} \end{cases} \tag{43.6}$$

Similarly to the genetically determined approximations $P_0^{(1)}$ and $P_0^{(2)}$, the analytical approximation $P_0^{(3)}$ is comparable structurally to the BAWMM formula. If the stock price S_0 lies below the killing price S^*, the value of the American put option on non-dividend paying stocks is ascertained by a correction of the corresponding European put option. The raw fitness value of the *ex ante* hybridised analytical approximation for the valuation of American put options on non-dividend paying stocks is 2.0043×10^{-5}. This is a further improvement when compared to $P_0^{(2)}$.

43.4   Experimental results

To give a first impression of the accuracy of the genetically derived analytical approximations for the valuation of American put options on non-dividend paying stocks as well as the killing price approximation we use the data sets of Geske and Johnson (1984) and Barone-Adesi and Whaley (1988) because these data sets are often used as comparisons. Furthermore, we use a huge sample of 20,000 randomly generated American put options (validation data set). This ensures that the assessment of the approximations will be highly accurate. The corresponding parameters are independent from those of the training sample and their domains are as follows: $10 \leq S_0 \leq 100$, $3 \leq r \leq 8$, $0 < T \leq 1$, $5 \leq \sigma \leq 50$, and $0.8 \leq \alpha \leq 1.2$. As can be seen the riskless interest rate and moneyness ranges are wider than those of the training sample. The enlargement of these value fields in the validation data set is, with particular regard to the genetically determined approximation formulas, aimed at highlighting the sensitivity of the approximation results to the input parameters. The numerically exact put option and killing prices P_0 and S^* were calculated using the finite difference method (with $\Delta t = (1/365) \cdot 5 = 0.00054795$, $\Delta S = 0.01$, and $S_{\max} = 2 \cdot S_0$) and MacMillan's (1986) procedure, respectively. For the *method-related* comparison we use the most frequently quoted analytical approximations P_{0J} of Johnson (1983), P_{0GJ} of Geske and Johnson (1984), and P_{0BAW} of Barone-Adesi and Whaley (1988) as well as MacMillan (1986).

In the following Tables 43.1 and 43.2 the genetically derived approximations $P_0^{(1)}$, $P_0^{(2)}$, and $P_0^{(3)}$ as well as the most frequently quoted approximations P_{0J}, P_{0GJ},

Table 43.1

Approximations for the value of American put options on non-dividend paying stocks and the killing price ($S_0 = 40$, data from [Geske and Johnson 1984, page 1519]).

r	T	σ	X	S^*	S^*_{proxy}	P_0	P_{0J}	P_{0BAW}	P_{0GJ}	$P_0^{(1)}$	$P_0^{(2)}$	$P_0^{(3)}$
0.0488	0.0833	0.20	35.00	31.9429	31.8309	0.0063	0.0062	0.0065	0.0062	0.0062	0.0062	0.0062
0.0488	0.3333	0.20	35.00	30.2079	30.1699	0.2001	0.1969	0.2044	0.2000	0.1981	0.1982	0.1988
0.0488	0.5833	0.20	35.00	29.3765	29.4087	0.4323	0.4205	0.4415	0.4318	0.4287	0.4284	0.4287
0.0488	0.0833	0.20	40.00	36.5062	36.3781	0.8509	0.8406	0.8503	0.8521	0.8485	0.8503	0.8504
0.0488	0.3333	0.20	40.00	34.5233	34.4799	1.5787	1.5262	1.5768	1.5759	1.5742	1.5760	1.5768
0.0488	0.5833	0.20	40.00	33.5731	33.6100	1.9894	1.8916	1.9888	1.9827	1.9887	1.9864	1.9879
0.0488	0.0833	0.20	45.00	41.0694	40.9254	5.0000	4.8403	5.0000	4.9969	5.0000	5.0000	5.0000
0.0488	0.3333	0.20	45.00	38.8387	38.7899	5.0875	4.7882	5.0661	5.1053	5.0779	5.0874	5.0886
0.0488	0.5833	0.20	45.00	37.7697	37.8112	5.2661	4.8584	5.2364	5.2893	5.2673	5.2585	5.2666
0.0488	0.0833	0.30	35.00	30.0958	30.0762	0.0777	0.0777	0.0780	0.0772	0.0772	0.0772	0.0774
0.0488	0.3333	0.30	35.00	27.2838	27.3136	0.6967	0.7056	0.7014	0.6972	0.6940	0.6938	0.6947
0.0488	0.5833	0.30	35.00	25.9326	26.0282	1.2188	1.2390	1.2281	1.2198	1.2165	1.2150	1.2154
0.0488	0.0833	0.30	40.00	34.3952	34.3729	1.3081	1.3047	1.3078	1.3103	1.3075	1.3078	1.3078
0.0488	0.3333	0.30	40.00	31.1815	31.2156	2.4810	2.4757	2.4783	2.4801	2.4781	2.4771	2.4782
0.0488	0.5833	0.30	40.00	29.6373	29.7465	3.1681	3.1634	3.1667	3.1628	3.1690	3.1637	3.1658
0.0488	0.0833	0.30	45.00	38.6946	38.6695	5.0590	4.9910	5.0470	5.0631	5.0602	5.0620	5.0564
0.0488	0.3333	0.30	45.00	35.0792	35.1175	5.7042	5.6090	5.6794	5.7017	5.7043	5.7009	5.7020
0.0488	0.5833	0.30	45.00	33.3420	33.4648	6.2421	6.1265	6.2150	6.2367	6.2463	6.2332	6.2392
0.0488	0.0833	0.40	35.00	28.2663	28.2812	0.2466	0.2499	0.2472	0.2461	0.2462	0.2462	0.2464
0.0488	0.3333	0.40	35.00	24.4943	24.5223	1.3447	1.3886	1.3491	1.3461	1.3421	1.3419	1.3428
0.0488	0.5833	0.40	35.00	22.7175	22.7826	2.1533	2.2475	2.1619	2.1553	2.1525	2.1513	2.1518
0.0488	0.0833	0.40	40.00	32.3043	32.3214	1.7659	1.7763	1.7659	1.7688	1.7660	1.7658	1.7659
0.0488	0.3333	0.40	40.00	27.9935	28.0255	3.3854	3.4494	3.3825	3.3863	3.3824	3.3816	3.3829
0.0488	0.5833	0.40	40.00	25.9629	26.0372	4.3506	4.4728	4.3494	4.3475	4.3518	4.3486	4.3500
0.0488	0.0833	0.40	45.00	36.3423	36.3616	5.2856	5.2706	5.2735	5.2848	5.2875	5.2867	5.2822
0.0488	0.3333	0.40	45.00	31.4927	31.5287	6.5078	6.5535	6.4875	6.5015	6.5051	6.5030	6.5048
0.0488	0.5833	0.40	45.00	29.2082	29.2919	7.3808	7.4874	7.3597	7.3695	7.3830	7.3766	7.3794
MAE					0.0553		0.0692	0.0082	0.0040	0.0020	0.0027	0.0016
MSE ($\times 10^{-5}$)					449.7680		1351.8420	15.4237	4.4433	0.7912	1.1971	0.3970
MAPE					0.0018		0.0217	0.0045	0.0025	0.0028	0.0029	0.0022

and P_{0BAW} are applied to the data sets of Geske and Johnson (1984) and Barone-Adesi and Whaley (1988), respectively. P_0 and S^* denote the numerically exact put option and killing price, respectively. S^*_{proxy} is the analytical approximation for the killing price, and at the end of each table the three error measures mean absolute error (MAE), mean squared error (MSE) and mean absolute percentage error (MAPE) are given for each approximation. The approximation results can be summarised as follows:

- When we look at the two data sets of Geske and Johnson (1984) and Barone-Adesi and Whaley (1988) it can be seen that Johnson's (1983) put pricing formula delivers less accurate approximations. The mean absolute errors are about 7 and 71 pence, respectively. The next best approximations come from Barone-Adesi and Whaley (1988), MacMillan (1986), and Geske and Johnson (1984) having mean absolute errors between about half a penny and one penny. In comparison, the genetically derived approximations are roughly speaking better than the others because their mean absolute errors are between about two tenths of a penny and one penny. Furthermore, it can be seen that the killing price approximations are close to the numerical ones. The mean absolute errors are about 6 and 28 pence, respectively.

Table 43.2
Approximations for the value of American put options on non-dividend paying stocks and the killing price ($X = 100$, data from [Barone-Adesi and Whaley 1988, page 315]).

r	T	σ	S_0	S^*	S^*_{proxy}	P_0	P_{0J}	P_{0BAW}	P_{0GJ}	$P_0^{(1)}$	$P_0^{(2)}$	$P_0^{(3)}$
0.08	0.25	0.20	80.00	89.3693	89.3528	20.0000	18.0909	20.0000	20.0012	20.0000	20.0000	20.0000
0.08	0.25	0.20	90.00	89.3693	89.3528	10.0353	9.0470	10.0130	10.0730	10.0232	10.0283	10.0343
0.08	0.25	0.20	100.00	89.3693	89.3528	3.2217	3.0378	3.2201	3.2115	3.2193	3.2203	3.2223
0.08	0.25	0.20	110.00	89.3693	89.3528	0.6642	0.6406	0.6810	0.6647	0.6615	0.6616	0.6660
0.08	0.25	0.20	120.00	89.3693	89.3528	0.0888	0.0865	0.0967	0.0879	0.0881	0.0881	0.0891
0.12	0.25	0.20	80.00	90.9923	91.8622	20.0000	17.1344	20.0000	20.0112	20.0000	20.0000	20.0000
0.12	0.25	0.20	90.00	90.9923	91.8622	10.0000	8.2620	10.0000	9.9811	10.0000	10.0000	10.0000
0.12	0.25	0.20	100.00	90.9923	91.8622	2.9225	2.6265	2.9251	2.9110	3.0298	2.9312	2.9347
0.12	0.25	0.20	110.00	90.9923	91.8622	0.5541	0.5189	0.5781	0.5541	0.5727	0.5587	0.5646
0.12	0.25	0.20	120.00	90.9923	91.8622	0.0685	0.0654	0.0789	0.0676	0.0712	0.0696	0.0712
0.08	0.25	0.40	80.00	75.4859	75.5369	20.3196	19.7588	20.2478	20.3699	20.3062	20.2974	20.3088
0.08	0.25	0.40	90.00	75.4859	75.5369	12.5635	12.4222	12.5142	12.5511	12.5537	12.5496	12.5513
0.08	0.25	0.40	100.00	75.4859	75.5369	7.1049	7.1204	7.0999	7.1018	7.0986	7.0968	7.1009
0.08	0.25	0.40	110.00	75.4859	75.5369	3.6968	3.7476	3.7120	3.7017	3.6927	3.6919	3.6970
0.08	0.25	0.40	120.00	75.4859	75.5369	1.7885	1.8310	1.8068	1.7892	1.7855	1.7852	1.7893
0.08	0.50	0.20	80.00	87.2480	87.4318	20.0000	16.6555	20.0000	19.9402	20.0000	20.0000	20.0000
0.08	0.50	0.20	90.00	87.2480	87.4318	10.2890	8.8392	10.2348	10.3712	10.3270	10.2661	10.2995
0.08	0.50	0.20	100.00	87.2480	87.4318	4.1885	3.7889	4.1933	4.1519	4.2082	4.1899	4.1983
0.08	0.50	0.20	110.00	87.2480	87.4318	1.4095	1.3140	1.4459	1.4121	1.4102	1.4057	1.4101
0.08	0.50	0.20	120.00	87.2480	87.4318	0.3969	0.3768	0.4244	0.3961	0.3945	0.3935	0.3948
MAE					0.2803		0.7083	0.0184	0.0173	0.0122	0.0055	0.0040
MSE ($\times 10^{-4}$)					1983.1964		14886.3928	7.3752	8.2725	7.1066	0.7473	0.3828
MAPE					0.0031		0.0721	0.0218	0.0034	0.0072	0.0030	0.0040

The application results just shown cannot be used for a general assessment of the accuracy of the approximation formulas because the underlying data sets are too small. If we use the 1,000 data records used in the genetic programming approach as a basis for a general assessment the problem arises that this data sample represents training data, and thus the assessment would be open to criticism of being a "self-fulfilling prophecy". Therefore, the definitive judgement of the approximation formulas is to be made from the above mentioned validation data set which has a much larger scope and is independent of the training data set, too. Let us first investigate the accuracy of the genetically derived killing price approximation.

The graph in Figure 43.1 is based on the validation data set and shows the cumulated frequencies of the absolute deviations between the numerically calculated exact killing price S^* and its approximation S^*_{proxy}. First of all it can be seen that the absolute deviations are always less than unity. If we look at the 90 % and 95 % probabilities we can see that the absolute deviations are always less than about 20 and 30 pence, respectively, and it can be estimated how well the genetically derived killing price approximation works.

Based on the validation data set the graph in Figure 43.2 shows the accuracy of the genetically derived approximations as well as Johnson's (1983), Geske and Johnson's (1984), Barone-Adesi and Whaley's (1988), and MacMillan's (1986) put pricing formulas. The accuracy is shown in terms of cumulated frequencies of the absolute deviations between the numerically calculated exact put option price and the approximations just mentioned.

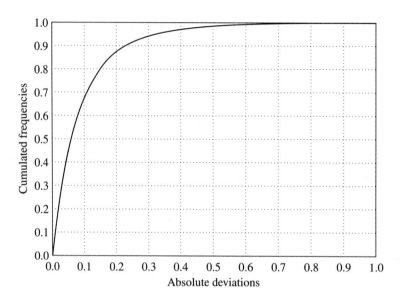

Figure 43.1
Cumulated frequencies of the absolute deviations between S^* and its approximation.

• Johnson's (1983) put pricing formula delivers the weakest approximation results. The next best approximations come from MacMillan (1986) and Barone-Adesi and Whaley (1988), and the best of the most frequently quoted approximations is Geske and Johnson's (1984) valuation approach.

• Whereas for the other approximations it can be said with almost 100 % probability that the approximated option prices differ from the numerically exact option prices by no more than 12 pence, deviation to this level is only found in Johnson's (1983) solution in 65 % of cases. Put another way, in 35 % of cases there is a deviation of more than 12 pence. Due to these poor results, Johnson's (1983) approximation is not considered in further discussions.

• If we focus on the 95 % probability we are able to say that the absolute deviations in MacMillan's (1986) and Barone-Adesi and Whaley's (1988) as well as Geske and Johnson's (1984) approach are always less then about 6 pence. Focusing on the 90 % probability we can say that the absolute deviations are always less than about 5 pence—if we look at MacMillan's (1986) and Barone-Adesi and Whaley's (1988) approach—and less than about 3 pence if we look at Geske and Johnson's (1984) approach.

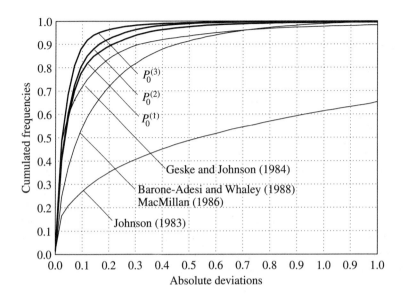

Figure 43.2
Cumulated frequencies of the absolute deviations between P_0 and the approximations.

- In comparison, the genetically derived formulas deliver better approximations than the most frequently quoted ones. The $P_0^{(3)}$-formula delivers the best approximation followed by $P_0^{(2)}$ and $P_0^{(1)}$.

- Focusing on the 90 % probability the $P_0^{(1)}$-, $P_0^{(2)}$-, and $P_0^{(3)}$-formulas always cause absolute deviations less than about one, two, and two pence, respectively. If we focus on the 95 % probability the absolute deviations of the genetically derived formulas are always less than about two, three, and three pence, respectively.

The above analysis shows that the genetically derived analytical approximations for the valuation of American put options on non-dividend paying stocks deliver better results, i.e., smaller deviations from the numerically calculated exact put option price, than the most frequently quoted analytical approximations. The presented figures result in an accuracy improvement factor of about three to four, and so we are able to say that the genetically derived put pricing formulas outperform the approximations of Johnson (1983), Geske and Johnson (1984), Barone-Adesi and Whaley (1988), and MacMillan (1986). The genetically derived $P_0^{(1)}$-formula has the additional advantage that it is a purely analytical approximation[3].

43.5   Concluding remarks

In this contribution we have shown that the genetic programming methodology can be used to derive accurate analytical approximations for the valuation of American put options on non-dividend paying stocks. Using sample data sets from the literature as well as a huge validation data set, it was possible to show that the genetically derived put pricing formulas outperform the most frequently quoted analytical approximations. Furthermore, we have seen that the killing price calculated with a genetically derived formula is very close to the numerically calculated one.

We introduced genetic programming as a data-driven, non-parametric method for generating option valuation models. In traditional parametric approaches, the derivation of the model is closely bound to those parameters that model the stochastic price process of the underlying asset, and incorrect specifications for these parameters or the stochastic price process will lead to systematic errors in the valuation model. In comparison, genetic programming methods have the following advantages. They need only a few assumptions with regard to the parameters mentioned, and are rather insensitive to the effects of specification errors in these parameters. As any mathematical or statistical function can be included in the set of terminal symbols, the methods of genetic programming are flexible enough with regard to the determination of option valuation models to be applied to a broad variety of derivatives and associated stochastic price processes of the underlying asset. This flexibility is sufficiently great so that option valuation models can be found by genetic programming even when the stochastic price process of the underlying asset is only given implicitly, e.g., by historical prices. The valuation of exotic options should be mentioned here in particular as a field of application. If the stochastic

---

3. When analytical approximation statements are referred to the literature, it is not very exact terminology. If the literature discussed in this paper, for example, is examined, only Johnson's formula may be accurately described as an analytical approximation, as only this one represents a purely analytical solution. Geske and Johnson's, Barone-Adesi and Whaley's, and MacMillan's formulas are indeed of an analytic nature, but include parameters to be determined numerically. In the case of Geske and Johnson's formula, at least the distribution function of the trivariate, possibly also the multivariate, standard normal distribution should be used which is normally calculated using numerical integration. For the approximation of Barone-Adesi and Whaley as well as MacMillan, the killing price is required which can only be determined numerically, e.g., with the Newton-Raphson procedure. This last point is of course also true for the genetically derived approximations $P_0^{(2)}$ and $P_0^{(3)}$.

price process of the underlying asset can be described correctly by appropriate parameters with the result that an analytically exact valuation model can be found, it is obvious that this model is to be preferred to the genetically determined one. However, it should be noted that such circumstances occur rarely enough, so that genetic programming can be seen as a reasonable alternative method for constructing derivative pricing formulas.

Appendix

The parameters contained in $P_0^{(1)}$ and $P_0^{(2)}$ are as follows (in alphabetical order, the calculation order is w, q, v, u, β, A or A', c, $D(Y)$, and $B(Y)$):

$$A = \Phi\left(\frac{\ln(\beta) + (r + \sigma^2/2)T}{\sigma\sqrt{T}}\right)\beta$$

$$A' = \Phi\left(\frac{\ln(S^*/X) + (r + \sigma^2/2)T}{\sigma\sqrt{T}}\right)S^*$$

$$B(Y) = \frac{1}{2}\left[e^{e^r-1} - \frac{2r}{\sigma^2} - \sqrt{D(Y) + \frac{8r}{\sigma^2(1 - e^{-rT})}}\right]$$

$$\beta = \left[\frac{r}{\sigma\pi\sqrt{T}(2 + 4\sigma T + \sigma^u)}\right]^v$$

$$c = \frac{1}{2}\left[0,955 - \frac{2r}{\sigma^2} - \sqrt{\frac{\ln(\alpha)}{T\sigma^3(r + rT + T\sqrt{p_0/X})} + \frac{8r}{\sigma^2(1 - e^{-rT})}}\right]$$

$$D(Y) = \left\{\frac{\left[\ln\left(\frac{T^2(\ln(Y)+rY+T^2/2-T)^2}{Y^3}\right) - r + 2\sigma^2 - T\right]T}{\Phi\left(\sigma\sqrt{\sigma\sqrt{(\alpha-T^2)^2}}\right)\Phi\left(T\sqrt{(\sigma-T^2)^2}/Y\right)}\right\}^2$$

$$q = T\pi + \frac{r}{\sqrt{T}} + r + 4\left[\sigma - \frac{r}{\sqrt{T^2\sigma + T}}\right] + 2$$

$$u = 4r\left[\frac{T\sqrt{T}\sigma}{(T^4 + r)^{r-T} - \pi} + r^2\pi^2 T\pi^\pi + 4r + 2\sigma^q\right]^2$$

$$v = \frac{\sigma}{4}\left[T^2 + T\right]^{\sigma/w}$$

$$w = \left[(\sigma\pi)^{\sigma^2 T^2 r\pi\pi^\pi/\sqrt[4]{T}} + \sigma\right]\left[(rT\pi^\pi)^{[2(T^6\sigma+r)^T]} + \sigma\pi - T^2\right] + 16T^2 r + \frac{4r}{\sigma} - T^2$$

The parameters contained in $P_0^{(3)}$ are as follows (in alphabetical order, the calculation order is D_1, E, B', and c; for A' see above):

$$B' = \frac{1}{2}\left[e^{D_1} - \frac{2r}{\sigma^2} - \sqrt{\left(\frac{E}{S^*/X}\right)^2 + \frac{8r}{\sigma^2(1-e^{-rT})}}\right]$$

$$c_1 = \frac{1}{2}\left[0,955 - \frac{2r}{\sigma^2} - \sqrt{\frac{\ln(S_0/X)}{T\sigma^3\left(r + rS^*/X + T\sqrt{p_0/X}\right)} + \frac{8r}{\sigma^2(1-e^{-rT})}}\right]$$

$$D_1 = \sigma^2\left[\frac{p_0}{X} + \Phi\left(2 - \frac{\sigma}{\Phi\left(\frac{\sqrt{T}[\ln(S^*/X)-(r-(p_0/X)^4)^\alpha]}{\sqrt{S^*/X S^*/X}}\right)}\right)\right]^2$$

$$E = T - \left[\sqrt{\left\{\frac{T\left[\ln(S^*/X) + r + T^2/2 - T\right]}{\Phi(S_0/X)S^*/X}\right\}^2 + r + \sigma^2 - T}\right]$$

The above formulas are as derived by the genetic programming algorithm without possible simplification.

References

Aho, A. V. and J. D. Ullman. 1972. *The Theory of Parsing, Translation, and Compiling*, volume I: Parsing. Prentice–Hall, Englewood Cliffs.

Alander, J. T. 1994. *An Indexed Bibliography of Genetic Algorithms: Years 1957–1993*. Report Series No. 94–1. Department of Information Technology and Production Economics, University of Vaasa.

Barone-Adesi, G. and R. E. Whaley. 1986. The valuation of American call options and the expected ex–dividend stock price decline. *Journal of Financial Economics*, pages 91–111.

Barone-Adesi, G. and R. E. Whaley. 1987. Efficient analytic approximation of American option values. *Journal of Finance*, pages 301–320.

Barone-Adesi, G. and R. E. Whaley. 1988. On the valuation of American put options on dividend–paying stocks. *Advances in Futures and Options Research*, 3:1–13.

Black, F. and M. Scholes. 1973. The pricing of options and corporate liabilities. *Journal of Political Economy*, 81:637–659.

Brennan, M. and E. Schwartz. 1977. The valuation of American put options. *Journal of Finance*, pages 449–462.

Cox, J., S. Ross, and M. Rubinstein. 1979. Option pricing: A simplified approach. *Journal of Financial Economics*, pages 229–263.

Fischer, E. O. 1993. Analytic approximation for the valuation of American put options on stocks with known dividends. *International Review of Economics and Finance*, pages 115–127.

Geske, R. 1977. A note on an analytic valuation formula for unprotected American call options with known dividends. *Journal of Financial Economics*, pages 375–380.

Geske, R. and H. E. Johnson. 1984. The American put option valued analytically. *Journal of Finance*, pages 1511–1524.

Goldberg, D. E. 1989. *Genetic Algorithms in Search, Optimization, and Machine Learning.* Addison Wesley, Reading, Massachusetts.

Hanke, M. 1997. Neural network approximation of option pricing: Formulas for analytically intractable option pricing models. *Journal of Computational Intelligence in Finance*, pages 20–27.

Hanke, M. 1999. Neural networks vs. Black–Scholes: An comparison of the pricing of two fundamentally different option pricing methods. *Journal of Computational Intelligence in Finance*, pages 26–34.

Holland, J. H. 1975. *Adaption in Natural and Artificial Systems.* The University of Michigan Press, Ann Arbor.

Hutchinson, J. M., A. W. Lo, and T. Poggio. 1994. A nonparametric approach to pricing and hedging derivative securities via learning networks. *Journal of Finance*, pages 851–889.

Johnson, H. E. 1983. An analytic approximation for the American put price. *Journal of Financial and Quantitative Analysis*, pages 141–148.

Kim, I. J. 1990. The analytic valuation of American options. *Review of Financial Studies*, pages 547–572.

Koza, J. R. 1992. *Genetic Programming. On the Programming of Computers by Means of Natural Selection.* The MIT Press, Cambridge, Massachusetts.

MacMillan, L. W. 1986. Analytic approximation for the American put option. *Advances in Futures and Options Research*, 1:119–139.

Margrabe, W. 1978. The value of an option to exchange one asset for another. *Journal of Finance*, pages 177–186.

Merton, R. C. 1973. Theory of rational option pricing. *Bell Journal of Economics and Management Science*, pages 141–183.

Roll, R. 1977. An analytic valuation formula for unprotected American call options with known dividends. *Journal of Financial Economics*, pages 251–258.

Stephan, J. A. and R. E. Whaley. 1990. Intraday price changes and trading volume relations in the stock and stock option markets. *Journal of Finance*, pages 191–220.

Stoll, H. R. and R. E. Whaley. 1986. New option instruments: Arbitrageable linkages and valuation. *Advances in Futures and Options Research*, 1:25–62.

Whaley, R. 1981. On the valuation of American call options on stocks with known dividends. *Journal of Financial Economics*, pages 207–211.

Contact Information

Chapter 2
Paul Glasserman: pg20@columbia.edu
Philip Heidelberger
Perwez Shahabuddin

Chapter 3
Matthew R. Morey
H. D. Vinod: vinod@murray.fordham.edu

Chapter 4
Ralph Neuneier
Dirk Ormoneit: ormoneit@stat.stanford.edu

Chapter 5
Art Owen: art@stat.stanford.edu

Chapter 6
Sebastian Schneider: sebastian.schneider@wiso.uni-augsburg.de
Manfred Steiner

Chapter 7
Catherine Shenoy
Prakash P. Shenoy: pshenoy@ukans.edu

Chapter 8
Filippo Altissimo: altissi@tin.it

Chapter 9
Andrea Beltratti: beltratti@econ.unito.it
Claudio Morana

Chapter 10
Engelbert J. Dockner
Georg Dorffner
Christian Schittenkopf
Peter Tiňo: petert@ai.univie.ac.at

Chapter 11
Jeff Fleming: jfleming@ruf.rice.edu
Chris Kirby
Barbara Ostdiek

Chapter 12
Juan del Hoyo: juan.hoyo@uam.es
J. Guillermo Llorente

Chapter 13
Amir F. Atiya: amir@work.caltech.edu
Malik Magdon-Ismail

Chapter 14
Zhi-bin Lai
Yiu-ming Cheung: ymcheung@cse.cuhk.edu.hk
Lei Xu

Chapter 15
Juan K. Lin: jklin@math.mit.edu
Peter Dayan

Chapter 16
Cornelis A. Los: cornelis.los@adelaide.edu.au

Chapter 17
John Moody
Howard Yang: hyang@cse.ogi.edu

Chapter 18
Min Qi: mqi@bsa3.kent.edu
Yangru Wu

Chapter 19
Ramazan Gençay: gencay@uwindsor.ca
Giuseppe Ballocchi
Michel Dacorogna
Olivier Pictet

Chapter 20
A. N. Burgess: N.Burgess@lbs.ac.uk

Chapter 21
N. Towers: ntowers@lbs.ac.uk
A. N. Burgess

Chapter 22
Zac Harland: zachar@dial.pipex.com

Chapter 23
Thomas Hellstrom: thomash@cs.umu.se
Kenneth Holmstrom

Chapter 24
David Hsieh: dah7@mail.duke.edu

Chapter 25
Raymond Tsang: Raymond_L_Tsang@nag.national.com.au
Paul Lajbcygier

Chapter 26
Michael de la Maza: RedfireGrp@aol.com

Chapter 27
John Moody: moody@cse.ogi.edu
Matthew Saffell

Chapter 28
Dirk W. Rudolph: drudolph@global.nacamar.de

Chapter 29
Spyros Skouras: Spyros.Skouras@econ.cam.ac.uk

Chapter 30
Benjamin Van Roy: bvr@stanford.edu

Chapter 31
Shareen Joshi: shareen@santafe.edu
Jeffrey Parker
Mark Bedau

Chapter 32
David Goldbaum: goldbaum@andromeda.rutgers.edu

Chapter 33
T. S. Raghu: Raghu.Santanam@asu.edu
H. R. Rao
P. K. Sen

Chapter 34
Edmar Martinelli: edmar@icms.sc.usp.br
André de Carvalho
Solange Rezende: solange@icmc.sc.usp.br
Alberto Matias

Chapter 35
Tor Jacobson: Tor.Jacobson@riksbank.se
Kasper Roszbach

Chapter 36
Kasper Roszbach: nekr@hhs.se

Chapter 37
Mikhail Chernov: mchernov@psu.edu
Eric Ghysels

Chapter 38
N. K. Chidambaran: chiddi@stern.nyu.edu
C. H. Jevons Lee
Joaquin R. Trigueros

Chapter 39
Peter Christoffersen: christop@management.mcgill.ca
Jinyon Hahn

Chapter 40
Les Clewlow
Russell Grimwood: phd96rg@cutlass.wbs.warwick.ac.uk

Chapter 41
Jorge Galindo-Flores: jorge_galindo_phd98@post.harvard.edu

Chapter 42
George J. Jiang
Pieter J. van der Sluis: P.J.vdrSluis@kub.nl

Chapter 43
Christian Keber: chris@finance.bwl.univie.ac.at

Keyword Index